The Which? Guide to Buying Antiques

The Which? Guide to Buying Antiques

PUBLISHED BY CONSUMERS' ASSOCIATION
AND HODDER & STOUGHTON

The Which? Guide to Buying Antiques
researched and written by **Rachael Feild**

Which? Books are commissioned by
The Association for Consumer Research
and published by Consumers' Association,
2 Marylebone Road, London NW1 4DX, and
Hodder & Stoughton, 47 Bedford Square,
London WC1B 3DP

First published 1982
Revised edition 1983
First paperback edition 1988

THE WHICH? GUIDE TO BUYING ANTIQUES
was researched and written by Rachael Feild
1988 revision by Cooper Dale,
1A Dalling Road, London W6 0RA

Typeset by Modern Word Processing, Hull and
Tradeset Ltd, London

Printed and bound in Great Britain by Jolly and Barber, Rugby

The publishers gratefully acknowledge the expert advice of the following in updating prices quoted in *The Which? Guide to Buying Antiques:* John Bly, Jack Franses, Charles Hajdamach, Henry Sandon and John Webster.

British Library Cataloguing in Publication Data

Feild, Rachael
The Which? guide to buying antiques
——1st pbk ed.
1. Antiques – Collectors' guides
I. Title II. Consumers Association
745.1

ISBN 0-340-49196-5

Frontispiece: Staffordshire $8\frac{1}{2}$-inch plate in the blue, white and rust colours of the Japanese Imari palette, c. *1840.*

Contents

Prices in this Guide

The prices quoted in this *Guide* can only be an indication of what a buyer should expect to pay an established dealer for a similar piece in reasonable condition. Every price has been checked by more than one expert, but in antiques as in many other areas, if you consult two experts you are quite likely to get two different opinions. However, the items priced are neither museum pieces nor junk, and there are enough of them around to allow fairly consistent pricing. You may well pay less at auction, but buying at auction is not recommended for significant purchases without expert advice or until you have a fair working knowledge. You must always expect to pay more for a piece in exceptionally good condition, and less for one that has been poorly treated. If you are selling, you must expect to take considerably less than the resale price – at least 20%, even if the piece is perfect, and it may well be more. Prices change with inflation and other market forces such as fashion; those quoted here are valid for 1988–9.

Introduction

The moment you say 'antiques' many people imagine big money and huge profits. This book is about neither. Nor is it about junk. It is about buying antiques of reasonable quality because you like them and because they may cost no more than buying new. It is about buying things to enjoy, with the added comfort that they are likely to benefit your pocket in the long run.

There are hundreds of areas of antiques to choose from. The ones we have selected are the most practical. We all need furniture, glasses to drink out of, china to eat from, cutlery and flatware to eat with and carpets on the floor. It is possible to have antique versions of all these things. It may take time, but it can be done. It will cost money, but think of what you have to spend on these items anyway.

Two things cannot be over-emphasized. You should *only ever buy things you like* and *this is not an investment guide.* Both require some comment.

There is no point in buying antiques that are widely recognized as being in good taste if that taste is not yours. You have to live with what you buy. On the other hand, tastes change. A style that ten years ago you might have rejected as unsympathetic you may now find more congenial and possibly even quite desirable in your own mind. This is where looking at antiques and handling them is valuable, because it is the only way to arrive at an appreciation of their virtues as well as of their faults.

Investment in antiques is a professional business. It is the domain of dealers and collectors. On the other hand there is an investment aspect to buying antiques for yourself. If you follow the *Guide's* advice, you will be buying recognized antiques fairly safely (nothing is absolutely safe) in an established market in which values have, on the whole, risen steadily. If you buy new, your purchases will have second-hand value; if you buy antiques you will, after a few years, probably see your money back and you may make a profit too. Why? Partly because of rarity value – the number of genuine antiques of a given period can only decline; and partly because of the quality of workmanship and materials – both, faced with mass-market pressures, have declined drastically. This is not to say that items of the highest quality are not made now, but that the skills and sometimes the materials are both inordinately expensive.

The focus of the *Guide* then is on those items which are useful and fairly readily available in the areas of Furniture, Glass, Pottery and Porcelain, Rugs and Silver. Nothing costs over £3,000 at current prices (except canteens of silver, but they can be bought in parts), most of the items mentioned cost a great deal less, almost all are of domestic manufacture (except rugs), and dealers stock them because they are the core of the market.

How the *Guide* Works

The purpose of the *Guide* is not to tell you what to buy but to help you buy wisely the sorts of objects you like and can afford. To that end, each section gives you:

1. An introduction that describes the particular features of that area of the market and gives any essential historical background.

2. An illustrated description of the styles made, together with, where relevant: the major influences that caused changes in style – therefore an explanation of why pieces were made to look as they do; the way they were made at that time or in that place – a vital clue to authenticity; the materials used – again, evidence of whether the piece under examination is likely to be genuine as certain materials are restricted to certain periods; what sorts of object were made in a given period – another way of checking that a particular piece could be genuine.
3. Care and restoration – it is perfectly reasonable to buy certain (but by no means all) articles in a damaged state and have them repaired. This tells you when you should and when you should not, what can be done, and how to clean up objects and look after them.
4. A price guide, giving not only likely prices for a range of exemplary items but pointing out which variations are likely to raise or lower that probable price. Prices of widely available modern reproductions are sometimes quoted to put antique prices in context.
5. Illustrated definitions of the specialist terms used in this book or commonly used in the antiques trade.
6. A reading list pointing the way to more detailed knowledge.

Antique Dealers

Antique dealers are only human and they are looking to make a profit just like every other retailer. They will seek to sell their stock for whatever the market will bear. What keeps prices down is competition between dealers and the fact that private buyers can also go to salerooms and bid against the dealers.

A dealer's mark-up has to cover the following things: rent, insurance, lighting, heating, labour, restoration, transport and profit. Profit = the dealer's income; if it is large enough, some of it will be ploughed back to expand the business or to buy better quality stock.

The best dealers are considerable scholars and will be leading experts in their fields. At the top end of the market they may be called in by museums to give advice on their collections. In the middle range, which concerns us, they should still be knowledgeable and should be able to substantiate their description of a piece from reputable sources. They do not like know-alls, but they do respond to intelligent questioning and to evident appreciation of their stock. You can learn a great deal by talking to dealers, and on the whole they are happy for you to learn.

Because there is no absolute price for any antique item, prices fluctuate even in the same shop. If an item is sticking, the dealer is likely to reduce its price. If he is selling to a fellow dealer he will give a trade discount. It is for these reasons that dealers often mark their goods with codes rather than simple price tags. The codes usually refer to the stock book, in which all the expenses associated with that piece are recorded. The code may also indicate the dealer's target price for selling to the trade and his target price for selling to a private buyer. Ask if the price quoted includes VAT.

Buying from a dealer

Bargaining is often possible, but to bargain properly you need to know what you are about: no dealer is going to sell for less than he thinks is justified. Bargaining is much more likely to be successful if you are paying cash and going to carry the piece away with you. If you pretend to be trade you can lose your legal protection as a consumer. Do remember that large cheques have to be cleared and that credit card companies take a percentage of the dealer's price, which he has to allow for in his prices if you are to get the advantage of the credit card service. Dealers will usually be able to arrange transport for you if an item is large, but you will have to pay for carriage.

Any purchase of a piece should be accompanied by a receipt which states the dealer's description of the article and the price paid. If when you get your purchase home you find you have made a mistake (it's the wrong size for your room, for example), take it back, explain your reasons and ask for a refund. As long as you have bought from a reputable dealer there should be no problem.

Selling to a dealer

Whenever you sell to a dealer you have to give him room to add his mark-up. If you have bought fairly recently at full market price (salerooms excepted) it will be several years before the piece has appreciated sufficiently to cover the mark-up. An example: you buy a piece from a dealer for £60; the next month you could sell it to a dealer for, perhaps, £40 and he would sell it again for £60. If, however, you wait two years or so, you might be able to sell at £60 to a dealer who might re-sell at £85. Even at this stage you have lost money because of inflation. If you hold on to the piece for five years you might well find that you could sell it for, say, £85, at which you would be around break-even. Thereafter the chances of your getting a profit in real terms increase steadily.

Antique dealers' organizations

There are two main trade bodies that cover the good middle- and upper-range dealers. The sign of either in a dealer's window should inspire confidence, as it means that the dealer is established and respectable and you can, *in extremis,* appeal to the organization if you get into an insoluble dispute with the dealer.

The organizations are:

British Antique Dealers' Association (BADA),
20 Rutland Gate,
London SW7 1BD.

and

London and Provincial Antique Dealers' Association (LAPADA)
112 Brompton Road,
London SW3 1JJ.

To become a member a dealer must be knowledgeable, have been operating honestly for three years or more, be registered for VAT at a fixed place of business and be vouched for by established dealers who are themselves members of the organization. Both BADA and LAPADA realize, as do most dealers, that it is important to regulate their business and maintain codes of conduct that are more than merely cosmetic. BADA members prefer to trade in goods made before 1830. LAPADA members have greater flexibility.

Salerooms and Auctions

It is assumed throughout this book that you will be buying from dealers, because it is much the easiest way to buy and also the safest. However, as you acquire knowledge and confidence, auctions may well become an attractive alternative source of pieces. This is what to expect.

An auctioneer is only an agent, who is not directly responsible to the buyer except in the general terms of auction-room procedure. His sole function is to raise as much money as he can for the seller, from whom he is getting a commission. Today, many provincial sale rooms have followed the lead of the big three in London – Christie's, Sotheby's and Phillips – in charging a buyer's commission of 5% or 10% as well as the vendor's commission, but this does not apply to all salerooms.

Buying at auction

It is vitally important to discover the auctioneer's conditions of sale as they vary from one auction room to another. You will find them printed in the catalogue of every sale. Here among other things you are likely to find a disclaimer which states that the auctioneer is not responsible for the authenticity, attribution, genuineness, origin, authorship, date, age, period, condition or quality of any lot and the 'imperfections are not stated' in the description. The only general clue to poor condition is the two letters 'a.f.' at the end of a description; they mean 'as found' – in other words, significantly damaged.

You should examine the pieces you are interested in during viewing hours – usually the day before or the morning of the sale. If, after looking at a piece you would like to bid for, you have doubts, ask the advice of the auctioneers. They are usually only too willing to give you the benefit of their experience and advice. The more specialized the sale and the more up-market the auction house, the more likely it is that the auctioneer will have an expert on hand. It cannot be stressed too often, however, that experts can rarely give you guarantees; the best they can offer is an opinion.

Before the sale check the duplicated list stating the auctioneer's estimated prices for the lots you intend bidding for. Write them beside the lot numbers in your catalogue together with your personal limits, which you should not exceed.

On the day of the sale, arrive in good time. Auctioneers can whistle through lots at an incredibly fast rate, and once bidding has started it may be difficult to find a good vantage point. Apart from that, it is a distraction to everyone if there are unnecessary interruptions to the sale.

Do not try and behave like a veteran. A nod is as good as a wink for the regular buyers, but the auctioneer has probably never seen you before and will not know that you are bidding unless you make a clear sign to attract his attention. Once you have done this however, keep your signals clear and don't fidget. The auctioneer will be looking to you for bids and may misinterpret an incidental gesture. If the bidding goes over your limit but the auctioneer looks in your direction for another bid shake your head clearly to indicate you are out of the running.

A word of warning. Do remember that in addition to the hammer price you will not only have to pay VAT on the auctioneer's commission and maybe a buyer's commission (these can put well over 10% on the hammer price) but you have to remove your purchase quickly. If you cannot remove it yourself you will have to pay for transport, and the auctioneers have the right to charge you storage until you have taken your items away. If the very worst happens and you do not arrange removal within the time stated by the auctioneer, he will have the right to sell the items again to defray his costs. It is no wonder then that large items can sometimes be picked up relatively cheaply at country auctions.

Reserves and commission bids

It is customary for the seller to put a reserve price on each lot. This reserve is the minimum price the seller is prepared to accept, and if the bidding does not reach the reserve the auctioneer must withdraw the lot from the sale. The reserve is confidential between the vendor and the auctioneer before the sale and should not be confused with the auctioneer's estimate.

You may very well bid up to the auctioneer's estimated price only to find the lot withdrawn. This is because the reserve price is above his estimate. If this happens, all may not be lost. As long as the piece remains on his premises the auctioneer is empowered to sell it at not less than the reserve price. You may be lucky if, at the end of the sale, you go to the auctioneer and ask what the reserve was, which he is now at liberty to disclose. If the price is still within your limit you can offer to buy the lot at the reserve price by private treaty – i.e. outside the sale. The auctioneer is not obliged to accept your offer.

The auctioneer's job is to get the bidding up as high as possible, but it sometimes seems that he or she is doing this by inventing bids, appearing to pluck them out of the air when no-one is bidding. This is because he has been given instructions to bid on commission by people unable to attend the sale. Here is an example of what might happen. A lot has an estimate of £70 on the auctioneer's list. The bidding opens at £10 and goes to £40. The auctioneer stares at the ceiling and adds '£45, 50, 55, 60,' and then looks down at the bidders in the saleroom again. Someone makes a bid of £70 and the auctioneer, again staring at the ceiling, adds '£75, 80'. A bidder in the saleroom takes it up to £90. The auctioneer adds another bid of £100 and knocks the lot down to an invisible buyer. What has happened is that the auctioneer has been instructed by one absent buyer to go to £60 and by another to go to £100. All quite open and above board if you understand what is happening, but confusing and even suspicious if you do not.

A word about 'the ring'. This is a bogey that belongs largely to the past, when a group of dealers agreed among themselves that only one of them would bid for a lot so that the price would not be pushed up by their bidding against each other. After the sale the group would hold a rough-and-ready auction between themselves known as a 'knock-out'. The highest bidder would take the piece, the saleroom bidder would get his money back and the members of the group would split the margin between them. The vendor in the saleroom lost out and so did the auctioneer, who was taking his commission on a smaller price than was appropriate. There is now a law against rings: the Bidding Agreements Act exists to protect both salerooms and their clients.

Selling at auction

It remains to explain how a saleroom operates if you are the seller and not the buyer. If the piece is portable, take it to the auctioneer and ask for a valuation. If it is too big, take a photograph. If you are dissatisfied with the auctioneer's estimate get a second opinion, either from another auctioneer or from a dealer. If you decide to sell through the saleroom be realistic about your reserve, as the auctioneer will charge a fee if the piece does not sell.

Find out what the auctioneer's total charges will be for storing, handling, insuring and selling and take them into account in your reserve. Some salerooms charge a flat fee, others a percentage of the hammer price. Try and ensure that your piece goes into a specialized sale, even if it means waiting, because specialist sales attract more attention than general sales and thereby (usually) higher prices. Finally, before committing your piece, read the conditions of sale and make sure you understand them.

Reproductions

There are two kinds of reproduction – period and modern. Period reproductions mean Edwardian, Victorian or earlier reproductions of previous styles. They are, if more than 100 years old, antiques in their own right. Modern reproductions are those that you can buy now, new. Anything in between is a matter of guesswork.

Certain period reproductions are just as well made as the pieces they imitate. They have the patina of age and are in every respect good pieces. They should not cost as much as the original, but as antiques of quality they still justify good prices.

A number of Victorian and Edwardian reproductions of earlier styles are not nearly as satisfactory. Machine-made of relatively inferior materials they should be viewed as secondhand when estimating their value.

Modern reproductions are, on the whole, the least satisfactory of all. Often they are even less well made than Edwardian reproductions and will not improve with use or age. Good modern reproductions are very expensive – so expensive in fact that it is probably cheaper to buy period reproductions. It is the quality of pieces that allows them to survive, become antiques and therefore valuable. If the quality is not present in a reproduction of any period it will be a poor buy in the long run.

To help assess whether something may be a reproduction – albeit a period reproduction – use the lists of characteristic products given under each period in the main chapters to see when that kind of object came into quantity production and use the notes on influences as a cross-check.

Limited Editions

Usually offered as 'the antiques of the future', limited editions are outside the purpose of this *Guide*. Limited editions are a speculators' market, to be compared more with the stock market than with the antique trade. This is not to say that some of them will not prove to be good investments, but all too often these attempts to create instant antiques are shoddy and not a little cynical. Manufactured in quantities which are so large they cannot guarantee the scarcity value implied in the promotional material, they may also suffer from poor design, inferior materials and second-rate workmanship. The best are very good indeed and will undoubtedly appreciate in value – sometimes far faster than antiques – but they are not antiques yet.

Insurance

There are some people who insure every single antique at valuation, buying peace of mind at a noticeable cost. Others underinsure and live to regret it. Which you choose depends partly on the kind of person you are but mostly on your insurance company.

Each insurance company can have different conditions and it is essential to be aware of the precise coverage of your home contents policy. Compensation for loss or theft of an individual item is usually limited either to a percentage of the total sum insured or to a fixed sum, whichever is the less. Valuables (such as pieces of silver) may have to be specified on the policy and the insurance company may demand evidence of value. Items can of course be insured individually if the general policy cover is inadequate. It is always a good idea to get and keep receipts for antiques, so that if they are lost or damaged you have not only proof of ownership but a valuation which can be scaled up as necessary.

Minimize the risk of burglary by putting things of value where they cannot readily be seen from outside. There is no point in owning beautiful things if you cannot enjoy them, but it is asking for trouble to flaunt them for any passer-by to see.

If you sell a piece, check your insurance policy and, if it was individually insured or specified, inform the insurance company.

Value Added Tax

Many dealers are registered under a special VAT scheme which means that they can charge VAT on their margin only, thus considerably reducing the cost to the customer. It is possible to sidestep this scheme and pay VAT on the entire cost, but it is worth doing only if you can claim back the VAT yourself. If an article is sold under the special scheme the dealer is not allowed to issue a VAT invoice. The invoice will state only the total price paid, but should describe the article as being over 100 years old. If you are buying at auction there is no VAT on the hammer price but it is payable on the commission.

Further Reading

The Lyle Official Antiques Review (annual)
Miller's Price Guide (annual)
British Art and Antiques Year-Book (annual)
Doreen Yarwood, *The English Home: A Thousand Years of Furniture and Decoration*, London, 1956
Bea Howe, *Antiques from the Victorian Home*, London, 1973
Official Descriptive and Illustrated Catalogue of the Great Exhibition of the Works of Industry of all Nations, London, 1851
David Benedictus, *The Antique Collector's Guide*, London, 1980

On care and restoration:

Michel Doussy, *Antiques: Professional Secrets for the Amateur*, London, 1973
Jaqueline Ridley, *The Care and Repair of Antiques*, Poole, Dorset, 1978

Furniture
Up to £2,500

Mahogany balloon back with over-stuffed serpentine seat and turned front legs, c. *1840.*

Introduction

Good modern furniture can be as well designed as reasonable antique pieces. It can even be as well constructed, though this is less likely. What then are the particular advantages of antique pieces?

First, there is the nature of wood. With age, wood acquires qualities that can never be properly faked. It acquires a patina that makes it glow. Thus of two identical pieces, one made today and the other 150 years ago, the old one will look better and feel better.

Second, there is the matter of cost. Quality for quality, antiques are often actually cheaper than new. The best materials now cost a fortune and craftsmen to work them are thin on the ground, with the result that top quality modern furniture has to be very expensive.

Third, there is the matter of resale value. All our present antiques were once new pieces and they went through a long period of having secondhand value only, before they began to grow steadily in value as antiques. The same thing happens with new furniture now. Even if it is a piece that is an antique of the future, it has almost certainly got to go through a long period as a secondhand piece before it can become valuable; your grandchildren may benefit but you are unlikely to. If you buy an antique piece from a dealer you cannot of course expect to get your money back on the open market until general price levels have absorbed the dealer's margin. It might therefore be five years before you reach break-even. Thereafter, even given the vagaries of the market, you are likely to be holding the value of your possession in real terms, and you may well make a profit if ever you come to sell.

The antique furniture trade is full of stories of made-up pieces and items that owe more to restorers than to their original makers. There are also tales of pieces worth thousands lying in barns and waiting to be picked up for a few pounds. These things do happen. However the information given in this section about the kinds of furniture described should safeguard you against the worst excesses of restoration and making up, and remember that price is on your side. A dealer who is shady is not going to spend good money having a piece made up unless he can see a large margin at the other end. He or she is better off taking honest pieces and selling them at honest prices. The market prices of the pieces described here do not allow a sufficient margin for wholesale fraud. The other side of the coin is not to expect to get spectacular bargains. They are as rare as first dividends on the football pools and there are a lot of knowledgeable people out looking for them.

The real key to the secrets of antique furniture lies in its construction. Designs can be copied, but the meticulous attention to detail and the way a piece of furniture was put together provide the best proof of its age and respectability. So this summary traces the developments in carpentry, joinery and cabinet-making, for it is here that the real clues are to be found. There is a logical thread running from period to period when furniture is looked at this way. Developments and changes in design are less arbitrary than they may, at first sight, seem.

There was very little free-standing furniture made in Britain until Elizabethan days. Chests, coffers, stools, chairs, beds and simply constructed tables were built on a box-frame principle: a square skeleton, nailed or pegged together, with board panels slotted into the frame. There was not much decorative detail and little finesse, for most movable pieces of furniture were held together with glue and thick iron nails.

By the end of the 16th century the joiner had replaced the carpenter, resulting in the 'joined stool' or 'joint stool', which heralded an entirely new kind of construction. Chairs and stools were made with proper legs instead of being glorified boxes with seats and backs. The legs were strengthened with stretchers and simply decorated with reel or bobbin turning. All this was made possible by slotting one piece of the frame into another and securing it with wooden pegs or dowels: the mortise-and-tenon joint.

Oak was the most common wood used. But in Elizabethan days most of the thick timbers were requisitioned for building the 'wooden walls of England' – and in order to give furniture an air of great solidity, decoration and carving was added instead of being an integral part of the piece. The huge carved 'bulbs' on court cupboards and four-poster beds were glued to the plain turned uprights; strips of decorative carving, known as strapwork, were also added in the same way. Steel and iron hinges were nailed on with thick clout nails.

The profligate use of so much of Britain's standing forests resulted in a shortage of timber, especially of oak, at the beginning of the 17th century. Rooms were no longer panelled, cupboards and linen presses once built into the panelling were now made as free-standing pieces of furniture. Chest furniture became more sophisticated and less clumsy in construction, single drawers were built in below chests, slotting into the main frame. Legs of chairs and tables were lightened with decorative swash-turning. Except for dressers and court cupboards there was still no case furniture. In grand houses there were corner cupboards and open shelves built into panelling to display plate and silver. The coarse, heavy grain of oak was not suitable for the new fine chests on stands and for the lighter lines of chairs. Nor was oak suitable for applying the decorative inlaid panels, rich in ivory and mother-of-pearl, which began to come into the country through Holland and in ships of the newly established East India Company. Walnut and beech were favoured for their finer grain. Carving and decoration were crisper as a result.

Thus far the basic construction of furniture had hardly changed at all except in refining the joints and improving the finish. Chests were raised on stands to lighten their appearance and to accord better with the proportions of high-ceilinged rooms. Metalworking techniques had improved, particularly among locksmiths and clockmakers, and fine furniture was decorated with ornamental hinges secured with hand-made, lathe-turned screws. Gate-legged tables with hinged flaps stood against walls when not in use, and there was a more spacious air to rooms.

The Restoration of Charles II in 1660 brought a major change in fashion as he and his returning court imported the French styles to which they had grown accustomed in exile. Six years later the Great Fire destroyed much of London. When the city was rebuilt, the new houses had separate dining rooms, parlours and bedrooms, each requiring different furniture. Coupled with this great social upheaval came the art of veneering, learned from the Dutch.

Veneer, parquetry and marquetry are all variations of the same technique: thin sheets of decoratively grained or patterned woods are applied to the surfaces of furniture made from less costly woods. The surfaces must be smooth and without joins or the veneer lifts off. The old frame construction was accordingly abandoned in favour of making carcases from close-grained Baltic pine, with as many of the joints as possible on undersurfaces or inside the piece. Drawer fronts could no longer be nailed to the sides, and a crude through-dovetail joint was used. This too proved to be unsatisfactory, since the veneer lifted off the end-grain of the through joint.

By the end of the 17th century lap-dovetailing, fairly chunky but effective, was in general use by cabinetmakers. Chests of drawers, chests on stands and early desk furniture were magnificently veneered with natural grains, such as oyster veneer, or richly intricate designs of fruit, flowers and birds in lighter woods which were often stained. Glass for windows was being made in quantity by the end of the 17th century, and the first pieces of case furniture were made with glass-fronted doors and thick glazing bars, in which the wealthy displayed their silver and their oriental blue-and-white porcelain.

In the 18th century market towns grew into provincial cities and expanding trade and victory in war increased the wealth of the entire nation. New customs of living and eating were adopted from the French. There were tall windows, and furniture was light, with graceful, well-proportioned lines. Walnut, imported from France and Virginia, was ideal for strong, springy legs to chairs and tables, known as cabriole legs, which did not need strengthening with stretchers. The old stool-with-back construction of chairs changed to a frame in which the back legs continued up in one piece, curving over into elegantly shaped backs. The cabinetmakers had finally rebelled against the inlaid and lacquered panels which were still being imported, and English lacquer ('japanning'), duller than the glossy oriental lacquer, was used to embellish important pieces of furniture.

Now the gentry needed bookcases and desks, display cabinets and glass-fronted cupboards to show off their collections of leather-bound books, beautifully decorated 'cabinet ware' and ornamental porcelain figures. By the mid-18th century the fashion for tea-drinking produced a whole new range of light, elegant tables, chairs and parlour furniture. Meals were now taken with all the guests sitting down on sets of matching chairs at dining tables which were still made on the gate-leg principle, but with straight or bowed legs ending, like chair legs, in crisply carved pad or ball-and-claw feet. As well as the servants' quarters and kitchen quarters there were boudoirs, morning rooms, breakfast rooms and bedrooms, all to be furnished and many of them on show.

Those who could not afford the very best scrabbled to keep up with the times. Provincial copies of fashionable furniture were made, not in subtle, springy and expensive walnut, but in elm, beech, fruitwood and even oak. As the 18th century wore on and the classical simplicity of taste and fashion came within the reach of the growing middle classes, the gentry built grander and grander houses and filled them with more and more ornate furniture. There was much ormolu and gilding, intricate swirling designs adapted from French rococo, and a fashionable passion for chinoiserie, calling for more and more delicate cabinetmaking. Bow-fronted chest and case furniture softened the simple classical lines of earlier designs as new processes of working timber were developed. But walnut was growing scarce and the fashionable designers of the day turned to an entirely new wood, coming in from England's new colonies.

Mahogany was the darling of the Georgians. Its immense strength and girth simplified construction, since it did not need supporting along its length. It needed no inlay or lacquer. It was a beautifully grained wood, ideally suited to the purity of proportion and line and to producing the plain glossy surfaces so desirable at this period. Enormous dining tables rested miraculously on central pillars with splayed tripod feet. Bookcases and display cabinets stretched the entire length of walls, their glass fronts supported by fragile-looking glazing bars in ornate geometric shapes. There were mirrors everywhere to reflect the light, and within the strict classical lines of Georgian architecture furniture took on an elegant serpentine curve.

The swirling, rococo gilt mounts on commodes and chest furniture of the earlier part of the century, so loved by William Kent and Thomas Chippendale, were at first expensively imported from France. By the 1760s Britain had caught up with and outstripped the rest of Europe in industrial progress. Ormolu, gilt metal, and brass screws, hinges, bolts, escutcheons, backplates and handles were all being made cheaply in Birmingham.

The Regency period combined all that was excellent in craftsmanship with important discoveries in engineering, both in design and construction. Newly discovered principles of load-bearing and stress were applied to furniture design, resulting in the sabre-leg and flush-sided chair, as well as a proliferation of furniture with concealed purposes, sliding tops, and ingenious construction. But if machines could be harnessed to make hinges and screws, they could also perform the most time-consuming work of the joiner and cabinetmaker. By the end of the 18th century machine-cut dovetail joints had begun to replace the slightly uneven handcut dovetails of earlier decades and thinner machine-cut veneer lay sleekly over Scandinavian pine carcases. In the first 20 years of the 19th century mass production came to the fore. After one last gigantic wave of ostentatious decadence, enshrined for ever in the Royal Pavilion at Brighton, machine-made, mass-produced furniture flooded the market and 'thin veneer' became a pejorative term.

One way or another, the Victorians reproduced and copied practically every style and every period, sometimes well, sometimes atrociously. In many ways 19th-century versions of 18th-century furniture are more solid, more soundly constructed than the originals. Good 'Victorian Chippendale' is exact in proportion though slightly differently constructed. It is often veneered instead of being cut from solid wood, and all the joints are regular because they are machine-cut. Bad Victorian Hepplewhite or Sheraton is awful, both in its failure to follow the right proportions and because the wood is cut across the grain. Eighteenth-century originals used the natural spring of the wood for strength; weaker Victorian versions are stretchered, which ruins the line.

The longing to return to the feel of natural wood and genuine craftsmanship of the Pre-Raphaelite Movement and the Victorian aesthetes, headed by William Morris and John Ruskin, led to 'Victorian Tudor' or 'Mediaeval', which is perfectly correct in its construction on the frame principle with mortise-and-tenon joints, except that both the holes and the pegs are machine-cut and neatly symmetrical instead of being hand-cut and oddly shaped. The same can be said of their rustic turned furniture, carved oak settles and refectory tables as they too were made by machine. A comparison of a genuine Tudor piece with a Victorian imitation will quickly show the difference in feel.

Imitation may indeed be the sincerest form of flattery, but too much of it debases the original and eventually renders itself practically worthless. At almost every sale, in almost every junkshop there is at least one piece of Edwardian satinwood furniture, a pale, sad reflection of the Adam original. There are Sheraton sideboards in every furniture store, made yesterday from thinly veneered chipboard, and Hepplewhite-style chairs by the hundred. But in antique shops there are country copies of fashionable furniture made perhaps 50 years after the original, beautifully constructed and with a resonance of the period which is unmistakable, though the proportions may not be quite right and the construction may be a little too sturdy.

Care and Restoration

Care

The chief enemy of antique furniture is central heating. Nothing will damage a good piece faster than bringing it into a fully insulated, centrally heated, double-glazed house without due precaution. Wood must have moisture to survive and improve, but efficient central heating produces a bone-dry atmosphere. The result is that wood shrinks and cracks.

The rule is to attune pieces slowly to their new atmosphere. Keep pieces in the coolest place in the house for months if need be, near

The construction of a chair. Note how every part is jointed – wooden blocks or metal brackets at the corners usually indicate repair or inferior manufacture. The parts are: a – *crest rail;* b – *splat;* c – *side rail;* d – *shoe-piece;* e – *seat rails;* f – *stretchers. If the shoe-piece is made in one with the splat, the chair is quite likely to be a reproduction. The joints would normally be held with glue and wooden pegs for maximum strength.*

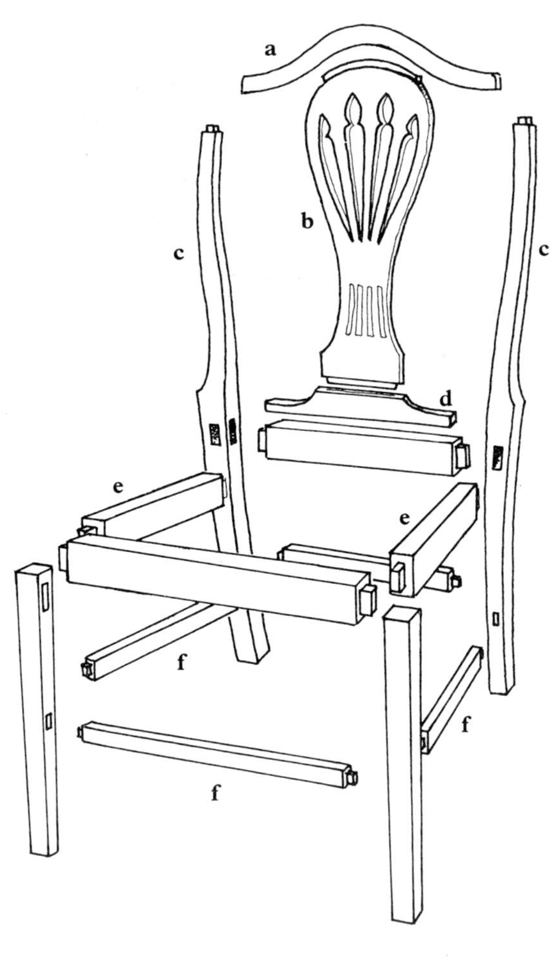

windows (but out of direct sunlight and out of draughts) and away from heaters.

The two secondary enemies are sunlight and worm. Direct sunlight bleaches wood and can raise veneer. Worm will first make furniture unsightly and then destroy it. It is however unrealistic to assume that you will always be able to buy pieces that have suffered from neither light nor worm, but make sure that you do not pay top price for something damaged in either of these ways. If you have any suspicion that the worm in a piece you buy may be still alive (fresh-looking wood and powder in the holes, sharp edges to the holes), treat it thoroughly and immediately with a proprietary woodworm killer and again the following summer. It is not just the new piece you are protecting but all your other furniture too. Sunlight damage can be improved a little by polishing and careful staining, but consult a book on restoration for this.

Wood needs feeding and you feed it by polishing. A lot of elbow grease and a little beeswax is the recipe. Too much wax and you are left with a dull finish that attracts dirt. Sheepskin buffers attached to power drills are seductive, but useless. They rotate so fast that they melt the wax and disperse it.

Restoration

Just about anything can be restored, but the question is whether it is worth it. Buying a chair cheap at £10 because it is damaged, spending £40 on it and finding that at the end the chair is worth £25 is counter-productive. Many repairs however are relatively easy and cheap, and as long as the cost of repair is reflected in the purchase price there is no reason why you should not buy.

Many chairs and tables in time will come apart at one or more corners. The glue may have given out (particularly on stripped furniture) and the piece simply then needs regluing. Joints sometimes break, in which case the solution is usually dowelling the parts back together. Upholsterers will often do this work on chairs, for a flat charge of a few pounds per wobbly corner. You will often come across pieces with blocks or metal angle brackets screwed into the corners. This works, but is not approved of on good pieces. If it has already been done, leave it, but do not add any more such repairs.

Veneers often bubble or lift, crack or become crazed. The skilled amateur can do a lot to improve these problems and professional restorers can put them right, with the exception of crazing, which should be left as an attractive feature and a good sign of age. It is fine to buy pieces with damage to veneer as long as the price is right.

Marks are really of two kinds: dents and stains. Quite a lot can be done about both, but it is necessary to be realistic. A piece that may be 200 years old is going to be marked from normal use and it would be foolish to pretend that it won't. That is why modern reproduction furniture is sometimes 'distressed' – pitted, stained and dented – to add a phony appearance of age. If the overall appearance of a piece is pleasant, leave it. If it is dirty, badly dented or badly stained, pay less if you are buying and get to work if you own it already.

Dents can be eased by placing a damp rag over the spot and applying the tip of an electric iron set at the coolest temperature. The warmth and moisture cause the wood fibres locally to swell. Work carefully and expect an improvement, not a total cure.

Stains are of various kinds, requiring different treatments. All of them require follow-up polishing.

Water stains: white rings left by glasses or bottles; carefully rub in linseed oil, turpentine or butter.

Heat stains: similar effect and similar treatment.

Grease marks: cover the mark with blotting paper or several layers of tissue and press with a cool iron; you want just enough warmth to get through to soften the grease and let the paper take it up; a sprinkling of talcum powder under the paper can help.

Alcohol stains: on polished surfaces treat as water stains; alcohol dissolves varnish, so on varnished surfaces rub down the affected area and re-varnish; on French polished surfaces you have to get the piece repolished.

The things to look for in a chest of drawers. Tops have often been scratched in use or bleached by sunlight; veneer may have lifted, cracked or been replaced – the thinner the veneer, the later the piece. Drawers can tell a lot about the date and authenticity of a piece. Look for wear on the runners. Look too at the dovetail joints – if they are perfectly regular they are machine made and therefore probably Victorian. If the grain of the drawer bottoms runs front to back it is likely to be pre-1730. In later pieces the grain runs from side to side and the bottom is likely to be in two or three pieces. Drawers run the full depth of chests from about 1770. Damaged moulding round drawer fronts is easy to replace. Handles and scutcheon plates (keyhole surrounds) are sometimes damaged or changed. An original undisturbed fitting will have a build-up of wax and dirt round its edges. If in doubt about the authenticity of handles, look on the inside – spare screw holes will indicate that a change has been made. Finally, the feet of an old piece will almost certainly show signs of scuffing, though if it is very bad on a veneered piece, the veneer may quite legitimately have been renewed.

Ink stains: if fresh, swab with water and then work in lemon juice carefully; if old, paint the stain only with vinegar, using a fine brush, and follow up with a solution of 1 part Milton (from a chemist) : 10 parts water; dab off and repeat as necessary; expect improvement, not cure.
Blood stains: bleach out with a solution of 1 part Milton : 10 parts water.
Burn marks: the only real cure is to sand out the burned wood; if you are (understandably) reluctant to do this, you may be able to bleach out some of the stain with 1 part Milton : 10 parts water, but do not hope for much.

Cleaning

So much for the obvious things. What affects a great deal of old furniture though is dirt, and you should always consider cleaning any wood that is not in obviously good condition. The first stage is to wash the piece with soapy water – ordinary washing powders are fine. If this is not strong enough use a mixture of 1 part methylated spirits : 4 parts turpentine : 4 parts white vinegar : 4 parts linseed oil. Wipe the dirt off rather than rubbing it in.

You may think that cleaning in this way will damage the patina. It will not. Dirt and patina are quite different things and the patina will be much more obvious and pleasing if the surface is clean.

Stripping

The extreme of cleaning is stripping off unwanted paint or varnish. It is not only cheaper furniture that has been maltreated in the past: some excellent pieces have been disguised with paint and given rougher treatment than they were meant to take. Pine is the most familiar wood for stripping at the moment, but any wood that has been inappropriately painted or varnished can be stripped.

A simple piece can be stripped at home – an old kitchen table or kitchen chair, for example – with a proprietary paint stripper such as Nitromors. The job is messy and time-consuming but manageable. Home-stripping, if it is done thoroughly and well finished, looks better than stripping in a bath, which is the alternative way of doing it.

Professional furniture strippers usually have a large bath or tank of caustic soda in which they immerse pieces. It is a very effective way of doing the job quickly and of getting into difficult corners and round carved or turned parts. It is also relatively cheap. The professionals, however, rarely take the trouble to finish their work well, and if a piece comes back looking clean but dull, it will pay to wipe it over with vinegar (to neutralize any vestigial caustic soda) and then to polish deeply with beeswax until the wood glows. One thing to watch for is whether the joints have been loosened in the course of dipping: the caustic soda often dissolves the glue and can stay in joints and rot the wood; it pays to go to someone whose finishing is thorough. If you have got a piece with weakened joints make sure it is really dry and then repair it or have it repaired as described above.

Incidentally, pine strippers today are as skilled at making up pieces as any of the craftsmen of the past. Pine is not a very durable wood and so cannibalization of the good bits of damaged pieces to make up whole ones is rampant. There is nothing wrong with this as long as it is well done and the result is good-looking, serviceable and sensibly priced. What you are buying in many cases is furniture made with mellowed old wood, not authentic antique pieces.

Stripping of quality pieces is a delicate task and you do need to know what you are doing. A lot can be done at home, but only after experimenting on cheap pieces and reading everything you can find on the subject. The better the piece, the more certain it is that you should go to a professional antique restorer.

And a word about restorers. Good restorers are fully capable of making new pieces of high quality that are perfect matches in craftsmanship and materials to Queen Anne, Georgian or whatever. They understand construction and decoration as well as the old makers did. A lot of people who work as restorers however are skilled at joinery and turning but little more. Their achievement is to make pieces serviceable again rather than restoring them to their original condition. Choose your restorer according to the quality of the piece.

Dealers' Restoration

If a piece has any real value and age, the chances are that it has been restored in some way at some time. It is quite likely, if you are buying the piece in good condition that the dealer from whom you are buying has had the work done.

Good restoration is entirely legitimate, but a lot of not so good work – some of it downright peculiar – is done. Misleading restoration is one of the tricks of the trade, which you can come to understand only by learning – and, very possibly, by getting caught at some time. Dealers get caught too.

There are literally hundreds of rules to learn, the wise application of which will tell you with reasonable certainty whether a piece is what is claimed or whether it has been restored. They can be learned, with assiduity and patience, over a period of years. The people who know them best are the dealers and restorers. If you can develop a good relationship with a good dealer you will not be deceived and you will learn a lot. Failing that, look at each piece from *every* angle to see if it is harmonious. If it is, it is either perfectly authentic or has been well restored – probably. Either way, it doesn't matter too much as long as the piece functions properly unless you are buying very expensive pieces, and do not do that until you know very well what you are doing.

Periods and Styles

We start early in the 18th century, with Queen Anne, because furniture from the earlier periods is both relatively rare and on the whole rather expensive. Tudor, Elizabethan, Jacobean, Restoration and William & Mary styles were however revived in the 19th century, but clear indications are given in the sections on the Victorian period to help you tell copy from original.

Period: 1702–27 - Queen Anne

(The prevailing style did not change much under George I, 1714–27)

Influences: Cabriole legs adapted from French; otherwise style of this period is pure English.

Materials: Walnut, walnut veneer, marble, gilt gesso, English lacquer (japanning); elm, beech, yew; yellow Baltic pine for carcases.

Characteristic types of furniture: Dressing tables, dressing mirrors, knee-hole desks, chests-on-chests, chests-on-stands, tallboys, lowboys, bureaus, desk-and-bookcases, glazed china cabinets, corner cupboards, chests-of-drawers, long-case clocks, tea caddies, side chairs, dining chairs, dining tables, kitchen dressers, carved walnut-framed mirrors, drop-leaf tables, card tables.

Construction: The main development was the cabriole leg, which depended for its strength on the natural spring of the wood and made stretchers unnecessary. The shape was found in the wood, meaning that sometimes pieces of considerable girth were used. Tongue-and-groove joints on folding tables and cabinet doors made edges join with a hairline crack. Wooden hinges with flexible dovetail construction produced card tables of great elegance with folding tops, rounded corners for candles and dished cavities for coins and counters. Joints were customarily hidden.

Chairs: Cabriole legs, some stretchers, drop-in seats or over-stuffed seats, central back splat slotted into shoe-piece separate from back seat-frame. Side chairs still made on the old frame principle, with over-stuffed seats. Matching sets of dining chairs now made in quantity.

Chest and case furniture: Chests-on-stands with turned legs and bun feet giving way to

chests-on-stands with X-stretchers and chests-on-chests with bun or bracket feet. Some glazing of display cabinet doors.
Drawers: Oak sides with rounded top edges made shorter than the length of the carcase to allow for ventilation inside. Around 1710 small lip mouldings were introduced to project round drawer edges to protect the veneer as the drawers were opened and closed.
Design and detail: Immaculate finishing to complement elegant, flowing shapes of furniture. Glazed doors and block-front doors to case furniture; architectural pediments to cabinets; pigeon holes and finials to desks; bun feet; ball-and-claw feet towards the end of the period; pad feet; friezes or aprons to conceal hingeing legs; rounded edges; cross-banding, feather-banding hid veneer edges; shell and scallop motifs; English lacquer, which is duller than oriental, particularly in red and gold with Chinese dragons for bureaux, dressing mirrors, chairs, small furniture; brass bail handles with solid backplates secured by iron pins split and flattened on insides of drawers; brass locks, keys and escutcheons.

Period: 1727–60 – Early Georgian

Influences: Classical, chinoiserie, rococo, Gothic. William Kent, John Adam; Thomas Chippendale senior published *A Gentleman and Cabinet Maker's Director* in 1754. It was used all over the country as a pattern book and Chippendale-style furniture was made for the next 50 years. Even after that date, country-made chairs with definitely Chippendale lines and proportions were still made and are legitimately within the period of direct influence.
Materials: Walnut, mahogany (San Domingo plain, Cuban curled or figured, Honduras 'baywood'), Virginia walnut; imported American red pine, white pine and Baltic yellow pine for carcases.
Characteristic types of furniture: Reading or 'cock-fighting' chairs, corner chairs, pillar-and-claw and tripod tables, console tables, hanging corner cupboards, tallboys, lowboys, secretaires, serpentine-fronted commodes or chests-of-drawers, rococo mirrors and brackets, fireplace mirrors and overmantels, piecrust tables, tripod tables, broken pediments to cabinets, glass-fronted bookcases and bureau-bookcases, tea tables, teapoys, tip-top tables, drop-leaf tables, knee-hole desks, writing tables, library tables, settees, sofas and couches, Windsor chairs, upholstered wing chairs.
Construction: The strength of mahogany, which now became the most fashionable wood, allowed construction to become far simpler. Mahogany did not warp, was immensely strong and was able to be cut in considerable widths of plank. Joins were unnecessary, table tops could be supported on a central column into which tripod legs and feet (known as pillar-and-claw) could be dovetailed; leaves of tables could be unsupported except for bolt-and-fork fastenings to secure them, glazing bars were more slender, surfaces were unbroken and, with the arrival of figured mahogany, undecorated. Bookcases, cabinets and display cabinets could be built of great height and beds could be made with slender columns to support canopies.
Chairs: Square-sectioned legs, drop-in seats. Chairs with cabriole legs terminated in paw or pad feet and were more slender. Overstuffed seats for some chairs; country and provincial chairs with wooden seats were shaped to take squab cushions.
Chest and case furniture: Bow-fronts or serpentine fronts, particularly commodes or chests-of-drawers. Spider joins replace tongue-and-groove for even more smoothly joining surfaces.
Drawers: Cockbeading fitting flush round sides and lip, drawer bottoms made of a single piece of wood, grain running front to back until *c.* 1730, when bottoms were made with the grain running side to side.
Design and detail: Classical architectural silhouettes of desk and case furniture softened by broken pediments; serpentine- and bow-fronted furniture; asymmetrical flowing shapes adapted from French rococo with almost every straight line broken, curved or ornamented; heavy use of gilt and ormolu,

giving way to more subtle furniture inspired by oriental design. Cabriole leg refined to delicately curving lines; other legs severely square-sectioned; development of pillar-and-claw pedestal supports for tables, with fluting and reeding much in evidence; marble tops for centre tables, console tables; bracket feet replace bun feet; castors with brass arms and leather disc rollers on small tables and some chairs; pierced backplates and bail handles secured at either side by screws through the thickness of the wood; cast brass rococo mounts and handles on grand furniture.

Period: 1760–1811 – Late Georgian

Influences: French and classical: the great age of classicism; Robert Adam *d.* 1792; George Hepplewhite *d.* 1786: his *Cabinet-maker and Upholsterer's Guide* published 1788; Thomas Shearer: *Cabinet-maker's London Book of Prices* 1788; also his *Designs for Household Furniture*; Thomas Sheraton's *Cabinet-Maker and Upholsterer's Drawing Book* published 1791–4; Thomas Chippendale junior *d.* 1822; Angelica Kauffmann. Manufacturers: Morgan & Sanders, George Seddon, Thomas Butler, William Ince, John Mayhew.

This was the greatest period of English furniture design: a closer study of the individual works of Adam, Hepplewhite, Sheraton and Shearer is essential in order to train the eye to all-important proportion and detail, both of which have often been bungled by later reproductions. Briefly, Robert Adam introduced classical symmetry, refined the cabriole leg to its ultimate grace, reintroduced inlay for swags, anthemions, urns, Greek key pattern. Hepplewhite was responsible for extremely graceful bow-fronted and serpentine chest furniture with curved aprons, bracket feet, and for the mercilessly copied shield-back chair, straight tapered legs and a wider use of marquetry employing satinwood and other pale coloured woods. Sheraton favoured square and rectilinear shapes, corner moulding and inlaid or veneered stringing, ornamental glazing bars to bureau-bookcases, display cabinets and corner cupboards. Sheraton probably influenced English furniture more than any other designer – as witness the endless reproductions of his work down to the present day. Sheraton also designed many ingenious multipurpose pieces in order to adapt to the severe shortage of both materials and money caused by the Napoleonic Wars (1793–1815). Thomas Shearer, though less of a household name, produced many items adapted from 'campaign furniture' designed for the houses of average families. Again, bear in mind the time-lag of around 50 years between London and the provinces: furniture made to the designs of the masters was still being made from their pattern books until well into the 19th century and cannot strictly be called reproduction.

Materials: Mahogany (flame-grain Cuban), satinwood, tulipwood, kingwood, harewood (stained sycamore), birch, chestnut, oak, beech, cheap 'baywood' (Honduras mahogany); imported Scandinavian red and white pine for carcases and built-in cupboard furniture. Gilding and gilt ornament; ormolu; revival of marquetry and parquetry.

Characteristic types of furniture: Clothes presses (wardrobes), Carlton House desks, cylinder desks, kneehole desks, pedestal desks, dining room furniture: sideboards, side tables, wine coolers, knife boxes; bachelors' chests, bonheurs du jour, campaign furniture, cane-seated painted birch and beech chairs, ladder-back, lyre-back, wheel-back and shield-back chairs, hall chairs, serpentine-front chest and case furniture, library steps, two-seater chair settees en suite with drawing room chairs, envelope tables, work tables, games tables, sewing tables, Pembroke tables, demi-lune side tables, draw tables, sofa tables, drop-leaf tables, bow-front commodes and chests-of-drawers, chiffoniers, Tunbridge ware, wash stands, side cupboards, pot cupboards, pine dressers, kitchen furniture.

Construction: The two principal constructional innovations in this period are the result of Matthew Boulton's Birmingham Brass Foundry which began making brass fittings and ormolu mounts from 1762, rendering it no longer necessary to import expensive brass fittings from the continent. The advent of lathe-turned screws and cast brass hinges produced a mass of furniture designed to conceal its function. Small furniture of all kinds appeared. Lighter construction of chairs, tables etc. brought back H-shaped stretchers for all but the finest mahogany shield-back chairs whose construction eliminated the central back-splat and shoe-piece.

Chairs: Tapering legs, straight, round or square in section, sometimes fluted, ending in spade feet or small plinths; towards the end of the 18th century horizontal back-splats replaced vertical back-splats. Hepplewhite chairs favoured over-stuffed seats, Sheraton chairs drop-in seats.

Drawers: In chest and case furniture they had bottoms made from oak with grain running side to side, usually in two or three pieces, fitting into grooves in drawer side from 1770. Drawers ran the whole length of the piece of furniture from about the same time.

Design and detail: Popular decorative motifs were lyre and shield, festoons, swags, masks, medallions; light-coloured woods used for small furniture of all kinds, much of it inlaid, painted or stained; marble tops inlaid with classical themes on more slender console tables, often fixed to walls so that the delicate supports did not bear the weight; lavish use of brass and ormolu.

Period: 1811–30 – Regency

Influences: French Empire, Graeco-Roman, Egyptian; Thomas Hope's *Household Furniture and Interior Decoration* published 1807; George Smith's *Cabinet Maker and Upholsterer's Guide* published 1828; Brighton Pavilion. Manufacturers: Gillows, Pratt & Sons, Morgan & Sanders.

Materials: Dark glossy woods: mahogany, calamander, amboyna, zebra-wood, Brazilian rosewood; imported Baltic pine (red and white) for carcases; French polish, imitation bamboo, japanned beech, ebonized wood.

Characteristic types of furniture: French sofa beds and couches, Grecian couches, bed-steps, Canterburys, Davenports, dumb waiters, fitted wardrobes with door mirrors, brass trellis-fronted bookcases and cupboards, brass inlaid writing boxes, sewing tables, work tables, card tables, foot stools, gout stools, music stools, pedestal desks, hanging bookcases, 'quartetto' tables, X-frame music stools, X-back chairs, sabre-legged chairs, lyre-back chairs, square-back chairs, S-arm chairs, marble-topped console tables and side tables, lyre-ended tables, sofa tables, leather-covered desks, writing tables, library and drum tables.

Construction: Changes lie in the increasing use of machines for planing, turning, moulding, grooving and brass inlay. Machine-cut veneer reduced the thickness from $\frac{1}{8}$in or more to less than $\frac{1}{16}$. Machine-cut dovetail joints are regular and uniform in size, with longer narrower tails. Evolution from pillar-and-claw to splayed feet from central pedestal or reeded column; round-topped tables on fluted pillars and tripod legs, massive monopodium central supports.

Chairs: Construction changed (with Thomas Hope 'Trafalgar' chair) to side-frames entirely flush; return of drop-in seat or square-edged cushion on cane seat; scoop-backed upholstered chairs; turned legs, stretchers and crest-rails.

Chest and case furniture: More massive, architectural in concept with broken pediments; breakfront bookcases; drawers uniformly made with machine-cut dovetail joints, cockbead, bottom runner now reaching full depth of carcase.

Design and detail: Typified by Egyptian, Graeco-Roman low lines to furniture; curves, scrolls; classical architectural pillar shapes (Doric, Ionic, Corinthian) echoed in furniture. The overall impression is one of flowing lines in dark woods highlighted with brass ornament, sometimes overdone and foreshadowing the excesses of Victorian ornamentation. Much Boulle work. Ebony and ebonized wood used to accentuate this very distinctive style. Particular to the Regency period are the nautical 'Trafalgar' or 'rope' motifs, commemorating the great naval victories of the day. Reeded, turned legs to tables and chairs; lion's paw brass feet, lion's head and ring handles, stamped brass backplates and keyplates; cast brass shoes to curved feet on sofas, couches, tables; much brass inlay, trellis, galleries, detail; square brass handles with two small backplates screwed through thickness of wood; brass rosettes and stringing.

Period: 1830–37 – William IV

(Late Regency or Early Victorian)
Influences: Continuing Regency, Louis XIV style, Pugin and the Gothic/Tudor Revival, late French Empire style; J.C. Loudon's *Encyclopaedia of Cottage, Farm and Villa Architecture and Furniture.* Manufacturers: Gillows, Holland & Co. (later '& Sons'), J.G. Crace & Sons, Pratt & Sons.
Materials: Veneers, French polish, brass decoration, padded upholstery, plain polished rosewood, solid mahogany, cast iron for conservatory furniture, beds and hall furniture; shell and mother-of-pearl inlay; imported Canadian/North American pine for carcases and kitchen furniture.
Characteristic types of furniture: Balloon-backed chairs, 'Grecian' chairs, couch-beds, prie-dieu chairs, button-back and upholstered spoon-back chairs, conservatory furniture, whatnots, plant stands, brass beds, decorative wrought iron beds, marble-topped washstands, side tables, servants' pine furniture, papier mâché chairs, small tables, trays, tea caddies, embroidered fire screens, pole screens, pier tables, console tables, marble-topped library tables.
Construction: This hitherto neglected period marks the divide between hand-made furniture and cabinet-makers' work and the beginnings of mass-produced machine-made furniture of all kinds. Improved steam-driven marble-cutting techniques brought pier tables and console tables into wider fashion. Coiled metal springs were patented by Samuel Pratt in 1828 and led to sprung seats for all kinds of seating furniture during this period. Thin machine-cut veneer now common.
Chairs: From the Thomas Hope flush-sided chair evolved a shape with a broad crest-rail over-running the frame and decorative horizontal splat with straight, turned or reeded legs; variations on this design had hooped backs and more decoratively carved horizontal splats, some chairs with 'waisted' back. Machine turning allowed the reproduction of 'Jacobean' chairs with swash-turned stretchers and uprights to backs, but with padded upholstered centres instead of cane. Return to over-stuffed seats for early balloon-back chairs.
Chest and case furniture: Bow-fronted or serpentine, as machine methods of shaping wood improved. Drawers were in cheap Honduras mahogany or oak-sided with mahogany fronts. Cheaper veneered furniture had pine runners.
Design and detail: William IV furniture styles overlap both Regency and Early Victorian, with heavy, solid woods, a tendency to over-ornamentation, the use of Greek and Egyptian motifs, heavy cast-brass ornament and rounded shapes as a result of the growth of the padded upholstery trade. Regency purity of line suffered, as upholstery caused Grecian lines to swell into over-emphasized curves. Stylized brass rosettes, used in the Regency with restraint, were added wantonly as were heavy cast-brass ornaments for mounts. The Victorian mania for copying shows with reproduction Restoration chairs, 'improved' by the substitution of upholstered panels in place of cane. Much veneering, use of tapestries, Berlin woolwork and printed fabrics of all kinds.

Period: 1837–60 – Early Victorian

Influences: Romantic, Gothic and Tudor, Louis XIV style, oriental, Indian, neo-Greek; William Morris, A. Pugin, E.W. Godwin; Strawberry Hill; Great Exhibition 1851; Scottish baronial style. Manufacturers: William Watt, Gillows, Collinson & Lock, W. & A. Smee, J.G. Crace & Sons, Holland & Sons.
Materials: Mahogany for dining-room fur-

niture, rosewood for drawing rooms; beech, birch, yellow-coloured ash, bird's eye maple; painted white and gilt furniture for bedrooms, boudoirs and ballroom chairs. Veneering, French polishing, japanning, papier mâché, ebonizing, stained birch, ash, bentwood; oak for 'Tudor' revival; imported North American softwoods for carcases; iron frames for some seating furniture after the Great Exhibition; iron strap hinges for 'romantic' oak furniture.

Characteristic types of furniture: Machine-carved 'mediaeval' chests, cabinets, Chesterfields, pegged and carved 'romantic' chairs, 'Bible boxes', dressing boxes, 'Tudor' cupboards, 'Jacobean' chairs, Walter Scott-inspired 'romantic' Abbotsford chairs, slab-topped 'refectory' tables with pegged stretchers, button-back tub chairs, deep-buttoned leather or upholstered framed sofas and settees, conversation seats, ottomans; painted deal servants', kitchen and cottage furniture; reclining neo-Greek chairs, flat-fronted chests of drawers, Sutherland drop-leaf tables, military chests, Wellington chests, work tables, sewing tables, loo tables, music stools, Canterburys, Windsor chairs, smokers' bow chairs, cutlery stands, butlers' trays, wine coolers, teapoys, tea caddies, fitted travelling boxes, writing boxes.

Construction: Characterized by two opposing trends: the harking back to romantically mediaeval methods of construction and the increasingly machine-made mass-produced ranges. Wooden dowels and pegs used in great profusion on suitably romantic furniture, which can be easily detected from originals by the fact that both dowels and dowel-holes were machine-made and uniform in size. Machine-turning brought a revival of swash- and bobbin-turned furniture, the former often proclaiming its late origins by the Victorian passion for symmetry resulting in opposing twists: 17th-century twists all turned the same way. Machine-turning is noticeably shallower than hand-turned. Lathe-turned steel and brass screws with sharp points used on almost all furniture, including one-piece bottom boards for drawers screwed to side-pieces. Cheap machine-made furniture was veneered with paper-thin veneer over coarse-grained softwood carcases; better furniture with knotty red pine or cheap imported Honduras mahogany carcases veneered with machine-cut Cuban mahogany or rosewood.

Design and detail: Heavy late Regency furniture lost its crispness by having corners rounded, pedestals made circular instead of triangular. Early modest turning on chair legs became more accentuated and bulbous. Balloon-back chairs developed more nipped-in waists and, for drawing rooms, were made with cabriole legs of short unhappy proportions. Lighter, beechwood, cane-seated bedroom balloon backs are more elegant than elaborately ornamented bulbous-legged parlour versions. Tendency to heaviness in all furniture. Heavy cast-brass ornament, oriental inlay, Berlin work, tapestries, Anglo-Indian ivory inlay, machine-grooved brass inlay, Victorian machine-cut Boulle. Carcase woods and thickness of veneer determine quality. Some fine detail and carving in solid woods. Great Exhibition of 1851 and subsequent exhibitions in Paris, Chicago etc. promoted 'novelty' furniture: cast-iron frames to upholstered seating furniture and papier mâché chairs for example. The Great Exhibition also led to a profusion of Indian-inspired use of fabrics: detailed study of articles from the Great Exhibition is rewarding. In contrast to the overstuffed look of almost all domestic furniture of the period, the clean simple lines of 'campaign' furniture are remarkable: strictly functional, brass-bound chests, desks and canvas-seated chairs in solid wood, unlike the veneered, French-polished drawing room furniture of the period.

Period: 1860–1920 – Late Victorian and Edwardian

Influences: Early Victorian influences continued – almost anything could be and was copied; strong element of 'art furniture' from Arts and Crafts movement, later from Art Nouveau which ran parallel but separate; William Morris, Bruce Talbert, E.W. Godwin, C.R. Ashbee, Ernest Gimson, C.F.A.

Voysey, C.R. Mackintosh, C.R. Eastlake's *Hints on Household Taste in Furniture* (1868), Ambrose Heal. Manufacturers: William Watt, Collinson & Lock, W. & A. Smee, J.G. Crace & Sons, Holland & Sons, Waring & Gillow, Liberty's, Heal's.

Materials: Light oak, stained oak, walnut for drawing-room furniture, ebonized woods, satinwood, machine-cut inlay panels, machine-made Boulle; ceramic and marble tiles, shell inlay, ivory, bone, mother-of-pearl, japanning, bird's eye maple, bamboo, cane, beech, ash; brass galleries, mounts and binding for campaign furniture. As period progresses, more incorporation into furniture of leather, metal, glass, mirrors and ceramics.

Characteristic types of furniture: Military chests and campaign furniture (Colonial and Crimean wars), pine chest furniture with oak-lined drawers, specimen chests, surgeon's fitted chests and cabinets, credenzas, bedside cupboards, pot cupboards, secrétaire-bookcases, bureau-bookcases, display cabinets, oriental lacquered display cabinets, serpentine-fronted inlaid glazed display cabinets, roll-top desks, Davenports, pedestal and ladies' kneehole desks, furniture 'en suite' for drawing rooms, bedrooms and dining rooms, pine washstands, fitted workboxes and travelling cases, writing slopes or lap desks, tantaluses, tea caddies, music stools, bedroom stools, bamboo and cane chairs, stands, conservatory furniture, garden furniture. Country ladder-back, wheelback, stickback, William Morris rush seat and bentwood chairs, Windsor chairs, dressers, Chesterfields. Eccentric furniture purpose-built in strange 'architectural' shapes for redesigned and new houses.

Construction: A schizophrenic period, with a huge output of machine-made furniture and a modest output of hand-made. On the one hand there was little change from the first half of the Victorian period, except for a general tendency to heaviness, bulbous turning, thin veneers and machine-made furniture. Campaign furniture and military furniture soundly constructed on traditional principles; handles and backplates, though machine-made, of fine quality. Tendency towards plain undecorated surfaces with the fashion for draping cloths and antimacassars over tables and chairs. Less sturdy, poorer quality woods for mass-produced carcases and drawers; furniture was screwed together with additional blocks where legs joined seats or table tops, producing an unstretchered line at the expense of durability. Wood was cut in any direction of the grain that suited the machines and much of it soon broke, cracked or warped: there was no time for timber to season. Much poor quality deal or pine furniture for servants' rooms. Hand-made furniture of the period was honestly and well constructed, though use of machine-cut joints and screws was common. Dowelling was frequently used, but its regularity shows the use of machines rather than hand-boring and cutting.

Design and detail: The late Victorian and Edwardian periods cannot be properly separated. Traditional designs, that is, yet more 'Queen Anne' and Regency-style pieces, flourished in the mass market while a design revolution, which is still having a direct impact on today's furniture, was taking place in parallel. In the mass market there was a whirlpool of design trends, in which there is a definite echo of Chippendale's chinoiserie, mixed with the overall design philosophy of the Adam period. Furniture was designed more to embellish and decorate the room than for its function, often resulting in pieces which, divorced from their original surroundings, seem to be made in extraordinary shapes. The mass-produced furniture of this period is characterized by a general decline in quality and design, with the original good intentions of early manufacturers sinking under the growing demand. With the establishment of the Empire, fragments of every culture were incorporated into designs of smaller furniture and used as motifs for decoration. Mother-of-pearl inlay, ivory, tassels, fringes – few things could be left alone, most were over-ornamented and exaggerated. Cast-brass ornament now often replaced with stamped copies in thin metal; ceramic knobs to pine furniture, turned wood knobs for bedroom furniture; ceramic rollers to castors. The best designed and made pieces were those in the oriental manner, though cheap British-made copies quickly debased richly ornate designs from India, China, Korea, Japan and Malaya. The use of ebony and ebonized wood, black lacquer and mourning cherubs' heads in sentimental grief was much in evidence for a considerable period after Prince Albert's death in 1861. Some good existing furniture was stained or painted black as the nation went into elaborate mourning.

In the same year William Morris founded a factory to produce furniture and ornaments with clean, clear lines and honest, simple traditional construction. This was in direct reaction to the mish-mash of derivative, heavy, veneered designs that swamped the market. The influence of Morris and his many collaborators in the Arts and Crafts and Aesthetic movements was powerful upon their successors in 20th-century design, but did little to influence contemporary mass-produced furniture. The inclusion of metal, glass, tiles and painting all into one piece did have some influence however, especially on bathroom and kitchen furniture. It is not properly accurate to label this design revolution Art Nouveau, which was properly a continental phenomenon. English Art Nouveau was much more restrained in its lines, at least in furniture. The decorative motifs of French and German Art Nouveau were however adopted with increasing frequency from continental models after about 1890. The simple 'country' styles reintroduced by the Arts and Crafts movement were to emerge, debased, in mass-market furniture with the Tudor taste of the 1920s.

The Late Victorian and Edwardian periods are interesting, if complex, and although the majority of their products are by definition not antique they are rapidly becoming so.

Price Guide

Chairs (£50–2,500)

Jacobean, Restoration, William & Mary. Oak: twist-turned legs, uprights and H-stretcher, carved front stretcher and crest rail, cane back and seat; often found with upholstered back panel, which means either a later replacement or Victorian copy. Singles in oak with cane backs, about £260; set of six: out of price range. Set of six 19th-century copies from £1,000–£1,800.

William & Mary country versions in beech, walnut, mixed woods, less elaborately carved with plain barred back instead of carved surround and cane back; in oak with wooden seat and plain flat stretchers can be found for £200–300; country walnut £1,200+ for six. Watch out for Victorian and later copies, machine-twist turned with upholstered backs: Victorian machine-twists usually are symmetrical—one leg twists one way, the other in opposite direction: originals have the twist going the same way on all legs.

Single chairs without arms about 70% less. Pairs more than double price of single chairs. Sets very rarely found: should be well outside price range if genuine.

Queen Anne. Walnut: spoon-back, centre splat fixed to backframe with shoe-piece, drop-in seat, curved back, crest rail discreetly carved, cabriole leg, ball-and-claw feet, no stretchers: singles well outside price range.

Oak singles from £450. Good country walnut versions: single £1,500+. Fruitwood, country-made, good quality, now not less than about £2,000 for six. Nineteenth-century walnut copies with ball-and-claw feet if they are of good quality will now be outside the price range for a set of six.

Georgian. Pre-Chippendale, (Virginia) walnut, with pierced splat, shoe-piece and drop-in seat, straight or slightly shaped crest rail, provincial made: £300 for singles.

Country-made oak-and-elm with wooden seats: about £50 single to £200 for pairs. Set of six in beech, ash or fruitwood over £1,000, but their size is rather against them.

Mahogany versions well outside price range. Nineteenth-century copies in mahogany can be found, often with unsightly back stretcher: around £1,000 for a set of six.

Chippendale: Mahogany well outside price range. High quality Victorian copies valued at £200 for six only 15 years ago now fetch up to £2,000, depending on quality. Look for fine carving, cabriole legs and claw-and-ball feet. Contemporary country Chippendale: elm, fruitwood, provincial in mahogany; set of six well outside price range. Wooden seats, saddle-shaped—set of six: £1,200. Surprisingly low appreciation so far. Oak with fretted back-splat—set of six: around £1,500.

Chippendale ladder-back: well outside price range. Country made, from original design, made around the turn of the 19th century, elm or oak with rush seats, set of six: £1,250; ash and elm with wooden seats: £600. Gothic designs—their size can be a drawback —go for about £200 each.

Hepplewhite: Mahogany, classic style, *c.* 1790, pierced splats, shoe-piece, over-stuffed seats, slightly tapered leg, pair: £750. Not so popular; low appreciation.

Wheatsheaf design, drop-in seat, shoe-piece, untapered legs, set of six: out of price range after recent good appreciation.

Camel-back country Hepplewhite 'wheat-sheaf' in elm originally stained or varnished to look like mahogany, have probably been recently stripped, set of six: £2,000.

Oak, wooden seat, full-width shoe-piece, untapered legs, country-made Hepplewhite, set of six: £1,800. Considerable appreciation over recent years.

Many copies made up to mid-19th century: beware Hepplewhite wheel-back reproductions; originals had dished or bowed seats and shoe-piece. Reproductions should be in the region of £850–1,000 for six.

Shield-back: legs should be unstretchered, back frame supports shield; spade feet, curved front seat frame, over-stuffed seats, well outside price range. Even good 19th-century copies are fetching over £1,200 for set of six.

Note: Correct proportions set out in Hepplewhite pattern book: depth of seat 17ins, front width 20ins, height of seat frame 17ins, total chair height about 37ins.

Sheraton: Mahogany, square shape to back, slightly curved and tapered legs, drop-in seats and stretchers, some reeding on crest rail and uprights: outside price range. Simplest provincial-made: around £1,250 for six, low appreciation. Oak-and-elm, country-made: around £700–800 for six with better appreciation.

'Suffolk' chairs with horizontal back-splat, plain or bobbined in mixed woods; elm seat with oak or sycamore can be found for around £1,250–1,500 for six with good appreciation. Rush seats less at £800–1,200 for six.

Sheraton X-back, unstretchered, square-sectioned, tapered front legs, reeded backs, over-stuffed seats: well outside price range. This design has been put together with Sheraton's delicate cane-seated painted white-and-gilt chair with round section reeded legs and X-stretcher to produce many later versions of the X-back, which was a far more solid chair. Victorian and Edwardian copies and reproductions abound with bad propor-

Good plain late Georgian country-made Hepplewhite chairs. Part of a set of one elbow chair and five singles, of consistently dark laburnum wood. Made about 1780, perhaps in Scotland.

tions and over-turned front legs and H-stretchers.

Modern reproductions in ebonized wood, turned spindle leg and H-stretchers cost from £150–200 each; S-arms around £200; the best are hand-made, in the upper price range.

Late 18th-century transitional design with tapering turned legs, broad crest rail and horizontal splat, often rope-twist, unstretchered round-section legs, slightly tapered with over-stuffed seats: now well outside price range with recent surge of appreciation.

Elm and beech wheelback Windsor chair with turned legs and arm supports, mid-19th century.

Thomas Hope 'Trafalgar': Mahogany, sabre-leg, flush-frame construction, rope-twist crest rail, unstretchered square-section tapered legs, drop-in seats: sets now well outside price range, though uneven rise in value, actually depreciating in the first five years of the last decade, then rising sharply.

Modern reproduction rope-backs are around £600 for a set of six second-hand, but note that sabre-legged chairs involved the careful cutting of timber, using natural spring; reproductions seldom have the same original thickness of timber from which the leg is cut, and legs break easily down the grain.

Lyre-backed chairs: with reeded legs and curved side-rail: example of vagaries of taste—sets of six rose in value early in 1970s to £650, then dropped in price and are now £1,000 +. If your heart is set on Regency chairs, consider making a harlequin set: the flush-frame construction and even height lends itself to near matches. Singles can be found at about the same price as modern reproductions second-hand: around £100. Sets of six are well outside price range except for the less popular lyre-back.

Quantities of 'rout' chairs in beech, birch and pine, painted, of X-back derivation, were made for Regency balls and social functions. Singles of these with recaned seats are around £50–60.

Windsor chairs. Yew, yew and elm, early Windsors with curved centre stretcher and cabriole legs rare and a long way out of the price range. Construction of solid, saddle-shaped seat into which legs and back were fixed. From 1755 attempts to make design grander by incorporating simplified versions of Chippendale, wheatsheaf, Prince of Wales feathers and wheelback. All chairs with yew arms are more expensive. Yew and elm, cabriole leg, curved stretcher: around £800–1,200 with considerable recent appreciation. Simple stick-back, elm and fruitwood: £400–600.

Late 18th-century yew and elm with decorative centre splat: £600–850. Original wheelback in yew, recent huge appreciation, now up to £1,500; plain comb-back yew have recently soared towards £850.

Nineteenth-century straight stretchers with reel-turned legs: from £250–400 depending on wood.

Smokers' Bow, 19th-century, with arm-hoop made from several pieces screwed together and not in a solid piece—correct construction of the period; elm, pine, beech: £250–400.

Single chairs: plain stick-back: £45–60; sets of six: £400–500.

Lancashire slat-back or turned stick-back, sets of six: £400–600.

Plain Victorian bar-back, matching sets of six if they can be found: £1,800+.

William IV. Rosewood, simulated rosewood, mahogany; crest rail over-runs chair frame of flush construction; legs were round-sectioned, unstretchered, reeded and turned; drop-in seat; carved horizontal splat: a recent and, to some, surprising increase in value has brought sets of six nudging the top of the price range. There was a time when the rather clumsy front legs were replaced with sabre legs to increase their value but this period seems to be doing very nicely in its own right today. Many versions of these chairs with original legs and undecorated horizontal splats can still be found. Set of four: £1,200–1,500, but a set of six will be out of the price range. Watch for those with replaced legs and other alterations.

If the crest rail over-runs and they are sabre-legged, examine closely as they may have been remade. Provincial-made genuine articles with original legs and with stretchers are a bit cheaper than London-made (no stretchers), £2,250 for six.

About 1830, more fluid, French-inspired chair with curving crest rail and upholstered back, seat often upholstered in leather: £2,400 for six; rather cheaper if needing new upholstery, cleaning off and polishing. Hoop backs £1,200 for six.

Awkward cabriole leg or heavier reeded leg, often with castors: £2,250 for six; mahogany or rosewood (but watch out for veneering as opposed to solid wood), plainer versions, often with happier scrolled feet or turned legs still have upholstered squarish seats; open-backed without upholstery are more expensive: around £2,400 for six, depending on quality of wood and carving.

Early Victorian. Early balloon-back with mildly nipped-in waist, curved seat frame and turned or cabriole leg with scroll feet, sets of six: around £2,250. Look for manufacturer's name 'Gillow' on good ones, but expect to pay more.

Later balloon-back with well-rounded, waisted backs and increasingly bulbous legs, decreasing in value according to design and proportion. Light plain versions in beech, originally for bedrooms, with stretchered legs, can be found for as little as £700–900 for six.

Round-backed chairs with circular panels of Berlin-type woolwork and seats are identifiably Early Victorian and, if needlework is original, value is increased. Singles around £250; sets of six (unusual as they were parlour chairs): around £2,250.

Prie-dieu high-backed chair: usually in not very good condition, but quite fun to have around in hall or living room; recent considerable appreciation, £250–300 in poor condition, £550–750 in good condition.

Late Victorian and Edwardian. William Morris stained beech with rush seats, no appreciable investment value, since these chairs have been made continuously since mid-19th century. Current prices for new ones best guide to a straight second-hand bargain.

Art Nouveau high back curiosity in inlaid oak, four for up to £1,000 with recent appreciation.

Clean-cut versions of classical mahogany dining chairs with dipped top rails, *c.* 1910, going up fast to around £2,000 for eight. If interested in this period, study works of movements, individual designers listed (on page 26) under this period and use a crystal ball. Investment value depends on fashion to a large extent.

Tables (£150–2,500)

Dining Tables

Mediaeval, Tudor. Oak: early oak refectory tables have soared well outside the price range from their modest prices of 15 years ago. The only available tables of this design are Victorian 'Tudor' with heavy bulbous legs and even they are nudging £2,500 or more. With some searching, country-made work tables can be ferreted out, plain trestle-type tables or plain square-stretcher tables for between £1,200 and £1,500 depending on size, the bigger the cheaper. Look for good stout worm-free timbers and good-condition top surfaces with few joints in the width. Ideally this type of table is made from as few planks as possible and for this reason they tend to be rather narrow for their length. Wood contracts across the grain, not along it: a guide to age for tables with a cross-piece at either end is that the width of the table has contracted with age: flush clamp ends and sides could mean that the top is new or has been cut. Tables in elm or fruitwoods such as apple are equally collectable.

Jacobean. Gate-leg tables in oak: here the price depends to a great extent on convenience of size: six-seater gate-legs being well outside the price range if they are of any quality. Smaller ones, measuring about 3ft across when closed, opening to 3ft × 4ft are around £600, rising to £1,200 depending on the quality of the turning, age and condition. Watch for replaced leaves: there should be signs of wear where the gate has held up the leaf, and handling will have caused parts of the underside to be darker with a slight patina compared with the rest of the underside which should be untreated, paler and slightly dusty. The tops should be pegged, not screwed, through the underframe. Larger sizes out of price range.

Queen Anne. Walnut, veneer, quartering, marquetry: well outside price range.

Georgian. Drop-leaf mahogany: £850+ depending on quality. Larger country Georgian period drop-leaf tables in oak can be found for £500–600, but watch for signs of restoration.

Late Georgian drop-leaf tables of smaller size, about 4ft × 4ft 6ins, can be found, also in oak, at £250+. Late 18th-century pine cottage tables, 7ft × 3ft, plain, £250+. 5ft × 3ft proportionately less, at £200+. *Note:* Modern reproduction drop-leaf tables 'in the Sheraton manner' cost over £400.

William IV and Early Victorian. The 19th century saw a proliferation of cheval-constructed drop-leaf tables known as 'Sutherlands' with tops which are often very attractive, in burr-walnut veneer or figured walnut. The ardent efforts of the Victorians to achieve 'authenticity' often resulted in swash-turned or bobbin-turned legs, albeit machine-turned, which may be preferable to the end-pillar legs, where turning, reeding and fluting is often on the heavy side. Still a good buy for £450–600. Appreciation has been considerable over the last five years.

Breakfast tables, supper tables, 'tip-top' tables, loo tables

Tilt-top tables suitable for use as small dining tables.

Late Georgian and Regency. Rectangular in solid mahogany with splayed legs and brass paw feet are out of the price range. Plainer versions around £2,000.

Late Regency, Early Victorian in rosewood or amboyna veneer, some just within the price range at around £2,250. *Note:* Copies of Regency splay-foot circular-topped tables made around 1900 are fetching £1,000+.

Victorian. The most spectacularly decorated marquetry tilt-tops have already slipped out of the price range. In burr walnut, rosewood, flame walnut, coromandel, mahogany veneer they are £400 upwards, depending on quality. Ovals fetch less than circular.

Loo tables in plain veneers of the same woods also show recent appreciation and are currently in broad band of £1,500–2,500 depending on quality, lightness of style and decoration. Round tip-top breakfast tables, measuring about 5ft across, are between £850 and £1,500. Shaped, oval and rectangular are less.

Centre tables
Not usually suitable for dining tables because of their deep frieze below the table top. Some ornately decorated 'oriental' Victorian examples lack this frieze and though the tripod base may be over-ornate are fair value at about £700–800.

Side tables
All side tables have blank backs because they were designed to stand against the wall.

Georgian. Good quality side-tables with walnut frames and marble tops, originally made in pairs, can be found as singles for £2,500.

Late 17th- and 18th-century with turned legs and stretchers in elm, oak, usually good proportions and solid craftsmanship: £850–1,850.

Country oak furniture following grand designs of Chippendale and Hepplewhite; side tables are still excellent value at around £600–850 but must be in prime condition with original tops for any investment value.

Mahogany, with plain square or chamfered legs, £800–1,200. Plain, in oak, same period, from £450.

Georgian pine functional side tables, often pleasantly proportioned and hard-wearing, £150. Beware Late Victorian softwood side-tables with replaced legs. Strictly kitchen pieces, they had turned bulbous legs and were made of inferior pine. Secondhand value only.

Victorian. 'Sheraton' side tables usually thinly veneered and too spindly for anything but display, which is what they were intended for. Often serpentine-fronted and quite elegant, fetching considerable prices nevertheless: £350–450. D-shaped or 'demilune' side tables, usually in pairs in satinwood veneer were made from Late Georgian to Edwardian. The catch is the Edwardian copy, imported in quantities from France, with machine-cut inlay which lifts very easily, warps, and is poor quality. Genuine Late Georgian satinwood, £2,000+, depending on quality.

Oak tip-top tripod table, late 18th century.

Pembroke tables
Two-flap tables with side drawer.
Georgian mahogany, very handsome and elegant, £1,500+.

Late 18th-century mahogany or rosewood with some inlay decoration: £1,500–2,000.

Sheraton period satinwood: out of range.

Early 19th-century in plain mahogany, undecorated, solid and stable: £550–800.

The Victorians preferred 'demilune' and reduced the pretty Pembroke to an uncompromising two-flap, often with castors, all-purpose household table.

Card tables
In general, anything before mid-18th century well outside price range, and 'demilune' or

Late 18th or early 19th century elm two-flap table in a simple country form.

halfmoon card tables can be more expensive than square.

Chippendale period: with straight chamfered leg and foldover top in solid mahogany still well within price range after little escalation in last five years: £800–1,500.

George II. Cabriole leg with pad feet and concertina action pull-out supporting legs are at the very top of the range, justifiably because of their beautiful craftsmanship, and are therefore unlikely to be found within the price range.

Versions of this neat and elegant table were made as tea tables with polished surfaces. If baize has been added, look for a poor quality cross-banded edge. All the same, they may cost as much as £1,500.

George III. Rectangular Hepplewhite and Sheraton designs in mahogany with spade feet: good value at £450–800, but suspect surfaces as in previous paragraph.

Regency. Satinwood veneer, opening to a square shape with rounded corners, were much sought after 15 years ago but became unfashionable until recently; now experiencing considerable appreciation: £800–1,500.

D-shaped: often originally made in pairs with fine satinwood cross-banding on mahogany veneer, not much under £2,000.

Good Regency card tables have soared outside the range, particularly those with fine design and inlay on both inside and outside surfaces. Even the late Regency splay-foot is at least £1,000.

William IV. Regency revival pillar-and-claw, noticeably heavier than originals, at a reasonable price of around £750, with quality marks added for fine figured wood veneer, mahogany veneer, carved solid rosewood centre pillar.

Victorian. Heavy pillar-and-claw pattern. Carving detail on the pillar and scrolled or paw feet increase value. Also quality of veneering, which can be fine and in a variety of woods: burr-walnut, figured walnut, rosewood. Machine-cut marquetry used to good effect, and prices still reasonable at £400–800.

Edwardian. Satinwood reproductions, inlaid or painted in the manner of Sheraton's finest work, were mass-produced over a long period and are easily identifiable by paper-thin veneer and unstable spindly legs. The only interesting revival was the envelope card table, first made in the 18th century. Some Edwardian versions were quite well designed and made and have recently appreciated quite considerably to lift them into the £500–700 bracket. However, many of them were made of unsuitable wood which tends to warp, thus lifting the thin veneer.

Sideboards (£550–2,500)

Sheraton: Genuine period sideboards may well be within price limit because of their enormous size, over 6ft 6ins long: £1,000+. Victorian 'Sheraton' often same price and therefore likely to be less good value. Do not be misled by lead-lined drawer, apparently a sign of genuineness: the Victorians used them too. Look for paper-thin machine-cut veneer, spindly legs, wrong proportions of the latter.

Smaller bow-front genuine period Sheraton well outside price range if dated before 1800.

Nineteenth-century Sheraton-style small mahogany bow-front at around £550–750; so ceaselessly copied that reproductions in veneered chipboard are still being manufactured today.

Dressers and Dresser bases (£500–2,500)

Nineteenth-century James I-type oak dressers, £1,200–1,500.

William & Mary oak dresser base and others from 18th century with original tops missing, still very handsome, from around £2,000.

Eighteenth-century oak low dressers measuring about 5ft 6ins with single drawer, from around £2,000.

Georgian oak low dresser with three drawers: now out of price range.

Welsh dressers: by definition country pieces, though the best are extremely grand and expensive. Even relatively humble ones are towards the top of the range, at between £2,000 and £2,500.

Parlour pieces in oak, beech and ash of varying quality range from £1,000 upwards for the very best. The lower prices often indicate considerable restoration.

Nineteenth-century heavy Lincolnshire-style dressers, usually on the large side, can be found in varying condition from £800 upwards.

Prices for pine dressers vary according to size, as with sideboards: the bigger the cheaper. 6ft wide × 6ft 6ins high with fielded panel doors below: £600–850. 6ft 6ins wide × 8ft high somewhat less. Plain 18th-century pine kitchen dressers with three drawers and two plain cupboards: £500–750. Good Georgian natural pine with moulding and decorations significantly more at around £1,500+. Should be less though if it has been painted and then stripped. Useful sign of age is that scrubbing of kitchen floors will probably have rotted the base: if there is no visible rot, look for repair pieces let in.

Side cupboards (£300–600)

Pine kitchen, passage or pantry pieces, but watch for remade dresser bases.

Nineteenth-century side cupboard with

A pine dresser, probably 19th century. Check the bottom corners for signs of wear indicating age.

flight of three drawers and single cupboard: £300–400.

60ins long with centre cupboard and two flights of drawers flanking: £400–600.

48ins long of similar design (better size for today's living): £500–700.

72ins long around £400–600.

Upholstered Furniture (£450–2,500)

Settees, sofas, couches

Settees, couches, daybeds and sofas, up to the late Regency period, with hard horse-hair upholstery, following designs in period pattern books, are outside price range because of their scarcity. This in part was due to their fragile construction, and in part to their wholesale scrapping with the advent of padded upholstery and sprung furniture.

Late Georgian settees in unrestored condition can be found at less than £1,500.

William IV and Victorian. The bulk of upholstered furniture within the price range comes from this period.

Most popular were the chaise-longue shapes in rosewood or mahogany with undulating back and scooped sides with serpentine front and cabriole legs. Solid walnut, rosewood or mahogany frames, considerably 'rescued' and reupholstered: £1,500–£2,000.

Grecian-style daybeds of this period, often with splay feet and brass inlay, have appreciated enormously over the last few years and are now out of the price range, but not very comfortable with old-fashioned horse-hair upholstery. The deep plain shape degenerated with the addition of bulbous turned legs; they are around in battered condition for second-hand prices.

Chesterfields were also popular, but there is little merit in acquiring one other than for its second-hand value, since the same model has been in almost continuous production since the early 1820s.

Easy chairs and button-backs

As with ballon-backed dining, salon, parlour and bedroom chairs, the appeal of these button-backs is partly their amazing comfort.

Mahogany, walnut, rosewood carved frame with open arms, cabriole legs and stuffed back and seat. Enormous appreciation over the last few years, now cost around £800–1,000. The first of the button-backs, not yet complicated by reproductions.

With upholstered arms, carved frame, cabriole legs but with less decorative framework: £450–750.

'Grandfather' or salon chair with scooped back, plain rounded back frame of rosewood, mahogany or walnut, the best with block arms, short cabriole leg: up to £1,250, fully restored and upholstered.

'Grandmother' spoon-backed ladies' chair without arms, decorative rosewood frame, still going up and costing anywhere between £800 and £1,200 depending on condition. Iron frames mean lower prices.

Horseshoe-backed 'smokers' chair' with open arms, turned rosewood supports and legs: up to £550; Edwardian versions with raised padded backs considerably cheaper.

Tub chairs, nursing chairs with low seats, padded spoon backs: around £450–£650.

Iron-framed tub chairs made following the Great Exhibition are of curiosity value at a slightly lower price. *Note:* Reproductions of these popular little chairs with foam upholstery cost from £100.

Chest Furniture (£80–2,500)

Note: Study drawer detail, frame and carcase construction, carcase woods of the period, thickness of veneer, drawer handle detail. Appearances often deceive. Many pieces of plain and honest country chest furniture have recently received veneering to add appeal and increase prices. Watch too for 'marriages,' particularly in early period of chest-on-chest or chest-on-stand: new tops on bottom halves of chests-on-chests, Victorian or later stands to chests-on-stands. Beware Victorian 'Tudor' at all times: its construction will give it away.

17th century: Small oak country-made chests from the 17th century are fairly common, usually with three flights of paired drawers (frame construction) but have been subjected to considerable restoration: new tops, drawers, feet. The best are in two halves, but marriages are common: between £500 and £2,500. Chest-on-stand in oak, 4ft 6ins high, stand replaced: £1,000–1,500. Country-made oak on restored original stand, rather more.

Queen Anne and Early Georgian. Walnut: outside price range. '18th-century' chests at low prices have often been made up from larger pieces. Good value for around £500–700 but little prospect of appreciation. 18th-century pine clothes presses: built-in wardrobes with double doors over three drawers of varying size, often originally built without backs, large (72ins high × 57ins wide): £500+. Late 18th-century with poorer workmanship, about the same size: around £500.

Georgian. Mid-18th-century flat-fronted chests of drawers in mahogany over £1,000. Lower prices most often indicate large size, much restoration, replaced tops, new aprons and feet. Searching can be well rewarded with country pieces of good proportions made in elm, fruitwood, oak with pine-lined drawers for around £400–600.

Eighteenth-century chests-of-drawers may well be bottom halves of chests-on-chests or tops of chests-on-stands with new feet. If the former, the outer line often flares slightly to match the original top. Between £500 and £650, but not worth the price if new top is added to bottom half of chest-on-chest.

Late 18th-century walnut 'marriage' of well-matching chest-on-chest: £700–850. Intact survivals should be well outside the price range.

Late 18th-century bachelors' chests now out of price range. *Note:* Reproduction bachelors' chests in 'yew wood finish' of thin veneer on chipboard are over £350.

Nineteenth-century reproductions of Chippendale-style chests-on-chests can be more than £1,000, but markedly less graceful of proportion than original design.

Regency. This period is governed by size except for the finest pieces. Most furniture was large. A George III chest-on-chest would be around 70ins high × 48ins wide: in handsome bow-front mahogany with satinwood cross-banding, well over £1,000. Smaller pieces by Sheraton and Shearer have been reproduced almost continuously; the originals are well outside price range.

Mahogany tallboys are around for low prices, not surprisingly with measurements of over 6ft tall and 3ft 6ins wide: £750 upwards, good value and appreciating recently.

Early mahogany wardrobes with mock drawers in doors to look like tallboys are interesting but large. 78ins high × 50 ins wide with interior fittings still intact: well in excess of £1,000. In order to accommodate full-length hanging space many presses have been stripped of interior fittings, bottom drawers have been removed and left false-fronted. Genuine bow-fronts and serpentine-fronts with handsome architectural pediments outside price range.

Military chests: flush-fitting drawer-handles, brass-reinforced corners, often made in two pieces fitting together: mahogany, teak, padouk, cedar and camphorwood. Prices of these soared in the early 1970s but reproductions and made-up pieces have brought values down. Best prices well over £1,000 for fitted details, helmet drawer, secretaire drawer etc. Some still around £400–600; more for good woods, detail etc. An awkward size for every-day use.

Victorian mahogany veneer bow-front chest with original handles.

William IV. Size keeps prices relatively low. Most linen presses, clothes presses, wardrobes are over 6ft tall. Preference for fitted built-in cupboards in today's houses keeps price down: between £500 and £800.

Victorian. Small furniture fetches more than more cumbersome though well-made Victorian chest furniture. Best value are plain bow-fronted mahogany-veneered chests-of-drawers on solid imported Honduras mahogany carcases from £250 with turned wooden knob handles and two top drawers. More for ones with finer detail: ivory escutcheons, stamped brass handles. Watch as usual for replaced tops due to cracking in over-heated rooms or re-veneering. Better quality: £850–1,250. Drawers with bottoms of one-piece pine—keep an eye out for veneered oak country carcases. Knotty red pine and mahogany were the only timbers used at that period. Oak carcases could indicate later veneering or Continental origin. Pine chests mostly date from this period, porcelain handles or turned wood, some quite prettily made with bracket feet, shaped aprons, often with new brass handles but none the worse for that: £150–400. Good modern reproductions are about the same price. Less functional, with fewer deeper drawers and bulgy turned legs: £80–150.

Late 19th-century pine wardrobes or linen presses: £250–500. Modern reproductions: about £300. *(Note:* Excellently made solid pine reproduction furniture recently on the market threatens the appreciation of less well made earlier pieces, although the reproduction is likely to cost a little more than the original.) Wellington chests; specimen cabinets with hinged side-pieces to prevent drawers opening in transit, from the

1850s in walnut veneer, plain rosewood, mahogany, maple and oak; value increased by specially fitted drawers, decorative veneers, bracket detail: big recent appreciation, probably because of their usefulness for storing papers: best between £600 and £1,800.

Fin de siècle, Edwardian. Mostly reproductions of 'Sheraton' in unlikely satinwood veneer or characteristic mahogany veneer cross-banded with satinwood. Thin veneers a giveaway. Also imported satinwood veneered furniture and considerable use of ormolu mounts. This period is generally easily recognizable by its over-refined and wavering line. Good quality workmanship and materials against contemporary prices best guide. Even the pine furniture of this age is poor.

Case Furniture (£100–2,500)

Display Cabinets

Earliest within price range are William IV or Victorian. Smaller pieces in these periods already climbing fast out of reach.

Victorian. Standing display cabinets, probably one of their happiest and best designs, just under 3 ft in height with brass gallery, ormolu or cast-brass mounts, glass doors and sides, in burr walnut, bird's eye maple or figured veneers in exotic woods: £600–1,000 with considerable recent appreciation. The most spectacular are Victorian Boulle or brass-inlaid rosewood or ebonized wood, with marble tops: still £1,400–2,000.

Also wide range of Indian and oriental small chest cabinets, trinket cabinets, notably handsome brass-mounted Korean in black lacquer with decorative strap hinges: £850–2,000. Many were mass-produced 'in the oriental manner' and are in poor condition, but a few decorative pieces are around for under £200.

Edwardian. Some of the best pieces of this period are the satinwood glass-fronted display cabinets, painted in the French classical manner with swags, drapes and medallions. The proportions are a little top-heavy because of the fashion for thin, tapered legs and most have been ignored until recently when good quality cabinets have become desirable and 18th- and even 19th-century pieces are out of reach. Take note of quality: best pieces over £1,000.

Later versions of Victorian standing display cabinets raised on the inevitable Edwardian spindly tapered legs, often with faint 'oriental' overtones; not so neat or so stable: £250 upwards with higher prices for ornament and veneer decoration.

Curiosities of this period are numerous: watch for 'art furniture' with curious combinations of woods, metal inlays, lacquers, enamels, often with a distinct Japanese air. They need hunting for and recognizing; very high prices are being paid for the best, well outside the price range but with erratic appreciation. Edwardian curiosities are now going for £500+. Taste and pocket are the truest guides.

Corner Cupboards

17th century. Not many made. Extant examples are usually large and carved in same style as dressers of the period. Standing, sometimes two halves, many built into panelling in custom of the day. If they survive intact, with original hinges, fittings, backs, well outside price range. More elaborately carved tops alone have often been converted to hanging corner cupboards with considerable restoration. No glazed fronts of this period, therefore utility appeal, limited investment value: £600–800, but at this price part of extensive panelled work and therefore not a 'whole' piece.

Queen Anne. Walnut with glazed doors well beyond reach. Country made, block-fronted, in oak, elm or fruitwood: from £700. More for original brass H-hinges, detail, patination, good woods. Veneered walnut, often bow-fronted, out of price range.

Bow-fronted English lacquer or japanning in chinoiserie taste of the day, probably the top halves of original tall standing cupboards; very decorative: £750–2,000.

Georgian. (Virginia) walnut, mahogany, fruitwood, country oak, probably originally designed for stands if below £500. Watch for lack of bottom mouldings and flares to fit former stand.

Mahogany, elegant architectural shapes with fluted columns, moulded or broken pediments: with glazed doors outside price range. Block-fronted can be found at £1,250–2,000. Watch for restoration, replaced backs. Late 18th-century block-front pine corner cupboards, often built-in originally and therefore with replacement backs (indicates part of larger suite of built-in cupboards) £850–1,500; less if stripped.

Small 18th-century hanging corner cupboards with block-fronts £250–450 and somewhat more for period country-made oak.

A full height pine corner cupboard, unusual in that it has just the one door. Probably 19th century.

Regency. Standing corner cupboards with brass grill-fronts are dubious. Many of them are French of a considerably later date. Also widely copied in ebonized wood and brass by Victorians. So too are the 'Sheraton' style mahogany corner cupboards inlaid with satinwood. Both should be viewed with suspicion if less than £750.

Pine standing corner cupboards with fan-shaped fluting, original shelves, often made with block-front doors for pantries, or plain glazed doors, from £1,500 to out of price range. This design has been subject to much plagiarism in a wide variety of sizes, which will tend to damage long-term appreciation.

Note: Small reproduction solid pine half-glazed standing corner cupboards: £250–500.

Victorian. Oriental lacquer flat-fronted corner cupboards, not to be confused with Queen Anne, usually over-ornate with lattice or decorated pierced hinges, block-fronted and decorative, many in the Anglo-Indian taste with inlaid ivory, mother-of-pearl, with good workmanship and materials: £150–450. Stripped pine: many hanging corner shelves, originally part of suite of kitchen or pantry fittings, without doors: £100 or less.

Note: Open-shelved solid pine modern reproduction corner cupboards: £50–150. Reproduction 'yew wood' finish glassfronted corner cupboards from £150.

Country-made 19th-century oak corner cupboards in considerable quantities and varying qualities: glazed doors more expensive at £700–950; block front: £550–800. Also in fruitwood at slightly higher prices.

Edwardian. Most interesting are the 'architectural' or Japanese-style corner cupboards often of eccentric shape and mixed materials; prices vary wildly according to condition and design, and can be anything from £150–1,500.

Standing corner cupboards, glazed doors, satinwood, painted or machine inlay, as for display cupboards (see page 39).

Kitchen pine corner cupboards: craftsmanship and materials best guide against current reproduction prices. Glass-fronted modern reproduction solid pine: £150–170. Look for non-functional glazing bars and yellowish tinge to wood: plain pine has a soft golden honey colour.

Desk and Writing Furniture (£80–2,500)

Desks, Secrétaires and Bureau-bookcases

17th century. Fall-front escritoires on stands, often of beautiful marquetry work well outside price range. Those desks that are within price range seem incredibly cheap before close inspection, when they turn out to be 'marriages' of writing slopes or travelling desks on top of side-tables or chest-of-drawers of same period. Appreciation potential low unless decorative. Around £750–1,000.

William & Mary and Queen Anne. Walnut desks and Queen Anne bureau-bookcases well outside range. Fall-front secrétaires of this period to be viewed with suspicion if within price range. Frequent marriages of Victorian 'Tudor' stands and fall-front top sections.

Georgian. Secrétaires with shallow fall-fronts often concealed as mock drawer. Should have top flight of drawers, but frequently replaced with glazed door bookcase top or block-front door of later date. If less than £1,000 this is probably the case. True bureau-bookcases with sloping fall-fronts well outside range. Eighteenth-century country-made oak, elm, or fruitwood slope-fronted desks around £500–1,500 with some appreciation. Less convenient than kneehole desks of the period, which are well outside price range.

Plain late Georgian nine-drawer kneehole desk with original handles. The drawers are oak-lined and their fronts are cock beaded.

Late Georgian, Regency. Genuine examples outside price range and are large, like other library furniture of the period. Country-made or provincial partners' desks also on the large side but reasonable at £1,500–2,500.

Best bet for small-sized desks (though hard to find) are early 19th-century campaign or military secrétaires at around £1,500–2,500.

Some nice later Georgian pine pedestal two-flight 6-drawer desks at around £1,500–2,000.

Regency rosewood writing tables: between £1,500 and £2,500; more with brass inlay.

Grand Carlton House desks, good quality 19th-century reproductions are now in excess of £2,000.

William IV. Most writing furniture large and sombre. Exceptions are ladies' pedestal desks of convenient size: £2,000+.

Knee-hole desks with heavy ormolu handles and mounts, often inlaid, out of price range. Plainer versions from £1,500.

Regency Davenports: compact low desks assumed to be designed for ladies, named after Captain Davenport who had this design made by Gillows in the late 18th century. It was repeated for 100 years or more. Earliest models straightforward with mock drawers at side, cupboard below, often with small brass gallery: veneered in satinwood, rosewood, mahogany, burr walnut: beware if priced under £1,000.

Victorian Davenports more ornate and less well proportioned. Best piano tops over £1,500; later, plainer versions £750–1,000.

Pine pedestal desks with two flights of four drawers: £400–700; poorer quality ones with three-drawer flights: £300–500.

Victorian. Ladies' cylinder desks or tambour fronts in rosewood or mahogany have pleasing proportions at the expense of stability; not much investment value: prices around £600–700.

Note: 4-drawer mahogany-finish writing desk modern reproductions (second-hand): about £400. Reproduction modern 'yew finish' bureau-bookcase: £700.

Library Tables

Library tables of late Regency design, elongated rectangular on central stretcher and cheval support are a little large at 5ft but provide plenty of desk-space if no drawers. Appreciating: £225 ten years ago, now out of price range.

Victorian writing tables, grandly called 'bureaux-plats', rather despised but better proportioned, unostentatious pieces which provide writing space and two drawers in frieze, good value at £1,500+.

Edwardian library tables not that much less: £800–1,000.

Writing Slopes, Writing Boxes

Travelling desks, often erroneously called 'Bible boxes', few of which survived. Slope-fronted oak copies made in Victorian 'Tudor' period and still around for under £100.

18th century. Resurgence of popularity of travelling furniture, usually made to fold up like a box, fitted inside, usually with at least one secret drawer. Rare to find in genuine hand-cut Boulle and expensive.

Regency. Writing slopes in rosewood or mahogany, often with elegant scrolled supports and fitted pigeonholes along the back, recently appreciating: now £175–500.

Plainer versions of campaign-style writing boxes with brass-bound corners: £80–175.

William IV. Some very fine examples in satinwood veneer inlaid with ivory or mother-of-pearl: around £300–600.

Early Victorian. Anglo-Indian and lacquer with decorative shellwork, Victorian Tunbridge ware and machine-cut brass inlay varying from £80–£300 depending on decoration and quality.

Brass inlaid rosewood, extremely decorative: £225–500.

Furniture Terms

Acanthus see **Decoration**

Anthemion see **Decoration**

Apron Panel immediately below frame of table-top or chair seat, or below chest of drawers between the front legs.

Arabesque see **Decoration**

Armoire Large cupboard of a kind originally made for storing armour, now used to describe many large cupboards with decorative panels, usually French.

Arts and Crafts Movement Movement away from mass-produced to hand-crafted designs, influential from 1860s under the aegis of William Morris.

Bachelor's chest Low chest of drawers, with top opening out to writing surface; from 18th century.

Back plate Brass or ormolu plate on to which the handle of drawer or cupboard is fixed.

Bail handle Half hoop like a slightly flattened miniature bucket handle.

Balloon back see **Chairbacks**

Baluster see **Legs**

Banding Strips of veneer set round the edges of tables, drawer fronts etc; when the grain of the banding runs at right angles to the grain of the main surface it is called 'cross-banding' and if the veneer is arranged in a herringbone pattern it is 'feather banding'.

Barleysugar twist Turned in the shape of twisted barleysugar; also known as twist-turned, swash-turned.

Baroque Ornate style, grandly ornamented, particularly of Restoration period and up to 1730s.

Baywood Mahogany.

Berlin work Pictorial embroidery in great popularity from 1830s almost to the end of the century.

Bible box Small lidded box, often oak, with some shallow carving, originally mediaeval but copied, heavily carved, by Victorians and Edwardians.

Block front Solid-fronted (cabinet, bookcase, bureau-bookcase) as opposed to glass-fronted.

Block foot see **Feet**

Board construction see **Construction**

Bobbin see **Decoration**

Bolt and fork Brass or steel plate and socket used to join leaves of tables together.

Bombé Term used chiefly of commodes and chests to describe fronts swelling out in a curve towards the bottom: a D-shape when seen from the side.

Bonheur du jour Small writing desk of light, elegant construction, with long tapered legs.

Boulle (boule, buhl) Originally tortoise-shell inset with brass or silver; later versions usually rosewood.

Bow front Convex shape of fronts of chests, commodes, etc.

Bracket foot see **Feet**

Breakfront Bookcases, display cabinets, etc. with centre section set forward from two side wings.

Chairbacks

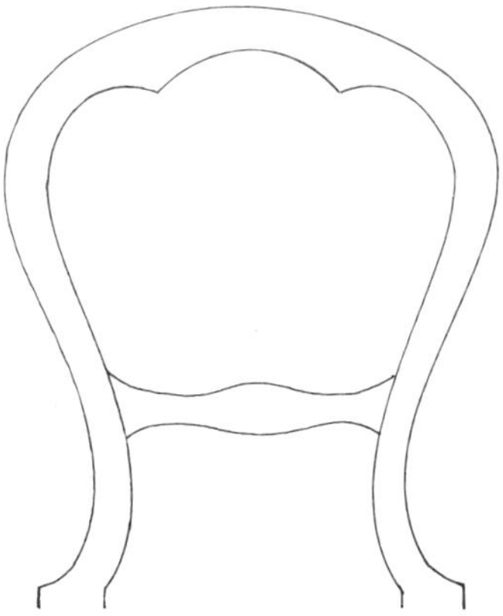

balloon

camel

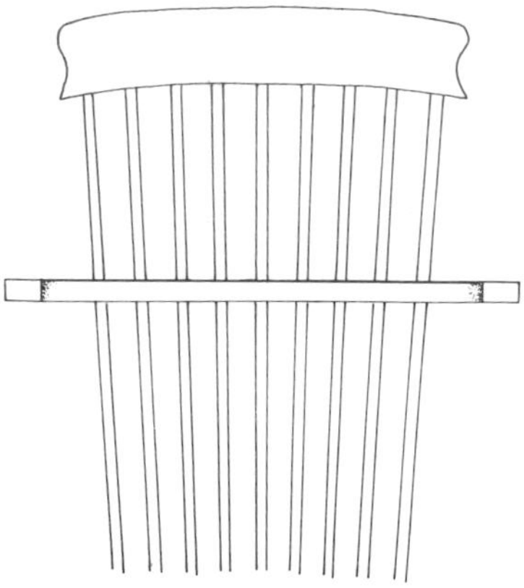

comb

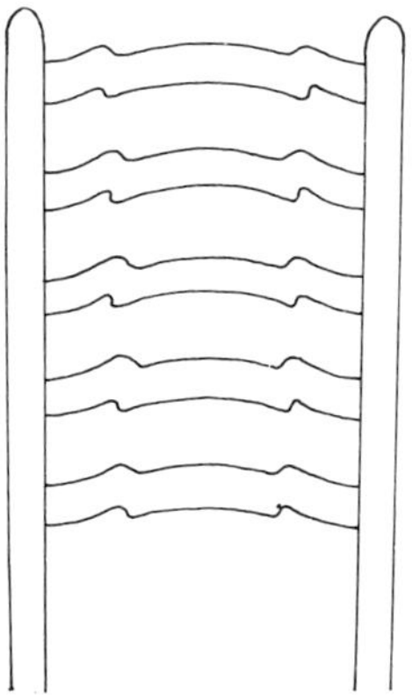

ladder

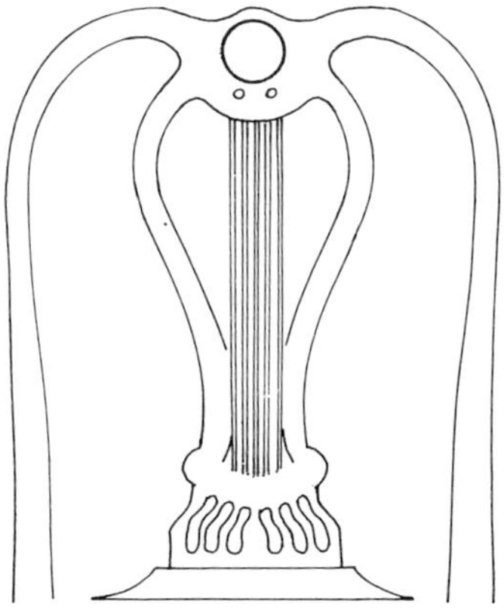

lyre

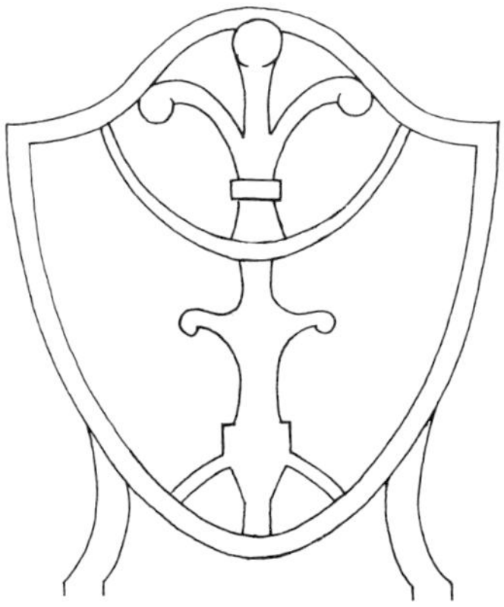

Prince of Wales' feather

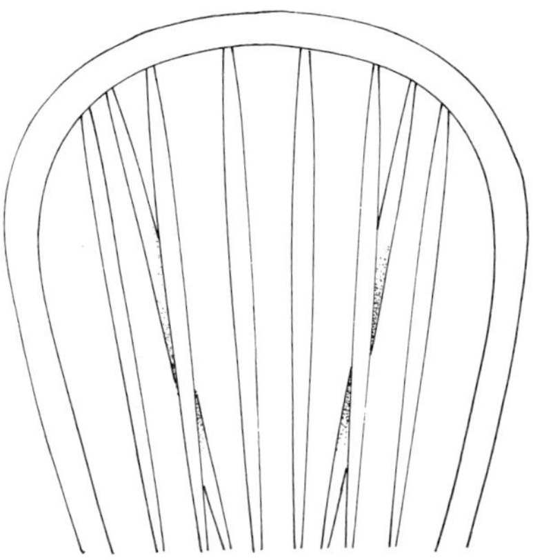

spindle

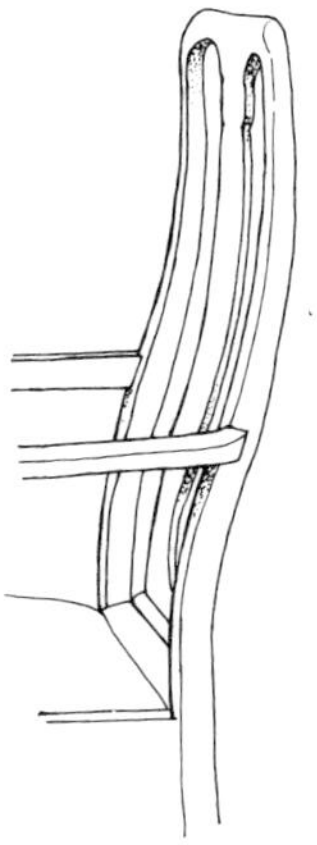

spoon

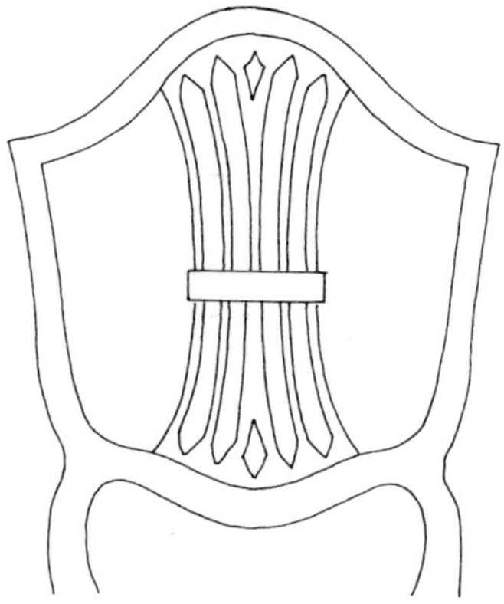

wheatsheaf

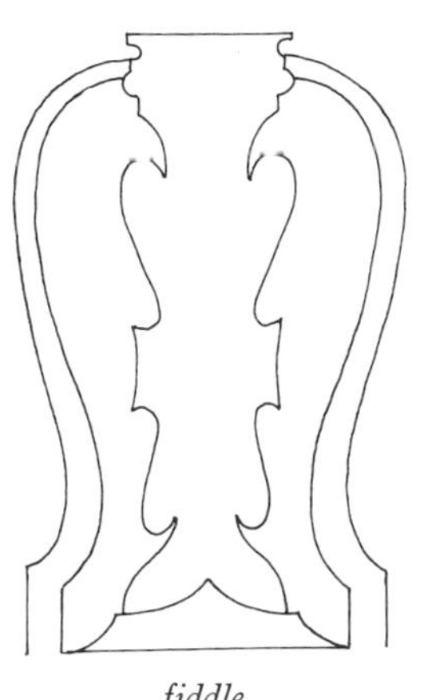

fiddle

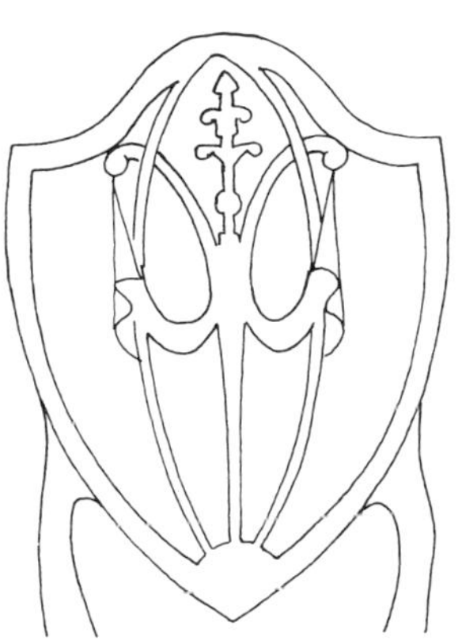

shield

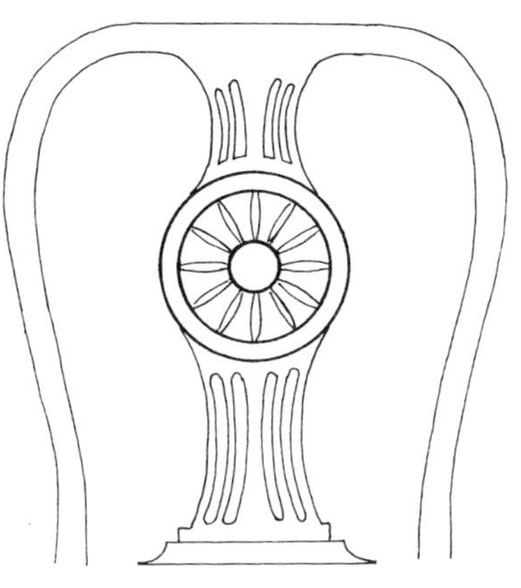

wheel

Broken pediment Top moulding to bookcases, cupboards etc, with symmetrical shape cut out in the centre.

Cabriole leg see **Legs**

Camel back see **Chairbacks**

Campaign furniture Portable furniture with straight lines, countersunk brass handles, particularly associated with Peninsular, Crimean Wars.

Canterbury Sheet music rack on castors, with divisions.

Carlton House desk D-shaped desk on legs with pigeonholes and drawers; late 18th century onwards.

Case furniture Any kind of cupboard, including bookcases and display cases.

Carcase see **Construction**

Chairbacks see illustrations, left.

Chest furniture Chests containing drawers as opposed to cupboards.

Cheval Type of construction depending on support at sides or ends only: large mirrors pivoting from standing frame, or tables supported at ends only.

Chiffonier Low moveable cupboard suitable as a sideboard, sometimes with shallow bookshelves above, sometimes with marble top; Regency examples often have brass lattice-front doors lined with silk.

Clothes press Early term for wardrobe.

Clout nail Iron nail with rough rectangular head.

Cockbeading Moulding which projects round the edge of drawers to protect veneer; from *c.* 1730.

Coffered panel Panel sunk into frame.

Commode Ornamental chest-of-drawers.

Console table A table supported by brackets fixed to a wall.

Construction
Board: Carpenters' work of nailed planks, pegged bars, flush surfaces back and front.
Carcase: Box construction in common timber, on to which veneer is added.
Frame: A solid skeleton of strong timber.
Joined: Solid joiners' work using mortise-and-tenon joints.

Conversation seat Two joined seats, facing opposite ways.

Pine chiffonier, showing appropriate signs of wear at the base, round the drawers, on the decoration and on the top. Probably Victorian.

Country furniture Two meanings: cottage-type furniture of local plain woods – Windsor chair the most famous example; alternatively, copies of fashionable styles made in the country of local plain wood, without veneer or inlay, often simplifying the model but retaining the true spirit of its design.

Court cupboard Two- or three-tiered display cupboard with heavily carved pillars: forerunner of both dresser and sideboard.

Credenza Credence table, originally used for Holy Communion, later small cupboard on legs.

Crest-rail The top rail of the back of a chair.

Cross-banding see **Banding**

Cylinder desk Roll-top desk, originally with one solid curved sliding top, not the later Victorian slatted construction.

Davenport Small desk with slant or piano top and side-drawers.

Deal Softwood.

Decoration see illustrations, right.

Demi-lune Half-moon shaped.

Desk see **Bonheur du jour, Carlton House, Cylinder, Davenport, Knee-hole, Pedestal**

Distressed Trade term for damaged surface; originally described badly cut veneer.

Dovetail Joint in which fan-shaped wedge fits into corresponding wedge-shaped slot at right angles; through-dovetails with tail-ends projecting from 1600, lap-dovetails which do not penetrate drawer-front from late 17th century.

Draw table Table with leaves that draw

Decoration

acanthus

anthemion

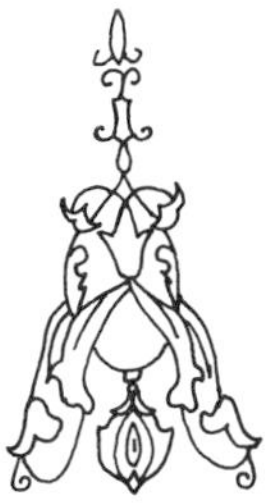

arabesque

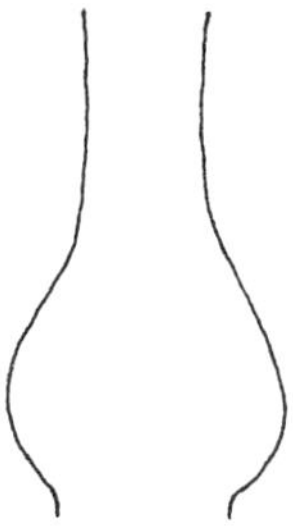

baluster

barleysugar

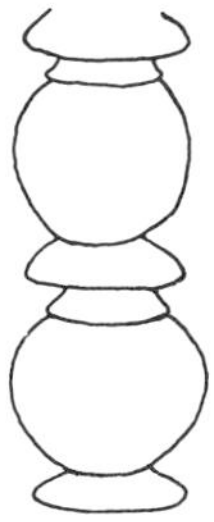

bobbin and reel

corinthian

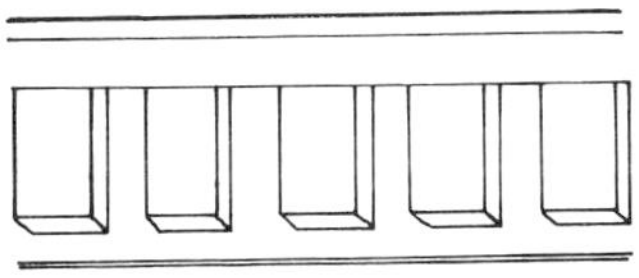

dentil

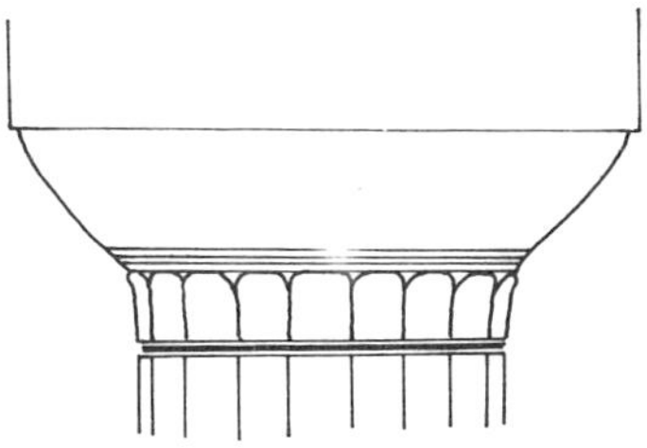

doric

egg and dart

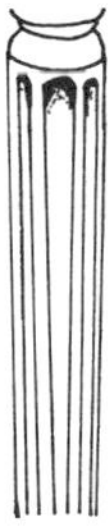

fluting

festoon/swag

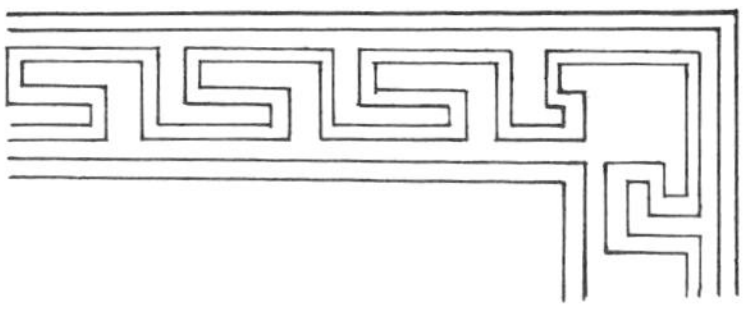

fret/Greek key

gadrooning

ionic

continued

Decoration *continued*

out from under the central section and are supported on their integral slides.

Drop front see **Fall-front**

Drop handle Brass tear-drop or pear-shaped handle hanging from backplate; late 17th century, much copied.

Drop leaf Any table with hinged supported leaves.

Drum table Round-topped table on centre pedestal with drawers in the frieze.

Dumb waiter Circular two- or three-tiered table on centre pillar with tripod legs; also a revolving drum-shaped stand for use in centre of dining table.

Egg and dart see **Decoration**

Envelope table Table with top which opens out from centre from small square to larger square.

Escritoire Secrétaire; desk with vertical fall-front, as opposed to sloping desk top; made both with cabinet above and as desk, particularly in the 18th century.

Escutcheon Originally shield-shaped

plate round keyhole; term used for all keyhole plates.

Etagère see **Whatnot**

Fall-front vertical flap to desk, opening outwards on hinges to horizontal surface, often supported by slides.

Feather banding see **Banding**

Feet see illustration below for some common kinds.

Fielded panel Opposite to coffered; with the central panel raised and bevelled.

Finial Decorative knob.

Fluting Concave grooves resembling those found on classical columns; the opposite of reeding.

Frame see **Construction**

Frieze Decorative border below cabinet cornice, table top etc.

Gate-leg Table with drop leaves supported on hinged swinging legs; usually oval or round with flaps up.

Harlequin A set of similar but not matching items: chairs, glasses, china etc.

Hinges
H-hinge: surface-mounted hinge on cupboards, cabinets, shaped like an H.
Rule: commonest kind of hinge for table-flaps etc. fixed to the concealed edges and invisible on surfaces.
Strap: long horizontal iron or steel basic hinge on face of doors to cupboards, often elaborately ornamental; typically 16th, 17th centuries.

Hutch table Cupboard with top which hinges down to form table.

Feet

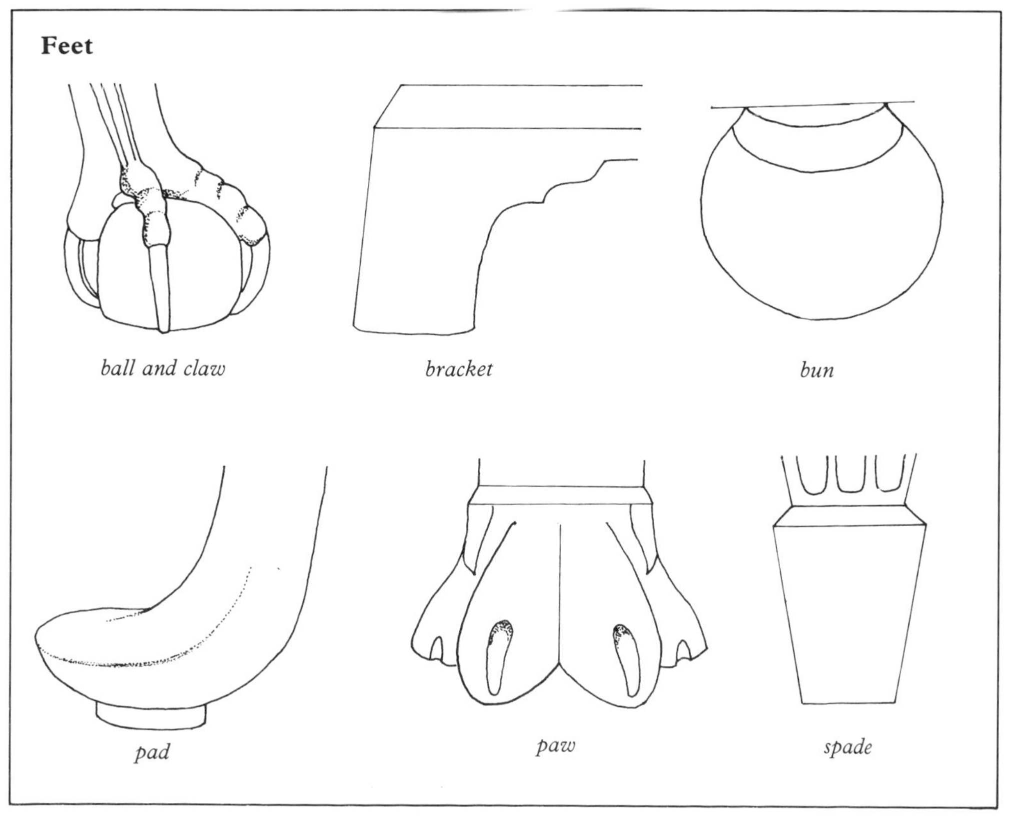

Japanning layers of varnish applied to form rich glossy surface, similar to but not identical with lacquering, which it imitated.

Knee-hole desk Desk with horizontal top and central recess to take the knees of the writer.

Knife box Veneered box with slots to take knives, sloping top for graduated sizes inside; from the 18th century onward.

Lap dovetail see **Dovetail**

Ladder back see **Chairbacks**

Legs see illustrations below.

Linenfold see **Decoration**

Linen press Old term for clothes cupboard.

Lip moulding Similar to **Cockbeading**

Loo table Tip-top table used for 'loo', a Victorian card game.

Lowboy Small toilet or dressing table without mirror (boy = *bois,* wood).

Lyre back see **Chairbacks**

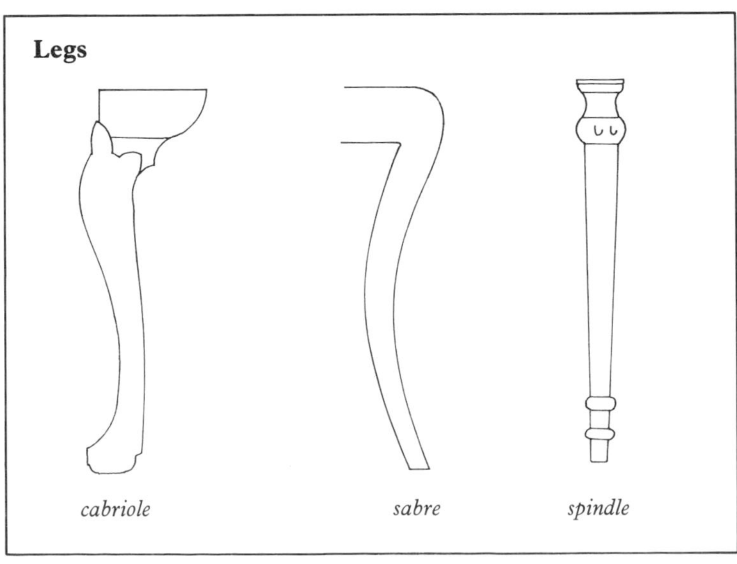

Marquetry Inlaid veneers in coloured woods, when the veneer is cut and fitted together in decorative motifs.

Marriage A piece of furniture made up from two or more parts of other pieces.

Military chest The most commonly known piece of **Campaign furniture.**

Monopodium Table supported on single central pillar.

Mule chest Recent term for wooden chest with one or two drawers in base: forerunner of chest-of-drawers.

Ormolu Cast brass decoration gilded to protect it from tarnishing.

Ottoman Most commonly a backless box with upholstered seat.

Over-stuffed (stuffed over) Upholstered seat secured on the outside of the chair frame.

Oyster veneer Veneer cut from knotty wood; the knots show as elaborate irregular rings resembling oyster shells in their shape.

Pad foot See **Feet**

Parquetry Veneer cut in geometrical shapes.

Patina Sheen or bloom on old furniture, built up through years of polishing and use.

Pedestal Desk or sideboard supported by separate pedestals or plinths at each end, usually containing drawers or cupboards.

Pegged see **Construction.**

Pembroke table Small light table with flaps, small drawer beneath top, usually squarish but sometimes oval; from 1750s.

Piano top Curved top shaped like the cover of a piano keyboard.

Piecrust Frilled edging to small pieces of furniture, usually tripod tables.

Pier table Table designed to be placed between two windows; often made in pairs.

Pillar-and-claw Tables, from 18th century, supported on central column ending in three splayed feet.

Prie-dieu Prayer chair: chair with very low seat and very tall padded back, usually over-stuffed; crest rail padded too.

Provenance History of a piece of furniture, therefore proof of its authenticity.

Quartetto tables Nest of three or four small tables made for drawing rooms from the end of the 18th century.

Rail The struts of a chair, e.g. seat rails: the front, side and back members of chair seats; also back rails. See illustration page 18.

Reading chair Chair with seat shaped for man to sit astride facing the back, sometimes with leather-padded curved back to rest the arms on and with a small ledge for book.

Reel see **Decoration**

Refectory table Long narrow table with solid stretchers which almost touch floor.

Rococo From French *Rocaille* = rock and shell; light, fanciful asymmetric decoration in vogue during early–middle 18th century; can best be seen in English form in Chippendale mirrors.

Rope twist Cable twist to chair backs and uprights; in celebration of the Battle of Trafalgar, 1805.

Rout chair, rout stool Light chair or long narrow stool, usually with caned seat, painted or gilded, for occasional use during routs or balls.

Sabre leg see **Legs**

Saddle seat Seat shaped with ridge to prevent the sitter sliding forwards; usual on Windsor chairs.

Secrétaire Fall-fronted desk with flap dropping down to rest on two pull-out supports, or held by curved brass hinges; forerunner of slant-topped desk.

Serpentine S-shaped.

Shield back see **Chairbacks**

Shoe Brass casing, usually paw foot design, with small brass castors, fitted to pillar-and-claw tripod legs.

Shoe-piece Separate, often shaped, slot-piece to house bottom of back splat on chairs, made separately and attached to back seat rail through 18th century; in one piece with seat rail on reproductions.

Smoker's Bow Variation on original Windsor chair, but with low hooped back in one piece with arms.

Spider join Matching concave and convex mitred edges, used in particular for hair-crack joins of gate-leg and flap tables, often continued right round edges.

Splat Piece of a chair, often decorated, connecting the back seat rail with the top or crest rail.

Spoon back see **Chairbacks**

Squab seat Loose padded cushion, originally fitting into depression in chair seat.

Stick back see **Chairbacks**

Stretcher Horizontal support between legs, used to strengthen construction and/or as foot rail.

Stringing Narrow inlaid strips of wood

(brass much used in Regency), sometimes chequered.

Sutherland table Narrow space-saving gate-leg table with deep flaps; from 1860s.

Swash-turned see **Barleysugar twist**

Tallboy Double chest-of-drawers, the upper one slightly narrower than the lower; made from 1700s (boy = *bois,* wood).

Tambour Roll-top or roll-front.

Tantalus frame for two or three square-sided decanters with bar to lock them up; Victorian.

Teapoy Originally a small tripod table in Georgian period; by Regency days applied to small tea-chest on tripod stand.

Tongue and groove Joint for two planks, one with groove, the other with shaped ridge, with the grain.

Trafalgar motif see **Rope twist**

Tunbridge ware Form of veneering in which different woods are bunched together and cut to show the endgrain; these small sections of variegated veneer are then applied to small wooden objects in highly intricate patterns.

Twist turned see **Barleysugar twist**

Wellington chest Tall narrow chest-of-drawers with hinged flap to prevent drawers from falling open in transit; originally a piece of **Campaign furniture.**

Welsh dresser Term used loosely for any kind of oak dresser. Properly there are three variations in dresser design native to Wales just as there are local variants in other parts of Britain.

Whatnot Etagère; small stand with several shelves or levels for displaying ornaments.

Wheelback see **Chairbacks**

Wine cooler Lead- or zinc-lined container to keep wine bottles cool; often in brass-bound mahogany from late 18th century; sarcophagus-shaped in early 19th century; zinc-lined only from early 19th century.

Writing slope Originally a box with sloping front to stand on table; with its own stand (forerunner of the desk) from late 17th century; portable 'lap desks' from 18th century often folding into brass-bound box; revived in many variations in Victorian period.

X-frame Two curved, often carved X-shaped frames for back and front legs of chair; seat, often leather, slung from side-rails joining the two back and front pieces; commonly associated with Carolean and Cromwellian periods.

X-stretcher X-shaped stretcher to chairs, stands for chests, often with central finial.

Further Reading

Joseph Aronson, *The Encyclopaedia of Furniture,* London, 1966

John Bly, *Discovering English Furniture,* Aylesbury, revised edition 1976

Victor Chinnery, *Oak Furniture–The British Tradition,* Woodbridge, 1979

Ralph Edwards, *The Shorter Dictionary of English Furniture,* London, 1964

Therle Hughes, *The Country Life Collector's Pocket Book of Furniture,* London, 1968

Geoffrey Wills, *English Furniture 1760–1900,* London, 1969

Glass
Up to £2,000

Ale glass of standard form engraved with hops and barley; folded foot and plain stem, c. *1740.*

Introduction

Dating and Authenticity

The dating of drinking glasses by identification of certain features such as stem and bowl shape, knop shape and position, or certain types of decoration such as air twist or engraving can be hazardous. Although general guidelines can be given there are numerous variations which bear witness to the individuality of the craftsman who made the piece. Weight, colour and workmanship are the best criteria for identification, but of course one needs to have some experience in order to be able to make the comparisons which indicate 'fine workmanship', 'good colour'.

There was a great deal of persuasive copying by the Victorians of 17th- and 18th-century pieces and, of course, copying continues today. Jacobite commemoratives, for example, with their characteristic and beautiful decorations of roses and legends extolling the Stuart cause are much sought after and expensive. Many originally plain 18th-century glasses were engraved with Jacobite motifs and passed off as authentic. It is very difficult for anyone other than an expert to spot this sort of clever doctoring.

The pontil mark is also taken as an irrefutable dating mark. Up to 1750 the pontil, an essential part of the making of drinking glasses, was left unground. It was not part of the piece being blown but was later attached to the blown but still molten piece while the mouth of the glass was cut and smoothed. In order that the uneven break point of the pontil would not affect the stability of the glass a raised foot was formed by folding or doming the foot in order to contain the pontil. Between 1750 and 1830 there was a tendency to grind off the jagged pontil of finer pieces while leaving lower-grade glasses unsmoothed in order to save production time and costs. With the introduction of blown moulded glass in about 1830 the pontil was again left unground, especially on copies of older styles. As the 19th century progressed most glasses lost their pontil mark. As such an obvious sign of age it is not surprising that the pontil has been used by many copyists in a misleading manner.

Wetting the rim of a glass and rubbing one's finger around it to make a musical note is no more a reliable test of 'good' glass than 'pinging' the rim with a finger-nail. Genuine crystal, heavy with lead (24% in 'half lead' and 30% in 'full lead' crystal glass), will make a fine, clear sound but so will a lot of non-crystal glass because the frequency depends, to a great extent, on the shape of the bowl. Even the common glass found in pubs can sound melodious.

Historical Background

English glass, and more specifically the drinking glass, owes its history and development as much to politics as to design and invention. In 1575 Elizabeth I granted a patent to the expatriate Venetian, Jacopo Verzelini, to make glass which would compete with the imported Murano drinking glasses which, hitherto, had dominated the market. George Ravenscroft (1618–81) was the first man to come up with a formula for making 'flint glass' of 'glass or lead'. His experiments at the Savoy, by the Strand in London in the early 1670s, and later at Henley-on-Thames as the offical glassmaker to the well established Glass-Sellers Company of London, resulted in English glass of a brilliance and hardness which quickly halted foreign imports. Once Ravenscroft's license had run out glass houses all over Britain began to make glass to his formula and quickly the old soda glass, with its characteristic bubbles and imperfections, was superseded.

Wine bottles in dark green or brown glass were made in England from about 1650 onwards. The coloured glass was partly the result of impurities in the raw 'metal' and partly because it was found that wine kept better if protected from the light. With the arrival of port wine in England as a result of the Methuen Treaty of 1703, which favoured Portuguese wine over French with 20% less duty, the shape of decanters changed and in order to keep port in good condition, stoppers had to be airtight. Unlike claret, which was often cloudy, port was a deep ruby colour which merited clear glass instead of dark-coloured bottles.

In Bristol, blue 'zaffre' or cobalt from Saxony was added to glass, thus producing the famous 'Bristol Blue', though Bristol was by no means the only place to make blue glass. Stourbridge also made it, as well as many other glass houses all over the West Country and the West Midlands. With the introduction of the cut Silesian stem from Germany around 1714, English glassmakers began to perfect the art of glass-cutting and faceting which reached its height in the luxuriously heavy glassware so typical of the Georgian period.

The swingeing tax on glass of 20% by weight which was imposed in 1745 proved to be both a blow and a stimulus to the British glass industry. The quality of glass was lowered because of the quantities of 'cullet' – scrap glass – added to the melting pots. Engraving and enamelling took the place of cutting for decorative purposes, since the glass could be thinner and lighter. Coloured glass, easily obtainable from the bottle houses and exempt from tax, was used for wine glasses and tableware, and flat-cutting was introduced to glasses as well as airtwist and colour-twist stems.

The Irish glass houses, hitherto a small and unremarkable industry mainly making tableware for the wealthy Anglo-Irish, now assumed an enormous importance, for Irish glass was free of tax. From the 1760s Irish glass became the synonym for heavy, deep-cut glassware of all kinds. By the 1780s Waterford and Dublin were paramount. Perhaps their most famous creations were the cascades of pendants, peardrops, icicles and fingers of cut glass – Waterford and Dublin chandeliers. The production of Irish glass continued in all its magnificence until 1825 when the Irish imposed their own tax on glass.

The production of English enamelled glass also petered out after a heavy tax was imposed on it in 1777. Yet again, though, the glassmakers found a way round the restrictions by combining splash-enamel with coloured glass, producing the highly distinctive Nailsea-type glass full of milky swirls and patterns, first made at the enterprising Nailsea glass houses near Bristol and then throughout the country as 'novelty' and 'fancy' glass became more and more popular.

The glass excise tax was finally removed in 1845, freeing the manufacturers from control and the designers from limitation. As with every other branch of antiques, the Victorian era is a mixture of the grandest and the worst. The Royal Pavilion inspired richness and decadent 'good taste' and a mass of cheap gimcrack copies of practically every style and period. In the field of glass, taste and fashion pursued two very different paths: the mass-produced products of the new industrial techniques, and the fine craft-made objects which drew their inspiration from the purity of the Arts and Crafts Movement, William Morris and John Ruskin.

British glassmakers and the British public in general were a conservative bunch, and though there was a rather vulgarized British version of Art Nouveau, most of it was imported from France, Austria and Bohemia. Yet one English glassmaker, Thomas Webb, was the inventor of one of Art Nouveau's most recognizable characteristics: the curiously metallic finish, originally known as Webb's Bronze, which had been inspired by the discoveries of chemically changed fragments of glass in the archaeological expeditions of the day.

Despite Ruskin's condemnation, cut glass not only survived but flourished at the end of the 19th century. 'Rock crystal cutting' had a tremendous vogue in the 1880s and 90s. With the inexorable march of progress, machines took over from craftsmen and by Edwardian days, slice-cut glass was monotonously decorated with deep daffodil-leaf shaped cuts in designs that were as mechanical as the machines which made them.

Care and restoration

Care

Carefulness is synonymous with care when dealing with glass. Glass is at its most vulnerable when it is being washed – not because of hot water (if it does not hurt your hand it will not hurt glass) but because of putting glass down clumsily or drying it carelessly. Many good drinking glasses have ended their days being washed up after a good evening's drinking. Rinse them after washing and put them on a drying rack or on a towel – never straight on to a hard surface. Do not economize on time by piling them higgledy-piggledy with plates and pans. Wash and dry them first.

Drying is important, as damp can spoil glass. A whitish cloudiness in glass is usually the result of not drying it properly or of storing it in a damp place. There is nothing that can be done, as the stain is the result of a chemical change in the glass itself.

Some stains however can be removed. Wine stains and stains in glass flower holders can be removed with a solution of one part nitric or sulphuric acid (from the chemist) to 20 parts water; use rubber gloves and rinse the glass very thoroughly. What appear to be cloudy stains at the bottom of old decanters can sometimes be loosened with a weak solution of domestic bleach.

Stoppers stuck in necks can be removed in one of two ways. First hold the neck and stopper in hand-hot water for a minute or so; different rates of expansion may loosen the stopper. If this does not work, mix glycerine (from the chemist) and methylated spirits in approximately equal parts, pour the mixture round the stopper and leave overnight.

Store glass in as dry conditions as possible. Wrapping it in newspaper is not a good idea as newspaper attracts damp.

Restoration

It is possible to repair broken glass after a fashion, but on the whole the pieces should go in the bin. If however you are very fond of the object and wish to keep it at all costs, epoxy resin is the normal answer, provided that it will dry and stay clear. You will have to resign yourself to having lost the value of the piece and you will probably not be able to use it again without being conscious of the repair.

When glass breaks it has smooth edges to which adhesives do not bond as easily as to rough surfaces. It is therefore necessary to support the piece perfectly while the adhesive works – you cannot simply push the pieces together and hold them for ten minutes.

If you are repairing a broken bowl use adhesive tape to hold the pieces in place while the resin sets. Drinking glasses can be treated the same way if the break is in the bowl, but if it is in the stem you will need to build a Plasticine cradle to support the glass until the adhesive has gone hard. Stems of very special pieces can be joined with glass dowels, but this is a difficult and highly professional job.

The old way of repairing broken glass was with white of egg; it will not stand up to use or hot water, but it dries clear and holds.

Glass is occasionally ground down to eliminate a chip in a rim or foot – this accounts for some of the eccentric shapes one occasionally sees. Grinding down is to be counted an alteration (lowering the value), not a repair.

Do not buy cracked or chipped glass. Be particularly careful, when buying decanters, that the rim has not been ground to eliminate small chips. Check too that the stopper matches and is a correct fit.

Periods and Styles

Glass dating from the 17th century is not only rare but very expensive too. We therefore start with the earliest 18th-century styles, though some of these are almost identical to those of the end of the 17th century.

Period: 1685–1714 – William & Mary, Queen Anne

Influences: Dutch, French, Huguenot. Glass tax of 20% weight levied 1695–98. Treaty of Utrecht 1713 permitted import of German glass. Glassmaking centres at Bristol, Stafford, Stourbridge, Newcastle, King's Lynn, Henley and London. More robust wheel-engraving used to fine effect on stronger, thicker English glass for commemoratives, royal and loyal.

Drinking glasses: Change in drinking habits as a result of the Methuen Treaty of 1703, allowing Portuguese wines into England at 20% less duty than French wines. Small heavy balusters, wine glasses with triple-ringed knop, plain knop, mushroom, cylinder and collar. Spiral-ribbed bowls ('wrythen'), multi-knopped and inverted baluster. King's Lynn peculiarity: ribbed rings and knops. Brief use of coloured glass, exempt from tax, for tableware. Bristol making blue glass from imported 'zaffre' (cobalt oxide) from Saxony.

Wine bottles, decanters: Distinction between claret jugs with handle, lip, cork, and clear-glass port decanters to show deep ruby-coloured wine. Wine bottles dark green to exclude light made in vast quantities. In 1695 it was computed that 240,000 dozens of bottles were made in England every year. Decanter jugs from 1685.

Other table, glassware: Beakers, fluted ales, tall flower holders, vases, tall small-bowled cordial glasses, bowls, dishes in silver shapes, applied decoration, stringing, punch bowls, stirrers, flattened cup-shaped tazzas or salvers, small finger bowls with folded rims, candlesticks in metal baluster shapes, taper sticks, plain dome-footed two- and four-arm standing candelabra, water jugs, ewers. Open lattice-work baskets, bowls, rims to plates, similar to salt-glaze patterns, often attributed to Bristol because of sapphire-blue edge.

Period: 1714–27–George I

Influences: 'German George' and introduction of Silesian stem. London Distillers' monopoly broken on sale of spirits and wines. Establishment of Newcastle-upon-Tyne as prime centre for wine glassmaking. Increased use of wheel-engraving, Newcastle glasses sent to Netherlands for diamond-point engraving.

Drinking glasses: Principal design change with introduction of four-sided pedestal-stemmed Silesian pattern. Widespread drinking of cheap spirits: sturdy 'tots', 'drams'. Tavern glasses and 'firing glasses' for rapping on tables at political meetings and clubs. Ale glasses plain-stemmed, trumpet-shaped, often engraved with hops, barley. 'Deceptive' glasses with thick glass at base of bowl for holding very small quantity of liquor. Tumblers with thick bases, broad mouths, tall-stemmed small-bowled cordial glasses for 'champaign' – still red wine, not sparkling white. Light balusters from 1724, particularly from Newcastle, centre for wine glass trade, many glasses of the period being called 'Newcastle glasses'. Distinctive for tall

baluster stems, thin bowls, very clear with high surface brilliance. Goblets, rummers with solid stems and broad footed for drinking hot rum and beer.
Wine bottles, decanters: Shouldered shape for wine bottles. Claret jugs with glass stoppers, port decanters with almost air-tight ground stoppers for better storage, many without handles.
Other table glassware: Sweetmeat glasses with Silesian stem, hexagonal, octagonal, popular over next 45 years. Candlesticks with variation on Silesian stem and wider drip pans. Jelly glasses, custard glasses with tall bowls on flat feet, no stems, one or two handles. Tazzas, fruit and punch bowls, small cream jugs, milk jugs, ewers, water jugs.

Early 19th-century fluted half ale glass.

Period: 1727-45 - Early Georgian

Influences: Classical, Adam brothers, some Jacobite, some Continental. Government regulations on spirit, alcohol measures 1736. Silesian stem shape encourages use of stem faceting. Air twists from 1740.
Drinking glasses: Light baluster glasses made in sections: bowl, stem and foot. Feet often double-thick, sometimes cut, sometimes scalloped or 'sewn', sometimes domed. Folded foot rarer than in earlier 18th century. Trumpet bowls, plain bowls, often with ridged foot, made in such quantitites they were sold by weight. Characteristic bowl-shapes: round funnel, ogee, cup, drawn and tapered, lipped cup (rare) and double ogee. Engraved festoon ornament echoing Adam designs. Cut stems increasingly fashionable: elongated diamond, close-scale faceting and grooving. Sometimes 'rose' continued to base of bowl as fluting to make pattern from inside bowl. Air-twists from 1740, at first with drawn bowl and air twist often not quite reaching base of bowl. Twists: mercurial, corkscrew, coil, silver rope. Also variations such as 'wrythen' or spiral grooves on outside of stem, similar to Venetian. 'Amen' glasses engraved with crown and Stuart legend, etc.
Wine bottles, decanters: Wine bottles with squarer shoulders and straighter necks. Plain glass decanters, mallet- or club-shaped, sometimes faceted, some with bullseye stoppers, all with ground glass close-fitting stoppers. Engraving themes: festoons, swags, floral, bird, butterfly, landscape, sporting.
Other table, glassware: Sweetmeat glasses, pedestal bowls with cut 'Vandyke' rims, serrated, looped, toothed. Small custard glasses, jelly or syllabub glasses, circular stands with galleries to hold fruit in pyramid with sweetmeat glass at top. Centrepieces, snake arms, baskets, cut-glass 'rose' bowls, plain or flat-cut cream jugs, water jugs, candle and taper sticks. Cut-glass designs: shallow flat diamonds, hexagons, vertical fluting, slice-cutting. From Bristol, imitation of soft-paste porcelain in opaque white glass for candlesticks, tea caddies, oriental-shaped flower holders, spill holders.

Period: 1745–60 – Mid-Georgian

Influences: Jacobite Rebellion 1745. Brierley Hill Glassworks opened 1740, at Stourbridge. William Beilby, glass enameller at Durham, then Newcastle. Glass excise duty imposed 1745. Chippendale's *Directory* 1754. Lighter weight glass to cut payment of tax, increasing use of 'cullet' or waste broken glass, less lead content. Growing use of green, blue bottle glass (exempt from tax) for tableware. Ruby red introduced in 1754.
Drinking glasses: Wine glasses with opaque spiral twists, mixed air and opaque, seldom with domed foot, nearly always folded. Standard bowl patterns: tapering or funnel, round funnel, bell, rectangular bell, bucket, waisted bucket, lipped bucket, ogee, double ogee, ovoid, trumpet, rounded or cup-shape, thistle, hexagonal, octagonal. Jacobite themes of rose and one or two buds, oak leaf, oak tree, star, thistle, compass, Bonnie Prince Charlie, many Latin tags such as 'Fiat', 'Audentior ibo', 'Reverescit', 'Redeat', etc. Jacobite loyalists' toasting glasses incriminating, hence symbols hidden beneath foot or in floral designs. From 1750s green glass for wines, blue for cans (tankards).
Wine bottles, decanters: Wine bottles more elongated, mallet-shaped. Decanter stoppers hollow, domed, with ribbed tops, button finial to 1750, spire-cut from 1750s. Label decanters from 1755 with vine, grape, fruit decoration round engraved 'Port', 'Marsala', etc. Engraving themes: hunting, sporting, landscape, birds, floral, classical buildings, architectural, masonic, vine leaf, hops, barley. Bristol blue-glass decanters usually half-pint size for cordials and other strong spirits.
Other table, glassware: Punch bowls, toddy lifters, ladles, tazzas with flattened rim, hollow stem and domed foot. From 1750s salt cellars, dishes, plates, bowls, basins, cruets, sugar casters, 'lining plates' for delicate porcelain. Water glasses, finger bowls from 1750s tumbler-shaped, straight-sided. Epergnes with snake-arms holding baskets, candle-holders. Candlesticks with air-twist stems, sweetmeat dishes with bucket-bowls, air-twist stems known as 'Master', 'Orange' or 'Captain' glasses. Sweetmeats with flat bowls, Vandyke or saw-cut edges, from 1760, sets of cruet bottles in stands, mustards, salts following boat-shaped silver designs. Ceiling chandeliers in metal shapes with flat cutting to arms and spheres.

Period: 1760–1800 – Late Georgian

Influences: Classical, Adam, Hepplewhite, Sheraton. Development of Irish glass houses outside jurisdiction of English excise tax: Dublin 1764, Belfast (Benjamin Edwards) 1776, Waterford (George & William Penrose) 1783. William Edkins, glass enameller at Bristol, Beilby family at Newcastle. Nailsea glass houses opened 1788. Tax on enamelled glass 1777. This period marks the height of English glassware, decorations, cutting, imaginative use for lighting, architectural detail and decoration. Decline of Bristol with tax on elegantly decorated enamelled ware.
Drinking glasses: Bowl shapes unchanged, but feet ground flat without pontil for most good glassware. Colour twists: combined transparent blue, pink or turquoise and air-twist, then opaque and colour-mixed twist. From 1770s cut and faceted stems. Fine green glass for wines, usually with baluster stem, some air-twist, Silesian cut. Champagne glasses deep with folded rim to bowl. Other air-twists: mercurial, corkscrew, coil. Enamelled heraldic, armorial, full colour or white by Beilby.
Wine bottles, decanters: Recognizably bottle-shaped bottles with almost straight sides and short necks. Decanters with diameter of base increased, drum-shaped, squared, or gently sloping shoulders, short necks, two to four neck-rings, flared mouths. Elaborate cutting for best quality, plain-shaped labelled decanters, also in sets, coloured glass with silver frames like cruet stands. Bristol blue labelled, decorated with gilding by William Edkins. Cutting: shallow flat diamonds, hex-

Left: Clear glass triple ringed mallet-shaped decanter, c. *1800, delicately engraved with grapes and birds around the sides; bullseye stopper. Right: Tapered clear glass club-shaped decanter with bevelled stopper,* c. *1790.*

agons, vertical flutes or slice-cutting, elongated diamond, close-scale facets, strawberry, hobnail. Ships' decanters ('Rodneys' for example) from 1780 with wide flattened bases and bodies. Spire-cut stoppers, partially cut flattened spheres, plain upright discs.

Lighting: High-quality cut glass stimulated idea of lustres, pendants, drops, prisms to increase reflection and refraction. Moulded glass candlesticks with wide drip pans hung with polished icicles, shallow-cut buttons, pear-shaped lustres. Table candelabra with glass arms, lustres, embellishments.

Other table, glassware: Sets of cruet bottles in stands, coloured, labelled or flute cut. Water glasses, finger bowls with curved sides. Bristol blue straight-sided, often with Greek key patterns. Wine-glass coolers, similar to finger bowls with one or two notches in rim to hold inverted stems of wine glasses. Flat-bowled sweetmeat dishes closely resembling today's champagne glasses, but many of them with serrated, decorated or saw-cut rims. From 1770 flat-cut geometric, diamond, with serrated, fan-cut, scalloped and Vandyke rims to boat-shaped fruit bowls, salts, sweetmeat and sugar bowls. Blue glass rolling pins, spirit flasks from Bristol.

Nailsea: Ingeniously using dark greens, browns, 'blacks' of bottle-glass free of tax, decorated, embellished with white splash-enamel, trailing, crinkling for purely ornamental glass, inspired by 'friggers' or small curiosities made for extra money by glass-blowers, sold to visitors. Rolling pins in coloured stripes, flask-shaped bottles, mugs, jugs, tumblers, jars, walking sticks, gemmel flasks, always with decoration in slight relief. Similar, less refined wares also made at Warrington and Midlands without relief effect. Dark green, blue 'witch balls' for superstitious sailors, gaudy polychromatic or blue splashed white for visitors.

Irish glass, Waterford glass: With the doubling of the glass tax in 1776 and the granting of free trade to Ireland in 1780, tremendous incentive for English glassmakers to set up business in tax-free potential export country. Most Irish glass, including Waterford, made to old Stourbridge formula and designs from England. Distinguished by excellence of workmanship, precision in cutting, particularly broad panels of miniature diamonds covering entire piece. Classical forms, Greek urns, boat shapes, turn-over rims to pedestalled fruit bowls, celery vases. Compared to contemporary English glass with lower lead content and lighter weight, Irish glass is heavier, richer, more brilliant; the cutting more profuse and precise. Today the long-held opinion that Waterford has a smoky metallic blue colour has largely been discounted, but nevertheless some pieces of undoubted provenance have blue-grey tinge.

Period: 1800–30 – Regency

Influences: Classical, Thomas Hope. Egyptian. Graeco-Roman. Height of popularity of cut glass, Waterford, Irish until Ireland imposed its own tax, 1825. Brighton Pavilion rococo an influence from 1817.

Drinking glasses: Cut and faceted stems, wheel-engraving to wines as well as ales, flutes and goblets. Return of the original 'roemer' shape with baluster stem as cider or beer glasses. Tumblers, beakers, considerable use of coloured glass, in particular deep blue and green, now made in many glassworks other than Bristol. Introduction of services or sets of glasses, same pattern, different sizes, with matching decanters. Square bases, hobnail cutting to large goblets, tumblers with rose-cut bases and fluted sides. Emphasis on using glass as material in its own right to add sparkle to dark woods of furniture.

Decanters: Whiskey decanters, square-shaped, often square-cut, with silver collars and faceted ball stoppers. Experiments with mixing patterns of strawberry, diamond, fluting, step-cutting on same piece. Applied neck-rings for easier grip while pouring. Rose-cut mushroom stoppers, flute-cut mallet, club shapes.

Lighting: Old methods of construction abandoned for ceiling chandeliers, now made with cascades of hanging drops, dramatic falls of close-set cut buttons, drops to conceal central shaft supporting gilt metal ring into which short, glass-embellished candle arms were set. 'Fingers' of cut crystal, diamond-shaped icicles used to great effect, following example of Royal Pavilion, Brighton. Girandoles, wall-lights, candlesticks, all dripping with lustres for refraction, glitter. Silvered witch-balls also used to great effect.

Other table, glassware: Straight-sided finger bowls with mouths slightly smaller than bases, wine coolers in plain cut glass rich dark green, amethyst, blue with gilded Greek key patterns. Complete sets of dishes, cruets, plates, urns and covers, fruit bowls on short stems with low pedestals, all heavy, deep-cut and lustrous. Decanter jugs, paperweights, scent bottles, toiletry articles, silver-mounted desk articles, rose bowls, punch bowls. Silvered glass salts, sugar bowls. Green glass 'floral' patterned solid door stops, sugar crushers, stirrers, Nailsea ornamental glass, coloured glass hand bells with clear flint-glass clappers, gemmel or twinned flasks, looped elegant decoration. Walking sticks, rolling pins, miniatures, sulphides or 'crystallo ceramics'.

Period: 1830–60 – William IV and Early Victorian

Influences: American press-moulded glass introduced to England 1825, commercially manufactured 'stained' glass, removal of excise duty 1845. Gothic, pseudo-Chinese, oriental, 'Venetian', 'Bohemian', 'Egyptian', 'Etruscan', 'Grecian' and proliferation of coloured glass.

Drinking glasses: Netherlands 'roemers' with hollow stems, prunts, copied in many sizes. Copies of 'façon de Venise' winged goblets, revival of Murano glassworks. Elegant flutes, flat cups both for champagne (now sparkling white) and 'foaming' wine. Wine glasses with coloured bowls, clear stems and feet, cranberry, green, ruby. Increasing manufacture of services, sets of glasses for individual wines, cordials and spirits. Ostentatious goblets, loving cups with trailing vine pattern, romantic themes. Cut, serrated edges to foot, return of domed foot for romantic-style goblets and glasses.

Decanters: Square-sided spirit decanters in sets of three, guarded by 'tantalus' frame with lock. Decanters with simple spire-shaped stoppers or hollow balls. Moulded square-sided square-cut decanters from 1830s. Cased glass stained over, then cut away to show clear; most popular in red. Neck rings tend to disappear. Cutting excessive, shapes more bulbous, heavier, though good-looking ships' decanters, many finely-cut Irish, in use during reign of 'Sailor Billy'. Fine pouring decanters on pedestal base with handle; embellished with delicate engraving.

Other table, glassware: As with furniture, taste extremely uneven with contrasting styles of simplicity and ostentation, excellent copies of early shapes, exuberant use of new techniques. Press-moulded glass first made in England at Newcastle 1833 and Stourbridge same year. Development slow until lifting of tax. Early English press-moulded glass excellent quality, almost as clear as true cut glass from which it was copied. Fire-polished to give crispness. Early press-moulded tumblers, goblets, glasses with pontil mark, but from 1850s bases held with claws, though pontil marks deliberately added to give authenticity to 19th-century copies of early Netherlands glass. With social changes and growing prosperity, increase in demand for glass of all sorts. Wine glasses, goblets, tumblers, sugar basins, butter dishes, coolers, salt cellars, honeypots, door and drawer knobs, domestic articles, kitchen articles. Coloured glass, cased or stained, gilding, enamelling, early machine-engraving, all much in evidence. 'Bohemian' and 'façon de Venise' both made in Birmingham. Stourbridge making 'Egyptian', 'Etruscan' and 'Grecian' and coloured. Ruby, oriental blue, chrysoprase, turquoise, black, rose, cranberry, opal-coated blue, cornelian, opal-frosted, pearl opal, mazarine blue, both plain gilded and overlaid, particularly red and brown overlaid clear. Accidental production of orangey 'carnival glass' due to imperfect staining. From 1851 injection of new ideas from Continent: black 'Etruscan' boxes, urns, opaline or milchglas, fashionable 1824–30. English 'millefiore' paperweights first made *c.* 1845, in Birmingham.

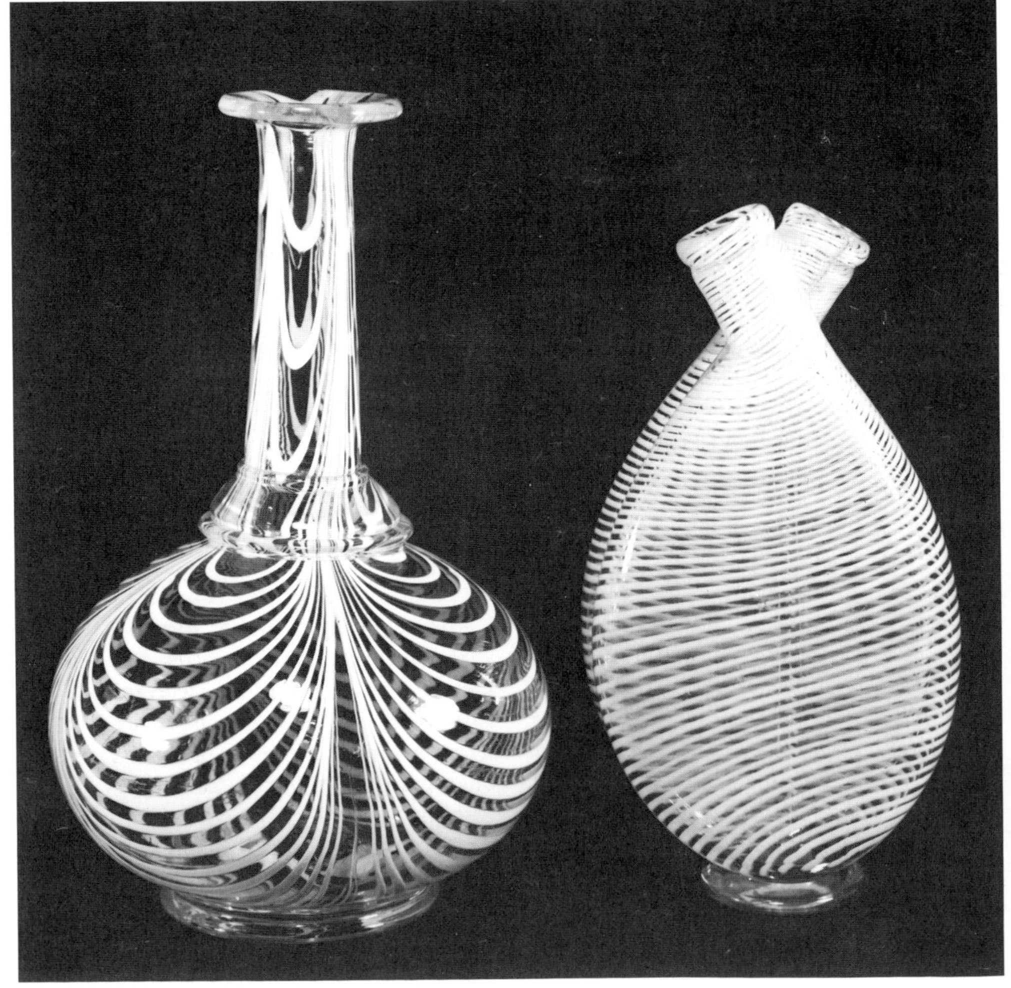

Left: Carafe of clear, colourless lead glass decorated with festoons or loops of opaque white glass common during the 19th century. Right: 'Gemmel' or double flask of clear lead glass decorated with trails of opaque white glass typical of the Nailsea style, c. *1845.*

Period: 1860–1900 – Late Victorian

Influences: France, America. Lalique, Emile Gallé. 'Façon de Venise', Bohemian, archaeological discoveries, American Tiffany glass. Reaction from heavy 'static' cutting and shapes to flowing, blowing to show texture. Leaves, swirls, pale tints, copied by Powells of Whitefriars from work of Salviati at revived Murano glassworks. Squared shapes from 1870s. Pressed glassworks of Sowerby, Gateshead, largest in world by 1880s. Greeners of Sunderland, Davidsons of Gateshead also producing pressed glass in quantity. Reintroduction of soda glass for copies of high technical skill and artistry.

Drinking glasses: Many mass-produced table glasses blown-moulded in ribbed, 'wrythen' and other earlier patterns. Drinking glasses with moulded stem, foot, blown bowl, joined after being made separately. Acid-engraving from 1870s. Machine-etching same date. Straw-coloured, greenish-tinged soda glass for 'Venetian' 'façon de Venise'. Some high-quality cut, engraved flint glass.

Decanters: Pressed glass blurred shadows of cut originals, 3-set square decanters for spirits in tantalus. Surprisingly good revival of Regency square shapes, elegant decanter jugs copied from 'Elgin' jug with pouring lip, narrow neck, handle, elegant engraved body on pedestal foot. High Gothic ecclesiastical shapes for ewers, claret jugs, many silver-mounted with silver lids.

Lighting: Distinct new departure with use of paraffin for domestic lighting in 1860s. Large production of oil lamps, shades, bowls, chimneys, inventive and decorative night-light holders. 'Queen's Burmese Ware' originating in America and also made at Stourbridge for lampshades, nightlights, small vases. Proliferation of moulded glass 'lustres' on light fittings of all kinds, wall, ceiling, standing, poor version of cut crystal with little reflection and dingy sparkle. Cut glass used excessively for lustres on better-quality light fittings.

Other table, glassware: 'Queen's Ivory Ware' by Sowerby's Ellison Glassworks *c.* 1870 as imitation of the pierced, lattice-rimmed salt-glaze and Wedgwood's 'Queensware'. Less happy developments included opaque 'vaseline' green glass for pierced, lattice, basket-weave, later in translucent pale pink, and blue from 1870s. 'Pearline' glass from 1889 in blue, greeny-yellow and brown. Milk-white opaque glass for pseudo-porcelain shapes, vases, flower holders, oriental vases. Also for fine pierced plates with grape design, loving hands, dishes, 'cow' butter dishes, little baskets. Transparent coloured glass made in blue, green, amber, puce, brown, black majolica, malachite, but lacking any subtlety, except for cranberry ranging from deep ruby to pale pink, rose. Artificial iridescence and 'metalling' used with abandon during the craze for Egyptology. All manner of novelty glass in their press-moulded millions: pin trays, cigar trays, spill holders, inkwells, candle- and chambersticks, nightlight holders and covers, decorative knick-knacks, 'bonnet' glass baskets, covered butter dishes, animal shapes, commemorative plates, figures, bottles and containers. Sowerby's 'Vitro-Porcelain' *c.* 1880 with new range of opaque white domestic, kitchen and tableware, opaque white and tinted dessert plates, dishes, 'fish jugs', shell-shaped covered basins, butter dishes, cream jugs. Press-moulded butter-dish covers, biscuit jars, water jugs, carafes and tumblers. True 'Bristol blue' and 'bottle green' relegated to the pharmacy as medicine bottles. Fashion for mixing clear and frosted

Press moulded Victorian custard cups.

glass for novelties, vases, celery vases, some tableware. 1885 Thomas Webb & Sons of Stourbridge got the licence to manufacture Queen's Burmese Ware, a tinted glass ranging from rosy-pink to pale yellow, which had first been produced in America. Webb & Sons also produced American 'spangled' or 'spattered' glass (given its name by the glittering effect of mica).

Period: 1870–1920 – Art Nouveau, Fin de Siècle, Edwardian

Influences: William Morris, Lalique, John Ruskin, 'Guild of Handicrafts', Arts & Crafts Movement. Ambrose Heal, Waring & Gillow, Liberty's.

Drinking glasses: Mass market supplied by Czechoslovakia, Bohemia and mass-produced, press-moulded, blown-moulded table glass. The Aesthetic Movement returned to clear, simple shapes of early Netherlands and Murano glass in classical shapes, little or no decoration except stringing and faded soda-glass colours. Slim tankards, beakers, flutes, hock glasses on tall thin stems, 'Elgin' shapes for glasses to match decanters. Sherry sets, plain well-proportioned whiskey tumblers, thistle shapes, some with cut bulbs. Use of rock crystal cutting, deeper than engraving with clear-cut line, intaglio cutting for similar effect. Some singles, sets using combined cutting, engraving and intaglios of impressively high artistic, decorative merit.

Decanters: The same applies, with elegantly-shaped decanters, decanter jugs made in matching sherry sets, whisky sets with outstandingly pure line and shape. Some heavy, hand-made, hand-cut decanters with flat rose-cut bases, fluted necks, rose-cut stoppers and return to traditional Waterford designs.

Other table, glassware: Main idea of Art Nouveau absorbed into English Arts & Crafts Movement, harking back to 'source' material. Marbled, agate glass similar to Whieldon/Wedgwood styles for vases, jugs, ewers, decorative spire-handled glass bells, tall tulip vases, loving cups, use of thickness of glass alone to shape and underline design. At the other end of the period, opulent sets of table glasses, finger bowls, side plates, rather stilted engraving and stiff daffodil-leaf slice-cutting, wide-mouthed, heavy-based iris vases, flower vases, toilet sets, writing sets, bathroom tumblers, carafes, powder jars, scent bottles. Domestic ware, kitchen ware, ovenproof 'Pyrex' from 1915 in America, 1919 in England.

Lighting: Imported Art Nouveau shades by Liberty's for oil lamps and electric lighting. English oil-lamp shades in frosted, engraved, opaque and frilled glass. This field is the only one which Art Nouveau proper penetrated, together with Tiffany glass lamps in petal shapes, bells and flowers.

Price Guide

Wineglasses (£100–1,200)

Plain teardrop stem, drawn trumpet, folded foot, 7ins, *c.* 1730, £180–220.

Light baluster, bell, teardrop, knopped stem 6½ins, *c.* 1740, £250–450.

Simplest Jacobite, *c.* 1745, £300–500.

Plain Newcastle with drawn trumpet bowl, 7½ins, *c.* 1750, £200–250.

Bell-shaped bowl, mercury corkscrew air-twist, domed foot, 7ins, *c.* 1750, £200–300.

Large tavern glasses with double knop, domed foot, 7ins, *c.* 1750, £240–300.

Large output of early Georgian glasses, 5ins, *c.* 1750–60, surviving in quantities, now risen to £150–200.

Mixed opaque and colour-twist, funnel and trumpets, rarer and not usually in mint condition, £200+.

Singles, pairs, late 18th-century bell-shaped with corkscrew air-twists, 6ins, also made in considerable quantities and to be found for

£250–300 a pair.

Heavy 3-piece baluster tavern glasses, heavy quality, 6½ins, *c.* 1750–60, very usable and solid from £150–200.

Same size, date, waisted bucket-shape with opaque double twists, £200–250.

Small, 4¾ins, ovoid bowl, with faceted, flute stems or twists, late 18th-century, £180–250.

Set of six early 19th-century blown-moulded, 5ins, from *c.* 1830–50, recent appreciation to £240–300.

Set of six Edwardian 5½ins wine glasses with dolphin stems, £240–300.

Coloured wineglasses. Late 18th-century rummers in blue with prunts, 5ins, hollow stems, £200–280.

Set of six, plain green Georgian glasses, 5ins, £800–1,000.

Set of six, Victorian cranberry bowls, 5ins, plain stems, £100–150.

Set of six, Georgian cup-shaped bowls, ribbed stems, *c.* 1750, £900–1,200.

Ales, Rummers (£80–300)

Mid 18th-century ale glass with vertical fluting. double opaque twist stem, 8ins, £180–240.

Ale glass, with barley, hop engraved motif and cut stem, 6ins, *c.* 1770, £250–300.

Tall elegant ale glass, with double air-twist, round funnel-shaped bowl, *c.* 1750, £220–280.

Engraved loyal and commemorative, 'deceptives', £300+.

Firing glasses, dram glasses, 4½ins, *c.* 1740, £150–180.

Thick heavy cordials, with folded foot, 5¼ins, *c.* 1730–60 £150–200.

Set of four, Victorian ale glasses, 7ins, £180–220 the set.

Plain rimmed-foot rummer, with engraved sailing ship, *c.* 1855, £200–240 (Sunderland 'nauticals' more, at £250+).

Regency capstan, cut-stem rummers, *c.* 1810, quite reasonable at around £80–120 depending on quality.

Late 18th-century nautical port glasses, 5ins, £150–250.

Tumblers, Water Glasses (£150–500)

Wide-mouthed, engraved Jacobite motif rose and two buds, 3½ins diam., late 18th century, £300–500.

Flower-engraved finger bowl, 3¾ins diam., 18th century, £150–300.

Commemorative finger bowl, 4½ins diam., early 19th century, £150–300.

Regency gilded key pattern, 'Bristol blue' wine coolers, £200 and up. Greens, simple bowl-shaped with or without lips, at £150 but many reproductions around.

Decanters (£100–2,000 singles)

Bottle decanter, with cork stopper, handle, body decorated with 'nipped diamond waics' design, *c.* 1680, £2,000+.

Pair late 18th-century shouldered decanters with stoppers, £350–400.

Pair late 18th-century club-shaped decanters with mushroom stoppers, £350–400.

Set of three 'Bristol blue' decanters with cut stoppers, probably originally with silver stand, *c.* 1790–1820, £400–500 without stand. Single, green, £100–140.

Single ale carafe, jug, engraved hops and barley, *c.* 1770, £450–500.

Single mid-Georgian early lime glass decanter with hollow stopper, £150–200. More than double for pairs.

Pair of Irish decanters, three applied neck rings, mushroom stoppers, *c.* 1800, £500+.

Late 19th-century heavy cut glass with square-cut stopper, £175–225.

Pair 19th-century imported Bohemian pinched glass with gold decoration, £150–200.

Bowls, Salvers, Tazzas (£50–700)

Pair of bowls and covers, early 19th-century strawberry, fan cut with faceted stems, 8ins, £300–400.
Cut-glass fruit bowl, mid-19th century, with turn-over rim, detachable raised pedestal stand not mint condition, £200–250.

Mid-19th-century two-handled cup and cover, heavy cut-glass, probably Irish, £250–300.

18th-century Irish cut-glass bowl with scalloped rim, square-cut pedestal base, 10ins, £400–600.

Plain tazza, with flattened rim, domed and folded foot, 10ins diam., *c.* 1790, £180–220.

18th-century jelly stand or tazza with domed and folded foot, 14ins diam., £200–250.

Victorian dish in milk glass with frilled edge, £50–80.

Late 19th-century wide-mouthed glass vase in pink overlay with cameo mark 'Webb', 6¾ins high, £400–700.

Pair Victorian cranberry glass vases, flute-shaped, frilled edge, clear glass foot, 10½ins high £200–300 pair.

Jugs, Ewers, Water Jugs (£100–800)

Pair of late Georgian claret jugs with stoppers, 13¾ins high, £350–450 the pair.

Victorian silver-mounted claret jug, engraved with scrolls, foliage, 1865, by Messrs Barnard, 11ins high, £600–800.

Mappin & Webb silver-mounted cut glass claret jug, 11ins high, 1902, £400–500.

Cut-glass ewer, with ribbed handle, pedestal foot, in Neoclassical style, 10½ins high, *c.* 1830, £350–450.

Heavy George III cut-glass water jug, 6½ins high, £150–200.

Heavy cut-glass ewer, with plain handle, decorated rim, foot, Neoclassical style, 10¼ins high, *c.* 1830, £300–350.

Nailsea baluster cream jug, with opaque white decoration, applied blue band to rim, 3½ins high *c.* 1820, £100–150.

Stourbridge 'satin glass' ewer, in two shades of amber, 5½ins high *c.* 1870, £130–180.

Glass terms

Acid engraving Nineteenth-century method of shallow line-engraving on glass using hydrofluoric acid.

Ale glass Drinking glass usually with deep funnel or bucket bowl, often on tall stem, decorated with hops, barley, for strong ale.

Amen glass Drinking glass *c.* 1745 with large trumpet bowl, a Jacobite engraving and the word 'Amen' beneath.

Air twist From *c.* 1740 threads of air bubbles drawn and twisted for stems of drinking glasses, later made with prepared rods or canes combining air, opaque and coloured glass. See **Stems.**

Baluster see **Stems.**

Blown-moulded Shaped, patterned vessels formed by blowing molten glass into metal mould. Widely used from the 17th century onwards for one-piece moulds, two-piece from 1800s, three-piece from 1820s. Unlike pressed glass, surface indentations are noticeable inside as well as on outer surface.

Bonnet glass Little baskets shaped like old-fashioned poke bonnets, in pressed glass from 1860s, known also as fancy glass or novelty glass.

Bowl shapes see illustration below.

Bullseye stopper Upright shaped disc similar in shape to a target, often crinkled, fluted towards the centre.

Burmese glass see **Queen's Burmese Ware.**

Captain glass Sweetmeat glass which topped elaborate pyramids of salvers and tazza of

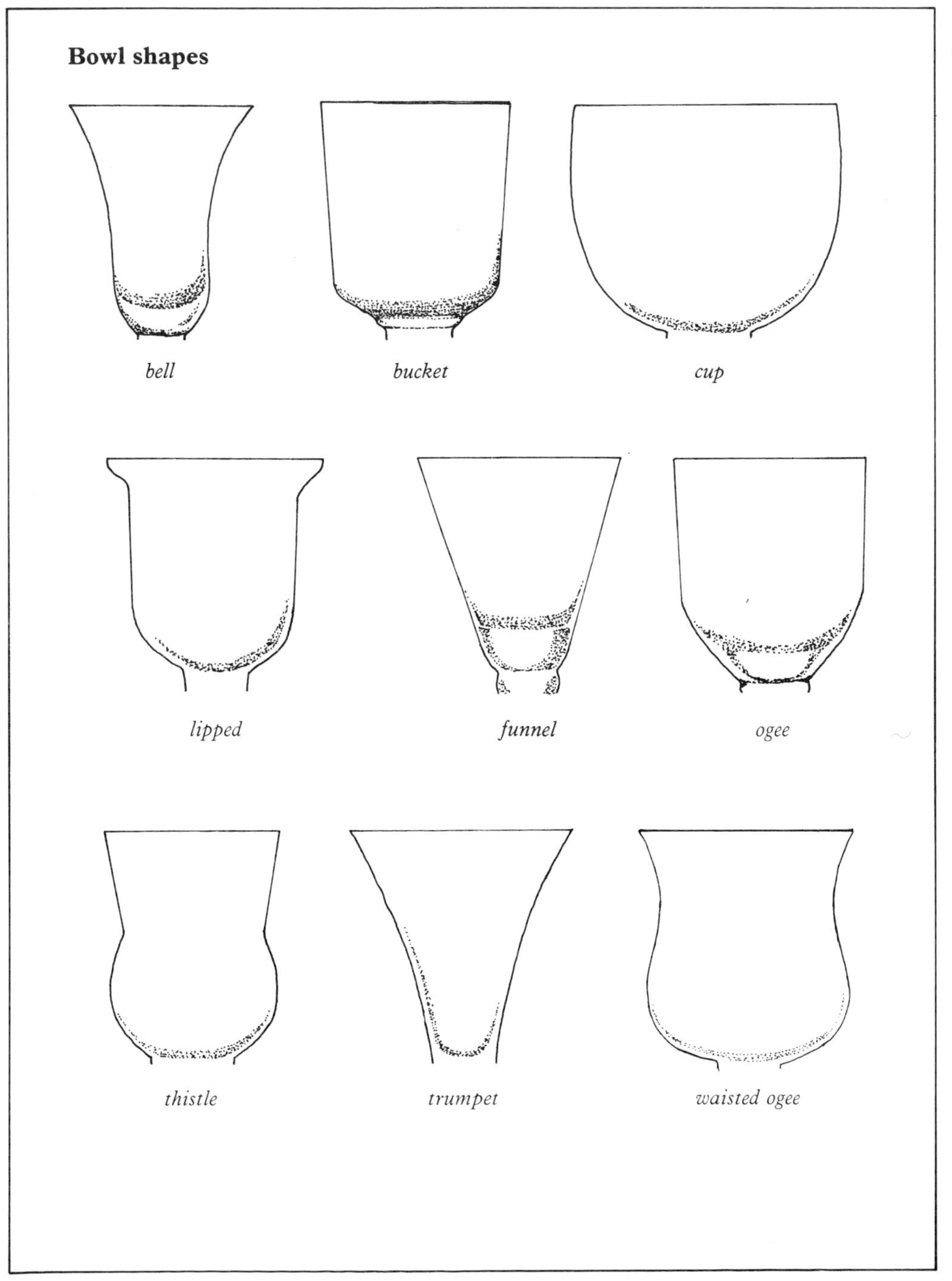

fruit. Known also as Orange glass, Master glass.

Cased glass From 1845 onwards in England, coloured and opaque glass overlaid and fused together, then cut away to form facets outlined in oblique stripes cut through layers. High quality 19th-century ware should not be confused with poor, coarse quality imported from Continent in 1920s and later.

Caudle cup Two-handled cup with cover and saucer, made in pairs as presentation sets for mother and child for rich warm drink. To Victorians, display pieces only.

Cordial glass Tall-stemmed glass with small bowl for strong liqueur-type drink.

Crisselling Network of fine cracks characteristic of 17th-century lead glass.

Crystallo-ceramic Crystal cameo. Patented in England 1819 by Apsley Pellat, developed at his Falcon Glassworks. Minute cameos embedded in clear flint glass.

Cullet Waste glass, scrap, broken glass, added to new meltings.

Deceptive glass Drinking glass with extra thickness in base of bowl, thus holding smaller quantity than it appears to.

Diamond point Engraving on glass using diamond 'blade' and tools. Highest craftsmanship achieved by Dutch in 17th, early 18th century, often on plain imported English glasses.

Domed foot see **Feet.**

Dram glass Heavy-footed stubby glass, often with no stem or short thick stem, holding 2oz of spirits. From 1736, after government regulations on spirit, alcohol measures.

'Elgin' shape Elegant decanter jug on classical lines inspired by the archaeological finds of the Victorian era.

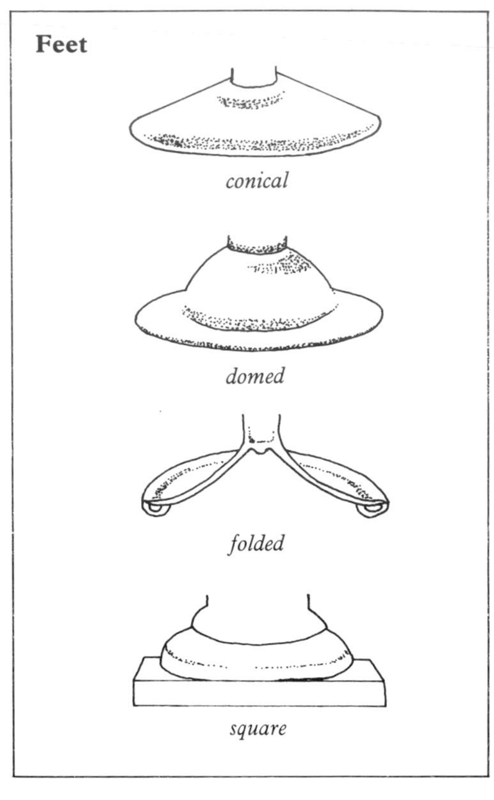

Epergne Table centrepiece with elaborate arms for candleholders, sweetmeat dishes, radiating from central tiers of bowls. Also in silver, less common in glass, ceramics.

Ewer Large water jug, usually to accompany basin for washing hands.

'Façon de Venise' Venetian glass from Murano and other glass houses, straw-coloured, yellow-greenish soda glass. Typical are glass goblets with elaborate covers and winged stems. Also gilded glass, coloured glass and white-opaque. Famous from 13–17th centuries after which English clear flint glass ousted it for most purposes. Romantic revival in 1850s–60s.

Faceting Facet cutting. Shallow hollows forming diamonds, triangles, to add refraction, brilliance. Shallow from 1720–40, then more elaborate until largely superseded by deep diamond cutting from 1790s.

Fan cut Cutting in the shape of a fan, often on scallops of rims and feet.

Firing glass Stubby dram glass with thick heavy foot to applaud toasts by rapping on tabletop with sound resembling firing muskets.

Flint glass see **Lead crystal.**

Flute glass Tall drinking glass with deep conical bowl to allow sediment in cider, ale, to settle.

Folded foot see **Feet.**

Feet Base of stemmed drinking glass. See illustration opposite.

Frigger End-of-day glass made up by glassworkers from odds and ends. Now used as term to cover all Victorian, Edwardian novelty glass, including Nailsea.

Gemmel Twinned flasks (less commonly other objects) as Nailsea spirit flasks, oil-and-vinegar bottles fused back-to-back.

Girandole Lustre-hung branched candle brackets, candlesticks, candelabra. Extremely ornate, often with mirror backing from 1750s, more functional from 1780s.

Heavy baluster Solid knopped stems to wine glasses taking lines from candlesticks and furniture of the 17th and 18th centuries in new quicker-cooling lead glass whose properties differed from soda glass. From *c.* 1673–*c.* 1715.

Hobnail cutting Deep cross-cut diamonds cut again into eight-pointed stars, from 1780s in heavy Irish glass, later in English after lifting of glass tax.

Intaglio cutting Incised design.

Kick-up base Pushed-up dome in base of bottles, decanters.

Knop Originally the ring connecting the bowl to the stem, changing to a decorative element in the design of drinking glasses. See below for the types of knop most commonly

Knops

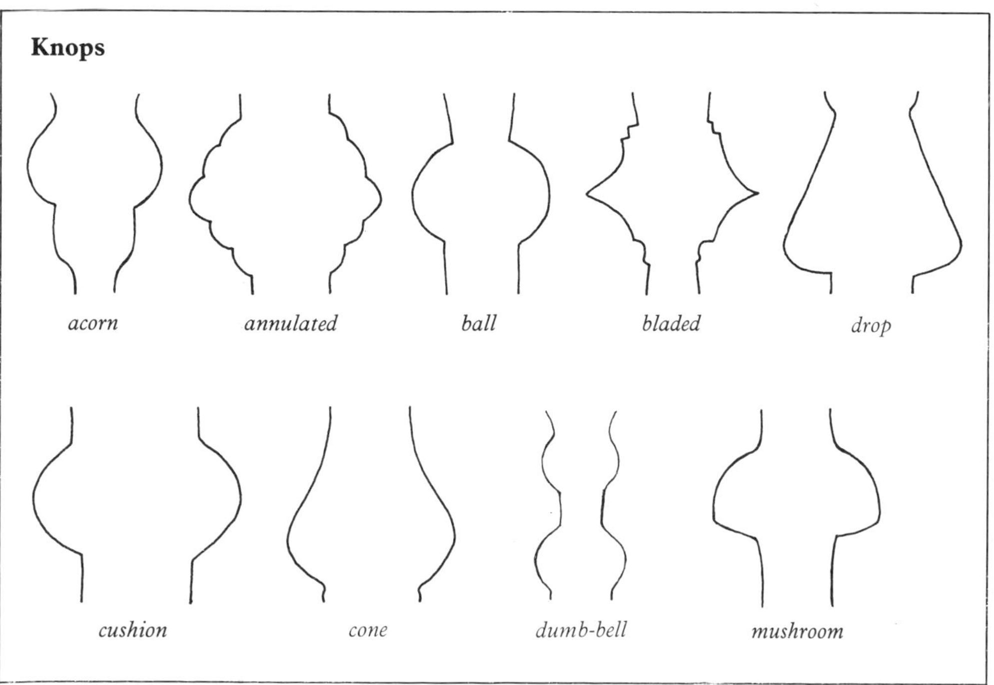

found, sometimes in conjunction with each other. 'Knop' is the old spelling of 'knob'.

Latticino Technique invented, perfected, by Venetian glassmakers: lace-like threads of white or coloured glass enmeshed in clear glass, used most successfully by Nailsea at end of 18th, early 19th century as well as Sunderland, Newcastle, Stourbridge and other glassmaking centres.

Lead crystal Lead glass, flint glass. Developed by George Ravenscroft *c.* 1673 by replacing lime with lead oxide for more brilliant, stronger glass and widely used by end of 17th century.

Light baluster Refined version of heavy baluster, particularly in Newcastle glass from *c.* 1724 onwards.

Lustres Polished, cut pendant drops, icicles, beads, usually hung from chandeliers, girandoles, candelabra etc. to increase refraction and reflection.

Master glass see **Captain glass.**

Milchglas Opaque, almost white glass imitating porcelain, made in Germany and France by adding tin oxide and decorating with enamel or transfer-printing. Similar ware also made in Bristol and Stourbridge.

Milk glass Not the same as the milchglas of Germany. Practically indistinguishable from slagware or vitro-porcelain.

Moulded see **Press-moulded, Blown moulded.**

Nipped diamond waies Bands of applied glass wound in diamond pattern over body of decanter-bottle and while still molten, pinched with disc-ended pinchers into raised diamond shapes.

Opal glass Semi-opaque ornamental glass much favoured by Victorians, in white and milky colours.

Opaque glass see **Milchglas.**

Orange glass see **Captain glass.** No political connotation as an orange was often used to top pyramids of fruit, dessert.

Pontil, punty Uneven mark left on base of glass vessel where dab of glass had attached it to iron rod used to hold the glass during finishing and shaping. Ground off from 1750. Reappeared for a while in early press-moulded glass *c.* 1830 and used to advantage in fakes.

Press-moulded Pressed glass. Cheap method of making decorative functional glass, originating in USA and taken up by English manufacturers *c.* 1830. Molten glass was pressed into a patterned metal mould with a plunger, giving characteristic smooth inner surface, unlike blown-moulded glass.

Prunt Applied ornamental glass disc, often stamped with strawberry, raspberry, lion's mask, often decorating hollow stems of Netherlands glass 'roemers'.

Queen's Burmese Ware American patent for heat-tinting opaque glass coloured pale yellow to deep orangey pink with uranium or gold. Made in England for some tableware, but principally for nightlight covers, light shades, lamp shades.

Queen's Ivory Ware Opaque glass known as vitro-porcelain, also made in other colours, between 1870 and 1890 by Sowerby's Ellison Works.

Rock-crystal cutting Deep wheel engraving in lead crystal glass with pattern polished free of matt engraving finish to a brilliant clarity. From 1878, associated particularly with West Midlands.

'Rodney' decanter Type of ship's decanter with wide flat bottom, named after Admiral Lord Rodney in 1780s.

Rummer, roemer, romer Originally

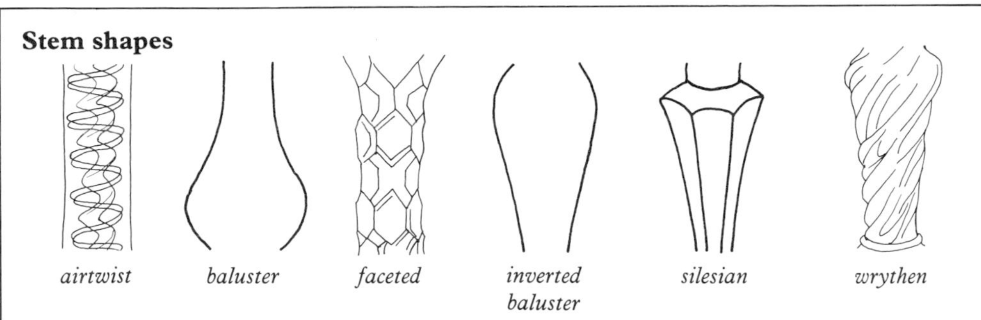

German, Netherlands pale green drinking glass with wide hollow stem, often decorated with prunts. The roemer or romer developed into the first English round-bowled thick-stemmed 'rummers'.

Salver Originally a flat dish with low raised edge standing on a low foot. Later simply a flat tray, usually silver, on three or four small feet.

Sconce Bracket candlestick, i.e. wall sconce.

Sewn foot Shape of glass foot which has been held, minutely gathered, by claw as opposed to pontil during shaping and finishing.

Ship's decanter Flat-bottomed decanter, fashionable from 1780s. See **Rodney decanter.**

Silesian stem Hexagonal or octagonal vertical cut stem for wine glasses introduced to English glassmakers from the beginning of Georgian period with German fashions, customs, designs imported with the Hanoverians. See **Stems.**

Slag glass A trade name of Sowerby – the so-called vitro-porcelain which incorporated steel slag, the waste from iron furnaces, to give a purple or green mottled effect.

Slice cutting Deep cuts tapering at one or both ends.

Soda glass Quick-cooling fragile glass characteristic of pre-17th century European glass, superseded by English lead or flint glass (q.v.). Revived by Victorians for romantic 'façon de Venise' winged goblets, drinking glasses, etc.

Spire cut Of decanter stoppers cut like a church spire.

Splash enamel Opaque glass incorporated into clear or coloured glass in random decorative splashes. Typical of Nailsea and its imitators from the end of 18th century.

Stem shapes see illustration above. The distinction between shapes and knops can at times be slight – as for example with baluster stems.

Stringing Glass threads wound round mould to make hollow stems for Netherlands 'roemers' and for decoration in all periods. Particularly favoured by Victorians as decoration to handles and stems of glass vessels.

Tantalus Set of three square decanters in wooden frame with locking bar.

Tazza Similar to the original salver shape – wide shallow bowl on low foot used as table centre-piece for fruit.

Tear A tear-shaped air-bubble trapped in the stem or base of the bowl.

Toddy glass Similar in shape to rummers for hot toddies (rum or whisky, lemon, nutmeg, sugar, hot water) from 1770s. Also giant goblet on thick stem, often square foot, for mixing and serving toddy.

Toddy lifter Small long-necked decanter-shaped glass instrument with hole at each end, operating on pipette principle. One end immersed in bowl, filled, top hole covered with thumb to retain liquid to be released into drinking glass.

Vandyke rim Lace-edged, taken from collars of Vandyke portraits of the time.

Wheel engraving From *c.* 1730, glass engraved with pattern cut by abrasive action of revolving wheel and sand-based powders.

Wrythen Surface twisting of stem, lower part of glass bowl in swirled ribbing, faintly distorting clarity of contents thus masking cloudy wines. See **Stems.**

Zaffre Prepared cobalt, originally imported from Saxony, for colouring enamels, glass and ceramics.

Further Reading

L. M. Bickerton, *Illustrated Guide to 18th-Century English Drinking Glasses,* London, 1971

John Brooks, *The Arthur Negus Guide to British Glass,* London, 1981

R. J. Charleston, *English Glass and the Glass Used in England c. 400–1940,* London, 1984

D. C. Davis, *English Bottles and Decanters 1650–1900,* London, 1972

G. Gross-Galliner, *Glass, A Guide for Collectors,* London, 1970

Harold Newman, *An Illustrated Dictionary of Glass,* London, 1977

Barbara Morris, *Victorian Table Glass and Ornaments,* London, 1978

FURNITURE

Left: *A Charles II period walnut open armchair,* c. *1670, with barleysugar turned supports. Look for fine, rich colour and coarse canework at this period.*

Above: *A late 17th-century oval drop-leaf gateleg table of attractive small size in oak. Look for corresponding signs of wear under the leaves and for original feet.*

Above: *A polescreen* c. *1760 on a mahogany tripod base with a contemporary needlework panel. Polescreens are still underestimated commercially. If the base is carved, it is preferable for the screen frame to be similarly treated.*

Right: *A mid-18th-century foldover top teatable with a shaped frieze and cabriole legs. Most curvilinear furniture of this period was plain, not carved, and still represents a good investment.*

Above: *A late Regency dining chair,* c. *1830, combining classicism in the legs and seat rails with a heavily carved, foliate back. Such combinations were to proliferate in the Victorian period, but were rarely handled with such style and originality.*

Above: *A late 19th-century or Edwardian period open armchair. Disregarded until recently as an important part of furniture history, this period has now become very collectable.*

GLASS

Right: *A ruby cased goblet, engraved with roses. English, mid-19th century.*

Above: *A late 19th-century jug in three layers of glass–yellow, white and pink–with a clear glass shell handle. English, probably made in Stourbridge.*

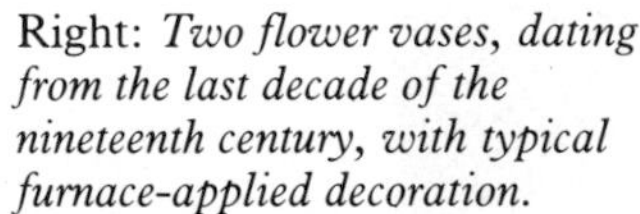

Right: *Two flower vases, dating from the last decade of the nineteenth century, with typical furnace-applied decoration.*

POTTERY & PORCELAIN

Left: *A Liverpool delftware plate, painted in lovely soft colours on a soft tin glaze,* c. *1760. Delftware is the one type of pottery in which some chipping around the rim is to be expected and is not greatly detrimental to the value.*

Right: *A porcelain 'mask jug' transfer-printed with the popular 'Fisherman and Cormorant' pattern in about 1780. Even the slightest damage will reduce the value greatly and collectors should watch out for repairs and restorations.*

Left: *A teacup, coffee can and saucer in the Imari style, Worcester; Barr, Flight and Barr period;* c. *1805.*

Left: *Two Royal Worcester candle extinguishers. The standing monk was in production for over 100 years, early examples being worth much more than modern ones. The praying friar, dating from 1855, is extremely rare.*

Below: *Wedgwood lustre decoration of the 1920s and 1930s is now keenly collected, especially if it shows fairies and elves. Lustre wares were also made at these dates by Crown Devon, Maling and Royal Worcester. They are less fine, but their prices are starting to climb.*

RUGS

Left: *An Indian 19th-century Agra rug, 7ft × 4ft 2in (2.13 × 1.27m).*

Right: *A fine Belouch prayer rug, measuring 2ft 6in × 5ft 8in (0.76 × 1.73m).*

Above: *A Turkoman Yumut hatchli, 5ft 9in × 4ft 6in (1.75 × 1.37m); note the cruciform quartered field with the four gardens of paradise.*

Right: *A Kurdistan 19th-century Kurd rug 6ft 6in × 3ft 10in (1.98 × 1.17m).*

SILVER

Left: *A pair of Victorian table candlesticks, marked for 1837, flanking a claret jug of 1882. Loaded candlesticks remain good value compared to the cast type. The Cellini pattern of claret jug shown here is greatly sought after–humbler designs are much cheaper. Glass-bodied examples are more popular at present than silver-bodied, making the latter relatively good buys. Never buy a glass jug with any damage to the body other than minor chips.*

Right: *A late George II tankard, made by Gurney & Cooke, London, 1752. The price will vary greatly according to quality and condition. Beware later armorials and initials, or erasures of them. Examples should preferably be marked on the cover as well as on the body or base.*

Below: *A collection of Georgian and Victorian wine labels. This is a good area for the collector, with prices starting at about £50, though rising to several hundred. Be fussy about the chains–it is all too easy to overlook them.*

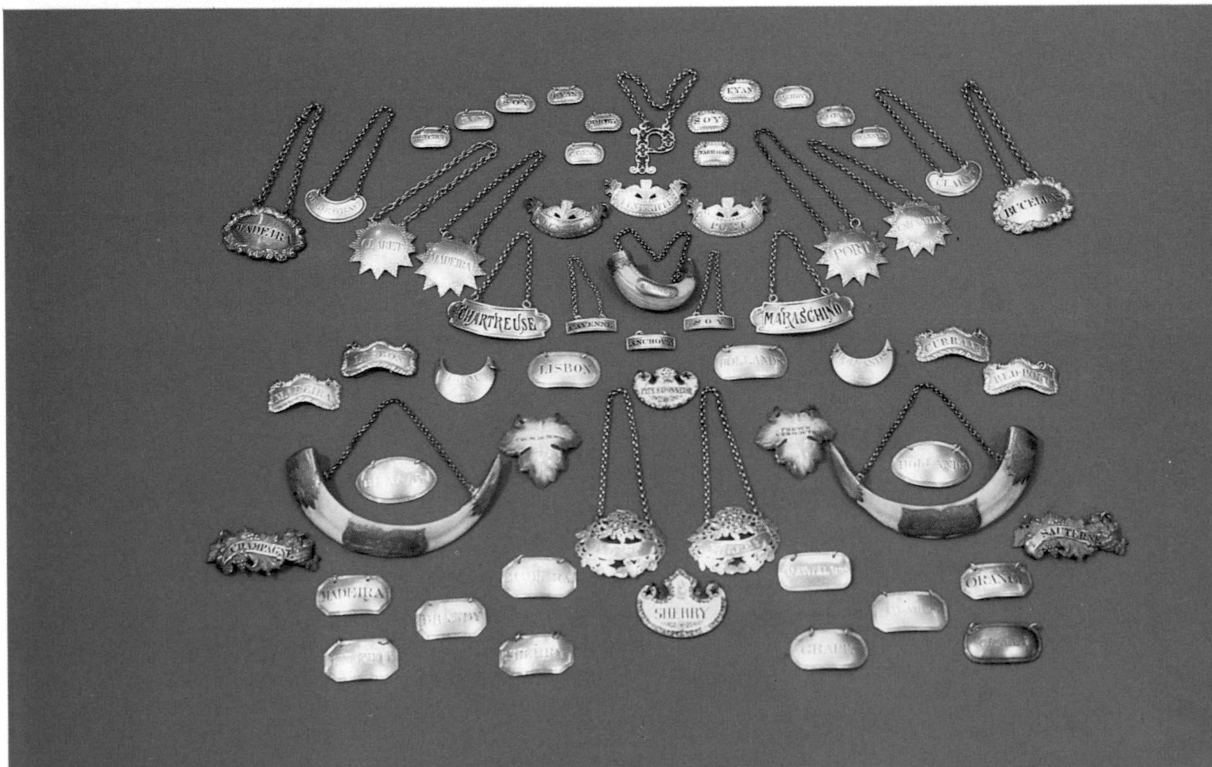

Pottery and Porcelain

Up to £2,000

Liverpool creamware jug printed with a harvesting scene with Palemon and Lavinia depicted in the foreground, c. *1790.*

Introduction

Buying

Old pottery and porcelain might well be reckoned the most complex area of all antiques. The literature, vast and impressively scholarly, is evidence of the collecting passions and historical detective work stimulated by this, somehow the most genteel of all the areas of antiques covered in this book.

Over the centuries, and particularly in the 18th, techniques changed quickly as an expanding middle class demanded more refined wares of different kinds. Manufactories rose and fell, sometimes to be resurrected by different owners (Royal Crown Derby is an example) with a change of emphasis on their products. Potters moved from factory to factory trading expertise, literally leaving their mark before moving on or setting up independently (the perambulations of William Billingsley of Nantgarw and the complicated story of Nantgarw-Swansea is a good example).

The documentation of old pottery and porcelain is often sketchy as many craftsmen, quite understandably, were much more concerned with making a living than ensuring that their records would be conveniently ordered for future historians.

Marks, which would seem to offer such an unequivocal way of dating and identifying a piece are not always as straightforward as they at first appear. Unlike silver hallmarks they were and are not legally regulated and enforceable and, as with the pontil mark on old glass, it is precisely because they are taken to be such an important means of dating and identification that they have been and are subject to copying. It is not wise, in a guide such as this, to attempt to explain the intricacies, the similarities and changes seen in the marks of the makers. Simplification can all too easily lead to confusion, and it is far better for the potential buyer to check marks in one of a number of excellent specialist publications listed on page 100. The range, diversity and complexity of the subject are precisely what make old pottery and porcelain such a good area for buyers and collectors at all sorts of levels. Here we are concerned primarily with pieces which, though special, are not too precious to use. Not many of us can afford or feel comfortable with a Chelsea cream jug of 1753 recently sold at auction for £2,860, or would be entirely relaxed pouring our coffee from a Worcester pot of 1760 sold for £3,520. But to build up a harlequin set of early 19th-century cups and saucers at £30 each, or to buy a Ridgway blue-and-white transfer-printed plate *c.* 1820 for £40 or an unmarked late Victorian willow pattern meat dish for £16 is within reach.

Damage will reduce the investment value of old pottery and porcelain considerably in all but the very early and rare earthenware where damage is almost inevitable, but it need not deter the buyer who really wants to build up, say, a dinner service of character which can be used rather than displayed, as long as the damage does not jeopardize the piece in use or make it impractical to use. Collectors at the highest level are fanatically fussy when it comes to damaged pieces and it is possible to buy good things reasonably because they have often quite slight damage. Even though such damage does not impair their function, it affects their value. Be prepared to accept, though, that your gain on the roundabouts might well be lost on the swings if you are buying with an eye on resale. A dealer who may have made light of damage when he sold the piece may suddenly announce that there just isn't a market for such pieces when you come to sell it back!

The vast production of enormous dinner, tea and dessert services from about 1820–1910 also provides a happy hunting ground. A 200 piece dinner service intact will be lucky to find itself a home, whereas it can profitably be split up by dealers (or even the private buyer who goes to a country house sale knowing unwanted pieces can be parcelled out to friends) into manageable parts.

Historical Survey

The very earliest history of pottery-making belongs more to the historian than those who want to buy things for use in the home and it is documented more fully elsewhere than this *Guide* can hope to do.

As far as most buyers are concerned the story of English pottery becomes interesting in the 16th century with the tin-enamelled earthenware introduced from the Netherlands; hence its name: delftware. Although English potteries made their own wonderful delftware, this sort of earthenware (although solid and robust-looking) is fragile and thus rare and comparatively expensive.

During the 17th century the crude and brittle pottery was coated with a clay and water solution (slip) to give it protection and decoration. This slipware was made in quantity at Wrotham in Kent, throughout Staffordshire, Sussex, North Wales and the West Country. It was also in the 17th century that the trade with the Orient being energetically pursued by the Dutch and English East India Companies, introduced what must have seemed the miracle of porcelain: light, translucent yet amazingly strong and beautifully decorated. Immediately English potters (along with their European rivals) began the search for a home-produced porcelain.

The debates about who discovered what, when, first, rage among historians of pottery and porcelain but there seems to be a grudging consensus that John Dwight of Fulham was the first to take out a patent in 1684 on something he called porcelain but which was, in fact, a fine salt-glazed stoneware resistant to hot liquids (unlike its earthenware predecessors, delftware and slipware). This breakthrough was quickly copied by other potteries and by 1715 the fine china clay of Devon and Cornwall was being used domestically and exported.

Continual experiment was spurred on by the increasing fashion for drinking coffee and tea which itself was part of the steady rise of a relatively wealthy middle class determined to cultivate 'taste' and refinement. Not for them the rough utility of coarse pottery, pewter or wooden plates and mugs of earlier and rougher times.

It was then discovered that if stoneware was fired at a lower temperature (750°C) than that previously used (1,200°C) a very adaptable creamware resulted which was lighter. It was then protected by a clear lead glaze. It began to replace other forms of pottery and was to be further developed in the 1770s and 80s by Josiah Wedgwood (who called his version Queensware). At about the same time Wedgwood was also foremost among a group of potters (including Miles Mason) in developing new forms of stoneware (a strengthening of earlier earthenwares) such as redware, brownware and saltglaze stoneware by adding vitreous – glass-like – materials and firing at very high temperatures. Wedgwood called his Black Basalte, Jasperware and Caneware whilst the company Mason founded in the 18th century was to market its Patent Ironstone China in 1813. Spode also made stoneware in the early 19th century.

All the foregoing are types of pottery, albeit pottery attempting to emulate the durability of porcelain, and the search for the secrets of porcelain is a parallel story. Porcelain is chemically different from pottery. It is a mixture of kaolin (china) clay (related to granite as a fine powdered form: hence strength and lightness) and china stone or petuntse (also related to granite). This paste is formed and fired first at 900°C and, having been glazed, is fired again at 1,300°C. The strength of the component clays and the vitrifying effect of the high firing temperatures produce toughness combined with lightness and translucency. This sort of porcelain is known as 'true' or 'hard paste' and the secret of its manufacture known previously only in China was broken by the Meissen factory, near Dresden, Saxony, about 1708. It took another 60 years or so before a passable hard paste formula was found in England (William Cookworthy of Plymouth is usually given the credit but Bristol and New Hall also made it during the 18th century).

In England, soft-paste porcelain proved a popular and often cheaper substitute for true hard paste. Local clay reinforced with sand or flint to boost the vitreous content were substituted for kaolin clay and potash or lead replaced china stone. It was fired first at 1,100°C and then glaze-fired at 900°C. Soft paste, as the name implies, scratches more easily than hard and more easily develops surface cracks when filled with hot liquid. The colours applied to the under-glaze of soft paste sank deeper and produced a softer and very attractive effect.

In the second half of the 18th century soapstone was also substituted for the kaolin clay of hard-paste porcelain because it was found to make pieces more resistant to changes of kiln temperature and therefore a better business proposition.

The addition of bone ash from reduced ox bones (as much as 50% in some cases) to soft-paste porcelain (Bow about 1749) and then to hard paste (Josiah Spode, 1794) created what was to be by 1800 the staple of fine English chinaware: bone china.

Left: New Hall hard paste coffee can enamelled in blue, pink and gilt, c. *1795. Centre: Fluted Coalport china coffee can,* c. *1820, painted and gilt with vines. Right: Crescent marked Worcester soapstone porcelain coffee cup, reeded and decorated in blue and gilt,* c. *1785. Note the characteristic straight sides of the cans compared with the rim-footed cup.*

Techniques and Terms

Agate ware Lead-glazed earthenware of brilliant-coloured glazes on improved cream-coloured salt-glaze body. Early Wedgwood/Whieldon partnership made agate, tortoiseshell and marbled stoneware while continuing to refine the body. Technically important as a turning point for English 'china'. In 1759 Wedgwood left the Whieldon firm and, using the refined earthenware body with cream-coloured glaze, began to make 'Queensware' or 'Creamware'. *Principal products:* tortoiseshell, marbled, plates, teapots, jugs, tureens, knife handles.

Applied relief Decorative shapes made separately and added to the basic shape, slightly raised on the surface.

Biscuit (or **bisque**) When pottery or porcelain clay has been fired once in the kiln it is hardened but porous and is still the original clay colour.

Black Basalt(e) ware Revived in the 19th century as Basalt or Black Basalte. Developed by Josiah Wedgwood in the 1770s and ultimately called 'Egyptian black' by him. Matt or shiny black stoneware made from ironstone and other ingredients. Extremely successful, highly prized during 18th and 19th centuries for vases, cabinet ware, tablets, plaques and as a silver substitute for writing and toilet articles. *Principal products:* teapots, cream jugs, sugar bowls, coffee pots, chocolate pots, medallions, plaques, cabinet-ware, articles for writing and toilet tables, vases, urns. *Principal producers:* Josiah Wedgwood's 'Etruria' works, E. Mayer & Son, Palmer & Neale, Thomas Whieldon, Lakin & Poole, Eastwood, John Turner, E. J. Birch, Joseph Twyford, Charles Green, H. Palmer of Hanley, Josiah Spode, David Dunderdale of Castleford. *Decoration:* Moulded, applied relief, classical and commemorative. Regency Adam style.

Blue-and-white The very high demand for imported Oriental blue-and-white porcelain stimulated the search for home-produced copies. Dr Wall, a Bristol merchant-chemist, succeeded in making a blue dye from cobalt (the supplies of which were previously dependent on Germany) and this breakthrough was commercially exploited by Dr Wall's Worcester Porcelain Company (which had started at Bristol). Other makers of pottery and porcelain also produced blue-and-white ware in the oriental manner.

By the last quarter of the 18th century transfer printing (introduced by Robert Hancock, 1756) on to pottery (Minton's fine Nankin ware is an outstanding example) was being developed. Much blue-and-white china was printed in underglaze blue whereby a pattern would be engraved on a copper plate, the plate treated with cobalt blue and an impression taken onto tissue-thin paper, and then transferred to the unglazed biscuit; the piece was then fired and glazed with the border being added separately (if one looks closely, some border patterns are seen not to meet accurately). Transfer-printed blue-and-white ware was immensely popular throughout the 19th century.

Willow-pattern blue-and-white is probably the best known. It was supposed to have been introduced by Thomas Turner of Caughley and then copied by Thomas Minton about 1785 when he left Caughley. Minton sold the pattern to several factories, the first of which may well have been Spode. There are many variants of the willow pattern and it has been estimated that there were over 200 potters turning out willow ware by 1865. The number of people on the bridge, the number of birds and trees varies greatly but they are not a reliable guide to dating.

Body Potter's clay, strictly a term used for earthenware and stoneware, but generally applied to all basic mixtures used by pottery and porcelain makers.

Spode transfer-printed bone china Italian pattern blue-and-white platter, early 19th century.

Bone china Adopted by most English potters at the beginning of the 19th century as an ideal formula for fine 'china'. Bone-ash from calcinated ox bones was added to hard-paste ingredients and was first produced commercially by Josiah Spode in 1794 from developments in 'bone porcelain' produced by Bow, Chelsea, Derby, Caughley, Liverpool. Due to its very white, translucent and durable characteristics it quickly became the standard English china. The great 18th- and 19th-century manufacturers made quantities of extravagantly decorated and gilded tableware for the nobility and by the middle of the last century were mass-producing many regular designs. *Principal products:* Tableware, tureens, vegetable dishes, dessert services, tea services, coffee services, breakfast services, ornamental and cabinet ware, vases. *Principal producers:* Derby, Rockingham, Minton, Liverpool, Coalport, Worcester, Copeland & Garrett (late Spode), Swansea, Davenport. *Decoration:* Initially copied from the French and German designs, but as technique improved, developed individual styles and colours of their own by which their wares are recognized.

Bone porcelain Soft-paste porcelain body strengthened with powdered bone ash.

Brownware Brown salt-glazed stoneware of the 17th and 18th centuries. Revived in the 19th century. It was made from sand-enriched clay, originating in Germany and known also as 'Cologne ware'. The first potter to make it in England was John Dwight of Fulham who also experimented with marbled effects, later taken up and developed by Thomas Whieldon and Josiah Wedgwood. *Principal products:* Jugs, mugs, functional bottles, spirit flasks, jars, harvest pitchers, Toby jugs, loving cups. *Principal producers:* Fulham, Lambeth, later Staffordshire, Sunderland, Derbyshire and many others. See also **Nottingham Stoneware.** *Decoration:* Turned rims, necks, incised flower, leaf decoration. Raised sporting, hunting scenes on buff-coloured body with dark-brown glaze to top half.

Cabaret set Usually porcelain or bone china tea set for one or two people, including matching tray in same material.

Cabinet ware Decorative pieces never intended for use but only for display and admiration.

Cane and bamboo ware Made by Wedgwood from the mid-1780s of tan-coloured unglazed stoneware with cane and bamboo imitation in relief. Used much for tea sets, jugs, pot pourri jars and candlesticks.

Castleford ware Late 18th, early 19th century. Moulded white salt-glaze ware with relief decoration and painted panels, usually landscapes. Castleford was near Leeds, the leading salt-glaze pottery of the period. Rare pieces marked 'Turner' for John Turner, or D D & Co. Castleford for David Dunderdale.

Caudle pot Two-handled bowl with lid and saucer, porcelain in 18th century, bone china in 19th. Often specially made in pairs as presentation gifts.

Cobalt Basic blue colouring, originally imported from Saxony in Germany (also known as zaffre or sapphire). Extremely important in early ceramics as it stood up to the extreme heat of the glazing kiln. Made in Bristol and Cornwall in the 18th century.

Combed decoration Simple method of decorating earthenware by combing the liquid 'slip' into wavy patterns.

Left: 'Opaque China,' late 19th century with Chinese decoration on a white ground. Right: Brown Nottingham stoneware jug, c. 1800, from the Morley factory.

Early 19-century Staffordshire pottery lustre cow creamers. A matching pair in blue and black with pink noses and green bases.

Cottages Also includes churches and castles in which tablets (called pastilles) were burned in order to give off a fragrant aroma – quite useful in the days before adequate sanitation. There are many modern replicas.

Cow-creamer milk jugs modelled to resemble, not surprisingly, a cow. The tail would be the handle, the mouth the spout, and milk was poured into the body through an opening in its back. Cow-creamers without a base are usually 19th century and early 20th century imitations.

Creamware From 1750s to the present day. Some authorities suggest it was invented by the Astburys and Enoch Booth; it was first developed commercially by Josiah Wedgwood using liquid cream-coloured lead glaze over an improved earthenware body fired at a moderate temperature and very similar to that used for saltglaze. In the late 18th century it displaced delftware as the principal earthenware product. Called 'Queensware' by Wedgwood in 1765 after a commission from Queen Charlotte. In its early stages its main drawback was that it was not hot water-resistant and could not be used for teapots, coffee pots etc. Once developed, taken up by many Staffordshire potters many of whom shamelessly adopted the name 'Queensware'. Creamware usually means plain undecorated ware, but much of it had simple decoration. *Principal products:* Sweetmeat and pickle dishes, bowls, cream jugs, serving dishes, sauce boats, tureens, pharmaceutical jars, jugs, dessert plates, centrepieces, cabinet pieces and display pieces. From 1760s teapots, coffee pots, chocolate pots, night lamps, food warmers and many domestic articles: mousse moulds, jelly moulds, shapes, ice-cream moulds, bowls and dishes. *Principal producers:* Wedgwood, Spode, Minton, Swinton (later Rockingham), Leeds, Swansea, Sunderland, Liverpool and many Staffordshire potteries. *Decoration:* Much pierced and lattice work similar to white saltglaze, low-relief lattice and decoration, painted scenes, nautical motifs, commemorative, royal and loyal, local views, export wares to America.

Delftware 16th, 17th and 18th centuries. Tin-enamelled earthenware with a white glaze. Brought into England by the Dutch, and was an attempt after contact with the Orient to produce a white-surfaced pottery which resembled 'china'. Naturally much of it was decorated to imitate Chinese and oriental patterns. *Principal products:* Wine bottles, pill slabs, drug jars, plaques, large shallow serving bowls or chargers, barbers' bowls, bleeding bowls, posset pots, vases, flower bricks, apothecaries' pots and jars, sauce boats, wine cups, caudle cups, syrup pots, spouted pots, fuddling cups, puzzle jugs, tiles. From 18th century: tea, coffee and chocolate pots. *Decoration:* oriental designs, sprigs, flowers, leaves, royal and loyal, commemorative and similar themes to slip-ware. London: White on white, blue and white, manganese purple. Bristol: Blue and white, green, brick red, brown, yellow, purple. Liverpool: Blue and white – in particular nautical scenes for deep large punch bowls, also polychrome enamels. Wincanton: Blue and white, blue and manganese, often covering the whole ground.

Earthenware Term used to refer to clay ware which remains porous after firing and for most purposes consequently requires glazing.

Engine turned Finely-shaped line patterns originally engraved on metal as decoration, used by Wedgwood and other potters from 1760s to decorate fine hard stoneware.

Faïence French tin-glazed wares originally named for pottery coming from Fayence.

Fairings Mementoes of a visit to the fair, they were small porcelain groups of figures manufactured mainly in Germany in the last half of the last century and the early part of the 20th for the English market. Often inscribed with slightly titillating mottoes ('Kiss me quick,' 'Last in bed must turn out the light') they are one of the classic examples (along with Staffordshire dogs and figures) of working-class knick-knacks which are now collected avidly and hence much copied.

Famille rose An exceptionally fine variety of Chinese decorative porcelain with a rose-pink glaze. The style was much copied by Meissen, Bow, Chelsea and Worcester, among others.

Felspar porcelain Another soft-paste substance based, as its name implies, on mineral as opposed to 'bone' base, contemporary with development of the more universally accepted 'bone china'. Thicker than hard-paste porcelain and was used in particular by Spode as base for transfer-printed wares.

Firing Baking clay-ware in kilns at high temperatures, baking glazed ware to fix the glaze. Twice-fired means fired again to fix the painting, decoration on once-fired ware.

Frit A vitreous mixture consisting of sand or calcined flint and potash or lead, added to local clay to give soft-paste porcelain its characteristic toughness.

Fuddling cup Three or more mugs, usually earthenware, joined together so that the liquid flows between them.

Glaze Coating made from silicate or glass-based substances to decorate, enhance and make pottery and porcelain non-porous.

Green glaze ware Tableware with a brilliant green liquid glaze over moulded shapes, first made by Whieldon in the 1740s, developed commercially by Wedgwood in the 1760s and popular ever since. Leaf-shaped dishes, cream jugs, serving dishes, dessert ware, tea ware, all with leaf theme. Made consistently by many imitators until the present day, as well as current Wedgwood products. Victorian green glaze was thicker, earthenware finer. *Principal producers:* Wedgwood and Whieldon. Imitated from 1860s by Poole, Stanway & Wood, Banks & Thorney of Hanley, Daniel & Son of Longton and many more recent imitators.

Hard-paste porcelain Pure white, translucent porcelain approximating to oriental 'china'. Has a metallic ring when struck and is immensely strong in spite of its apparent delicacy. The strength is acquired by ageing the paste, kaolin and china stone (petuntse), before firing at high temperature. The Chinese stored their paste for decades; to the English potters seven or eight months was enough. Called 'hard paste' because it requires a 'hard fire', i.e. a high temperature. First made commercially in England by William Cookworthy at Plymouth in 1768 but Richard Champion of Bristol had a monopoly on the Cornish clay essential to its manufacture. 1770 Plymouth potteries transferred to Bristol where Champion's Hard Paste Porcelain was manufactured. *Principal English products:* Copies of Dresden figures, Four Seasons, Four Elements, etc. Vases, cabinet pieces, decorative ware, tea ware in the oriental manner. *Principal producers:* Plymouth, Bristol, New Hall. *Decoration:* Inevitably, much decoration in the Chinese manner, blue-and-white for articles associated with tea-drinking. Copies also from Bristol of Meissen ware, marked with Meissen crossed swords and the letter 'B'. See also **Soft-paste porcelain.**

Imari Name used by.18th-century English potters for export Japanese ware, with patterns derived from brocaded silks, hence considerably gilded.

Incised Decoration made by cutting or engraving into the body.

'In the white' Undecorated ware.

Ironstone Tough earthenware made from mineral base.

Jackfield ware A generic term for any ware glazed with a glossy black finish. Coffee and teapots, jugs etc. made by several Staffordshire potteries including Whieldon. Originally a variety of red pottery covered with a brilliant black glaze made at Jackfield in Shropshire in the 18th century (sometimes called 'jetware').

Lambeth earthenware (Majolica ware, Mintonware) Only superficially resembling delftware because of common roots in antiquity via Italian maiolica. Made in the 1850s by Herbert Minton for a line of cheap wares, mugs, jugs, platters etc. Adopted by the 'Art Movement' of the Victorians and made from 1872 at John Doulton's pottery, decorated by many artists from the Lambeth School of Art. Continued production until 1914. *Principal products:* Traditional ware, the ground colour is distinctly yellow, the painting more elaborate than delft ware.

Lead glaze Powdered lead ore sprinkled on ware which turned yellow when fired in the kiln, producing familiar greenish-yellow 'Tudor green'. Colourless lead glaze from 1750s.

Low relief Decoration slightly raised from surface.

Lustreware A form of ceramic decoration using very small amounts of gold (for 'copper' lustreware) and platinum (for 'silver' lustreware) in the pigment. Although developed in Sunderland in the 1740s, its main production dates from about 1800 when it was used to imitate gold and silverware, an intention frustrated by the introduction of electroplating in 1840. Modern reproductions abound (especially copper lustre jugs and wall plaques). *Principal products:* All-silver tea services, coffee pots, chocolate pots, candlesticks, silver pieces, tankards, goblets etc. Lustre decoration for tableware, cups, saucers, jugs, mugs. Copper lustre for large-lipped jugs in sets, commemorative ware, royal and loyal, local views, souvenir pieces, plaques, motto jugs and mugs. Very popular with Victorians. *Principal producers:* Wedgwood as silver substitute, Sunderland and many Staffordshire potters for copper, purple etc. *Decoration:* As with gilding to highlight and band pieces of tableware, silver on white ground for tankards, mugs. Copper lustre, purple lustre with medallions of views, mottoes etc.

Majolica English derivation of 'maiolica', majolica was colourful moulded ware with opaque buff-coloured or white ground vividly painted. Developed in Minton factory in 1850s.

Martinware Jugs modelled in grotesque animal forms with spooky human expressions or human heads with leering clownish faces made by the Martin brothers first at Fulham and then at Southall, London, 1873–1915 in salt-glazed stoneware. This distinctive grotesqueness has created a collector's market but also effectively puts off many others.

Mazarine blue Rich blue colour developed in France, imitated by Chelsea, Derby, Worcester.

Mocha ware From 18th century, but mainly 19th century. A range of cheap tableware principally made for coffee houses, taverns, public houses. Its name variously attributed to 'Mocha' coffee, and to the moss-like decoration which resembles trees. Early Mocha ware is highly collectable, but by the 19th century, it was thick, crude earthenware with a cream glaze and 'Mocha' decoration and jugs, mugs, tankards, coffee pots, plates of various sizes were made in great quantities. *Principal producers:* Edge & Malkin, Burslem; T. G. Green & Co., Derbyshire; Leeds Potteries, by 19th century most potteries in Britain, also in France.

Moulded Tableware and figures made from pressing the body (stoneware, earthenware, porcelain etc.) between two moulds, allowing great freedom of shape and variety of decoration which could be repeated identically.

Nankin ware Common name loosely applied to 18th century pseudo-oriental blue-and-white ware.

Nottingham stoneware A finer quality brown salt-glazed stoneware particular to this town, made throughout the 18th century. Peculiar to Nottingham was double-walled hollow ware made in late 18th century, with inner vessel to contain liquid and outer pierced wall, punched or perforated to give an illusion of lightness in weight not otherwise achieved in this heavy material. *Principal products:* Loving cups, puzzle jugs, mugs and punch bowls, 'Bear jugs' with surface covered with clay shavings to represent fur. Made again at the end of 18th century with bear squeezing Napoleon. *Principal producers:* Nottingham, also Chesterfield and Brampton. *Decoration:* Turned and incised.

Parian Primarily a fine-grained unglazed, white variety of soft-paste porcelain used for figurines by Copeland and Garrett, Minton and Wedgwood, its cheaper hard-paste variety was used for moulded jugs, vases and dishes. Differs from biscuit or unglazed porcelain by its characteristic silkiness. Biscuit has a chalky appearance.

Pearl ware A harder-bodied earthenware with a slightly iridescent appearance. Developed by Josiah Wedgwood, resistant to hot water and considered by him simply as an improvement on Queensware. *Principal products:* Dessert services, tableware of all sorts until 1770s. After that date, confined mainly to ornamental work. *Principal producers:* Many other potteries used pearlware while experimenting with basic creamware, including Josiah Spode, Leeds.

Piecrust ware Dates from 1790s and outbreak of Napoleonic Wars when a flour tax prohibited English cooks from making standing crust pies and raised pies. Josiah Wedgwood produced a range of vitrified stoneware to substitute for pastry cases, brought to the table as 'crock pies'. Elaborately decorated, often in the shape of a hare, pheasant, duck etc. with sprigged ornament, leaves and flowers in relief. Not heatproof, purely decorative. Chesterfield potters developed an ironstone ware which was less crisply decorated but withstood oven heat and boiling in water. By the 1830s this ceramic was being made by several potteries.

In 1850 Wedgwood developed a new range of ovenproof glazed stoneware pie dishes in four sizes designed to be placed inside the ornamental piecrust. *Principal products:* Imitation piecrusts with crisp relief modelling of game, birds' head finials to lids, leaves, ferns, swags, etc. *Principal producers:* Wedgwood, John and William Turner, Elijah Mayer, William Adams & Son, John Davenport, Swansea. *Decoration:* Relief moulded, uncoloured. Swansea decorated theirs with sprigs of fruiting ivy.

Pill slab Tile, often delftware, used by pharmacists for mixing powders, potions and for rolling pills. Also used as shop signs.

Pipeclay Fine white substance made from 'china clay' used as decoration, particularly by Wedgwood.

Porcelain see **Bone china, Bone porcelain, Hard paste, Soft paste.**

Pot lids The decorative tops of glazed stoneware jars which originally contained men's hair pomade, fish-paste spreads, toothpaste or shaving cream were first produced in the early years of 19th century by such makers as Mayer, Maling and, most notably, Pratt of Fenton who pioneered a multicoloured printing process. Many reproductions can be found, of which the collector should beware.

Posset pot Two-handled, lidded, sometimes spouted pots made in slipware, delftware, stoneware in 17th, 18th centuries.

Prattware William Pratt (1753–99) made a highly coloured Staffordshire earthenware of folksy charm made also by many other potteries. Tea caddies, teapots, plaques, jugs with rustic themes in high relief are characteristic, as are Toby jugs, cow-creamers, watchstands, commemorative busts and naive ornaments. Dessert and tea services with distinctive malachite borders of intricate oak-leaf pattern borders and colour-printed pots lids were made until the last quarter of the 19th century.

Queensware Name granted to Wedgwood's range of creamware, later adopted by many other potteries for similar ware of their own manufacture. See **Creamware.**

Red stoneware Late 17th and 18th centuries. Developed by John Dwight of Fulham in imitation of Chinese red stoneware imported into England with cargoes of tea. Also made by John Elers of Vauxhall and by several early 18th-century imitators, among them Josiah Wedgwood. Unglazed hard red stoneware later improved upon by Samuel Bell of Newcastle-under-Lyme and polished to high gloss. Josiah Wedgwood in early 1760s produced attractive 'rosso antico' with engine-turned and 'famille-rose' enamel type decoration. Proved highly suitable material for tea, coffee, chocolate pots in mid-18th century. The red clay base later proved an ideal substance for Staffordshire lustreware. *Principal products:* Tea ware, pots, bowls, cream jugs, sugar boxes, teapoys. *Principal producers:* Fulham, Lambeth, Wedgwood, Coalbrookdale, Enoch Wood, Spode, Samuel Hollins, Robert Wilson and other Staffordshire potters. *Decoration:* Impressed, stamped, pierced and engine-turned. Applied raised decoration, imitation Chinese sprig ornament, decorative handles, spouts. Some with imitation Chinese stamps on base.

Relief A raised decoration modelled on to the pottery or porcelain body.

Salmon scale Fine gilt lattice decoration resembling fish scales, used notably by Worcester.

Saltglaze First developed by John Dwight of Fulham in 1671, rock salt was thrown into the kiln, where it volatilized together with silicon and aluminium oxides in the clay to give a slightly pitted glaze. During the mid-18th century bright enamel colours were used to make striking contrasts with neutral-coloured body. It was moulded, and a high degree of intricacy was achieved in pierced ware, basket-work and low relief decoration. Being neither thrown nor turned, all manner of curious shapes were used for teapots in particular, including houses and animals. *Principal products:* Teapots, coffee pots, chocolate pots, dishes, plates, puzzle jugs, mugs, food warmers, night lamps, cream jugs, sauce boats, dessert baskets, serving dishes, tureens, chestnut dishes, domestic ware, flat ware. *Principal producers:* Burslem, Leeds, Liverpool, many Staffordshire potteries. *Decoration:* White pipeclay moulded relief, lattice, pierced, basket-work, moulded relief. From 1740s blue cobalt-stained clay was rubbed into incised decoration, known as 'Scratch blue'. Blue-and-white oriental enamelled overglaze with clear colours, crude painting. Agate, tortoiseshell and marbled also made for knife handles, teapots, ornamental figures, particularly by Whieldon and Wedgwood in 1740s.

Scratch blue Scratches or incisions filled with cobalt blue powder before firing. 18th century.

Sgraffito After the pottery has been coated with a creamy slip it is scratched ('sgraffito' in Italian) to make a pattern. The piece is then glazed. Although this is an ancient tradition it was particularly popular on Staffordshire mugs and jugs. When the scratched part was coloured in with cobalt it was known as Scratch blue.

Slip A cream-thick mixture of clay and water which was either used to completely cover a piece or was dribbled over it for decorative effect.

Slipware Plain earthenware decorated with slip and then glazed. Made in the 17th and 18th centuries, with country potteries continuing well into the 19th century. The ground colour of lead and manganese glaze is yellowish, or yellowish-green. The natural clay colour depends on the district, varying from light buff to dark terracotta red. Sometimes an entire piece is dipped in slip which is then cut away into patterns before firing and glazing. *Principal products:* Jugs, posset pots, flat plates, dishes, chargers, pitchers, flasks, wine jugs, puzzle jugs, fuddling cups, tygs, naive ornamental pieces. *Principal districts:* Wrotham in Kent, Harlow in Essex, Staffordshire, Tickenhall in Derbyshire, Bolsover near Chesterfield, Buckinghamshire, Cambridgeshire, Hampshire, Nottingham, Somerset, Bristol, Warwickshire, Wiltshire, Yorkshire, Glamorganshire, Devon.

Soapstone porcelain A divergence from earthenware in the search for white, hot water-resistant substances for tea ware, tableware, soapstone porcelain is a soft-paste porcelain which bridges the gap between earthenware and 'bone china' which was finally developed in the late 18th century. *Principal producers:* Worcester, Bristol, Liverpool and Caughley 1748–80.

Soft-paste porcelain White-bodied base also known as 'bone porcelain' and transitional development before 'bone china'. First made at Bow in the 1750s, followed by Chelsea, Derby, Liverpool and Lowestoft. Early soft-paste porcelain was very fine and the nearest then yet achieved by English potters to oriental 'china'. It could not withstand hot water and was at first confined to cabinet pieces and ornamental ware. *Principal products:* Ornamental figures, candlesticks, writing and toilet table articles, decorative ware, bowls, boxes, figures. From 1760s when Bow developed a hot-water resistant soft-paste porcelain, dessert services, tea services, coffee services, breakfast services, flatware and tableware of all kinds. *Principal producers:* Bow, Chelsea, Derby, Liverpool, Lowestoft, Longton Hall, Worcester. *Decoration:* Early ornamental figures made at Derby, Chelsea, Bow, were influenced by Meissen, Sèvres, Dresden, pastoral, animal, finely decorated and sculpted, though colouring was still relatively crude compared to European work.

Spill vase, spill jar Wide-mouthed, often straight-sided jar to hold strips of wood, paper, etc. to light pipes from the fire.

Staffordshire blue White earthenware, bone china, painted or transfer-printed, made in great quantities by numerous potteries in 18th and 19th centuries.

Stoneware Stone or flint was added to the clay used to make earthenware and fired at a high temperature (1,300°C) to produce a hard non-porous pottery. Salt was thrown into the kiln at its highest temperature to produce salt-glazed stoneware.

Tazza Originally from the Arabic for basin, they were dishes on a raised foot or pedestal which held fruit or sweetmeats. A necessary part of most Victorian and Edwardian dinner and dessert services, they were grandly positioned at the centre of the dining table or on the sideboard.

Teapoy In ceramics, a lidded container for preserving tea.

Terracotta Ancient, soft, unglazed, slightly porous ware, material for flowerpots etc. In 18th century developed by Josiah Wedgwood into intricate classical urns, plant pots, boxes, jardinières. Victorian terracotta highly popular for conservatories etc. made at Lambeth, Wedgwood, Doulton, Coalbrookdale, Lowesby in Leicestershire and F & R Pratt of Fenton.

Tin-enamelled, tin-glazed Opaque substance with tin base, particularly associated with Delft.

Toby jugs First produced about 1760 and made by many factories, they represent genre-types such as hearty squires, national heroes and historical characters. Although modelled with great vitality in the 18th century they had by the end of the 19th century degenerated into crude copies. Very early jugs tend to be unglazed with non-gaudy colours.

Transfer-printing Stoneware, bone china, decorated by transferring pattern or picture from engraved and inked copper plate onto a sheet of tissue paper, a process which could be repeated many times with each engraving. See **Blue-and-white.**

Turned Hollow ware shaped and made on a lathe.

Tyg A drinking pot often with more than one handle.

Wemyss ware Vases, mugs, tea sets bowls, candlesticks, with underglazed painting of fruit, flowers, cocks and hens, made at the Fife Pottery by the Heron family from 1817.

Willow pattern See **Blue-and-white.**

Principal Pottery and Porcelain Factories

Belleek: 1857– present day

Established at Fermanagh, Northern Ireland, it specialized in a lustrous mother-of-pearl effect on rather elaborate openwork baskets, or dishes decorated with modelled marine motifs such as seahorses and sea-shells. Tea services were often decorated with finely modelled flower-clusters.

Bow: 1745–75

Soft-paste porcelain developed by Thomas Frye and others in competition with Chinese imports. Blue-and-white from 1753 for tea ware etc. Dessert services, tableware from 1759. Pastoral scenes, fruits, birds on useful and decorative wares. Octagonal plates and pot-bellied mugs were typical. Blue ground from 1765, then rose pompadour, rich cobalt blue, turquoise, copper red, yellow, tiny gold leaves. Its vast output varied in quality and appearance, making identification difficult sometimes. Some Bow soft paste has poor translucency, is heavy for its proportions and is strongly absorbent on unglazed areas. In the later years a decline was marked by increasing elaboration and gilding.

Bristol: 1600s–1770s

Tin-enamelled delft from 1600s. Buff tinted body, slatey blues, reddish-white glaze. Also 'quaker green', dull yellow, brownish orange, manganese purple and pale turquoise blue. Symmetrical flowers characteristic. Much Oriental-style blue-and-white. Soft-paste porcelain from 1750s. Firm acquired by Dr Wall of Worcester in 1752. See Champion's Hard-Paste Porcelain below for last period.

Caughley: 1775–99 (Pronounced 'calf-lee')

Established as The Salopian China Manufactory by Thomas Turner, formerly of Worcester. Soapstone porcelain, transfer-printed in black, sepia and blue. Much blue-and-white, blue with characteristic violet tinge. Plain tableware in all-over blue with gilding. Chinese-style landscapes, fisherman and pleasure-boat designs. Gilding for edge bandings, highlights, sprays of foliage picked out in gold. There is also a great deal of confusion with Worcester which worked closely with Caughley. 1799–1814: traded as Coalport/Caughley. Caughley manufactory acquired by Coalport in 1814.

Champion's Hard-Paste Porcelain: Bristol, 1770s–1782

Richard Champion acquired William Cookworthy's patent, improved on the hard-paste and adopted fashionable Sèvres neo-classical decoration. Champion concentrated on tea and coffee sets both for grand families and as 'cottage' ware but also made figures and small oval plaques modelled with flowers. Beset by litigation from rivals and the failure of his North American trade, Champion was forced to sell his patent to the group of Staffordshire potters who founded New Hall.

Chelsea: 1745–69

1745–49 Triangle period
1749–52 Raised Anchor period
1752–56 Red Anchor period
1756–69 Gold Anchor period
Leader in the field in fine porcelain in the Sèvres and Meissen style. The Raised Anchor and Red Anchor wares are most prized, the better the piece the smaller the anchor. Some oriental styles also produced. Colours are exceptionally brilliant and have been copied by almost every other pottery with greater or lesser success. Famous Chelsea claret and turquoise, mazarine blue, pea green, well-balanced gilding. Later ware fell in with the fashion for landscape, exotic birds, fruit and flowers.
Chelsea–Derby: 1770–84. See Derby.

Coalport: 1795 to present day

Considerable output of willow pattern and transfer-printed ware from 1814. 1822 felspar porcelain production for fine translucent tableware. Characteristic rich maroon ground colour; rich, ornate services, many in the Sèvres and Meissen manner. Great copyists: Derby mazarine blue, Sèvres turquoise and rose pompadour, Chelsea claret ground colour. In 1926 Coalport moved to Stoke, Staffordshire. See also Caughley.

Copeland

See Spode

Davenport: 1793–1885

Earthenware and moulded stoneware. Bone china in similar colouring and decoration to

Derby. Large table services, some fine decoration.

Derby: 1749–1848 (Royal Crown Derby 1876 to present day)

Under William Duesbury, mainly figures in the Meissen manner but also useful wares of variable quality, often thickly potted with pitted glaze. After Duesbury bought the Chelsea factory in 1770 there was an improvement in the production of both figures and useful wares, especially tea and dinner wares. Known as Crown Derby (1786–1811), it was during this period that the introduction of bone china meant an increased emphasis on tableware, quantities of which were decorated with the Japanese Imari pattern. Between 1811 and 1848 the factory was known as Bloor Derby and quantity replaced quality - opaque, heavy china with glazes tending to crack; poor, gaudy colouring and heavy-handed use of the Imari pattern to hide defects and appeal to a popular if vulgar taste for strident colours. Old Crown Derby China Works (1848–1935) was established by ex-employees using old Derby moulds. An entirely separate concern - the (Royal) Crown Derby Porcelain Co. - was established in 1876 and continues to this day.

Doulton & Co: 1815 to present day

Established as a manufacturer of sanitary earthenware, after the Great Exhibition of 1851 moved into 'craft' pottery in association with the Lambeth School of Art, producing ornamental pottery, grotesque heads, commemorative mugs. In 1872 production began of Lambeth faïence, based on the Minton series of majolica ware and very popular with Victorians. Royal Doulton from 1902. Work by many famous artists from this pottery: deserves further study.

Fulham 1671 - present

Founded by the remarkable John Dwight in 1671 to make, salt-glazed earthenwares, later developed by John Astbury and Ralph Shaw into white salt-glazed stoneware. The family remained in control until 1861 making a range of salt-glazed stoneware domestic and sanitary ware and tankards and jugs decorated with hunting scenes and celebrities of the day. In the 1860s the decoration changed to favour the Japanese style.

Leeds: 1760–1878

Salt-glazed stoneware. Creamware, blue-and-white in Chinese designs. Among the finest manufacturers of creamware which is particularly fine and light in weight. Lattice, trellis, patterns cut by hand with hearts, diamonds, circles, handles of inter-twined strips ending in flowers, leaves, berries. Pierced candlesticks, table centre-pieces. Also made agate, pearlware, tortoisehell and lustre. Engine-turned red stoneware.

Liverpool: 17th century - 1800

Tin-enamelled delft ware by 1710. Blue-and-white oriental teaware. Creamware from 1780s, light in weight, decorated in blue and other enamelled colours, and blue and black transfer printing. Soft-paste porcelain from mid-18th century to 1800. Soapstone porcelain resistant to hot water from 1756. Much blue-and-white Chinese design to 1770s. Some red and black transfer-printed ware, not very high quality. Excellent tableware in soapstone porcelain with high-quality enamelled decoration. Of the group of Liverpool potteries of the 18th century, the Herculaneum is the best-known, founded in 1796. Heavy quality fine tableware and flat ware with duck-egg greenish glaze from Herculanaeum is distinctive, also punch bowls decorated with brilliant blue enamel.

Mason's Patent Ironstone transfer-printed side plate in 'India Grasshopper' pattern, c. *1820.*

Lowestoft: 1757–99

Soft-paste porcelain domestic wares, souvenirs, commemorative, blue-and-white and polychrome, also small flowers painted inside bowls as well as on the outside. Reds are very purplish, mauve-pink.

Mason's *c.* 1792 – present

Strong, hard plebian earthenware development by Miles Mason *c.* 1792 and patented 1813 but used in slightly adapted forms by many potteries. Mason's Patent Ironstone China was extremely popular, mass-produced, brought pseudo-Oriental polychromatic designs to the general public who had only been able to buy monochrome transfer-printed wares. By the mid-19th century designs were peonies, roses, birds of paradise, butterflies, all lavishly painted, the more expensive services embellished with generous gilding. Most typical are Mason's octagonal jugs with reptilian handles, sold in sets of three to 14. From 1848 until recently the firm traded under the name of Geo. L. Ashworth and Brothers, but has recently reverted to Mason's Patent Ironstone.

Minton: *c.* 1793 – present

Thomas Minton was a pupil of Thomas Turner of Caughley and at one time an employee of Jeremiah Spode. He founded his own firm about 1793 and by the turn of the century had begun production of bone china with fine blue transfer printing of 'Nankin' patterns. Regency Greek key patterns on simply decorated rims to 1820s; thereafter designs became more exotic with increasing use of gilding for foliage, vines and tendrils. Japan colouring introduced for patterns with blue and pink peonies and variegated leaves. From 1823 Minton cups had decorated inner rims and by 1825 scalloped edges to cups and saucers. Thomas died 1836 and was succeeded by his son Herbert, who produced a wide range of excellent transfer-printed ware from the 1840s. In the 1850s developed English 'majolica' resembling Dutch Delft with a warmer, creamier ground. From 1848 began new range of exotic cabinet ware and enormous output of dinner services and tableware from the most opulent to the humblest. Minton's used a year code from 1842 to 1943, continuing thereafter with last two digits of the year only.

Nantgarw-Swansea: 1813–20

After an abortive attempt to produce a soft-paste porcelain to rival Sèvres, William Billingsley moved from Nantgarw near Swansea to the better-equipped factory of the Cambrian Pottery at Swansea. A distinctive and fine duck-egg porcelain was one of the results of this period at Swansea (1816–17) but Billingsley went back to Nantgarw to produce his own soft-paste porcelain. Whether from Nantgarw or Swansea, the wares were famous for high-quality painting, especially of flowers. However, a lot of Nantgarw-Swansea ware was decorated in London from

Minton bone china teacup and saucer, late 18th century.

the white. Much faked and much copied, especially by Coalport.

Rockingham: 1745–1842

From 1745 making earthenware, tea and coffee services; from 1785 under the name of Swinton. 1787–1806 the firm was in partnership with Leeds and making identical wares under the name of Greens, Bingley and Co. Creamware, Queensware, Nankin blue, tortoiseshell, Egyptian black and brown china. From 1807 traded under the name Brameld, making brown domestic china, domestic ware, cane-coloured stoneware from 1820. 1826 with financing by Earl Fitzwilliam began trading under the name Rockingham for fine bone china. Rich clientele and consequently ornate rococo designs, heavily gilded, with superb colouring: opaque apple green particularly characteristic, also deep violet blue, deep pinks, deep yellow, maroon, peach and gilded pink. Relief-moulded edges to dessert services, dinner services in Georgian silver shapes. Tea-table ware with engraved views on base and sides. Massive table services were stock-in-trade but nobility deserted the firm after the death of William IV with catastrophic results.

Spode: 1770–1833

Copeland & Garrett 1833–47
Copeland 1847–1970
Spode Ltd 1970 - present
Creamware from 1770. Transfer-printing from 1780s. Pearlware from 1780s - richer, more lustrous blue than 'Staffordshire blue'. Felspar porcelain, ironstone china from 1800s. Fine transfer-printed ware with Oriental, pastoral, Indian, 'new Nankin', Italian and in 1826 'Blue Imperial'. Table

One of a pair of Spode's 'New Stone' sauce tureens decorated in famille rose *coloured enamels applied over a printed outline pattern, c. 1825.*

Brameld (which later became the great Rockingham factory) parroquete *pattern. Twelve-sided dish with gadrooned edges, 1820–30.*

services, richly coloured and often gilded. Distinctive blue with splashes of scarlet, many of them in fashionable Japanese patterns. Early period to 1797 when Josiah Spode died most highly regarded. From Copeland & Garrett more run-of-the-mill table services as well as made-to-order, but did not aspire to the rich heights of Rockingham. Now trades as 'Spode Ltd.'

Wedgwood: 1759 to present day

Most prolific and inventive of all English potters, though the firm only ventured into bone china for a brief period. Original partnership with Thomas Whieldon experimenting with fine-quality stoneware, producing range of agate, tortoiseshell and marbled wares together prior to Wedgwood's independent firm. 1759 began to produce creamware and green glaze. Unlike most other potters who swiftly began to copy Wedgwood's creamware, Wedgwood's was usually decorated, at its most simple with rim band, leaves in relief, from 1770s transfer-printed decorative bands. Creamware named 'Queensware' from 1765 after commission by Queen Charlotte. Red stoneware, black basalte from 1760s called 'rosso antico' and 'Egyptian black'. Cane ware or bisque porcelain from 1770s. Brown-glazed pie dishes from 1793. Piecrust ware from 1790s. Bone china from 1812 to 1822. First oven-proof pie-dishes from 1850s. Other products include terracotta urns, flower pots, jardinières, kitchen ware, jelly moulds, mousse moulds, ice-cream shapes, green leaf-shaped dessert ware.

Worcester: 1751 to present day

First Period (Dr Wall) 1751–76
Davis, Flight 1776–92
Flight and Barr 1792–1804
Barr, Flight and Barr 1804–13
Flight, Barr and Barr 1813–40
Chamberlain and Co. 1840–52
Kerr and Binns 1852–62
Royal Worcester Porcelain Co. 1862 – present day

Blue-and-white soapstone from 1751. Dinner services, dessert, tea and coffee services from 1763. Particularly recognizable mazarine blue and gold, sky blue, pea green, French green, sea green, purple, scarlet. Japanese in-

Pieces from an impressed Wedgwood creamware dessert service with cream-coloured body painted in rust, yellows and oranges, c. 1820. The service includes a comport (centre), two square dishes (example right) and 12 plates (example left).

fluence, in particular Imari pattern, modified colour palette, lattice gilding known as salmon scale, often on a blue ground, very recognizable. Much work commissioned during 1770s, 1780s by royalty and nobility.

Transfer-printing from 1757 as underpattern for artists, later with pastoral scenes of milkmaids, shepherds, romantic ruins, usually transfer-printed in black, deep red, lilac or pale purple till 1770, then blue and sepia, hand-finished with touches of gilding. Bone china from 1798 with wide range of impressive flatware, often with borders, rims of raised rococo decoration, enamelled or gilded. Fine soft-paste from 1811, translucent, fine clear surface, for matching dinner, dessert and breakfast services. This range was known as 'Regent China' and continued in production until about 1820.

Bone china from that date frequently depicted views of castles, houses, each piece different in the set, with location printed on underside. Recognizable Worcester apple green dates from the second half of the eighteenth century, as well as resurgence of Japanese patterns, notably Imari, popular in 1830s. The firm has continued to make highly prized bone-china tableware until the present day, with many private commissions from the rich and noble; gilded, crested, particularly during Victorian and Edwardian periods.

Price Guide

Teapots (£40–£200)

Red stoneware, engine-turned, simple 18th century, £80–200. With applied relief, decorative handles, over £150.

Black basalte: Elijah Mayer 18th-century, £150–200. Early minimal decoration Wedgwood £150+. Square silver-shape, *c.* 1805, £70–140.

Early Staffordshire named potters (Astbury, Jackfield, Pratt, Wood), all out of price range.

Leeds, Liverpool late 18th-century, simple shape and decoration, £150 upwards after good recent appreciation.

Smear-glazed Wedgwood stoneware £40–70.

Leeds and Liverpool 'bamboo' creamware is all out of the price range, likewise Wedgwood bamboo.

Late 19th-century Wedgwood, classical with medallions £60–150.

Saltglaze: plain white 18th-century, tubby shapes now out of range.

Flower pattern Worcester blue-and-white around £150–300.

Bone china: Early 19th-century printed and painted as little as £40 for florid gilded Rockingham-type to as much as £1,000 for rare Swansea. Taste and pocket best guide here but good condition is essential. 'Novelty' teapots shaped like animals, houses, etc. now fetching high prices, even relatively poor-quality coarse Staffordshire around £100. Victorian lustre at a premium, also Mason's Ironstone and Herculaneum (Liverpool).

Early 19th-century Wedgwood 'Etruria' teapots from £120.

Huge kitchen and barge Staffordshire teapots now fetch £70–200.

'Cottagey' crude painted squat shapes around £40 with recent appreciation but made in vast quantities and not scarce.

Tea and Breakfast Services (£150–£1,200)

'Cabaret' sets for one or two (early morning tea services) late 19th, early 20th century, Coalport, Royal Crown Derby and others, £200–500+. Larger sets, same period, comprising 12 small plates, 12 cups and saucers, sucrier and milk jug made by most leading bone china manufacturers, often without teapots which would have been silver, £200–500+ depending on quality, decoration. If complete and in mint condition they are likely to be outside the price range.

Copeland 1830s breakfast/tea service of 12 teacups and saucers, 12 breakfast cups and saucers, 12 plates, milk jug, cake plate, teapot, simple £180, elaborate £800.

Extraordinary value: late 19th-century breakfast services, Derby Crown Porcelain Company, not very high quality for collectors and with little value as singles, 12 cups, saucers, plates, teapot, jugs, bowls etc. can be found for £150. Elaborate examples £600 + .

Bloor Derby not considered high quality, similar service to Copeland, 60 pieces, £350–1,000 + . When rare with very fine decoration single bone china cup and saucer fetches £100 + but run-of-the-mill items little value in terms of investment.

Royal Crown Derby post-1890 tea service for 12 people, about the same at £200–1,200. Special collectable individual items with rich decoration fetch good prices at around £70–250 for single cup and saucer.

Worcester 'Imari' pattern, early 19th-century, £100–200 per piece.

Coalport tea service, six cups and saucers, teapot, milk jug, sucrier, mid-19th-century £400–1,000.

Royal Worcester 1880s tea service for 12 totalling 40 pieces, £150–1,000. Designs made over long period, with replacements to service over the years, often worn with use, considered fairly low investment value but beautiful quality.

Coffee Pots (£25–£1,000)

Black basalte *c.* 1800 Wedgwood, £75–200. Unmarked pieces same period, less. Earlier dates £100–300.

18th-century Worcester blue-and-white surprisingly rare: £250 + .

Creamware, printed and painted, recently appreciating, now at £400–1,000 + depending on quality, pottery, design.

Bone china, major manufacturers from 1870 to recent times £30–50 for standard shapes, designs. Earlier dates less common than continental. English coffee pots usually made in silver and quality of bone china usually not very desirable with few exceptions. Thick coffee-house Mocha ware recently climbing from a few pounds to £25 and much more.

Coffee Sets (£150–£2,000)

In England the custom of after-dinner coffee drinking was not widespread until the late 19th, early 20th centuries and so early coffee sets are rare and collectors' items. Late sets usually made without jugs and pots which would have been silver. In the price range are Wedgwood bone china and characteristic jasper ware with white relief. Edwardian fashion for presentation sets of coffee cups, saucers and spoons in satin-lined boxes produced enormous quantities of these rather ostentatious sets between 1900 and 1935 from all major potteries. Scarcely dish-washer-proof, with such heavy decoration, not suitable for too much regular use because insides of cups were frequently gilded, patterned, but most attractive, good potential investment value at around £150–300 complete sets with spoons. Birds, fruit, collectable themes rising slowly and steadily, the best already reaching £1,500–2,000 + .

Mugs (£12–£1,000)

Collectable, expensive. Not made in bone china until the 19th century.

Stoneware 18th-century Fulham mugs £200 + . Excellent Victorian copies cost much less.

Nineteenth-century Royal Doulton harvest beakers, £40–60.

Nottingham stoneware outside price range.

Saltglaze plain tavern mugs not less than £40.

Creamware: early transfer-printed £100–1,000. Early commemorative mugs outside price range.

Pearlware: recent fashion has pushed this outside price range. Simple tavern tankards *c.* 1800 £60–200.

Blue-and-white: many outside price range but 18th-century Worcester £200–500. 19th-century Staffordshire lustre decoration with mottoes £40–200. Nautical themes, Sunderland, Liverpool from £60. Early Staffordshire over £80. Victorian Staffordshire less.

Staffordshire bone china 1850 onwards £30–60. Prices largely unchanged in recent years, but elaborate examples now over £200.

Coronation, commemorative bone china souvenir mugs, Victoria Jubilee, £25–100. Beakers around £20–100. 1900s Edward VII, George V, Edward VII, £20–25+, George VI £12–15+.

Jugs (£15–£2,000)

Delft puzzle jugs and other jugs, outside price range.

Stoneware tavern jugs, 18th-century, £100–600. Famous 'bear' jugs *c.* 1750, now £2,000 even with some restoration.

Nineteenth century Royal Doulton harvest pitchers, £45–100.

A Chamberlain Worcester fluted cream jug, c. *1795, the shape influenced by silver designs of the period.*

Basalt 19th-century cream jugs £30–70.

Creamware: cream jugs with minimal decoration, Wedgwood and other potters, 1770–1800, around £60–200.

Pearlware: rising, with single sauceboats at £50–100.

Blue-and-white Liverpool cream jugs £50–300+. 19th-century blue-and-white transfer-printed cream jugs £35–50.

Transfer-printed Staffordshire commemorative mostly over limit. Large tavern jugs £100+. With special themes (nautical etc) mostly outside limit.

Lustre small jugs £25–60. Early silver lustre decorated tavernware well over £100; small copper lustre cream jugs, 19th-century, £15–75.

Victorian, Edwardian washbasin and jug sets from £40. Jugs only £20–50 with good decoration, though some can be considerably more expensive. Bone china: late Victorian heavily painted commemorative jugs from £25, some attractive shapes, views, scenes, worth hunting for.

Worcester cabbage-leaf mask jugs from £250. Mason's Ironstone octagonal-shaped jugs, which were made in sets (smallest 3ins high), have been appreciating so that the smallest are now £50–70. Victorian Mocha coarse tavern ware is now upwards of £30 and is rarely to be found in good condition.

Serving Dishes (£50–£1,000)

Large dishes made before the 1800s were not necessarily intended for use with hot foods or hot water, and should be treated with circumspection. Many of them are not ovenproof and will not stand up to today's detergents and hot washing-up water. This said, they were made to be used: it is only the manner of use which has changed and providing they are treated with care they remain attractively serviceable for cold buffets, cakes, fruit and so on.

Most covered soup tureens, vegetable dishes, date from the 1820s and were part of huge complete services, together with smaller sauce tureens, side dishes and the full panoply of the 19th-century table. Unless they are French or German of earlier date, these dishes can be highly priced. Most originally had matching dishes on which they stood with little depressions for footrims. Covered dishes are considerably more valuable if they are still together with their stands. All of these items are greatly in demand. Prices start at about £50 and can rise to more than £1,000 for exceptional pieces.

Delft single dishes with simple pseudo-oriental patterns are from £70 depending on condition, and seldom under £100. Since they were fetching £40 ten years ago, they have showed little appreciation.

Saltglaze stoneware: plain white lattice-work dishes under £200. Oval dishes can be more at £150–350.

Late 18th-century Liverpool punchbowls, £200 to well over £1,000.

Blue-and-white: rare, collectable and if it is before 1800, outside the price limit. Early 19th-century blue-and-white rising quickly—£40–100 for good florals, more for good scenes such as Indian and European. The common Willow Pattern is in the same price range as the florals.

Nineteenth-century Staffordshire blue printed meat dishes from £60 for simple, small examples to £200–300 and more for large dishes with scenic decoration and gravy wells.

Pearlware, simple feather edge, £30–80; with Chinoiserie centres, £50–100; more for rare patterns or fine quality, less for damage or wear.

Mason's Ironstone now heavily collected, huge mock Japanese gilded sets of meat dishes and serving dishes used to go for a song, now strictly for collectors.

Dinner Services (£200–£2,000)

These are usually massive and comprise at least 60 pieces: 24 plates, 12 soup plates, 8-10 meat dishes, serving dishes, soup tureen, sauce tureens, vegetable dishes. This amount sounds daunting until the possibilites are realized.

From a full set at around £750 two sets with considerably more pieces than an equivalent set of today's manufacture can be made. It is possible to split sets between two households and for the middle to lower range would by no means be considered a crime by purists and collectors. With this in mind, the initial outlay is more than reasonable for a dinner service that will at least hold its value if not increase, though investment value depends to a large extent on fashion.

Coalport 1820s dinner service of average decoration, incomplete, anywhere from £200–£2,000. If particularly well-decorated, single plates are around £40 and upwards each, the same or more than when bought in a full service.

Davenport, same date, similar prices, with fine examples going for as much as £80 for a single plate.

Incomplete early Royal Crown Derby, originally privately commissioned with armorial decoration, considerably more. Even incomplete they can be as much as £700 or more.

Minton 1870s standard services with sparse decoration: 12 dinner plates, 12 soups, 12 desserts, serving dishes, vegetable dishes, slightly smaller with 50 pieces to be found for £300–600.

Royal Worcester and others: 1900s game services (decorated with birds, animals): 12 plates, serving dishes, sauce boats, more expensive at £700 or more. Smaller sets £300–500 with singles fetching from £30.

Well-known 'Imari' pattern Derby early 1900s mass-produced dinner services of 60 pieces at around £900–1,500 and appreciating.

Copeland services at second-hand value mainly. Not one of the 'great' houses for specially commissioned work. On the other hand, Rockingham is well out of reach.

Note: Full coats of arms add to the value; crests only or monograms tend to lessen the value.

Plates: Singles (£10–£400)

Two sizes only until mid-19th-century, roughly 9ins and 11ins described below as 'small' and 'large'. Soup plates begin in the late 18th century; covered bowls and porringers were the rule in some households until well into the 19th century. Side plates are a Victorian addition to the English table. Until after 1830 when sizes standardized, 'small' and 'large' are very variable.

Delft: Simple pseudo-oriental blue and white, small unexciting examples £40–100.

Creamware 1770–1800: unmarked pierced rim, small, around £30–60.

Leeds, Wedgwood small and large, up to £100 undecorated except for lattice rims.

Pearlware: Early Wedgwood 'botanical' dessert plates, around £200–400 and increasing rapidly. Davenport pearlware more heavily decorated desserts around £40–200.

Blue-and-white: late Caughley, of inferior quality, now over £75. Bristol and Worcester out of price range.

Monochrome transfer-printed early Spode, Minton, £35–100.

Unmarked pre-1800 Staffordshire blue small and large around £25–50.

Early series patterns, notably American views, can be beyond limit.

Spode, Minton and others, 1800 onwards, simple, £15; more elaborate £150+.

Pearlware chinoiserie, including early willow pattern, *c.* 1800, £25–100.

Victoria themes: ruins, overblown roses, flowers, 'series' from £10. Polychrome from £12–15 with birds more than some other subjects. *Note:* Polychrome heavily decorated 18th-century 'cabinet ware' never intended for ordinary use. Plates, cups, saucers, etc. still very reasonable because of this, unless highly prized themes and collectable rarities. From £10–50 with earlier dates more expensive than Victorian, though recent vogue is

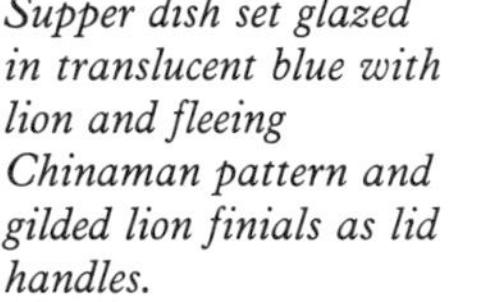

Supper dish set glazed in translucent blue with lion and fleeing Chinaman pattern and gilded lion finials as lid handles.

pushing up Victorian 'narrative' themes, scenes based on contemporary novels etc.

Bone china: 19th-century dessert plates not much used nowadays: some not resistant to hot water. If of no particular interest to collectors, cheap at £10–15 per plate but decorative value only.

Special named potteries: Rockingham, Derby, etc., out of range unless bought as part of dismantled service at around £20–150 per plate.

Cups and Saucers (£25–£120)

This is a highly complex field and very specialized: collecting harlequin sets of tea or coffee cups which will have some investment value requires special study. This is primarily a collectors' field as a glance in any antique shop which deals in porcelain will indicate. Many designs which typify named manufacturers have been made continuously for 100 years or more and a knowledge of marks is essential to know the date of any given piece. Cups and saucers in bone china from 'broken' tea services may be in worn condition or be of different dates, having been replaced at a later date. Transfer-printed ware is full of pitfalls; as much can be learned from the shape of the cup as from a maker's mark and here again, though at first glance the pattern may appear to match, closer inspection may reveal minute differences which mean a 'bad buy'. However, if it is the intention to become a serious collector, this is an extraordinarily rich field to study and providing you stay within a strict price limit, though you may make mistakes, you will still have some very pretty cups and saucers to use.

Late 18th-century Caughley and Worcester tea ware single fluted cups and saucers from £40–60, with blue-and-white highly collectable and some out of price range.

Nineteenth-century Spode, Minton, from £30–120 for tea cups and saucers.

Bone china: singles from dismantled tea services, early 19th-century Worcester, Coalport, Derby, Minton with fine decoration from £45.

Coffee-drinking in private houses was also limited to richer establishments until the late 18th century and some early coffee cups were shaped like miniature tankards and are known as 'cans'. Individual pieces, even without saucers, start at around £25, but coffee cups before late Victorian can be less than £65. Once they were mass-produced their value decreased, from a collector's point of view, and many single coffee cups from broken sets can be picked up for a few pounds, but are unlikely to appreciate.

Breakfast cups and large-sized cups were made in small numbers and Staffordshire named potteries now fetch up to £40 with limited appreciation in recent years.

'Bizarre' 1930s patterns have risen fast.

Care and Restoration

Care

Ceramics, like glass, are at greatest risk when being washed. Always wash one piece at a time, lift it out of the water carefully, put it on a drying rack or cloth and dry it immediately. It is not the washing that will harm a piece but careless handling.

Wash pottery and porcelain in hand-hot water with a little detergent. The more elaborately decorated the piece (particularly if it is gilded) the less detergent you should use. For terracotta use hot water and soda crystals. Leave terracotta to dry naturally, but dry glazed ware with a soft cloth, then rub it over with a little methylated spirit and when the spirit is dry polish with a soft cloth. This should be used for display pieces only, as methylated spirit does not enhance the taste of food!

Restoration

The biggest problem is breakage. If the piece is valuable (financially or sentimentally) or if the repair is complex, use a professional restorer. They can do an enormous amount, not just in sticking bits together but in filling and retouching, removing old rivets, dowelling, tinting adhesives and so on to produce a near-perfect result.

Straightforward breaks in pieces of modest value can be repaired quite easily with epoxy resins (either two-part or contact). It is essential that the surfaces to be joined be spotlessly clean and that no dribbles of adhesive be left – they are practically impossible to remove. Broken-off parts can be remodelled with plastic resins or ceramic pastes, but on the whole this will be a job for a restorer, who will know not only how to remodel, but how to repaint and glaze to disguise the repair.

If you are buying an old piece always check for rivets and signs of poor modelling of replaced parts. If the piece is cheap and attractive enough, you can have rivets removed and poorly remodelled parts taken off and done properly. If the piece looks sound, balance it if you can on three fingers and ping it with a nail of the other hand. An unrepaired piece will have a clear note, and so can a piece that has been repaired properly with epoxy resin. If the note is flat or dull look again for signs of repair.

Old pottery, whether glazed or not, can show a white deposit on the surface as a result of salts in the clay or paste working out to the surface. If the surface is flaky as well, take the piece to a restorer. If the surface is sound, half immerse the piece in distilled water. The water will gradually permeate the piece and soak out the salts. Change the water daily. After a few days, take a teaspoon of the soaking water, hold it over a flame and evaporate all the water. If the water is salt-free there will be no deposit on the spoon, but if salts are still leaching out of the piece there will be a mark of sediment on the spoon.

Further Reading

M. Berthoud, *An Anthology of British Cups*, Broseley, 1982

A. W. Coysh & R. K. Henrywood, *Dictionary of Blue and White Printed Earthenware*, Woodbridge, 1982

J. P. Cushion & W. B. Honey, *Handbook of Pottery and Porcelain Marks*, revised edition, London, 1980

Geoffrey Godden, *Encyclopaedia of British Pottery & Porcelain*, London, 1966

—*The Handbook of British Pottery & Porcelain Marks*, London, 1968

—*Staffordshire Porcelain*, London, 1983

P. Miller & M. Berthoud, *An Anthology of British Teapots*, Broseley, 1985

Henry Sandon, *Royal Worcester Porcelain*, 3rd edition, London, 1979

Rugs
Up to £2,500

Kashan made in the 1920s for the European market. Note the Isfahan palmette and arabesque.

Introduction

Rugs old and new

By comparison with modern fitted carpet old rugs are not an outrageous self-indulgence. Old rugs will cost more, square metre for square metre, but fitted carpet has the hidden costs of fitting and so on. Also, a rug can be turned and turned, to give it even wear and make it last longer; a fitted carpet that has worn badly in just one place will need patching or replacement. A well made and reasonably cared for old rug can have a great deal of life in it, and remain attractive throughout.

We refer deliberately to 'old' rugs rather than to 'antique rugs'. A genuine antique rug - 100 years old or more - is unusual; it will almost certainly be well outside our price range and will be a collector's piece. The majority of rugs in dealers' shops will be a mixture of old rugs - perhaps 30 or 50 years - and rugs of new or nearly new manufacture. Certain dealers of course will stock only genuine antiques or rugs that are at least very old.

The value of a rug depends on a mix of factors: age; size; condition; materials used; whether it is hand- or machine-made; and provenance - some traditional rug-producing areas no longer manufacture or no longer export their goods, and the resulting scarcity puts up the value of those rugs that are on the market.

We have adopted a price ceiling of £1,500 and have given detailed descriptions of rugs within that range. Some rugs that are well beyond the price range are mentioned because their names will crop up in dealers' shops and in salerooms. Modern production under traditional names is mentioned from time to time, partly to point out the general decline in quality and partly to indicate which designs and types are widely reproduced.

Where do they come from?

There are five groups of prime importance (see map p. 109). 1 Persian; 2 Turkish; 3 Caucasian; 4 Afghan; 5 Turkoman. In addition we have included China and India, which are of lesser importance to collectors, as well as Pakistan, Tibet and the Balkans. Each has its distinctive traditions and patterns, construction, materials, colours, design, which all go to make up the 'language' of rugs. Although complex, this vocabulary is fascinating and its rudiments need to be mastered if you are thinking of buying.

There are three basic types of rug (for the sake of simplicity the word 'rug' is used throughout, although technically speaking a rug becomes a carpet when it is over 5 × 8 feet —1.5 × 2.4 metres):

1 *Nomad or tribal* There are two types within this group, irrespective of which area they come from. The mountain or pastoral nomads with their rich pastureland produce lustrous wool which makes thick long-pile rugs affording good insulation in the extreme cold of the mountains. Desert animals, on the other hand, on their more arid land produce dry, brittle wool and the rugs tend to have short, tight pile woven on thick backing to compensate for the relatively poor quality of the wool. All tribal nomadic rugs tend to be small as the looms have to be transported with the tribe. The colour range is also fairly

limited by available natural dyes.

2 *Village* rugs have a shorter pile than most mountain nomadic rugs, which allows more detailed design (longer pile tends to favour simpler, more geometric patterns). They can be larger because rugs are woven on fixed looms, and the range may include sets of room rugs as well as runners of considerable length.

3 *City or town* rugs are characterized by a very fine, dense, short pile resulting in rich design and colour and very fine knotting.

In Turkey and some parts of the Caucasus, carpet-producing centres are better-known for the purpose of their rugs, i.e. prayer rugs, room rugs, runners and room sets and where this is the case they are classified in this way under the sub-heading 'Type', under their place of origin.

Structure and Materials

The diagram shows the three principal types of knot which are one of the main indicators of authenticity. Gently fold the rug back in a line parallel to the weft. If the ends of the knot appear together and the knotting thread covers both warp threads then the knot is the Turkish (T) or Ghiordes. If a warp thread can be seen between two upright ends of the knot then it is Persian (P) or Sehna. If the knot is wound round three, four or more warp threads it is the Djufti (Dj). A Djufti knot will allow a thread to be pulled away easily from the groundweave because it is so loosely tied. It will wear quickly because of the lack of density of the pile. Machine-made carpets and rugs are easy to identify for they have no knots, the pile being held in by glue or rubber backing.

The pattern of the rug should be clearly visible on the back. Handmade rugs are knotted with the wool being taken round and over the warp thread and then back again to the front. Machine-made rugs will not normally show the pattern on the back.

Rugs are made on horizontal and on vertical looms, and are made up of the warp, weft, side cords and overcasting. Jute, animal hair, cotton and wool are all used for the warp

Knots

Ghiordes

Persian

Djufti

and weft. Wool tufts knotted individually form the pile, as well as silk, which does not come into this price guide because of its very high cost.

Kelims (see page 123) are a type of woven cloth rather than a carpet, and indeed were intended for use as hangings.

Dyes

One of the most contentious subjects in the world of rugs and carpets is that of dyes. Many dealers, buyers and collectors will turn up their noses at any rug whose wool has been dyed with anything other than natural vegetable dyes. To a certain extent this is an excellent rule, but it does not hold good entirely. There are two kinds of synthetic dye: aniline and chromatic. It is the aniline dyes which provoke disparagement because they are not colourfast or lightfast and fade quickly to a drab shadow of their original. Aniline dyes were used indiscriminately in harsh colours for about 70 years from 1880 to 1950 with the result that there is a sad trail of beautifully-knotted and woven rugs and carpets with some colours almost bleached out where these dyes were used. Chromatic dyes, first used in the 1920s and 30s, have a good range of subtle colours, fast to light and water, and today, particularly in Turkey, many rug-weavers use a mixture of wools, some dyed with natural dyes and some with chromatic.

A quick though by no means entirely reliable test to discover whether aniline dye has been used is to spit on a clean white handkerchief and rub it fairly briskly over each colour in turn. If none of the colours show up on your handkerchief, the carpet is almost certainly not guilty. If there is a suspiciously bright stain, one of three things has happened: aniline dye has been used; the wool has been dyed and insufficiently rinsed so that it is not completely 'fixed' and may either run or fade drastically; or if the rug is over 40 years old it may have been 'painted' to restore its faded colours. Many rugs woven with aniline-dyed wool have been given this treatment.

How to Buy

Rugs and carpets need examination before you decide to buy. The rug should be laid on the floor to make sure that it lies flat. Many dealers hang rugs from batons or frames, and you should insist that they be taken down. The weight of a hanging carpet will conceal any lumps and humps caused by years of rolling or folding, ruckling, or faults in warp, weft and weaving. Again it should be stressed that the salerooms are no place for a novice, particularly in this field. Even on viewing day it is often difficult to lay out a rug or carpet properly, and it is difficult to judge one rug's effect among many others. Most reputable dealers will allow you to take a rug home on approval.

The value of a rug or carpet lies in the degree to which it is handmade. A rug can be hand-knotted, but if the yarn has been machine-spun or the dyes are uniform as a result of controlled vat-dyeing the appeal and value will be less than those of a piece in which every stage has been carried out without benefit of machines. Hand-spun yarn and domestically dyed wool add not only to the value but to the extraordinary depth of colour and design which gives so much lasting pleasure.

It comes as a surprise to many people embarking on buying old rugs to find that often the pile is worn down so that it looks more like a thick flat stitched fabric. At the first viewing, examine the rug carefully and note the overall condition. Remember that if you buy in the salerooms, mistakes such as buying an original which on closer inspection turns out to be a copy cannot be rectified. If buying from a dealer make sure you have a full description on the receipt and be certain to keep it. It is your insurance – if, on getting home you find you have made a mistake with size or colour the dealer should take it back for the price you paid. The potential buyer of an oriental rug or carpet may be persuaded to buy something which is not what it seems; the traditions of the bazaar are nowhere more persuasively practised. At least it is as well to go armed with the right questions, to be confident enough to ask them and to insist on clear answers.

Care and Restoration

Cleaning

A vacuum cleaner is a mixed blessing for good rugs and carpets. It will only remove surface dust and dirt and, if allowed to run over the fringes, will slowly damage them irreparably. The best method is to hang the rug over a line and to beat it gently with a bamboo or garden cane to dislodge the grit which has worked its way into the fabric and which can eventually cut it like a knife. Care must be taken to avoid picking the rug up by one end in the case of smaller pieces in order to shake them, as the weight of the rug may pull at the places where it is gripped. If it is not possible to beat your rugs, then once every two or three months turn them over and vacuum the back as well as the front. If the vacuum cleaner beats at the same time, this will help to dislodge grit on to the floor where it can be swept up. Gentle rubbing with a cloth dipped in a very weak solution of ammonia and warm water – about a tablespoonful to a gallon – will help to restore the brilliance of the colour. On no account should the rug be allowed to get more than very slightly damp. If proprietory brands of carpet cleaner are used for more extreme cases of dullness and dirt, try a small section of the back with the solution first to make sure your colours are fast and will not run. Some brands of carpet cleaner are only suitable for modern machine-made carpets and advice should be sought before embarking on cleaning rugs with them.

Stains. In every case, speed is of the essence, since once a stain has dried into the fabric it is often extremely difficult to remove. Fresh ink should be mopped with a wet cloth, turning to a fresh piece with each dab in order to dilute the ink and avoid spreading the stain. Wine stains should be well diluted with soda water and then mopped quickly, again turning the cloth each time. Salt, which is often the remedy for spilt wine on table linen, should not be used because it has a bleaching action. Pets' urine (and children's) will mark rugs badly, removing or discolouring dyes by its acidity. The quickest remedy and the most effective is to sprinkle the whole area liberally with an antacid or bismuth stomach powder which will neutralize the chemical action by alkalinity. Rub it in very gently with the fingertips, wait until it is dry and then brush off with a soft handbrush. Grease stains will respond to a light brushing with talcum powder which should be left for at least 24 hours before gently wiping it off. Alternately, a layer of thick brown paper, the coarse furry kind, can be laid over the grease spot and a hot iron passed quickly over it. The heat will melt the grease and the brown paper will absorb it as it melts and lift it out of the pile, but this should be done with considerable care. Dry cleaning grease solvents such as benzene and ether should first be tried on a corner of the carpet before using to remove stains. In all cases, remember that each colour is composed of a different dye and treatment should be tried on a penny-sized patch of the same colour before attempting to remove the stain.

Care

If you are storing your rugs or carpets, they should never be folded but always rolled, if possible round a cardboard cylinder or a roll of cloth stiffened with a broom handle. Ideally, lay an old sheet over the rug before rolling it so that it protects the pile from the backing. Brush the rug well before storing, and spray the old sheet with an anti-moth preparation to protect it from attack.

If moth, silverfish or carpet beetles do get into a carpet during storage or use, the traditional cure is to take it to a carpet dealer and ask him to 'beat and bake'. Baking in an oven kills the larvae and beating removes them. A home cure for smaller rugs is to put them in a freezer for about four days in the spring when the eggs are hatching and then beat.

Strong sunlight eventually fades even the most colourfast dyes. If your rug is in pride of place in a living room with large windows, turn the rug as often as you can to ensure even exposure. Better still, avoid areas of strong sunlight altogether. Runners are an ideal shape and length for passages, but they

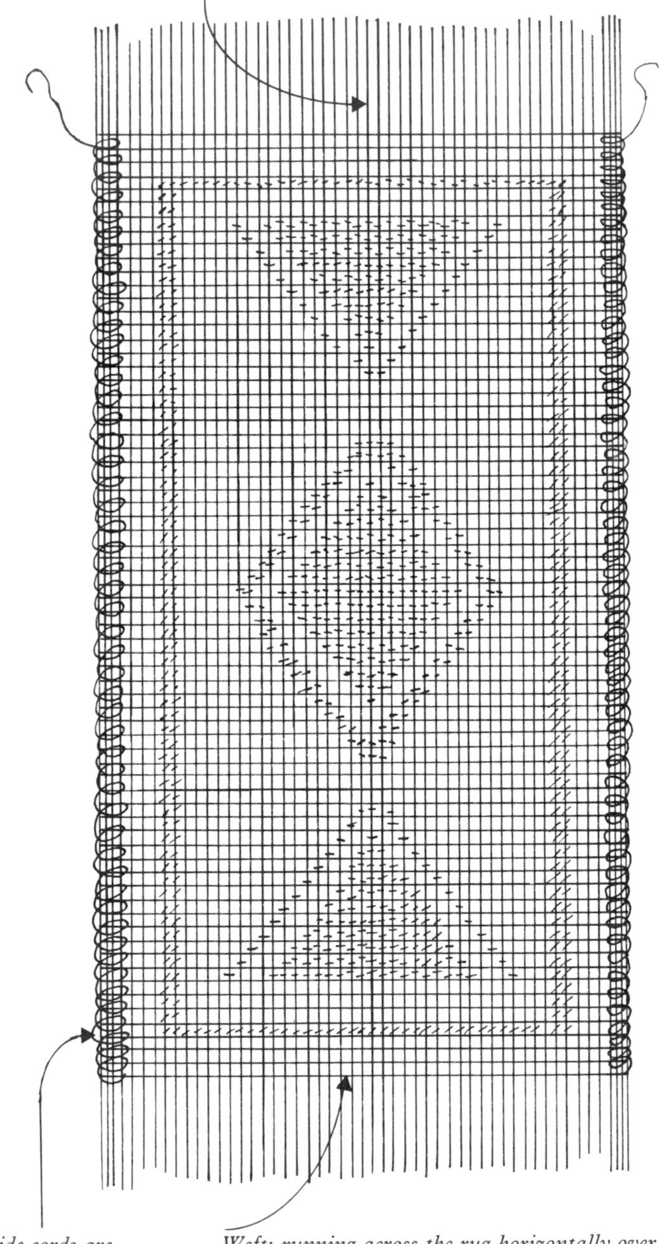

will wear badly, as will all rugs where the wear is constantly in the same place. If your floor has an uneven surface use an underlay. Stitch a strip of the same underlay at either end of rugs which are lying directly on a smooth floor to prevent them from ruckling up and wearing thin on the folds. Turn rugs, runners and carpets regularly so that the wear is on different parts near doors, etc. Small cups can be purchased from most iron-mongers in which to stand legs of heavy furniture such as tables and sideboards. If you cannot track these down, use pads of felt, particularly under castors or metal feet.

Repair

The fringes are the most vulnerable part of a rug. If there are signs of disintegration, act quickly and with a large blunt needle either oversew or blanket-stitch between each clump of warp threads using carpet twine or thick button thread. Side cords may pull away from the edges, and as long as they are only the additional decorative edges, the matter is not serious. Repair them by oversewing with several strands of embroidery wool matched as closely as possible to the original colour and a thick blunt needle or curved carpet needle which can be bought at most haberdashers' departments. If a careless person has dropped a cigarette or a small coal has burnt a hole in your rug, it is possible for the worst of the damage to be concealed, but the art of knotting is difficult and expert advice should be sought if the damage is bad. A small hole should be carefully ringed with stitching to prevent the damage spreading, and then darned by taking your blunt-ended needle well into the warp and weft threads with loose threads so that you do not make the damage worse by pulling the fabric.

Hanging rugs

If you do not wish to expose your rug to heavy wear, hang it like a tapestry from the wall. Fix a baton to the wall on to which tack a length of Velcro. Stitch a matching length of Velcro to the rug below the fringe and press the two surfaces together. If this proves difficult, using small stitches sew webbing to the top and bottom of the rug, kelim or hanging. Slide a bamboo rod or thin pole between the rug and the webbing, and hang it on a couple of hooks in the wall. The weight is thus distributed evenly and the carpet will not pull out of shape.

Kelims should really be hung as, with the exception of Soumaks, they were not intended to be used on floors; if you do use them as rugs, always use underlay on a bare floor.

Sources, Styles and Prices

Persia

One of the most prolific of all carpet-producing areas, Persia has been supplying the European market for over 200 years. From here came the fabulous silk Persian rugs made for the courts of kings and emperors, with rich, velvety pile woven into patterns in imitation of gardens, as well as the mosque carpets with hanging lamps and central medallions and the long runners which flanked them. Every motif woven into a carpet has a symbolic meaning: the vase of cut flowers, reminding man of his ephemeral existence; the tree of life; the cyprus and weeping willow; the garden of Paradise; the Herati pattern, said to symbolize the world surrounded by the four elements, looking like a rosette encircled with leaves (see p. 128). From Persia too comes the palmette, as well as the Serabend or Saraband, which in its continuous convoluted form makes the Paisley pattern. Persia is the home of many tribal nomads who weave small rugs with fresh, naive designs, many of them traditional, with their own symbolism of desert and plain, mountain and high pastureland. Designs, shapes and symbols occur and vanish, only to reappear in a different form hundreds of miles away.

Afshar
Type: Desert nomad.
Construction: Knot: T or P. Warp: wool or cotton. Weft: cotton. Double or treble side cord, multicoloured overcast wool.
Colours: Typically nomad dark red or indigo blue. Natural wool, white, cream.
Design: 'Boteh' resembling Caucasian pecking bird, lozenges, two or three angular medallions with stylized floral grounds – animals, little figures, 'akstafa' or stylized cockerel.
Price: Inflated prices due to fashion for ethnic work. Long-term investment value offset by their relatively short lifespan due to poor quality of desert wool. Nomad Afshar 6ft 6ins × 4ft 6ins, £900–2,200; same size village-made rather less: £600–900.

Ardebil
Famous 'Ardebil' carpet dated *c.* 1540 now in Victoria & Albert Museum shows clearly origins of antique Tabriz medallion design and rich blue ground colour. Today Ardebil is particularly known for runners made in villages surrounding towns.
Type: Town, village.
Construction: Knot: T. Warp: cotton or wool. Weft: cotton. Single side cord overcast cotton.
Colours: Deep reds, blues, traditional Persian palette. Cream field characteristic.
Design: More angular, almost more Caucasian than Persian, though more rigid and formal than true Caucasians. Coarse wool. Many carpets of poorer quality, rougher work from outlying districts sold through Tabriz, particularly 'Ardebil runners', made in villages, often reaching considerable lengths, sold as stair-carpets to Europe, America.
Price: Good rugs outside price range. Care should be taken if offered one of this name under £1,500; it is likely to be a coarse Tabriz copy. Caucasian-type room rugs made in the

district may be worth considering though, in their eagerness to simulate genuine Caucasians, the blacks and browns have been chemically corroded to make them look older and purchases should be made with this in mind. They are not as old as they look. 6ft 6ins × 3ft 10ins for around £700.

Birdjend (Birchend, Birjand, Birchand)
Type: Village.
Construction: Knot: P, T and Dj. Warp: cotton. Weft: cotton. Single cord overcast wool.
Colours: More vivid, but same dark plums, greens, blues as Meshed (see page 111).
Design: Thicker pile, fresher design, though more formal than nomad. Geometrical patterns, stylized flowers, Herati pattern, often covering whole ground.
Price: Hand-knotted prayer rugs 6ft 1in × 4ft 2ins, about £1,000.

Fars (also known as Gabeh, Gaba)
Type: Nomad.
Construction: Knot: T. Warp: wool. Weft: wool. Thick single cord, overcast brown or cream.
Colours: Undyed, untreated wool, natural colours, cream to dark brown.
Design: Simple geometrics, diamond-shaped medallions, dark on light ground or vice versa. Two main qualities: those made in foothills of Khorassan mountains finer, often with little red embellishments; poorer quality from district around Shiraz, often with similar stylized birds, animals, figures to Afshar. Can be confused at first sight with Northern Persian and Caucasian rugs.
Price: Khorassan around £600 for 6ft × 4ft. Poorer quality from Shiraz should not be much above £300 for same size. Not particularly special, but considering political situation and possible future rarity of such work, investment value may be quite good. Too new on the market for many precedents.

Fereghan (Ferahan)
Type: Town, village.
Construction: Knot: P. Warp: cotton. Weft: cotton. Single cord overcast wool. Cotton ribbed kelim ends.
Colour: Typical celadon green border, pale lustrous colours.
Design: The best work of this district of plains villages shows all-over floral patterns like rich pasturelands. Unusual feature is that distinctive celadon green often corrodes because it is copper-based.
Price: Much prized in the Edwardian country house, and increased in value by over 250% between 1951 and 1961 when pale colours were very fashionable. The rise over next ten years was only 150% and today's more vivid modern colour schemes tend to make these rugs look a little drab. Large room rugs can be found for around £1,500. Increased demand for runners has lowered standards in this, one of the largest carpet-exporting districts of Iran today.

Hamadan
One of Iran's largest carpet-making centres with thousands of fixed looms turning out almost every possible mixture of design. Loose knotting, heavy-handed use of chemical dyes partially disguised by long thin pile.
Type: Town, village.
Construction: Knot: T. Warp: cotton. Weft: cotton. Single cord wool overcast.
Colours: Traditionally natural camel-coloured ground. Now wide and indiscriminate palette.
Design: Once traditional designs of zigzag diamond medallions on natural camel ground with broad camel-coloured edging, easily recognizable. Today, unsuitable floral designs, crude because of coarse knotting, hybrid 'boteh' designs which are flat and dead. Recent attempts to improve both quality and design have produced Malayer, Sehna-Hamadan, with many copies of Caucasian patterns.
Price: Very wide differences in quality, so great care should be taken when confronted with this name. Good quality rugs in traditional patterns can be found for as little as £300 for 6ft 6ins × 4ft 6ins but the name alone is no guarantee. There is a large output of Caucasian-type rugs which sell for high prices. Hamadans with Caucasian designs, known as Hamadan Kurds, may be as much

as £900 for a rug measuring 8ft × 4ft; 6ft 6ins × 4ft 6ins start at £400. More runners are made in the Hamadan area than anywhere else, and again, vary in quality from poor to very good. Prices for a 10ft × 3ft vary from about £400 to about £800.

Isfahan (Isphahan)
Old carpets knotted with Turkish, recent ones with Persian knot. Noted for very high knot-density, but the quality of the wool is often inferior.
Type: City.
Construction: Knot: P. Warp: Cotton or silk. Weft: cotton or silk. Single cord wool or silk overcast.
Design: As befits the one-time site of Persian Court carpet manufactory, designs are exquisite. On short velvety pile, they derive from tooled leather of Koran covers with ivory-cream ground and all-over Herati stemmed pattern. Today these designs are also woven in Nain which has no long tradition of weaving.
Price: Good value for one of the finest modern carpets made to traditional standards. New Isfahan or Nain rug 6ft 6ins × 4ft 6ins £1,000 upwards. Carpets £300–1,000 per sq.m.

Kermanshah
Type: Manufactory.
Construction: Knot: T or P. Warp: cotton. Weft: cotton. Single cord wool overcast.
Colours: Wide range but dull.
Design: Derivative, copies of traditional patterns, an unvarying flat texture even when handknotted. Coarse versions of traditional Hamadan, Kirman, Sehna. Floral-patterned European-style carpets.
Price: As with Hamadan, Mir Serabend and Malayer, derivative designs mean they are less expensive. If you find them attractive they could turn out to be a reasonable investment. 6ft 6ins × 4ft 6ins from £900.

Kurd (Kurdistan)
Type: Mountain nomad.
Construction: Knot: T. Warp: wool. Weft: blue wool. Multiple sidecord, coloured wool overcast, often blue.
Colours: Dark, vibrant, lustrous due to high-quality wool. Dyes are often chemical but harsh colours will fade to pleasant shades.
Design: Simple geometrics, very distinctive. Kurdish rugs particularly recognizable by erratic warp tension resulting in lumpy carpets which will not lie flat and wear unevenly. Saddle bags, small rugs, common output of tribes.
Price: Beware copies made in Mossul. Look for small pieces which are more likely to be genuine. Typical are small marriage rugs, made as wedding presents for brides: under £100 for 2ft × 1ft 6ins. 6ft × 4ft £400–600.

Mahal (Sultanabad)
Type: Town, manufactory.
Construction: Knot: T or P. Warp: cotton. Weft: blue cotton. Single cord overcast wool or cotton. Characterized by large knots and soft pile. The good ones can be very silky.
Design: Pressure of demand forced too many changes on traditional industry resulting in speedy deterioration; dead, meaningless patterns. Some improvement recently and Saruk-Mahal made to better standards.
Price: Saruk-Mahal worth considering, or Mahal rugs, carpets over 50 years old at around £1,500 for 11ft × 8ft. Recent manufacture a poor investment.

Malayer (Mazlaghan)
Type: Village (modern).
Construction: Knot: T. Warp: camel or goat hair and cotton. Weft: the same. Single cord wool or, if fine quality, camel overcast.
Colours: Traditional Hamadan-type camel-coloured ground with blue borders. Red grounds with dark red borders.
Design: More tribal version of 'boteh' than manufactured carpets, stylized Herati pattern on red ground with dark red border, rosettes. Characteristic zigzag lines along the length of the field. Sadly these good quality carpets are much in demand and already are becoming stereotyped with repetition.
Price: May be found of smallish room rug size for less than £1,500 but do not look for spectacular appreciation.

Meshed (Mashad)
Type: City.
Construction: Knot: P, T, Dj. Warp: cotton. Weft: cotton. Single cord overcast wool.
Colours: Plum, purple-rose, dark greens.
Design: Mainly medallion designs on covered ground, also all-over Herati pattern with never-ending repeat. Palmette often as border design. Djufti knot used, leading to much poorer, less dense work. Turkish knots also used in recent years. East Persian rugs have more guard stripes and broader borders than other regions. Meshed Belouch (see page 120) rugs also sold through Meshed. Prayer rugs with flowery hunting scenes very occasionally found.
Price: Fair quality Persian designs around 50 years old, 11ft × 8ft start at about £1,000. Smaller rugs, 6ft 6ins × 4ft 6ins, from £500.

Mossul
Iraqi trading centre for Kurdish tribal rugs. Recently looms set up here to mass-produce rugs strongly resembling Baktiari work. Mossul carpets bear most of the identifying marks of factory-produced work. Worst Baktiari traits copied, including use of harsh bleached whites, bright unsubtle colours, as well as traditional dull brownish red. Mossul copies use Persian knot.
Price: Today's production of pseudo-Baktiari work is harsh in colour and quality. A surprising development is recent arrival of machine-made 'Mossul' rugs from Brussels. The colours are less crude, wool slightly better quality, but more stereotyped and muted than copies of tribal work from Mossul. £150–250 for a 4ft × 3ft rug from either source.

Qashqai (Kashkai, Kashkay)
Type: Desert village, nomad.
Construction: Knot: T. Warp: wool. Weft:

OPPOSITE *Malayer rug, c. 1900, of small room rug size with stylized floral pattern field with broad palmette and leaf Herati border.*

wool. Double, triple side cord multicoloured overcast wool.
Colours: Typically desert nomad spectrum, sombre reds, greens, blues, indigo, natural.
Design: Exuberant to point of hysteria. 500 or even more animals, birds, in single centre ground, as well as 'boteh' borders, stylized tree-of-life patterns. Recent settlement of tribes by Iranian government has led to decline in spontaneous design, sad loss of embroidered kelim ends to rugs.
Price: Since much-publicized TV coverage of these tribes, prices have rocketed. Village Qashqai, 7ft × 5ft, £950. Twenty to 30-year-old rugs have real character. Brittle wool limits their long-term potential, however. Mock Qashqais now made in pale colours and soft wool in Pakistan are attractive and well made, but expensive at £1,500 for 11ft × 8ft.

Qum (Kum)
Type: Town, manufactory.
Construction: Knot: P. Warp: cotton. Weft: cotton. Single cord overcast wool, often red.
Colour: Lustrous, varied, white and ivory most common field colours.
Design: Serabend pattern in pyjama stripes on natural ground, also known as 'cane pattern'. 'Boteh' pattern shows clearly how Paisley pattern evolved. Short pile, lustrous wool. Also delicately patterned medallion rugs, copies made since the 1930s of antique Persian hunting carpets.
Price: Quality of wool, workmanship has always been high, hence much in demand. In good condition, elongated room rugs of about 7ft × 4ft 6ins over 30 years old will not be less than £1,000.

Saruk (Sarouk, Sarug)
Type: City, town.
Construction: Knot: P. Warp: cotton. Weft: cotton. Single cord overcast wool.
Colours: Rich red, blue for grounds.
Design: Koran cover, large medallions, Herati pattern in simplified flowing version much in evidence in borders. Rich and spontaneous decoration. So finely knotted and dense, it is not unusual to find old Saruk carpets cracked through stiffness of texture. Inferior designs exported, especially to America.
Price: These more traditional carpets have not appreciated as much as other more popularly designed carpets of other districts. Room rugs of 7ft 6ins × 4ft 5ins were £1,500 ten years ago. Today they are still to be found in good condition for £2,800. Smaller rugs are just within the price limit.

Serabend
Type: Town, village.
Construction: Knot: T, or recently P. Warp: cotton. Weft: cotton. Single cord often overcast madder-red wool.
Colours: Blue, red, ivory grounds.
Design: Almost exclusively 'boteh', resulting in this design being named 'Serabend' or 'Saraband'. Crests or feathers of 'boteh' usually change from left to right in alternate rows. Used in every size from large to very small version known as 'flea pattern'.
Price: Rugs £500 up to £1,600; carpets now from £900–£2,500. Pakistan copies, often natural ground or washed-out reddish pink good value at £200–300 for a runner measuring about 8ft 6ins × 2ft 3ins but do not expect them to wear too well as the wool is soft. Machine-made copies of same designs from Brussels may be better buy in terms of quality at £225 for similar size.

Shiraz
Type: Desert nomad (see Afshar, Qashqai).
Construction: Knot: T or P. Warp: cotton or wool. Weft: wool. Double, triple side cord, multicoloured overcast wool.
Colours: Sombre, typically nomad.
Price: Nomad work selling through Shiraz: small rugs 5ft 6ins × 3ft 6ins start at £500 and go up to £1,200. Persian designs from village looms, 6ft 6ins × 4ft 6ins, range between £700 and £3,000.

Tabriz
Type: City, town, manufactory.
Construction: Knot: T. Warp: cotton. Weft: cotton. Double flat side cord wool or cotton overcast.

Colours: Traditional deep red, deep blue ground.
Design: Traditional antique Tabriz carpets have all-over patterns of flowers, never-ending foliate trails overlaid with rich, dark medallions. Local wool can be poor quality. resulting in tired colouring without depth or brilliance. Today, about 15 per cent of the output is of high quality, but if an attractive design appeals, watch out for irregular cotton wefts, flat matt pile – indicators of low standards of materials and manufacture.
Price: Recent production not likely to be an investment unless outside price range. Those from the first half of the century from £2,000 for 11 × 8ft £3,500 for 13 × 9ft 6ins. 6ft 6ins × 4ft 6ins start at £900.

Turkey, Anatolia

Turkish rugs are less sophisticated than Persian, their designs less elaborate. By far the greatest quantity of rugs imported into England during the Victorian and Edwardian eras came from Turkey. 'Turkey rug' conjures up old-fashioned standard patterns in red and blue, with thick pile, large medallions, rich floral patterns. Turkish carpets are woven on a wool groundweave and are more pliable than Persian ones which are more tightly woven on unyielding cotton groundweave. They almost always have geometric, abstract designs, because the Moslem religion forbids the depiction of living creatures in lifelike manner. There is a very high output of prayer rugs of all kinds, each one basically consisting of a prayer arch (mihrab) in the centre surrounded by decorative border, with corner-pieces which are often elaborate. Saphs or family prayer rugs with several mihrabs are also widely made in many regions of Turkey. However, it must be remembered that many fine Persian carpets came through Turkey on their way to Turkish ports, and many of the early Turkish carpet-producing centres based their designs on rich and rare rugs from Persia.

Bergamo (Bergama)
No carpets made in town itself, but in surrounding countryside.
Type: Room, prayer rugs.
Construction: Knot: T. Warp: cotton or coarse wool and hair. Weft: the same. Double flat side cords overcast blue wool. Woven kelim end with diagonal central pattern. Low knot density.
Colours: Typical dark reds, blues, some yellow.
Design: Geometric, not unlike traditional designs from Caucasian Kazak-Gendje area. Unusually, red dye corrodes. In general, work sold from Bergamo today is fairly undistinguished though of reasonable if coarse quality, redeemed by handsome woven kelim ends.
Price: These attractive geometric rugs have escaped current boost to prices of anything with a Caucasian look. Prices have remained steady over past two decades at around £600 for 6ft 3ins × 4ft 3ins. Investment potential does not look good on past evidence.

Ghiordes
Once-flourishing centre for very recognizable prayer rugs, today makes sad, poor-quality copies of famous traditional design.
Type: Prayer, room rugs.
Construction: Knot: T. Warp: wool. Weft: red wool. Double flat side cords red wool overcast.
Colours: Reds, yellows, blues and pale green.
Design: Typical larger Ghiordes rugs have giant stylized carnations and geometric leaves. Traditional Ghiordes prayer rugs have columned prayer niche, usually on natural ground, tending to be small because of encroaching decorative borders, corner-pieces.
Price: Proper antique Ghiordes rugs command a high price – well outside the price range. Old, but not antique, Ghiordes can be found at between £500 and £1,000 for 6ft 6ins × 4ft 6ins. Copies from Konya are about £400 and are of good quality. Modern Ghiordes-looking rugs are around from Romania and Bulgaria – beware.

Kars
Near Russian border, trading centre for

nomad rugs more Caucasian than Turkish.
Type: Nomad.
Construction: Knot: T. Warp: Blue wool. Weft: wool. Single cord wool overcast.
Colours: Bright, primary – use of both vegetable and synthetic dyes.
Design: Bold geometrics, lozenges, zigzags, hooks. Quality of wool and knotting varies considerably from tribe to tribe.
Price: The eye should be best guide for preference, the price should not exceed £300–400 for about 5ft 6ins × 3ft 6ins.

Kayseri
Type: Large room rugs, short-piled wool, made to order, prayer rugs.
Construction: Knot: T or P. Warp: cotton or silk. Weft: cotton or silk. Fine side cords, cotton or silk overcast.
Colours: Wide palette, often pale, with pale pistachio or celadon green very typical.
Design: Many niched prayer rugs or 'saphs' made here for export as well as traditional ones for home market. Old designs, patterns still used, and both Persian and Anatolian designs copied. Kayseri carpets have no particular style of their own.
Price: Well outside price range (£1,800) but artificial silk, rayon and mercerized cotton 'flosh' Kayseri can be attractive and good value at £400 or less for 5ft 6ins × 3ft 3ins but doubtful investment value.

Kirshehir
Type: Room rugs, prayer rugs.
Construction: Knot: T. Warp: wool. Weft: wool, often red or greenish-yellow. Double side cord overcast greenish-yellow wool.
Colours: Yellow, olive-green grounds most typical among wide spectrum.
Design: Rich floral carpets much influenced by European designs with rococo swirls on white ground. Prayer rugs, saphs and cemetery rugs with sketchy mihrabs overlaid on yellow, olive-green grounds. General effect a little drab compared with other districts.
Price: Prayer rugs only within price range, with less appreciation in last decade than previous ones. Perfect condition around £750. 4ft × 2ft good value at £300–500.

OPPOSITE A mid-19th-century Kirshehir prayer rug with stepped mihrab. Note abrach.

Konya
Type: Room rugs, prayer rugs, village.
Construction: Knot: T. Warp: wool. Weft: red wool. Double cord overcast wool.
Colours: Reds, yellows, blues and pale greens.
Design: Today Konya reproduces 'Ghiordes' and 'Ladik' prayer rugs. Work is good, much of it still made by peasants in outlying villages using traditional red-dyed weft, or undyed brown wool or goat hair.
Price: Good quality copies of Ghiordes and Ladik (beyond our price range) prayer rugs, but copies all the same: £500 up to £800.

Kula
Type: Prayer rugs, room rugs.
Construction: Knot: T. Warp: wool. Weft: thick wool. Double flat side cord wool overcast.
Colours: Apricot most distinctive in wide palette.
Design: Tends to be hotch-potch of features from other districts. Traditional Mudjur tiled border, central floral pillar or column which is weak version of three-column Ladik.
Price: Antique distinctive prayer rugs well outside price range. Fifty to 60-year-old pieces at about £600–900. Modern copies of Mudjur and Ladik rather cheaper –£400–600.

Melas (Milas)
Type: Prayer rugs.
Construction: Knot: T. Warp: wool. Weft: red wool. Double flat side cord overcast red wool.
Colours: More yellowish than other Anatolian prayer rugs, with distinctive rust-red often predominating.
Design: Instantly recognizable by waisted prayer niche often with red, yellow centre. Saw-edged leaf pattern often used in border.
Price: Outside price range for antique prayer rugs. However, good-quality rugs for overseas buyers are also made. 6ft 6ins × 4ft 6ins £700–950. Danger that Melas will

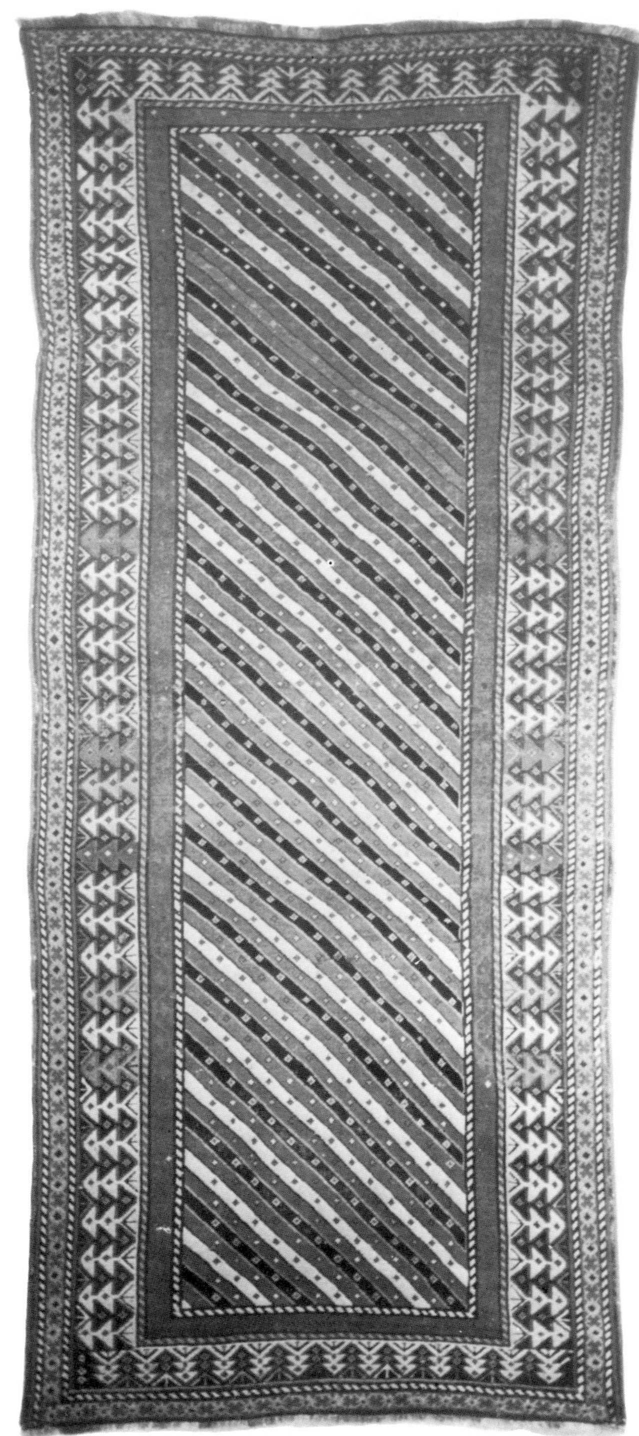

Daghestan runner with Gendje diagonal stripes, multi-coloured ground design. Today Daghestan has been absorbed by the Soviet-controlled Derbend manufactory, with a consequent loss of vivacity.

fall prey to imitation because of distinctive design and suffer consequent depreciation.

Mudjur

Type: Prayer rugs.

Construction: Knot: T. Warp: wool. Weft: red wool. Double cord overcast wool.

Colours: Unusually bright, rich colour range, in particular distinctive red ground for prayer niche.

Design: Traditional prayer rugs had subdued, tiled-effect borders and stepped prayer niches with red grounds instead of usual Anatolian blue. Today this design still being made, but many copies elsewhere. Particularly wide borders are characteristic.

Price: Mudjurs cost between £600 and £800 for 6ft 6ins × 4ft 6ins. There are many copies around, in particular from Kula, which are also colourful and decorative.

Panderma (Banderma)

Misleadingly, fine 'silk Pandermas' are not made here but in Kayseri.

Type: Saphs, prayer rugs, room rugs and export goods.

Construction: Knot: T. Warp: silk, rayon or mercerized cotton. Weft: the same. Double or single flat side cord silky overcast.

Colours: Wide range, including pastel colours for silks.

Design: Copies of ancient Turkish and Persian antique designs most skilfully made, often artificially aged by rubbing with brick to bruise pile and make it soft and silky. May often be identified by cotton overcast instead of silk. Source of multiple-niched prayer rugs in pale-coloured silky materials, recently popular in Europe and America to hang on bare walls. Rayon as well as silk is used in pile to give silky soft appearance.

Price: Mixed wool and cotton pile and their soft, unfashionable slatey colouring may be the reason for low appreciation over last decade. Recently-made Panderma 5ft 8ins × 4ft 3ins, around £600, same price as 10 years ago. Saphs high at £400–600 with little resale value at present.

Sparta

British Oriental Carpet Company set up at Smyrna at turn of century to produce Sparta carpets. Tremendous output. Sparta carpets could be ordered by the yard, of any pattern or size – durable and hard wearing.
Type: Room rugs and export goods.
Construction: Knot: P. Warp: cotton. Weft: cotton. Heavy double side cord often overcast cotton.
Colours: Typical slatey blues and blue-tinged reds, but muddy and dull.
Design: Carpets from this district used to be known as 'Smyrna' carpets because of their port of export. Some quite reasonable copies of old designs still made in the local gaol using traditional methods and materials.
Price: Rugs made in local gaol are only ones with investment potential and even then appreciation has not been that high over last two years. Too much 'carpeting' as opposed to 'carpets' has been made here for any great investment value. Condition and comparable price for new carpets should be your guide to second-hand Sparta carpets.

Ushak

Type: European shapes, sizes, room rugs, carpets.
Construction: Knot: T. Warp: green wool. Weft: wool. Double flat side cord overcast wool. Not particularly durable due to widespread use of mercerized cotton for groundweave, also sometimes mixed with wool for pile.
Colours: Deep reds, blues typical ground colour.
Design: Persian-based, but dark blues and reds are harsh and shallow, often due to chemical dyes.
Price: Early Ushaks have soared to millionaire prices, but modern copies do not bear much relation and are made in most carpet-making centres. Not particularly fashionable in design at present, and not particularly durable. They compare well for price alone with brand new tufted carpets as alternative floor covering in second-hand condition and were almost standard Victorian dining-room carpets. 'Turkey' rugs made in 1920s are sound value at £600–900 for 11ft × 8ft in good condition.

Yajebadir (Yakebedir)

Type: Room, prayer rugs.
Construction: Knot: T. Warp: cotton or coarse wool and hair. Weft: the same. Double flat side cords, overcast blue wool.
Colours: Dark-blue grounds, reds and whites.
Design: Similar in many way to antique Bergamo rugs in concept and colour. Geometric patterns, motifs, knotted in good-quality lustrous wool.
Price: Probably due to appreciate; 20 to 40 years old, 6ft × 4ft should be around £600.

Yuruk

Type: Pastoral nomad, prayer rugs.
Construction: Knot: T. Warp: wool. Weft: wool, often brightly coloured. Triple or quadruple cord weft-coloured wool overcast.
Colours: Very vivid but limited palette as with most nomad work.
Design: Two important factors distinguish work of Yuruk: long pile and simple patterns, usually geometric, with hooked or zigzag outlines. Often extra strands of long hair woven into pile, or a glass bead, believed to ward off evil eye.
Price: Genuine Yuruk about £300 for small prayer rugs.

Caucasian

Although Caucasian rugs and carpets have recently gained tremendous popularity in the West, it should be remembered that at the beginning of this century it appeared as though half the total population of the Caucasus was knotting carpets for the Russians and for export. They were not considered of any great importance to the European rug collector.

The centre of carpet-making in the Caucasus was the wild districts of mountain and plain on the Eastern side which shelves down to the Caspian Sea. The western side of the Caucasus has always been an area of settled people and rich crop-growing communities. Cotton has long been grown in

Shirvan, and in both Shirvan and the Karabagh districts silk has been cultivated for centuries. In the 18th century the Caucasus was divided into Khanates, and their names used to identify the carpet producing centres.

A common feature of Caucasian rugmakers is a childlike delight in bold primary colours and simple shapes. Every pattern, flower, leaf, animal and human is reduced to a geometrical shape.

Caucasian rugs and carpets are worth a little judicious speculation even when not in prime condition. This is because genuine work from these districts has ceased altogether and restorers of old rugs and carpets will pay a reasonable price for those which are not past redemption. That said, do not plunge into this field without considerable experience, nor without thoroughly comparing the many copies being offered. Caucasian carpets were not considered in the same league as Turkish or Persian, and right up to the 1950s the highest prices paid were in the region of £35–50. It is still possible to pick up a poor-condition Caucasian from a contents-of-house sale for under £500. Good-condition Caucasians have appreciated by over 300% in the last decade and are seldom to be found for under £3,000. Even then, as long-term investment they will continue to appreciate because they will never be made again and cannot be copied successfully. Look at the Soviet-made work and compare it with a genuine piece and you will understand the value of Caucasians made before World War II. Some of these are still seeping on to the European market from Israel, in mint condition with their woven, knotted kelim ends still intact.

Baku (Azerbaijan)
Recent attempts to resuscitate traditional designs, resulting in forlorn shadows of once-bright geometric, 'boteh', Persian-influenced designs of old production.
Type: Manufactory.
Construction: Knot: T. Warp: wool. Weft: wool. Double flat side cords overcast wool.
Colours: Washed-out indigos, pale greens and blues, dull colouring looking faded even when new.
Design: Persian-influenced, 'boteh' similar to Persian 'feather serabend' and striped medallions with fine outline, usually on dark-blue grounds. From Baku are sold carpets with similarity to Turkomans and other octagonal lozenge patterns, not to be confused with genuine nomad work.
Price: Turkoman-type patterns made in manufactories without lustre, fluidity. Do not confuse deliberately faded colouring with genuine old Turkoman. Prices should be in the region of £350–650 and not a bargain for quality.

Derbend (Derbent)
Recent Soviet control of production has resulted in poorer quality.
Type: Village, nomad.
Construction: Knot: T. Warp: undyed wool. Weft: cotton. Double side cord overcast dark brown wool.
Colours: More muted palette than those of other districts.
Design: Many motifs borrowed from neighbouring Kuba, adapted and mixed with some Shirvan motifs. Not uncommon to find 'running dog' borders, small tribal symbols mixed into town versions of more formal stepped polygon designs. Large Derbends are common, reaching sizes of 19ft × 7ft.
Price: From £650 for 7ft × 4ft.

Genje (Kazakh Gendje)
Type: Village, nomad.
Construction: Knot: T. Warp: undyed wool. Weft: natural reddish-brown wool. Double and triple side cord overcast red, brown or multicoloured wool. Village-made distinguished from nomad by shorter pile.
Colours: Unusually subdued for Caucasian.
Design: The 'crab' border is quite common, more controlled geometric designs from villages. Room sets or 'dast khali gebe' were made in this more settled area. Some carpets have tiled or diagonally striped ground.
Price: 7ft 6ins × 4ft 6ins £900–1,000. Soviet-made small room rugs, 7ft × 4ft, industrially manufactured with lifeless design, around

£350–800 per sq.m. Copies from Turkey start higher at £620–650. Prayer rugs from borders of Anatolia and Bordjalou sometimes labelled Kazak but are the work of mountain nomads and fetch similar prices to Turkish mountain nomad work. Few prayer rugs are made in Soviet Russia today.

Karabagh (Garabagh)
Area now mainly in Soviet province of Armenia. Wide use of chemical dyes in modern production.
Type: Formerly village, now manufactory.
Construction: Knot: T. Warp: undyed brown wool. Weft: dyed red wool or cotton. Double flat side cord overcast reddish wool.
Colours: Cochineal reds and vermilions, rich to the point of violence, combined with the widespread use of black.
Design: Bold geometric shapes and immense stylized flowers sometimes know as 'Sunburst Kazaks' or 'Eagle Kazaks'. Crab border is common, also Chinese-influenced 'cloudband' motif in border. The swastika also found in more fluid form, as well as interlocking T-border stemming from farthest eastern territories of Cenral Asia. Many very floral pieces with large cabbage roses.
Price: Old Karabaghs 6ft 6ins × 4ft 6ins from £500 to £1,000. 'Carpet of roses' still produced but lacking exuberance of older versions: from £350 per sq.m.

Sejur (Seichur)
Type: Room rugs, larger sized than usual.
Construction: Knot: T. Warp: thick natural wool. Weft: white cotton. Single or double side cord overcast blue wool or cotton. Fine net-like knotted blue cotton kelim ends.
Colours: Clear soft tones of red, blue and yellow, with unusually flat browns.
Design: Giant sunburst or cross-shaped medallions and huge diagonal crosses. 'Running dog' border with more sinuous, less angular shape. Rugs from this province often called 'Kuba Sejur'.
Price: around £800 for 7ft × 4ft.

Shirvan
Although Shirvans have been exported main-

Shirvan runner, c. 1880, with indigo field, four medallions, an ivory lovebird border and three guard stripes.

ly since 1850 (and indeed produced since the 16th century), since the 1920s huge carpet manufactories have produced thousands of carpets every year.
Type: Village, manufactory.
Construction: Knot: T. Warp: thick natural wool, or cotton. Weft: undyed cotton. Single or double side cord overcast dyed blue or brick-red cotton. White plaited cotton kelim ends.
Colours: Traditionally vibrant, now flat.
Design: 'Perepedil' has uniform ram's horn motifs. 'Snake Caucasian' is a lifeless interpretation, copied in Ardebil, of 'Cloudband Kazak'. 'Karashli' is a modern Soviet-produced design using traditional forked leaves, and scrolls.
Price: Reasonably priced at £800–1,000 for older rug 7ft × 4ft or from £350 per sq.m.

Shusha
One-time capital city of Karabagh Khanate. Small city manufactories producing more formal, disciplined versions of exuberant Karabagh designs.
Type: Room rugs.
Construction: Knot: T. Warp: natural wool. Weft: cotton. Single or double side cord often overcast coloured wool or cotton.
Colours: More judicious use of flaming cochineal reds, bright, luminous but disciplined.
Design: Finely knotted, short pile, silky wool with more intricate patterns with Persian, European influence. Fixed looms allow stricter control, larger sizes.
Price: around £1,000 for new 6ft 4ins × 4ft 7ins.

Turkoman (Bokhara, Afghanistan, Belouchestan)

Turkoman rugs and carpets, tent trappings and camel trappings are easily identifiable as a group and impossible to subdivide without considerable study. Colouring is distinctive: brown shading to dark red and plum, often with a faint blue overtone. Unlike any other Oriental rug, Turkoman work keeps the same ground colour in the border as in the central field. The Persian knot is used and the work is short-piled and incredibly fine and dense, for rugs and trappings must withstand the constant abrasive action of sand and be closely-woven enough to prevent the sand from penetrating, even in desert storms.

East of the Caspian Sea, the Turkoman 'gul' is to each tribe of Central Asia what heraldry is to the West. Each has its own particular 'gul' with which it marks all its possessions: horses, tents, bags – even women.

Afghan
Common ancestry with Turkoman work, though 'guls' are larger, symmetrical octagon, sometimes known as 'elephant's foot'.
Type: Carpets, prayer rugs. Tribal mountain nomad hatchli, tent trappings, bag faces, camel trappings.
Construction: Knot: T or P. Warp: brownish wool or goat hair. Weft: undyed wool. One to three flat side cords overcast dark goat hair. Long red kelim ends, occasionally with diagonal striped pattern.
Colours: Similar to Turkoman but reds are more scarlet, browns more chestnut.
Design: Afghan hatchlis are less rigid, panels and cross-pieces often broken with stylized tree of life, decorated with miniature border patterns.
Price: Good genuine Afghan 'gul' room rug 11ft × 8ft can still be found for £800–1,000 with recent high appreciation. Quarquin cheapest (around £750 for 13ft 6ins × 8ft 6ins), Pendiq medium quality, Davlatobad best. Recent changes in the political situation may reduce genuine production drastically, with consequent rise in likely investment value. Tent and camel trappings, bag-faces, seeping on to market from displaced tribes: £100 upwards, with totally modern added decoration of bullet cases and beercan ringpulls as sad but authentic record of current events. Mass produced 'Red Afghan' runners from Pakistan are around £350 for 11ft 6ins × 2ft 3ins. See also Golden Afghans, p. 122.

Belouch (Belouchi, Balouchi)
Type: Prayer rugs, room rugs, tent trappings,

camel trappings.
Construction: Knot: P. Warp: natural wool and goat or camel hair and, more recently, cotton. Weft: the same. Two or three side cords, overcast two-colour check pattern.
Colours: Subdued, sombre browns and natural beige, smoky blue-reds, occasional use of bleached white.
Design: Combination of Caucasian and Afghan smaller motifs, including hooked lozenges and 'running dog' borders. Uneasy marriage of Caucasian 'botehs' with Herati pattern in the border. Little animals and birds are often incorporated as well as the 'akstafa' cockerel met with in other nomad work. Prayer rugs may have hand shapes each side of the niche.
Price: Belouch rugs are made on both sides of the Iranian-Afghan border and differ considerably. Iranian rugs sold in Meshed and known as Meshed Belouch: 6ft × 3ft: £400–600. Those made in Afghanistan are sold in the town of Herat and are known as Herat Belouch. These tend to be smaller; 5ft × 3ft can be anywhere from £100 to £1,000. 'Belouchi' rugs with mercerized cotton or rayon pile are produced in Soviet manufactories. They sell for about £300.

Beshir (Yagbeshir, Kabul)
Settled in communities longer than any other Turkoman tribe, possibly with different ethnic origins. The Turkish knot is used as well as the Persian. Sold through Kabul as well as other trading towns.
Type: Prayer rugs, hatchli, room rugs.
Construction: Knot: T and P. Warp: coarse wool or goat hair. Weft: the same. Four side cords overcast black-brown goat hair or double cord overcast red and brown.
Colours: The exception to Turkoman work, with very rare blue ground, packed with red motifs, the results looking almost purple, or red-on-red, with judicious use of yellow. Narrow bands of alternating colours are distinctive in the borders.
Design: The 'gul' is subordinate, and many designs come from recognizably Chinese motifs, such as the cloudband, as well as the Herati pattern. Small 'guls' may be incorporated into stylized flower-shapes, or in borders which are unusually wide.
Price: Attractive old Beshir rugs can be had for between £400 and £1,000, 6ft 6ins × 4ft 6ins. Recent production of similar size sell at the lower end of this price range.

Bokhara (Tekke, Yummut)
Old misnomer for Turkoman rugs sold through the bazaar of Bokhara. The practice of dyeing brown wool with indigo to make black once earned them the misleading name of 'blue Bokharas'. Today the vague category of 'Bokhara' is to be viewed with suspicion, as the name itself has been largely discredited by specialist Turkoman dealers.
Price: Old Bokharas of genuine tribal origins can be found for £300–700 for 5ft 6ins × 3ft 6ins and £500–1,000 for 6ft 6ins × 4ft 6ins (£300–500 sq.m.). There are however copies from many sources—Meshed, Hereke, Sivas, Russia, Rumania and large quantities from Pakistan. Modern Soviet Bokharas with part silk content—a sure sign of manufactory work—sell for £900–£1,000. Small copies of quite good quality from other sources: about £200.

Ersari
Originally made all the so-called Afghans. Their territory ranges as far as the Caspian Sea to the Afghan border and they are more truly Turkoman than the Beshir.
Type: Bag faces, room rugs, trappings.
Construction: Knot: P (sometimes single row of T before kelim ends). Warp: undyed dark goat hair. Weft: the same. Single or double side cord overcast undyed goat hair. Cotton is never used.
Colours: Yellows and greens as well as plums and browns of Turkoman palette.
Design: The 'gul' is often arranged in trellis or diamond pattern; some Ersari work is typical of mountain nomads in its liberal sprinkling of flowers, leaves, in random fashion over the ground colour.
Price: Genuine Ersari work scarce, fetching higher prices than Beshir. Recent good reproductions of old designs from Afghanistan, chemically washed to pale smokey pink,

reasonably priced at around £250–500 for room rug but of doubtful investment value.

Golden Afghans (Washed Afghans)
Originally occurred in 1920s by accident when harsh red dyes were chemically washed to tone down colour. French interior design and fashion made these 'washed Afghans' extremely popular and they have been made in quantity ever since. Recently 'made golds' have come on the market, made from wool specially dyed to the same palette, but which will hold their colour and last longer than chemically washed products. 'Washed golds' can be detected by red at the roots of tufts.
Type: Same range as Afghans.
Construction: Knot: T or P. Warp: coarse goat or camel. Weft: the same. One to four flat side cords overcast wool or camel hair.
Colours: Pale beige-golds, faded reds.
Design: Identical to Afghans.
Price: Chemical washing lessens the life of the wool and the colours are currently out of favour, so Golden Afghans tend to be on the cheap side: £300–500 for 6ft 6ins × 4ft 6ins and £300–700 for 10 × 7. 'Made golds' may or may not appreciate from current £450 for 5ft × 6ft.

China

In the 1920s there was a surge in popularity for 'chinoiserie' and a consequent increase in Chinese carpet imports into Europe and America. As demand increased the previously high standard seen in excellent hand-knotting, subtle pale colours, often with flowers, and patterns embossed by clipping the pile, declined, leading to low-grade 'boudoir' carpets. Today there are huge carpet industries in Sinkiang, Peking and Tientsin, mass-producing carpets of every size and design. Patterns are derivative, owing more to French Savonnerie and Aubusson designs, though Chinese symbols in standardized forms are often incorporated.
Type: Mass-produced, any size or shape.
Construction: Knot: P. Warp: machine-spun cotton. Weft: the same. Single cord overcast cotton. Low knot density.
Design: Embossed, clipped pile, circular, half-moon, and many copies of European, Caucasian, Persian, made in unconvincing colours. Symbols incorporated into designs include the cloud, the dragon, the lotus, the fish and the flower vase.
Price: 1920s 6ft 6ins × 4ft 6ins £300–1,000 for top quality; otherwise second-hand value.

Tibet

Sold through China, India, Ladakh. Hand-knotted by mountain people. Colours are cruder than Caucasians, but these are less tame than many other derivative rugs, though the quality of wool is coarse, knotting looser.
Price: Caucasian-type, a far better bet than many other copies at £450–550 for 8ft × 5ft. Must not be confused with factory-made Chinese Caucasians, which have little resemblance to originals.

Pakistan

Thriving carpet industry established in last 30 years, making Turkoman-type rugs with quick economical 'Djufti' knot. Also 'Red Afghans' and 'Pakistan Bokharas', Turkomans. Some genuine Belouch work sold through Pakistan to West.
Type: Runners in Turkoman patterns, room rugs, prayer rugs.
Construction: Knot: P or Dj. Warp: cotton. Weft: mercerized cotton, rayon. Single cord overcast silk, mercerized cotton. Often very high knot density.
Colours: In Turkoman copies the reds are too cherry, blues too dull.
Design: Derivative, some well-made to high standards of knotting, but wool too soft, pile flattens quickly.
Price: Danger area. All qualities from top quality Pakistan 'Bokhara', tightly knotted, excellent quality workmanship, to lower quality 'Djufti' knots, even machine-made tufteds. Addition of Australian wool gives soft finish, chrome dyes used, but mostly colourfast. Purists, specialists, tend to dismiss all Pakistan work but some good dealers with sound knowledge of this work will guide you

to the best. Prices for 'Bokharas' about £230 for 6ft × 4ft handmade. Recent production of identical copies of Persian rugs with Kashan designs, the best hard to tell from originals. Half the price of Persian, but still outside our limit.

India

Originally 'Indo-Isfahans' were excellent, of high quality, good craftsmanship. Mirzapur, largest carpet-producing centre, produced enormous quantities of carpet in 1920s with consequent decline in quality; miserable Persian-derivative designs. Since 1950 quality has risen, wool imported from Australia has improved texture, pile. Today Amritsar produces carpets, rugs, textiles in staggering quantities, variable qualities, nothing of aesthetic interest.
Price: Apart from small rugs made in Agra gaol which are now collectors' pieces and well over £1,000, prices should be calculated against same area-covering for European equivalents. Little hope of investment value even of best quality, because of gigantic output from Mirzapur, Amritsar.

The Balkans

Historic tradition of carpet- and rug-making throughout the Balkans since occupation under Ottoman Empire.

Rumania
Today Rumania has enormous carpet industry, copying almost every known design, using Turkish knot and coarse cotton groundweave.
Construction: Knot: T or recently P. Warp: hemp or cotton. Weft: coarse cotton. Single heavy side cord overcast thick wool.
Price: Reasonable copies of Caucasians, but on coarse cotton groundweave, harsher, more uniform colouring, around £230–250 for 6ft 6ins × 4ft 6ins. Persian-type room rugs more genuine. Many Iranian emigrants using traditional patterns, European colour palette, identifiable with experience. 6ft 6ins × 4ft 6ins, Persian-type, around £360.

Bulgaria
As for Rumania, also with addition of emigrant carpet weavers from Iran using genuine Persian patterns, unhappily with European palette. Copies of Turkoman, Caucasian, with strange dead look of misunderstood symbols, antique designs.
Construction: Knot: P and T. Warp: hemp or goat hair. Weft: cotton or cotton and wool mixed. Single side cord overcast thick coarse wool or cotton.
Price: Fine pre-1939 Kirmans very hard to tell from real Persian Kirmans and outside the price limit. Modern copies of Caucasian and Turkoman rugs better than those from Pakistan – Bulgarian mock Caucasian 6ft 6ins × 4ft 6ins about £400.

Kelims

This is a general name given to flat-weave woollen textiles which are more like coarse cloth than a carpet. Indeed, except by desert nomad tribes, they were never used as floor-coverings, but instead served as coverings for chests and boxes, tent hangings and wall-hangings. Kelims in general were considered of such little account until recently that thirty years ago shipments of carpets were wrapped in kelims and no charge was made for them, nor for their Indian equivalent – the cotton 'dari'. In rug markets in Turkey and Persia, kelims were sold by the kilo. Only the Soumak flat-weave is really suitable for floor

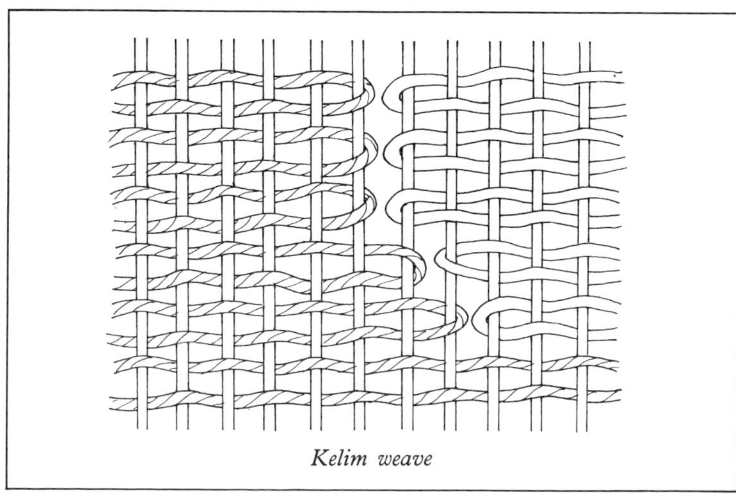
Kelim weave

use because it is thicker, though its embroidered face wears less well.

Anatolian kelims

The finest of these is the Karaman or Karamanli which comes from the region around Konya. The weft thread of each colour is woven to and fro in its own part of the pattern and no weft runs the entire width of the piece. Thus small slits separate each part of the pattern, usually staggered so that the slit is as small as possible. Anatolian kelims are reversible. The weft is usually dyed red.

Sehna

Finest of all kelims, woven by the Kurds on very fine warps, sometimes of silk. The best known pattern is the Fereghan or Sehna, but there are others with roses packed tightly overall. Kurdistan kelims are never large because of the delicacy of their construction. It is said that the women of the tribe wrapped themselves in Sehna kelims in the bath houses – hence these kelims' particular elegance. 6ft × 4ft £300.

The Balkans

Bright and decorative kelims are traditionally made all over the Balkans, but almost all are modern: 7ft × 4ft £220 or £85 per sq.m.

Caucasian

Flat-weaves from this area are made differently from Anatolian and Iranian kelim-weave. Instead of the under-and-over technique, the weft thread is taken in a loose over-and-over stitch like a herringbone. New colours are introduced and worked in, and the ends are left loose at the back to make them warmer and thicker. This technique, known as Soumak, is also found in parts of the Balkans, but takes its name from a town in the Eastern Caucasus. Particularly fine are the Kuba-Soumaks. They are also made in Shirvan, Daghestan and Derbend, many of them with the familiar hooked lozenge motif.

Sileh

Sileh kelims are woven with a refined version of the Soumak weave, so that the back looks more like a knotted carpet back, except where the threads are carried over to the next part of the pattern with the same colour. Sileh kelims come from the Southern Caucasus, notably Karabagh, Kazak and Baku. The most beautiful are the 'Dragon' kelims with huge scrolled S and Z shapes. White cotton is always used in Sileh kelims for the white parts of the pattern. They are woven in narrow (12–14inch) strips. For wider pieces, two or more strips are sewn together with the pattern matched.

Verneh

Large curtain-like hangings, native to Karabagh and Kazak, recognizable for their brick-red, yellow-brown, dark yellow or brown-black groundweave. These hangings are also known as 'shadda'.

Azerbaijan

Like other nomad work, these kelims often include little stylized birds, animals, humans.

Shiraz

Some of the brightest and boldest of all, with great lozenge shapes and zigzag motifs.

Kis-kelims

Kis-kelims formed part of a girl's dowry and were suitably large and grand, often with silver or metallic foil threads woven into them.

Price: Fine kis-kelims with much detail may cost as much as £500 or more, but there are excellent ones with some age to be found in large sizes for about £125. Sehna, Shiraz and particularly Caucasian kelims have so far established investment value. Owing to their fragility there is a scarcity value as well as an aesthetic one. Some more sombre-coloured Sehnas are to be found at around £300, but paler colours – rose, ivory, pale yellow and pale green – in good condition can go from £500 to well over £1,000 for 6ft 6ins × 4ft 6ins.

With the general rise in price and value of so much nomad work, specialist dealers have recently been acquiring kelims of such excellence that they should be valued on the

OPPOSITE Turkish prayer kelim with narrow mihrab filled with tree-of-life motif.

same scale as rugs from the tribes from which they originate. These fine pieces of work should never be put on the floor, and should be hung properly if they are not to be pulled out of shape.

Kelims of recent make from the Balkans and Turkey are bright and colourful, but should not be more than £125 for a reasonable size. Owing to the ethnic trend, there are shops, usually not regular dealers in textiles and carpets, who sell them at a much higher price than is justifiable.

Rug Terms

Abrach (Abrash) An uneven line across a rug where the colour of dye changes due to new hanks of wool being used from different dyeing. Once a sign of authentic age and hand-dyeing, now frequently deliberately incorporated to mislead. Artificial abraches can be recognized because they run evenly across a row of knotting. With genuine work the change is uneven and the same variation of colour will appear in other parts of the carpet.

Akstafa A stylized bird pattern.

Aniline dye A chemical dye which replaced vegetable dyes in the 1880s much to the detriment of many carpet-making centres. It is not lightfast or colourfast – most easily seen from the back of the rug where it has not faded.

Aubusson A French carpet-making centre with a distinctive pattern and colour.

Backing General term for the weave on to which the pile is knotted.

Bag face The patterned, knotted front of a nomad saddle bag or other bag. The backs of these pieces are plain.

Baktiari Nomad tribe living mainly on border mountains between Iran and Turkey. A name often inaccurately applied to indeterminate nomad work from the area.

Belouch, Beluchi Nomadic tribes living on the Pakistan/Iran/Afghanistan borders.

Bleached white Most nomad work and genuine handmade rugs use the natural wool for white – bleached white is often a sign of more commercial manufacture.

Bokhara Misnomer for Turkoman tribal work, originally so-called because it was sold through the trading centre of Bokhara.

Border The 'frame' or border pattern surrounding the central motif. Characteristic of place of origin.

Boteh A tribal and Caucasian pattern, shaped like an inverted comma, ranging from a fluid shape to an angular one, which is often known as the 'pecking bird'. The basis of the Paisley design.

Caucasian Rugs and carpets made in the Caucasus with such distinctive colours and patterns that the term 'Caucasian' also denotes these as well as the place of origin. Since Soviet control of this area, true Caucasians are no longer made.

Celadon Pale green often made with a copper-based dye which may corrode the wool.

Cemetery rug Graveyard rugs: common to many districts, used for funerals, usually incorporating a cypress tree or a weeping willow, with one or two houses, the whole being repeated several times.

Chemical wash Rugs with too-hard colours washed in a chemical solution to soften them.

Chromatic dye As distinct from the crude aniline dyes, chemical dyes with far more subtlety of colour, lightfast and colourfast, introduced in the 1920s.

Cloudband Design probably originating from China, found in Persian and Caucasian work, sometimes also known as 'ram's horn'.

Cochineal Red dye originating from China where it was made from the carapace of a beetle. More brilliant and rose-coloured than other red dyes.

Corrode, corrosion Some dyes have a natural chemical content which in time eats away the wool pile of a rug. Most commonly a black or dark brown, but also copper-based celadon and some other dyes.

'Crab' border A Caucasian version of the **Herati** pattern resembling a crab. Found in work from districts near Black Sea.

Dari Indian cotton drugget or flat-weave.

Dast khali gebe A set of rugs for a room, also known as a **room set.**

Djufti knot A rather loose knot, most common in Pakistan work. See **Knots.**

Elephant's foot Often used to describe the Turkoman 'gul' pattern.

Embossed Pile clipped to make patterns in relief.

Engsi Nomad tent-flap or opening.

Everlasting knot Chinese motif often found in Eastern Turkoman and Turkmenistan nomad work.

Fereghan pattern A flowing version of the Herati pattern developed by the Fereghan and Sehna carpet makers.

Field Background colour. See **Ground.**

Flosh Cotton mercerized to look like silk.

Foliate Composed of leaf-patterns.

Ghiordes knot Turkish knot, found mainly in Turkey and the Caucasus, with notable exceptions among nomads and displaced carpet weavers. See **Knots.**

Golden Afghan Afghan rugs which have been chemically washed to give them a golden appearance.

Ground The background colour of the central part of a rug.

Ground-weave The warp and weft.

Guard stripe Thin stripes separating borders from each other, or from the main part of the design.

Gul An eight-sided motif used in a similar way to heraldic shields by the Turkoman tribes. It also means 'flower' and 'lake'.

Hatchli A nomad tent flap or opening with a design resembling a simple wooden door, with the cross-pieces giving them the name 'hatchli', and a broad band at the bottom forming a skirt, often a kelim-weave with a thick fringe. Hatchlis also doubled as prayer mats, and some have simple niche-shapes at the top. Hatchlis are symmetrical from side to side, but asymmetrical from top to bottom.

Herati pattern A classic pattern appearing in many variations, such as the 'crab' and the 'lion's mask'. Basically composed of a rosette encircled by four curved leaves, it is also found as a continuous pattern in the central field as well as in borders.

Hook motif A rectangular hook shape characteristic of many Caucasian designs. In borders it is known as 'running dog'.

Jap silk Poor quality 'seconds' of silk from silk cocoons.

Kelim A flat-weave used for tent hangings and coverings, made in most carpet-producing areas.

Kelim ends The ends of a carpet which have been flat-woven to form a broad band between the pile and the fringe.

Kis-kelim Flat-weave tent hangings of more grand design which formed part of a girl's dowry. Often with metallic threads interwoven in the fabric.

Knots Persian or Senneh, Turkish or Ghiordes, and Djufti. See p. 103.

Motifs

Herati

palmette

Turkoman gul

boteh or sarabend

running dog

Knotted Confusingly carpets are usually described as 'woven' but the pile is knotted into the groundweave.

Lanceolate Shaped like a spearhead, leaves tapering at each end.

Leaf scroll Curled leaf motif forming scroll.

Lion's mask A broad palmette with the look of a lion's face.

Lozenge Diamond-shaped.

Machine-made Carpets made on machines are not knotted but tufted – the pile is simply looped round the weft thread without being secured.

Machine-spun Wool spun by machine lacks the depth and unevenness of hand spun wool and does not bush out to form a thick pile but remains in its individual yarn form.

Madder Red dye made from madder root, most typical in Turkoman and tribal work, distinguished by a faint blue overtone which originally gave its name to 'Blue Bokharas'.

'Made gold' Rugs made of wool dyed to the same shade as Golden Afghans, as opposed to being chemically-washed to soft colouring.

Manufactory Not to be confused with 'manufactured'. Small or large carpet-making centres where knotted carpets are made in quantity by hand.

Medallion Circular central motif.

Mihrab Prayer niche.

Mordant Literally 'eating'. Those dyes which corrode the woollen pile.

Motif Design.

Natural dye Those dyes made from natural and vegetable extractions and not from chemicals.

Niche Arch-shaped design at the top of a prayer rug and enclosing the main part of the rug.

Overcast Whip stitch usually in wool, which covers the side cords of a rug.

Painted Literally means painted with paint or dye where the original colour has faded.

Palmette One of many patterns originating from Shah Abbas' workshops in Iran in the 16th and 17th centuries. Palmettes are based on flower shapes.

Pastoral Nomad tribes inhabiting the foothills as opposed to the mountainous territory.

Pecking bird Angular Caucasian version of the boteh pattern.

Persian knot Senneh knot, predominating in Iran, Central Asia, Pakistan, Turkmenistan, Afghanistan and used by many scattered nomad tribes. See **Knots.**

Pile The surface of a knotted rug formed by closely-packed individual tufts knotted on to the groundweave.

Pistachio A particular pale olive green dye.

Prayer niche The church-window shape in the centre of a prayer rug, arched at the top. Proper name: mihrab.

Prayer rug Traditionally made for Moslems, the arch of the mihrab or prayer niche must always point towards Mecca when in use.

Ram's horn Curled motif like a Greek Ionic capital, roughly similar to a cloudband.

Room rug A rug usually measuring about 15–18ft by 6ft and made as part of a room set. Now describes any rug larger than about 5ft × 8ft.

Room set See **Dast khali gebe.** A set of rugs comprising a central rug 15–18ft × 6ft; a principal rug set like a T across the top of the central rug and measuring about 10 × 5ft 6ins. These two main rugs are flanked by two runners measuring about 17 × 3ft.

Rosette Stylized flower pattern.

Runner Long thin rug, originally forming part of a room set, measuring about 15–18ft by 3ft.

Running dog Repeated hook motif resembling heads of animals used as a border pattern.

Saph Prayer rug with many mihrabs, for family prayer.

Serabend, Saraband Design motif also known as the pine or leaf pattern, shaped like an inverted comma or tear-shaped boteh repeated all over the ground, from which the Paisley pattern was derived.

Savonnerie French carpet manufactory with distinctive pattern and colour.

Saw-edged leaf Serrated edged angular leaf.

Sehna knot see **Persian knot.**

Shadda Large pieces of flatweave tent hangings native to parts of the Caucasus.

Shirazi The overcasting to the side cords on silk rugs.

Shah Abbas 16th–17th century ruler of Iran whose workshops originated many of the now-traditional patterns of Persian carpets.

Side cord The thick cords on either side of

a rug round which the weft is woven. Many rugs have more than one side-cord to add strength and these are often overcast in coloured wools as a decorative finish.

Sileh kelim Flatweave hangings woven in narrow strips and sewn together. The most famous are the 'dragon' Silehs with huge scrolled S-shapes over several narrow widths.

Smyrna Name given to many Turkish carpets at the end of the last century which were shipped through the port of Smyrna.

Soumak A much more sturdy form of flatweave with a thick undersurface where the weft threads are left loose – a technique which makes them the only kelims or flat weaves at all suitable for floor coverings.

Stem wave Boteh design linked by a waving line.

Trappings Decorative bands, camel harness, etc.

Turkoman A group of desert nomads whose territory extends from the Caspian Sea across the deserts of Central Asia. These tribes are not Turkish. The name derives from the Turkic language.

Turkic Not to be confused with Turkish or Turkey – generic term for nomad tribes speaking the Turkic language.

Turkish knot see **Ghiordes knot.**

Vat-dyed Wool or yarn dyed in huge batches without variation of colour.

Verneh Large curtainlike tent hangings, also known as 'shadda'.

Warp The lengthwise threads of groundweave which are attached to the loom at the top and bottom.

Warp threads The ends of the carpet, often fringed plaited or knotted.

Washed Afghan see **Golden Afghan.**

Washed gold Chemically washed Golden Afghans as distinct from 'made golds'.

Weft The threads woven crosswise between each row of knots which are on the warp threads.

Wineglass pattern Alternating wineglass shape inverted and upright, often used in a border.

Further Reading

Ian Bennett, *The Country Life Book of Rugs & Carpets of the World*, London, 1979

Cecil Edwards, *The Persian Carpet*, London, 1983

Nicolas Fokker, *Persian Carpets for Today*, London, 1976

Jack Franses, *European & Oriental Rugs*, London, 1973

Janice Summers Herbert, *Affordable Oriental Rugs*, London, 1980

Reinhard G. Hubel, *The Book of Carpets*, London, 1971

Georges Izmidlian, *Oriental Rugs & Carpets Today*, Newton Abbot, 1983

Yanni Petsopoulos, *Kilims*, London, 1979

English Silver

Up to £3,000 for single pieces

Pear-shaped cream jug with scalloped rim and double scroll handle on three splayed feet, 1796.

Introduction

People often think that silver can only be for the rich. This is not true. Admittedly, it is not for the poor, but everyone in between can collect worthwhile silver as long as it is done with patience.

Georgian coffee pots at several thousand pounds are, on the whole, out of the question. Sets of cutlery, however, can be bought whole for under a thousand pounds or pieced together over the years without ever spending as much as a hundred pounds at any one time. There are in addition thousands of small single pieces available, some of them at quite modest prices. Silver to use is still accessible, and it is still possible to form a collection which is of interest and value.

Silver wisely bought has proved a spectacularly successful investment over the last decade; it would be most unwise to imagine that this success will be repeated. On the other hand, silver is likely to remain precious for the foreseeable future, so sensible buying for the pleasure of using and owning it now is unlikely to be disappointing as an investment in the long run.

Sterling Silver

English silver or 'sterling silver' is an alloy of pure silver and a small amount of copper without which it would be too soft and too malleable to work. Precious metals are weighed in Troy weight which differs from standard avoirdupois and is measured in ounces and pennyweights or 'dwts'. A troy ounce (20 dwts) is 0.9115 of an avoirdupois ounce.

The standard proportion of pure silver to alloy which constitutes sterling silver is 11oz 2dwts pure metal to 18dwts alloy. Scottish silver up to 1836 contained minutely more alloy.

Silver can be adulterated with an almost equivalent weight of base metal before the alloy can be visibly detected – hence the practice of hallmarking and assaying, which was first enforced by an Act of Edward I in 1300 when the King's Mark or leopard's head was first stamped on silver which had been assayed. The leopard's head later became the hallmark of the London Assay Office, and the lion passant or walking lion was universally adopted in England as the assay mark for all sterling silver. It is now illegal to describe as silver any piece not properly marked.

Apart from a brief period from 1697–1720 when a higher 'Britannia' silver standard was in force, full sterling hallmarks since 1543 have consisted of the sterling silver lion passant, a single letter of the alphabet to denote the year, the mark of the assay office, between 1784 and 1890 the head of the monarch to whom duty was paid, and the initials or symbol of the silversmith who made the piece. Silver made during the period of the Britannia standard contains a higher proportion of pure metal and is therefore more costly. The Britannia standard is still used occasionally, with its own marks. In 1790 certain articles of less than 5dwt of silver were exempted from payment of duty and consequently may only bear the lion passant mark, sometimes even without the maker's mark.

In 1890 the duty on silver was no longer

A sterling hallmark: from left – the maker's mark; the sterling lion passant; the George III London leopard; the date letter (1808) and the monarch's head.

payable and the monarch's head was dropped from the hallmark of all but special commemorative pieces such as coronation souvenirs.

Provincial assay offices used their own marks in place of the London Assay Office mark of the leopard's head. For quick reference there is a small booklet which can be bought from most silversmiths; larger books on the detailed hallmarking of silver are listed in the bibliography at the end of this section. The provincial, Scottish and Irish assay office marks most commonly found are:

Birmingham: an anchor
Chester: a shield with three half-lions and wheatsheaves until 1779; after that date three wheatsheaves and a sword
Dublin: a harp
Edinburgh: a triple-towered castle
Exeter: three towers
Glasgow: a tree and a salmon
Newcastle-upon-Tyne: three towers, two above and one below
Norwich: a castle above a lion, a crowned Tudor rose, both rare
Sheffield: a crown, sometimes combined with the date-letter
York: a cross incorporating five lions.

The date-letters for provincial assay offices did not run concurrently with those of the London Assay Office.

Cutlery was made in large quantities in the provinces, particularly Birmingham and Sheffield, the centres of steel and blade-making. Even if it was made with silver handles, in the 18th century it was often unmarked, having been made by a cutler rather than a silversmith.

Plate

The word 'plate' can be very misleading to the beginner. Plate is an old term used to denote objects made in silver and gold, and the trade continues to use the word in this sense, meaning articles made in sterling silver. There are, however, at least three processes also described as 'plate', 'plating' or 'plated'.

Sheffield Plate

The first of these is 'Sheffield Plate', also known as 'Old Plate' or 'Old Sheffield'. Sheffield Plate was first made in the early 1740s and consists of a thin layer of silver which has been fused to a sheet of copper by heating the two metals and rolling them out to the required thickness. At first the metal was plated with silver on one side only and then silvered or tinned in the case of hollow ware: molten silver or tin was swirled around inside the vessel in order to protect the contents from coming into contact with the copper, which can be poisonous. By the 1770s Sheffield Plate was coated with silver on both sides for making a wide variety of objects. In this form it is often referred to as 'double plated', and the seams where the two coats meet are a good test of genuineness.

The Britannia mark

Sheffield Plate is a little cheaper than sterling silver, is much collected and has proved to be an excellent investment. It is still looked down on by some dealers and collectors, but that does not alter the fact that Sheffield Plate can be very desirable from all points of view. Incidentally, proper Sheffield Plate is not marked 'Sheffield Plated': that was a dodge resorted to by later electroplaters.

EPNS

The second use of 'plate' is to denote electroplated silver, a technique first used in 1840 and a timely invention for an age which gloried in ostentation and display. An alloy or base metal was thinly coated with a layer of silver by electrochemical action. Between 1840 and 1860 pieces were made using both processes: fused silver-plated copper for the main body of larger pieces, and detail and decoration in electroplated cast metal. Such silver is sometimes referred to as 'Transitional Plate'. Many alloys and metals were subjected to electroplating, the best-known being EPNS or Electro-Plated Nickel Silver, sometimes known as 'German Silver'.

Neither Old Sheffield Plate nor electroplated silver was subject to the same rigorous laws as sterling silver and there are many, many unmarked pieces. Some control was achieved between 1784 and 1836, when

An EPNS mark

an Act required makers of articles resembling silver within a hundred miles of Sheffield, 'who desired to place a mark thereon', to register that mark at the Sheffield Assay Office, but this did not by any means cover all the makers or all the articles made between those two dates.

British Plate

Between 1836 and 1840 another version of Sheffield Plate, replacing the copper core with nickel alloy, was patented under the name of 'British Plate'. It often bore marks which at first sight seem to be silver hallmarks but which, on closer inspection, turn out to have a dog, for instance, instead of the genuine lion passant.

British Plate was soon replaced by electroplated nickel silver, cheap and easy to manufacture in enormous quantities, particularly for the growing hotel, restaurant and catering trade of the second half of the 19th century. An entire range of tea services, coffee services, tableware and flatware was actually called 'Queen Anne' by its Victorian manufacturers, who copied 18th-century silver lines openly and innocently at the time.

EPBM: Electroplated Britannia Metal, a form of silver plating despite the lavishness of its mark.

This electroplated 'Queen Anne' silver can be very misleading.

The fourth and perhaps most misleading development in 'plate' occurred after the end of World War II, when the price of nickel rose to such an extent that it was no longer economical to use for electroplating. Manufacturers of plated silver went back to using copper as the base metal now that it was cheaper than nickel. Electroplated copper can be worked in exactly the same way as Old Sheffield, unlike nickel which can only be cast. EPNS was used almost exclusively for tableware and flatware. A little knowledge is a dangerous thing: too many people assume, when they see the copper base showing where the silver deposit has begun to wear off, that they are looking at a genuine piece of 'Old Sheffield' and pay a high price for it. Disillusionment can be painful and expensive.

Although some genuine 18th-century Sheffield Plate is less expensive than heavily decorated 19th-century silver, the only advice must be to steer clear of the entire field until you have made a proper study of it and sought the advice of one of the very few specialists and experts in Old Sheffield.

Silver Gilt

Silver gilt is what it says: a silver piece coated in gold. Because it contains more silver (much more silver) than gold it counts (and is hallmarked) as the lesser of the two metals and is described here whenever it occurs frequently in a given period. An attractive variant on gilding silver all over was partial gilding, known as 'parcel gilt'.

Appreciation

The price of silver has risen by 600% in the last ten years, with one great leap in the late 1970s which was exceptional (and when, incidentally, quantities of heavy Victorian silver were melted down and sold at a profit by dealers as bullion). On average, the increase has been from 40–60% per annum. This does not, sadly, mean that your investment will show an immediate profit on this scale. The minimum profit margin of most dealers is in the region of 30% and is often higher. When you buy you pay the value of the piece plus the dealer's profit margin. When you sell, you sell at the dealer's buying-in price only. It will take several years for this gap to be wiped out before you even sell at the price you buy at, unless of course you have been very lucky – or clever.

Caution before buying silver

No one wants to make a bad buy but it is not difficult to make a mistake when buying silver. Hallmarks can be faked, or even cut out of one piece and transferred to another. Some fakes are very well done indeed, but many can be spotted by someone with sufficient knowledge. That is why it is best, until you have acquired a really sound working knowledge of silver, to go to a recognized silver dealer.

All this is not to say that you should never buy from other sources: the point is always to buy with knowledge, and if you haven't got it you want to be sure that the person you are buying from has. If you know what you are doing you can buy considerably more cheaply at auction. If you know what you are doing you can buy well or even get a bargain in ordinary mixed antique shops or from market stalls: the relative ignorance of more general dealers can work in your favour, and do not forget that the specialist silver dealers are buying some of their stock from the markets and the general shops.

Care and Restoration

Care

Silver is easy to care for as long as you do not mind polishing. Polish*ing*, not polish; elbow grease, not a patent product. Old, well cared for silver has a soft bloom that makes it both more attractive and more valuable. The only way to achieve a good patina is by polishing and use. There are no short cuts.

The way to care for silver is to wash it in hot, soapy water, dry it thoroughly on a soft cloth and then polish it either with a soft cloth or a chamois leather. Whatever you polish with must be absolutely free from grit, as silver scratches very easily. One important point about polishing: go easy on hallmarks, because they should remain as crisp as possible. It is enough to keep them clean.

All silver will tarnish if exposed to the air, and though washing and polishing is the kindest treatment, cleaning agents do need to be used from time to time to remove tarnish. Many of the silver cleaners on the market are abrasive and therefore harmful; they will succeed in bringing up brilliance but they will damage the patina. The cleaning agents favoured by the trade because they are effective and harmless are Goddard's Silver Dip for major work and Goddard's Long Term Silver Polish for occasional removal of tarnish. Don't use cleaning agents on plated articles. The old folk remedy for removing tarnish, incidentally, is to immerse the piece in skimmed milk, leave it for some minutes, remove, leave to dry and then polish with a cloth or leather.

Sterling silver that has been neglected for a very long time can occasionally become coated with verdigris. This is the natural result of the small amount of copper mixed with the silver oxidizing and can be cured quite readily by a silversmith.

Silver that is to be put away for a long time should be stored perfectly dry. The silver itself should be bone dry and it should be wrapped in bone dry cotton wool or fresh, acid-free tissue paper and then put in a sealed polythene bag. Never use newspaper, which attracts damp.

Always empty silver salt cellars and clean salt spoons after use. Salt corrodes silver.

Restoration

Whereas the care of silver is a relatively simple matter, the restoration of damage is not.

Many pieces you are likely to come across will have been repaired at some time. Feet break off, thin areas crack, arms or initials may be removed, tea and coffee pots are liable to part company with their handles. All these things should be looked for when examining a piece before buying. Repairs do lower the value if clumsily carried out (a visible line of solder round a cartouche, for example); they reduce its attractiveness too. On the other hand it would be silly to suggest that quality items should be melted down rather than repaired.

Some parts of pieces can be soldered back on without anything showing on the outside. Hollow pieces (teapots, for example) can often be repaired very effectively from the inside – a point you should always check before buying hollow ware. In this regard, be wary of pots that are so badly stained inside that you cannot see whether they have already been repaired. It is of course a straightforward matter to glue handles back on to cutlery and flatware.

Until, then, you have sufficient knowledge of your own, be guided by an expert dealer on what is worth repairing and do not attempt to do it yourself. By the same token, do not pay top prices for repaired pieces.

Periods and Styles

The periods into which the history and design of silver is divided are wider than those of furniture. Changes were not entirely based on the whim of fashion, and though silver shapes altered in detail from period to period, revolutionary changes in design occurred only when there was a major upheaval in the world of architecture, fashion, lifestyle or custom.

A particular feature of silver is that it has often been engraved with armorial bearings. The decoration surrounding the bearings varies from period to period and from style to style. The ensemble of bearings and surrounding decoration is known as a cartouche, and since it is such a prominent feature, is noted separately in the descriptions of period and style that follow.

The lists of Principal Products for each period are designed to help you see if an item is likely to be genuine. The lists cannot pretend to be all-inclusive, but you will find, on the whole, that if you are looking at an item whose kind is not listed in the appropriate period you are considering a piece that is unusual or rare (and therefore expensive) or a 'misunderstanding'.

Period: Up to 1700 and William and Mary

Influences: Dutch silver of the 17th century, which was ornate and fanciful; some oriental influence as well.
Decoration: Sheet silver, embossed and chased. Flowers – tulips in particular – and acanthus. Engraved Chinese motifs from 1680. Partial gilding of decoration and ornament.
Cartouches: Crossed plumes with rather coarse engraving – feathery plumes from 1680.
Principal products: Drinking beakers; apple corers; patch boxes; serving spoons; basting spoons; eating spoons; straight-sided spice and sugar casters; chocolate and coffee pots with ebony or fruitwood handles set opposite straight spouts; goblets; snuffers; two-pronged forks; box-shaped inkstandishes; pocket nutmeg graters; hammered, hand-embossed and chased candlesticks, usually 6-7ins high; ladles; monteiths; small tankards; one- and two-handled porringers, salts and footed trencher salts, meat skewers, apostle spoons; rat-tailed spoons; straight-sided lidded tankards; two-handled cups with covers.

Period: 1700–40 – Queen Anne, Early Georgian

Influences: Plain Dutch shapes and a simplified French style giving what was later called the 'Queen Anne' style. Later in the period silver became more ornate under the influence of rococo, but the plain shapes were continued as well. Famous silversmiths: Jean Berain, André-Charles Boulle, Paul de Lamerie, David Willaume.
Decoration: Elaborate ornament in the French manner, embossed and chased with cast-silver orament. Punched, fluted, with applied cast strapwork of shells, leaves, female heads, masks.
Cartouches: Baroque, architectural, scallop shells or masks with scrolled surrounds, symmetrical flowing shapes often incorporating animals unrelated to the coat of arms depicted on the shield proper.
Principal products: Lidded claret and other wine jugs, pear-shaped with silver scroll handles denoting their use for cold liquids; pocket apple corers; bread and cake baskets in pierced work; bells; snuff boxes; tobacco boxes; marrow scoops; spoons; pear-shaped low-footed sugar and spice casters; lidded chocolate and coffee pots with ivory, ebony or fruitwood handles at right angles to the body and curved spouts, sometimes with spout lids; creamers with moulded feet, rimmed and turned; pierced épergnes; three-pronged forks; inkstandishes; cast candlesticks; douters; small-sized round-bellied teapots; kettles on stands; silver-handled steel knives; straight-sided tankards; mustard pots; pap boats; punch bowls; punch ladles with ebonized whalebone handles; small-footed salts, pedestal-footed trays or salvers; double-lipped two-handled sauceboats; oval rim-footed sauceboats; matching sets of table, dessert and tea spoons; basting spoons and mustard spoons; covered sugar bowls; scroll-handled tankards; tea caddies; small pear-shaped teapots, two-handled soup tureens, porringers; wine-tasters (often called bleeding bowls).

Period: 1740–60 – Georgian

Influences: French rococo, asymmetric forms derived from rocks *(rocaille),* seashells, ripples, waves. Famous silversmiths: Juste-Aurèle Meissonier, Paul de Lamerie, Nicholas Sprimont, Paul Crespin.
Decoration: Piecrust rims to trays and salvers coinciding with Chippendale period. Shell-bases, swirl-bases, oval feet and plinths; beading, gadrooning. Embossed chinoiserie decoration, pierced and punched work.
Cartouches: Asymmetric, rococo swirling shapes.
Principal products: Pierced swing-handled cake baskets, épergnes, snuff boxes, tobacco boxes; straight-spouted coffee and chocolate pots; creamers; sauceboats on cast scrolled legs; cruet sets on frames; four-pronged forks; candlesticks with removable drip pans; three-footed salts; three- and four-footed trays and salvers; three-footed boat-shaped sauceboats; sugar bowls; sugar tongs; baluster-shaped tankards; spherical 'bullet' teapots. Old Sheffield Plate makes its entrance, initially for smaller items, but gradually extending through the range.

Georgian crested silver sauce boat with hoof feet and C-scroll handle; one of a pair.

Period: 1760–1800 – Late Georgian

Influences: Robert Adam and symmetrical, neo-classical motifs. Josiah Wedgwood's classical designs. Famous silversmiths: Hester Bateman, Bateman family, Matthew Boulton and John Fothergill.
Decoration: Severe, less flowing; leafed, palmate feet to sauceboats and creamers; festoons, ribbons, swags, anthemion, acanthus, symmetrical elegant elongated lines, teapots, jugs, sugar bowls and hollow ware raised on pedestal foot; embossing, gadrooning, reeding, fluting, 'bright cut' engraving, particularly from Birmingham; silver-gilt for important pieces.
Cartouches: Neo-classical with masks, swags, medallions, rams' heads, urns, acanthus, reed and ribbon until 1785; bright-cut, deeply engraved, simplified classical from 1785 to 1805.
Principal products: Asparagus tongs; cheese scoops; vinaigrettes; caddy spoons; cruet sets; pear-shaped and baluster coffee and chocolate pots with pedestal bases; helmet-shaped creamers; cow-creamers; jugs; branched standing candelabra; taller loaded candlesticks up to 12ins high; dish crosses; covered serving dishes; goblets; egg cups; fish slices; ice pails; hot water jugs; four-footed oval salts; oval trays, often with pierced galleries and handholds; covered sauce tureens; square-based or plinth sauceboats, creamers and jugs; barrel-shaped tankards; straight-sided, straight-spouted, oval, drum-shaped teapots; toast racks; tableware; flatware; plates and serving dishes; wine labels.

Period: 1800–20 – Regency

Influences: Classical to about 1810, then more massive styles deriving from Egyptian, baroque, rococo and French Empire patterns. Famous silversmiths: Bateman and Chawner families, Paul Storr, Benjamin Smith, Robert Garrard.
Decoration: Minimal, restrained decoration for classical revival: pure elegance of line with fine bands of delicate chasing and engraving, precise cast relief work. Sculptured forms for more elaborate work, chinoiserie and romanticism. The most prolific period for English silver, with new wealth and increased ability of rising middle classes to buy and display silver resulting in considerable quantities of poor workmanship, thin gauge and bad construction as well as the very best. Birmingham excelled in pierced, elaborate work. Victory for England at the end of the long Napoleonic wars in 1815 brought much commemorative work into fashion. Beginning of factory production, with simplified lines of average pieces. Excellence of handmade silversmithing rose to new and elaborate heights as a result of this competition. Vine leaves, scrolling, gadrooning and beading all prominent.
Cartouches: Sometimes absent altogether, with plain shield only engraved or bright cut. Otherwise flowery, leafy scrollwork, similar to but more delicately executed than that of the early 17th century.
Principal products: Massive table silver, matching entrée dishes, soup tureens, meat dishes; desk and dressing-table sets; toilet articles; tea trays; goblets; wine coolers; biscuit boxes; vinaigrettes; egg cruets; tea-kettles on stands; melon-shaped teapots; matching teasets comprising teapot, sugar bowl, milk jug; canteens of heavy table silver; wine labels; cast paw feet to sauceboats, salts; cruets; fine fluted candlesticks; standing branched candelabra with heavily decorated bases; table centre-pieces.

Period: 1830–50 – Late Regency, William IV and Early Victorian

Influences: Rococo revival, chinoiserie revival of Chippendale style, romantic, baroque and Gothic Revival.
Decoration: The exaggeration of all that was fine in the previous period into overblown, ostentatious designs in keeping with the taste of the time; much fine simple silver of previous periods given florid embossed ('late-embossed') decoration in pseudo-rococo

designs, or fluted and reeded to emulate earlier Regency style; some good simple copies of Georgian and Dutch shapes; Adam designs in semi-mass-produced wares. Much silver of this period is engraved with flamboyant quasi-heraldic motifs. Old silver engraved, with consequent decrease in value. Monogramming and initialling very fashionable. Gothic Revival motifs.

Cartouches: Florid, romantic, gothic with curving central shield, flamboyant crests and supporters.

Principal products: Return of straight-sided drum-shaped and oval teapots; plain shapes for entrée dishes, serving dishes and for less expensive pieces to suit pockets of expanding market of buyers of silverware; heavy handles to cutlery, massive sets with much larger spoons, forks and knives than previous periods; soup spoons added to canteens of matching silver; wine coolers, ice buckets.

Period: 1850–1900 – Victorian, Late Victorian

Influences: French Empire, German Gothic, neo-classical, pseudo-Chippendale chinoiserie and rococo, Pre-Raphaelite romantic, Japan, William Morris and the Arts and Crafts movement.

Decoration: Heavy embossing, florid shapes, bulbous lines, many elaborate silver mounts to claret jugs, use of silver mounts for glass bowls, pierced silver much in evidence with new stamping techniques; much silver of this period considerably lighter in spite of heavy appearance, due to thinner metal with advent of machine-made spun silver. Proliferation of ornate, stamped, embossed lids to desk and toilet articles, silver mounts to most insignificant objects such as shoe-horns, button hooks. Card cases for engagement and visiting cards exceptionally well designed in a

Victorian silver-plated teapot of a 'half-reeded' design.

period not noted for its taste, even though die-stamped and not hand-embossed, and with shallow, acid-etched engraving; best made by Nathaniel Mills of Birmingham. Interesting square designs with clean lines and simple shapes (Japanese influence), especially for tea ware; domed lids identical with potteries' shapes for coffee pots, teapots, hot-water jugs.

Cartouches: Widespread engraving of armorial bearings on silver of this period may actually reduce value, even if contemporary. Only interesting, well-known armorials of famous people add to value.

Principal products: Anything and everything.

Period: 1900–20 Edwardian

Influences: The great age of machine copies. Only the English Arts and Crafts movement, similar to but not truly Art Nouveau, has any real design interest in this period, but many lower and middle range Art Nouveau pieces were produced in England, though the majority come from the Continent.

Principal products and Decoration: Shallow, acid-etched engraving, lightweight pieces, much electroplated cutlery, tableware, particularly for now well-established catering trade; coffee and teasets in plain, dull versions of early fine shapes. Good cutlery, tableware, flatware. Travelling cases, fitted toilet cases, writing table accessories, presentation sets of flatware in satin-lined boxes, christening spoons, fish slices, fish knives and forks, all glitter and little value at the time. In new designs, silver beakers, goblets, vases, baskets, bowls, rose bowls with swirling 'natural' designs similar to Art Nouveau shapes. Many copies of column candlesticks, varying sizes and quality. Curious mixture of lavish ostentation and rich simplicity.

Price Guide

The price of old silver is only governed by the world market price of bullion to a limited extent: during the great silver boom of recent years the price of all silver rose tremendously, but unless there is another similar surge, lesser fluctuations do not really affect the prices paid for antique or second-hand silver. Obviously though, the greater the weight of a piece the higher the price. Eighteenth-century teaspoons, for example, were often extremely thin and lightweight and consequently, unles made by a famous maker (Hester Bateman, for example) will be proportionately cheaper than heavy Georgian or early Victorian teaspoons, simply because of the weight of the silver.

Plain versus decorated

Articles in pure, simple plain silver are more expensive than those which are decorated with embossing or engraving for the simple reason that any blemish stands out. Decoration hides a multitude of sins. At the same time, fashion has pushed up the price of more ornate, elaborate ware against plain simple shapes, so it could be said that these two factors almost cancel each other out, except that plain silver is a better and safer investment than embossed. Sins of omission are meant to be covered by the Trades Descriptions Act, but there are dealers who neglect to add the vital information that a piece has been 'late-embossed' and often repaired in the process. Any large piece offered under £1,000 should be treated with suspicion. Remember too that much silver of the Regency period, though of good shape, was of poor quality and light gauge: prices are often unwarrantably high for actual value.

Note: Many people buying silver for weddings, christenings or anniversaries think it delightful to add a personal touch and have pieces engraved with initials or names.

DON'T. Your thoughtfulness will reduce the value of the item by 20% or more if it has any age at all. Better to hunt for old pieces engraved at the same period with appropriate initials.

Canteens of Cutlery and Flatware (£2,250–9,000)

For the purposes of this *Guide*, canteens are the most expensive items, but then to buy new would cost probably not less than £6,500 for a canteen with 12 place settings of an average of six pieces per place setting: two forks, two spoons, two knives per setting, plus two or more serving spoons.

Watch for wear on tines (prongs) of forks and on spoon bowls, for denting and for filing down of worn forks to an even length of prong. Old canteens of silver can be found in almost mint condition, having been put in the bank or only used on special occasions. Their excellent condition should encourage you to resist the blandishments of dealers offering less than top quality. For long-term antique investment value all pieces should bear the same hallmark – for bargain buys canteens which have had odd pieces replaced over the years cost less but will appreciate less.

Victorian canteens often have large place-settings, including teaspoons and coffee spoons as well as fish knives and forks and soup spoons. Edwardian canteens were most elaborate, often with seven or eight pieces for each place setting, plus four or more servers: they are sometimes still to be found in their original cabinets lined with green baize. Very often old knives have been replaced with new dishwasherproof ones with stainless steel blades, silver handles and modern cement-compound fillings. Old table knives had handles in ivory, green-stained bone or silver, with blade tails set in pitch or resin, steel or silver collars, and steel blades worn down with constant sharpening. Unless otherwise stated, prices are for matched canteens.

12 place settings:
Mid 19th-century King's pattern or Sandringham, £4,500–7,500. Irish bright cut, £4,500–7,500. Beaded £6,000–9,000. Fiddle, £3,500–5,000.

Late 19th-century, just under 100 years old, £3,500–5,000.

Mixed hallmark canteens over 100 years old as low as £2,250, depending on the number of replacements and condition; they need searching out.

12 place settings hovering around 100 years old can be found from dealers specializing in flatware for around £3,500 and upwards.

Edwardian Old English 60-piece service, some replacements, just under £3,000.

1930s all matched, heavy reeded pattern, £2,500; beaded or feathered always more.

Cutlery patterns

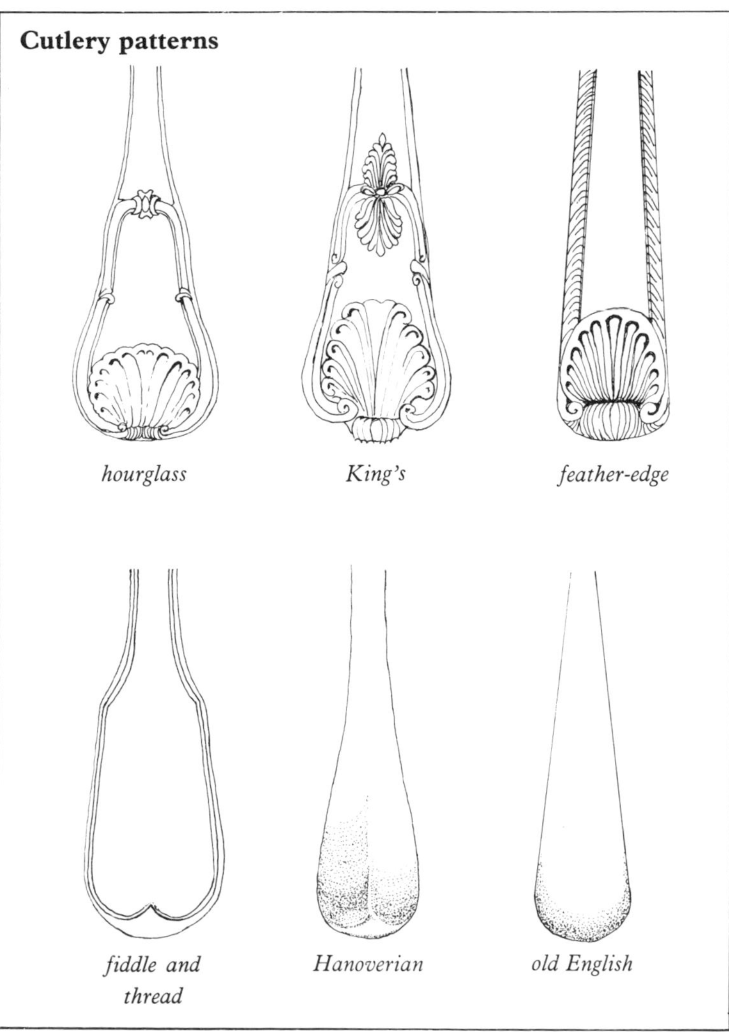

If such a large outlay is out of the question, sets of six settings are well worth considering, particularly if bought from a specialist dealer who can often make them up to sets of a dozen at a later date, providing you choose a date and pattern they advise. A 34-piece sterling silver canteen with six place settings all the same mark dated 1910 can be found for £1,200–1,500.

Additional items of tableware, such as large serving spoons and ladles, are almost half the price of brand new: soup ladles, sauce ladles, £100–200, whereas new ones nudge £250.

Separate sets of teaspoons, coffee spoons, often in presentation boxes (particularly Edwardian) are good value–

Six matching:

London mark, 1760, £150–200.

1790, bright cut, thin gauge, around £80–120.

1800, heavier gauge, bright cut, £150–200.

1860, London mark, undecorated, £100–150.

1920–30, dozen boxed silver coffee spoons from £100.

1930, dozen boxed silver teaspoons, Sheffield mark, £120.

Fish Servers (£150–500)

Considered out of date and ostentatious to use, but very reasonable to buy and great fun to own.

Georgian, slice only, pierced, with silver handle, £150–300.

Victorian, ivory or bone handles, more ornate the better, £200–500 per pair, often still in presentation satin-lined boxes. Edwardian period, a little lower priced.

Water Jugs (£1,500–2,500)

1775, pear-shaped, lidded, silver handle, gadrooned rim and pedestal base, £1,500–2,500.

About 1785, more elongated shape, beaded pedestal and borders, £1,500–2,500.

Low demand for silver jugs with handles not insulated against heat with ivory or ebony collars. Water jugs more commonly made in china from the late 19th century onwards.

Coffee Pots (£450–3,000)

Seventeenth and 18th-century coffee pots of traditional shape are well outside the price range.

Teapot-shaped coffee pots, originally made in sets with tea services, not considered very collectable until recently, unless by named maker, now just under £1,500 *c.* 1790–1815. Victorian copies £1,000–1,250.

True coffee pot shape, ebonized handle, *c.* 1855, undecorated, just under £1,500.

Same date, semi-melon, some decoration, around £1,200.

1810–30, Adam-style, formal engraving, acorn finial, simple shape, £1,800 upwards.

Later, half-fluted, less attractive shapes, just under £1,500.

1830–50, heavier, more ornate, silver handles with ivory or bone insulating collars, originally parts of sets, £800–1,200. Pre-1830, £1,000 upwards. Same date embossed, £800–1,200. Engraved, appreciating recently, £800–1,200.

1870–90, wide variety of quality, weight, shape; better ones appreciating recently as 100-year band extends to this period; from £800.

Recent 'second-hand' coffee pots in good copies of mid-18th-century shapes are at once good value and a snare. Made in quantities in London, Birmingham and Sheffield between 1900 and the 1930s, at first glance they look like the real thing. Prices of between £450 and £750 should indicate what they really are.

Sets of coffee and hot water or milk jugs were rarely made in silver until very recently. Breakfast coffee sets were stoneware or bone china; after-dinner coffee pots had matching cream jugs and silver bowls for sugar, but only from the Edwardian period. Pre-1900

OPPOSITE *Pieces from a mixed fiddle and thread service. The full set, most of which is 1859, includes six each of tablespoons, dessert spoons, table forks and a pair of sauce ladles.*

coffee pots matched four- or five-piece tea and coffee sets. Where sets are broken, usually the milk jug and sugar bowl are put together with teapots as three-piece sets, not with coffee pots.

Coffee Biggins (£,1,000–1,800)

Biggins are cylindrical coffee pots on stands with spirit lamps (now frequently missing). Cover usually not hinged (check it has same hallmark). Bone, ebonized fruitwood or ivory handle, from £1,300–£1,800 with stand. Even without stand, sturdy, well-proportioned, reasonably priced at around £1,000–1,500.

Chocolate Pots

Original chocolate pots, being 17th- or 18th-century, are way outside the price range. Early designs have not been extensively copied or revived, meaning that one rarely comes across them.

Teapots (£500–1,800)

The earliest teapots falling within the price range are: *c.* 1765–80, drum-shaped, straight-sided, straight low-set spouts, unhinged lids (check for same hallmark), flat tops, plain ebonized finial, elegantly engraved, often with swags or medallions, from £1,200–1,800.

1780–90, oval, straight-sided, straight-spouted, flat-topped, with engraved decoration, £800–1,200.

1790–1800, bright cut. tapered spout, slightly more curvaceous, hinged lids (check hallmarks all the same), around £1,000–1,750.

1800–10, embossed, less expensive, hinged, slightly domed lids, starting at around £600.

1804, embossed, boat-shaped, domed or curved hinged lids, curving spouts, also reeded, half-reeded, from around £500–700.

More rectangular, sometimes with curved, fluted corners, often originally with stands, around same price. More with original stands, starting at £1,000.

About 1810, more boat-shaped, curving spout, ball feet, around £600 and upwards, depending on weight.

About 1815, undecorated, squatter, curved spout, ball feet, much copied by Victorians, not much sought after at present, around £450 starting price. Same period, heavily decorated, if thick gauge with good modelling, up to £900.

1820–35, melon-shaped teapot, recent high appreciation mostly due to fashion trends, now starting at around £700–900 in good condition.

1830–50, Victorian version, thinner metal, cast scrolled feet, high-set spout, silver handle, around £500–700.

1835–60, more ornate half-melon with heavily embossed decoration, now much sought after for export; used to be around £250 not so long ago, now up to £750.

1850, rich rococo or Japanese decoration, heavy pieces from £700–900.

1870, good Victorian copies of plain Dutch shape, plain, round-bellied with curved spout, from £600–800.

1860, heavy-quality, round-bellied, with acorn or decorative finial, excellent Victorian copies of earlier shapes, from £500.

Tea Sets (£500–4,000)

About 1865, good quality Regency, Adam, classical shapes, originally four- and five-piece sets, now teapot, milk jug and sugar bowls from around £1,200–1,800.

1870–90, 'bachelor's' small-capacity three-piece sets, baluster and Japanese-influence shapes, suitable for early morning tea, £700–1,000.

Same period, more ornate, gothic, cast decoration often original and interesting design £2,000–4,000.

1880-1900, often wildly ornate embossing, at first sight rich and rare, but more likely to be spun low gauge silver, stretched paper-thin with embossing, which will wear and crack quickly. Prices should not be more than

Teapot shapes

£800. Good copies of Georgian sets, same date, from £900.

Just under 100 years old, Edwardian copies of traditional patterns made as three-piece tea sets: bullet-shaped, half-reeded, boat-shaped, but the silver looks more metallic and has less sheen than earlier models, around £500–750.

Candlesticks (£60–2,500)

From the end of the 18th century, candlesticks were made in large quantities in Birmingham and Sheffield as well as in London, with techniques that required very little hand-finishing. Thin sheet silver was die-stamped, then soldered together and filled with pitch or resin, often with an iron bar up the centre to add strength. This method continued to be used right through the 19th century, but as demand for silver increased, makers became less fastidious and continued to use die-stamps which were blurred and blunted, resulting in poor modelling and detail. These candlesticks are known as 'loaded' or 'filled' and are the most common. Seventeenth- and 18th-century candlesticks are now very expensive.

1820–30, late Georgian styles, taller than any other period, usually 11–12ins, Adam shapes or versions of Greek columns, less ornate designs, just over £2,500 a pair, with sets of four more than double the price.

First in reasonable range are Victorian copies, made in Sheffield or Birmingham, copies of Corinthian column type, 5–6ins, around £700 for pairs.

About 1830, Sheffield Plate, singles to £60.

About 1895, variety of classical shapes: square-based Georgian, oval-based Adam, round-based with gadrooning or beading, £750–1,250.

Some good copies of 18th-century shapes made around 1890–1910, just under 100 years old, around £600–800 a pair and better long-term investment than copies from previous two decades. Watch always for wear at corners, bruising, frilled bottom edges due to wear. Sheet silver is very susceptible to damage which can only be repaired by 'unloading' and is costly. Where very thin gauge silver has been used, it is often stretched by die-stamping to the point of wearing through completely. If it is already very thin it will deteriorate quickly with consequent drop in value. Occasionally odd little chambersticks, Birmingham made, copies of 18th-century rococo styles, turn up at around £450–650.

Edwardian, well-made copies of Adam shapes but slightly taller, around 7–8ins £400–700 depending on condition.

Warning: It is not unknown for a pair to be made up by casting a second candlestick from the first one, marks and all. If the placing of marks and minute imperfections seem suspiciously twinned, this is certainly the case and the pair is not worth investing in unless offered very cheaply for what it is.

Caddy Spoons

These charming little objects have been made since the days of Queen Anne. Their purpose was to take tea from the tea caddy and put it into the teapot, and they were originally shell-shaped in imitation of the shells that

---

OPPOSITE (a) Silver plated double struck King's pattern soup ladle, 19th century.
(b) Silver plated fiddle and shell pattern basting or stuffing spoon.
(c) One of a pair of Georgian bright cut engraved dessert spoons, c. 1783.
(d) Embossed Dutch commemorative spoon with cherub on the stem, late 19th century.
(e) Georgian silver embossed spoon.
(f) Small Georgian mustard spoon.
(g) Silver plated jam spoon with mother-of-pearl handle, 19th century.
(h) French sifter spoon, 19th century.
(i) Dutch parcel gilt spoon (19th century copy of a 17th century style).
(j) Victorian silver christening spoon with engraved initial.
(k) Georgian silver egg spoon with characteristically shaped bowl gilded to prevent tarnishing on contact with egg yolk.
(l) Silver salt spoon, 1908.
(m) Silver caddy spoon, 1834.

a
b
c
d
e
f
g
h
i
j
k
l
m

came as scoops in teachests. Prices start at £40, but there is a very wide variation in price to match the wide variation in styles and decoration that developed. Early examples can be very expensive. Collecting caddy spoons demands detailed knowledge.

Cream or Milk Jugs (£200–500)

Originally part of matching tea and coffee sets, considerable numbers to choose from of all qualities and designs.

Unlidded, 1770s, similar shape to pear-shaped pedestal coffee pots, £300–450.

1775–1806, helmet-shaped cream jugs, often very fine gauge silver, but nevertheless most desirable, now fetching from £300–500 and more in fine, unrepaired condition; handles in particular have often been completely replaced with consequent drop in real value: approach them with care.

1795–1810, more practical, flat-bottomed, often with punched decoration, £280–350.

1815–55, half-reeded, squatter, typical teaware patterns, £200–300.

1855–80, embossed, engraved, often with Chinese, Japanese motifs, £280–350: danger area for 'late-embossed' and thin Victorian spun silver.

Cruet Sets, Salts, Mustard Pots

Given the size of the objects, prices of these items are very high—often little less than very adequate pairs of candlesticks. Commonplace items less than 100 years old can be found from about £100 upwards (in these cases taste and pocket are the best guides) but serious collecting in this area is so specialized that it is desirable to study detailed books before starting.

Tankards

The weight of silver required to make a good tankard of any date puts the large pint-sized tankards at around £750. Lidded tankards and good quality heavy gauge tankards of any age are therefore effectively outside the price range. Prices start at £900; lidded: anywhere from £1,500–3,000.

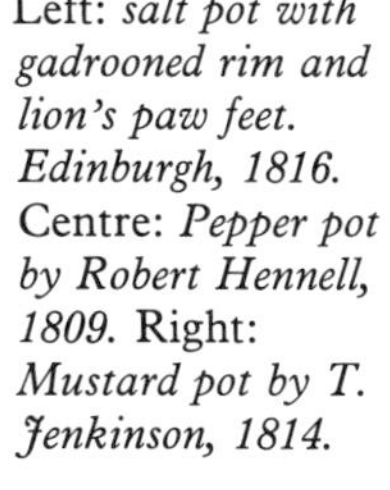
Left: *salt pot with gadrooned rim and lion's paw feet. Edinburgh, 1816.* Centre: *Pepper pot by Robert Hennell, 1809.* Right: *Mustard pot by T. Jenkinson, 1814.*

Christening Mugs (£250–600)

Half-pint and child-sized drinking mugs are a happy hunting ground for people wanting to invest a little money for the future. Single initials, monograms and names tend to lower prices; with a bit of searching the appropriate one can sometimes be found at a very reasonable price.

1790–1800, turned barrel-shaped small tankard, around £280–350. George IV, similar shape, heavier gauge, £300–400.

About 1840, children's mugs embossed with nursery or children's scenes, from £400–600.

About 1870, plainer embossing, small shields, swags, flowers, £200–400.

About 1890, Gothic mugs with animal handles, though often light gauge, can cost more at £300–500 because of today's fashion.

Good bet: plain tankard shapes first made by Garrard *c.* 1860; around £250–350 (but they still make identical ones today).

Goblets (£350–550)

1790–1810, plain, good shapes, round foot, used to be around £500 a pair, now not less than £400 a single. With square, beaded plinth base, classical Georgian shape, singles around the same price.

1850–70, thinner gauge, embossed, around £350–550 each. Some excellent plain shapes with engraved bands, glass shapes at around £300–500. Better, more decorative Victorian Tudor and Romantic more and can reach £600. Compare the price of modern manufacture and the prices will seem extremely reasonable.

Napkin Rings and Miscellanea (£20–200)

Napkin rings are largely a Victorian/Edwardian addition to the table, fun to collect and give. Set of six matching, over 100 years old, from £200. Singles of all sorts of dates and prices: plain band with milled edge, £20; engine-turned, £25; reeded edge, £25.

Good quality heavy silver spoons from £25–50, sugar tongs from £35, wine labels with maker's mark from £50, often very decorative: pierced, vine-leaves, rococo designs.

Silver boxes are no longer pretty little nothings: if considering any of these, brace yourself for a starting price of £200 for an undistinguished, unmarked piece. If serious, study books on the subject before proceeding further. It is amazing what can be made from remnants of larger pieces with early hallmarks.

Silver Terms

Acanthus Elegantly scrolled leaves originally used as decoration in classical architecture, later by 17th- and 18th-century woodcarvers and metalworkers. See illustration page 47.

Acid-etched Adaptation of copperplate engraving techniques where acid bites into unprotected parts of metal to form shallow patterns; used to decorate late 19th-century silver; recognizable by shallowness and lack of crispness of line.

Anthemion Stylized form of honeysuckle flower originally used in Greek decoration. See illustration page 47.

Apostle spoon Spoon with a figure of an apostle as the end of the handle; in sets of 12 or 13 (Christ and the twelve).

Assay Analysis of gold and silver to assure that it has no more than the legally permitted proportion of alloy, before being hallmarked by an assay office.

Baluster Characteristic shape in late 17th and early 18th centuries for candlesticks, glass stems, silver, with slender form swelling out to a pear shape below. See illustration page 47.

Beading Edging of small raised domes like beads.

Beaker Straight-sided, slightly tapering drinking vessel without stem or handle; slimmer, taller than a tumbler.

Blade tail Metal shank of knife blade running down centre of knife handle, secured by pitch or resin.

Bleeding bowl See **Wine taster**

Bright cut Method of engraving silver and

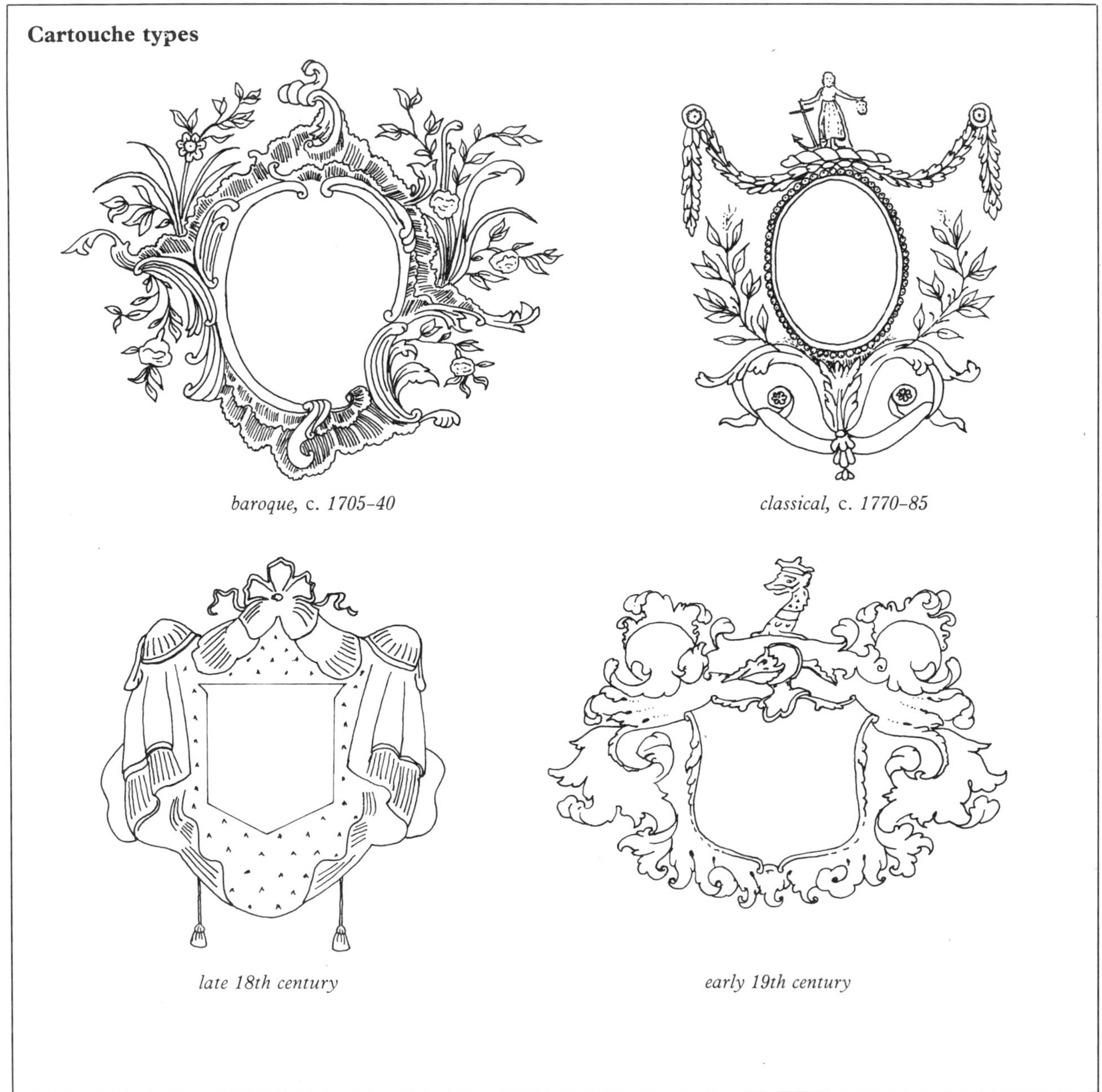

Cartouche types

baroque, c. *1705–40*

classical, c. *1770–85*

late 18th century

early 19th century

brass, with V-shaped or bevelled cut giving extra brilliance.

Britannia standard Higher silver content (95.8%; sterling is 92.5%) required by law from 1697–1720; still in occasional use.

British plate Version of Old Sheffield using nickel instead of copper as core; very short period of manufacture, from 1836.

Bullet Spherical-bodied; a teapot shape.

Caddy spoon Spoon with (usually shell-shaped) bowl and short stubby handle for measuring tea from tea caddy.

Cartouche Scrolled decoration forming part of armorial engraving. See opposite.

Caudle cup Usually two-handled cup with lid and (maybe) saucer, often in presentation sets of two for mother and child for warm drinks; also known as caundle cups, porringers and posset cups.

Chamberstick Low-stemmed candlestick with integral wide dish base, sometimes fitted with conical snuffer.

Chased Sheet metal decorated with punches, chisels, hammers for fine raised designs; often combined with embossing in 18th century to sharpen detail; flat chasing in low relief was popular in the 18th century combined with engraving.

Chocolate pot Distinguished from coffee pot (sometimes) by small hole in lid for the 'moliquet' or whisk. Usually early 18th-century with straight side-handle.

Close plating Sheet, cast metal, usually steel, plated with thin sheets of silver by means of solder; used from around 1805 mostly in association with flatware, table knives and domestic tableware likely to rust, e.g. meat skewers.

Demi-melon See **Melon**

Die-stamping Method of embossing metals and coins mechanically with an engraved metal stamp.

Dish cross X-shaped frame, sometimes with small burner in centre, to hold dishes and plates and keep them warm.

Douter Candle snuffer shaped like a dunce's hat; also scissor-shaped snuffers with coin-shaped ends.

Electroplate Nickel or copper thinly coated with layer of silver by electrochemical action; patented in 1840, largely ousting Sheffield Plate.

Embossed Decoration beaten out from the back of the metal with punches or, by the end of the 19th century, semi-mechanically.

Epergne Elaborate table centrepiece dating from 18th century with central bowl and arms for candles, sweetmeat dishes; a great showpiece for silversmiths.

EPNS Electroplated nickel silver.

Filled see **Loaded**

Finial Knob as terminal decoration for lids of teapots, coffee pots etc.

Flatware Forks and spoons; knives are cutlery.

Fluting Parallel concave grooves; the opposite of reeding.

Gadrooning Similar decoration to beading, consisting of raised domes but on a slant; originally deriving from knuckles of a clenched fist. See illustration page 47.

Gallery Raised border in pierced silver to trays etc.

German silver Also known as Argentan and Argentine: a form of electroplated nickel silver.

Part of a set of Old English flatware of various dates between 1783–1819. All are marked with the same family crest. The set consists of 12 each of tablespoons, table forks, dessert spoons and dessert forks.

Hollow ware Vessels, jugs, pots, etc. as distinct from flat tableware.

Inkstandish Ink stand dish: tray for ink, sealing wax etc.

Late-embossed Prevalent particularly in early 19th century, the practice of embossing plain shapes from the previous century, often of relatively thin gauge, with lavish decoration.

Loaded Sheet silver embossed, stamped with decoration and filled with pitch or resin, particularly for candlesticks and candelabra; also known as 'filled'.

Marrow scoop Long, narrow-bowled implement for scooping marrow from bones.

Melon Shaped like a canteloupe melon; also demi-melon or half-melon, with the segment shapes on the lower half only.

Milled Ground fluted edges as on coins.

Monteith Large silver vessel, usually of heavy oval shape, with scalloped rim for cooling wine glasses; said to have derived its name from the Earl of Monteith's scalloped-edged cloak.

Mount, mounted Bases, rims and handles of silver added to wood, ceramics and glass (claret jugs, coconut cups etc.) to cover raw edges and add decoration; in cast silver from 1780s, stamped, often with alloy fillings, from 1790s, and with elaborate decoration from 1815; on Sheffield Plate to hide the copper core of the sheet metal on exposed cut edges.

Old Sheffield see **Sheffield Plate**

Palmate Design originally based on the shape of the palm of a hand.

Pap boat Small lipped or spouted vessel shaped like an invalid's feeding cup; often elaborately engraved with commemorative designs for an infant.

Parcel-gilt Partially gilded silverware.

Patch box Small shallow box with polished underside to lid serving as a mirror, used for keeping 'beauty spots' worn by fashionable 18th-century ladies to hide spots or skin blemishes.

Pedestal foot Originally of columns, the raised base of a vessel, usually in stepped or classical shapes.

Pierced Decorative patterns cut with punches to the end of the 18th century, stamped from 19th century.

Pitch Thick tarry resin, originally used to caulk ships, used for loading and filling knife-handles.

'Plate' Trade term for English objects made in silver and gold; not to be confused with 'plated' or 'plating' which describe electroplate and silver-plate.

Porringer see **Caudle cup**

Posset cup see **Caudle cup**

Punched Decorative strengthening rows of raised beads formed by using a punch on undersurface.

'Queen Anne' Usually meaning Queen Anne style, not Queen Anne period; of late 19th-century manufacture.

Reeding Parallel lines of convex decorating, as in classical pillars; the opposite of fluting.

Repoussé Relief decoration to sheet metal made with punches and hammers on the reverse side, using a block of pitch as an anvil; often finished by chasing to sharpen detail.

Semi-melon See **Melon**

Sheffield Plate Also known as Old Sheffield, a method of plating copper with thin sheets of silver, invented by Thomas Bolsover of Sheffield about 1742 and used by him for small objects such as snuff boxes and buttons; first made into candlesticks by Hoyland of Sheffield shortly after. The recognizably warmer colouring of Sheffield Plate compared with electroplate is due to a minute alloying of the two surfaces of copper and silver. The highly skilled techniques of Sheffield Plate were gradually superseded by the advent of electroplating in the 1840s, though for a time the bodies of large pieces continued to be Sheffield Plate with the smaller parts electroplated.

Silver gilt An object made in silver and then gilded.

Silver plate Technical term properly meaning articles made of silver; see **Plate**

Spun silver Mechanically shaped hollow ware in thin silver made by pressing a disc of metal against a shaped block revolving on a lathe.

Sterling Silver of the standard British value of purity (92.5%), assayed as such and then hallmarked.

Strapwork Strictly, ribbon-type applied ornament, but the term is used to describe any applied ornament.

Swag Looping curve of flowers, foliage, fruit or drapery used on silver during Neo-classical period, particularly Adam in latter half of 18th century.

Tine Prong of a fork or tooth of a comb.

Trencher salt Small low bowl on three or four feet or low pedestal for holding individual salt, as opposed to the grand, standing table salts.

Turned Silverware made, decorated or finished on a lathe.

Vinaigrette Small double-lidded box to hold sliver of scented sponge, originally soaked in aromatic vinegar; inner lid always pierced, exquisitely decorated; the whole of the interior should be gilded; forerunner of the smelling bottle, popular and fashionable 1770s–1880s, often in shapes of miniature fruit, nuts, books etc.

Wine taster Small dish with (usually) one looped or flat handle, often mistakenly called bleeding bowl.

Further Reading

Frederick Bradbury, *A History of Old Sheffield Plate,* Sheffield, 1912

Frederick Bradbury, *Book of Hallmarks,* Sheffield, published annually

Vanessa Brett, *The Sotheby's Directory of Silver, 1600–1940,* London, 1986

Michael Clayton, *The Collector's Dictionary of the Silver and Gold of Great Britain and North America,* London, 1971

John Culme, *Nineteenth-Century Silver,* London, 1977

John Culme, *The Directory of Gold and Silversmiths, 1838–1914,* Woodbridge, 1987

Arthur Grimwade, *London Goldsmiths 1697–1837, Their Marks and Lives,* London, 1976

T. R. Poole, *Identifying Antique British Silver,* London, 1988

Peter Waldron, *The Price Guide to Antique Silver,* Woodbridge, 1982

Index

This index is designed to help you reach the main subjects of this *Guide*. Many points of detail and many definitions are given in the lists of terms appended to each chapter: Furniture, pages 43–52; Glass, pages 66–72; Pottery & Porcelain, pages 77–86; Rugs, pages 126–130; English Silver, pages 149–154.

A

B

L

M

N

O

P

Q

R

S

T

U

V

W

Y/Z

Photographic Acknowledgements

The publishers gratefully acknowledge permission to reproduce photographs as follows: The National Magazine Co. Ltd and, for the frontispiece, Jean Sewell (Antiques) Ltd; p. 13 Sotheby's Belgravia: p. 29 National Magazine and Whytock Reid, Edinburgh; p. 30 National Magazine; pp. 33-34 National Magazine and Suffolk Fine Arts, Bury St Edmunds; p. 36 Ann Lingard, Rope Walk Antiques, Rye; p. 38 National Magazine; p. 40 Ann Lingard, Rope Walk Antiques, Rye; p. 41 National Magazine and Farmhouse Antiques, Stoke Ferry, Norfolk; p. 46 Ann Lingard, Rope Walk Antiques, Rye; for photographs appearing between pages 55 and 98 National Magazine in conjunction with: for p. 53 Delomosne & Son Ltd, London: p. 58 A. & J. Stuart Mobey, Oxford; p. 60 Maureen Thompson, London; p. 62 Delomosne & Son Ltd, London; p. 63 Lacquer Chest, London; p. 73 Joanna Warrand, London; p. 76 Hemingway Antiques, London; p. 78 Lacquer Chest, London; p. 79 Torstore, Glastonbury; p. 80 Lynn's Antiques, Sheffield; p. 89 Sue Norman, London; p. 90 Delomosne & Son Ltd, London; p. 91 Belinda Coote, Hartley Wintney, Hants; p. 92 Libra Antiques, London; p. 93 Jean Sewell Ltd, London; p. 96 Joanna Warrand, London; p. 98 Libra Antiques, London; pp. 101, 110, 115 Sotheby Parke Bernet; p. 116 National Magazine and Smith-Woolley and Perry, Folkstone; p. 119 Sotheby's; for photographs appearing between pages 124 and 152 National Magazine in conjunction with: p. 124 Alaadin Ozutemiz Halici, Ankara; p. 131 D. & B. Dickinson, Bath; p. 137 Manchester Auction Mart; p. 139 John Roe Antiques, Finedon, Northants; p. 140 Shrubsole Ltd, London; p. 147 Knightsbridge Silver Co., R. S. & S. Negus, Robin & Valerie Lloyd, John & Janet Simpson; p. 148 Hennell Ltd, London; p. 152 Kate Green, Bath.

14

Effects of Food Production and Processing on Nutrients

In This Chapter

- Farm Production and Harvesting Influence the Nutrient Content of Foods
- Processing and Storage Affect Nutrients
- Handle Food Properly at Home for Most Nutritional Benefit

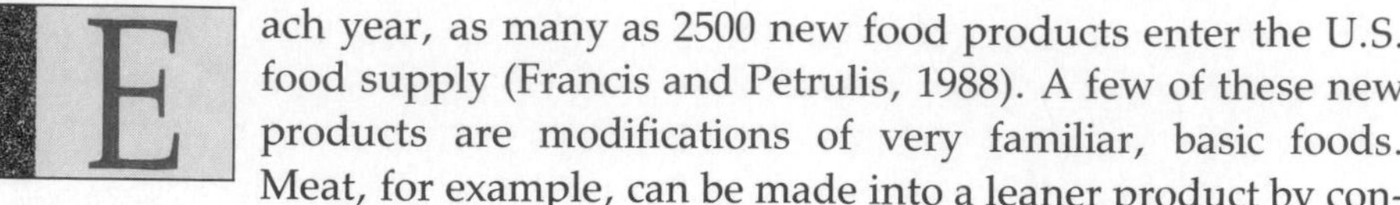

Each year, as many as 2500 new food products enter the U.S. food supply (Francis and Petrulis, 1988). A few of these new products are modifications of very familiar, basic foods. Meat, for example, can be made into a leaner product by controlling the body fat content of livestock. But the great majority of new products are processed foods designed for convenience—foods that are cleaned, cut up, combined, cooked, seasoned, preserved, and packaged so they can go from the shelf to your stomach in minutes.

Few of the many new food items that annually enter the market prove profitable enough to remain on the market. Food companies whose products do survive are those that keep up with changing domestic consumer preferences—as well as international food needs, technological advances, and organizational innovation (Veblen, 1988). When food industry marketing specialists survey consumers to determine what factors influence their selection of food, three out of four shoppers rate taste, nutrition, price, product safety, storability, and ease of preparation as important (Figure 14.1) (Food Marketing Institute, 1989). Consumers are also increasingly interested in foods that *appear* to be minimally processed while they offer the convenience of highly processed items (Lund, 1989).

Some of these preferences are easy for food producers to define, while others—like taste and nutritional value—are open to a variety of interpretations. Making foods more nutritious, for example, presents quite a challenge to food producers when a consensus on the definition of good nutrition is virtually impossible. A person whose primary interest is to lose weight will look for low-kcalorie products that taste sweet and feel rich without containing the sugar or fat that the traditional versions of such foods contain. Somebody else might regard products with added vitamins and minerals or fiber as nutritious. Another group of consumers might rate nutritional value by

Figure 14.1 When consumers talk, food processors listen. Urban consumers have the most clout in effecting changes in our food system today. The fast-paced urban lifestyle has encouraged the huge expansion of kcalorie-controlled, microwavable entrees in single-serving packages.

the purity of the product—foods that are grown without the use of fertilizers or pesticides and appear fresh or only minimally processed. Someone else again might believe nutrition is found in foods that contain less salt. From these examples you can see why food processors have to develop quite an array of different foods just to satisfy the public's interest in "good nutrition," to say nothing of the additional characteristics consumers want.

In the final analysis, how nutritious *are* today's foods, given our new food processing techniques? The mission of this chapter is to consider how nutrients in food are affected by various phases of production and processing, from the farmer's gate to your plate. Our discussion on the impact of production and processing on food will emphasize fats and cholesterol and minerals and vitamins, and will specifically address salt (sodium) because these are the substances about which consumers have the greatest concerns (Food Marketing Institute, 1989).

Farm Production and Harvesting Influence the Nutrient Content of Foods

The manner in which an animal is fed and managed or a plant is grown can affect its nutrient composition. Fats and cholesterol are more likely to be changed in animal products, since they usually contain more fat than plants, and because plants contain no cholesterol. Although both animal products and plants contain vitamins and minerals, production factors generally have more of an effect on the levels of these nutrients in plants and only an indirect influence on the nutrient content of the animals that consume them. Therefore, plants will be the focus of our discussion on vitamins and minerals. We will focus first on fat content.

Effects of Farm Production on Fat and Cholesterol in Animal Products

As mentioned above, because fat and cholesterol are a greater constituent in animals than in plants, the effort to lower lipid content in farm commodities has been centered on investigating how farm practices can effect changes in animal products. Although scientific advances have worked together with genetic factors to reduce the level of fat in meats and poultry, the industry must also consider consumer preferences in determining just how far to go with their technological capabilities.

Meats and Poultry The amount of fat and lean tissue on animals—whether beef cattle, hogs, lambs, or poultry—depends first of all on genetics. Inherited traits establish the patterns, limits, and types of growth that can be obtained (Byers et al., 1988), but the types and amounts of food given as the

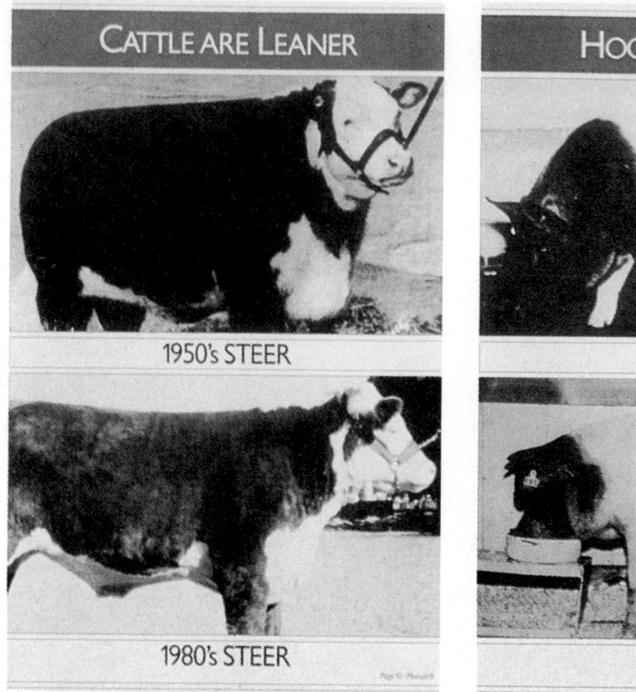

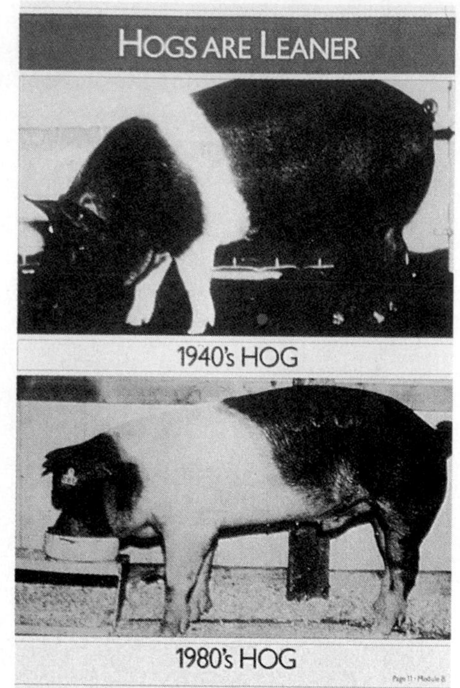

Figure 14.2 Fatness of meat animals "then" and "now." In recent decades, cattle and hogs have been genetically selected and raised to be less fat than formerly.

animal grows can affect proportionate gains in fat and lean tissue. And, by altering the character of the feed, it is possible to change the proportion of saturated and unsaturated fats produced in some animals. Further, the animal's own hormone system can be stimulated or additional hormones can be administered to promote the development of more lean and less fat. These techniques are selectively used, since not all are equally effective with all types of animals, and some have not yet been accepted for commercial use (Committee on Technological Options, 1988). The manipulation of hormones, for example, has not yet been accepted (Schelling and Byers, 1988). On the whole, though, the efforts to lower fat content of animal products have paid off. Today, beef cattle and lambs average about 6% less body fat than their counterparts of three decades ago, and pork has about 30% more lean meat per animal (National Livestock and Meat Board, 1987). Figure 14.2 shows some "before" and "after" pictures of this development.

Such technologies could be used to lower fat content even further, but there are factors that stand in the way of widespread adoption of these practices. One is the issue of acceptability by consumers. Because leaner meats are often perceived as less tender, juicy, and flavorful than fatter meats (Savell and Cross, 1988), it will be important to establish a lower limit of fatness below which it will not be an acceptable product to consumers.

Another stumbling block to decreasing fat content to the lowest possible degree is the grading system established by the United States Department of Agriculture (USDA). Since they were developed many decades ago before we understood the connection between high fat intake and heart disease, grading standards have placed a premium on higher fat content of meat.

Meats earning the higher quality designations (e.g., *prime* and *choice*) bring higher prices to the farmer; therefore, the grading system has been an incentive to overfeed and excessively fatten animals before slaughter (Committee on Technological Options, 1988).

A positive step was taken in 1987 when a lower-fat grade of meat, formerly labeled *good,* was renamed *select,* which has a more positive connotation to the consumer. Experts suggest, however, that more changes are necessary to remove grading biases that currently favor production and marketing of fatter meats. For the time being, by choosing select meats or meats with less marbling in the tissue and by trimming the fat around the cut of meat, consumers can effectively reduce their fat intake from animal products.

Milk As with meats, the current milk pricing system favors production of milk that contains the maximum content of fat and protein. But the dairy farmer has little control over the natural variation in the fat content of milk; the percentage of fat ranges from 3.4 to 5.6% of the milk's total weight, depending on the breed of the cow.

Experiments have shown that cows can be made to produce milk containing as low as 1% fat by modifying their diet (Gorewit, 1988). This method also increases the proportion of unsaturated fatty acids in the milk. It was found, however, that the experimental diet introduced certain health risks to the cow and is regarded as unacceptable practice. It seems much more practical at this point to lower the fat content of dairy products after they have left the farm. This will be discussed in the section on food processing.

Eggs Because egg yolks are high in cholesterol (see Chapter 7), some poultry scientists have developed methods to lower the cholesterol content of eggs by altering the hens' diets. Such diets tend to have negative effects on other nutritional values of the egg or on the hen's egg production. Drugs added to hens' diets can reduce cholesterol in eggs, but the products tested thus far also have harmful side effects and are therefore not a solution (Gyles, 1988). So far, it appears that lowering the cholesterol in eggs during subsequent processing can be more successful than trying to get hens to produce eggs low in cholesterol.

Effect of Farm Production on Sodium

The sodium content of foods as produced on the farm is very modest: it is estimated that only about 10% of the sodium we consume is naturally present in foods (National Academy of Sciences, 1989). The vast majority of sodium in our diets is added during commercial and home processing and at the table; therefore, it makes most sense for the individual to exercise control over his or her sodium intake. This will be addressed in later sections of this chapter.

Effects of Farm Production on Vitamins and Minerals in Fruits and Vegetables

In large part, the micronutrient content of animals and plants depends, again, on genetics. That is, the tissues of an animal in a given species generally have a vitamin and mineral content similar to that of other members of that species. Conditions under which they are grown, however, can also affect vitamin and mineral makeup. This is especially true in regard to plants.

Plants and Vitamin Content In studies that measure the effects that production factors have on the vitamin content of fruits and vegetables, the vitamin C level is often used as an indicator; vitamin C is more sensitive to changing conditions, and it is a nutrient we count on obtaining when we consume this group of foods. As we shall see, environmental conditions such as climate, soil, and fertilizer will influence vitamin levels of plants. For example, tomatoes that are vine-ripened outdoors in summer sunlight have twice as much vitamin C as tomatoes grown in greenhouses in winter (Agricultural Research Service, 1977), and grapefruit grown in the cooler coastal areas of California contain more vitamin C than those picked on the same date in the hotter desert areas of Arizona (Nagy and Wardowski, 1988).

The *mineral content of soil* can influence the *vitamin content of plants* as well. For example, when citrus fruits are grown on sandy Florida soils (which are naturally deficient in zinc, magnesium, manganese, and copper), the vitamin C levels in the fruits are lower than when soil minerals are present in adequate amounts (Nagy and Wardowski, 1988). Only moderate adjustments may be necessary to optimize vitamin C levels; overcompensating cannot force them to be higher than genetic limits allow.

In vegetable farming, the application of *too much* nitrogen can decrease the vitamin C content in some vegetables by as much as 30% (Salunkhe and Desai, 1988). On the other hand, *adequate* nitrogen is necessary for achieving healthy crops with a good yield and nutritive quality. Nitrogen deficiency is unquestionably the most common chemical deficiency of soils. Carrots that were *not* fertilized with nitrogen, phosphorus, potassium, or magnesium were found to have lower carotene levels than those that were fertilized (Salunkhe and Desai, 1988). Just as in earlier discussions about nutrient supplementation for humans, here we see that plants need an *adequate* amount of minerals present in the soil, but *more is not better; in fact, it becomes a negative factor when excessive.* It is important that farmers periodically have their soil evaluated so they can control the levels of minerals important for healthy crops (Figure 14.3).

Does it matter whether the origin of the minerals is an organic fertilizer (such as decomposed plant material or animal manure) or whether it is a synthetic fertilizer (specific pure chemicals)? Apparently not. In studies done with cabbage and carrots, there was no difference in vitamin C or carotene contents whether they were fertilized with organic or synthetic materials (Salunkhe and Desai, 1988).

Figure 14.3 Soil composition affects crop growth and nutrient content. This farmer is taking a sample of soil to have it analyzed for mineral content. No matter what kind of agricultural methods are used—whether conventional or alternative—it is important to monitor soil composition, because it can have a dramatic effect on total yield and on the nutritional quality of crops.

Maturity of fruits and vegetables at harvest can also affect vitamin levels. Research has shown that some fruits and vegetables reach their highest nutritive value while they are still immature, others when mature, and still others when overripe (Nagy and Wardowski, 1988; Salunkhe and Desai, 1988). Most often, though, a just-mature fruit or vegetable has nutritional value that is superior to products that were harvested either long before they were ripe or well past their prime. Very often, fruits and vegetables marketed as "fresh" may have been harvested and transported from a distance several weeks before they are purchased and consumed. Their nutritional values are very likely to be lower than a ripe, freshly picked product.

Plants and Mineral Contents Plants need certain minerals, such as potassium and magnesium, for survival; the level of these minerals found within a given variety of plant is quite constant. If there are not enough of these minerals in the soil to achieve those levels in the plants, the plants will not thrive.

The genetic makeup of some plants allows them to take up and store certain minerals for later use; for example, legumes store phosphorus in a form called phytate, but grasses do not. Some plants can accumulate minerals, such as selenium and aluminum, in amounts that would be highly toxic to other plants. Tea plants grown in aluminum-laden soil, for instance, may contain levels of aluminum high enough to impair or kill other kinds of plants.

As pointed out in Chapter 13, when certain minerals are in low concentration in soil, plants grown in that soil will be low in those minerals. Some elements that occur in plants in levels relative to those present in their soils are iodine, copper, manganese, cobalt, chromium, and molybdenum. While the lack of these minerals apparently is not a problem to the plants themselves, mineral deficiency can become a problem to animals (including humans) that eat the plants. For example, ruminants that feed on forage grown in soil deficient in cobalt are thin and "poorly fleshed" (Ockerman, 1988), and people who consistently eat food grown in soil low in iodine develop goiters, as you saw in Chapter 13.

Since most people now eat foods that were produced in many different regions, it is far less likely that they will experience mineral deficiencies due to low levels in some soils. Eating foods of *different geographical origins* adds another dimension to the advice that we should eat a varied diet.

Processing and Storage Affect Nutrients

food processing—any method of food handling that discourages spoilage of food or enhances its safety, nutrition, palatability, and/or convenience

Food processing is a very broad term that includes anything done to food after harvest to delay spoiling or to make food safer, more nutritious, more palatable, or more convenient. Processed foods technically include, therefore, everything from a fresh fruit or vegetable that has been waxed to a convenience food such as a frozen entree.

Although the number of processed foods has skyrocketed in the last few decades, the practice of food processing is older than we can document. Grinding grain into flour and making cheese from various animal milks are processes of prehistoric origin, as is the salting and drying of meat. Evidence of bread-making dating back to about 5000 BC has been found in Europe and Asia. Examples of later food processing methods include **canning,** which was developed in the late 1700s by Nicholas Appert in response to the French government's offer of a prize to whoever developed a method of preserving food for Napoleon's army. **Freezing** became commercially feasible about 1930, when Clarence Birdseye invented a process for freezing

canning—heating a food and its rigid container sufficiently to commercially sterilize the contents

freezing—lowering a temperature of a food so far that enzymes and microorganisms are almost inactivated but not destroyed

Figure 14.4 Food processing is not new. Although technology has advanced, this ancient limestone sculpture from a tomb at Giza, Egypt, of a woman grinding grain shows that food processing has been common practice for thousands of years.

packaged foods quickly, and **pasteurization** was commercially implemented during the 1930s for improving the safety of milk.

Food processing has benefited from many technological advances over time. In 1989 the Institute of Food Technologists, which is the professional organization for food scientists, celebrated its 50th anniversary. In connection with this observance, their members identified the following to be among the most important developments in food processing during their organization's half-century of existence:

- *High-temperature–short-term* ***(HTST) processing*** *and packaging* This method is used primarily for "boxed" fruit juices and allows for greater retention of aesthetic and nutritional quality; progress in plastics technology helped make it possible.
- *Refinement of commercial canning methods for vegetables* To ensure safety, specific procedures have been developed for different types of vegetables.
- *The microwave oven* By the year 2000, 90% of U.S. households are expected to have this convenient appliance.
- *Frozen concentrated citrus juices* This technology makes possible year-round access to food with a high vitamin C content.
- ***Controlled-atmosphere packaging*** *for fresh fruits and vegetables* This process delays ripening and spoilage.
- ***Freeze-drying*** This moisture removal process helps preserve product quality and retention of nutrients to a greater extent than other methods of drying.
- *Frozen meals* Specific conditions have been developed for different foods to maintain aesthetic and nutritional quality.
- *Food* ***fortification*** Fortification makes it possible to improve the nutritional status of large groups of people.
- *Ultra-high temperature* ***(UHT)****, short-term sterilization of milk* This variation of pasteurization allows milk or cream to be stored unopened at room temperature for more than 90 days.

A process the food scientists did not put on their list is **irradiation,** which can be used to rid food of pests or to preserve food for longer-term storage. When food is irradiated, it is exposed to gamma rays, x-rays, or electron beams; this controls various food spoilage factors, is more conservative of nutrients than some other processes, and does *not* make the food radioactive (IFT, 1986).

Irradiation has been approved in the United States for very limited uses: disinfecting spices and herbs, controlling insects in wheat and wheat flour, inhibiting sprouting of potatoes, controlling maturation and insects in fresh fruits and vegetables, and reducing the risk of trichinosis from pork (Newsome, 1987). These processes require lower dosages of radiation than do longer-term preservation uses.

Although studies of irradiation of food began in the late 1940s, applications to the U.S. food supply have been very few for a number of reasons: government regulations have not been fully developed; other effective and

pasteurization—heating a product at a temperature below its boiling point for less than a minute to kill most pathogens

HTST processing—the use of higher temperatures and shorter times than are used in conventional processes; precise conditions used vary with the product

controlled-atmosphere packaging—process in which proportions of oxygen and carbon dioxide within a storage facility or package are modified from proportions in air; delays ripening and rotting

freeze-drying—removal of moisture from food at very low temperatures

fortification—any addition of nutrients to foods during processing

UHT processing—sterilization of food by using higher temperatures than for HTST processing

irradiation—using gamma rays, x-rays, or electron beams to kill microorganisms and control certain factors that cause food spoilage

less expensive technologies for food preservation can be used; some scientists have reservations about certain chemicals formed in irradiated foods; and the general public has its own concerns about the process (Schutz et al., 1989). Further, effective regulation would be very difficult, since irradiation leaves no easily measurable unique markers and inspectors would not be able to identify irradiated foods. Irradiation is used more extensively in some other countries, especially in the processing of seafood.

Food technologists claim that many of these processes help maintain nutritional quality as well as convenience, safety, and aesthetic quality. But other people dispute the claim that commercially processed food is of good nutritional quality; their conviction is that nutritional value is better in unprocessed or minimally processed foods.

Who is right? Let's examine the effects of these and other processing methods on the food constituents we identified at the start of the chapter—fat and cholesterol, sodium, and other vitamins and minerals—to see what significant changes occur.

Food Processing Can Affect Fat and Cholesterol

During processing, the level of lipids in foods can increase or decrease. There are several ways to reduce fat in foods during processing; some are simple, such as trimming fat from the edge of a cut of meat, and others require sophisticated technology.

Meats and Poultry Whereas it has been customary to leave a border of approximately half an inch of fat around a cut of fresh meat, it is now more typical to find about one-eighth of an inch. This new practice has been adopted in response to consumer demand for less fat. Producers of processed meat have also responded to this trend. Products such as hams and sandwich meats that are 95% fat-free (by weight) have been very popular; the small amount of fat that remains is within or between the meat cells (Rust, 1988). But not all products easily lend themselves to fat reduction; the fat content of sausages is much more difficult to modify. In cooked sausage, such as a frankfurter, fat usually comprises 25–30% of the weight of the product, and if the fat is significantly lowered, the texture becomes rubbery. One way to correct this would be to substitute water for some of the fat, but current USDA regulations do not allow this. Another approach to reducing the fat in sausages is to use a lower-fat meat. For example, frankfurters made from poultry contain 18–22% fat (by weight), which is lower than the amount in beef frankfurters, but this percentage is still relatively high (Mast and Clouser, 1988). The Critical Thinking section in Chapter 7 pointed out that sometimes people do not understand what they are getting when they buy these products.

Fried chicken products have been a mainstay of restaurants, carry-out food shops, and retail frozen foods for many years, but traditionally breaded and fried chicken can obtain as much as 60% of its kcalories from fat. In response to consumer interest in eating less fat, the food industry is developing new cooking systems—such as removing the skin of the chicken and cooking it in hot air, reducing the amount of kcalories derived from fat to 27% (Mast and Clouser, 1988).

Prepared Meals and Entrees Combination dishes can be high or low in fat, depending on the ingredients and the method of preparation. For example, a portion of frozen lasagna could have around 20 grams of fat, whereas a serving of chicken teriyaki with rice might have only 6 grams. The market expansion of low-kcalorie frozen meals has made a greater number of low-fat entrees available, but not all low-kcalorie items are low in fat. The only way to know is to check the nutrition label. (Sometimes the major means of controlling kcalorie value has been to restrict the portion size.)

Not all the fat in prepared meals comes from ingredients obviously of animal origin. For example, the pastry crust on a pot pie may contribute more fat than the meat and gravy it contains; and the dessert in a frozen dinner may be high in fat.

Eggs Various methods are used to lower the cholesterol content of processed eggs (out of the shell); about 15% of all eggs consumed are such products. Since the yolk of the egg contains the cholesterol, removing the yolk is a common way to eliminate the cholesterol. In products of this type, the separated egg white is mixed with vegetable oil, food coloring, and other ingredients to yield a product that resembles blended whole eggs. Other approaches are to extract some of the cholesterol from a whole-egg mixture by using a solvent, or to add extra egg white to a whole-egg mixture. These latter processes accomplish only a partial reduction in cholesterol; you need to read food labels to determine the content of a given product (Mast and Clouser, 1988).

Milk and Dairy Products Milk fat can be separated easily from the non-fat substances in milk, and the dairy industry has responded to consumer interest by producing milk, yogurt, cheese, and frozen desserts with varying fat levels. For example, although natural cheeses generally have 7 to 9 grams of fat per ounce, **imitation** cheese products are available that contain only a few grams of fat or almost none. Such products may have a different **mouthfeel** and may behave differently from traditional cheeses when used as ingredients in recipes. The fat content of frozen dairy desserts ranges from 24 grams per cup for "premium" ice creams to almost no fat in some frozen yogurts.

Dairy products are also a source of cholesterol: a cup of whole milk contains 33 mg. Since 85% of the cholesterol in milk is associated with the milk fat, removing all or part of the fat also reduces the cholesterol. A cup of skim milk has an insignificant 5 milligrams of cholesterol.

imitation food—product that has less of one or more nutrients than the food it imitates, or that contains substitute ingredients

mouthfeel—term used by food scientists to collectively encompass the sensations of texture and consistency provided by a food in the mouth

Baked Grain Products Baked grain products vary considerably in fat content, from 1 gram in a slice of most yeast-raised breads to more than 20

grams in a piece of rich cake. Besides the quantity of fat in these products, consumers must be aware of the *type* of fat they contain. Some products use coconut oil, palm oil, or butter, all examples of saturated fat; other vegetable oils are less saturated (unless they are hydrogenated, in which case they are more saturated). When producers are aware of consumer concern about certain food constituents (as they are regarding saturated fat), the market usually diversifies to provide a wider range of products to choose from. Again, label reading is key to getting what you want (Figure 14.5).

Effect of Food Processing on Sodium Content

Various sodium compounds are present in food. Sodium chloride (ordinary table salt) is the most common and accounts for the vast majority of sodium in the diet, and fully 75% of this salt comes from processed food (National Academy of Sciences, 1989). Other sodium compounds—such as monosodium glutamate, sodium nitrite, sodium bicarbonate (baking soda), and sodium citrate—are thought to contribute less than 10% to the overall diet. They serve various functions, such as enhancing flavor, preserving food, leavening, and controlling pH. In this section, we will discuss attempts that have been made to lower sodium in some processed foods.

Processed Meats The level of sodium in processed meats today is approximately 15 times the level in fresh meats, largely owing to the addition of salt and sodium nitrite. Salt has three major functions in these products: preser-

Figure 14.5 Want to stay in control of what you're eating? Then read labels: with lots of choices on the market, you can often find a convenience food that contains what you want. The cake mixes below are made with different kinds of shortening.

CONTAINS: SUGAR, ENRICHED BLEACHED FLOUR [BLEACHED FLOUR, NIACIN, IRON, THIAMINE MONONITRATE (VITAMIN B1), RIBOFLAVIN (VITAMIN B2)] PARTIALLY HYDROGENATED SOYBEAN OIL WITH BHA, BHT AND CITRIC ACID ADDED TO PROTECT FLAVOR, CORN STARCH, DEXTROSE, MODIFIED TAPIOCA STARCH, BAKING POWDER (BAKING SODA, SODIUM ALUMINUM PHOSPHATE, MONOCALCIUM PHOSPHATE), PROPYLENE GLYCOL MONOESTERS, SALT, MONO- AND DIGLYCERIDES, ARTIFICIAL FLAVOR, SODIUM PHOSPHATE, CALCIUM ACETATE, CELLULOSE GUM, XANTHAN GUM, POLYSORBATE 60, LECITHIN, ARTIFICIAL COLOR AND FD&C YELLOW NO. 5.

INGREDIENTS

ENRICHED FLOUR (BLEACHED FLOUR, NIACIN, REDUCED IRON, THIAMINE MONONITRATE, RIBOFLAVIN), SUGAR, ANIMAL AND/OR VEGETABLE SHORTENING (CONTAINS ONE OR MORE OF THE FOLLOWING PARTIALLY HYDROGENATED FATS: COTTONSEED OIL, BEEF FAT, LARD, PALM OIL) FRESHNESS PRESERVED WITH BHA AND CITRIC ACID, DEXTROSE, LEAVENING (BAKING SODA, SODIUM ALUMINUM PHOSPHATE, DICALCIUM, PHOSPHATE), MODIFIED CORN STARCH, SALT, PROPYLENE GLYCOL MONO ESTERS, MONO AND DIGLYCERIDES, GUAR GUM, ARTIFICIAL FLAVOR, SOY LECITHIN, FD&C YELLOW NO. 5 & 6.

vation, promotion of binding, and flavor enhancement. Nitrites aid in preservation and coloring. Because these compounds serve multiple purposes, and because consumers seem to prefer the taste of foods that contain them, the industry has been disinclined to reduce their levels to a very great extent.

The level of nitrites in most processed meat products was voluntarily reduced by processors in the late 1970s, when it was questioned whether nitrites were safe. (More on this in Chapter 15.) In the last decade, there has also been considerable emphasis on reducing sodium in the food supply, and the industry has responded by reducing the levels in cooked sausage by an estimated 20% (Rust, 1988). Another approach to reducing sodium is to use other compounds such as potassium chloride as a partial substitute for sodium chloride. Substituting more than about one-third of the salt, however, results in unacceptable flavors (Mast and Clouser, 1988).

Canned Soups and Vegetables In 1980, USDA published data stating that the amount of sodium per 8 ounces of ready-to-eat canned soup ranged between 900 and 1100 mg. This is a large amount of sodium for one food item, considering that the recommended limit for sodium intake is 2400 mg per day from salt (Committee on Diet and Health, 1989).

Some commercial soup companies claim to have lowered the sodium content of their products since 1980 when the data were published; information from the labels of one popular brand now shows them to range between 700 and 900 mg per serving. The same soup maker markets an additional line of soups with one-third less salt, but even these products are significant sources of sodium (450–600 mg/serving). Reconstituted dehydrated soups, according to USDA data, usually contain 1000–1300 milligrams of sodium per serving.

Most fresh vegetables contain less than 10 mg per $\frac{1}{2}$-cup serving, but canned vegetables generally have about 300 mg, most of which is due to added salt. Some processors also market vegetables canned without salt so that consumers can add whatever amount they like. Vegetables pickled in brine are very high in sodium. A dill pickle, for example, contains about 750 mg of sodium.

Prepared Meals and Entrees Generally speaking, prepared meals and entrees contain quite a lot of sodium, although there is considerable variation from one brand (and even products of the same brand) to another. Many frozen and canned products fall within the range of 700 to 1200 mg of sodium per serving. That also holds true for many controlled-kcalorie frozen meals, although there are now several product lines with sodium content restricted to 500–600 mg per serving.

Before you judge commercial processors too harshly for loading their entrees with what may seem to be an excessive amount of salt, consider that most home recipes for similar items call for adding just as much sodium. Of course, when you prepare an item at home, you *can* control the amount of sodium it contains.

Read Critical Thinking 14.1 and consider how this matter relates to you and your choices.

Effects of Food Processing on Vitamin and Mineral Contents

A huge body of scientific literature has been generated regarding the effects of processing on nutrients. A respected reference on these matters, *Nutritional Evaluation of Food Processing* by E. Karmas and R.S. Harris, is a volume of almost 800 pages, and it claims only to summarize the work in this field. Our approach here will be to address general principles that affect micronutrients rather than deal with the details of particular products processed under specific conditions.

Generally speaking, a portion of vitamins and minerals is lost from a product during processing, and the losses are cumulative when multiple processes are used. Vitamins are more vulnerable to destruction than minerals are; of the vitamins, vitamin C and thiamin break down and lose their function most readily. Losses can occur from exposure to oxygen, light, or heat; a particular pH; the passage of time; or physical separation. Table 14.1 indicates which micronutrients are unstable in the presence of some of these conditions.

Notice that heat negatively affects the greatest number of nutrients. This is an important point, because most methods of food processing involve heat in some way. (An exception is irradiation, which involves little increase in temperature.) But heat is widely used because it serves many very beneficial purposes: it is the most common way of killing pathogenic organisms and controlling spoilage; it makes many foods more digestible; and it may protect against "off" flavors, loss of color, and poor texture (Dietz and Erdman, 1989). Commercial processors are careful to use only enough heat to achieve the benefits, because energy is expensive. This financial thrift results in nutritional savings as well.

Commercial processors not only govern the amount of heat they apply, but they also carefully choose the best packaging materials and storage conditions to retain sensory and nutritional quality. Because of the advanced technology and precise controls processors use, commercially processed food is likely to contain a higher proportion of its original nutrients than the same food processed at home.

Passage of time is another factor that affects nutrients. The micronutrient content of processed foods tends to decrease gradually during storage, but these losses occur much more slowly than would have occurred in the fresh food. Losses in processed foods can be minimized by storing products at temperatures that are not excessive. Canned foods retain over 90% of their vitamin C during one year of storage, provided storage temperature does not exceed 68°F (Gilbert, 1988). Frozen foods should be stored at 0°F or below; if stored at 20°F, losses of vitamin C are substantially higher (Fennema, 1988).

Table 14.1 Stability of vitamins. Different vitamins are vulnerable to different environmental conditions.

	Effect of pH					
Vitamin	Neutral pH	Acid pH	Alkaline pH	Air or Oxygen	Light	Heat
Vitamin A	S	U	S	U	U	U
Carotene (pro-A)	S	U	S	U	U	U
Vitamin D	S		U	U	U	U
Vitamin E	S	S	S	U	U	U
Vitamin K	S	U	U	S	U	S
Thiamin	U	S	U	U	S	U
Riboflavin	S	S	U	S	U	U
Niacin	S	S	S	S	S	S
Vitamin B-6	S	S	S	S	U	U
Folic acid	U	U	S	U	U	U
Vitamin B-12	S	S	S	U	U	S
Biotin	S	S	S	S	S	U
Pantothenic acid	S	U	U	S	S	U
Vitamin C	U	S	U	U	U	U

S = stable (no important destruction)
U = unstable (significant destruction)

Adapted from Karmas, E. and R.S. Harris, eds. 1988. *Nutritional Evaluation of Food Processing*. New York: Van Nostrand Reinhold Company.

Although nutrient loss is characteristic of processing, there are also situations in which nutrient contents of processed foods actually *increase*. The primary circumstance is when nutrients are deliberately added, a process called fortification. A broad array of products now contain added nutrients—from many baked products to some soft drink mixes (see Chapters 12 and 13 on the micronutrients).

An increase in some of the B vitamins in certain products can also be caused by the process of **fermentation.** For example, in the production and aging of cheese, niacin and folic acid increase; and in the production of tempeh (an Asian food) from soybeans, riboflavin and niacin increase five-fold over original values (McFeeters, 1988).

fermentation—process in which microorganisms metabolize components of a food, changing the composition and taste of the product

Probably the greatest positive impact of food processing on nutritional value relates to the content of the overall diet; processing enables many foods to be year-round commodities rather than just briefly available after harvest. This means that our diets can be more varied during all twelve months of the year, and a varied diet is likely to be a more nutritious diet than one that relies only on foods in season. In this light, it has been suggested that the development of the canning process was the most significant advance toward the eradication of nutritional deficiency diseases (Dietz and Erdman, 1989).

With these general principles in mind, let's take a look at some types of foods whose micronutrients are particularly affected by processing.

Sodium in Processed Foods: Is It a Problem?

The situation

Alan is 23 and in excellent health. His major form of recreation is participating in sports, and he wants to keep himself as healthy as possible so he can continue these activities. He realizes that good nutrition is part of this.

Recently, he has been trying to improve his eating. He has noticed that many dietary guidelines recommend cutting down on fat and salt. It has been fairly easy for him to make some changes to lower his fat intake, but cutting down on salt has been more difficult. Although he does not usually salt his food at the table, he eats in restaurants and uses a lot of convenience foods, which he has heard is high in salt. He wonders whether he really needs to do anything about salt, since the major concern is its relationship to blood pressure, and his blood pressure was fine when it was checked about a year ago.

Is the information accurate and relevant?

- Many dietary recommendations for the general public do suggest that people reduce their sodium intake (see Chapter 2).
- Epidemiological studies have found a connection between high sodium intake and elevated blood pressure (Chapter 13).
- While it cannot be said that all restaurant foods are categorically high in salt, many probably are; data show that many fast-food entrees and convenience entrees are high in sodium.

What else needs to be considered?

The epidemiologic evidence that correlates salt intake with blood pressure deals with averages for large population groups, but such correlations often do not hold up when you look at salt intakes and blood pressures of individuals within a group. Some people's blood pressure is not much affected by their salt intake, no matter how much they consume; others are noticeably *salt sensitive*, although the degree to which it affects their blood pressure is individually variable.

Genetics play a big role, too: some ethnic groups have a much higher incidence of hypertension than others, and it tends to be more prevalent in some families. Furthermore, many other factors have been shown to affect blood pressure, such as levels of intake of some other minerals (Chapter 13), body weight, alcohol intake (Chapter 18), and stress.

Alan is black, and adult blacks in this country have a higher incidence of hypertension than the 18% in the U.S. population overall. His mother and father both have high blood pressure, and his 30-year-old brother was diagnosed with it recently.

Alan's eating habits are an outgrowth of his lifestyle. He is single, has a desk job, and wants to spend most of his spare time on sports. He has never learned to do more than "survival cooking," mostly making sandwiches or microwaving frozen dinners, and he catches a lot of meals on-the-run, often fast foods. His first impression is that this lifestyle—which he intends to continue—makes it impossible for him to lower his sodium intake.

Gradually, Alan notices some ways to cut down on salt. He hears a person ahead of him at a fast food restaurant order a hamburger without salt; he learns that most fast food restaurants salt their hamburgers as they cook them, and many places are willing to omit the salt on request—but they can't do anything about the salt in pre-seasoned items like breaded fish and chicken. And one day, when Alan is on one of his quick trips to the grocery store, he sees a new product promotion for a brand of frozen dinners that has only about half the amount of sodium as those he had been eating. Then, when he is at a friend's place one night and is helping fix dinner, he realizes that it is fairly easy to broil meat in the oven and cook frozen vegetables in the microwave oven.

What do you think?

How important is it for Alan to be concerned about his sodium intake?

Does his reliance on restaurant and convenience food make it feasible to reduce his sodium intake, even if he wants to?

If you were Alan, which of the following alternatives would you consider?

- Option 1 You make no change in salt intake, recognizing that even though you are *statistically* at risk of developing hypertension, there is no sure way of knowing whether you will get it. Further, there is no guarantee that cutting down on salt would prevent hypertension anyway.
- Option 2 You make no change in salt intake, recognizing your risk, but believing that you are already doing enough of the right things—such as exercising regularly and reducing your intake of fat—both of which help keep your weight under control and thereby reduce risk of hypertension.
- Option 3 You reduce your salt intake when it is convenient, but are not slavish about it; this could mean buying the lower-salt frozen dinners but allowing yourself to eat what you want when you are out for meals.
- Option 4 You eat only at restaurants that are willing to fix foods on request with little or no salt.
- Option 5 You learn to cook for yourself so you can limit the salt. At first this will be learning to broil meat, fish, and chicken; fix salads; and microwave vegetables.
- Option 6 You ask your doctor or a dietitian for advice.

Do you see other options, or combinations that are workable? What do you think would be the best choice for Alan? What is your own situation, and what makes most sense for you?

GOOD 'N' QUICK

CHICKEN CACCIATORE

INGREDIENTS: TOMATOES, COOKED VERMICELLI, CHICKEN TENDERLOINS, WATER, ONIONS, MUSHROOMS, GREEN PEPPERS, RED WINE, TOMATO PUREE, MARGARINE, MODIFIED CORNSTARCH, SALT, CHICKEN FAT, COOKED CHICKEN, SUGAR, MONOSODIUM GLUTAMATE, SPICES, PAPRIKA, CORN OIL, LEMON JUICE, SODIUM PHOSPHATES AND LEMON JUICE SOLIDS, DEHYDRATED ONIONS, DEHYDRATED GARLIC, CHICKEN BROTH, ONION SALT, TURMERIC, NATURAL FLAVORINGS.

NUTRITION INFORMATION	PER SERVING
SERVING SIZE	10 1/2 OZ.
SERVINGS PER CONTAINER	1
CALORIES	270
PROTEINS	21g
CARBOHYDRATE	26g
FAT	9g
SODIUM	1180mg

PERCENTAGE OF U.S. RECOMMENDED DAILY ALLOWANCES (U.S. RDA)

PROTEIN	30	RIBOFLAVIN	10
VITAMIN A	10	NIACIN	25
VITAMIN C	20	CALCIUM	4
THIAMINE	8	IRON	6

Usual sodium in many convenience entrees

HEALTHY GOURMET

WHITE MEAT OF CHICKEN IN PEANUT SAUCE OVER LINGUINI AND VEGETABLE

INGREDIENTS: COOKED MACARONI PRODUCT, MILK, CHICKEN TENDERLOINS, SNAP PEAS, WATER, WATER CHESTNUTS, ONIONS, PEANUT FLOUR, PEANUT OIL, CARROTS, PEANUTS, SUGAR, COOKED CHICKEN, SOY SAUCE, MODIFIED CORNSTARCH, LEMON JUICE, SALT, CORN OIL, ENRICHED WHEAT FLOUR, GINGER, CORN SYRUP, GARLIC, FLAVORING (NATURAL FLAVORS, PARTIALLY HYDROGENATED SOYBEAN AND COTTONSEED OIL), POTATO STARCH, SPICES, LIME JUICE, WHITE WINE VINEGAR, DEHYDRATED ONIONS, SUGAR CANE SYRUP, ROASTED CHICKEN FLAVOR (NATURAL FLAVORS, DEXTROSE, PARTIALLY HYDROGENATED SOYBEAN AND COTTONSEED OIL), DEHYDRATED GARLIC, TURMERIC, NATURAL FLAVORINGS, SODIUM PHOSPHATES AND LEMON JUICE SOLIDS.

NUTRITION INFORMATION	PER SERVING
SERVING SIZE	9 1/4 OZ.
SERVINGS PER CONTAINER	1
CALORIES	330
PROTEINS	27g
CARBOHYDRATE	32g
FAT	10g
SODIUM	570mg

PERCENTAGE OF U.S. RECOMMENDED DAILY ALLOWANCES (U.S. RDA)

PROTEIN	40	RIBOFLAVIN	10
VITAMIN A	6	NIACIN	35
VITAMIN C	10	CALCIUM	8
THIAMINE	15	IRON	10

Less sodium in some new products

Vegetables Fresh vegetables, harvested at their prime and consumed soon after, offer the best possible nutrient quality. But the micronutrients in vegetables are more vulnerable than those in other types of foods because of their non-acidic nature. Their less stable vitamins start losing activity quickly, even when vegetables are kept cool after harvest: after two days of refrigeration, nutritional values of fresh vegetables generally have fallen below what the same vegetable, preserved right after harvest, would contain (Fennema, 1989).

dehydration, drying—removal of moisture from food; can be accomplished by various methods

Does it matter what method of food preservation was used—whether canning, **dehydration,** or freezing? Not much, if you compare the nutritional contents of different processed forms of the same vegetable *when they are ready to eat.* Figure 14.6 shows that although common commercial processing methods differ somewhat in destruction of nutrients, after vegetables have been cooked or heated to eat, they are quite similar in nutritional content. Because the data in this figure are for highly destructible vitamin C, they show more substantial losses than would occur with most other nutrients.

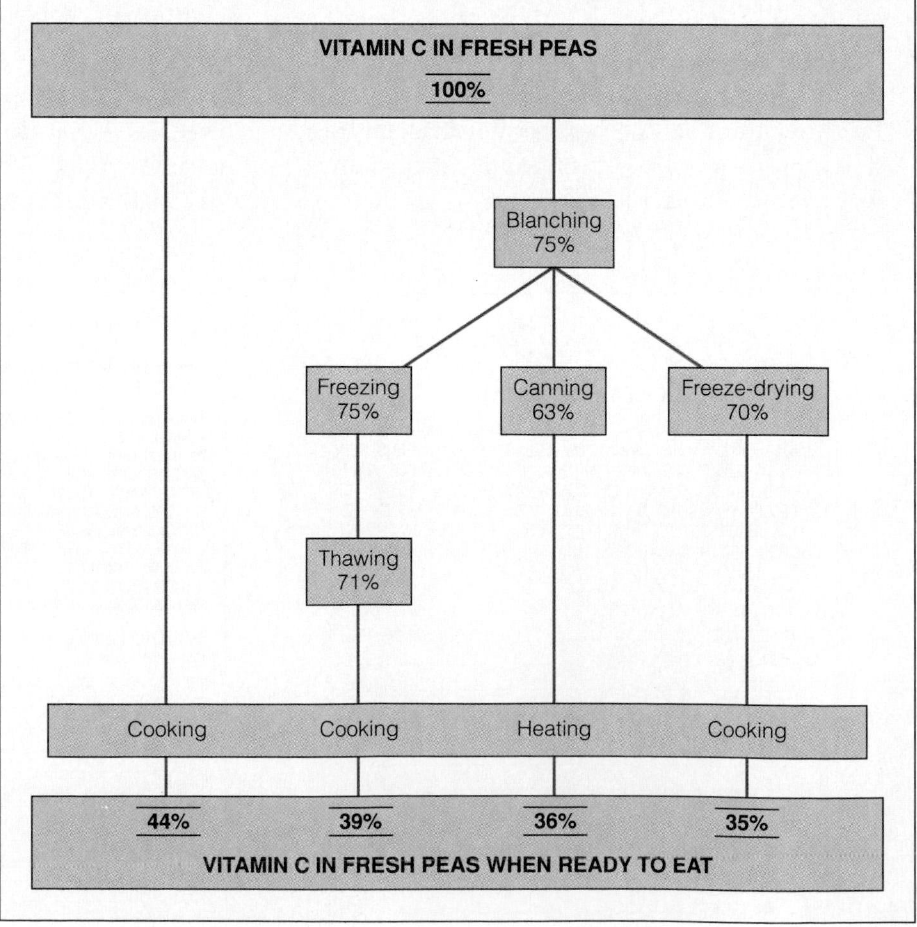

Figure 14.6 The bottom line: the nutrient value of a food as you eat it. Although different food preservation techniques decrease nutrient content by varying amounts, by the time you have cooked the food and are ready to eat it, there may not be much difference in nutritional value. This illustration indicates the percentage of vitamin C retained in peas processed by currently common methods and then prepared for eating. Remember that fresh peas that are not used immediately after harvest start losing vitamin value quickly; after two days of refrigeration, fresh vegetables are likely to have *lower* values than their commercially preserved counterparts. (Tannenbaum/Young/Archer: "Vitamins and Minerals." In *Food Chemistry* by O.R. Fennema (ed.), Marcel Dekker, Inc., NY, 1985.)

Fruits Processed fruits in general retain higher levels of vitamins because of their acidic nature, and freezing does a better job of retaining vitamin activity in these foods than does canning or dehydration. Frozen orange juice, one of the most commonly consumed processed fruit products, loses only 5% of its vitamin C; most other frozen fruit products retain over 70% of their original amounts (Fennema, 1988). Losses of vitamins in canned fruit are generally somewhat higher.

It is more difficult to generalize about vitamin activity losses in dried fruits, because there are many different processes, and they cause different amounts of loss. A major factor is the amount of water removed: the *drier* the final product, the *better* the vitamin C retention. Therefore sun-drying, which does not dry a product very thoroughly, leaves little vitamin C intact (Adams and Erdman, 1988). Certain commercial processes such as freeze-drying result in far less vitamin C loss (Bluestein and LaBuza, 1988); but a great deal of vitamin C loss can occur in dehydrated products that require an elaborate series of processes, not so much from the removal of moisture itself as from the processes that precede dehydration. For example, apple flakes are made by slicing, **blanching,** pureeing, and finally drying the product between hot drums; after this sequence, only about 30% of the apple's original vitamin C is left (Bluestein and LaBuza, 1988).

blanching—heating a food with boiling water, steam, and/or microwaves just for long enough to destroy many of the enzymes that reduce palatability and nutritive value

Grain Products The way grain is processed has a major impact on its nutritional value. Grains in their whole form have three major portions. The tough, darker, outer layers are the bran layers; the region toward one end of the kernel from which sprouting occurs is the germ; and the lighter, larger, inner starchy portion is the endosperm. Figure 6.4 showed these areas in a kernel of wheat.

Milling is the grinding of grain into flour. The bran layers and the germ do not break down as readily as the endosperm does, which makes them relatively easy to separate from the powdered endosperm early in the milling process. Such separation is called **refining.**

milling—the grinding of grain into flour

refining—separation of the coarser bran and germ particles from the endosperm early in the milling process

Different types of flour are produced by controlling the relative proportions of powdered endosperm, ground bran layers, and germ. Whole-grain flour contains all parts; refined flours have had some or all of the bran and germ sifted out. This is significant since the germ and bran layers contain most of the vitamins, minerals, and fiber that are in the grain, whereas the endosperm is largely starch.

The method of milling wheat in the United States results in overall nutrient losses of 40–60% in white flour (Institute of Food Technologists, 1986). Figure 14.7 shows the percentages of micronutrients found in white flour compared with whole-wheat flour. You can see from this illustration why the Basic Food Guide promotes the idea that at least two of the grain servings consumed per day should be whole-grain products. Commonly available whole-grain products are whole-wheat (graham) flour, brown rice, dark rye flour, and rolled oats.

Some of the nutrients lost during milling and refining of flour are replaced

enrichment—the addition of nutrients already present in a food to levels that meet a specific FDA standard

by the process of **enrichment.** In this process, thiamin, riboflavin, niacin, and iron are added to specific levels established by FDA standards. In the United States, refined grain products such as wheat flours, bread, rolls and buns, farina, cornmeal, corn grits, pastas, and rice are commonly enriched.

Figure 14.7 also shows how enriched wheat flour compares nutritionally with refined and whole-wheat flours. Enriched products are clearly second best to whole grains, because only four nutrients are added back. However, enriched products are a nutritional improvement over refined products, which have less than half the level of most nutrients that are present in whole wheat.

Milk Fresh milk is typically pasteurized, a process that kills most pathogenic organisms but does not destroy all microorganisms or their spores. Because the treatment is not very severe or very long, nutrient damage does not exceed 10% for vitamins present in significant quantities. Using high-temperature–short-time (HTST) processing achieves the same safety with even lower losses. Because these two processes do not produce sterile products, the milk must be refrigerated to discourage growth of remaining microorganisms.

Ultra-high temperature (UHT) processing, because of the higher temperature used, produces a sterile product; this allows fluid milk to be stored at room temperature for months as long as it is unopened. Because of the very short time for which heat is applied, nutrient losses are as low as those of

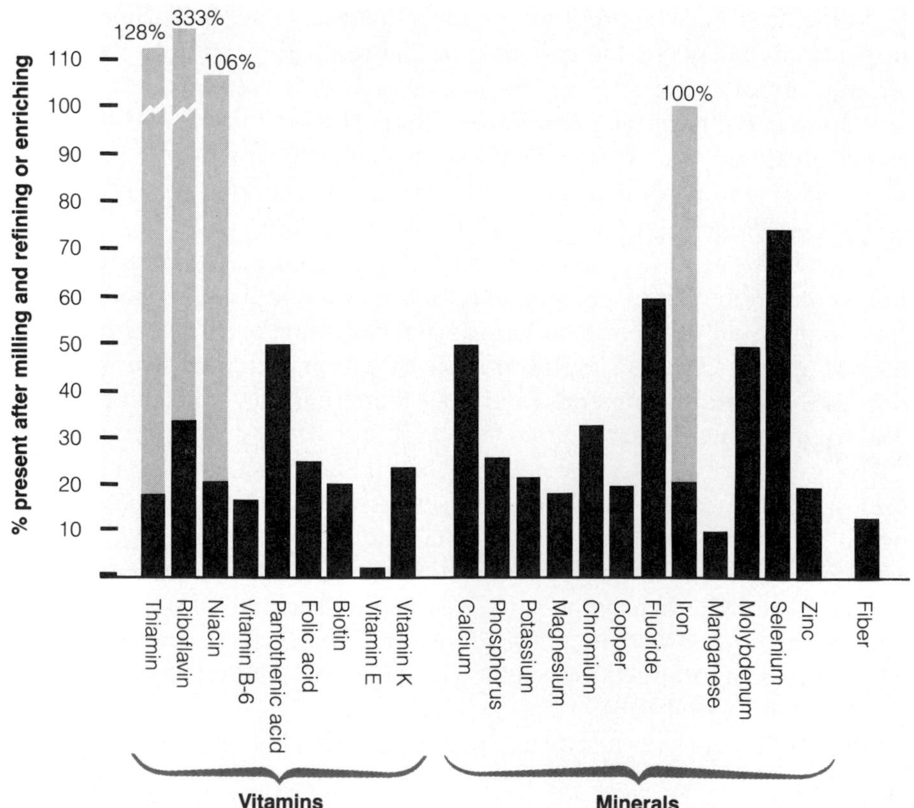

Figure 14.7 Proportions of some nutrients present in wheat flour after refining and enrichment. On this graph, 100% represents the nutrients found in whole wheat. The most commonly used refined flour (darker bars) contains less than half the amount of many nutrients present in whole wheat. Enriched flour (lighter extension of bars) has had only four nutrients added: thiamin, riboflavin, niacin, and iron.

traditional pasteurization (Lund, 1988). UHT milk is more heavily marketed in Canada and Europe than in the United States.

Meats Meats retain more nutrients if they are frozen rather than canned or dehydrated (Fennema, 1988). Most of the nutrients lost from frozen meat are in the thaw exudate, the liquid that pools during thawing. It is possible to recover some of these nutrients by heating and serving it with the juices lost from meat during cooking.

Prepared Meals and Entrees Prepared meals and entrees are important to consider because the use of these foods has increased tremendously. Canned combination foods have long been available; frozen meals and entrees have increased most dramatically; and now foods processed in a **flexible retort pouch** or similar flat, laminated container that can be stored at room temperature are also available (Figure 14.8).

flexible retort pouch—a multilayered package capable of being sealed by heat; can withstand high temperatures needed to sterilize contents

Generally when you eat these foods, whether they have been frozen, canned, or sealed in a retort container, you should expect to get somewhat lower levels of nutrients than you would have received from consuming a comparable product that was freshly made and immediately served. That is because processing the product and reheating the food before serving both take a toll on nutrient content.

Some people think of flexible retort containers as similar to cans; in both processes, the product is sealed into the container and they are sterilized as a unit. The retort container is quite flat compared with a can, however, and heat can completely penetrate the product in only half to two-thirds the time needed for the same item in a can. This shorter processing time has been shown to enhance nutrient retention significantly (Dietz and Erdman, 1989).

Imitation Foods and Formulated Foods Advances in food technology have enabled the food industry to produce "food clones" that really are different substances than the foods they are attempting to imitate. For example, you can buy a product that looks and tastes like crabmeat but is actually a less expensive type of fish, or something that seems like mayonnaise but isn't.

Figure 14.8 A new form of packaging that helps preserve nutrients. The food pictured here was packaged in a flexible, laminated retort container and sterilized as a unit, making the product storable at room temperature. Because these packages are quite flat, less time is required to heat the contents, and less loss of heat-vulnerable nutrients occurs.

Such foods are often produced as a cheaper alternative to the real thing, or may be designed to avoid an undesirable constituent, such as the fat in mayonnaise. In any event, the new product may have considerably different nutritional value than the food it resembles.

If a food producer markets a product that has significantly less nutritional value (usually 10% of the RDA) than the food it looks like, and the producer wants to use the name on the label of the food it mimics, then the product must be labeled "imitation." For example, pizza is commonly topped with a shredded dairy product that looks like mozzarella cheese, but it is made from milk protein derivatives, partially hydrogenated vegetable oil, and various additives to color, flavor, and preserve the product. Look at the list of ingredients on the label, and if the "cheese" is really an imitation, it must say so.

It is not possible to make a blanket statement about whether imitation foods are better or worse for you than the foods they resemble. It depends on what the particular product is, your needs, and how much of it you eat.

For example, the imitation egg mixture that is made without yolk loses much of the vitamin A, folic acid, vitamin B-12, iron, and zinc as well as all of the cholesterol found in the original egg. Although some of these losses are restored with additives, the imitation eggs still are nutritionally inferior. However, the major users of this product are likely to be people who, for medical reasons, have been advised to avoid cholesterol; for them, consuming this product is a far better alternative than having no eggs at all.

Sugars Some people believe that "less refined" or "more natural" sources of sugar are substantially more nutritious than white sugar. Although it is true that there are differences in the nutritional values of various sweeteners, they are minor. Table 14.2 shows that white sugar, brown sugar, honey, maple syrup, and molasses are all very low in nutrients and contribute only a tiny amount of the nutrients we need every day.

Handle Food Properly at Home for Most Nutritional Benefit

Once you bring food home, what happens to it nutritionally is up to you. The remainder of the chapter considers how home food handling affects fat and cholesterol, sodium, and other minerals and vitamins in food.

Fat and Cholesterol

The Nutrition for Living section near the end of Chapter 7 suggests how to reduce fat and cholesterol in your diet. Review that section for pointers on how to prepare food with less fat as well as suggestions for making leaner choices at grocery stores and restaurants.

Sodium

Since experts estimate that about one-third of the sodium in the food we eat is added during home preparation or at the table, there is much we can do to reduce the sodium content of our food. For many people, ordinary table salt (sodium chloride) is the major source of sodium added at home. A teaspoon of salt has approximately 2000 mg of sodium. Reducing the amount of salt in a recipe would not lead to failure of the product—as would, for example, reducing the leavening or thickening. In most cases, you can reduce the salt by half and still have an acceptable product.

For people who like quite a lot of salt in their food, the prospect of cutting down is an unhappy one. However, people who have had to reduce their salt intake for medical reasons testify that after several weeks of adaptation to a lower salt intake, the foods they previously ate seem excessively salty when they taste them again.

People who have been successful at reducing sodium intake find it help-

Table 14.2 Nutritional Content of One Tablespoon of Various Concentrated Sweets

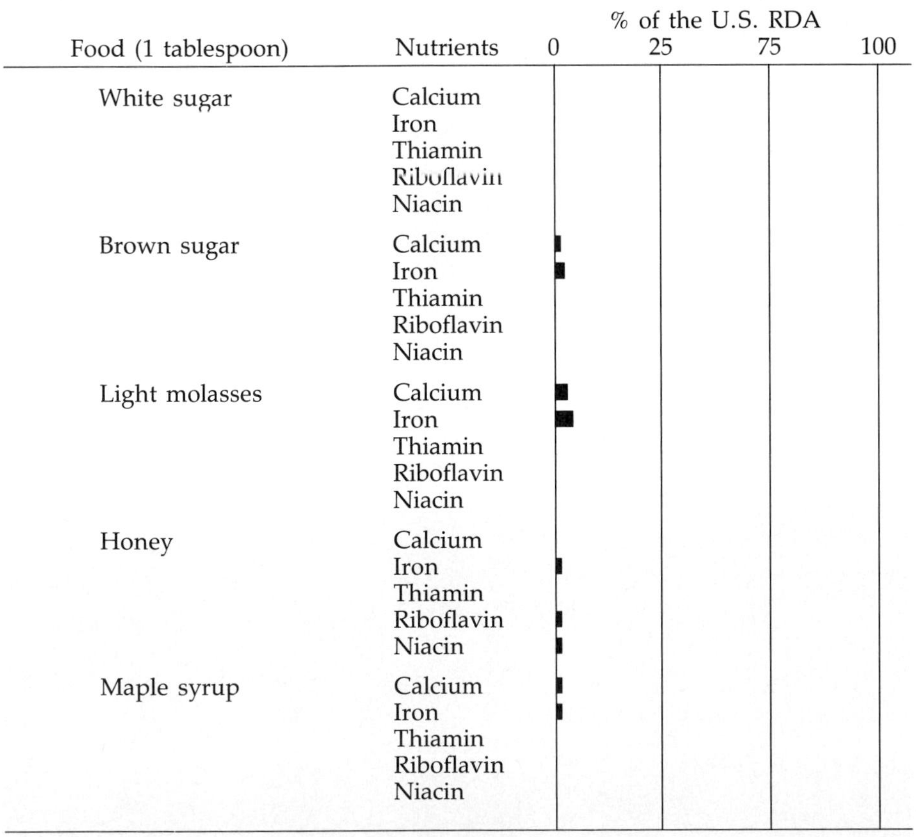

Food (1 tablespoon)	Nutrients	% of the U.S. RDA (0 – 25 – 75 – 100)
White sugar	Calcium	
	Iron	
	Thiamin	
	Riboflavin	
	Niacin	
Brown sugar	Calcium	
	Iron	
	Thiamin	
	Riboflavin	
	Niacin	
Light molasses	Calcium	
	Iron	
	Thiamin	
	Riboflavin	
	Niacin	
Honey	Calcium	
	Iron	
	Thiamin	
	Riboflavin	
	Niacin	
Maple syrup	Calcium	
	Iron	
	Thiamin	
	Riboflavin	
	Niacin	

Of the foods commonly used as sweeteners, none is a significant source of protein, vitamin A, or vitamin C—but they all contain from 42 to 65 kcalories per tablespoon.

Data sources: (1) Pennington, J.A.T. 1989. *Food values of portions commonly used.* New York: Harper & Row. (2) Science and Education Administration. 1985. *Nutritive value of foods.* Home and Garden Bulletin No. 72. Washington, DC: United States Department of Agriculture.

ful to use more of other non-salt seasonings. Most regular supermarkets carry an assortment of spices that contain negligible amounts of sodium; wines also offer interesting flavors. Monosodium glutamate, a flavor-enhancer marketed as Accent®, is an option that contains sodium but not nearly as much as salt does: it has approximately 600 mg per teaspoon.

In Asian meals, a major contributor of sodium is soy sauce, which has approximately 1000 mg per tablespoon, as do other products that include it such as teriyaki sauce. People accustomed to using generous amounts of soy sauce who want to cut down on sodium either could simply use less or could buy recently developed varieties with less sodium.

Other condiments can add substantial sodium to a meal if too much is used (Figure 14.9). A tablespoon of catsup, taco sauce, or prepared mustard has about 200 mg of sodium, but in the amounts some people eat, these products can add significantly to sodium intake.

Vitamins and Minerals

Various conditions lead to micronutrient loss: exposure to oxygen, light, and heat; a certain pH; passage of time; and/or discarding nutritious parts of food (physical separation). Attention to storage and methods of preparation, therefore, are important for retaining these nutrients.

Storage of Fresh Foods We are accustomed to refrigerating fresh foods such as milk, meat, and fruits and vegetables in order to keep them safe to eat. At the same time, refrigeration helps retain nutrients. When they are at room temperature, vegetables can lose three to four times the amount of vitamin C that they would when refrigerated. Similarly, the faster a product loses moisture, the greater the micronutrient losses will be, which is why it is important to keep fresh vegetables wrapped as air-tight as possible for storage.

As we mentioned in our discussion of commercial processing, the micronutrients in fresh vegetables are more vulnerable than those in meats and

Figure 14.9 Sodium in condiments. Some condiments are quite high in sodium, and others have more moderate levels. If you flood your stir-fry with soy sauce or drench your hamburger in catsup, condiments may add a substantial amount of sodium to your diet.

fresh fruits. When fresh vegetables are not consumed immediately after harvesting, progressive vitamin degradation will occur; vitamin C and the fat-soluble vitamins are particularly vulnerable to loss in typical oxygen-containing environments. Therefore, it is important to wrap food properly. The most important advice for getting maximal nutrition from refrigerated foods is to eat them as soon as possible.

Preparing Food When you are doing final preparation of food, continuing care needs to be taken to preserve micronutrients. Some experts believe that in most homes the greatest nutritional losses occur during this stage.

Removing edible parts of plant foods results in nutrient losses. This occurs partly because some of the food is thrown away and partly because the rest is exposed to oxygen. Sometimes it is also the case that the vitamin values of the discarded parts are higher (per unit weight) than those of the parts kept to eat. For example, the vitamin C in potatoes is present in highest concentrations in the layer just beneath the skin, and the vitamin A content of leafy green vegetables is highest in the outer, darkest leaves.

Any vitamins that are vulnerable to oxygen will be partially destroyed when food is cut or chopped. Dividing food into smaller pieces produces a larger total surface area; consequently, more oxygen exposure and vitamin destruction occur. It makes sense to wait as long as possible before cutting foods up for a meal.

Cooking or heating food just before serving is the final assault on its micronutrients. Heat, as we have discussed, has a destructive effect on most nutrients; the higher the temperature and the longer the heat is applied, the greater the losses. The best approach for protecting nutrients is to use as low a temperature for as short a time as possible, but you have to cook hot enough and long enough to ensure that what you have prepared is safe to eat. (More on this in Chapter 15.)

Because a food's water-soluble nutrients can dissolve into the water it's cooked in, it is better to cook food without directly putting it into water, especially if the water is to be discarded. **Steaming** and **pressure-cooking** allow for greater nutrient retention. If it is possible to produce a high-quality product with dry heat (roasting, grilling, stir-frying, or baking), doing so is also better than cooking in water.

steaming—using vapor from boiling water to cook foods while keeping the food out of the water

pressure-cooking—using superheated steam under pressure in an airtight utensil to cook foods quickly

microwave cooking—using short electromagnetic waves to cook foods quickly

How does **microwave cooking** rate? Studies show that the effects of "microwaving" vary with the product type, cooking time, internal temperature, and oven size, type, and power (Institute of Food Technologists, 1989). Because microwave cooking usually requires less time than other methods, however, nutrient retention is favored. Studies done with vegetables show higher vitamin C retention than conventional methods when cooking time was shorter and when the ratio of vegetable to water was less than 1 (Klein, 1989). Overall, the best general statement about the microwaving of all types of products is that it is no more destructive than conventional cooking methods and in some cases is much less so.

This chapter's Nutrition for Living section lists several ways to minimize nutrient loss caused by food processing.

Nutrition for Living sections in many previous chapters have emphasized that the *kinds of food you eat*—chicken, tomatoes, chocolate cake, corn chips, broccoli, cheese, apples—determine the nutrients you get. There's no question about that.

But other factors also affect the levels of nutrients you ultimately get from food—*how the food was produced* and *what has happened to it from the time it or its ingredients were harvested until you consumed it.* Here we will summarize suggestions for dealing with the nutrition issues of greatest consumer concern: controlling fat, cholesterol, and sodium in the food you eat and maintaining its vitamin value.

- Practical suggestions for dealing with fat and cholesterol were given in the Nutrition for Living section in Chapter 7.
- If you want to lower your sodium intake, remember that processed foods are the major source; nutrition labels can help you determine how much is in a given product. Traditionally, canned soups and prepared entrees have been very high in sodium, but now many reduced-sodium products are available.
- If you are concerned about your sodium intake and you generally use a lot of salt and salty relishes and condiments, reduce the amounts you use. You may want to try the lower-sodium versions of these products.
- When in restaurants, ask about items that can be prepared without salt or salty condiments.
- To get the best vitamin value from food generally, use foods as soon as possible. During storage, keep them from becoming too warm, and protect them from loss of moisture. Frozen foods retain vitamins best at 0°F and below.
- Fresh fruits and vegetables provide their optimal vitamin values if kept cool and consumed within two days of harvest. After that, preserved versions may have higher levels of vitamins.
- When cooking vegetables, heat them for the shortest possible time in the least possible amount of water to retain vitamins and minerals. It may take a while to get used to tender-crisp vegetables; trying new recipes, such as stir-fried items, may help.
- Whole-grain products have higher nutritional value than refined grain products; enriched grain products are in between; and fortified cereals have variable micronutrient values. Grain products need to be kept dry during storage. When cooked, they should be cooked in just enough water and long enough for the water to be absorbed.
- Meats need to be kept cold during storage. Methods of cooking that do not involve water help retain micronutrients. Natural meat juices (minus the fat) contain nutrients and should be consumed.

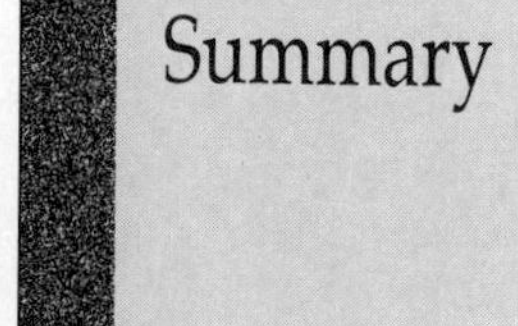

▶ Advances in agricultural and food processing technologies have led to a rapid expansion of the number of products available. The food industry is responsive to consumer interest in good taste, nutrition, affordable price, safety, storability, and convenience. More and more, it is becoming possible to create foods that have the characteristics we want.

▶ We can affect the nutritional properties of raw agricultural products to some degree. Animals are now fed in ways that yield leaner meats. Plants vary somewhat in certain vitamin and mineral values depending on environmental conditions and soil mineral content.

▶ Beyond the farm, food is subjected to various **food processing** methods designed to delay spoilage and to make food more safe, nutritious, palatable, and convenient. Among the processes used to preserve foods are **canning, blanching** and **freezing, pasteurization, high-temperature–short-term (HTST) processing, ultra-high temperature (UHT) sterilization, irradiation, controlled-atmosphere packaging,** and **freeze-drying,** as well as other methods of **dehydration.** Food preservation provides year-round access to a wide variety of foods thereby making better nutrition possible.

▶ However, every processing technique, whether done commercially or at home, inevitably causes some loss of micronutrients. Losses occur as a result of physical separation, heat, oxygen, light, certain conditions of pH, and the passage of time. Food preservation techniques control these factors and substantially slow down nutrient losses. Without preservation, a harvested "fresh" product might be nutritionally inferior to its commercially harvested and preserved counterpart within a couple of days. The vitamins most vulnerable to destruction are vitamin C and thiamin.

▶ Some foods *gain* nutrients during processing. In **fortification,** nutrients are deliberately added; **fermentation,** originally designed to preserve food, incidentally increases certain nutrients. Grains that have undergone **milling** and **refining** may later be **enriched** to restore the levels of thiamin, riboflavin, niacin, and iron that the whole grain had originally. Salt is often added to meet taste expectations; processed foods account for most of the salt in our diets, and eating large amounts of them may result in excessive intakes. Because there is increasing interest in less salty foods, some processors of lunchmeats, soups, canned vegetables, and frozen entree items have created new product lines with less salt.

▶ There are differences between the nutritional values of a fresh food and those of its various processed forms, and final preparation methods also cause different amounts of nutrient destruction; **steaming** and **pressure-cooking** cause the least nutrient losses. Nonetheless, by the time different process forms of a food have been prepared for the table, nutritional values are quite similar. Attention to home storage and preparation are important, since the largest nutritional losses can occur here.

▶ Food technologists have developed various **imitation foods,** which resemble traditional products but are made from different ingredients. They do not have the same nutrient values as the items they mimic. Nonetheless, imitation foods are not necessarily inferior products; each should be evaluated on its individual merits.

▶ New packaging techniques that help conserve nutrients may represent the next wave of changes in food processing. An example is the **flexible retort pouch,** which allows for greater nutrient retention and convenience over the metal can.

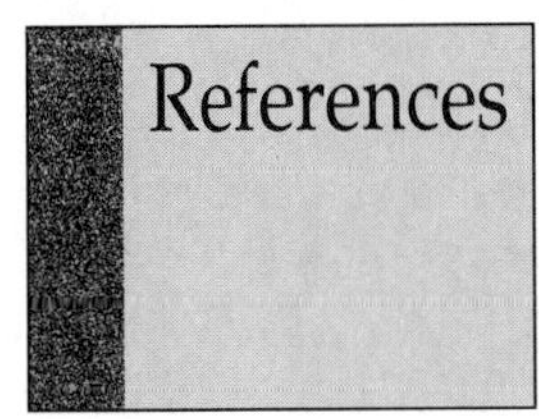

Adams, C.E. and J.W. Erdman, Jr. 1988. Effects of home food preparation practices on nutrient content of foods. In *Nutritional evaluation of food processing,* eds. E. Karmas and R.S. Harris. New York: Van Nostrand Reinhold Company.

Agricultural Research Service. 1977. *Conserving the nutritive values in foods.* Home and Garden Bulletin No. 90. Washington, DC: United States Department of Agriculture.

Bluestein, P.M. and T.P. LaBuza. 1988. Effects on moisture removal on nutrients. In *Nutritional evaluation of food processing,* eds. E. Karmas and R.S. Harris. New York: Van Nostrand Reinhold Company.

Byers, F.M., H.R. Cross, and G.T. Schelling. 1988. Integrated nutrition, genetics, and growth management programs for lean beef production. In *Designing foods.* Washington, DC: National Academy Press.

Committee on Diet and Health. 1989. *Diet and health: Implications for reducing chronic disease risk.* Washington, DC: National Academy Press.

Committee on Technological Options. 1988. *Designing foods.* Washington, DC: National Academy Press.

Dietz, J.M. and J.W. Erdman. 1989. Effects of thermal processing upon vitamins and proteins in foods. *Nutrition Today* 24:6–15.

Fennema, O. 1988. Effects of freeze preservation on nutrients. In *Nutritional evaluation of food processing,* eds. E. Karmas and R.S. Harris. New York: Van Nostrand Reinhold Company.

Food Marketing Institute. 1989. *Trends: Consumer attitudes and the supermarket 1989.* Washington, DC: Food Marketing Institute.

Francis, W. and M. Petrulis. 1988. Food processing and beverage industries: Moving toward concentration. *National Food Review* 11:23–27.

Gilbert, S.G. 1988. Stability of nutrients during storage of processed foods. In *Nutritional evaluation of food processing,* eds. E. Karmas and R.S. Harris. New York: Van Nostrand Reinhold Company.

Gorewit, R.C. 1988. Lactation biology and methods of increasing efficiency. In *Designing foods.* Washington, DC: National Academy Press.

Gyles, R. 1988. Technological options for improving the nutritional value of poultry products. In *Designing foods.* Washington, DC: National Academy Press.

IFT (Institute of Food Technologists' expert panel on food safety and nutrition). 1986. The effects of food processing on nutritive values: A scientific status summary. *Food Technology* 40:109–116.

Institute of Food Technologists. 1989. Microwave food processing. *Food Technology* 43:117–124.

Klein, B.P. 1989. Retention of nutrients in microwave-cooked foods. *Contemporary Nutrition* 14 No. 2.

Lund, D. 1988. Effects of heat processing on nutrients. In *Nutritional evaluation of food processing,* eds. E. Karmas and R.S. Harris. New York: Van Nostrand Reinhold Company.

Lund, D. 1989. Food processing: From art to engineering. *Food Technology* 43:242–247.

Mast, M.G. and C.S. Clouser. 1988. Processing options for improving the nutritional value of poultry meat and egg products. In *Designing foods.* Washington, DC: National Academy Press.

McFeeters, R.F. 1988. Effects of fermentation on the nutritional properties of food. In *Nutritional evaluation of food processing,* eds. E. Karmas and R.S. Harris. New York: Van Nostrand Reinhold Company.

Nagy, S. and W.F. Wardowski. 1988. Effects of agricultural practices, handling, processing, and storage on fruits. In *Nutritional evaluation of food processing,* eds. E. Karmas and R.S. Harris. New York: Van Nostrand Reinhold Company.

National Academy of Sciences. 1989. *Recommended dietary allowances,* 10th edition. Washington, DC: National Academy Press.

National Livestock and Meat Board. 1987. *Exploring meat and health.* Chicago: National Livestock and Meat Board.

Newsome, R.L. 1987. Perspective on food irradiation. *Food Technology* 41:100–101.

Ockerman, H.W. 1988. Effects of agricultural practices, handling, processing, and storage on meat. In *Nutritional evaluation of food processing,* eds. E. Karmas and R.S. Harris. New York: Van Nostrand Reinhold Company.

Rust, R.E. 1988. Processing options for improving the nutritional value of animal products. In *Designing foods.* Washington, DC: National Academy Press.

Salunkhe, D.K. and B.B. Desai. 1988. Effects of agricultural practices, handling, processing, and storage on vegetables. In *Nutritional evaluation of food processing,* eds. E. Karmas and R.S. Harris. New York: Van Nostrand Reinhold Company.

Savell, J.W. and H.R. Cross. 1988. The role of fat in the palatability of beef, pork, and lamb. In *Designing foods.* Washington, DC: National Academy Press.

Schutz, H.G., C.M. Bruhn, and K.V. Diaz-Knauf. 1989. Consumer attitude toward irradiated foods: Effects of labeling and benefits information. *Food Technology* 43:80–84.

Veblen, T.C. 1988. Food system trends and business strategy. *Food Technology* 42:126–130.

15

Beyond Nutrients: What Else Is in Your Food?

In This Chapter

- Toxicology Offers a Perspective on Harmful Substances in Food
- Microorganisms Are the Most Common Foodborne Problem
- Environmontal Contaminants Are Common but Not Always Harmful
- Naturally Occurring Substances Can Be Toxic
- Additives Pose Risk to Only a Small Number of People

In 1989 and 1990, food safety issues made headlines. People became alarmed about arsenic in Chilean grapes, Alar in apples, and benzene in Perrier water. As one food industry executive stated, "Food safety and food labeling are *the* issues of the 90's" (Boynton, 1990).

Many people feel a generalized anxiety about "the chemicals in our food." But as you know from preceding chapters, the essential nutrients themselves are chemicals, as are thousands of other naturally occurring substances that do not usually cause us harm.

Food safety issues have become big news. (© 1989 Newsweek, Inc. All rights reserved. Reprinted by permission)

There are also potentially harmful substances in foods. If we could produce two lists of chemicals—hazardous and safe—we could advise people to avoid the foods in which the harmful chemicals occur. Unfortunately, this is not possible. For one thing, we haven't yet identified all the substances in common foods. For another, now that laboratory equipment is sensitive enough to test for minute amounts of certain substances, scientists find trace amounts of these chemicals in almost everything they test. In other words, ensuring an absolute zero amount of a given chemical in food is probably unrealistic. We can detect 1 part per million, which is equivalent to 1 ounce in 32 tons of food; we can even detect 1 part per trillion, which is 1 drop in 10,000 gallons. Depending on the substance, such concentrations may be harm*less,* even if higher concentrations are harm*ful*. The question therefore, often is not "*Could* we experience problems from a given substance?" but "*At what level* might we experience problems?"

Potentially dangerous substances can enter food by various routes. Sometimes such chemicals occur naturally in plants as they grow; they might find their way into the food supply through manufacturing or packaging or they might be added to foods deliberately (in small amounts) to accomplish an important and useful purpose, such as preservation. In some instances it may be difficult to determine by what means—singly or in combination—a harmful amount of a substance gained entry; therefore, it may be difficult to know how to prevent it from happening again.

While food safety is not a particularly straightforward topic, it is an important one to address here, because we will be hearing much more about it in the future and because as consumers, we need to have enough scientific background to put food safety concerns into perspective. Let us emphasize from the start that many experts believe the food supply in North America to be generally the safest in the world. However, this does not mean it is risk-free or that it is even possible to be totally risk-free. In recent years, consumer groups and the media have chosen to focus on certain food safety issues. The questions that they raise call for explanations and sometimes changes on the part of regulatory agencies and the food production, processing, and service industries. Such questioning is beneficial because it ultimately strengthens the system and improves the food supply.

Another major purpose of this chapter is to explain what *you* need to do to keep your own food safe. The consumer is responsible for careful selection, storage, and preparation of food to ensure that it is safe to eat. A food that met standards for safety at the point of purchase can become unsafe with subsequent improper handling.

Toxicology Offers a Perspective on Harmful Substances in Food

Food toxicology is the science that establishes the basis for judgments about the safety of foodborne elements (Hall and Taylor, 1989). Toxicology includes detection of toxicants, identification of actions of toxicants, and the treatment of conditions they produce. The following are some terms commonly used in toxicological discussions:

food toxicology—the scientific study of harmful substances in food, including their detection and definition of action

- *safety*—a practical certainty that a substance will not cause injury
- *hazard*—the *probability* that injury will result from use of a substance, considering the dose and conditions of exposure
- *toxicity*—the capability of a substance to produce injury at some level of intake
- *toxicant, toxin, poison* (used almost synonymously)—a substance with the ability to cause harm
- *detoxification*—the process of converting a dangerous substance into a harmless one
- *mutagen*—a type of toxicant that causes a change in the cell's genetic material (These changes are called *mutations*.)
- *carcinogen*—a type of toxicant that stimulates a cell to multiply out of control, eventually resulting in cancer (Even if the risk of cancer is small—such as one case resulting per million exposures—a substance that has this effect is still called a carcinogen.)

A key concept is that *all substances are toxic at a certain level of intake, but most are not hazardous under normal conditions of use.* The types of problems that hazardous chemicals may cause range from such minor symptoms as a slight, short-term skin rash to permanent damage of the nervous system, kidneys, or liver.

Possible Relationships Between Dosage and Effect

Toxicologists view substances as having one of the four following effects:

- *no effect*—there is no negative effect at any practical level of intake
- *threshold effect*—the substance can be ingested without effect up to a certain amount; after that, negative effects increase with increasing amounts of intake
- *no threshold*—all levels of intake produce harm; the greater the intake, the greater the harm

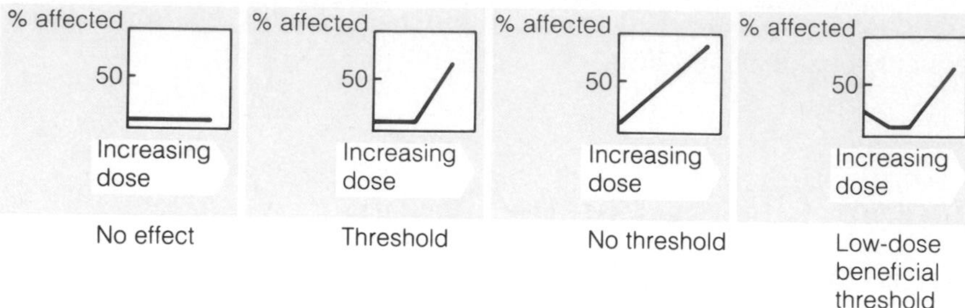

Figure 15.1 Possible forms of the dose-response curve. (Adapted from: Murphy, S.D. Toxicological assessment of food residues. Reprinted from *Food Technology*. 1979. 33[6]:35–42. Copyright © by the Institute of Food Technologists.)

- *low-dose beneficial threshold*—low levels of intake produce desirable effects; increasing levels eventually cause negative effects

dose-response curve—graph that shows the relationship between the dosage of a substance and its effect

Figure 15.1 illustrates these four possibilities, which are called **dose-response curves.**

Many nutrients have a low-dose beneficial threshold: vitamins and minerals that are essential for life at low levels of intake can be very toxic at higher levels. A large number of food toxicants are substances that show a threshold effect. For many chemicals, however, scientists do not know which curve best describes responses to a particular substance.

Testing for toxic effects is a complex issue, and results can be difficult to interpret. Scientists can feed or inject high doses of a substance and monitor acute effects, or they can feed low doses of the substance for years and monitor the gradual development of chronic effects. The advantages of the former types of trials is that clearly definable responses are generally noted more quickly, but these symptoms may be different than those induced in chronic feeding trials in which the bodies of the test animals have had time to adjust to the substance. Moreover, as already mentioned, substances can be essential or harmless at one level of intake and toxic at another. The advantage of the latter trials is that they resemble more closely the way people are usually exposed to substances in food; but chronic toxic effects are occasionally missed in these studies. Generally, scientists use a combination of both types of trials in several species of animals to try to define the toxicity of a substance.

Additional Factors That Influence Toxicity

In addition to the level of intake, a number of other factors influence the activity and effects of food toxicants.

Detoxification One reason that low levels of some toxicants cause no harm is that the body has a means of detoxifying small amounts of them. The liver is most directly involved in changing toxicants into harmless metabolites.

Time The liver is able to detoxify substances at only a limited rate. As an extreme example, we can safely ingest 10,000 mg of the toxicant solanine, which is present in the 120 pounds of potatoes the average American consumes annually, provided the consumption is spread out over a year. The same amount of solanine in one dose, on the other hand, would be enough to kill a horse.

Storage Toxicants that cannot be degraded easily by the body can slowly accumulate in the liver, bones, or adipose or other tissues over many years until eventually they are present in large enough amounts to cause serious problems. Cadmium and PCBs are examples of toxicants that the body stores.

Nutritional Status A person whose diet is deficient in either energy intake or specific nutrients (for instance, protein) has an impaired ability to deal with toxicants.

Growth and Body Size Rapid growth in children and during pregnancy can increase the body's absorption of some toxicants. Furthermore, when a given amount of toxin is ingested by two people of different body sizes, the toxin will have a greater effect on the smaller person because there is more toxin present per unit of body weight.

Interactions Among Substances The toxicities of individual substances are generally not additive; that is, if you ate $\frac{1}{100}$ of the lethal dose of each of 100 different toxic food components, the mixture would probably be harmless.

Some toxicants have **antagonists** that render the toxicants ineffective. For example, the presence of selenium in fish tends to decrease the potential toxicity of any mercury present. And the addition of calcium, iron, and other trace elements to the diet has been found to depress the absorption and therefore the toxicity of cadmium and lead.

antagonist—a substance that can render a substance inactive

There are also components of food that counteract the effect of cancer-causing substances. These are called **anticarcinogens;** one of the goals of current cancer research is to identify these chemicals and learn how they work. For example, foods of the cabbage family are believed to contain anticarcinogens. Also, vitamin A (at least carotene), vitamin C, and vitamin E have anticarcinogenic functions.

anticarcinogen—a compound in food that can counteract the effect of cancer-causing substances

Ranking of Food-Related Problems

A practical ranking of major food-related public health problems, based on the number of people affected by them, was suggested by a past director of the FDA's Bureau of Foods. Problems caused by microorganisms head the list, with environmental contaminants and naturally occurring food toxicants near the middle, and food additives—interestingly enough—at the bottom (Wodicka, 1977). Let's look at these factors in that order.

Microorganisms Are the Most Common Foodborne Problem

An expert panel of the Institute of Food Technologists (IFT) estimated that between 24 and 81 million cases of foodborne diarrheal disease occur each year in the United States, and that they cost between 5 and 17 billion dollars in medical treatment and lost productivity (IFT, 1988).

As high as these estimates seem, the true numbers are even higher; it is probable that only 10 to 15% of cases are reported. But when compared with the number of times people eat, even this incidence of illness is very low.

Foodborne bacteria can cause problems through either *infection* or *intoxication*.

Common Foodborne Infections

foodborne infection—illness produced by food containing large numbers of bacteria or viruses

gastroenteritis—inflammation of the stomach and intestines

If environmental conditions are favorable for their growth, bacteria can reproduce in food in large numbers, surpassing the threshold tolerated by most people. The resulting illnesses are called **foodborne infections.**

In the past, *Salmonella* was believed to be the most common cause of foodborne infection. However, *Campylobacter jejuni* causes even more **gastroenteritis** in the United States than *Salmonella* (Doyle, 1988). Other organisms implicated in foodborne infections are *Yersinia, Vibrio,* and even certain strains of *Escherichia coli (E. coli),* a bacterium that normally inhabits human GI tracts (Ryser and Marth, 1989).

These bacteria are fairly ubiquitous (widespread), occurring in human and animal intestines, skin, soil, and water. They thrive in any setting that provides essential nutrients (high-protein foods in particular); moisture; oxygen (or absence of oxygen, depending on their particular needs); and suitable temperature (especially 40–140° F).

All of these organisms produce GI distress in the form of nausea, vomiting, and diarrhea, anywhere from 12 hours to 5 days after ingestion (Ryser and Marth, 1989). The rapidity of onset of symptoms and their severity differ with the various bacteria and with the overall health of the victim. Although these illnesses tend to be short-term and are not usually severe, they occasionally cause death to a person already in weakened health.

The primary symptom of at least one foodborne infection, *Listeria monocytogenes,* is not GI distress but a systemic infection that leads to death in 30% of patients whose immune systems are not functioning normally and in fetuses that are infected (Lovett and Twedt, 1988). This means that it is of primary concern to people who are very ill (such as AIDS patients) and to pregnant women (for the sake of the fetus). It is not generally dangerous to healthy adults. One food to which a number of cases of this disease was traced was non-aged cheese made from unpasteurized milk.

Foodborne Intoxications

Some bacteria cause illnesses by producing *toxins.* These illnesses are called **foodborne bacterial intoxications.** *Staphylococcus aureus* is the most common cause of food intoxication. *Clostridium perfringens* frequently causes foodborne illness by both infection and intoxication. These organisms are most often found in cooked foods that were cross-contaminated with the bacteria from raw foods and then not stored properly. (For example, if you use the same cutting board to cut cooked potatoes for potato salad as you used earlier to cut raw chicken—without washing the board and knife thoroughly with detergent in between—you cross-contaminate the potato salad.) Both organisms cause abdominal pain and diarrhea; but *Staphylococcus* will also cause nausea and can cause symptoms more rapidly than other foodborne bacteria—anywhere from 30 minutes to 8 hours after ingestion (Newsome, 1988).

foodborne bacterial intoxication—illness produced by food containing bacterial toxins

One form of bacterial intoxication is particularly important because of its severity. The *Clostridium botulinum* organism, when it produces its toxin in food, may cause the sometimes fatal disease **botulism.** *C. botulinum* is found in soil and in the sediments of many freshwater lakes and rivers. The organism by itself is not hazardous: probably everybody has consumed it at one time or another without dire consequences. Problems occur when it is present in an environment where circumstances allow it to thrive: anaerobic conditions (no oxygen), the presence of low-acid foods, and room temperature. In time the bacteria, or their protected resting forms called spores, become active and produce the potentially deadly toxin. The affected food will not necessarily look or smell unusual, making the toxin impossible to detect.

botulism—an uncommon but sometimes fatal food intoxication

Low-acid canned foods that have been improperly processed are most often the cause of botulism. Foods with a pH higher than 4.6 are regarded as low-acid; Figure 15.2 shows the acidity of various foods. Products improperly canned at home are more often the source of this toxin than commercially canned foods.

A type of botulism can also occur in babies less than a year old. Unlike an adult's mature gastrointestinal tract, a baby's stomach or colon seems to provide the conditions that allow *C. botulinum* to produce toxins. Botulism in infants produces neurological distress; the condition is sometimes called the "limp baby disease." Although more than 500 cases have been reported, there have been very few deaths (Liska et al., 1986). The means by which babies get this disease is not known, but honey and corn syrup were believed to be the sources of *C. botulinum* spores in a couple of cases. Therefore, these sweeteners should not be given to infants.

Prevention Strategies

Just how much responsibility should be taken by industry or by the consumer for controlling the microorganisms in a particular food product is not

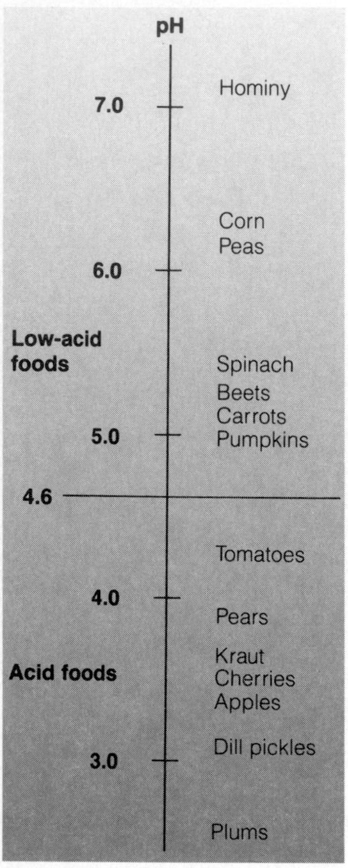

Figure 15.2 The pH values of various canned foods. Low-acid foods must be processed under pressure at temperatures greater than 212°F to ensure the destruction of *Clostridium botulinum*. (Reference: Leveille, G.A., and M.A. Uebersax. 1979. Fundamentals of food science for the dietitian: Thermal processing. *Dietetic Currents* 6(no.3). Columbus, OH: Ross Laboratories.)

always clear. Critical Thinking 15.1 serves as a basis for discussion of this issue. It is imperative, however, that the food industry and consumers share the responsibility for food safety. For both, the way to make food safe is to practice the "three Ks" in regard to microorganisms: *K*eep them out, *K*ill them if you can, and *K*eep them from growing.

Start with Clean Food Choose food that looks clean. Wash produce thoroughly. Foods that are good hosts for microbial growth should be well wrapped or packaged in closed containers at the time of purchase. Food cans should not show evidence of leaky seams or bulging ends. Eggs should not have cracks in them. Drink only pasteurized milk. Drinking raw (unpasteurized) milk—whether certified or uncertified—increases a person's risk of getting microbial infections. (Interestingly, some people who drink raw milk regularly appear to develop immunities to its pathogens [Blaser, Sazie, and Williams, 1987]. But why take such a risk when there are no proven advantages to drinking raw milk over pasteurized milk and when the benefits of pasteurization are well known?)

Cook Animal Products Adequately Raw meats, poultry, fish, and eggs should be cooked thoroughly before they are eaten, since the raw forms can harbor disease-causing microorganisms. Traditionally, consumers have been advised to cook pork to an internal temperature of 170°F so that parasites called *Trichina* that occasionally are found in muscles of swine are destroyed (Figure 15.3). This protects against the possibility of the painful disease *trichinosis*. Although trichinosis is rare today, this is good advice and still should be followed.

There is a much greater risk of getting sick from eating inadequately cooked chicken. In one study 23% of 862 raw chicken samples purchased from grocery stores tested positive for *Campylobacter jejuni* (Harris et al., 1986). Some officials estimate the percentage of chicken contaminated with this and other bacteria to be *much* higher. Chicken should be handled properly before cooking and then cooked thoroughly; refer to cookbooks for cooking times and temperatures.

In the past, the contents of uncracked eggs have been assumed to be sterile; therefore, it was regarded as safe to use them in foods and beverages that were not cooked, such as eggnog. Now it is known that eggs can be contaminated with *Salmonella* by the hen (St. Louis et al., 1988), and that it is risky to eat any uncooked (or less than thoroughly cooked) egg product. The risk is particularly high for people whose immune system function is compromised by already being ill or by being elderly.

The risks of eating raw or incompletely cooked seafood also have been highlighted in recent years. For example, in 1982 outbreaks of gastroenteritis associated with eating raw clams and oysters reached epidemic proportions in the state of New York—1017 people reported becoming ill with diarrhea and vomiting (Morse et al., 1986). A type of virus was believed to have caused these acute illnesses. When clams are cooked, care must be taken to heat them long enough (DuPont, 1986). The usual procedure—to steam them until the shells open—may be inadequate to inactivate viruses they contain. Most cookbooks don't take this new information into account.

Parasitic roundworms that can infect fish may cause chronic gastroenteritis in humans who eat raw fish (such as that in sushi and ceviche) or inadequately cooked fish. Freezing and holding fish at −10°F for seven days can make fish safe from these parasites (Jackson et al., 1990), but freezing does not prevent all the ills that can be associated with ingesting raw fish. For example, hepatitis has been contracted by people who ate raw oysters from polluted oyster beds.

Once you have properly cooked a food, *it is critically important to keep from recontaminating it.* Cooked food, with its low population of microorganisms, provides a medium in which newly introduced organisms can thrive without significant competition. To prevent this, thoroughly wash cutting boards, knives, blenders, and any other equipment that contacts food between uses. Plastic or glass cutting boards are easier to keep clean than are wooden cutting boards.

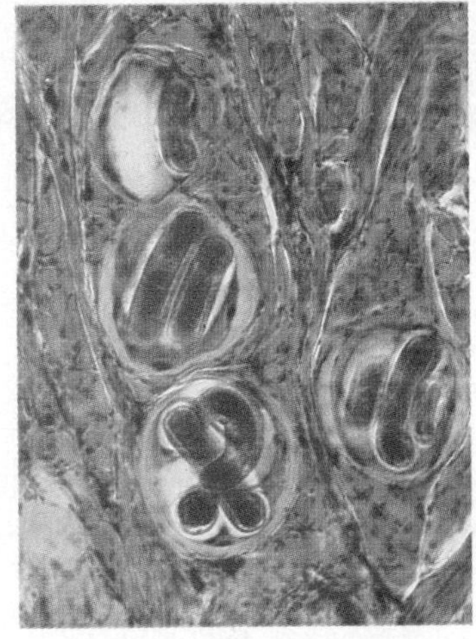

Figure 15.3 *Trichina.* The curled worms shown in this micrograph are the parasite *Trichinella spiralis* encysted in pig muscle. Cooking pork to 170°F destroys these parasites, should they be present. If they are alive when pork is ingested, they can result in the disease trichinosis.

Recontamination of food can also be caused by careless personal sanitation practices. When preparing food you need to wash your hands before handling food and after you have touched your clothes, face, hair, the baby, the dog, or anything else likely to carry organisms. Avoid sneezing and coughing onto food, and do not handle food if you have cuts or sores on your hands.

Keep Food Out of the Temperature Danger Zone The temperature range most conducive to the reproduction of microorganisms that cause foodborne illnesses is called the *danger zone.* The types of foods most likely to promote growth of microorganisms are those that are moist and high in protein. For storage and holding purposes, 40–140°F is the range to avoid. Figure 15.4 shows the effects of different temperatures on microorganisms.

Between preparation and consumption, food should be kept either hotter than 140°F or colder than 40°F. When cooling large amounts of cooked foods for cold storage, it is best to spread the food out in thin layers, which allows faster cooling. Of course, there are times when foods do sit out at room temperatures, such as when they are on the table during meals or are part of a buffet. If you have the right equipment, it is possible to maintain safe temperatures in these situations by using ice-lined bowls for cold food and warmers for hot food.

Most often, though, people do not use such precautions, and foods are exposed to danger zone temperatures for a while. It is impossible to know exactly how long they are safe to eat, but two hours has been suggested as a practical limit of safety for foods kept in the danger zone (Food Safety and Inspection Service, 1984). After that time, it is sensible to throw them away. Keep in mind the old adage, "When in doubt, throw it out."

The Slice of Life on page 509 gives an example of food poisoning caused by food left at room temperature.

Figure 15.4 Effects of temperature on microorganisms. (Adapted from Food Safety and Inspection Service. 1984. *The safe food book*. Home and Garden Bulletin No. 241. Washington, DC: United States Department of Agriculture.)

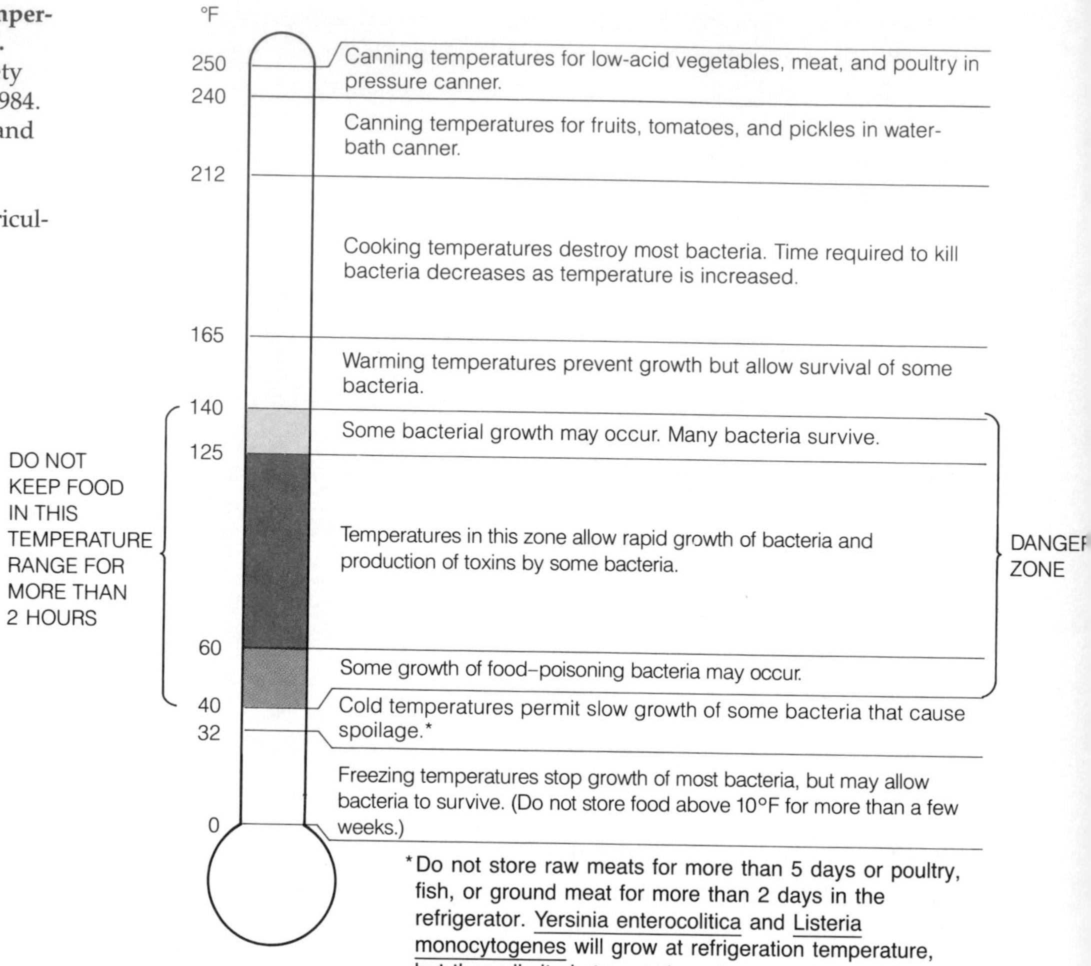

°F

250 — Canning temperatures for low-acid vegetables, meat, and poultry in pressure canner.

240 — Canning temperatures for fruits, tomatoes, and pickles in water-bath canner.

212 — Cooking temperatures destroy most bacteria. Time required to kill bacteria decreases as temperature is increased.

165 — Warming temperatures prevent growth but allow survival of some bacteria.

140 — Some bacterial growth may occur. Many bacteria survive.

125 — Temperatures in this zone allow rapid growth of bacteria and production of toxins by some bacteria.

60 — Some growth of food–poisoning bacteria may occur.

40 — Cold temperatures permit slow growth of some bacteria that cause spoilage.*

32 — Freezing temperatures stop growth of most bacteria, but may allow bacteria to survive. (Do not store food above 10°F for more than a few weeks.)

0

DO NOT KEEP FOOD IN THIS TEMPERATURE RANGE FOR MORE THAN 2 HOURS (40–140°F)

DANGER ZONE (40–140°F)

*Do not store raw meats for more than 5 days or poultry, fish, or ground meat for more than 2 days in the refrigerator. *Yersinia enterocolitica* and *Listeria monocytogenes* will grow at refrigeration temperature, but these limited storage times have not generally been associated with problems.

Foods in the danger zone. Microorganisms multiply very rapidly in moist, high-protein foods at environmental temperatures. After two hours, food that has not been refrigerated or maintained at over 140°F should be discarded.

Follow Canning Instructions to the Letter If you are canning foods at home, be sure to use methods recommended in the brochures published by the United States Department of Agriculture. This is particularly important for protection against botulism. Such brochures are available through the Cooperative Extension system in your state. If you have information from a previous year, check to be sure that it is still current; important changes are made in the instructions from time to time. It is critical to use the right method for each product you are preserving. Recommended substances to add to the product, processing times, and whether to heat in boiling water or in a pressure cooker may seem like picky details, but they may literally make the difference between life and death.

This section has emphasized the harm that can be caused by some bacteria present in food. It is only fair to point out that certain microorganisms

Slice of Life

An Easter Egg Hunt That Led to the Hospital

The fun and excitement of an Easter egg hunt turned into a day of gastrointestinal misery for almost 300 children who developed food poisoning from eating the festive hard-boiled eggs (Merrill et al., 1984).

A neighborhood church invited area children to an Easter egg hunt. Three to five days before the hunt, a cook boiled and dyed numerous batches of eggs and rinsed them in cold water. While most were still warm, he removed them from the water and left them unrefrigerated in the church kitchen.

The day of the hunt, the eggs were hidden on the church grounds, and approximately 850 children turned out to retrieve them. Many eggs were eaten at the hunt or on the way home.

Several hours later, children began showing up at local hospital emergency rooms with severe gastrointestinal symptoms. Some required intravenous fluids and electrolyte replacement. Although most children did not get so sick that they went to the hospital, an estimated one-third of the children who attended the hunt experienced some GI symptoms from eating the eggs.

County health department officials, on learning of the outbreak from an emergency room physician, began their sleuthing. Their investigation revealed that *Staphylococcus aureus* organisms were present in the eggs; the same type of bacteria were cultured from various sites on the cook's body.

Apparently, staphylococcus organisms from the cook got into the rinse water and through the shells of the cooked eggs. With the hospitable environment of a nutritious food supply and room temperatures, the organisms thrived and multiplied. By the time the children ate the eggs, they were heavily populated with the bacteria and their toxin.

It is advised that immediately after hard-boiling eggs for later consumption, you should run cold water over them and refrigerate them until they are eaten. We should seriously consider substituting plastic or wooden eggs for the real thing during the hunt. Don't give the Easter bunny—or yourself—a bad name by taking an avoidable risk.

can also play a positive role and are deliberately and safely added during processing. Bacteria are used to make yogurt, some cheeses, vinegar, and wine; yeast is used to make beer; and specific molds are cultured on certain varieties of cheese. Keep in mind, though, the important difference in safety: the time-tested, deliberate use of microorganisms in food processing is likely to be safe, but random or accidental introduction of microorganisms into food is more likely to create hazards.

Food Safety of Poultry: Whose Job?

The situation

The *Washington Post* of May 2, 1990, carried an article entitled "FDA Approves Irradiation of Poultry." Here are excerpts from the article:

> The Food and Drug Administration yesterday approved the use of irradiation to control salmonella and other bacteria in fresh and frozen poultry products. This is the first time the process has been approved in this country to control bacteria that cause illness in humans.
>
> According to the Centers for Disease Control (CDC), there are approximately 40,000 reported cases of salmonella poisoning a year. But since most foodborne disease outbreaks are not reported, the CDC estimates the actual number of annual cases could be anywhere from 400,000 to 4 million.
>
> . . . The poultry industry is not anxious to use the technology. "It amounts to consumer acceptance. At least at this time we do not have a sense that there's wide consumer demand for irradiated foods of any kind," said Stephen Pretanik, director of science and technology for the National Broiler Council.

In short, irradiation can now be used to lower the risk of a disease that has become an increasing problem; yet, the industry hesitates, because it fears loss of business in reaction to the process.

What action would you, the consumer, like to see taken?

Is the information accurate and relevant?

- It is true that the FDA approval of irradiation for poultry is the first attempt at reducing risk from bacteria; however in 1985, irradiation was approved for control of another pathogen, the *Trichina* worm, in pork. It has also been approved for selected other purposes of food safety and pest control.
- It is true that reported *Salmonella* infections have reached 40,000 cases per year and have been increasing at a rapid rate; unreported cases are probably many times higher.
- It is likely that the increase in the use of poultry is part of the reason for the increase in *Salmonella* infections; however, there may be other reasons, such as an increase in the use of delicatessen foods, or inadequate cooking or handling of food in restaurants or at home.
- There is evidence that some consumers reject the idea of eating food that has been irradiated; New York, New Jersey, and Maine have banned the sale of irradiated foods.

Environmental Contaminants Are Common but Not Always Harmful

Environmental contaminants can enter food from cookware and other food containers; vehicular wastes such as auto exhaust; industrial products and wastes; and agricultural wastes and products such as fertilizers, pesticides, and antibiotics.

What else needs to be considered?

Salmonella organisms are present on much raw poultry. Estimates range from one-third of poultry purchased to virtually all raw poultry. Current mass-production and processing methods are thought to contribute to the spread of contamination in poultry processing plants. Changing these processing methods would cost a great deal of money, and this cost would ultimately be borne by consumers.

Irradiation of foods is a process that has been approved by 33 countries around the world and is used more extensively in many countries than it is in the United States. Irradiation of food does not make food radioactive; the major scientific question that is raised about the process is whether other potentially dangerous chemical compounds might be formed in the food as a result of irradiation. (See Chapter 14 for more information on irradiation as a food preservation technique.)

Proponents of irradiation point out that traditional processes such as canning also produce some of these same chemical substances and that irradiation produces similar amounts. Furthermore, some of these chemicals also *occur naturally* in foods. Since the doses of irradiation approved for poultry are lower than are approved for some other applications, they are less likely to lead to the production of these chemical substances.

Because of the low levels of irradiation that have been approved, the number of *Salmonella* organisms on poultry would be reduced but not eliminated. With *Salmonella* organisms still present, proper refrigeration and cooking of poultry would still be critical in order to ensure a safe product. *Salmonella* organisms are destroyed when poultry is cooked to an internal temperature of 185°F.

What do you think?

There are a number of possibilities of how the concern about *Salmonella* infection from poultry could be addressed. Taking all of the above points into consideration, what do you think is the best action to take?

- Option 1 You decide that low dose irradiation of poultry at the processing plant as approved by the FDA is the best action to take; it offers a good cost/benefit ratio.
- Option 2 You decide that the poultry industry should change to smaller operations with slower production lines and more inspection to reduce contamination, despite higher costs to the consumer.
- Option 3 You decide that since *Salmonella* are killed by adequate cooking, uncooked poultry in the retail market should be labeled with instructions for safe cooking.
- Option 4 You decide to urge the expansion of relevant educational programs of the Cooperative Extension service and other agencies that teach consumers about safe food handling and preparation.
- Option 5 You decide that the status quo is satisfactory.

Do you see other options or combinations of options? Which makes the most sense to you?

Environmental contaminants vary greatly in their composition. Minerals, organic compounds, and even radioactivity can all contaminate the food supplies of people and animals, but only a relatively small number of these contaminants ever enter the food and water supply in sufficient quantities to be of practical significance.

Mineral Contaminants

Minerals such as lead, aluminum, tin, and iron can migrate into foods in varying amounts from food preparation equipment and metal storage containers. More minerals are leached if foods are liquid and acidic and stored for long periods in metal containers. Minerals can also gain entry from the larger environment, such as the air, soil, or industrial wastes. Diverse routes of entry can make it difficult to control the levels of these substances in food.

Lead Lead can cause anemia, kidney disease, and damage to the nervous system. There is particular concern about the exposure of children to lead because they absorb a higher percentage of the lead they ingest than adults do. The effects of exposure to low levels of lead in childhood persist into young adulthood. Children exposed to low (but nonetheless excessive) levels of lead have a greater incidence of reading disabilities, lower class standing in high school, and poorer eye-hand coordination as young adults (Needleman et al., 1990).

Data on lead levels in children from a recent Health and Nutrition Examination Survey (HANES—a major study of nutritional status in the United States) are shown in Table 15.1. A significant number of black children, especially from low-income urban homes, had high enough levels of lead in

Table 15.1 Percent of American Children with Elevated Lead Levels in Blood

	% of Children	
	White	Black
Annual Family Income		
Under $6,000	5.9	18.5
$6,000–14,999	2.2	12.1
$15,000 or more	0.7	2.8
Degree of Urbanization of Place of Residence		
Urban, 1 million persons or more		
Central city	4.5	18.6
Non-central city	3.8	3.3
Urban, fewer than 1 million persons	1.6	10.2
Rural	1.2	10.3

This table gives the percentage of children ages 6 months to 5 years who have blood lead levels of 30 micrograms or more per 100 ml (1976–1980). Adapted from Annest, J.L., K.R. Mahaffey, D.H. Cox, and J. Roberts, 1982. Blood lead levels for persons 6 months–74 years of age: United States, 1976–80. NCHS Advance Data 79:1–24.

their blood that medical treatment was advisable. Experts currently consider 25 micrograms of lead per 100 ml of blood to be the amount that indicates excessive exposure, but infants with little more than 10 μg of lead per 100 ml of cord blood (from the umbilical cord at birth) were found to have permanent mental impairment. Mental development index scores for these children at 12 months and 24 months of age were below average, even though their lead levels were then below 10 μg per 100 ml of blood (Bellinger et al., 1987). Where did this lead come from?

Lead can get into soil and water from such sources as paint chips from buildings being demolished, solid waste sludges used as fertilizers, and the airborne products of fuel combustion. The exhaust from vehicles requiring leaded gasoline also contributes lead to the air. Contaminants in soil, water, and air can, in turn, accumulate in food.

Many children, especially those living in old, low-income areas, are believed to ingest lead by chewing paint chipped from walls. (Indoor paint sold in the United States no longer contains lead.) Of course, prevention of pica would be the best strategy, but adequate nutrition helps somewhat: sufficient calcium intake reduces the amount of lead absorbed (Mahaffey et al., 1986).

Another way lead can get into food is via food containers. Some historians have suggested that toxicity caused by lead leaching from lead-lined cooking pots, wine goblets, and water pipes may have contributed to the decline of the Roman Empire. A more likely modern source of lead is from glazed pottery. FDA regulations prevent the sale in the United States of ceramicware that can leach significant amounts of lead into food; if you are shopping for pottery or ceramicware in another country, you need to determine whether the dishes have been glazed with products containing lead. If in doubt, use such tourist treasures for decoration—never as food or beverage containers.

Currently, containers of foods commercially processed in the United States add very little lead to food. In the 1970s, the FDA encouraged the food industry to make the following changes that ultimately resulted in cutting the lead levels in common adult foods almost in half, putting them within the safe range for intake. Food processors reduced the amount of solder used by rolling seams instead of soldering them, by developing a can with no side seam, and by packaging more foods in glass. All baby foods, except for infant formulas, are now sold in glass containers. People who make their own baby food are advised to avoid making it from ordinary canned food.

Drinking water can contain lead if the pipes or solder with which they were joined contain lead; building codes in many jurisdictions are being modified to prevent this problem. The Critical Thinking in Chapter 4 (on water) discusses lead and other contaminants in drinking water.

Aluminum Some people have become concerned that ingestion of aluminum will lead to neurological damage. At this time, researchers believe that levels of aluminum commonly present in the diet do not have adverse effects on people who are healthy. There are several ways aluminum may become part of food. Aluminum is one of the most common elements in the earth's crust, and it is therefore naturally present in plant foods. Although some aluminum enters the diet as a component of additives in certain processed cheeses and some baked goods, people who routinely take aluminum-containing medications can consume 100 times more aluminum than can be obtained through food. Aluminum-containing drugs, for example antacids, have been found to affect nervous function in some people with kidney failure (Greger, 1987).

Last on the list of contributors to aluminum intake are cooking implements and foil. Only a very small amount of the aluminum estimated to be in the average adult American diet can be attributed to aluminum cookware or aluminum foil (Greger, 1987).

Tin The main source of dietary tin is the coating on "tin" cans (which are really mainly steel). The tin content of foods increases dramatically if cans are opened and the foods are stored in them in the refrigerator (Greger, 1987). Ingestion of this excess tin may depress absorption of essential minerals, such as zinc and copper. For this reason, it is a good idea to remove any unused food from its can and store it in a glass or plastic container. If cans are lacquered or polymer-coated, however, only barely detectable levels of tin leach into food.

Iron Iron may also get into food from cans and kettles. Since this nutrient is low in many people's diets, there is generally little reason to worry about increased intake from this source. In fact, some nutritionists promote the practice of cooking in iron cookware as a means of increasing iron intake; but since iron from this source is believed to be very poorly utilized (Hallberg et al., 1983), we do not predict much nutritional benefit from this practice.

Mercury The burning of fossil fuel and the production of compounds including industrial chemicals, electrical apparatus, dental preparations, pharmaceuticals, and paper can add considerable amounts of mercury to the environment. There are government standards that limit the exposure of industrial workers and the general population to mercury. This has not always been the case; the phrase "mad as a hatter" is derived from the symptoms exhibited by hat makers who treated furs with mercury during the 1700s and 1800s.

Fortunately, very little industrial mercury waste enters the food supply; but problems can occur if microorganisms in soil and water add organic compounds to inorganic mercury. This produces an organic form known as **methyl mercury,** which is much better absorbed by and more toxic to biological systems (Tollefson and Cordle, 1986). The ingestion of methyl mercury in toxic quantities can cause progressive loss of coordination, vision, and hearing; mental deterioration; and death. Infants born to mothers who ingested large amounts of methyl mercury during pregnancy suffer from a variety of neurological disorders. One of the most publicized outbreaks occurred several decades ago in Japan among the people living near Minamata Bay (Figure 15.5).

methyl mercury—an organic form of mercury, highly toxic to biological systems

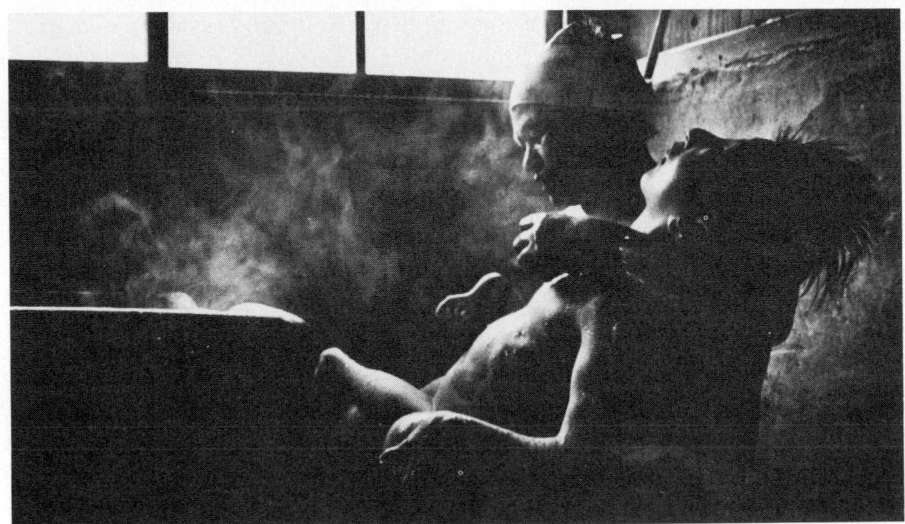

Figure 15.5 The effects of methyl mercury intoxication. The woman in this photograph ate fish contaminated with methyl mercury from Minamata Bay, Japan, when she was pregnant with her daughter; the girl is severely and permanently handicapped as a result.

Cadmium Cadmium enters the environment through its use in the manufacture of batteries, plastics, and paints. It is a common contaminant of phosphate fertilizers and sewage sludge. Cigarette smoke can be a major source of cadmium for some individuals.

Most foodstuffs contain little cadmium naturally (Kostial, 1986). However, oysters and other seafood, especially those grown in industrially contaminated water, can contain very high levels of cadmium. Some vegetable crops can also accumulate cadmium when grown in soil to which sewage sludge has been heavily applied.

Ingested cadmium damages the kidneys and reproductive organs and interferes with absorption of essential elements, such as zinc and iron (Kostial, 1986). In laboratory animals, it causes hypertension, but it is not known whether the same effect occurs in humans.

Organic Contaminants

Agricultural and other industrial technologies add many different organic contaminants to the food supply. Some can be toxic in certain situations.

Antibiotics In addition to their use in treating human infections, antibiotics are used to treat animal infections and to increase the weight gain of food-producing animals. This makes it possible to produce greater quantities of meats and eggs at lower cost.

There is some concern that antibiotic residues may remain in animal tissues and cause allergic or other adverse reactions. The USDA, particularly the Food Safety and Inspection Service (FSIS), conducts more than $1\frac{1}{2}$ million analyses annually to check for residues of antibiotics and pesticides in meats, poultry, and eggs. Less than 1% of tests show excessive levels; the limits generally provide a 100- to 1000-fold safety margin, according to USDA officials (Russell, 1990).

A more far-reaching concern is the buildup of antibiotic-resistant bacteria—*Salmonella* for example—in the intestinal tracts of humans. It is likely that the fairly indiscriminate use of antibiotics in treatment of patients and livestock is a more important contributor to resistant strains of bacteria than the inclusion of low levels of antibiotics in animal feedstuffs (DuPont and Steele, 1987). This practice needs to be studied more thoroughly and will continue to be a source of controversy.

Hormones A variety of hormones are naturally present in animal and plant tissues. As mentioned in earlier chapters, bovine somatotropin (BST) or bovine growth hormone (BGH), is a naturally occurring hormone that increases milk production. Scientists using biotechnology have developed ways to commercially manufacture large quantities of this hormone by splicing the gene for BST into bacteria; cows injected with the synthetic BST produce more milk, without any detectable increase in the levels of BST in the resulting milk (Sun, 1989).

Some consumers and activists have not been reassured by the available data; they wonder whether synthetic hormones, if present in milk, could cause harm to humans. In addition, farmers facing already surplus milk production doubt its economic value, and questions remain on its long-term effects on cows. (Chapter 9 mentions some other considerations.) Therefore in 1989 and 1990, several state legislatures restricted the use or sale of milk produced in this way. The future use of milk from BST-injected cows appears questionable even though in 1990, the FDA reported it to be safe.

Pesticides The need to produce sufficient food for a growing world population has led to increased global use of pesticides. Worldwide sales increased almost fivefold between 1970 and 1980 (Table 15.2). Pesticides (including insecticides, herbicides, fungicides, and rodenticides) vary greatly in their chemical structure, their mode of action, the manner in which they are applied, and their potential toxicity to humans.

There are many things to consider when evaluating the effects of these products on the public's health. The amount of residues that remain in food as consumed is important; these residues can be due to direct application of

Table 15.2 World Agrochemical Market

	1970	1980	(estimated) 1990
Total Expenditure ($U.S. billion)	2.7	11.6	18.5
Percentage of Total Expenditure			
Insecticides	37	35	33
Herbicides	35	41	39
Fungicides	22	19	21
Other	6	5	7

Adapted from Lotti, 1987. Production and use of pesticides. In: *Toxicology of Pesticides*, eds L.G. Costa, C.W. Galli, and S.D. Murphy. Berlin: Springer-Verlag.

pesticides to growing plants and animals or can be due to environmental contamination resulting from previous applications. The effect of pesticides also depends on the ability of animals to absorb, excrete, and/or detoxify the pesticides, and on the breakdown products and metabolites that remain in the body (Coats, 1987). In large doses, some pesticides are neurotoxins; other pesticides or impurities within them have been demonstrated to be carcinogens or **teratogens** (capable of inducing abnormalities in the fetuses of dosed animals).

teratogen—an agent or factor (such as industrial chemicals, drugs, radiation, excessive level of a nutrient, or disease) that causes a physical defect in an embryo

Consumers are generally not exposed to large doses of pesticides; often the amounts in food are barely detectable. But if a pesticide accumulates over time in body tissues, gradual effects may occur in behavior or immune function. In other cases, threshold doses of toxins are never reached. Extensive testing is needed to evaluate each pesticide.

In order to compare the risks of various substances, scientists have proposed a variety of toxicity indices. Bruce Ames, a well-known cancer researcher, and his associates have developed HERP scores; HERP is the acronym for *h*uman *e*xposure dose/*r*odent *p*otency dose. These scores express the human daily lifetime dose per kilogram if body weight as a percentage of the dose that induces tumors in half of the animals tested. Table 15.3 gives HERP scores for a number of substances; it suggests that the risks from commonly used pesticides at doses generally used are very small. In fact, compounds naturally present in foods are much more potentially carcinogenic (Ames and Gold, 1989).

It is important to be aware that plants and animals naturally produce compounds that act as pesticides to aid in their survival. Experts have estimated that 99.99% of the pesticides we consume have been naturally produced, not added by farmers and food processors (Ames and Gold, 1989).

Another important point is that the use of some pesticides or spoilage inhibitors may reduce the need for others. For example, Alar is a growth regulator that delays ripening of apples so that they do not drop prematurely and overripen in storage. The use of Alar is being phased out because it has been determined to be unacceptably carcinogenic. However, the use of Alar also made apples less susceptible to molds that are much more carcinogenic than is the Alar. Another substance or storage method will need to be developed to protect against the danger of the mold. Critical Thinking 15.2 on page 522 looks at some of the factors involved in the Alar issue.

Our concerns about pesticide toxicity change as new data become available. For example, ethylene dibromide (EDB) is a compound that was used in the United States to control insect infestation in stored grain and citrus fruit (Sun, 1984). After forty years of use, however, new information caused the status of this additive to be changed. Originally this compound was assumed to dissipate quickly after application, making it completely safe for use; later evidence showed that residues last for many months in agricultural products and foods made from them and that the residues may be carcinogenic. Beginning in 1984, the federal government began to change regulations governing EDB use. In this issue as in so many others, scientific judgment, political considerations, and consumer responses together have played roles in determining the new regulations; several states created more stringent regulations than the federal government finally settled on. Note in Table 15.3 that the risk from consuming EDB in food is small; but risk to people being exposed to large amounts of the compound in an industrial setting is very great if adequate precautions are not taken.

polychlorinated biphenyls (PCBs)—types of industrial compounds, some of which have entered the food supply by accident; are of concern because they may accumulate in biological tissues over time

Other Organic Contaminants Extensive use has been made of **Polychlorinated biphenyls (PCBs)** and related compounds for a variety of industrial purposes. Through improper disposal and accidents, many of these compounds have entered the food chain. Fish—especially sport fish—serve as

Table 15.3 Ranking of Possible Carcinogenic Hazards: The HERP Index.

The *H*uman *E*xposure/*R*odent *P*otency index is calculated as human exposure (daily lifetime dose per kg body weight) as a percent of the dose found to induce tumors in half of the rodents tested.

Possible Hazard: HERP %	Daily Human Exposure	Potential Carcinogen
Environmental pollution		
0.0008	Swimming pool, 1 hour (for child)	Chloroform
0.6 0.004	Conventional home air (14 hr/day)	Formaldehyde Benzene
2.1	Mobile home air (14 hr/day)	Formaldehyde
Pesticides and other residues in food		
0.0002	PCBs: daily dietary intake	PCBs
0.0003	DDT and related compounds: daily dietary intake	DDT
0.0004	EDB: daily dietary intake (from grain products)	Ethylene dibromide
0.0017	Alar from 6 oz. apple juice per day	Breakdown product of Alar
Natural dietary toxicants		
0.0003 0.0006	Bacon, cooked (100 g)	Dimethylnitrosamine Diethylnitrosamine
0.03	Peanut butter (one sandwich)	Aflatoxin
0.1	Mushroom (one raw)	Hydrazines
2.8	Beer (12 ounces)	Ethyl alcohol
Food additives		
0.06	Diet cola (12 ounces)	Saccharin
Drugs		
16	Phenobarbital, one sleeping pill	Phenobarbital
Occupational exposure		
5.8	Formaldehyde workers' average daily exposure	Formaldehyde
140	EDB workers' daily exposure	Ethylene dibromide

Adapted from: Ames et al., 1987. Ranking possible carcinogenic hazards. *Science*, 236:271–280. Additional reference: Ames and Gold, 1989. Pesticides, risk and applesauce. *Science*, 236:755–757.

an example. Being high on the ecological food chain, they pick up high levels of PCBs if they live in polluted water. Although PCBs are no longer manufactured in the United States, they continue to be a problem because they do not degrade easily (Sawheny and Itankin, 1985). (DDT, a highly effective pesticide, is another example of a chlorinated compound that has been banned but still occurs in the environment. Its persistence is due to its slow rate of degradation [i.e., its long *half-life*] and its continued use overseas; some DDT enters the United States in imported products.)

PCBs are not only persistent in the environment, but they also accumulate in body fat and are not easily excreted, except in breast milk (Jacobson et al., 1989). Therefore, many federal and state agencies monitor fish and the lakes from which they come (particularly the Great Lakes) for PCB contamination and then advise citizens of the degree of risk (Foran et al., 1989). Pregnant women who have routinely consumed fish caught in PCB-polluted waters are advised to plan to feed commercial formula to their infants rather than breast milk.

The effects of chlorinated compounds are many. Some are toxic to the liver and can thereby adversely affect the metabolism of some nutrients, drugs, and other toxicants. PCBs and related compounds have also been found to produce skin lesions and to adversely affect animals' nervous systems and immune systems, potentially making them more susceptible to carcinogens.

Radioactivity

More than 40 naturally occurring kinds of radioactive atoms have been identified in rocks and soil; many occur in the cells of plants and animals as well. We are all also exposed to cosmic radiation.

There are now sources of radioactivity other than nature. Fallout from tests of nuclear weapons, mining of certain ores, nuclear fuel processing, reactor installations, and applications of radioisotopes in medicine, industry, and agriculture can also add radioactivity to the environment. Figure 15.6 shows relative exposure from natural and other sources of radiation.

The nuclear accident at Chernobyl in the USSR in 1986 demonstrated that accidents at nuclear power plants greatly increase the radioactivity in foods over a wide region (Ansbaugh et al., 1988). Experts estimate that radiation-induced cancer mortality rates will increase 0.02% in excess over natural occurrence in the USSR and will increase 0.01% in the rest of Europe because of this accident.

Naturally Occurring Substances Can Be Toxic

Among the myriad of natural chemicals present in almost any foodstuff there are potentially toxic substances, as is suggested in Table 15.3. Because

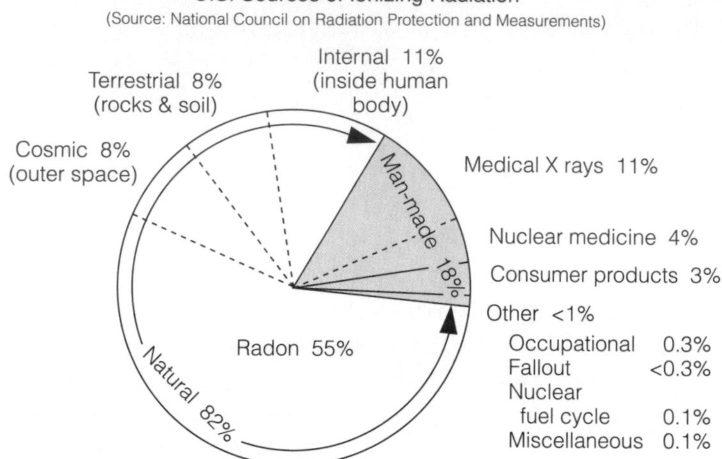

Figure 15.6 Where radiation risk begins. Most of the radiation hazard, as far as public health is concerned, comes from natural sources such as radon. (Figure reproduced from Marshall, 1990.)

people usually consume only low levels of these substances, however, they are not generally regarded as a problem.

Even so, there are certain situations in which injury can be caused by ingestion of compounds that occur naturally in plant and animal materials. Injuries can occur if toxicant-containing foods are consumed in abnormally large quantities; if foods contaminated with highly toxic substances from fungi or algae are consumed; if food look-alikes containing highly toxic substances are consumed; and if toxicants are consumed by individuals who are unusually sensitive to their effects.

Consumption of Abnormally Large Quantities of Natural Toxicants

If people eat large amounts of a single food (especially if they eat less of other foods at the same time), they may experience effects from naturally occurring toxicants. This can happen if individuals deliberately emphasize just a few foods in their diets, or it can occur in large numbers of people during a famine, when minor foodstuffs may of necessity become major dietary components. Certain naturally occurring toxicants have caused problems at times, but there are often ways to avoid such problems, as the rest of this section explains.

methylxanthines—group of compounds that occur naturally in many plant species, with coffee, tea, and cola beverages being common sources

Caffeine and Related Compounds Caffeine, theophylline, and theobromine are members of a group of compounds known as **methylxanthines.** They occur naturally in about 63 species of plants. Products containing these compounds are used daily in almost all cultures worldwide. The most common sources of these compounds are coffee, tea, chocolate, cola beverages, and a variety of over-the-counter prescription drugs. Caffeine has been the most thoroughly studied of these compounds. Table 15.4 indicates the amounts of caffeine in many commonly used substances.

Caffeine is a drug. It is well documented that low doses of it enhance alertness and increase the amount of time it takes for a person to fall asleep.

Table 15.4 Caffeine Content of Selected Food Products

Product	Amount	Range (mg)	Average (mg)
Roasted and ground coffee (percolated)	5 ounces	39–168	74
Roasted and ground coffee (drip)	5 ounces	56–176	112
Instant coffee	5 ounces	29–117	66
Roasted and ground coffee, decaffeinated	5 ounces	1–8	2
Instant coffee, decaffeinated	5 ounces	2–8	3
Tea	5 ounces	8–91	27
Instant tea	5 ounces	24–31	28
Cocoa	5 ounces	2–7	4
Milk chocolate	1 ounce	1–15	6
Chocolate milk	8 ounces	2–7	5
Baking chocolate	1 ounce	18–118	60
Soft drinks	12 ounces		
Regular colas		30–46	—
Decaffeinated colas		trace	
Diet colas		2–58	—
Decaffeinated diet colas, orange, lemon-lime, root beer, tonic, ginger ale, club soda		0–trace	

Adapted from Roberts, H. R., and J. J. Barone. Caffeine content of food products. Reprinted from *Food Technology*. 1983. 37(9):32–39. Copyright © by Institute of Food Technologists

Some studies in the 1970s indicated that caffeine can also aid performance in prolonged, exhaustive exercise, but research in the 1980s found that caffeine did not improve performance by well-trained marathoners during treadmill running (Casal and Leon, 1985).

The average adult American consumes 3 mg of caffeine per kilogram of body weight daily (Roberts and Barone, 1983). (A 150-pound person who consumes two to three cups of coffee per day gets approximately this amount.) Doses at this level (3–5 mg/kg/day) can produce mild anxiety, respiratory stimulation, cardiovascular effects, diuresis (increased urine production), and increased gastric secretions. But you can develop a tolerance to methylxanthines if you consume them consistently over a period of time. Long-term intake of more than 600 mg per day may lead to chronic insomnia, persistent anxiety, paranoia, depression, and stomach upset.

The results of studies on the role of caffeine or coffee as risk factors for cardiovascular disease are inconsistent. Caffeine causes blood pressure to rise slightly; but most people develop a tolerance to continued ingestion of caffeine, and blood pressure then returns to baseline (Myers, 1988). Several investigators have reported an association between coffee consumption and blood cholesterol levels, although they do not find the same association with tea or cola (Davis et al., 1988).

Studies attempting to link coffee consumption and cancer have also yielded mixed results. One study found an association between coffee

How Should Carcinogenic Agricultural Chemicals Be Regulated?

The situation

On May 6, 1989, National Public Radio (NPR) aired a feature about a proposal to ban the agricultural chemical Alar. The following are excerpts from that program. Scott Simon was the NPR reporter; participants were William Jordan, Chief of the Policy and Special Projects Staff in the Office of Pesticide Programs at the Environmental Protection Agency (EPA), and Janet Hathaway, a Senior Program Attorney with the Natural Resources Defense Council.

> SIMON: The Environmental Protection Agency announced earlier this year that Alar, which is sprayed on some red apple trees to keep the fruit on the trees until it's ready to be picked, posed a significant risk of cancer. The agency decided to propose a ban on the chemical, but it's allowing that chemical to remain in use for at least 18 months. . . .
>
> Mr. Jordan, . . . can you explain to us the process by which Alar was determined to be bad enough to ban by 1990 but not so bad that you could keep it on the market until then?
>
> JORDAN: Well, it's a long story that really has its roots back in the 1970s. EPA first became concerned about Alar when tests of the chemical showed that it might cause cancer. We began studying it intensively in the late 70s and . . . 80s; we got the results of a preliminary report on Alar in last fall, and those results were ones that raised concern at EPA, and based on them we propose to cancel the pesticide in 1990. . . . EPA is only able to take a pesticide off the market immediately if there is an imminent hazard. While we think there is a concern about Alar, we don't think it rises to the level of imminent hazard, an emergency.
>
> SIMON: Miss Hathaway, let me ask you: . . . can't the argument still be advanced that it's still safer to eat a red apple now that may have been the product of a growing process that included Alar than it is to drive somewhere on the Memorial Day weekend?
>
> HATHAWAY: Yes, that probably could be argued, but that's beside the point. The EPA does have an obligation to try to make our food supply as safe as possible, and when EPA finds a chemical that is so hazardous that even by their own standards and studies, they conclude that it is 45 times what they say is an acceptable level of carcinogenic potential, they ought to take it off the market immediately.
>
> JORDAN: . . . We don't believe that there is an imminent hazard. Miss Hathaway has said that there [is] 45 times the risk level; that's over a lifetime of exposure. We're looking at the risk that would occur over the next 12 to 18 months, and that's a considerably lower level. . . . With regard to Alar, . . . the most heavily exposed group, infants, . . . would have an increased chance of getting cancer, but a very, very small increase—1 in 100,000 . . . over the next 18 months. And we weighed that risk against the disruption that it would bring to the food supply if apples were removed from the marketplace, if applesauce were destroyed and apple juice were destroyed, and it did not seem to us, looking at that, . . . that it really came to the level of an imminent hazard.
>
> HATHAWAY: I don't think we should be posing risk against benefit. . . . We should simply draw a bright line and say, "If a chemical is very dangerous, if it is posing degrees of cancer on the order of Alar or anything approaching it, it simply ought not to be used.
>
> JORDAN: I wish it were so simple. First of all, EPA is required, no matter what Miss Hathaway says, to look at both the risks and the benefits of a pesticide use. And second of all, the data are often mixed, and that's the case that we're looking at with regard to Alar. And to weigh those squishy risk numbers against benefits is a very, very difficult job.

Is the information accurate and relevant?

- We have no basis on which to confirm or dispute the risk estimates. Note that Jordan referred to these numbers as "squishy"; in other words, they are not absolutes but involve a considerable amount of scientific judgment.

- On the question of relevance, that's really the whole issue to be explored here: what factors are relevant to the allowable use of an agricultural chemical?

What else needs to be considered?

We are exposed to many carcinogenic substances via the food supply and the larger environment; there is virtually no way to totally escape them. However, the risk from many of them is very small.

The risk from daily lifetime ingestion of 6 ounces of apple juice made from apples treated with Alar is calculated to be less than the risk from a daily peanut butter sandwich, or a mushroom, or a diet cola, or a beer (Table 15.3). Higher risks are also thought to come from daily exposure to the air in a typical home.

What is also important to consider is the risk that would prevail if the chemical were *not* used. Alar, in addition to delaying ripening of apples, retards the growth of molds during storage. If molds were to grow, some would be more highly carcinogenic than the Alar.

Regulations governing the acceptable levels of carcinogens in foods vary considerably, depending on how the chemical came to be there. We do not usually regulate against the *naturally occurring* carcinogens in traditionally consumed foods such as the hydrazines in mushrooms. However, the level of aflatoxin in a food can vary markedly, depending on the weather conditions at the time the agricultural product was grown and harvested. Therefore, products likely to contain aflatoxin are monitored by the Food and Drug Administration; if aflatoxin exceeds designated "action levels," the crop is unacceptable for sale.

Intentional *food additives* are more carefully regulated. According to the Delaney Clause of an amendment to the Food, Drug, and Cosmetic Act (which governs the activities of the FDA), *no amount* of a substance that can cause cancer to man or animal can be added to food. In recent years, there has been discussion about adopting a "de minimus" rule that would allow additives to be used if they would cause no more than 1 case of cancer per million people over a lifetime of use; as of mid-1990, this had not been adopted.

Pesticides are regulated by the EPA. The general guideline is that a chemical is allowable if its specified use would cause no more than 1 case of cancer per 100,000 or per million over a lifetime of exposure. When more recent estimates regarding Alar came in higher than this, the EPA proposed the ban discussed above.

What do you think?

If you could make the rule by which Alar or any other agricultural chemical currently in use were to be reevaluated, what would that rule be?

- Option 1 Disallow any agricultural chemical that has been found in any studies to be carcinogenic in any amount.
- Option 2 Establish a cutoff above which the risk of cancer is deemed unacceptable; *immediately* ban any chemical that, under normal conditions of use, is estimated to have higher risk.
- Option 3 Proceed as in Option 2, except allow continued short-term use of the chemical (resulting in minimal increase in risk) if its immediate withdrawal would have serious consequences to the food supply or to the producers.
- Option 4 If the consequences of *not using* the chemical are estimated to be worse than the consequences of using it, allow the continued use of the chemical no matter what the level of risk until a safer method can be identified and made available.
- Option 5 If new studies suggest that a particular chemical creates more risk than original studies showed, run a third series of studies before taking action.

Do you see other options or combinations of options? Which option makes the most sense to you?

intake and pancreatic cancer (MacMahon et al., 1981), but later research did not find an association (Nomura, Heilbrun, and Stimmermann, 1986). It is important to keep in mind that studies done on *coffee* are not necessarily indicative of the effects of *caffeine,* since there are many other compounds present in coffee, some of which may have toxic effects. Also, since some individuals habitually smoke when they drink coffee, some investigators believe that the cancer incidence may be related to the cigarettes rather than the coffee (Nomura et al., 1986).

Methylxanthines may be implicated as factors affecting other diseases as well. Some physicians have suggested that caffeine and related compounds may promote symptoms of cyclical fibrocystic breast disease in women who are susceptible to it (Boyle et al., 1984). This condition involves the development of hard, nonmalignant breast lumps that become enlarged and painful premenstrually. On the other hand, investigators doubt that methylxanthine consumption is related to breast cancer (Phelps and Phelps, 1988).

To protect against excessive intake of methylxanthines, it is best to follow the basic rule to consume all foods and beverages in moderation. Becoming dependent on large amounts of any substance is dangerous. For most individuals, a few cups of coffee or tea per day cannot be considered a real threat to health.

nitrate,nitrite—compounds of nitrogen and oxygen that occur naturally in many foods, and can also be added during processing

nitrosamines—chemical products of certain reactions involving nitrates or nitrites

Nitrates, Nitrites, and Nitrosamines Elemental nitrogen and oxygen combine in various proportions to form **nitrate** and **nitrite.** Both occur *naturally* in foods and in your body, where some interconversions occur between them. (The major difference between these compounds is that nitrate has more oxygen in its structure.) Nitrite is also used as a food additive to cure meats and prevent the growth of *Clostridium botulinum.* These compounds can react with other substances in food or in your body to form other compounds called **nitrosamines.**

Levels of nitrate and nitrite vary widely among foods (Table 15.5). A number of factors including agricultural practices and storage conditions can affect the nitrate levels in food. In the average diet, vegetables contribute 87% of the *nitrate* ingested. Although many people assume that all the nitrite in foods is added during food processing, only about 39% of the nitrite in the United States food supply is added intentionally, mainly to cured meats (Committee on Nitrite and Alternative Curing Agents in Food, 1981). The rest occurs naturally.

Actually, all the figures on dietary sources of nitrite and nitrate are somewhat misleading in that the human body also produces nitrate. Internal production of nitrate may be greater than the amount of nitrite and nitrate in an individual's diet (Lee et al., 1986).

In 1981, the Committee on Nitrite and Alternative Curing Agents in Food of the National Academy of Sciences reviewed the scientific literature on the links between nitrites, nitrates, nitrosamines, and cancer. They concluded that circumstantial evidence from epidemiological studies has implicated foods containing high levels of nitrate, nitrite, and nitrosamines in the development of cancer, particularly of the stomach and esophagus. Animal studies, however, indicated that the real carcinogens are the nitrosamines. The committee also pointed out that enhancers and inhibitors influence the occurrence of cancer. For example, the presence of vitamin C, α-tocopherol, and other antioxidants (substances that prevent reactions between oxygen and certain food constituents) can inhibit the activity of carcinogens by blocking the formation of nitrosamines from nitrites.

Currently, the food industry in the United States uses smaller amounts of nitrite to cure foods and, through the use of antioxidants, keeps the formation of nitrosamines at minimal levels (IFT, 1987). Therefore, concern about carcinogenic risk from consuming cured meats is much less than it was in 1982 (Committee on Diet, Nutrition, and Cancer, 1982).

The ingestion of large amounts of nitrate is sometimes a health concern for another reason. It can cause a condition called *methemoglobinemia,* which involves the production of abnormal hemoglobin unable to carry the usual amount of oxygen. This condition is most likely to occur in infants, who may become cyanotic (turn blue from lack of oxygen) if they consume well water contaminated with high levels of nitrate (Committee on Nitrite and Alternative Curing Agents in Food, 1981). In most states, there are county and/or state facilities that can test well water for its nitrate content.

Polycyclic Aromatic Compounds One difficulty in assessing the cancer risk from exposure to nitrate and nitrite in food is that these compounds do not

Table 15.5 Estimates of the Average Concentrations of Nitrate and Nitrite in Vegetables and Cured Meats

	Concentration, mg/kg fresh weight			Concentration mg/kg fresh weight	
	Nitrate	Nitrite		Nitrate	Nitrite
Asparagus	44	0.6	Melon	360	nd
Bacon, fried	32	7.0	Mushroom	160	0.5
Beans: green	340	0.6	Onion	170	0.7
lima	54	1.1	Peas	28	0.6
Beet	2,400	4.0	Pepper: sweet	120	0.4
Broccoli	740	1.0	Potato: white	110	0.6
Cabbage	520	0.5	sweet	46	0.7
Carrot	200	0.8	Pumpkin and squash	400	0.5
Cauliflower	480	1.1	Radish	1,900	0.2
Celery	2,300	0.5	Rhubarb	2,100	nd
Corn	45	2.0	Salami	78	13
Cucumber	110	0.5	Spinach	1,800	2.5
Endive	1,300	0.5	Tomato	58	nd
Ham, nitrite cured	150	10.0	Turnip greens	6,600	2.3
Lettuce	1,700	0.4	Wieners	96	10.0

nd = no data reported

Adapted from *The health effects of nitrate, nitrite and n-nitroso compounds,* 1981, with the permission of the National Academy Press, Washington, D.C.

necessarily occur in isolation. Other potential mutagens and antimutagens may also be present.

polycyclic aromatic hydrocarbons, polycyclic aromatic amines—common classes of mutagens produced in foods by certain types of dry heat cooking, especially if charring occurs

For example, some carcinogens may be introduced into foods by normal cooking procedures. Two common classes of mutagens produced in foods by cooking are **polycyclic aromatic hydrocarbons** and **polycyclic aromatic amines.** Both are groups of complex organic structures that are also found in some uncooked foods.

Polycyclic aromatic hydrocarbons are most likely to be produced in high-protein foods such as meats, particularly when they are pan-fried or broiled, and especially if charring occurs. Some experts believe consumers should think twice before ordering well-done charbroiled meats on a very frequent basis (Bjeldanes, 1983).

However, other experts note that these mutagenic compounds cause fewer cancers in test animals than might be expected on the basis of other laboratory tests. This may mean that there are anticarcinogens also present in cooked food that lessen the risk from the polycyclic aromatic compounds (Hargraves, 1987). One such substance appears to be a derivative of linoleic acid, called *conjugated linoleic acid* or *CLA,* which occurs naturally in grilled ground beef and milk products (Ha et al., 1990).

cyanogenic glycosides—compounds that can release the poison hydrogen cyanide; found in many types of fruit pits

Cyanogenic Glycosides Lima beans and the pits of almonds, apples, apricots, cherries, peaches, and other fruits contain **cyanogenic glycosides,** compounds that can release hydrogen cyanide in certain situations. This well-known poison is a potent respiratory inhibitor, and in large quantities it can cause death. Chronic consumption of small quantities of cyanogenic glycosides can affect the nervous system, vision, and hearing.

Generally, people don't eat fruit pits, so these are not a common source of trouble. As far as lima beans are concerned, breeding programs have reduced the levels of these compounds in commercially available varieties in North America. The people most likely to put themselves at risk from this substance are desperate cancer patients who sometimes consume a concentrated source of cyanogenic glycosides called *laetrile* or *amygdalin.* No claims for the effectiveness of laetrile have been substantiated in controlled clinical trials (Moertel et al., 1982).

Consumption of Toxins from Molds and Other Fungi

Certain fungi that can grow on food may produce toxins. These toxins lead to different consequences from the bacterial toxins discussed earlier in this chapter.

ergot—a fungal toxin that can cause hallucinations and blood vessel constriction

For example, **ergot** is a toxin produced by a fungus that can grow on grains, especially rye. The toxin can cause hallucinations; ergot is a natural source of LSD. It also can constrict capillaries and cause gangrene.

Before the development of modern milling processes that remove the part of the plant harboring the fungus, there were periodic outbreaks of the disease *ergotism.* Some historians believe that ergotism may have been the cause of the peculiar behavior of colonial Americans in the Salem witch trials. It probably was not "the devil" that made them act erratically; moldy rye may have been the cause.

Mold toxins of current importance are the **aflatoxins,** which are produced by some molds of the genus *Aspergillus;* many experts believe them to be the most potent liver toxins and carcinogenic agents known. Although aflatoxins have been found in many different foods, they most commonly contaminate peanuts, grains, and vegetables.

aflatoxins—a group of mold toxins believed by some to be the most potent liver toxins and carcinogenic agents known

Note in Table 15.3 the slight theoretical increase in the risk of cancer from eating a peanut butter sandwich every day of your life. This does *not* mean that you should quit eating peanut butter, but it emphasizes the importance of carefully monitoring the food supply for aflatoxin. Accordingly, sensitive tests are used routinely in North America to monitor peanuts and grains for aflatoxin concentration. As a result of these tests, your exposure from commercially processed foods is low. However, aflatoxin contamination is thought to be more prevalent in developing countries.

Some other mold toxins are also thought to be very hazardous, although they have not been as thoroughly studied as aflatoxin. It is often best to simply discard food that has become moldy, since it is difficult to estimate how far into the food's interior the mold's toxin may have penetrated. (If you want to salvage a large solid block of refrigerated cheese that has a slightly moldy surface, cut away at least ½ inch of cheese from every moldy surface to avoid the toxin [IFT, 1986].)

Consumption of Toxic Substances in Nonfood Materials

Young children are the most common victims of poisoning by nonfood materials. If you've ever watched a baby or toddler explore his or her environment by seeing, touching, and tasting everything, this will not surprise you.

In recent years, state health departments and the CDC have also received data on a number of adults who have been poisoned by natural products that resemble food products but are not foods themselves. Consuming poisonous mushrooms or herbs for tea that are "look-alikes" of edible varieties can be a fatal mistake.

Those who are interested in collecting and consuming natural products should obtain authoritative information from the experts in state hygiene laboratories and state horticultural cooperative Extension offices concerning which wild foods are safe to eat. If there is any doubt about a plant you are considering for use as food, do not consume it.

Treatment of people who ingest toxic plant material is often difficult because the poisonous substances in plants and the symptoms they produce vary so greatly. Some substances may irritate the gastrointestinal tract and rapidly induce nausea and vomiting; others damage the liver or central nervous system. This variety of consequences makes diagnosis difficult. If somebody starts to become ill after consuming an unusual natural product, call your local poison control center immediately. It is likely to be listed with other emergency telephone numbers on the first page of the phone book. If you are advised to go to the hospital emergency room, take along a sample of the plant material if you have it; this will aid in diagnosis and treatment.

Additives Pose Risk to Only a Small Number of People

The Food and Drug Administration defines additives as "substances added directly to food, or substances which may reasonably be expected to become components of food through surface contact with equipment or packaging materials, or even substances that may otherwise affect the food without becoming a part of it" (Jukes, 1981). The discussion that follows concerns substances that are directly and deliberately added to food.

Government Monitoring

The federal government has concerned itself with food additives since 1906. In that year, the Pure Food Law and the ensuing regulations that were drawn to enforce it provided the first means for protection of American food consumers. These documents established some early product and packaging standards, called for truth in labeling, and prescribed the testing methods to be used for evaluating the wholesomeness of foods. It also gave the government the authority to seize and destroy hazardous foods.

A primary concern at that time was to rid the food supply of foreign or misrepresented substances that some food processors were using in lieu of the pure, more expensive product they claimed to be marketing. For example, pepper sometimes was polluted with ground wood, raspberry jam with alfalfa seeds, ground mustard with flour, and candy with plaster of paris.

In 1938, the *Federal Food, Drug, and Cosmetic Act* improved on the earlier law, with stronger and more specific prohibitions against adulteration and misbranding. It also contained a method for establishing federal food standards, which identify the ingredients that must be present in particular foods. Over 200 such *standards of identity* exist for products including ice cream, catsup, and mayonnaise, to name a few common examples. Products for which standards exist are not required to carry ingredient lists on their labels at this time, but those without standards of identity must. Regulations are pending that will tighten these labeling requirements.

In 1958 and 1960, with hundreds of additives already in use, the Food, Drug, and Cosmetic Act was amended in several important ways:

GRAS list—list of thousands of additives in current use that are generally recognized as safe, based on their long-standing innocuous presence in the food supply

- Proof of safety had to be presented to the FDA by any company wanting to use a new food additive. The additive could not be used until the FDA gave its approval.
- A listing was made of hundreds of additives already in use that were generally recognized as safe **(GRAS)**, based on their innocuous presence

in the food supply for many years. (The list has now grown to thousands and includes items such as salt and sugar.) A list of *prior sanctioned substances* was also prepared, consisting of additives that FDA or USDA had approved before 1958. (The status of additives on these lists can be challenged by new evidence; some substances have lost their places on the original lists in that way.)

- A *margin of safety* was established. For most additives, there is an *acceptable daily intake* of $\frac{1}{100}$ of the amount thought to be hazardous. This applies only to substances that are not carcinogenic.
- The **Delaney Clause** specified that no substance could be added to the food supply if it had been shown to cause cancer in people or animals. Now that sensitive testing can identify minute, probably inconsequential levels of carcinogens in common foods, this legislation is not logical (Curran, 1988). Modifications of the Delaney Clause are often discussed, but no changes in legislation have occurred, probably because consumers and legislators do not really understand that defining zero amounts of substances in foods is becoming increasingly impossible as the sensitivity of techniques increases by more than a thousandfold.

Delaney Clause—law specifying that no substance can be added to the food supply if it has been shown to cause cancer in people or animals

Purposes and Prevalence of Additives

Additives must have purposes that will benefit the consumer. Four broad categories of legitimate use are to maintain product quality, to help in processing or preparation, to make food more appealing, and to maintain or improve nutritional value. Since the addition of nutrients has been discussed in earlier chapters, this section will focus on the first three purposes.

There are currently over 2800 additives approved for use in the United States. The average American consumes approximately 160 pounds of additives per year: over 140 pounds of sweeteners including sucrose, 15 pounds of sodium chloride (table salt), and 5–10 pounds of all the others. This means that all the flavorings, colorings, and preservatives ingested by Americans comprise about 0.6% of the estimated 1670 pounds of food we each consume in a year (Welsh and Marston, 1982).

Figure 15.7 shows examples of additives as they might appear on labels of processed foods.

Additives That Maintain Product Quality We benefit from the addition to foods of substances that eliminate or control microorganisms and other living contaminants, and substances that prevent oxidation of food compounds. For example, sodium and calcium propionate, sodium benzoate, potassium sorbate, and sulfur dioxide are used in baked goods and other products to prevent growth of bacteria, yeast, and mold.

Another important group of additives that preserve product quality are the *antioxidants*, which prevent chemical reactions between oxygen in the air and various constituents of foods. The additives BHA (butylated hydroxyanisole), BHT (butylated hydroxytoluene), propyl gallate, and vitamin E protect against oxidation of fats (rancidity). The former ones are often used in

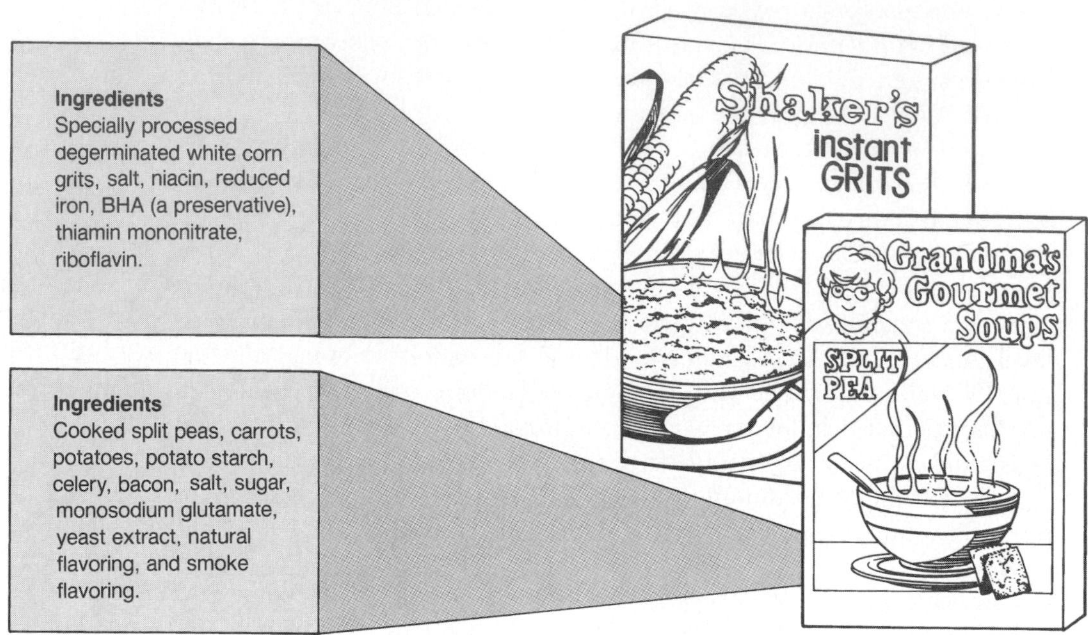

Figure 15.7 Examples of additives in two processed foods.

baked products. Antioxidants often function by being easily oxidized themselves, thereby sparing other compounds in the food.

Other additives are used to inhibit the enzymes that cause browning reactions in fruits and vegetables. Vitamin C is sometimes used for this purpose, especially to prevent the browning of fruits.

One group of compounds used to prevent browning—sulfites—has gained notoriety in the last decade. Since 1982, the Food and Drug Administration has received more than 20 reports of deaths alleged to be due to ingestion of food processed with sulfur dioxide, sodium sulfite, sodium or potassium bisulfites, or metabisulfites (Taylor, 1987). The people who died were known to have *asthma,* a condition in which the airways constrict under certain conditions. When people with asthma eat a food that contains a substance to which they are sensitive, an asthmatic attack can occur.

The experts believe that only a small percentage (5–10%) of severe asthmatics are sensitive to sulfites; most of those who are sensitive develop hives and shortness of breath that is not life-threatening. Nonetheless, anybody who is sulfite-sensitive should avoid sulfated food.

Packaged foods most likely to be treated with sulfites are light-colored dried fruits such as apricots and pears, dried potatoes, and wine. FDA regulations require all packaged foods containing significant sulfite residues (10 micrograms per gram of food) to be labeled accordingly. Over-the-counter medications may also contain sulfites; therefore, a sulfite-sensitive person must read labels of packaged consumables very carefully.

The FDA has also banned the use of sulfites on fresh fruits and vegetables. This means that most fresh salad bar items are safe for the sulfite-sensitive person. In the past, sulfites were used to treat some potatoes such as hash browns, which are difficult to keep from discoloring; their use in refrigerated hash browns was being debated by the courts in 1990. Since regulations regarding sulfites in foods continue to change, the safest strategy for the sensitive person is to read all labels carefully and ask about restaurant items you consider ordering.

Additives That Aid in Processing or Preparation Leavening agents, anticaking agents, emulsifiers, stabilizers, thickeners, pH control agents, humectants (moisturizers), maturing and bleaching agents, and dough conditioners are all types of additives used to achieve processing or preparation benefits.

Sodium bicarbonate (baking soda), calcium phosphate, and sodium aluminum phosphate are leavening agents used in all baked products raised without yeast, such as biscuits, muffins, cornbread, and cakes. Calcium and aluminum silicate and iron-ammonium citrate are anticaking agents used in salts and many powdered products. Emulsifiers, such as mono- and diglycerides, lecithin, carrageenan, and polysorbates, are used in salad dressings, processed cheese, and ice cream. Various gums, pectin, and alginates are used to thicken jellies, candies, and ice cream.

Acidity is adjusted in such foods as pickles and carbonated beverages by using acetic acid, citric acid, lactic acid, phosphates and phosphoric acid, and sodium acetate.

Additives That Make Food More Appealing Any additive that makes food more pleasing to taste or look at is a member of this group. *Flavorings* include condiments, spices, concentrated fruits and juices, process flavors (such as "roasted"), or flavor elements concentrated from the above. Whether such compounds have been extracted from food sources (natural flavorings) or produced in the laboratory (artificial flavorings), they are often chemically identical. In such cases, they are also indistinguishable in terms of their safety (Smith, 1981). Flavor enhancers, such as monosodium glutamate (MSG) and hydrolyzed vegetable proteins, heighten existing flavors in foods (see Chapter 8).

A large group of additives are flavors and sweeteners, including beet and cane sugars, syrups, honey, molasses, and purified sweet carbohydrates such as sucrose, glucose, fructose, sorbitol, and mannitol. All these sweeteners offer energy as well as flavor. Sweet additives that provide little or no energy are saccharin, aspartame, and acesulfame-K.

Saccharin has had a checkered past. Although it was included on the GRAS list in 1958 because of its longstanding use without apparent problems, its status was challenged in 1977 by evidence that it caused bladder cancer in rats (Lecos, 1981). Such evidence should be enough to require the removal of saccharin from the food supply, according to the Delaney Clause.

However, saccharin is still on the market as of this writing. Each time the FDA proposes a ban on its use, Congress declares a moratorium on the ban in response to public pressure to keep it available (Miller and Frattali, 1989).

This has occurred because of saccharin's widespread popularity, and because most experts regard saccharin as only a weak promoter of cancer.

Some of the public pressure to allow continued use of saccharin may ease off now that aspartame and acesulfame-K are on the market. Many experts believe that the best policy is to have several low-kcalorie sweeteners available for public use to lessen the chance of overuse of any one product (Gelardi, 1987).

Aspartame is a sweet dipeptide whose component amino acids are metabolized like those naturally occurring in food. Aspartame was approved for certain uses in the United States in 1974, but before it entered the market, the FDA stayed the approval because the validity of several toxicological studies was questioned. Subsequent reviews of the data and additional studies led to approval in 1981.

However, the controversy has not ended. Although more recent studies continue to support its safety when consumed in moderation (Stegink, 1987), some scientists and consumer groups continue to question whether there may be some risks if the product is heavily consumed.

Aspartame clearly constitutes a hazard for people with the rare genetic condition phenylketonuria (PKU). (PKU results in mental retardation if it is not diagnosed and treatment initiated within a few days of birth. There are infant-screening programs to test for PKU.) People born with this disorder are unable to metabolize phenylalanine, one of the amino acids in aspartame; if the intake of phenylalanine is not carefully controlled, it builds up in the blood, causing neurological damage. For this reason, a warning must appear on aspartame and all products that contain it, cautioning of the danger for those with PKU.

Colorings are the final group of additives that improve sensory appeal. There are approximately 30 food colorings in use in the United States, and some others that can be used in specified circumstances.

There have been more questions raised about the safety of colorings than about most other categories of additives. Many synthetic dyes formerly used in foods are no longer allowed, in some cases because they were found to be carcinogenic. Future use of other synthetic dyes will hinge on individual tests. Natural colorings are not as popular with the food industry, because they do not generally hold up as well in foods as the synthetic colorings do (Meggos, 1984).

Just as with some other scientific quandaries, the experts disagree over how to interpret studies on food coloring. For example, at about the same time that the FDA banned Red No. 2 and suggested using Red No. 40 as a substitute, Canada banned Red No. 40 and in its place used Red No. 2 (IFT, 1980).

Tartrazine, or Yellow No. 5, is a food coloring of current interest. It has been found to produce hives, itching, runny nose, and/or asthma in some people. The federal government now requires tartrazine to be mentioned specifically on food labels when it is used, a regulation that makes it unique among food colorings.

This chapter's Nutrition for Living summarizes how best to avoid taking in a hazardous amount of any toxicant.

Nutrition for Living

It is almost impossible for consumers to be aware of all toxic substances in food and conditions under which harm would be likely and to plan their food intakes on that basis. Fortunately this is unnecessary, because a few guidelines can help you avoid most problem substances:

- Eat a wide variety of foods, and avoid consistently large intakes of any one item. This makes it less likely that you will take in a hazardous amount of any toxicant.
- Consume a diet that supplies adequate levels of all nutrients. Good nutrition helps the body deal with stresses induced by toxicants. (Trying to avoid foods that contain potentially harmful substances could so limit a diet that undernutrition might result.)
- Carefully follow instructions for use on labels of pesticides, fertilizers, and all household and yard chemicals to keep them out of your food supply. Do not dispose of unused chemicals in your household trash. Contact your local sanitation department for more information on proper disposal of household hazardous waste.
- Keep informed about public health matters. The print and electronic media are sources of information on food recalls and food-handling practices.

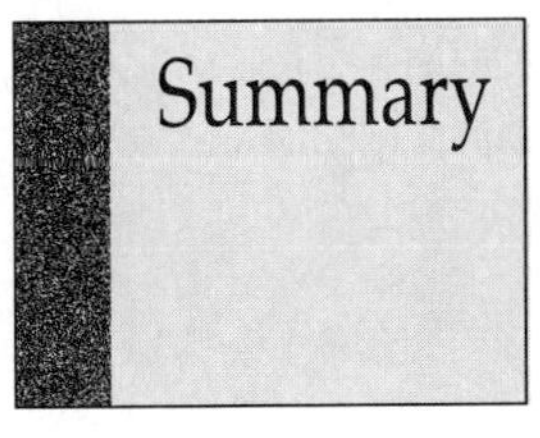

Summary

► Thousands of substances besides nutrients occur naturally in foods, and most are harmless in the amounts typically consumed. Among those substances that do have the potential to cause harm, some occur naturally, others find their way into the food supply by accident, and still others may be added intentionally to achieve some other effect. Unfortunately, it is not possible to simply make lists of harmful and harmless chemicals and avoid the former; it is not necessary to avoid all potentially harmful substances entirely, because at low levels of intake and under typical conditions many are harmless.

► **Food toxicology** is the science that establishes the basis for judgments about the safety of foodborne chemicals. Common toxicological terms are *safety, hazard, toxicity, toxicant* (also *toxin* or *poison*), *detoxification, mutagen,* and *carcinogen.* It is important to remember that all substances comprising foods are toxic at a certain level of intake, but most are not hazardous under normal conditions of use.

► **Dose-response curves** illustrate the relationship between the dosage of a substance and its effect. Some substances have no effect; others have a threshold effect or no threshold (are harmful at all levels of intake). Most nutrients have a low-dose beneficial threshold. Many factors influence toxicity, including detoxification processes, time, storage in the body, nutrition status, growth and body size, and interactions among substances.

► Microorganisms are responsible for the majority of food-related health problems, such as **gastroenteritis. Foodborne infections** (caused by large numbers of bacteria in food) and **intoxications** (caused by bacterial toxins) can be very unpleasant but are not usually severe. **Botulism,** a less common intoxication, can be fatal, as can infection with *Listeria monocytogenes.*

► Environmental food contaminants are common but not always harmful. Lead, aluminum, tin, and iron can migrate into food from metal food preparation equipment and storage containers, and from other environmental sources. Mercury (in the form of **methyl mercury**) and cadmium can also enter the food supply in various ways. The harm they produce depends on many factors including chemical form, dosage, length of exposure, and age and health status of the person(s) involved.

▶ Organic contaminants such as antibiotics, hormones, pesticides, and other industrial organic compounds such as PCBs can be toxic in certain situations, particularly if they accumulate in animal tissues over time. The effects of these compounds vary greatly. Some are toxic to nervous tissue, some to liver, some to the immune system, and some are carcinogens.

▶ Radioactivity is another possible food contaminant. Natural radiation comes from the soil and cosmic sources. Other sources are radioactive substances from medical and industrial uses and from nuclear power generation.

▶ Many naturally occurring substances can also be toxic. Problems can arise if an individual consumes abnormally large quantities of such substances as **methylxanthines** (including caffeine), **nitrosamines** and related compounds, **polycyclic aromatic hydrocarbons** and **amines,** and **cyanogenic glycosides** such as laetrile. Consuming the mold toxins **ergot** and **aflatoxins** can have dire consequences. Poisonings resulting from the ingestion of nonfood items such as misidentified mushrooms and certain herbal teas also occur periodically.

▶ Governmental monitoring of the North American food supply is routine and ongoing. Federal laws regulate the introduction of new additives and their margin of safety. The **GRAS list** includes thousands of additives that are generally recognized as safe, and the **Delaney Clause** specifies that substances shown to cause cancer in animals or humans cannot be added to the food supply. Regulations are continually being reviewed and revised.

▶ Additives must benefit food consumers in at least one of the following ways by: (1) maintaining product quality (controlling microorganisms, preventing oxidation); (2) aiding in processing or preparation (leavening, emulsifying, thickening); (3) making food more appealing (flavoring, sweetening, coloring); or (4) maintaining or improving nutritional value.

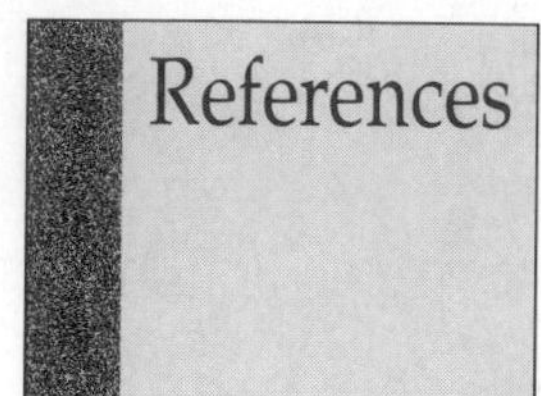

References

Ames, B.N. and L.S. Gold. 1989. Pesticides, risk and applesauce. *Science* 236:755–757.

Ames, B.N., R. Magaw, and L.S. Gold. 1987. Ranking possible carcinogenic hazards. *Science* 236:271–280.

Anspaugh, L.R., R.J. Catlin, M. Goldman. 1988. The global impact of the Chernobyl reactor accident. *Science* 242:1513–1519.

Bellinger, D., A. Leviton, C. Waternaux, H. Needleman, M. Rabinowitz. 1987. Longitudinal analyses of prenatal and postnatal lead exposure and early cognitive development. *New England Journal of Medicine* 316:1037–1043.

Bjeldanes, L.F. 1983. Hazards in the food supply: Lead, aflatoxins and mutagens produced by cooking. *Nutrition Update* 1:105–119.

Blaser, M.J., E. Sazie, and L.P. Williams. 1987. The influence of immunity on raw milk-associated *Campylobacter* infection. *Journal of the American Medical Association* 257: 43–46.

Boyle, C.A., G.S. Berkowitz, V.A. LiVols, S. Ort, M.J. Merino, C. White, and J.L. Kelsey. 1984. Caffeine consumption and fibrocystic breast disease: A case-control epidemiologic study. *Journal of the National Cancer Institute* 72:1015–1019.

Boynton, R. 1990. *California Farmer,* June 2, 1990.

Casal, D.C. and A.S. Leon. 1985. Failure of caffeine to affect substrate utilization during prolonged running. *Medicine and Science in Sports and Exercise* 17:174–179.

Coats, J.R. 1987. Toxicology of pesticide residues in foods. *Nutritional Toxicology,* volume II, ed. J. Hathcock. Orlando, FL: Academic Press.

Committee on Diet, Nutrition and Cancer. 1982. *Diet, nutrition and cancer.* Washington, DC: National Academy Press.

Committee on Nitrite and Alternative Curing Agents in Food. 1981. *The health effects of nitrate, nitrite, and N-nitroso compounds.* Washington, DC: National Academy Press.

Curran, W.J. 1988. Cancer causing substances in food, drugs and cosmetics: The de Minimis Rule versus Delaney Clause. *New England Jour-*

nal of Medicine 319:1262–1264.

Davis, B.R., J.D. Curb, N.O. Borhani, R.J. Prineas, and A. Molteni. 1988. Coffee consumption and serum cholesterol in the hypertension detection and follow-up program. *American Journal of Epidemiology* 128:124–136.

Doyle, M.P. 1988. *Campylobacter jejuni*. *Food Technology* 42(4):187–188.

DuPont, H.L. 1986. Consumption of raw shellfish—is the risk now unacceptable? *New England Journal of Medicine* 314:707–708.

DuPont, H.L. and J.H. Steele. 1987. Use of antimicrobial agents in animal feeds: Implications for human health. *Review of Infectious Diseases* 9:447–460.

Food Safety and Inspection Service. 1984. *The safe food book*. Home and Garden Bulletin Number 241. Washington, DC: United States Department of Agriculture.

Foran, J.A., M. Cox, and D. Croxton. 1989. Sport fish consumption advisories and projected cancer risks in the Great Lakes basin. *American Journal of Public Health* 79:322–325.

Gelardi, R.C. 1987. The multiple sweetener approach and new sweeteners on the horizon. *Food Technology* 41:123–124.

Greger, J.L. 1987. Aluminum and tin. *World Review of Nutrition and Diet* 54:255–285.

Ha, Y.L., J. Storkson, and M.W. Pariza. 1990. Inhibition of benzo(a)pyrene-induced mouse forestomach neoplasia by conjugated dienoic derivatives of linoleic acid. *Cancer Research* 50:1097–1101.

Hall, R.L. and S.L. Taylor. 1989. Food toxicology and safety evaluation: Changing perspectives and challenge for the future. *Food Technology* 43(9):270–279.

Hallberg, L., E. Bjorn-Rasmussen, L. Rossander, R. Suwanek, R. Pleehachinda, and M. Tuntawiroon. 1983. Iron absorption from Asian meals containing contamination iron. *American Journal of Clinical Nutrition* 37:272–277.

Hargraves, W.A. 1987. Mutagens in cooked foods. In *Nutritional Toxicology*, volume II, ed. J.N. Hathcock, Orlando, FL: Academic Press.

Harris, N.V., D. Thompson, D.C. Martin, and C.M. Nolan. 1986. A survey of *Campylobacter* and other bacterial contaminants of pre-market chicken and retail poultry and meats, King County, Washington. *American Journal of Public Health* 76:401–406.

Institute of Food Technologists (IFT). Expert Panel on Food Safety and Nutrition and the Committee on Public Information. 1980. *Food colors*. Chicago: Institute of Food Technologists.

———. 1986. Mycotoxins and food safety. *Food Technology* 40(5):59–66.

———. 1987. Nitrate, nitrite and nitrosocompounds in food. *Food Technology* 41(4):127–135.

———. Expert Panel on Food Safety and Nutrition. 1988. Bacteria associated with foodborne diseases. *Food Technology* 42(4):181–200.

Jackson, G.J., J.W. Bier, and T.L. Schwarz. 1990. More on making sushi safe. *New England Journal of Medicine* 322:1011.

Jacobson, J.L., H.E.B. Humphrey, S.W. Jacobsen, S.L. Schantz, M.D. Mullin, and R. Welsh. 1989. Determinants of polychlorinated biphenyls (PCBs), polybrominated biphenyls (PBBs) and dichlorodiphenyl tricholorethane (DDT) levels in the sera of young children. *American Journal of Public Health* 79:1401–1404.

Jukes, T.H. 1981. Organic foods and food additives. In *Controversies in Nutrition*, ed. L. Ellenbogen. New York: Churchill Livingstone.

Kostial, K. 1986. Cadmium. In *Trace elements in human and animal nutrition*, 5th edition, ed. W.J. Mertz. Orlando, FL: Academic Press.

Lecos, D. 1981. The sweet and sour history of saccharin, cyclamate, aspartame. *FDA Consumer* 15(no. 7):8–11.

Lee, K., J.L. Greger, J.R. Cansaul, K.L. Graham, and B.L. Chinn. 1986. Nitrate, nitrite balance, and de novo synthesis of nitrate in humans consuming cured meats. *American Journal of Clinical Nutrition* 44:188–194.

Liska, B.J., E.M. Foster, J.H. Silliker, and D.L. Archer. 1986. New bacteria in the news: A special symposium. *Food Technology* 40(8):16–26.

Lotti, M. 1987. Production and use of pesticides. In *Toxicology of pesticides: Experimental, clinical, and regulatory perspectives*, eds. L.G. Costa, C.W. Galli, and S.D. Murphy. Berlin: Springer-Verlag.

Lovett, J. and R.M. Tweat. *Listeria*. *Food Technology* 42(4):188–191.

MacMahon, B., S. Yen, D. Trichopoulos, K. Warren, and G. Nardi. 1981. Coffee and cancer of the pancreas. *New England Journal of Medicine* 304:630–633.

Mahaffey, K.R., P.S. Gartside, C.J. Glueck. 1986. Blood lead levels and dietary calcium intake in 1- to 5-year old children: The second National Health and Nutrition Examination Survey, 1976 to 1980. *Pediatrics* 78:257.

Marshall, E. 1990. Academy panel raises radiation risk estimate. *Science* 247:22–23.

Meggos, H.N. 1984. Colors—key food ingredients. *Food Technology* 38(no. 1):70–74.

Miller, S.A. and V.P. Frattali. 1989. Saccharin. *Diabetes Care* 12:75–80.

Moertel, C.G., T.R. Fleming, J. Rubin, L.K. Kvols, G. Sarna, R. Koch, V.E. Currie, C.W. Young, S.E. Jones, and J.P. Davignon. 1982. A clinical trial of amygdalin (laetrile) in the treatment of human cancer. *New England Journal of Medicine* 306:201–206.

Morse, D.L., J.J. Guzewich, J.P. Hanrahan, R. Stricof, M. Shayegani, R. Deibel, J.C. Grabau, N.A. Nowak, J.E. Hermann, G. Cukor, and N.R. Blacklow. 1986. Widespread outbreaks of clam- and oyster-associated gastroenteritis. *New England Journal of Medicine* 314:678–681.

Myers, M.G. 1988. Effects of caffeine on blood pressure. *Archives of Internal Medicine* 148:1189–1193.

Needleman, H.L., A. Schell, D. Bellinger, A. Leviton, and E.N. Allred. 1990. The long-term effects of exposure to low doses of lead in childhood: An 11-year follow-up report. *New England Journal of Medicine* 322:83–88.

Newsome, R.L. 1988. *Staphylococcus aureus*. *Food Technology* 42(4):194–195.

Nomura, A., L.K. Heilbrun, and G.N. Stimmermann. 1986. Prospective study of coffee consumption and risk of cancer. *Journal of the National Cancer Institute* 76:587–590.

Phelps, H.M. and C.E. Phelps. 1988. Caffeine ingestion and breast cancer. *Cancer* 61:1051–1054.

Roberts, H.R. and J.J. Barone. 1983. Biological effects of caffeine: History and use. *Food Technology* 37(9):32–39.

Russell, L. 1990. Consumers face little danger from residues in meat and poultry. *Food News* 6(4):10–11.

Ryser, E.T. and E.H. Marth. 1989. "New" foodborne pathogens of public health significance. *Journal of the American Dietetic Association* 89:948–954.

Sawheney, B.L. and L. Hankin. 1985. Polychlorinated biphenyls in food: A review. *Journal of Food Protection* 48:442–448.

Smith, M.V. 1981. Regulation of artificial and natural flavors. *Cereal Foods World* 26:278–280.

Stegink, L.W. 1987. Aspartame: Review of the safety issues. *Food Technology* 41(1):119–121.

St. Louis, M.E., D.L. Morse, M.E. Potter, T.M. DeMelfi, J.J. Guzewich, R.V. Tauxe, and P.A. Blake. 1988. The emergence of grade A eggs as a major source of *Salmonella enteritidis* infections. *Journal of the American Medical Association* 259:2103–2107.

Sun, M. 1984. EDB contamination kindles federal action. *Science* 223:464–466.

Sun, M. 1989. Market sours on milk hormone. *Science* 246:876–877.

Taylor, S.L. 1987. Allergic and sensitivity reactions to food components. In *Nutritional Toxicology*, volume II, ed. J.N. Hathcock, Orlando, FL: Academic Press.

Tollefson, L. and F. Cordle. 1986. Methylmercury in fish: A review of residue levels, fish consumption and regulatory action in the United States. *Environmental Health Perspectives* 68:203–208.

Welsh, S.P. and R.M. Marston. 1982. Review of trends in food use in the United States, 1909–80. *Journal of the American Dietetic Association* 81:120–125.

Wilson, R. and E.A.C. Crouch. 1987. Risk assessment and comparisons: An introduction. *Science* 236:267–270.

Wodicka, V.O. 1977. Food safety—rationalizing the ground rules for safety evaluation. *Food Technology* 31(9):75–79.

PART VI

NUTRITION THROUGH YOUR LIFE

16

Nutrition for Pregnancy and Lactation: Mothers and Infants

In This Chapter

- A Pregnant Woman Needs to Gain Enough Weight
- A Pregnant Woman Needs a Nutrient-Dense Diet
- There Are Ways to Cope with Physiological Changes of Pregnancy
- Pregnant Women Should Avoid Toxic Substances
- Rapid Growth During Infancy Calls for High Nutrient Intake
- Both Breast-Feeding and Bottle-Feeding Have Certain Advantages
- Older Infants Need Nutrients That Solid Foods Provide

"You're *what?* You're *pregnant?*"

Take a few moments to speculate on the rest of this scenario. A happy young husband could be responding to the news from his elated wife, both delighted that their plans for starting a family are on target. Or a couple could be facing the news with mixed reactions—anticipating that parenthood will enrich their lives, but wondering how much they will need to change their career-oriented lifestyle. A teenage boy could be recoiling in fright and anger at the news from his panicky girlfriend. Or an older father who has enjoyed his parenting role but is now looking forward to having the children go out on their own could be reacting in shock to the announcement of his equally astounded middle-aged wife.

Pregnancy has a substantial emotional impact on the lives of the prospective mother and father and the people close to them. It also has a considerable physiological impact that affects nutritional needs. During pregnancy all the raw materials for the development of what becomes the baby must be taken from the supply of nutrients circulating in the mother's bloodstream. Protein for the newly forming organs and muscles, for example, and minerals for the bones and teeth are supplied from the mother's food intake and body stores. (For a newborn baby, the phrase "You are what you eat" may be more appropriately stated "You are what your mother ate.") At the same time, the mother must meet all her own nutritional needs. During pregnancy, then, the mother is truly eating for two. She will be reminded of this by her increased hunger, but she may need information about what foods will best satisfy her greater nutrient needs.

The decision whether to breast- or bottle-feed is an important one that the mother and father must make before delivery. After birth, breast-fed infants continue to rely on their mothers' bodies as their main source of nourishment. Bottle-fed babies consume substitutes for breast milk in the form of various specially designed formulas created by modern technology.

The questions of when to start adding other foods and what these other foods should be are also important parental considerations. In the past, most parents simply adopted the usual practices of their culture, but now we have scientific data to help shape our thinking about the best way to feed babies. Not only do we know more about nutritional needs, but we have developed an appreciation for the impact of the feeding relationship on a child's social development as well.

This chapter deals with all of these topics.

A Pregnant Woman Needs to Gain Enough Weight

Although nutrition has a great deal to do with a healthy baby and mother, it is not the only thing that matters. The age of the mother and her health, lifestyle, and history of previous pregnancies also influence the birth outcome. Table 16.1 lists major factors present during the course of pregnancy and/or at conception that pose a risk to the developing fetus.

Obviously, some of these factors—such as the age of the mother—apply only to some women. But one factor that is of great importance in every pregnancy—and one over which the mother has a great deal of control—is the matter of appropriate weight gain. Gaining enough weight is essential: if a mother doesn't gain sufficient weight during **gestation,** the baby may be too small. This puts the infant at risk of death or, if it survives, increases the risk of various health problems. Infant birth weight is more closely related to infant mortality than is any other variable (Brown, 1989). Therefore, in this opening section, we will focus on appropriate weight gain.

gestation—development of the future baby from fertilization to birth; pregnancy

The Right Amount of Weight to Gain During Pregnancy

Research has shown that poor birth outcomes are likely to occur with mothers who have gained too little or too much weight. Generally speaking, for a mother who was at her recommended weight at conception, a weight gain of 25–35 pounds for a single pregnancy will produce the healthiest babies (Committee on Nutritional Status, 1990).

There are many exceptions to this standard. If a woman is very underweight, it might be best for her to gain more weight than is advised for

Table 16.1 Risk Factors in Pregnancy

Risk Factors Present at the Beginning of Pregnancy
Age
15 years or younger
35 years or older
Frequent pregnancies: three or more during a 2-year period
Medical problems during previous pregnancies
Poverty
Bizarre or faddist food habits
Use of nicotine, alcohol, or certain other drugs
Therapeutic diet required for a chronic disorder
Abnormal weight
Less than 85% of standard weight
More than 135% of standard weight

Risk Factors Occurring During Pregnancy
Low levels of iron in blood (according to special standards for pregnancy)
Any weight loss during pregnancy
Inadequate weight gain: less than 2 pounds/month after the first 3 months
Excessive weight gain: more than 2.2 pounds/week after the first 3 months

Adapted from Williams, S.R. 1988. Nutrition for high-risk populations. In *Nutrition throughout the life cycle,* eds. S.R. Williams and B.S. Worthington-Roberts. St Louis: Times Mirror/Mosby College Publishing.

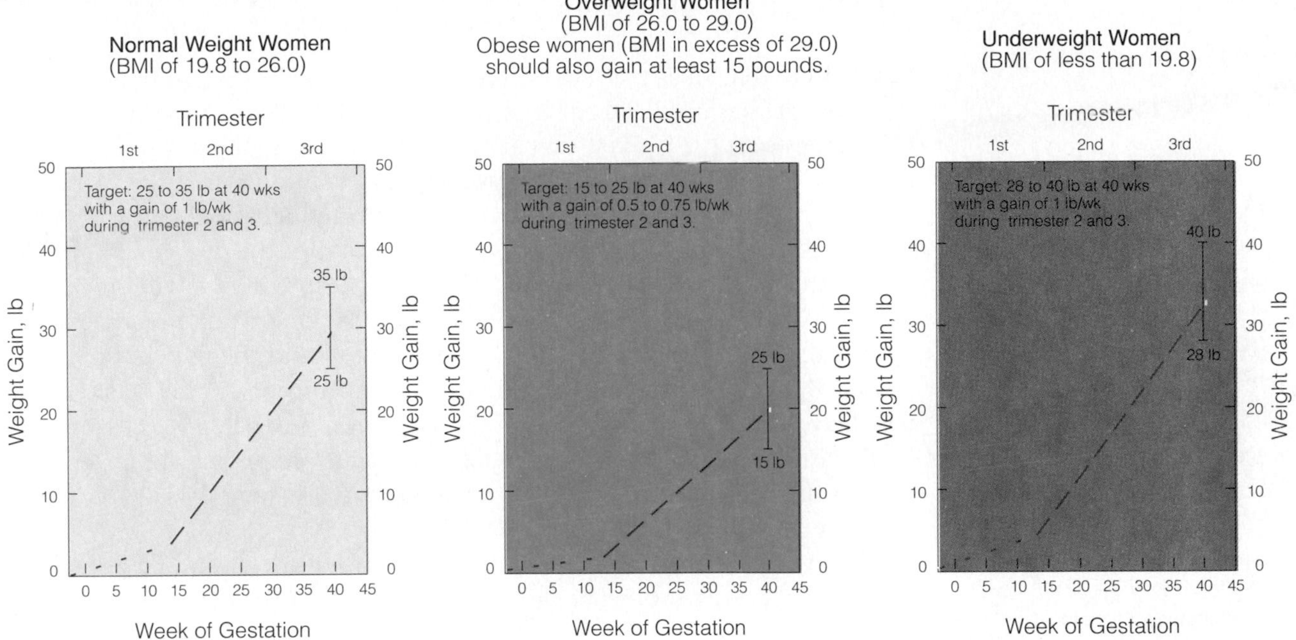

Figure 16.1 Recommended Weight Gain Ranges for Single Pregnancies Based on Body Mass Index (BMI). A mother's weight status at conception determines how much weight she should gain during pregnancy. The highlighted graph represents gains recommended for normal weight women with a prepregnancy BMI of 19.8 to 26.0. Recommended weight gain ranges for overweight and underweight women are shown in graphs at right. (Adapted from Committee on Nutritional Status During Pregnancy and Lactation. 1990. *Nutrition During Pregnancy,* Appendix B. Washington, DC: National Academy Press.)

women of normal weight. Women who are 10% or more below standard weight for height are more likely to have problems during pregnancy and, consequently, poor birth outcomes. On the other hand, if a pregnant woman is either very overweight or quite petite, a somewhat lower weight gain may be recommended.

Figure 16.1 shows what amounts and patterns of weight gains are recommended for pregnant women, depending on their prepregnancy body mass index (BMI). Note that even an obese woman needs to gain some weight during pregnancy; *this is not the time to try to shed excess pounds,* because it may have a negative effect on the development and health of the fetus.

Notice in the figure that the pattern of weight gain during pregnancy is not a straight line from conception to delivery. There is likely to be little (perhaps 2 to 4 pounds) if any gain in the first **trimester,** but the weight gain in the second and third trimesters should make up for it. During those phases, the mother should gain an average of almost a pound per week. It is not unusual for the weekly gain to be slightly higher in the second trimester than in the third.

trimester—the first, second, or third 3-month period of pregnancy

Individual cases may deviate somewhat from this pattern and still be safe, but it is important that a health care professional monitor a mother's progress and recommend action if there is any indication of a problem. The following Slice of Life gives an example of the pattern of weight gain in one woman's pregnancies.

For multiple pregnancies, the mother needs to gain more weight than when she is carrying a single fetus. The recommended weight gain for a woman carrying twins is 35–45 pounds (Committee on Nutritional Status, 1990).

What Makes Up the Weight

The growth that takes place between conception and birth is truly phenomenal. A single fertilized egg cell is so small and multiplies so rapidly that after only four weeks it is 7000 times larger than its original size, yet is only one-fifth of an inch long and still weighs less than an ounce.

During the first two weeks after conception, the fertilized egg is called a **zygote.** Approximately two weeks after fertilization, the zygote attaches itself tightly to the wall of the **uterus,** the chamber in which it will grow until delivery. At this stage it is called an **embryo.** In the area of attachment, an organ called the **placenta** develops; this organ contains the network of blood vessels that allows for the exchange of oxygen, nutrients, and waste products between the blood supplies of the mother and developing baby. Eight weeks after fertilization, when the fetus's organs are beginning to develop and tissues are assuming distinct functions, the organism is called a **fetus,** the term used until birth (Figure 16.2).

zygote—the name given to a fertilized egg during the first two weeks after conception

uterus—the organ in which the baby develops during gestation

embryo—a zygote that has attached to the wall of the uterus

placenta—organ that forms at the site of embryo attachment and contains the blood vessel network that supports the developing baby

fetus—a developing baby from eight weeks after egg fertilization until birth

The average infant at birth weighs 7 to 7½ pounds (3.2 to 3.5 kg). Then why does the mother need to gain 25 to 35 pounds? The answer is that many additional materials are needed to support healthy development.

The weight of the *uterus* increases by almost 2 pounds by the time of delivery. The *amniotic fluid* surrounding the developing baby takes up another 2 pounds. By the end of the pregnancy, the *placenta* accounts for an additional 1 to 2 pounds.

That's not all. The mother's *blood supply* increases by about 3 pounds. Her *breast tissue* increases in preparation for **lactation.** In addition, she needs to store *extra body fat* so that late in pregnancy, when its need for kcalories is

lactation—milk production

Slice of Life

Weight Gain During Pregnancy

In her book *Child of Mine,* Ellyn Satter, who is both a registered dietitian and a mental health worker, describes the pattern of her own weight gain during pregnancy:

> I found in my pregnancies that I lost two or three pounds immediately when I became pregnant, probably because of a shift in water balance, then gained seven pounds in each of the fourth and fifth months. I blamed that on a shift in body fluid as well, because I know I wasn't overeating, at least to that extent. I kept my fingers crossed and tried not to do any mathematics in my head (you know, the type where you say "seven pounds times four more months is—") and just kept on eating. Sure enough, by the sixth month the monthly gain had leveled off to a nicely respectable three pounds, and it actually dropped during the last trimester to only about two pounds per month. (Source: Satter, E. 1986. *Child of mine.* Palo Alto, CA: Bull Publishing Company.)

Although her weight wavered slightly above and below the standard gain during her three pregnancies, she gained about 25 pounds each time, and all three babies were in excellent health. ▲

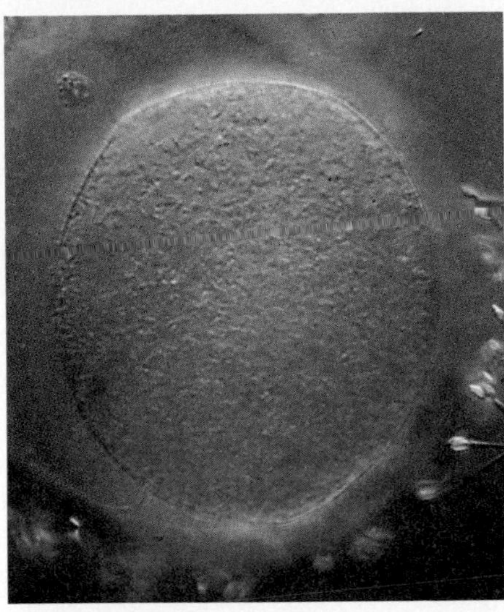

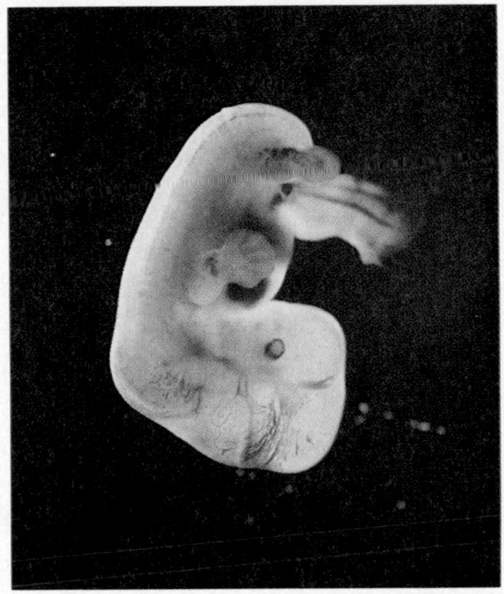

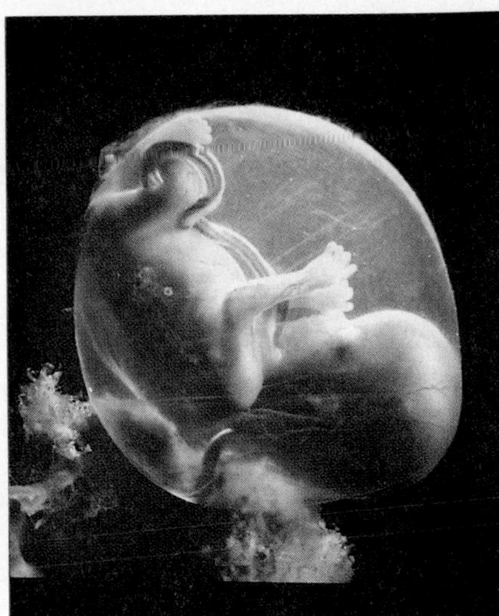

Figure 16.2 Stages of development between conception and birth. Human sperm surrounds a human egg (left). The organism pictured in the center is five weeks old, representing the embryonic phase. The photo on the right was taken during the fetal stage at 14 weeks.

very high but the mother is not likely to be able to eat enough to entirely meet these needs, the fetus can draw from her body fat reserves; the fat also provides energy that may be needed for breast-feeding the baby later. Finally, the mother is likely to accumulate more extracellular fluid (which, if excessive, results in edema). Table 16.2 summarizes these values.

Sometimes women attempt to restrict their weight gain during pregnancy in order to avoid the accumulation of extra fat. This is not a good idea, because such restriction can simultaneously affect the normal development of the fetus (Worthington-Roberts, 1988).

When the baby is born, the typical mother loses less than half of the weight she gained during a normal, healthy pregnancy. With labor and delivery, the amniotic fluid and the placenta leave the mother's body. The added maternal tissues take a longer time to shed. Sometimes a new mother is upset that she is not at her prepregnant weight immediately after delivery, even though she is definitely at the "right" weight for that time. In the

Table 16.2 Composition of Weight Gain at the End of a Single Pregnancy

Type of Tissue	Weight Gain (Pounds)
Fetus	7–7½
Amniotic fluid	2
Placenta	1–2
Increase of	
Uterus	2
Maternal blood supply	3
Breast tissue	1
Other materials (fat, extracellular fluid, and possibly some lean mass)	9–17
TOTAL	**25–35 pounds**

weeks after delivery, she will lose fluid her tissues retained during pregnancy (Committee on Nutritional Status, 1990). Loss of accumulated fat generally occurs more gradually.

Possible Problems from Inadequate Weight Gain

As we mentioned earlier, if the mother does not gain enough weight, her baby could be too small, and very small babies may not live. If they live, they may have serious problems; inadequate weight gain by the mother can result in abnormal tissue formation in the fetus.

low-birth-weight babies—infants that weigh less than 2500 grams at birth

Effect on Birth Outcome Babies weighing less than 2.5 kg (about $5\frac{1}{2}$ pounds) at birth are referred to as **low-birth-weight babies.** These infants are 20 times more likely to die in their first year than babies of higher birth weight.

Some babies who have a low birth weight even though they were carried to term are known as small-for-age babies. Infants who are premature didn't have the chance to develop fully in the womb. The premature infants are more likely than the small-for-age babies to die at birth or in their first few weeks of life.

The low-birth-weight babies carried to term exhibit two types of growth retardation. Some of these babies have poorly developed muscles and almost no body fat but are of typical length, with normal head circumference and skeletal development. Others are growth-retarded in both length and weight. Studies of low-birth-weight laboratory animals show that body organs, such as the liver and brain, often exhibit growth retardation as well, resulting in biochemical and developmental impairment (Worthington-Roberts, 1988). Low-birth-weight human babies can have the same fate.

Not only does weight gain during pregnancy have a critical influence on the weight of the baby; the *mother's prepregnant weight* is also important. If a mother is underweight when she becomes pregnant, she is more likely to have a small-for-age baby. One study showed that 18% of the babies of underweight mothers were small-for-age at birth. The risk was somewhat lower if they gained at least 1 pound per week during the last two trimesters, but even then the risk of having a small baby was three times higher than for normal-weight women (van der Spuy et al., 1988).

The effects of being a low-birth-weight baby can extend into the next generation. Mothers *who themselves were low-birth-weight babies* are at greater risk of *having* low-birth-weight babies. Their babies are more likely to require intensive care, to have respiratory difficulties, and to die (Hackman et al., 1983).

Effect of Timing The problems that occur as a result of malnutrition depend to some degree on the phase(s) of pregnancy during which nutrition is inadequate. The normal sequence and rate of tissue formation in the fetus are intricate and methodical. Typically, the basic tissue structure is estab-

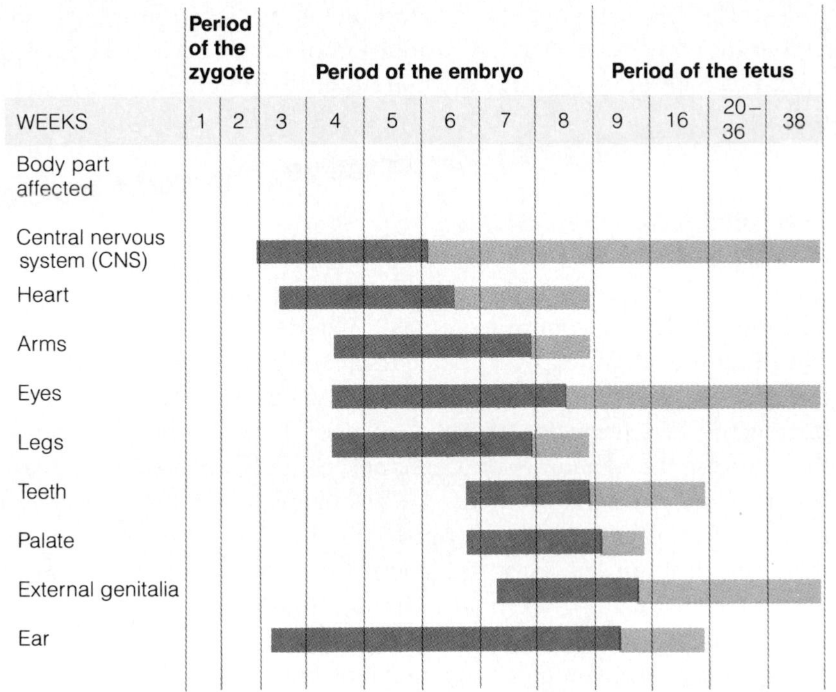

Figure 16.3 Vulnerable periods for various parts of the developing body. Different tissues, organs, and systems develop at different times during pregnancy. The critical period theory of development states that injury from nutrient extremes or teratogenic agents is more likely to occur during these periods of rapid development. The red parts of the bars indicate when damage is likely to be more severe than when the bars are blue. (Adapted from Moore, K.L.: *The developing human*, 4/e. Philadelphia: W.B. Saunders Co., 1988. Reprinted by permission.)

lished first by cells dividing rapidly (hyperplasia). In the next phase, cell division continues, and existing cells simultaneously increase in size. Finally, increase in cell size (hypertrophy) predominates.

Some experts believe that malnutrition is more likely to have serious consequences during the stages of *rapid cell division.* Since the basic structures of body organs are being developed by **cell differentiation** and proliferation during the embryonic phase, this stage is often referred to as a **critical period.**

cell differentiation—progressive development of the features of specific types of cells

critical periods—developmental stages involving rapid cell division, during which maternal nutrient intake can have the greatest consequences for the fetus

Figure 16.3 shows during which weeks of pregnancy some body structures are most vulnerable to injury. Although the embryonic period is obviously of primary importance, it is certainly not the only time during which damage can occur. At later stages, for example, although the *structure* of an organ may not be noticeably affected, malnutrition may result in less than optimal *function.*

The effects of maternal malnutrition on babies have been studied in women who experienced food shortages during war and famine. Generally, if poor nutrition is limited to the early months of pregnancy when cell division should be rapid, the embryo does not develop normally, and it is less likely to survive. If deprivation occurs only toward the end of pregnancy when cell enlargement takes place, the survival rate is better, although low birth weight can occur.

A Pregnant Woman Needs a Nutrient-Dense Diet

During pregnancy, as mother and fetus undergo change and development, the mother's need for most nutrients increases. But simply to eat more is not necessarily the solution; the proportion of the extra nutrients needed is higher in many cases than the proportion of extra kcalories needed. For the health of both mother and baby, therefore, the pregnant woman must eat a diet that is high in nutrient density.

The Need for Extra Kcalories

The energy cost of supporting a full-term pregnancy is approximately 80,000 kcalories (RDA Subcommittee, 1989). This is the approximate number of extra kcalories required over the course of nine months for gaining the recommended 25 to 35 pounds. Since little if any weight gain is anticipated during the first trimester, there is no need for additional kcalories at this time; during the remainder of pregnancy, though, an average increase of 300 kcalories per day is recommended. This means that if a woman before pregnancy ordinarily consumed approximately 2200 kcalories per day, she would need about 2500 kcalories (about 14% more) during pregnancy. Scientists have made these estimates based on certain assumptions about the amount and type of tissue gained during a typical pregnancy, about the average pregnant woman's basal metabolic rate (it is likely to increase), and about her usual activity level. If an individual's pregnancy doesn't follow the norm, her need for extra kcalories may be either higher or lower than 300 per day. For example, although appropriate physical activity is encouraged during pregnancy, some women become considerably less active, especially during the last trimester; at that time, the number of extra kcalories needed may not be as high.

The Increased Need for Specific Nutrients

The Recommended Dietary Allowances for almost all nutrients increase during pregnancy, although the allowances for some nutrients increase more than others (Figure 16.4). For vitamin A, vitamin D, calcium, and phosphorus, the recommendations for the pregnant woman are the same as for the nonpregnant 19- to 24-year-old woman. This conservative approach for vitamins A and D reflects the safety margins built into the RDAs; excess levels of these fat-soluble vitamins can cause toxicity.

During pregnancy, the need for most other nutrients (that is, protein and many vitamins and minerals) increases by between 10% and 38% above the needs of nonpregnant 19- to 24-year-old women. The extra nutrients are required to supply the raw materials for building all of the fetal and maternal tissues and for the metabolic needs of increased energy production. Since the recommended increase in kcalorie intake is only 14%, the pregnant woman needs to choose her extra kcalories carefully to achieve these higher nutrient intakes.

The recommended intakes of folic acid and iron increase by 100% or more. The large increase in usage of folic acid is accounted for by its function

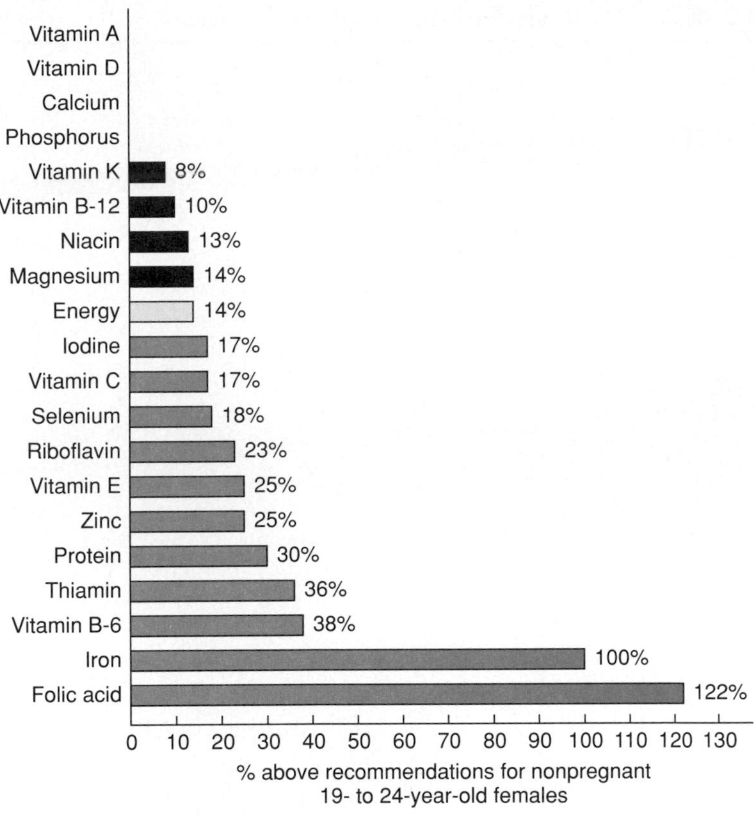

Figure 16.4 Increased nutrients recommended for adult pregnancy. During pregnancy, intakes of most nutrients should increase above prepregnancy recommendations. Since the needs for some micronutrients and protein increase substantially more than the recommended energy intake, the mother should choose more high-nutrient-density foods. (Data from National Research Council. 1989. Recommended dietary allowances. Washington, DC: National Academy Press.)

in production of red blood cells and in cell division in general. The extra iron is needed for several tissues: the expanded maternal blood supply, the fetal blood supply, and the fetal liver.

Eating to Meet the Increased Needs

In order to meet the higher recommended intakes for pregnancy, women need to eat more (although not as much as some might wish!). While some women experience nausea, which may interfere with meeting increased needs, most women will eat more without problems. A pregnant woman's appetite often increases naturally in the second and third trimesters, when the needs are highest.

Women not only find themselves eating more, but they often also acquire new food preferences. In a study done on a middle-income American population, pregnant women substantially increased their intake of milk; they frequently craved ice cream, sweets and candy, fruits, and fish. The foods to which they most often developed aversions were coffee, red meat, poultry, and certain sauces (Rosso, 1988). Although some of these inclinations help meet nutritional needs, others do not. Therefore, it is best to follow guidelines for meeting recommended intakes.

The Basic Food Guide for Pregnancy and Lactation (Table 16.3) can be used for selecting an adequate diet. Since the need for many micronutrients

Table 16.3 Basic Food Guide for Pregnancy and Lactation

	Minimum Servings Daily		
Food Group	Nonpregnant 19- to 24-year-olds	Pregnant and Lactating Females	Pregnant Vegans[d]
Fruits and vegetables	5[a]	5[b]	8
Grain products	6	6 or more	6
Milk and milk products	3	4[c]	4 (as soy milk)
Meats and meat alternates	2	2	3 (as legumes, nuts, and seeds)

[a] Includes one vitamin C-rich and one vitamin A (carotene)-rich food daily.

[b] Includes two servings of vitamin C-rich and one vitamin A (carotene)-rich food daily.

[c] For pregnant teenagers, increase to at least five servings daily.

[d] Adapted from Mutch, 1988; and 1989 RDA.

increases proportionately more than the need for extra energy, extra food should be of high nutrient density, and limited extras should be de-emphasized. The Basic Food Guide suggests eating an additional serving of vitamin-C-rich food each day, drinking an additional glass of milk, and eating enough grain products to produce the recommended weight gains.

Vegans, who avoid all foods of animal origin, need to be especially careful to eat foods that will provide enough energy, protein, vitamins, and minerals during pregnancy. (Bioavailability of the minerals is also a concern, because the insoluble fiber content of vegan diets is high.) Vegans, who often avoid fortified and enriched foods and/or do not take vitamin and mineral supplements, are particularly at risk of nutrient deficiency.

Recommendations for food intake for pregnant vegans are also given on Table 16.3. Nonetheless, to be sure that her diet is nutritionally adequate, a pregnant vegan should seek the advice of a qualified nutritionist or dietitian.

Are Supplements Needed During Pregnancy?

Most pregnant women (especially omnivores) can meet their needs for almost all nutrients by eating a balanced and varied diet. Even the RDA for folic acid during pregnancy can be met from ordinary foods. But the one nutrient unlikely to be obtained from foods in the amount suggested by the RDA is iron: the recommended intake increases from 15 mg before pregnancy to 30 mg during pregnancy. Since it is a challenge for many women to take in even 15 mg from the diet, the RDA recommends a daily iron supplement during pregnancy.

Although a well-chosen diet can fulfill the other nutritional needs of most pregnant women (Committee on Nutritional Status, 1990), many physicians also recommend that all their pregnant patients take a moderate multivitamin and mineral supplement. Doing so may be useful and is not hazardous unless the amounts of nutrients are excessive or unbalanced; vitamin supplements that are too potent can be toxic to the fetus.

The moderate supplement recommended by the doctor must not be regarded as a replacement for a balanced diet, though. Since some essential nutrients are not likely to be included in supplements, a nutritious diet is still of critical importance.

A Special Program for High-Risk Pregnant Women

The **Supplemental Food Program for Women, Infants, and Children (WIC)** is a nationwide, federally funded program that provides access to particular foods, nutrition education, and medical referral services to low-income women who have high-risk pregnancies. Several studies have demonstrated its effectiveness in decreasing the incidence of premature births, stillbirths, and maternal anemia and in increasing birth weight (American Dietetic Association, 1989).

Supplemental Food Program for Women, Infants, and Children (WIC)—national federally funded program that provides nutritional and medical support for low-income women who have high-risk pregnancies

The most positive effects of the WIC program are seen among women with the poorest nutritional status at the time they joined the program. Adequate length of time in the program is also important; a study of the program in Missouri showed that mothers needed to receive benefits for at least seven months before increased birth weights were seen (Stockbauer, 1987).

One group of people served by the WIC program is pregnant teenagers. In the next chapter, after normal adolescent development has been discussed, we will focus on this group.

There Are Ways to Cope with Physiological Changes of Pregnancy

During pregnancy, physiological changes take place in virtually every system of a woman's body to accommodate and support the pregnancy. Some of these changes are related to nutrition and occasionally become of sufficient magnitude to constitute medical problems. This section discusses how pregnant women can cope with the lesser problems and discomforts; it also emphasizes the importance of medical intervention for more serious conditions.

Nausea and Vomiting

Over half of pregnant women experience some degree of nausea and vomiting during pregnancy, whether it occurs as "morning sickness" or at other times of day. Many women who are troubled by this problem report relief if they keep some food in their stomachs much of the time. They do this by eating small, frequent meals; by drinking fluids between meals rather than with them; and by eating something bland like a few crackers or toast before getting out of bed in the morning.

For a very few women, these suggestions do not help. If a pregnant woman cannot keep anything down, she should get in touch with the health care professional who is monitoring her pregnancy. Without intervention, the risk of having a low-birth-weight baby is many times higher than in women with less severe vomiting. If nothing else can be found to ease her problem, nutrients in solution can be delivered intravenously to provide what she and her fetus need (Levine and Esser, 1988).

Heartburn

Heartburn (reflux of acidic stomach contents into the lower part of the esophagus) also bothers some women during pregnancy. It is most likely to occur in the later stages of pregnancy, when the fetus is large enough to exert pressure on the stomach. Avoiding fatty or greasy foods, heavily spiced dishes, and caffeine can help reduce heartburn. Eating smaller meals and not lying down soon after eating can also help.

Constipation

Constipation is common during pregnancy, especially in the later stages when the rapidly growing fetus crowds the colon. In addition, hormonal changes during pregnancy relax the muscles of the colon, slowing down the movement of solid waste. Some pregnant women believe that iron supplements contribute to constipation. Usually, increasing the amount of fiber in the diet by eating more fruits, vegetables, and whole grains and by drinking more fluids solves the problem. Moderate exercise, such as walking, also helps.

Pregnancy-Induced Hypertension (PIH)

Some pregnant women develop a unique form of hypertension. Along with the increase in blood pressure, they are likely to excrete abnormally high levels of protein in the urine and experience fluid retention. Intervention is important to prevent more serious consequences, such as death or damage to the fetus or, in rare cases, death of the mother. PIH may also put the mother at increased risk of cardiovascular or renal disease later in life (Zeman and Ney, 1988).

Although it is not known for certain why this condition occurs, we know that certain groups of pregnant women are at higher risk of pregnancy-induced hypertension. It is most common in women who are pregnant for the first time and who are under 20 or over 35 years of age. Because it is also seen more often among low-income groups and among underweight women, experts believe that poor general nutritional status and quality of prenatal care may contribute to its development (Zeman and Ney, 1988).

In the past, sodium was commonly restricted during pregnancy in the belief that this would help women avoid PIH. We now know that *severe* sodium restriction can interfere with the development of the fetus and that it is not effective in preventing the condition. *Moderate* sodium restriction (avoiding added salt and obviously salty foods) and bed rest can usually help control PIH if it develops (Zeman and Ney, 1988). Fortunately, the condition resolves after delivery of the baby.

Pregnant Women Should Avoid Toxic Substances

Just as it is important to provide enough of the essential nutrients for fetal development, it is also critically important to avoid taking in substances that could cause fetal damage; such substances are known as teratogens. Alcohol, tobacco, and many other drugs are known teratogens.

The safety of ingesting caffeine during pregnancy has been called into question. Also, the effects on the pregnant woman of consuming non-food items (a common practice in some cultures) has been evaluated. In this section, we will discuss what is known about the consequences of these behaviors.

Alcohol

Like many other substances, alcohol in the mother's bloodstream will cross the placenta and circulate in the baby's bloodstream. At some level, alcohol interferes with the growth processes in the embryo or fetus, possibly by reducing the supply of oxygen flowing through the placenta and/or by blocking the activity of essential nutrients. It is estimated that as many as 2% of all babies born alive in the Western world may be suffering from the effects of alcohol exposure in utero (Miller, 1986).

The effects of alcohol are thought to increase in severity in proportion to the amount of alcohol consumed and to vary in effect depending on the stage of pregnancy. Excess alcohol during the first three months of pregnancy is thought to be most often associated with the development of physical abnormalities in the fetus. Animal studies and observations of humans indicate that one or more episodes of binge drinking during the early stages of pregnancy are most likely to produce low-birth-weight babies and children with impaired mental functions (Wright et al., 1983). Alcohol in the second three months can increase the risk of miscarriage. And during the third trimester, alcohol abuse is most likely to reduce the rate of growth of the fetus (American Medical Association, 1983). Even heavy alcohol use before conception has been associated with low birth weight (Little et al., 1980).

fetal alcohol syndrome (FAS)—condition occurring in some children of alcoholic mothers, involving certain characteristic abnormalities

In the 1960s the name **fetal alcohol syndrome (FAS)** was given to the set of abnormalities seen among some children of women who consumed large amounts of alcohol during pregnancy. FAS is now considered a prime cause of mental retardation in the Western world. The typical abnormalities of FAS include characteristic facial features as seen in Figure 16.5; poor growth before and after birth; and central nervous system disorders, including mental retardation and deficiencies in fine motor skills.

Although experts agree that frequent heavy drinking during pregnancy is dangerous to the developing fetus, studies regarding the effect of light-to-moderate use of alcohol have produced conflicting results. This is due in part to difficulty in separating the effects of alcohol from those related to other factors such as smoking and poor diet.

A recent study found that consumption by mothers of 1.5 ounces of alcohol per day (about three drinks) before they knew they were pregnant resulted in lower IQ scores in their children than were achieved by the children of nondrinkers. Measured at the age of 4 years, IQ scores were 5 points lower in the children of the mothers who drank early in their pregnancies (Streissguth et al., 1989).

It is important to note that no threshold level has been defined; that is, *there is no level of alcohol consumption known to be completely risk-free during pregnancy*. The American Medical Association advises: "*Physicians should be explicit in reinforcing the concept that, with several aspects of the issue still in doubt, the safest course is abstinence*" (American Medical Association, 1983). Other reports concur: the *Dietary Guidelines for Americans* (USDA and USDHHS, 1990), *The Surgeon General's Report on Nutrition and Health* (1988), and *Diet and Health* (National Research Council, 1989) recommend the avoidance of alcohol during pregnancy.

Recent data suggest that the father's habits of alcohol consumption before conception may be related to his child's birth weight. Infants whose fathers drank two drinks or more per day in the month prior to conception weighed almost 6 ounces less than the babies of those who drank only occasionally (Little and Sing, 1986). This topic deserves more study.

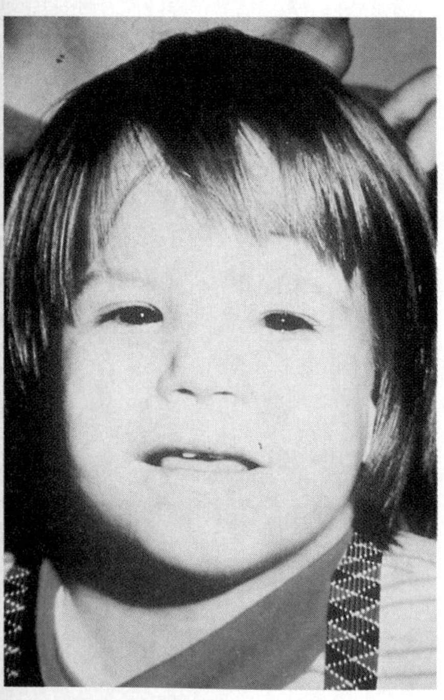

Figure 16.5 A child with fetal alcohol syndrome (FAS). This child shows several facial characteristics of FAS: wide space between the eyes, small nose, and thin upper lip.

Other Drugs

Various pharmaceuticals can damage the developing fetus. Some of these are prescription medications, and others are over-the-counter drugs. The pregnant woman should check with her health care professional about any medications she is considering using.

Street drugs can also have serious negative effects. For example, data are accumulating that pregnant women who use cocaine are more likely to have spontaneous abortion, premature labor, or small-for-age babies; teratogenic effects are less clear (Committee on Nutritional Status, 1990). As with alcohol, it is difficult to separate the effects of illicit drugs from the effects of other lifestyle factors that may be practiced simultaneously, such as smoking tobacco, use of other drugs, poor nutrition, and inadequate health care.

Caffeine

Caffeine is a drug naturally present in coffee, tea, and chocolate. It is also added to colas and other soft drinks and to certain medications (see Chapter 15).

Because caffeine is a stimulant that crosses the placenta and circulates in the fetal bloodstream, there has been concern that its use during pregnancy may have detrimental effects on the fetus. Animal studies using *very* high levels of caffeine have shown that it can cause abnormalities.

Several studies have been conducted to determine whether these effects can occur in humans as well; the results have generally been negative. Studies have shown that women who consume relatively large amounts of caffeine during pregnancy have smaller, less healthy babies; but this may actually be a result of other factors common in the same women, such as smoking and alcohol use (Linn et al., 1982).

Most experts believe that alcohol and smoking cause more damage to unborn children than caffeine, but the potential for adverse effects of high doses of caffeine still exists during pregnancy. Therefore, the Food and Drug Administration recommends that pregnant women avoid high intakes of caffeine from food and drugs during pregnancy (Lecos, 1980).

Smoking

Smoking during pregnancy has many negative effects. Babies of mothers who smoked are shorter and lighter and have a higher prevalence of signs suggesting growth retardation in utero. One study showed that infants of mothers who smoked weighed 5% less than those whose mothers did not smoke (Brooke et al., 1989). Complications of pregnancy—bleeding, premature rupture of membranes, abortion, and infant death—are also more likely (Hoff et al., 1986). In addition, children of mothers who smoked during pregnancy are at greater risk of developing cancer as young children (Stjernfeldt et al., 1986). These effects are dose related; that is, the more a woman smokes, the higher the risk of these negative consequences.

Pica

Another dietary practice thought to be potentially dangerous during pregnancy is pica. Pica is often defined as a pathological craving for substances that are not food, such as clay, laundry starch, or chalk. It is sometimes practiced by members of certain socioeconomic and racial groups, especially black women from the rural South; it may be culturally influenced as well. Some people believe that pica is a *response* to a deficiency of iron or other nutrients; many others believe pica is the *cause* of the poor status of iron that is often associated with the condition (Blinder et al., 1988).

The significance of pica in nutrition depends on the type and amount of nonfood items consumed. Some items (such as starch) have a significant effect because they provide empty kcalories and displace foods that could have provided additional nutrients. Other substances (such as clay) can bind dietary minerals into a nonabsorbable form. Clay, chalk, and paint chips may contain dangerously high levels of toxicants such as lead; further, ingested clay may result in intestinal obstructions or may be the source of parasites that cause disease (Blinder et al., 1988).

We cannot anticipate all of the nonfood items people might choose to eat; who would have thought that someone could develop an appetite for burnt matches, hair, mothballs, tire inner tubes, or air-freshener blocks? Yet, those are among the items that have been consumed (Worthington-Roberts, 1988). Certainly, the ingestion of any nonfood items should be discouraged; at worst, death of the mother and fetus can result from pica.

The many factors that can have positive and negative effects on pregnancy are condensed into brief guidelines in the Nutrition for Living: During Pregnancy section.

Rapid Growth During Infancy Calls for High Nutrient Intake

During the first year of life, growth in both length and weight is more rapid than at any other period of life outside the womb. A normal infant doubles his or her birth weight by about four months and triples it by the end of the first year. The child's height at one year is usually 150% of his or her birth length. This rapid growth causes infants to have the highest nutrient needs per unit of body weight of any age group. Therefore, the decision of what to feed a baby is an important matter.

Continuing Growth

The growth taking place in the infant involves all types of tissue and requires adequate levels of nutrients; insufficient nutrient intake during the first few months after birth can result in a slowing of growth. If adequate feeding is restored later in the first year, part of that deficit can usually be made up. Sometimes, but not always, catch-up growth is complete (Pipes, 1989).

Body growth is important for its own sake, but it is also critical because of its relationship to brain growth. One expert asserts that the best way to assure good *brain* growth is to encourage optimal *body* growth from conception until the second birthday (Dobbing, 1984).

Physical Status

At birth, although the healthy baby is sufficiently developed to survive as an independent biological entity, its tissues, organs, and systems are still developing. Therefore, what the baby consumes must not only meet its nutritional needs but also be consistent with its physiological and metabolic capabilities.

Because the gastrointestinal tract is immature and of small capacity at birth, the production of gastric secretions, stomach acid, and certain enzymes may be low. The stomach, which will be able to hold about 7 ounces of food at 1 year of age, holds less than 1 ounce at birth. Nor are the kidneys fully developed at the time of birth; they do not have the ability to concen-

During Pregnancy

There's a great deal in folklore about what a pregnant woman should and shouldn't eat. Science offers more reliable guidelines:

- The Basic Food Guide (Table 16.3) suggests an increase in minimal intakes from most food groups: one more milk serving, an additional vitamin C source, and probably more grain products. There is no one right way to add the extra food: it can be consumed either as larger meals or as snacks. Some women like to eat more frequent, smaller meals to satisfy their hunger and limit the volume in the stomach, which may be more comfortable.
- This extra food intake should amount to about 300 extra kcalories per day in the second and third trimesters, which means that limited extras should be especially limited during pregnancy. Chances are, if a pregnant woman eats more of the nourishing foods she needs, she will have less appetite for "junk food."
- Alcoholic beverages, smoking, and pica should be avoided entirely during pregnancy.
- Some foods may become unexplainably appealing during pregnancy, like the classic combination of ice cream and pickles. Such appetites do not relate to specific nutritional needs. There is no harm in giving in to strange cravings as long as the items make a reasonable contribution to the total diet and are not consumed to the exclusion of other foods.
- Certain foods, on the other hand, may become distasteful. During pregnancy many women find coffee nauseating, though at this time, any food can become unappealing. Somebody who ordinarily loves Italian food might not be able to abide it—even the smell of it—during pregnancy. We don't know why this happens, but there's no need to worry; there are plenty of other good things to eat, and old favorites will have appeal again.

trate urine that the older child's and adult's kidneys do. Therefore, infants require about $1\frac{1}{2}$ ml of water per kcalorie ingested, compared with the 1 ml/kcalorie that will be adequate later in life.

These factors suggest that during the first four to six months of the infant's life, it is wise to limit its intake to fluids that are sufficiently dilute and easy to digest. Breast milk and formulas that simulate it are the best choices.

Nutritional Status

A healthy full-term infant (one who was born to a well-nourished mother after nine months of normal gestation) has a reserve supply of some nutrients. For example, iron stored in the newborn's liver can meet its needs for several months if the baby's intake of iron is low.

Even so, a steady supply of energy and nutrients is essential for proper growth and development. Estimating the infant's needs for individual nutrients is based on the average amount consumed by thriving infants breastfed by healthy, well-nourished mothers (RDA Subcommittee, 1989). Energy requirements of the normal infant, per unit of body weight, are three to four times that of the normal adult (Heird and Cooper, 1988). Adequate intake of nutrients is especially critical for babies who are born without adequate reserves; low-birth-weight babies are usually more susceptible to the effects of poor diet and disease.

Psychosocial Status

The infant's social development begins at birth, with its first human contact. Since so much of the time spent with a baby involves feeding him or her, the feeding relationship is the primary route by which the baby finds out about itself and the world during the first year of life.

At birth, it is thought that infants can distinguish between positive and negative sensations but not what caused them. It takes a sensitive caregiver to identify what is causing a negative sensation (such as hunger), to get rid of the cause (feed the baby), and to read the cues from the baby that the problem has been solved (satiety). Such two-way communication between the infant and caregiver helps the baby gain self-awareness, assures it that it can make known what it wants, and teaches trust (Satter, 1986a).

If, on the other hand, babies are consistently frustrated or thwarted in their demands for food or have food forced upon them when they do not want it, they learn a very different lesson about their world: they may perceive it as a hostile place. For them, hunger is associated with anxiety rather than with pleasurable anticipation.

The best way to promote healthy psychosocial development through the feeding interaction is for the caregiver to feed the infant "on demand"; that is, when the baby gives cues that it is hungry. One cue is persistent crying; of course, an infant may also cry because of some other discomfort, but if the crying continues after other needs have been met, the baby probably needs to eat. Another cue may be when the baby sucks on anything available—its fist, the blanket, your shirt, etc. Caregivers need to learn to be responsive to each individual baby's cues; the rigid feeding schedules that have been promoted for infant feeding in the past are not now thought to foster the best psychosocial development.

Both Breast-Feeding and Bottle-Feeding Have Certain Advantages

An infant's needs can be successfully supported in the first few months by mother's breast milk or formulas that simulate it. From a biological point of view, if the mother and baby are both healthy, the best choice is for the mother to nurse her baby. In addition to being nutritionally optimal, mother's milk is less likely to cause allergies in the baby. If there is a history of allergies in either the mother's or father's families, breast-feeding is clearly the best choice.

Human milk also contains substances that protect the infant from gastrointestinal infections. This is an important safeguard to infants' health, especially in the developing countries, where sanitation is often poor; but its importance in the industrialized nations where babies are less exposed to pathogens is debated (Bauchner et al., 1986). There is evidence that breast milk also contains substances that promote the maturation of the infant's GI tract (Sheard and Walker, 1988). These substances are not present in formulas.

Today's standard commercially produced infant formulas are made to mimic human milk as much as possible; from a nutritional perspective, they run a close second to mother's milk. Therefore, if allergies are not in the family history, bottle-feeding the baby is a reasonable option. The next section considers in greater detail what breast milk and formulas can provide for the infant.

Considerations Regarding Breast-Feeding

From the time of delivery, the mother's mammary glands produce fluids for the infant. For the first few days, a fluid called **colostrum** is produced; this is a watery substance that is higher in protein and some minerals than the milk that will come later. It also contains antibodies and special cells that increase the baby's immunity to several diseases.

colostrum—watery liquid produced by the breasts (mammary glands) of mothers during the first few days after delivery

Nutrients and Immune Factors in Mature Milk Colostrum is replaced by mature breast milk about four or five days after delivery. Mature breast milk, too, provides unique benefits for the infant beyond supplying nutrients needed for growth.

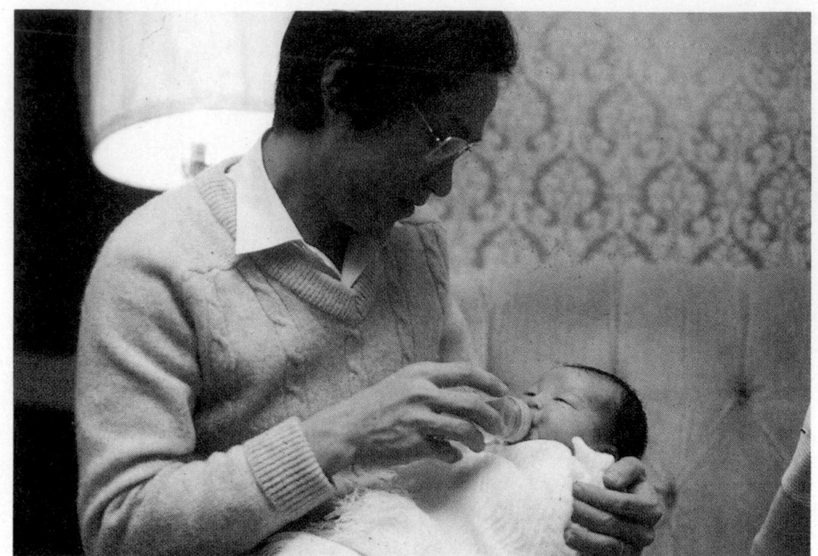

Infant feeding—breast, bottle, or both? Nutrition and immunological factors are important, but many other considerations enter into this decision as well. For example, bottle-feeding allows greater participation by the father.

- Human milk contains several substances that help protect the baby against various types of infections. Antibodies from the mother, certain proteins in her milk, and certain other substances contribute to this immune function.
- The proteins in breast milk are less likely to provoke allergic reactions than the milks of other animals. This is an especially important consideration for the infant with a family history of allergies.
- The proteins in breast milk are mostly lactalbumins, which are easier for the infant to digest than the casein proteins of non-heat-treated cow's milk.
- Lactose is the main carbohydrate in human and animal milks. It is present at a higher level in human milk than in cow's milk, and it promotes the absorption of calcium and some other minerals.
- Fats supply about half of the kcalories in breast milk, and the structure of the triglycerides makes them highly absorbable.
- The mineral content of breast milk is likewise well suited to the infant's needs. The ratio of calcium to phosphorus is approximately 2:1, which facilitates absorption. Although the iron content is low, it is very readily absorbed by the infant.
- If the mother is well nourished, the vitamin content of her milk usually will be adequate for the baby's needs, but inadequacies in the mother's diet will be reflected in lower quantities of some vitamins in her milk. This has been shown for a number of the water-soluble vitamins (Whitehead, 1988).

The Breast-Fed Infant's Need for Supplements Although breast milk from a well-nourished mother is generally thought to meet the nutritional needs of her infant, there are a few exceptions and qualifications.

At birth, most infants are given an injection or oral supplements of vitamin K. This is because their bodies initially do not have enough vitamin K for normal blood clotting in the unlikely event they might be injured. In the weeks after birth, as they consume vitamin K in breast milk and develop colonic microflora that produce it, their needs for vitamin K are met without further supplementation.

Supplemental vitamin D is usually recommended for the breast-fed infant, because breast milk does not supply an adequate amount. Although sun exposure leads to some internal production of vitamin D, dark-skinned babies in northern climates are unlikely to produce enough and therefore should be given the supplement (Fomon, 1986). Whether or not light-skinned babies who get some sun exposure need a supplement is debatable, but vitamin D is often recommended as a safeguard (Pipes, 1989).

Fluoride supplements also should be given to breast-fed infants. This is necessary because very little fluoride transfers from the mother's plasma into breast milk. Fluoride is important for developing healthy teeth and probably bones as well.

A case can be made either for or against iron supplementation. Because of the high bioavailability of iron in breast milk, fewer breast-fed than bottle-fed babies become anemic. Some pediatricians, however, may recommend iron supplements to provide some reserves.

Composition Change During the Feeding The composition of mother's milk changes somewhat within a feeding period. The water content of breast milk is initially high; thus, the baby gets relatively dilute milk at the beginning of the feeding session when he or she is very thirsty. This provides the amount of water that the infants' kidneys need. As the feeding continues, the fat content increases, the milk is more concentrated, and the baby's hunger is satisfied more quickly.

Volume Influenced by the Baby's Intake The amount of milk the lactating mother produces changes in response to the baby's needs. During the first six months, the nursing infant consumes an average of 750 ml (approximately 3 cups) of breast milk per day. Wanting to eat more often, the baby signals this need by thoroughly emptying the mother's breasts. Emptying the breasts causes them to make more milk. From 6 months to 1 year of age, the baby is likely to decrease its intake to an average of 600 ml (about $2\frac{1}{2}$ cups) per day as it begins eating solid foods (RDA Subcommittee, 1989). The decreased emptying of the breasts causes them to make less milk. That's why a mother who feeds her young infant with formula in place of breast milk on frequent occasions may find that her supply of milk decreases so much that it becomes difficult to resume more regular breast-feeding later. However, some mothers find it very satisfactory to combine the use of formulas and breast milk to feed their infants.

Because milk production increases with frequent and thorough emptying of the breasts, some mothers of twins have even been able to breast-feed their babies. The combination approach mentioned above can work well for these mothers too.

Volume Influenced by the Mother's Diet In some instances the mother may not produce enough milk to satisfy her baby's needs. If her energy intake is inadequate (because of poor eating habits, dieting to lose weight, or being "too busy to eat"), her milk output may be low despite her infant's deliberate message about wanting more (Satter, 1986b). This is less of a problem in the developed countries than in the developing countries, where food shortages and poverty can compromise the ability of some mothers to nourish their children adequately by breast-feeding.

Mother's Increased Needs During Lactation Just as production of new tissue during pregnancy calls for additional energy and nutrients, so does production of milk. A breast-feeding mother is advised by the RDA to consume 500 kcalories more each day than she needed before pregnancy. Note that this is even more food energy than is recommended for the latter part of pregnancy. Some research has demonstrated that it is possible to lactate successfully on less than this (Butte et al., 1984; Prentice and Prentice, 1988; Sadurskis et al., 1988), but cutting back too far will result in lower milk production, suboptimal infant growth, and maternal fatigue.

The lactating woman's needs for protein, vitamins, and minerals increase; recommended intakes of these nutrients increase by as much as 65% above the amounts needed *before pregnancy.* Compared with recommendations *during pregnancy,* most of the nutrient recommendations for lactation are slightly higher; others stay the same, and those for iron and folic acid are lower. The RDAs for the nursing mother during the first 6 months are slightly higher than from 6 months to 1 year, reflecting the decrease in the baby's intake of breast milk as it starts consuming solids (between 4 and 6 months of age).

The mother's need for water increases according to the volume of milk the baby drinks—anywhere from $\frac{1}{2}$ quart (for a newborn) to over one quart per day. Nutrition for Living: During Lactation summarizes intake recommendations for food and fluids. Normally, nutritional supplements are not needed by lactating women.

Effects of Lactation on the Mother's Body Lactation has effects on the mother's whole body just as pregnancy does. When a baby nurses, the suckling stimulates muscle contractions in the mother's uterus. This helps the uterus to return to its prepregnant size. Lactation generally decreases the mother's fat stores; many mothers, during the first few months they are nursing their babies, experience a gradual loss of 2–3 kg (4–6 lb) of the extra fat they accumulated during pregnancy. How much fat is lost, however, depends on the individual's physiological makeup, on the amount of milk the baby takes, as well as on all the usual factors in the energy balance equation: energy intake, resting metabolic rate, thermic effect of exercise, and thermic effect of food.

Mothers who nurse their babies have a slightly better chance of losing some of their excess fat than mothers who bottle-feed. Fifty-six well-educated middle-income women were studied in the six months after childbirth. Mothers who exclusively nursed their babies lost an average of 18.3 pounds; those who exclusively bottle-fed their infants lost 15.9 pounds; those who used a combination of breast- and formula-feeding lost 18.0 pounds (Brewer et al., 1989).

Lactation may also decrease bone mass. Although there is no evidence that a lactation period of up to six months adversely affects the bone mass of the mother, a longer nursing period could. One group of investigators studied the bone status of women who had nursed three or four children. Reduced bone mass was found in those who had nursed their babies for almost a year (Wardlaw and Pike, 1986). Much more study is needed to determine whether such effects are consistent and to determine how long and how many periods of lactation can be undertaken without affecting bone mass. (Reduced bone mass increases the risk of osteoporosis; see Chapter 13 [on minerals].)

What Formulas Have to Offer the Infant

If an infant's parents have family medical histories of allergies, breast-feeding is the best option until the baby's immune system and gastrointestinal system are more mature; this development takes place throughout the first year of life. For a variety of reasons, however, some parents might decide that bottle-feeding is a better option for them, or they might alternate between breast- and bottle-feeding. For these parents, a variety of infant formulas can take the place of mother's milk.

The nutritional makeup of the standard commercially prepared infant formula is a satisfactory substitute for breast milk for most infants. Although these substitutes do a good job of imitating mother's milk, each formula has slightly different characteristics, and they cannot provide the immunity or reduce the likelihood of allergies as breast milk can. Let's take a look at some

During Lactation

A woman's diet during lactation can remain much as it was during pregnancy, with the exceptions noted below.

- Fluid intake should be increased by approximately a quart a day, or more if the baby takes more milk than that. If a mother does not get naturally thirsty for it, she should drink a glass of fluid every time she nurses her baby.
- Traces of anything the mother eats can transfer into her milk. Most babies don't appear to mind the changing flavor of milk, but if they seem distressed whenever the mother has consumed a certain food, avoiding it could solve the problem.

of the options available to parents who decide to feed their babies infant formulas.

Cow's Milk Formulas Most infant formulas are made from cow's milk that has been modified to resemble breast milk as closely as possible. However, the major protein in cow's milk—casein—is difficult for a baby to digest: it makes a tough curd in the stomach. For that reason, most milk-based formulas have been heat-treated in a way that makes the casein easier to digest. The butterfat is replaced by polyunsaturated vegetable oils that are more readily absorbed. Additional lactose or other carbohydrate is incorporated; vitamins and most minerals are also added to resemble the levels in human milk.

One ingredient in formula about which there is some debate is iron; the availability of both iron-fortified formula and formula without iron reflects this difference of opinion. Some experts believe that because a normally healthy newborn is thought to have enough iron stored in the liver to last for approximately six months, no extra iron is needed in infant formula. They suggest that extra iron may actually have a negative effect. Some parents report that infants who have been fed iron-fortified infant formula, for instance, may experience gastrointestinal distress, although this is not supported by recent research (Nelson et al., 1988). Another concern is that high iron intakes seem to encourage the growth of pathogenic organisms in some infants. This latter observation has been made in developing countries, where iron deficiency is often accompanied by low-grade infections; when iron was supplemented, the infections quickly *worsened.*

In the United States, iron deficiency has been a problem in some infants, especially those who are bottle-fed. To prevent anemia, the American Academy of Pediatrics now recommends that iron-fortified formula be used for all formula-fed infants (Committee on Nutrition, 1989).

A choice to make in buying formula involves its dilution. Most formulas are available as a powder, a liquid concentrate, or a ready-to-use beverage. The first two need to be reconstituted with appropriate amounts of water before use, which is less convenient but also less expensive. It is critical that the formula be of the correct concentration when given to the baby. If it is not dilute enough, the baby's body can become stressed; if it is too dilute, the baby will not be adequately nourished.

Soy Formulas Some commercially produced infant formulas are made from soybeans. Such formulas tend to have a slightly higher protein level and a slightly lower carbohydrate level than cow's milk formulas. Also, the bioavailability of some minerals may be lower, since these products are of plant origin. Because of such differences, these products should be used only on a pediatrician's advice.

Soy formulas may be recommended for infants who are potentially allergic to milk or milk formulas and for the management of conditions in which lactose must be avoided. However, soy formulas are not recommended for infants who have already shown signs of allergy. Soy protein, like cow's milk protein, is a common allergen. Infants who have reacted strongly to cow's milk protein may react strongly to soy protein as well.

Other Formulas *Whole cow's milk or formulas made from it at home are not recommended for the first six months of life.* After the baby drinks from a cup and consumes a significant proportion (about one-third) of kcalories from solid foods that provide iron, vitamin C, and carbohydrate, whole cow's milk may begin to replace breast milk or formula. Before that time, using whole milk may result in inadequate intake of some nutrients. Furthermore, some young infants become anemic on cow's milk because it is a poor source of iron and it may cause low-level intestinal bleeding (American Academy of Pediatrics, 1983a).

Low-fat milks (2%, 1%, or skim) are not recommended for use in the first year, because they do not provide sufficient energy value or essential fatty acids. Furthermore, they have larger concentrations of electrolytes and proteins that cannot easily be handled by immature kidneys; the **renal solute load** is too high.

renal solute load—amount of dissolved substances processed by the kidneys

Infants should not be given raw milk or imitation milks. If parents want to use the milk of other animals for their infants (e.g., goat's milk) they should thoroughly discuss whether this is advisable with their pediatrician.

The Bottle-Fed Infant's Need for Supplements As we mentioned earlier, all newborns should receive supplemental vitamin K initially. In addition, babies fed commercially produced infant formula may benefit from supplemental fluoride if they do not get adequate amounts from water they drink. Because fluoride intake from water can vary widely with the infant's intake and with the fluoride content of the local water supply, and because excess fluoride is toxic, it is not added to infant formulas. Parents should follow the advice of a pediatrician on whether or not to supplement, and if so, how much.

Precautions About Bottle-Feeding Some precautions need to be taken with bottle-feeding. As has been mentioned before, it is important that the formula be at the proper dilution when given to the baby. If you have mixed the formula in advance, store it in the refrigerator until you use it. Then, if the baby prefers it warmer, take the chill off of it by putting the bottle into a container of warm water for a few minutes. *Do not heat the formula in a microwave oven;* it is easy to overheat the contents of the bottle. Also, because the heat may be unevenly distributed, "hot spots" may occur in the formula. Some infants have suffered burns in the mouth and/or esophagus from drinking microwaved formula.

With bottle-feeding, there is the possibility of **baby bottle tooth decay** (sometimes called nursing bottle caries). This condition is characterized by rampant dental decay in children around the age of 2 years (Figure 16.6), but it is avoidable. It is most likely to occur in children who are put to bed with a bottle containing sweet liquids such as milk, juice, soda pop, or any sugar-

baby bottle tooth decay—tooth decay resulting from prolonged exposure to sweet beverages (even infant formula) consumed from baby bottles

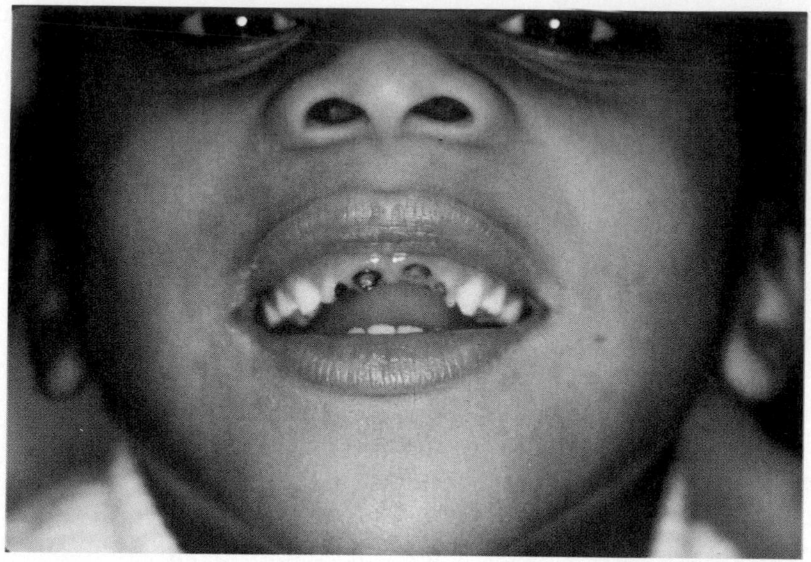

Figure 16.6 Baby bottle tooth decay. Infants who are put to bed with bottles of sugar-containing fluids may develop rampant dental decay.

sweetened drink. Decay occurs because as the child falls asleep, saliva flow (which ordinarily helps cleanse the teeth of sugar) diminishes; with sweet liquids pooled in the mouth, mouth bacteria have the opportunity to metabolize the sugars, producing acids that cause decay.

Parents can prevent this tooth decay in their children by *not* putting their babies to bed with bottles and by weaning their children from the bottle at about 1 year of age (Johnsen and Nowjack-Raymer, 1989).

Other Factors in the Breast Versus Bottle Decision

Since infant formulas match the nutritional content of human milk so well, bottle-feeding is a reasonable nutrition option for parents to consider if there are no allergies in the family. But there are many other factors that legitimately come into play in making this decision.

The mother needs to consider her availability and time and schedule constraints. Given her circumstances, does she think of breast-feeding as a convenience or an inconvenience? For example, if she works outside the home and would find it difficult to be with her baby at some feeding times, is she willing to pump her breasts so she can leave breast milk for the baby in her absence? Alternatively, is she willing for the baby to receive formula when she is gone, and nurse it when she is at home? Or does formula-feeding seem overall to be the most manageable situation?

If the parents are concerned about the possibility of toxicants being secreted into the mother's milk, then formula-feeding should be considered. Nicotine, alcohol, and caffeine are all partly secreted from the mother's body into her milk. Certain medications, some of which could have harmful effects on the baby, also can pass into breast milk; a breast-feeding woman should check with the baby's doctor about using any of these substances.

If a lactating mother is exposed to high levels of certain environmental contaminants, they may be secreted into her milk as well. This is particularly true of chemicals that are stored in the mother's fatty tissues, such as PCBs and some insecticides. When a woman is lactating, she should follow public health guidelines for avoiding environmental toxicants. If an expectant or lactating mother thinks that she has been exposed to high levels of such substances, she should inform her baby's physician.

Breast-feeding can promote emotional **bonding** between the mother and the baby, but bonding is also possible when a caregiver bottle-feeds a baby. The father's feelings—either negative or positive—about breast-feeding the baby should be taken into account. The father's support of breast-feeding is very helpful.

bonding—special feelings of love and attachment that can occur between caregiver and baby

Finally, if cost is an issue, parents may not opt to buy formula. If she eats a normal diet of ordinary foods, a mother can usually breast-feed for less money than she would spend for formula.

Not all of these issues will be of equal importance or will be viewed from the same perspective by all parents. Critical Thinking 16.1 on page 560 gives you a chance to consider what you would do if you were in one couple's circumstances.

Older Infants Need the Nutrients That Solid Foods Provide

Introducing Solid Foods

Several decades ago, when convenient baby foods were new on the market, proud parents looked on a baby's early eating of solid foods as a sign of accelerated intellectual and physical development. (It was also believed that eating solid foods would encourage a baby to sleep through the night—a theory that has been disproved by many babies.) However, getting solid foods into a young child was found to be no proof that he or she was ready for them. Some parents actually resorted to using "feeders" that squirted food into the back of the mouth because the baby was unable to swallow it otherwise.

Now we believe that the introduction of solids to infants' diets should be based on when they need the nutrients that such foods can provide *and* when they are physically ready to handle those foods. These two conditions occur at approximately the same time—four to six months of age. If there is a family history of allergies, parents should be careful when introducing new foods.

Nutrient Needs At four to six months of age, the infant's iron stores are likely to be running low, especially if the baby has not received iron supplements or iron-fortified formula. The rapidly growing infant can now benefit from eating some solids, which tend to be more concentrated in energy and protein than breast milk or formula.

To Breast-Feed or to Bottle-Feed?

The situation

Angie and John are expecting a baby in 3 months. John is a policeman, and Angie is an elementary school teacher. They both intend to continue to work after the baby is born, although Angie will take a maternity leave of 2 months.

When they first started talking about having a family, they had planned that Angie would breast-feed their baby for about a year. They believed the adage that "Breast is best"; they believed that besides providing good nutrition, breast-feeding would promote bonding between Angie and the baby, and that the baby would be less likely to be "colicky," get sick, or have allergies if he were breast-fed.

Now, as the time is getting closer and Angie is coping with the rigors of teaching plus the stresses of late pregnancy, she privately wonders whether she will have the time or energy to nurse the baby. She knows that she herself was bottle-fed as an infant, and she was healthy; couldn't bottle-feeding work for their baby too? But she assumes that John is counting on her, and she thinks that her best friends, who breast-fed their infants, will think less of her if she doesn't nurse her baby. She feels guilty even thinking about bottle-feeding.

John also remembers their commitment and still basically believes in their decision. However, he's been thinking about the fact that breast-feeding will make it more difficult for him to be as involved with the baby as he would like. He's reluctant to bring this up; it seems pretty self-centered. Furthermore, he doesn't want Angie to misconstrue his motivation; he doesn't want her to think that he has lost confidence in her ability to breast-feed the baby and to be a "good mother."

Is the information accurate and relevant?

- It's true that the milk of a well-nourished mother sets the standard for nutrition for the baby. However, commercial infant formulas closely mimic the nutrients in human milk.
- It's true that breast-feeding does encourage bonding, which can promote an infant's healthy development; but if a caregiver holds and interacts with the baby during feeding, bonding can be fostered during bottle-feeding as well.
- It is not true that breast-feeding prevents **colic;** up to 30% of *all* babies, both breast-fed and bottle-fed, experience these periods of crying caused by spasms of abdominal pain. In some cases, breakdown products of cow's milk in formula or in mother's milk have been thought to be the cause of colic (Nutrition Reviews, 1988); however, changing the feeding techniques (Davidson, 1983) or trying various responses to the baby's crying (Taubman, 1988) are usually more effective than changing the nature of the milk feeding.
- The immune factors in breast milk are very important for infant health in the *developing* countries; but in the *developed* countries where sanitation is generally good and infections not as common, breast-feeding does not provide the same clear advantage (Bauchner et al., 1986).
- It is true that allergies are less likely in breast-fed babies; this is an important factor in families with a history of allergies. There is no such history in either Angie's or John's family.

colic—periods of crying apparently from spasms of abdominal pain in an otherwise healthy infant

What else needs to be considered?

When Angie and John made their decision about breast-feeding some time ago, they planned that Angie would quit working when they had a baby. As things are turning out, as happy as she is about having the baby, she now realizes how committed she is to teaching . . . and how much they like the double income. They decided together that Angie should continue teaching. Since their circumstances will be different than they originally thought, and since their thinking and feelings about breast-feeding are in flux, they should reopen the topic for discussion.

There are things that they didn't consider earlier when they thought Angie would be at home with the baby. Angie knows that some mothers who work away from home also breast-feed their babies. Although she would not find it possible to come home for feedings as one of her friends did, she knows that some mothers pump their breasts and leave the milk for the baby. She does not know how this is done, so she decides to ask the obstetrician about it. Another source of information would be a local chapter of the La Leche League, an international organization that provides education about and promotion of breast-feeding. They have clearly written print materials, well-informed leaders, and members who share their experiences and encourage each other.

Angie and John are also somewhat concerned about the issue of toxins in breast milk. Angie has totally avoided alcohol during her pregnancy, but one of the things she has been looking forward to when she is no longer pregnant is being able to relax with friends and have a beer. She makes a mental note to ask the baby's doctor whether her drinking one or two beers would pose a problem for the baby. Pediatricians give different advice on this question.

She and John are also beginning to wonder whether there is any problem with the fact that about once every two weeks she has been eating fish that John caught in the local lake. The lake is fed by a river that flows through agricultural areas, and they wonder whether runoff chemicals could have been in the fish they've been eating. If so, were they absorbed into her body, and would they be secreted into her milk? In some states, departments of natural resources periodically publish recommendations regarding the safety of consuming fish taken from state waterways. John plans to check on this; such information could help in estimating whether Angie has been accumulating levels of toxins in her body that could get into her breast milk. Angie will talk with her doctor about this too.

As they discuss again the issue of how to feed their baby, they realize that their early decision to breast-feed was based on some correct information, some misinformation, and some emotion. They are learning that there are other responsible feeding options from which "good parents" can choose. They still both appreciate that breast-feeding has certain physical and emotional benefits, but now understand that bottle-feeding is also a healthy option. It is legitimate to take practical matters into account as well when making their decision.

What do you think?

If you were advising Angie and John, what would you recommend? Some options are listed below; do you see others?

- Option 1 You advise Angie and John to exclusively breast-feed their baby for the first year, as they had planned. You suggest ways to ensure that Angie gets enough relaxed time to nurse the baby and that John gets regular quality time with the baby as well.
- Option 2 You advise that the baby should be exclusively breast-fed while Angie is on leave for two months; then, as she prepares to go back to work, she should make a transition to formula-feeding.
- Option 3 You advise that the baby should be breast-fed during the first year whenever Angie is home and be given a bottle of either breast milk or formula when she is away.
- Option 4 You advise that the baby should be formula-fed exclusively from the beginning.

Adding solid foods to an infant's diet. The appropriate time to begin giving solid food to infants is between four and six months of age, when they are physically ready and need the nutrients.

A separate set of RDAs applies to babies in the latter six months of the first year. In most cases, the RDAs are higher for the older infant—sometimes as much as double the recommendations for newborns. This reflects the larger size of the older baby.

Physical Readiness Physical development is the most reliable indicator of a child's readiness for solid foods. Somewhere between four and six months of age, many changes occur that enhance a baby's ability to eat solid foods from a spoon. First, a baby can learn to swallow solids at about this time. His kidneys can concentrate urine more efficiently. He can sit in a high chair. He can show his eagerness for more food when he is hungry, keeping an eye on the food and opening his mouth as the spoon approaches. He can also turn his head away or otherwise refuse food when his hunger is satisfied. It is important to respect these cues in order to avoid overfeeding.

Social Implications When the baby starts on solids, the feeding routine changes somewhat. Now the baby's tasks are to experience the food, move it back in his mouth, swallow it, sense how it feels to have it in his stomach, and then communicate whether he wants more or not. But the caregiver still needs to give the same time and attention as before to the baby's signals of hunger and satiety and respond appropriately to them.

If the caregiver short-circuits the process by simply spooning food into the baby until the dish is empty (irrespective of cues from the infant), the baby gets the message that his hunger and satiety signals are not being taken seriously. Depending on the baby's personality, there are different responses he or she might have. If a placid baby is overfed, he may accept the situation and open his mouth each time the spoon advances; a more determined infant might resist the spoon frantically in a fight for her right to self-determine her intake.

The risk in overfeeding or restricting food during infancy is that children are likely to learn not to trust their internal messages. Some experts believe that when children learn to override their internal hunger and satiety signals, they may initiate lifelong problems with eating behaviors.

Sequence and Timing Because of the increased need for iron as the baby grows, it is a good idea to feed iron-fortified infant cereals as the first solid food. Some pediatricians recommend that rice or barley cereals be used until seven to nine months of age since they are less likely to provoke an allergic response than wheat, corn, or mixed cereals.

Once cereals have been successfully incorporated into a child's diet and the infant has mastered the skill of getting semisolid food from a spoon and swallowing it, he or she is ready for more challenging textures. Cooked, fork-mashed, or diced fruit and vegetables fed by spoon or self-fed by fingers offer a developmentally and nutritionally logical next step. The addition of meat can be postponed until a child begins eating from the table, somewhere near the end of the first year.

When a new food is added to an infant's diet, it should be included in small amounts for several days before another new food is tried. In this way, if there are allergic reactions, the offending food can be easily identified.

When solid foods represent a large part of the child's food intake, caregivers should offer extra liquids, since solid foods contain less water than the breast milk or formula that they are partially replacing.

Table 16.4 summarizes the recommendations for the introduction of solid foods to the infant diet. This table does not need to be followed slavishly, because normal babies develop at different rates. The important consideration is to match the diet to the baby's nutritional needs and developmental readiness.

Commercial Versus Homemade Baby Foods Many parents rely on commercial baby foods until the child can eat with the rest of the family. The commercial products come in ready-to-eat form, and some are also available as dehydrated flakes to which liquid must be added. Others prefer to prepare their own baby foods "from scratch."

The commercially prepared foods are convenient and safe but are often more expensive than home-prepared foods. Furthermore, because of their smooth texture, they don't offer much developmental challenge to the child who is ready to progress to a more mature eating style.

Many people believe that commercially prepared baby foods are high in sugar, salt, and preservatives, but most manufacturers now use little or none of these ingredients in their basic pureed foods. If you make your own baby food out of foods being prepared for the rest of the family, you can take out the baby's portion before adding seasoning or sauces. In this way, you will minimize the level of sugar, salt, and spices that the baby receives. For future convenience, freeze some in ice cube trays and then store in plastic bags. Do not make baby food from canned food: most canned vegetables and meats contain added salt, and most canned fruit has added sugar. Furthermore, canned foods may contain lead if lead solder was used in making the can (see Chapter 15).

Table 16.4 Recommendations for Feeding Infants

Age	Foods to Introduce	Physical Development	Comments
Birth	Breast milk or formula.	Baby can suck liquids from birth, but thrusts tongue forward to push solids from mouth (extrusion reflex). Kidneys cannot concentrate urine. Digestive secretions produced at low levels. Little control of head and neck.	Breast-feeders should get supplemental fluoride and vitamin D. Formulas are usually adequate in vitamin D, although fluoride may need to be supplemented.
4–6 months	Iron-fortified cereal[a] mixed with formula or breast milk.	Baby learns to swallow solids. Control of head and neck allows child to sit up for eating and to indicate hunger and satiety. Kidneys are able to concentrate urine.	Delay wheat cereals until 7–9 months if there is family history of allergies.
8 months (or 6 weeks after cereal)	Strained, mashed, or diced fruits and vegetables. Either bottled baby foods or table foods prepared without sugar, honey, or seasonings.	Baby can grasp and route food from hand to mouth. Teeth begin to come in.	Babies at this age accept many tastes and can learn to accept a variety of textures. Allow 3–4 days between introduction of new items.
9 months	Juices from a cup. Finger foods, whole pieces of soft fruits and vegetables. Pureed, milled, or finely chopped meats. Eggs. Casseroles from family table. Bread and crackers.	Chewing pattern has begun. Child can drink from cup.	This is a transitional period from soft, mushy foods to table foods. Older babies usually prefer to feed themselves and to examine their food by handling it.
12 months	Table foods. Finely cut meats. Most finger foods, except items that are hard to chew (such as popcorn, nuts, and raisins), or small, slippery, rounded foods (such as hot dogs, grapes, and candy), because of the risk of choking.	Biting, chewing, and swallowing are well developed. Pincer grasp (thumb and fingers) enables child to pick up small objects. Good spoon control begins.	Delay use of honey and corn syrup until after 12 months: they may cause infant botulism. Infant should be weaned from the bottle and may be weaned from the breast.

[a]Continue iron-fortified infant cereal until at least one year of age, to help restore dwindling iron reserves.

A good rule of thumb for those who buy baby food is to stick to simple, single-ingredient items in glass jars or use dehydrated flakes. If the food does not agree with the baby, it is easier to identify the problem. Furthermore, foods like strained chicken are cheaper and more concentrated in nutrients than fancier combination foods like chicken dinners.

Safety Baby foods prepared from the family's meals can be just as nutritious as commercial types, but special care is required to make them as safe. One potential problem is microorganisms. The safest approach to avoiding microorganisms is to make and serve the baby's food, on the spot, from what is being served to the rest of the family. Family fare can be changed to baby food by grinding, fork-mashing, or dicing. Baby food that is pureed or ground in quantity ahead of time and not properly stored is a perfect medium for bacterial growth because of its large surface area. Make sure that all equipment used in preparation is scrupulously clean; keep hot foods hot and cold foods cold until they are ready to serve. Do not reheat leftover baby foods more than once, and if a baby food has been at room temperature for more than half an hour, throw it away.

Two commercial products sometimes given to infants, honey and corn syrup, have been found to contain spores of *Clostridium botulinum* (see Chapter 15). Since the infant's immature gastrointestinal tract in some cases allows the spores to become active and produce their lethal toxin, these products should not be given to children under one year of age.

A final safety issue has to do with the form of the food served to young children. Data have recently been collected on children who choked to death on food. In a study of over 100 cases involving babies through nine-year-olds, the most common offending foods were hot dogs, candy, nuts, grapes, cookies, meats, and carrots (in that order). This indicates that small, slippery, and thin or rounded foods are risky for the young child (Harris et al., 1984). Caregivers must be especially attentive if they allow children to eat such foods. The safety of some items can be improved by cutting them into pieces that will not block the child's airway. For example, carrots or hot dogs cut into thin strips are safer than big cylindrical chunks.

Self-Feeding Another milestone in a baby's development is usually reached between seven and nine months, when the baby starts to feed herself. Self-feeding begins with easy-to-hold foods like teething biscuits and progresses to soft foods like pieces of cooked vegetables. Anything that sticks together long enough for the baby to get it from the high-chair tray to her mouth is fair game.

At about this time, the baby can also begin to drink liquids from a cup. Many experts recommend waiting until this stage to give the baby fruit juices, because fruit juices from a bottle are a possible cause of baby bottle tooth decay.

How Much Is Enough?

Parents are chronic worriers about whether their baby is getting enough or too much to eat. This can be a particular concern when there is strong influence from grandparents, who are more likely to believe that a fat baby is a healthy baby. On the other hand, a new generation of parents wants to keep its children too slender.

The soundest approach is to abandon preconceived ideas about how thin or fat a particular child should be and to provide, from the beginning, appropriate food in response to the child's hunger and satiety messages. Babies fed in this way have the chance to attain their individually appropriate body weights. Some babies will be naturally fatter or leaner than others, but this does not predestine their size for life: a fat baby usually does not become an obese child (Shapiro, 1984). We will discuss this topic more thoroughly in the next chapter.

Babies differ in the quantity of food they require for their normal growth and in the frequency with which they demand to be fed. Many newborns need to be fed every two to three hours until their stomach capacities increase enough to have fewer and larger feedings. A month-old infant will take about 20 ounces of formula or breast milk each day, although the amount may vary considerably from day to day. This often increases to well over a quart per day by around four to six months, the time at which a few teaspoons of solid food are added to the diet. By the time a child is a year old, a variety of table foods accounts for a large part of the diet, and milk intake should have decreased to about 20–32 ounces ($2\frac{1}{2}$ to 4 cups) per day (Satter, 1986b).

The best way to check whether a baby's intake of food has been appropriate is to measure his or her growth in length and weight. Parents should take their babies to health care providers for regular health checkups, which will include growth monitoring. Charts from the National Center for Health Statistics (Figure 16.7) show the typical length and weight distributions for American children. The 50th percentile for weight is the point at which half of the infants weigh more and half weigh less. The 90th percentile is the point at which 10% weigh more.

Figure 16.7 **(a) Normal growth curves for girls. (b) Normal growth curves for boys.** The bold lines in part (b) show one child's poor growth. (Adapted from National Center for Health Statistics: NCHS Growth Charts, 1976. Monthly Vital Statistics Report Vol. 25, No. 3, Supp. (HRA)76-1120. Health Resources Administration, Rockville, Maryland, June 1976. Data from The Fels Research Institute, Yellow Springs, Ohio. 1976 Ross Laboratories, Columbus, Ohio 43216.)

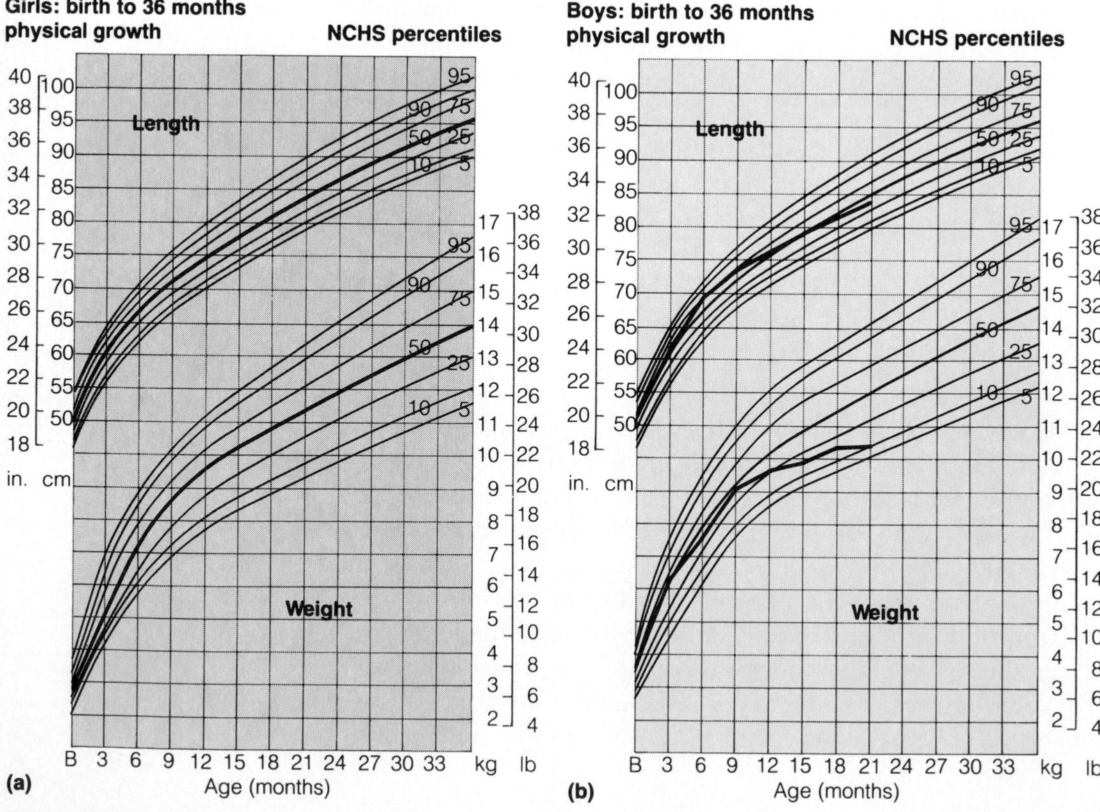

Every child's medical chart should contain a growth chart so that changes in length and weight can be monitored. Once a child has settled into particular bands on the growth charts, she is likely to progress along in those "canals" or close to them.

Babies are very individual in the rates at which they grow and in the eventual body sizes they attain. You need not be alarmed if a child does not keep up with the growth of a neighbor youngster of the same age; what is important is that the child keeps up with himself—that is, the pattern he established previously. Most babies do this naturally, but there are occasional exceptions.

Figure 16.7(b) shows an example of a child who "fell off his growth curve." Such **failure to thrive** is serious and can be the result of an underlying illness, an organic problem, or misunderstanding on the part of the caregivers about how to feed the baby. In any case of failure to thrive, it is extremely important that parents seek the help of health care professionals to determine the cause and aid in the treatment of poor growth.

failure to thrive—inability to maintain a previously established growth curve

This section's Nutrition for Living: During Infancy offers some practical pointers for this stage.

During Infancy

These points summarize what to do to optimize a baby's nutrition:

- Consider which method of feeding the baby is best (breast or bottle), keeping in mind the needs and lifestyle of all family members.
- Keep a growth chart for the baby. If the child's growth fails to progress, consult a pediatrician without delay.
- Between four and six months, offer solid foods that are consistent with the baby's nutritional needs and development. Progressively provide foods with more interest and challenge as the baby seems ready, but guard against foods that could cause choking.
- When you add something new to an infant's diet, wait several days before introducing the next new item. This will allow you to identify a food to which the child is reacting if food sensitivity occurs.
- Relax and enjoy the humor in a child learning to eat!

The baby should be ready to eat cut-up family fare before his or her first birthday.

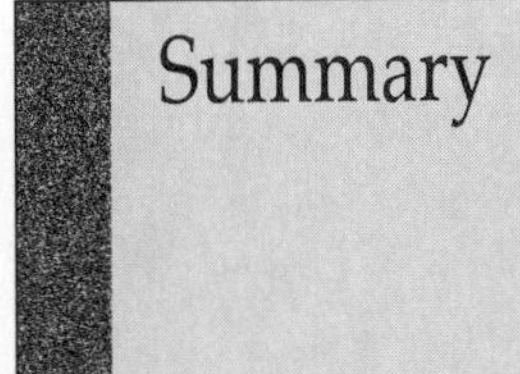

► Nutrition plays a critical role during pregnancy because so much new tissue is formed at this time. Some of the new tissue becomes the baby, after progressing through several developmental stages. For the first two weeks it is called a **zygote,** and then an **embryo** once it becomes implanted in the wall of the **uterus.** The term **fetus** refers to the developing baby from eight weeks after fertilization until birth. Other types of new tissue, such as the **pla-**

centa, support and nourish the embryo and fetus, and still others become part of the mother.

► Certain stages of **gestation** are characterized by rapid cell division and **cell differentiation;** it is during these **critical periods** that the mother's nutrient intake and exposure to other substances (including **teratogens**) can have the most dramatic consequences.

► The weight of both the mother-to-be and the new baby are important; total desirable gain for the normal-weight mother is 25–35 pounds, although a fairly wide range can be normal, depending on the woman's pre-pregnant weight and height. The birth weight of the baby should be at least $5\frac{1}{2}$ pounds; an infant weighing less is a **low-birth-weight baby.** The foods eaten to achieve these weight gains should be chosen for nutritional adequacy, balance, and variety, since the need for many nutrients is high at this time, especially in the last two **trimesters.** A carefully planned diet can meet these needs, and while vitamin/mineral supplements are advised in some cases, the principle of adequate but not excessive intake should be kept in mind. Good nutrition also provides reserves for **lactation.**

► Pregnant women should be careful to avoid ingesting dangerous levels of dietary toxicants. A set of abnormalities called **fetal alcohol syndrome** has been shown to appear in the children of women who consumed alcohol heavily during pregnancy. (Less is known about the risks of drinking alcohol in smaller amounts.) Practices such as pica and smoking may also affect the fetus, so pregnancy calls for an evaluation of many lifestyle factors besides nutrition.

► The rapid growth of infants causes them to have the highest nutrient needs per unit of body weight of any age group, so the decision of what to feed a baby is an important matter. The immature gastrointestinal and urinary tracts of infants do not handle adult foods well for the first few months of life. Healthy full-term infants do have reserve supplies of some nutrients that can meet their needs during the time when milk is their only food.

► Infants should be fed on demand until they are satisfied. This practice not only allows them to establish their own natural growth pattern but also allows for development of trust.

► Both breast-feeding and bottle-feeding have certain advantages. Breast milk is uniquely adapted to the infant's nutrition needs, and the **colostrum** contains factors that increase immunity to several infections. Both the composition and volume of milk produced can vary in response to the baby's demands. Formulas can provide nutritionally satisfactory substitutes for breast milk and are available in several different varieties. Factors other than nutrition—such as psychological factors (e.g., **bonding**), convenience, economy, safety, and lifestyle of the parents—can also influence the decision of how to feed a baby.

► Older infants need the nutrients that solid foods provide; such foods should be introduced when the baby is physically ready for them, as usually happens between four and six months of age. Iron-fortified cereals are often the first solid food and can be followed by others introduced gradually. Commercially prepared baby foods are convenient and safe, though often more expensive than those prepared at home. Between seven and nine months of age, a baby is usually able to begin feeding itself and to drink from a cup. At this stage of life (as at others) it is probably best to provide appropriate food in response to the child's hunger and satiety messages. A reliable way to check on whether this provides enough nutrients is to keep track of the baby's height and weight, which can then be compared with population norms and the child's own past growth pattern. A few children will exhibit **failure to thrive,** but most grow normally.

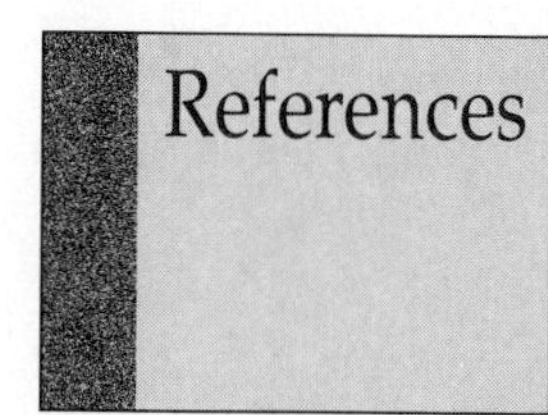

References

American Academy of Pediatrics. 1983. The use of whole cow's milk in infancy. *Pediatrics* 72:253–255.

American Dietetic Association. 1989. Ambulatory nutrition care: Pregnant women. *Journal of the American Dietetic Association 89 (Supplement)* S10–S14.

American Medical Association. 1983. Fetal effects of maternal alcohol use. *Journal of the American Medical Association* 249:2517–2521.

Bauchner, H., J.M. Leventhal, and E.D. Shapiro. 1986. Studies of breast-feeding and infections. *Journal of the American Medical Association* 256:887–892.

Blinder, B.J., S.L. Goodman, and P. Henderson. 1988. Pica: A critical review of diagnosis and treatment. In *The eating disorders*, eds. B.J. Blinder, B.F. Chaitin, and R. Goldstein. New York: PMA Publishing Corp.

Brewer, M.M., M.R. Bates, and L.P. Vannoy. 1989. Postpartum changes in maternal weight and body fat depots in lactating vs nonlactating women. *American Journal of Clinical Nutrition* 49:259–265.

Brooke, O.G., H.R. Anderson, J.M. Bland, J.L. Peacock, C.M. Stewart. 1989. Effects of birth weight of smoking, alcohol, caffeine, socioeconomic factors, and psychosocial stress. *British Medical Journal* 198:795–801.

Brown, J.E. 1989. Improving pregnancy outcomes in the United States: The importance of preventive nutrition services. *Journal of the American Dietetic Association* 89:631–638, 641.

Butte, N.F., C. Garza, J.E. Stuff, E.O. Smith, and B.L. Nichols. 1984. Effect of maternal diet and body composition on lactational performance. *American Journal of Clinical Nutrition* 39:296–306.

Committee on Nutrition, American Academy of Pediatrics. 1989. Iron-fortified infant formulas. *Pediatrics* 84:1114.

Committee on Nutritional Status During Pregnancy and Lactation. 1990. *Nutrition During Pregnancy*. Washington, DC: National Academy Press.

Davidson, M. 1983. Causes and management of colic in infancy. *Nutrition and the M.D.* 9(no. 11):1–3.

Dobbing, J. 1984. Infant nutrition and later achievement. *Nutrition Reviews* 42:1–7.

Fomon, S.J. 1986. Breast feeding and evolution. *Journal of the American Dietetic Association* 86:317–318.

Hackman, E., I. Emanuel, G. vanBelle, and J. Daling. 1983. Maternal birth weight and subsequent pregnancy outcome. *Journal of the American Medical Association* 250:2016–2019.

Harris, C.S., S.P. Baker, G.A. Smith, and R.M. Harris. 1984. Childhood asphyxiation by food: A national analysis and overview. *Journal of the American Medical Association* 251:2231–2235.

Heird, W.C. and A. Cooper. 1988. Nutrition in infants and children. In *Modern nutrition in health and disease*, eds. M.E. Shils and V.R. Young. Philadelphia: Lea & Febiger.

Hoff, C., W. Wertelecki, W.R. Blackburn, H. Mendenhall, H. Wiseman, and A. Stumpe. 1986. Trend associations of smoking with maternal, fetal, and neonatal morbidity. *Obstetrics and Gynecology* 68:317–321.

Johnsen, D. and R. Nowjack-Raymer. 1989. Baby bottle tooth decay (BBTD): Issues, assessment, and an opportunity for the nutritionist. *Journal of the American Dietetic Association* 89:1112–1116.

Lecos, C. 1980. Caution light on caffeine. *FDA Consumer*, October, 1980:6–9.

Levine, M.G. and D. Esser. 1988. Total parenteral nutrition for the treatment of severe hyperemesis gravidarum: Maternal nutritional effects and fetal outcome. *Obstetrics and Gynecology* 72:102–107.

Little, R.E. and C.F. Sing. 1986. Association of father's drinking and infant's birth weight. *New England Journal of Medicine* 314:1644–1645.

Little, R.E., A.P. Streissguth, H.M. Barr, and C.S. Herman. 1980. Decreased birth weight in infants of alcoholic women who abstained during pregnancy. *Journal of Pediatrics* 96:974–977.

Miller, M.W. 1986. Effects of alcohol on the generation and migration of cerebral cortical neurons. *Science* 233:1308–1311.

Mutch, P.B. 1988. Food guides for the vegetarian. *American Journal of Clinical Nutrition* 48:913–919.

National Research Council. 1989. *Diet and health*. Washington, DC: National Academy Press.

Nelson, S.E., E.E. Ziegler, A.M. Copeland, B.B. Edwards, and S.J. Fomon. 1988. Lack of adverse reactions to iron-fortified formula. *Pediatrics* 81:360–364.

Nutrition Reviews. 1988. Is colic in infants associated with diet? *Nutrition Reviews* 46:374–376.

Pederson, A.L., B. Worthington-Roberts, and D.E. Hickok. 1989. Weight gain patterns during twin gestation. *Journal of the American Dietetic Association* 89:642–646.

Pipes, P.L. 1989. Nutrition in infancy and childhood. St. Louis: Times Mirror/Mosby College Publishing.

Prentice, A.M. and A. Prentice. 1988. Energy costs of lactation. *Annual Reviews of Nutrition* 8:63–79.

RDA Subcommittee. 1989. *Recommended dietary allowances.* Washington, DC: National Academy Press.

Rosso, P. 1988. Regulation of food intake during pregnancy and lactation. In *Control of appetite,* ed. M. Winick. New York: John Wiley & Sons, Inc.

Sadurskis, A., N. Kahir, J. Wager, and E. Forsum. 1988. Energy metabolism, body composition, and milk production in healthy Swedish women during lactation. *American Journal of Clinical Nutrition* 48:44–49.

Satter, E. 1986a. The feeding relationship. *Journal of the American Dietetic Association* 86:352–356.

———. 1986b. *Child of mine: Feeding with love and good sense.* Palo Alto, CA: Bull Publishing Company.

Shapiro, L.R. 1984. Obesity prognosis: A longitudinal study of children from the age of 6 months to 9 years. *American Journal of Public Health* 74:968–972.

Sheard, N.F. and W.A. Walker. 1988. The role of breast milk in the development of the intestinal tract. *Nutrition Reviews* 46:1–8.

Stjernfeldt, M., K. Berglund, J. Lindsten, and J. Ludvigsson. 1986. Maternal smoking during pregnancy and risk of childhood cancer. *Lancet* (no. 8494): 1350–1352.

Stockbauer, J.W. 1987. WIC prenatal participation and its relation to pregnancy outcomes in Missouri: A second look. *American Journal of Public Health* 77:813–816.

Streissguth, A.P., P.D. Sampson, H.M. Barr, B.L. Darby, and D.C. Martin. 1989. IQ at age 4 in relation to maternal alcohol use and smoking during pregnancy. *Developmental Psychology* 25:3–11.

Surgeon General. 1988. *The Surgeon General's report on nutrition and health.* Washington, DC: U.S. Department of Health and Human Services.

Taubman, B. 1988. Parental counseling compared with elimination of cow's milk or soy milk protein for the treatment of infant colic syndrome: A randomized trial. *Pediatrics* 81:756–761.

USDA and USDHHS. 1990. *Nutrition and your health: Dietary guidelines for Americans.* Washington, DC: U.S. Government Printing Office.

Van der Spuy, Z.M., P.J. Steer, M. McCusker, S.J. Steele, H.S. Jacobs. 1988. Outcome of pregnancy in underweight women after spontaneous and induced ovulation. *British Medical Journal* 296:962–965.

Wardlaw, G.M. and A.M. Pike. 1986. The effect of lactation on peak adult shaft and ultra-distal forearm bone mass in women. *American Journal of Clinical Nutrition* 44:283–286.

Whitehead, R.G. 1988. Pregnancy and lactation. In *Modern nutrition in health and disease,* eds. M.E. Shils and V.R. Young. Philadelphia: Lea & Febiger.

Williams, S.R. 1988. Nutrition for high-risk populations. In *Nutrition throughout the life cycle,* eds. S.R. Williams and B.S. Worthington-Roberts. St. Louis: Times Mirror/Mosby Publishing Company.

Worthington-Roberts, B.S. 1988. Maternal nutrition and the course and outcome of pregnancy. In *Nutrition throughout the life cycle,* eds. S.R. Williams and B.S. Worthington-Roberts. St. Louis: Times Mirror/Mosby Publishing Company.

Wright, J.T., I.G. Barrison, I.G. Lewis, K.D. MacRae, E.J. Waterson, P.J. Toplis, M.G. Gordon, N.F. Morris, and I.M. Murray-Lyon. 1983. Alcohol consumption, pregnancy and low birth weight. *Lancet* 1(no. 8326):663–664.

Zeman, F.J. and D.M. Ney. 1988. *Applications of clinical nutrition.* Englewood Cliffs, NJ: Prentice-Hall.

17

Nutrition for Growing: Children and Adolescents

In This Chapter

- Children's Eating Patterns Through the Elementary School Years Are Related to Many Changing Factors
- There Is Room for Improvement in the Nutritional Status of Today's Children
- Growth and Increased Independence Influence Adolescent Nutrition
- Food Assistance Programs Can Help Nourish Children and Teens

Change is the hallmark of the growing years: taking the first steps at about one year; developing thought processes and language during the preschool years; finding an identity within the wider society during the teens. Such changes make these first two decades of life very dynamic and exciting. At the same time, these years are also potentially very frustrating and filled with conflict, as the child and the caregivers repeatedly adjust to new circumstances.

Eating behaviors often reflect these changes. For example, fluctuations in appetite roughly parallel growth and plateaus in growth. Changes in food preferences may reflect an increasing self-awareness. And new eating styles may well be a consequence of the influences of peers, advertising, and increasing independence and mobility.

When conflicts over eating occur between children and their caregivers, the issue is usually one of control: who will make the decisions regarding what, how much, and when (or how often) to eat. Although the matter of how much to eat should be determined by the child from the beginning, he or she should gradually take on the other decisions as well. Of course, the rate at which a child assumes responsibility for various aspects of eating has to be worked out individually, depending both on the child's needs and capabilities and on the family's situation.

How can the adults in a child's life—in their roles as older brothers or sisters, parents, teachers, coaches, health care providers, neighbors—help the child cope with these changes? An important starting point is to become informed about what is normal for each stage in a child's development. Such information provides guidelines for parents to help children develop sound

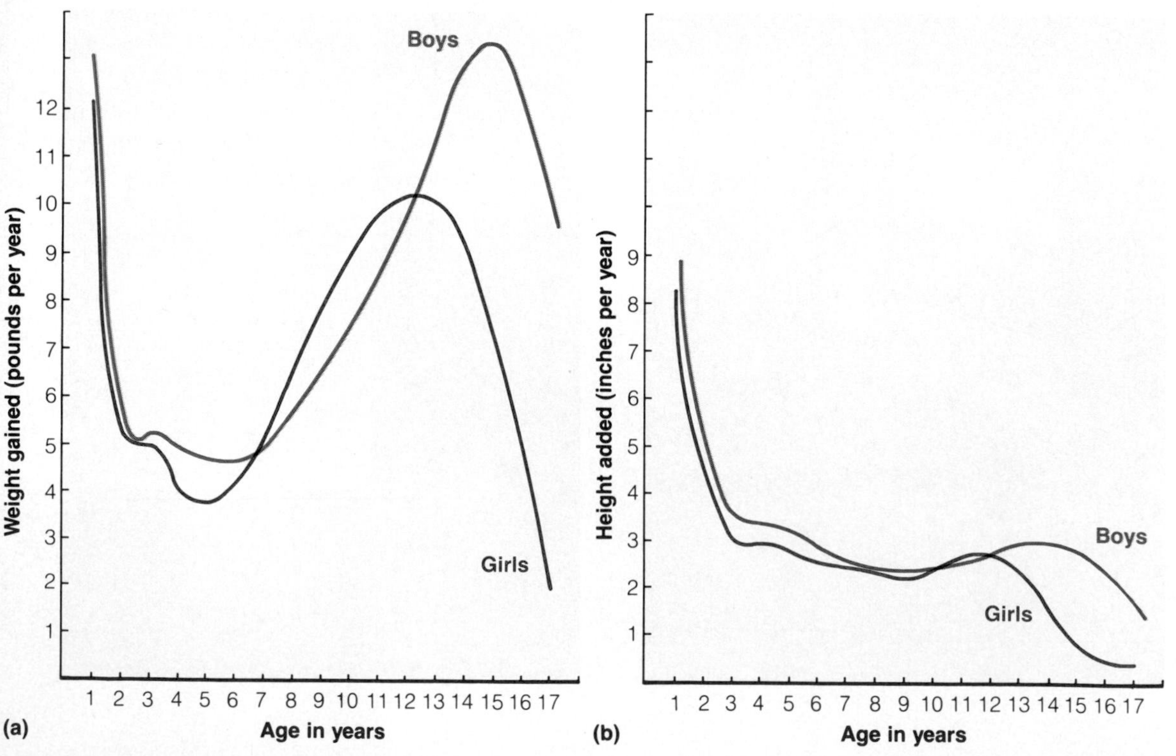

Figure 17.1 (a) Average gains in weight for girls and boys. (b) Average additions to height for girls and boys. (Data source: National Research Council. 1989. *Recommended dietary allowances.* Washington, DC: National Academy of Sciences.)

eating habits. This is the most important influence a caregiver can have on a child's nutrition during these years.

Children's Eating Patterns Through the Elementary School Years Are Related to Many Changing Factors

Food and eating are closely interwoven with a child's development. Of course, foods provide energy and nutrients the body needs for physical growth, development, and activity. But foods and meals also continue to be an important part of the socialization process through which feelings and behavior patterns are formed. A growing child undergoes complex physical, psychosocial, and emotional changes. During the prenatal period and the first year after birth, physical growth takes place at a very rapid pace, but during early childhood (ages 1–7) the overall rate of growth is much slower. Figure 17.1 shows average gains in weight and height for girls and boys.

Physical Development and Activity

During these years, body tissues and organs also continue to develop (Figure 17.2). For example, the gastrointestinal tract matures so that it can handle complex foods. Gastric secretions and most enzymes are present at nearly adult levels by the end of the first year, making it feasible for the young child to consume a wide variety of foods. The presence of eight molar teeth by about 2 years of age and four permanent molars around age 6 allows a child to break apart meats and other chewy foods. The nutrient content of the diet is very important during these years, because in addition to meeting immediate needs, nutrients must be stored in preparation for the accelerated growth that will take place during adolescence.

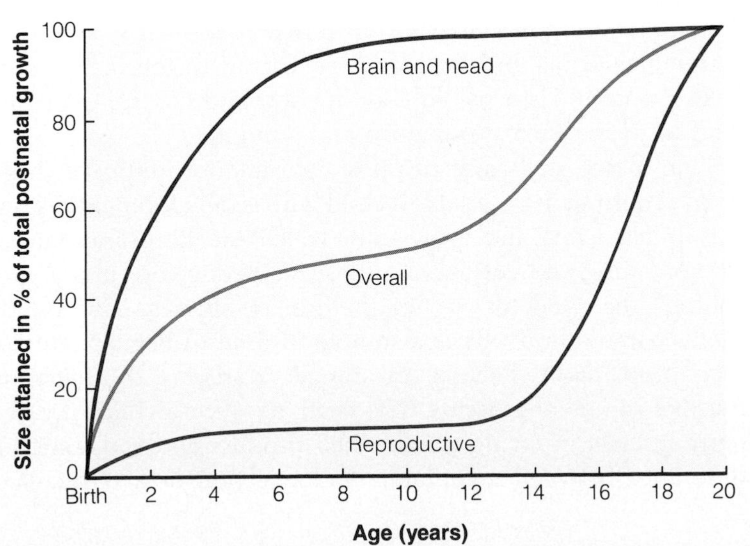

Figure 17.2 Growth of body components. (Adapted from Scammon, R.E. 1927. The measurement of the body in childhood. In *The Measurement of Man* by J.A. Harris, C.M. Jackson, and R.E. Scammon. Minneapolis. MN: University of Minnesota Press.)

The food intake of young children is extremely variable, with peaks and valleys in appetite. Before and during a period of rapid growth, a child may seem like an eating machine, but during the periods of slow growth, it sometimes seems that he or she cannot possibly be eating enough to stay alive. In general, the appetite of children during their first year of life is regarded as excellent or good by over 80% of parents. However, between the ages of 3 and 4, less than 20% of parents rate their children's appetites that way. By the time their children are age 7, though, over half of parents again think of their children's appetites as excellent or good (Beal, 1957). It may help parents who worry about their child's lagging appetite to know that such fluctuation is normal and is usually not a danger sign. Not surprisingly, these natural changes in appetite result from and are reflected in the changes in weight gains and linear growth shown in Figure 17.1.

Children's energy needs are also partly determined by activity levels. Because physical activity varies greatly among children, some need more food than others, even when they are the same size. As a child's total daily energy needs increase as he or she gets older, so does food intake. But because metabolic rate drops with age, these increases are not proportionate: a 40-pound preschooler needs approximately 1600 kcal/day to fuel his or her energy needs; at 80 pounds (about age 11), this child will need roughly 2000 kcal/day. During the first several years of life, infants and preschoolers need between 40 and 45 kcal/lb; at age 11, their needs are down to 20–25 kcal/lb. (The trend does not stop there: for people over the age of 50, energy needs are less than 15 kcal/lb.)

These values seem to suggest that children's energy intakes are highly predictable and consistent from day to day, but this is hardly the case. Although the *trends* suggested above are reliable, an individual child is likely to vary his energy intake considerably over the course of several days.

Coordination

Physical development in children generally takes place from the trunk to the extremities (arms and legs) and from head to toe. Large muscles develop before smaller muscles, so coordination and control over fine movements tend to follow increases in size and strength.

Fine motor skills and physical coordination improve throughout childhood. These changes enable a child who is developmentally 3 years of age to manipulate a fork and spoon quite well at mealtime and, later, to use a knife for spreading and cutting. As these skills develop, it is a good idea to encourage the child to practice them at mealtimes. This builds confidence. Many parents find this is also a good time to begin involving children in food preparation. Peeling an orange or stirring the batter for a batch of muffins can be engrossing new challenges for a child. It can also give him more interest in trying the finished product and can sometimes mean the difference between acceptance and rejection of a particular food (Figure 17.3).

Figure 17.3 Fixing food = trying food. Children are more likely to try a new menu item if they have helped prepare it. The activities must be matched to the child's developmental level. Here nursery school children demonstrate some kitchen skills. (Source: Ann A. Hertzler, Extension Specialist in Food and Nutrition. Virginia Polytechnic Institute and State University; Blacksburg, Virginia.)

Psychosocial Development

Psychosocial changes also occur during childhood. Throughout the growth years, the child is building her own self-image, learning how to cooperate with others and gradually establishing her independence from her parents. The process of gaining independence can truly be a struggle, since it often conflicts with the need to be, at least in part, cared for by adults. This is especially true for preschoolers. A four-year-old may resist any parental efforts to help or control her ("Let *me* do it"), and then suddenly demand that her parents do everything for her ("Daddy, *you* put butter on my bread. I can't.") Another way of showing independence is food rejection. Refusing to eat certain foods is one way in which a child sometimes exercises control over her own behavior.

Children may also use their eating behavior to control others. For example, a child who senses his parents' concern over whether he eats his vegetables may learn that agreeing to eat them is a way of negotiating for things he wants. He may even go so far as to insist on a reward *before* eating them. Maintaining a sense of humor and anticipating children's table behavior may help parents during these confrontations. Fortunately, emotions usually stabilize during the elementary school years.

Understanding who should attend to which aspects of eating also can help substantially to lessen food-related hassles (Satter, 1987). Essentially, *parents and other caregivers are responsible for providing nutritious, appealing, regular meals and snacks. Children are in charge of deciding how much to eat.* If this division of responsibility is carried out, a healthy child will usually eat adequately and with minimal fuss. (A chronically sick child may need special help, but that is outside the realm of this book.)

Pressuring a child to eat more or to eat less simply is *not* in the best interest of the healthy child. Pressure from a caregiver tells the child that her own sense of how much food she needs is not to be trusted, that it is OK to regularly override her sense of hunger and satiety, and that she needs to check with an outside source (the caregiver) about how much she needs. This can undermine the child's self-confidence and emerging sense of self-control.

Training a child to ignore the inner signals about how much to eat can also set the stage for a lifetime of weight regulation problems. A child who complies with the pressure to eat more may become too fat; a very assertive child under the same circumstances may resist and eat less than ever. On the other hand, a compliant child whose intake is restricted may mutely accept the limitation and consequently fail to gain weight or grow in a normal fashion; his more assertive sibling might continually insist on more food and become overweight as a result.

Let us put aside this focus on the negative influences of pressure and focus instead on a *positive* and *desirable* eating situation. The best interest of the child is served when the parents or other caregivers provide food:

- that is nourishing and that the child will eat
- in forms that are manageable and safe for the child's developmental level
- at regular intervals, such as three meals and two snacks, or in whatever pattern meets the particular child's needs
- in an environment that encourages appropriate attention to eating (generally in a chair at a table)

After the parents have provided these things, the child's job is to eat as much as he or she is hungry for. This means that if a child is not particularly hungry at a meal and eats less than usual, that should be accepted without a fuss. However, if the child claims to be hungry an hour later and asks for ice cream to eat, then the answer is "no"; the child has to wait until the next usual meal or snack time for something to eat, and cannot expect a bottomless bowl of ice cream. It is the responsibility of the parents or other caregivers to offer appropriate food to the child. Even young children can learn to function within these limits.

The Child's Food Environment

Environmental factors include the type and amount of food available, the kind of setting in which it is provided, and various other outside influences surrounding the child regarding food. In Chapter 9, we discussed a wide variety of environmental factors that affect the eating behaviors of us all; these apply to children as well. In this section, we will point out a few that are especially important to children.

What a child eats is primarily affected by the type and amount of food available to the child; these are influenced by the family's income, economic status, family structure, and the parents' employment status. Single-parent families and those in which both parents are employed outside the home often have different eating practices than the "traditional family," much less common now than several decades ago. In an earlier era, the mother usually made the food choices for all members of the household. Most meals were eaten by all family members together and were prepared by the mother from groceries she had selected. Lunch, the meal most often eaten away from home, was likely to have been packed by her. Except on rare occasions, family members had little opportunity to select what they were going to eat.

Typical meals . . . then and now. Decades ago, most meals were major family social events: several generations gathered for home-prepared meals. Now, the average household size is much smaller, and most families eat together less often. More food is eaten away from home or purchased as convenience items.

The family situation today is dramatically different, since over half of mothers with school-age children work outside the home. With fewer hours available for householding, parents prepare and serve fewer meals to the family; they utilize convenience foods and fast-food restaurants more often than families with more traditional parental roles. Research shows that people who eat one of the day's meals away from home tend to have lower intakes of some nutrients (Bunch, 1984). Increasingly, family members (even young children) select their own meals. When parents are getting ready for work, everyone may choose his or her own breakfast from what is in the cupboards and refrigerator. Some children do not even eat breakfast at home—the first meal of the day may be eaten at the babysitter's house, at a day-care center, or at school.

Although many families no longer eat all meals together, it is nonetheless critical that children have the assurance that they will get enough satisfying food at regular intervals to meet their needs. Even though a parent may not directly share every eating occasion with his or her child, parents still have the responsibility of being sure it happens for the child. When making day-care, school, or after school arrangements, it is important to be sure that the child will be offered food at reasonable times and that the food will contribute to a nutritious diet. Then, when parents pick up the child at the end of the day, asking what and how much a child actually did eat helps them plan for what the child might need later at home.

Not only can environmental factors influence what is *available* to the child, but they can also influence the child's *preferences.* The expanding number of people with whom a child comes into contact can affect what he or she wants to eat. A child in school or day care also experiences peer influences on his eating behavior. Johnnie may think that broccoli is a perfectly delicious food until he realizes that his friends say it's "yucky" or that one of his adult role models (a teacher, or Uncle Tim, or a hero from a comic book) doesn't like it. Parents who sometimes fault their own poor eating habits when their child rejects certain foods should take heart: experts say that parents' food preferences have only a weak influence on their child's food preferences (Rozin, 1988).

Television, on the other hand, can be a strong influence on what a child wants to eat. The average child in elementary school spends more time in front of a television set each year than he or she does in the classroom. The child watches about 20,000 television commercials each year, many of which unfortunately promote foods that are high in sugar, salt, and/or fat. A 1988 study analyzed 225 commercials during 12 hours of Saturday morning children's TV programming; 80% of those ads were for foods of low nutritional value (Cotugna, 1988).

For many children, TV and other media are a significant part of the process of nutrition socialization; that is, their values concerning food and their concepts about what foods are appropriate to eat and when they should be eaten are partly determined by what they see on television. Parents who watch TV with their children can help them understand that TV programs don't always show things as they are in real life and that food commercials are designed to make them want a particular item whether or not it has any nutritional merit.

The food ads on TV may also suggest to children that they *eat while watching TV* and thereby encourage excessive intake. Watching TV can spell trouble for the balance of energy intake and expenditure as well: sitting in front of the TV takes less energy than almost any activity in which a child might otherwise be engaged. It is little wonder that research has found an association between overweight children and the number of hours spent watching TV per week (Dietz and Gortmacher, 1985).

Nutrition education at school can influence a child's nutritional intake somewhat; however, nutrition education experts often find that increased nutrition knowledge does not necessarily lead to better food choices. These findings are complicated by the fact that the quantity and quality of nutrition education offered in the classroom varies substantially from one location and time to another.

There Is Room for Improvement in the Nutritional Status of Today's Children

The recommended intakes of nutrients for children according to age and sex are shown in the 1989 RDA table. Figure 17.4 shows how the RDAs for various ages compare to the adult male RDA. In general, the older the child, the higher the nutrient intake recommendations. These increases reflect the demands of maintaining a larger body in addition to furnishing raw materials for further growth.

Notice that even young children sometimes need as much or more of a nutrient than an adult male needs; that is true for vitamin D and calcium. These nutrients are important for promoting the greatest possible bone mass that the child's genetic limits will allow.

Nutritional Status of North American Children

Compared with children in other parts of the world, children in North America do quite well in meeting minimum nutritional requirements. A 1986 national survey evaluated the nutritional intakes of young children in

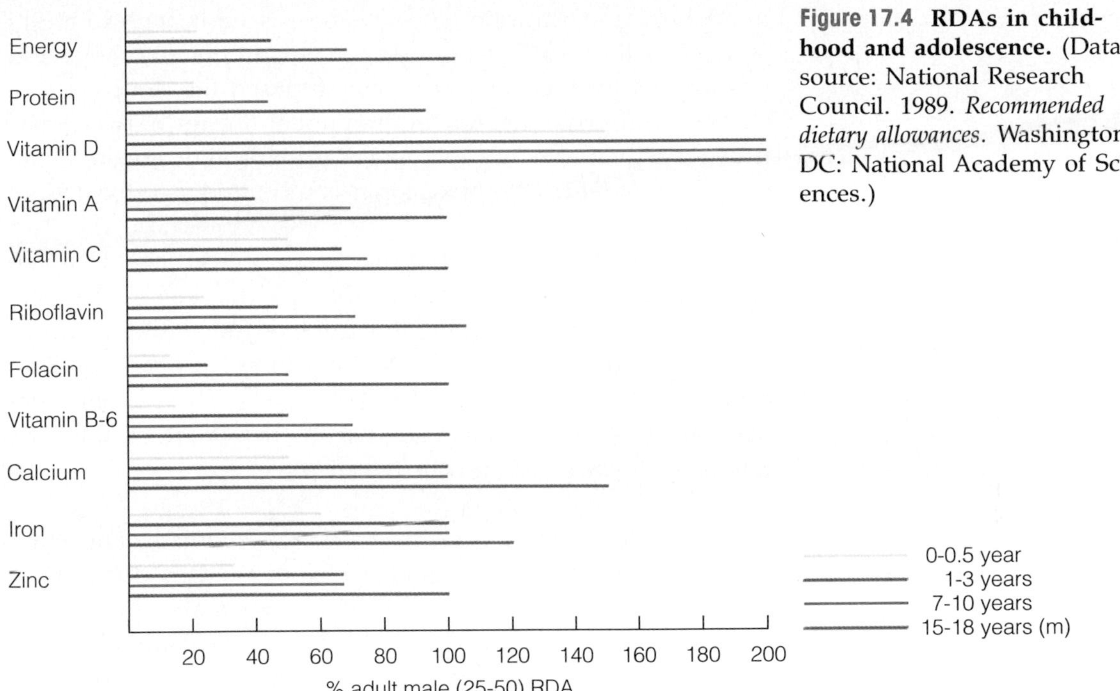

Figure 17.4 RDAs in childhood and adolescence. (Data source: National Research Council. 1989. *Recommended dietary allowances.* Washington, DC: National Academy of Sciences.)

the United States. Information was collected from mothers on as many as six separate occasions. The study found that the average intakes of children ages 1 to 5 met the RDA for all nutrients except iron and zinc, which were 82% and 79% of the RDAs, respectively. The average intakes of calcium for nonwhite groups of children were 80–88% of their RDAs (HNIS, 1988). Even for children of impoverished families, average intakes were at least 100% of their RDAs except for iron (84%), zinc (78%), and calcium (97%) (HNIS, 1988). Of course, averages being what they are, these data do not show that all the children in the survey were well-nourished. Furthermore, homeless children were not included in this survey because of the difficulty in collecting data (see Chapter 9); it is unlikely that their needs are consistently met. Let us take a look, then, at the consequences of undernutrition—whether we are considering our own hungry children or the 14 million beyond our borders who die each year due, in part, to shortage of food.

Children who have been severely malnourished in infancy experience growth deficits. Usually children who have been nutritionally deprived have also lacked social stimulation, so experts are not sure to what extent each influences poor growth. Some growth deficit may be partly made up for in early childhood; how much can be corrected depends on the developmental age at which adequate nutrition is provided, the length and severity of the previous inadequacy, and the composition of the rehabilitation diet. Similarly, the intellectual impairment that results from malnutrition in early childhood may be partly or mostly restored when nutrition improves, if it takes place soon enough and if it is accompanied by adequate social stimulation.

Poor and homeless children are not the only ones who may be undernourished; undernutrition also has been seen in mid- to high-level income families in the U.S. For example, some parents who have adopted a strict low-fat diet for their own use have imposed the same diet on their young children. A low-fat diet for children under the age of two years old does not provide enough energy for proper growth and development. After that, restriction of fat to 30% of kcalories is recommended for the normal healthy child.

Physicians have also noted that some preteen children, especially girls, are so afraid of becoming fat that they restrict their food intake to very low levels. Over a period of time, this can interfere with linear growth and sexual maturation, even if such children do not progress to the extreme disorder of anorexia nervosa (see Chapter 11). The problem emphasizes the need for children to develop good eating habits and establish realistic expectations of themselves and their bodies.

Less Anemia In the past, iron-deficiency anemia has been a serious problem in children, involving almost 15% of children one year old, the most seriously affected group. Fortunately, this situation has been changing.

A study of low-income U.S. children ages 1–5 found that the overall prevalence of anemia decreased from almost 8% in 1975 to approximately 3% in 1985 (Yip et al., 1987). This decrease has been attributed to the use of iron-fortified formulas for bottle-fed infants (Committee on Nutrition, 1989).

In children who are no longer being given iron-fortified formula, anemia may result from the lower level of iron in milk. Further, if children drink so much milk that they do not eat enough solid foods, which are better sources of iron, they may develop "milk anemia."

Decreasing Dental Decay Dental caries are another significant problem in children. As discussed in Chapter 6, tooth decay is most likely to occur in susceptible teeth with the presence of fermentable carbohydrate and acid-producing bacteria. Important factors in the control of dental caries are adequate fluoride intake (from water or appropriate supplements) or topical application; restricted intake of fermentable carbohydrates such as sticky sweet snacks; and adequate dental hygiene to remove carbohydrates, acid, and bacteria.

The prevalence of caries has declined in the last 20 years. In the early 1970s, children 5–17 years of age had an average of 7 decayed, missing, and filled teeth. A decade later, this number had dropped to less than 5. Statistics show the prevalence of caries to be highest in the Northeast, in females, and in lower socioeconomic groups for both sexes (National Research Council, 1989).

Increasing Obesity The body weight status of American children is alarming. In a 15-year period, the percentage of obese 6- to 11-year-olds has increased by more than 50%; the number of superobese children has increased by almost 100% (Gortmacher et al., 1987). (In this study, the 15% of children with the largest skinfolds at the beginning of the study were regarded as *obese;* the top 5% were *superobese.*) In the first 11 years of the Bogalusa Heart Study, the prevalence of overweight among 5- to 14-year-olds increased from 15% to 24% (Shear et al., 1988). (Here, children above the 85th percentile for body mass index were regarded as *obese.*)

Obesity in children is a matter for concern because even at young ages, overfatness has both physiological and psychological consequences. Just as with adults, obese children are at greater risk for high blood pressure and high blood cholesterol (Shear et al., 1988). They are also at increased risk of obesity in adulthood. Obese children often experience a great deal of psychological distress because they are often teased or even socially isolated by their peers; this can be very detrimental to the child's self-concept.

The incidence of obesity among children is increasing. In a recent 15-year period, the incidence of obesity increased by over 50%.

Intervention for Overweight in Children

A child who is overweight should be evaluated by a physician to make sure there is no underlying physical problem. Next, a plan should be developed for dealing with the weight issue.

If the child is not severely overweight, most experts think it is better to *stabilize* his or her weight rather than lose the excess. They believe that as the child gets taller, the height/weight relationship becomes more normal and relative body fatness decreases. On the other hand, if the child is severely overweight, a weight reduction program is in order. Moderate programs are more successful than very aggressive programs at any age, but with children, moderation is more crucial; it is important not to interfere with normal linear growth (Dietz and Hartung, 1985).

If the cause(s) of the obesity can be determined, it will suggest what emphasis the treatment program should have. When *inactivity* is a problem, the most logical and satisfactory intervention is to encourage physical activity that the child will find pleasurable and not regard as punishment for being overweight. In some instances, it may be feasible to bring together a number of overweight children for exercise, but such groupings need to be done with considerable tact to avoid negative labeling. One of the best approaches is for the child's family to find activities they enjoy doing together and can do often. Walks after supper, frequent bike rides, and regular backyard volleyball games would be excellent, but the nature of the activity is not as important as simply getting away from sedentary activities (Dietz, 1988).

Some obese children overeat for comfort, for self-reward, or to relieve boredom. Eating is a reliable and convenient source of pleasure, and some children are not very resourceful about finding other positive experiences for themselves. In such cases, it is useful to help the child find alternative gratifications to substitute for the excessive eating. Although it is important to help a child not to *overeat,* he or she should be allowed to eat enough to satisfy hunger at regular meal and snack times. As is recommended for all children, the obese child needs to determine how much to eat at each eating occasion. Pressure on the child to restrict eating is likely to backfire, as the Slice of Life on p. 588 demonstrates.

The issue of *what* the child eats requires more parental involvement, particularly for the younger child. The child should be encouraged to eat fewer foods that are high in fat and sugar; fried potato chips and other snacks, candy, most cookies and cakes, sugar-sweetened beverages, butter or margarine, and oil-based salad dressings should not be a regular part of the child's diet. The best way to accomplish this is to avoid having these items in the house, or to provide lower-fat substitutes.

There are ways to increase the chances of successful weight control for children without professional intervention. If a parent is concerned about a child's weight and the issue has not become a highly emotional one, it is possible that between themselves, the parent(s) and child can work out some changes that will address the problem. It may be helpful for the parent first to get an outside resource, such as the booklet produced by the University of California's Cooperative Extension Program (Ikeda, 1989). Publications such as this help parents to talk about the issue with their children without hurting their self-concepts, to provide the best kinds of foods, and to plan activities their children might enjoy.

Slice of Life

Withholding Food from the Overweight Child Can Backfire

(From Satter, E. 1987. *How to get your kid to eat . . . but not too much.* Palo Alto, CA: Bull Publishing Company.)

When Melissa was three and a half, they visited their pediatrician, who told them she was too fat and they should do something about it. They started cutting back on her food, and over the next eighteen months her rate of weight gain again increased. It appeared their attempts to withhold food, which I'll call restrained feeding, was currently at the heart of the problem. Her preoccupation with food that was resulting from the restrained feeding was making her eat more and actually making her gain more weight than when they had just been feeding her normally.

We set out to reestablish normal feeding and get rid of the restrained feeding. The first step was to reassure Melissa that she would get enough to eat. We let her know she could have snacks and what times those snacks would be. We told her she could have as much as she wanted at meals and at snacks. And we told her she would not be allowed to eat between times.

Melissa's parents were ahead of the game, because they were doing a good job of having good meals. However, they were giving food handouts instead of having planned snacks, so they started to work on that. They set up regular snack times, and started choosing some food for snacks that she liked and was likely to [find] filling and satisfying.

The structure and reassurance worked. At first she ate quite a bit, and she pestered them for food in between. But they held firm and kept their bargain about allowing her to eat as much as she wanted, and after a couple of weeks her pressure on food began to drop off. She still wanted a lot on her plate (it seemed she needed that to reassure herself she would get enough), but she often didn't finish it. She would go off and play, and occasionally she would even play through snack time.

Now Melissa's eating is more positive and relaxed, and her weight has leveled off. ▲

In some homes, the problem can escalate to the point where emotions are highly charged and family members cannot deal with them effectively on their own. It is possible that the child's problems stem from deep-seated difficulties within the family. A practitioner who treats children with eating disorders notes, "Eating is a sensitive barometer of emotional state and parent-child interaction" (Satter, 1986). For example, a parent who is very concerned about his or her own body weight may be determined to prevent a similar problem in a child. The overweight parent may prohibit the child from eating enough to satisfy hunger in a misguided attempt to make him thin. The hungry child, then, looks for every opportunity to get more to eat to satisfy his hunger and even to hedge against anticipated deprivation later on.

In such cases, the family may well profit from family counseling or from a program designed to help overweight children and their families. SHAPEDOWN is one such comprehensive program that is available around the country; the program addresses issues of nutrition, exercise, self-concept, the child's food environment, and family interactions (Mellin, 1988). Many programs for overweight children will not accept a child for treatment unless the parents participate as well; this greatly increases the child's chances of success.

Basic Goals and Common Questions

The overall goals in feeding children are straightforward: to regularly provide food that will meet nutritional needs, be safe and appropriate to the child's stage of development, and be appealing to the child. Parental support for children as they develop their own good habits is also important.

The Basic Food Guide advises caregivers about what kinds and amounts of foods are likely to meet a child's nutritional needs. Children benefit from a variety of foods just as adults do, although portion sizes are different. Table 17.1 recommends numbers of servings and serving sizes for children at various ages. An easy standard to keep in mind when serving an item to a young child is that about 1 tablespoon (standard measuring tablespoon size) per year of age is a reasonable amount with which to start. The child may not eat it all or he may want more, but until he is old enough to serve himself or tell you how much he wants, this ratio can serve as a guideline.

Because a child has a small stomach capacity, she needs to eat more often. Depending on the child's current size and growth rate and on the family's schedule, a child may need one, two, or three snacks per day. Caregivers need to plan snacks that will make a nutritional contribution, since snacks usually provide 15–20% of a child's energy intake (HNIS, 1988).

Nutrition for Living: The Toddler and Elementary Years suggests what specific kinds of food to provide to avoid the nutritional shortfalls sometimes seen in young children. It also considers some safety issues for children at this age. Most of the time, these simple guidelines provide sufficient

Table 17.1 Basic Food Guide for Various Ages

	Include at Least This Many Servings Daily				
	Child ½–9 Years	Child 9–12 Years	Teen[a]	Young Adult[a]	Older Adult
Fruits and vegetables[b]					
Vitamin A rich	1	1	1	1	1
Vitamin C rich	1	1	1	1	1
Others to make a group total of . . .	4	4	5	5	5
Grain products (preferably whole grain; otherwise, enriched or fortified)	4[c]	4	6	6	6
Milk and milk products	2–3	3	3	3	2
Meats and meat alternates	2[d]	2	2	2	2

[a] Here, define "teen" as a person who has added height in the past year and is at least 12 years old; an "adult" has not added height in that time. The young adult includes people through 24 years of age.

[b] For preschool children, serving size is 1 tablespoon per year of age.

[c] Give smaller servings, depending on age.

[d] For preschool children, serving size is half of the standard Basic Food Guide serving.

information for feeding a healthy child well. With all the changes that children experience as they grow, however, and with children gradually assuming more responsibility for themselves in all realms, there may be occasional conflicts over eating. This is normal; it calls for reevaluation of the situation, possible adjustments in the division of responsibility, and usually results in progress. Nonetheless, caregivers often find it challenging to deal with and may wonder what to do, if anything. The rest of this section discusses some of the questions most often asked by parents and people who work with children.

Won't kids get what they need if you just let them eat what they want? This idea probably originated from the studies of pediatrician Clara Davis, who in the 1920s and 1930s published at least a dozen papers on the self-selection of diets by infants and children up to the age of about 5 (Story and Brown, 1987). The young children she studied were orphans housed in a hospital unit in Chicago; they did amazingly well at meeting their nutritional needs by choosing each meal from a tray of 10 foods and 2 types of milk. An essential point that most people are not aware of is that the children were choosing from simply prepared, uncombined, basic foods such as oatmeal, beef, eggs, haddock, bananas, spinach, peaches, and carrots. No sweeteners were added to any of the foods. Moreover, the children had no exposure to TV or to fast foods.

The foods from which these children chose were very different from what is available to most children today. Many of our foods are combinations of

The Toddler and Elementary Years

Although children need to eat foods from the same groups as adults do, that does not mean that kids can or should eat all of the same food items. Children's stages of development and common nutritional shortfalls should play a role in what specific food items are offered.

- For **fruits and vegetables,** be sure the form in which they are offered is safe for the child's stage of development. For example, at a very young age a whole raw carrot would be a hazard, but cooked carrot sticks would be manageable. Whole grapes would be unsafe, but a child would not be likely to choke on quartered grapes.
- Children usually like **grain products,** and these foods are nutritionally important. Offer whole-grain and enriched breads, pastas, crackers, and cereals. The typical American breakfast based on ready-to-eat cereal is nutritious: a study of breakfasts of 5- to 12-year-old children showed that kids who had these cereals with breakfast at least three mornings per week had higher nutritional intakes than those who ate other foods for breakfast (Morgan et al., 1981).
- Offer enough **milk and milk products;** sometimes calcium is low in children's diets. Children who do not drink much milk may better accept other dairy products such as cheese, lowfat yogurt, or puddings.
- **Meats and meat alternates** provide some nutrients that tend to be low in children's diets, particularly iron and zinc. It makes sense to regularly offer these foods, but be sure they are prepared in ways that make them easy for young children to eat. Children may eat more when meats are very tender, ground up, or cut small and thin enough to make them easy to chew.
- Many **combination foods** that are safe for children to eat are available. Children are more likely to accept simpler combinations in which they can readily identify the ingredients, such as spaghetti, but reject mixtures that have many or unfamiliar components.
- Do not assume that combination foods targeted at children are necessarily in their best nutritional interest. Some kid-centered frozen entrees, for example, are high in fat and sodium.
- Now there are single-serve combination dishes marketed for young children *to heat for themselves.* We urge parents and other caregivers to think twice about turning over the heating of food to young children, either stove-top or microwave cooking. Not only does the equipment offer hazards, but overheated or unevenly heated food can cause severe burns. This may indeed be "the 'zap' generation," but we believe it should start at a later age than those suggested on many current food product labels.
- **Limited extras** are popular with children. Although it is wise to underplay highly sweet, fatty, or salty foods in a child's diet, it is not necessary or practical to prohibit children from ever touching a potato chip, piece of candy, or glass of pop; doing so simply increases the appeal of these foods considerably. Using these foods as a reward for eating foods the child doesn't like as much has the same effect.

Moderation is the key. This can usually be achieved by not bringing many such foods into the house and by making sure that there is an adequate amount and variety of nutritious and appealing foods to eat.

ingredients and have sugar added to them; since children like sweetness, they would undoubtedly favor such foods if they were included in a study like Dr. Davis'. Because these foods would not necessarily provide the levels of micronutrients children need, we can't count on a hunger-satisfied child being a well-nourished child, especially if the types of foods provided for selection are not of reasonably high nutrient density.

How can I convince my child to try new things? First of all, we have to acknowledge that children prefer familiar foods; they eat best when they are offered foods they know and accept. But it is important to expose children gradually to an expanding assortment of nutritious foods so that more and more foods *become* familiar.

There is no way you can *make* a child eat something, and the use of force is unlikely to work. That does not mean you can't try some subtle techniques to overcome their neophobia (fear of something new). Sometimes, special treatment of a new food may encourage a child to try it. Cutting sandwiches into interesting shapes, decorating the food, or telling a story about it may help the child overcome initial resistance. Letting a child taste the food without having to swallow it is another possibility; if they want to, they can spit it into a napkin. Try reintroducing that same food after a few weeks or months; most children will be more willing to try it.

Another strategy is to involve children in helping prepare the food. This often heightens their interest; they take pride in seeing others eat what they have fixed and therefore are more willing to eat it themselves. Of course, the activity has to be appropriate to the child's developmental level, but as early as age 2 there are things they can do to help. Figure 17.3 shows some children intent on their culinary tasks.

We should also caution against bribing a child to eat something. If you do, you may win the battle but lose the war: a child *bribed to eat* a food ("If you eat your peas, you can watch TV") is less likely to eat the food again later. When a food is used *as a bribe* ("Be good while I'm on the phone and I'll give you a cookie"), it makes the food (cookies) more appealing in the future (Nutrition Reviews, 1986). It also may impress upon the child that food is a suitable reward, distraction, or time-filler.

Are "food jags" a serious problem? Sometimes children like a food so much that they want it to be the mainstay of every meal. Such temporary food fixations are common during the toddler years as a child begins to discriminate between different sensory characteristics of food and develop preferences. But nutritious though it may be, peanut butter for breakfast, lunch, and dinner cannot be accepted as a balanced diet. Thankfully, children themselves usually limit a food jag so parents do not have to make an issue of it unless it persists for more than a couple of weeks.

What foods are good for snacks? Snacks should make a good nutritional contribution to a child's diet. Since foods from the basic food groups are the most nutritionally dense, they offer good snack possibilities. Every food group has some items that lend themselves to being convenient as well as nourishing. Fresh fruits and vegetables (what could be more convenient than a half of a banana?), milk and crackers, cereal in big enough pieces to pick up by hand, cheese curds, and a quarter or half of a peanut butter sandwich are some of the easiest to prepare. You're not looking for whole meals, just something to tide the child over until the next meal. Also, kids may not want the same foods that they eat at mealtimes, so it may help to have certain items that are specifically used for snacks at your house—maybe particular kinds of cereal or crackers that you don't otherwise bring to the table.

Table 17.2 shows how some commonly used snacks rate nutritionally. Notice that sugared foods are generally at the bottom of the list because of their lower nutrient density. Although it's fine to have a cookie *with a meal* when there are a lot of other things to help satisfy hunger, at snack time kids may be more inclined to overeat when given sweets. It may be better to offer the less-sweet foods for snacks.

Table 17.2 Snack Food Rankings

Food Class	
Raw vegetables	
Fruit or vegetable juice	**High nutrient density**
Cereal	
Milk	
Fresh fruit	
Pumpkin or sunflower seeds	
Yogurt, flavored	
Cheese	
Milkshake	
Peanuts	
Rolls, bread, bagels	
Pudding	
Peanut butter	
Graham crackers	
Ice cream	
Dried fruit	
Crackers, pretzels	
Cookies or cake	
Canned fruit	
Granola bars	
Potato chips	
Pies, pastry, doughnuts	
Jello	**Low nutrient density**
Candy	
Soft drinks	

Adapted from Gillespie, A. 1983. Assessing snacking behavior in children. *Ecology of Food and Nutrition* 13:167–172.

Should all children take supplements? Many parents believe that their children should take supplements to make up for their poor eating habits. A multivitamin and mineral supplement at RDA levels can be useful for making up minor deficits, but they should not be counted on to correct major dietary flaws. As a source of nutrients, supplements are an inferior second choice to a well-balanced diet. Of course, if a qualified health care provider diagnoses a medical condition (such as a malabsorptive disease) and recommends appropriate supplements, the advice should be followed.

Does sugar affect children's behavior? Some popular articles have claimed that refined sugars cause behavioral and emotional problems in children. The authors of such articles often suggest that parents should put their children on "natural" or "sugar-free" diets.

Let's examine this recommendation by looking at some facts and some evidence. When high-carbohydrate foods are eaten alone—whether the food is sucrose or any other readily digestible carbohydrate—digestion and absorption are relatively rapid, and blood sugar rises. This stimulates the pancreas to secrete extra insulin, the action of which causes glucose to move from the bloodstream into the body's cells, and brings about a decrease in blood sugar that is generally still within the normal range. These physiological changes may be accompanied by some perceived energy differences but do not normally involve major mood changes. On the other hand, people who have reactive hypoglycemia (a rare condition described in Chapter 6 in which blood glucose drops to abnormally low levels after eating carbohydrates) may experience anxiety along with the physical symptoms of this condition.

Some uninformed individuals have tried to make a connection between the possible emotional effect of carbohydrate ingestion in people with hypoglycemia and the effects of carbohydrates on children's emotions and behavior. To support their claims, they use theories and anecdotal reports rather than evidence from well-designed scientific double-blind studies. The theories remain unproved (Gans, 1989).

When well-controlled studies have been conducted to determine the relationship between sugar consumption and behavior, the association has usually been found to be very weak if present at all. As of 1989, at least a dozen studies had been done to examine the effects of sugar on children's behavior and mental performance. They did not find that sugar significantly increased children's level of activity; in most of the studies, sucrose ingestion had no effect. In some studies, it actually had a calming effect (Greenwood, 1989). Of five studies that included cognitive measures, three found no differences in mental performance, one found improvement, and only one found poorer performance (Kruesi and Rapoport, 1986). These findings are hardly an indictment of sugar as the culprit in altering children's moods and behaviors.

Do other food substances affect attention deficit disorder? Another popular theory linking food to behavior was published in 1975 by the late Dr. Benjamin Feingold, an allergist with the Kaiser-Permanente medical system in California. Among his patients were children with **attention deficit disorders** (also called ADD, *hyperkinetic syndrome,* or *hyperactivity*). Children with this condition are more physically active, fidgety, excitable, impulsive, and distractible, and they have shorter attention spans, lower tolerance for frustration, and more difficulties in learning than most children of their age. (These children are nonetheless of normal or above normal intelligence according to standardized tests.)

attention deficit disorder—condition occurring in some children who tend to be more physically active, excitable, and distractible than their peers

According to his theory, certain food additives and *salicylates* (which are naturally occurring chemicals in many fruits, vegetables, herbs, and spices and also constitute the drug aspirin) are responsible for these behaviors. Dr. Feingold reported that 50–70% of hyperactive children improved when they were placed on a diet free of foods containing salicylates and artificial flavors and colors (some of which are chemically related to salicylates). This type of diet received so much publicity that many controlled scientific experiments were conducted to determine whether such a relationship does exist. An analysis of 23 studies, however, provided negligible support for the effectiveness of the Feingold diet (Gans, 1989).

Megavitamin therapy has also been suggested to be useful for reducing hyperactive behavior in children, but well-designed experiments fail to support this hypothesis. In one double-blind study, behavior during megavitamin therapy actually worsened (Nutrition Reviews, 1985).

Some experts believe that there is no harm in trying to treat hyperactivity with special diets, but others do not recommend organizing the lives of a child and his family around a special diet. Blaming behavior on an outside influence can decrease the child's sense of mastery over his own behavior and adversely affect his personality development.

Do children really need breakfast? Some children would rather sleep late than get up in time to have breakfast before school. Does it matter if kids have breakfast, as long as their overall intake for the day is adequate? Some studies suggest that skipping breakfast has a negative effect on the quality of children's schoolwork.

On a test that involved matching familiar figures (Pollitt, Leibel, and Greenfield, 1981), investigators have found that skipping breakfast impaired children's late morning problem-solving performance. Another study showed poorer performance in arithmetic and in continuous performance tasks on days when breakfast had not been eaten (Kruesi and Rapoport, 1986). Although the studies have varied in their methods and the ages of children tested, they show that, even with well-nourished children, hunger can have significant, measurable, negative impacts on their school performance (Meyers, 1989).

Are vegetarian diets healthy for children? The diets of lacto and lacto–ovo vegetarians can provide adequate amounts of nutrients for most children when they are carefully planned. Milk, cheese, eggs, and legumes usually can provide the protein, vitamins, and minerals that are provided by meat in the omnivore's diet.

However, strict vegetarian (vegan) diets are not recommended for preschool children because these diets make it difficult to provide adequate protein, vitamins, minerals, and energy for normal growth. One problem is that a large volume of food must be eaten to get the recommended amounts of nutrients. An additional problem is that the bioavailability of minerals from plant sources is relatively low. However, older children can usually thrive on properly planned vegan diets. Vegan children will need to eat three meals and three snacks every day to get enough nutrients. Their growth should be carefully monitored to ensure that their diet is adequate (Jacobs and Dwyer, 1988).

When Day-Care Snacks Ruin Dinner

The situation

Elise and Sam, both of whom work full-time, take their four-year-old daughter Mollie to a day-care center. Overall, Elise and Sam are very happy with the arrangement: Mollie likes it there; the staff relates very well to the children; and the environment is safe, it is comfortable, and it provides indoor and outdoor space and equipment for creative play.

There's just one sticking point. Sam picks Mollie up at the end of the day, and when they get home, Elise is generally already there fixing dinner. They eat about 15 minutes later, but Mollie usually just picks at her dinner without eating much. Recently they have been asking Mollie what kind of snack she had in the afternoon, and invariably she says it was cookies or candy.

It appears to Elise and Sam that Mollie may be eating a lot of sugary things in the afternoon that spoil her dinner. They are not sure what to do about the situation.

Is the information accurate and relevant?

- It's hard to know whether Mollie's report of the snacks is totally accurate; preschoolers can have an active imagination, or they might report their favorite things rather than what was actually served that day. It would be a good idea to check with the day-care providers regarding what was actually served for snacks.
- Elise and Sam have noticed that on weekends, when they provide all of Mollie's meals and snacks, she eats well at the evening meal. This adds to their belief that her day-care snacks may be the problem during the week.

What else needs to be considered?

The problem might have more to do with the *timing* of the snack than the *nature* of it. If the snack is served late in the afternoon, Mollie may be so hungry that she eats enough to interfere with her ap-

What can parents do if they are not happy with the food being served to their child by others? Some parents are concerned about the quality of the food served to their children in day-care, nursery school, or after school care. They may not agree with the kind or amount of food being served, or they may find it difficult to coordinate the care provider's schedule with their family schedule.

These are legitimate concerns. The quality of care programs is inconsistent, as is the food they provide (Spedding, 1989). It is not uncommon that the food served provides less energy and other nutrients than parents would expect (Briley et al., 1989). In other circumstances, enough food is provided, but parents may have other concerns such as you will note in Critical Thinking 17.1.

petite for dinner. If the snack were eaten earlier, she might eat less and therefore be hungrier for her evening meal.

Another condition that can negatively affect a child's appetite is being overtired. It is possible that Mollie is more tired after playing all day with other children than she is from being at home with her parents on the weekend. Maybe what she needs is a chance to rest quietly before dinner.

To begin, Sam decides to find out what snacks are actually being offered. When he picks up Mollie, he asks one of the day-care workers or the college student helper what the snack was that day. After a week, he has found that they had cookies twice, peanut butter and crackers once, birthday cupcakes one day, and candy that was provided by a parent for an upcoming holiday on the other day. He asks about the timing of the snack, and finds that it is usually between 3:30 and 4:00. One of the day-care workers mentions that Mollie enjoys the snacks a lot, especially when they have something sweet.

With this information, Elise and Sam consider some options.

What do you think?

If you were in their situation, which of the following alternatives would seem best to you?

- Option 1 Explain your concern to whoever plans the snacks, and ask that they consider serving fewer sugary things; have some examples in mind of items you would find more acceptable, or volunteer to be part of a parent committee that plans the snack menu.
- Option 2 Suggest that the center use candy, birthday treats, or cookies as a dessert item with lunch rather than as a snack, when children might want to eat more of it.
- Option 3 Suggest that a memo be sent to parents recommending which items make good treats (for birthdays, holidays, etc.) but are not excessively sugary.
- Option 4 Ask whether the snack could be served earlier.
- Option 5 Postpone dinner for an hour, allowing everybody some time to relax after the day and allowing Mollie time to get hungry for dinner.
- Option 6 Leave things as they are if Mollie seems to be growing normally; even without much dinner, she may be getting enough to eat during the rest of the day.

Do you see other options or combinations of options? Which do you think makes the most sense?

Growth and Increased Independence Influence Adolescent Nutrition

The adolescent years are unique in many ways. During this time, teenagers make a concerted effort to separate themselves from younger children and their parents by identifying with a "teen culture" that looks, acts, and functions differently. Along with these lifestyle changes, eating habits also change during the teen years.

Influences on Needs and Intake

The adolescent years are a period of increased vulnerability in regard to nutrition. First of all, the rate of physical growth is greater than at any time since infancy. Approximately 20% of adult height and 50% of adult weight are added during these years (Lucas et al., 1989). Second, this is the very time when other factors tend to compromise nutrient intake.

Growth The average American girl adds more than 10 inches in height and 40–50 pounds in body weight during the five adolescent years of greatest growth, from ages 10 through 14 (see Figure 17.1). The average adolescent boy experiences his greatest growth from ages 12 through 16, during which time he is likely to add approximately 12 inches in height and 50–60 pounds in weight (see Figure 17.1).

As many junior-high school students have observed with dismay, the growth spurt in girls generally occurs two years earlier than it does in boys, although there is tremendous individual variation. In fact, the age at which puberty begins and growth spurts occur in teens is so variable that growth charts based on age are of limited value for teenagers. Some health care providers who work with adolescents find it more useful to evaluate growth in relation to sexual maturation rather than chronological age.

Another generalization is that the gains in weight are much more marked than the increases in height. At the end of the growth spurt, teens weigh 65% more than they did at the beginning and have gained 15% in height. Weight gain in girls is attributable to increases in blood volume, muscle mass, skeletal mass, and adipose tissue. Boys have greater increases in blood volume, skeletal mass, and muscle mass than girls and actually become leaner during adolescence (Figure 17.5).

The increased blood volume and muscle mass raise the requirement for iron (for hemoglobin and myoglobin). Although girls add less of these materials than boys, they have a high need for iron to replace what is lost in menstrual flow.

There is some evidence that nutritional status affects the age of puberty in females. Within any culture, there is a range of ages during which it is normal for a woman to begin to menstruate. But young women from Western cultures, who are generally better nourished, usually begin to menstru-

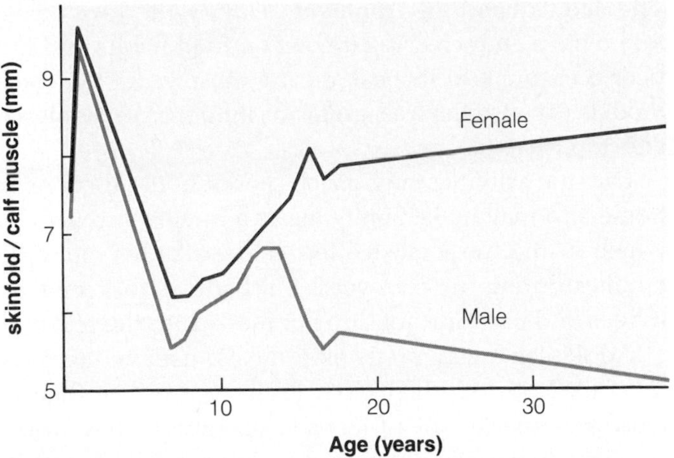

Figure 17.5 Fat accumulation between childhood and adolescence. Measurements of skinfold thickness in the calf indicate that the deposition of fat during adolescence varies greatly according to sex. (Adapted from Valadian, I., and D. Porter. 1977. *Physical growth and development from conception to maturity: A programmed text.* Boston: Little, Brown.)

ate at an earlier age than women in less developed countries. Also, girls who have minimal levels of body fatness—such as runners, gymnasts, ballet dancers, swimmers, and cyclists—have been reported to begin menstruating later or to menstruate less often than other young women who have a greater percentage of body fat (Loucks and Horvath, 1985). This is often associated with abnormal levels of certain hormones and can be a result of kcaloric restriction, excessive activity, or both. There is concern about the long-term implications of this condition; some preliminary studies suggest that the low hormone levels may allow larger losses of calcium from the body, increasing the later risk of osteoporosis. Further studies are needed to determine whether this is a consistent effect (Loucks and Horvath, 1985).

Just as body weight seems to affect reproductive capability, the reverse may also be true. One group of researchers has documented that women who start to menstruate at a younger age are almost twice as likely to be obese later in life. Data revealed that women who had started menstruating before age 11 had nearly 30% more fat by age 30 than those who began menstruating after age 14 (Garn, 1986).

Psychosocial Development During the teen years, children not only grow bigger, stronger, and more mature physically, but they also develop mental characteristics that are not common in younger children. They push for greater independence but still seek reasonable and supportive limits. Emotional volatility often replaces the more easygoing disposition of the elementary school years. The tendency to reject traditions in the search for their own identity can lead to some bizarre eating habits. In some teens, decreased growth or even eating disorders such as anorexia nervosa may be caused by fear of becoming fat, by fear of the physical and social consequences of maturing, or by a sense of ineffectiveness (see Chapter 11).

Teens tend to think in terms of the present; they are not much influenced in their behavior by what might happen in the future. When trying to educate them about nutrition, it makes more sense to promote good nutrition on the basis of what it can do for current appearance and performance than how it can reduce risk of heart disease, cancer, and osteoporosis at age 50.

The Teen's Food Environment During the teen years, factors outside the home have an increasing impact on food habits and nutrition beliefs. While peer pressure is at its peak during these years, coaches and other adult role models can also have a significant influence on adolescents' nutrition beliefs and food habits.

Outside activities such as jobs and school functions keep teens away from home and may make family meals a rare occurrence. Even the dinner meal, which is the meal most often eaten together, may be disrupted in some families during the teen years if schedules for teenagers' extracurricular activities and part-time jobs do not mesh with the rest of the family's program.

Adolescents commonly skip meals, usually breakfast or lunch. Girls are most likely to skip breakfast. Partly because of their irregular meals, most teenagers snack; 80% of teens in one survey had from one to seven snacks per day (Bigler-Doughten and Jenkins, 1987). Typically, snacks account for approximately 20% of an adolescent's energy intake (Story, 1989).

Fast foods are popular with adolescents and often are a major source of meals and snacks. Traditional fast-food menu items have been criticized for being high in fat, kcalories, salt, and sugar. Most entree items still are relatively high in fat, kcalories, and salt—especially the breakfast sandwiches and sandwiches with special sauces (Mayo Clinic Nutrition Letter, 1989a and b). Many fast-food operations have responded to some degree to these concerns and now offer some entrees that are lower in fat than the traditional items; for example, a broiled chicken sandwich is markedly lower in fat than a fried one. Some also have expanded their menu to include salads, low-fat salad dressings, and low-fat milk, and some will prepare certain items to order without salt.

Despite all the factors that tend to separate the teen from his or her family, there is still some degree of interdependence in the nutrition realm. Most teens value eating dinner with the family, although it is not always possible. In some families, teen-aged children participate in routine food-related tasks such as grocery shopping and food preparation.

The best ways for parents to influence the nutrition of their teenagers are to provide family meals that are nutritious, relaxed, and enjoyable as often as possible; to be good models of healthy eating behaviors; and to be sure there are plenty of healthy, convenient, appealing snacks in the house. This is as far as a parent can go at this stage in overcoming the barriers that teens say interfere with their eating well—lack of time, inconvenience, lack of self-discipline, and lack of a sense of urgency about reducing the risks of developing chronic diseases (Story, 1989).

Other Influences on Teen Eating

Many other factors determine teenage eating habits. At this time in life, a child is trying to find out what he or she thinks for himself or herself and is likely to be more experimental about eating than he or she was at an earlier age. Some of the factors that influence a teen's eating behaviors include his or her physical appearance, acne, physical performance, substance use and abuse, and pregnancy.

Appearance At no time in most people's lives is physical appearance of greater concern than during adolescence. The majority of teenagers are unhappy with their bodies. In one study, 70% of the girls surveyed wanted to lose weight, although the proportion that was obese was 15% (Lucas et al., 1989). It is not known how attitudes favoring thinness have developed (Feldman et al., 1988); even the thinnest girls want to be thinner (Moses et al., 1989). Among boys, 59% want to gain weight to achieve a strong, muscular look.

The strength of these concerns is such that fad diets and special body-shaping products have great appeal to many teens. Furthermore, the psychological discomforts associated with maturing and the impatience of many teenagers have made them a target for quackery. Bogus products are being marketed that promise to speed teens' development and ease their growing pains. The fact that many teens have discretionary money to spend makes them prime targets for quacks (FDA and BBB, 1988).

Acne The hormonal changes that trigger the onset of puberty are also largely responsible for acne, a common teenage problem that affects about 85% of teens and young adults to some degree.

Acne begins with the excessive secretion of sebum, an oily substance that lubricates the skin. This fosters the proliferation of bacteria that cause inflammation in ducts and glands beneath the skin. Anxiety, lack of sleep, and hormonal fluctuations during the menstrual cycle can aggravate the condition.

acne—skin condition especially common during adolescence; caused by proliferation of bacteria that produce inflammation in ducts and glands beneath the skin

Scientific studies have not found over-the-counter products to be cures for acne; similarly, most dietary changes do not bring about significant improvement. However, since certain products and food restrictions have been known to help some people, physicians may suggest this approach, making sure that the diet is nutritionally adequate at the same time. Fortunately, whether acne is treated or not, spontaneous improvement occurs in almost all cases before the end of the teen years.

For people with cystic acne, a severe form of the disease in which large abcesses cause pits and scars, help is now available. A synthetic form of vitamin A called **13-cis-retinoic acid** has proved helpful in many of the most serious cases. This drug is not as toxic as other forms of vitamin A, but it can produce side effects including elevated levels of blood lipids, reduction of normal body secretions, and possible birth defects. For these reasons, it is available by prescription only, and its use should be carefully monitored by a physician. It should not be used by any female at risk for becoming pregnant.

13-cis-retinoic acid—synthetic form of vitamin A that has been helpful in treating some serious cases of acne

Physical Performance Physical performance is another common motivator of adolescent eating behavior. Many teens try to boost their athletic capabilities by using food supplements or eating "good-luck" foods before an ath-

letic event. The degree to which such approaches are useful or not (or dangerous or not) varies considerably.

A staggering number of special sports nutrition products and supplements are available; most have no demonstrable benefit beyond what is obtainable from a well-balanced diet (Kris-Etherton, 1989; Williams, 1989). Furthermore, they can be very expensive; taken as directed, they can cost over $100 per week (Kris-Etherton, 1989). Participants in some sports are more likely than others to use supplements; one study found that weight lifters most often used them (Schultz, 1990). For some athletes, such products may contribute to the athlete's *psychological* preparation; using foods to "psych up" may have a placebo effect. Nutrition is among the four very important factors critical to top-level performance: anatomical structure, training state, motivation, and nutrition.

When people physically exert themselves, especially in endurance activities, they need to increase most markedly their intakes of water and carbohydrate (see Chapters 4 and 6). Their need for micronutrients also increases. Generally, since many athletes consume more food than their less active peers, it is easy for them to meet these micronutrient needs; however, for activities in which people try to maintain low body weight (such as gymnastics, volleyball, dancing, running, cheerleading, and waterskiing) it should not be assumed that nutrient intakes are adequate. If an athlete's food intake is low, it would be a good idea to evaluate that person's nutrient intake.

Some of the regimens athletes use can be very dangerous, such as the fasting or restricting of fluids that some wrestlers practice in order to "make weight." In their "Position Stand on Weight Loss in Wrestlers," the American College of Sports Medicine points out the risks of such practices: a reduction in muscular strength; a decrease in endurance; lower blood volume; a reduction in cardiac functioning during submaximal work conditions; lower oxygen consumption, especially with food restriction; an impairment of body heat regulatory processes; decrease in kidney function; a depletion of liver glycogen stores; and an increase in the amount of electrolytes being lost from the body (American College of Sports Medicine, 1976). Such effects not only jeopardize athletic performance but could interfere with normal growth and development as well. It has also been suggested that the wrestler who has repeatedly fasted and overeaten ("weight-cycled") may be a candidate for problems with overweight later in life. A study that compared the resting metabolic rates (RMRs) of wrestlers who weight-cycled with those who did not found that the weight-cyclers averaged 12% lower RMRs (Steen et al., 1988).

Since nutrition is often badly abused by athletes, and since it can have an important effect on performance, how can athletes be convinced of what really is in their best interest? Nutrition counselors acknowledge that simply advising athletes to eat from the four food groups doesn't have much appeal when compared to the glitzy testimonials of famous athletes paid to promote special products (King, 1989; Loosli, 1990). Alvin R. Loosli, a physician who does research on the nutritional practices of athletes, also counsels Olympic athletes. He has found that discussing *eight food-nutrient groups* meets the special concerns of athletes better than talking about four groups (Loosli, 1990). These eight groups are complex carbohydrates, simple sugars, protein, fats, vitamins, minerals (especially calcium and iron), fiber, and water.

Alcohol and Other Drug Intake The use of alcohol and street drugs may occur in the teen years. By 18 years of age, over 90% of teenagers have had some experience with alcohol (Lucas et al., 1989).

Alcohol can interfere with nutrient absorption and utilization, in addition to providing empty kcalories that displace nutritious foods. Because nutrient needs are high during the teen years, alcohol-induced nutrient shortages cause the classic ill effects of alcohol to be accentuated among teenagers. (These effects are discussed in Chapter 18.) Another serious concern regarding alcohol consumption is that approximately 50% of fatal automobile accidents involve a driver who is intoxicated. The interaction between nutrients and street drugs has not been as thoroughly studied as the relationship between nutrition and alcohol; generally, though, frequent drug users have poorer nutrient intakes.

Teenage Pregnancy One of every five infants born in the United States has a teenage mother. Almost 1 in 5 of those babies is a low-birth-weight (LBW) infant (Stevens-Simon and McAnarney, 1988). LBW babies are more likely to be a product of pregnancies that occur within two years of **menarche** (Olson, 1987). Chapter 16 discusses the problems of low-birth-weight infants in greater detail. Other medical consequences of teenage pregnancy include infant respiratory distress, pregnancy induced hypertension (PIH; see Chapter 16), difficult deliveries due to small pelvic size, and higher maternal and fetal death rates.

menarche—the onset of menstruation

Many factors make teenage pregnancy more likely to have a poor outcome. One is the mother's physical immaturity; pregnancy puts great demands on the teenager's own body, which is undergoing its own rapid growth. In addition, the teen mother may have other kinds of problems such as inadequate medical care; tobacco, alcohol, or drug abuse; or various sociological problems.

Sociological difficulties common in early pregnancy include interrupted and incomplete education, poverty and welfare dependence, social disapproval, unstable families, and child abuse and neglect. Since most teen births occur out of wedlock, another disruptive factor is the lack of emotional and financial support from the baby's father. Alienation from family and friends may be another problem for the pregnant teenager.

Nutrition is often a significant problem; teenage girls are the most poorly nourished age/sex group in the United States. Like other teens, pregnant teenagers may choose food based more on what they like and what their peers eat than on what is best for them. Furthermore, in the teen mother, there seems to be reduced transfer of nutrients to the fetus, so the developing infant probably derives less benefit from a given nutrient intake than would the fetus of an adult mother (Stevens-Simon and McAnarney, 1988).

And teen mothers, who often live in impoverished circumstances, may not have access to adequate food.

Teenage mothers can increase the likelihood of delivering a healthy baby by gaining enough weight during pregnancy. Fetal mortality from teenage mothers who gain 26–35 pounds during pregnancy is only half the rate as for those who gained less than 16 pounds (ADA, 1989). Although it is probably better for young teenage mothers to gain more weight than pregnant adult women, experts do not agree on how many pounds they should gain (Stevens-Simon and McAnarney, 1988). A committee of the National Academy of Sciences suggests that young adolescents should strive for weight gains at the higher end of the ranges recommended for adult mothers (Committee on Nutritional Status, 1990). The American Dietetic Association suggests that weight goals should be individually determined; they should take into account what the mother's expected weight gain from her own growth (without pregnancy) would have been in addition to the gains needed for a healthy pregnancy. Her prepregnant weight status—whether underweight or overweight—is an important consideration as well (American Dietetic Association, 1989).

People who work with teenagers should be alert to the possibility of teenage pregnancy and help the pregnant teen seek prenatal health care at the earliest possible opportunity. In addition to medical and social services, care should include two important nutrition goals: to ensure adequate access to food and to encourage the consumption of nutrient-dense foods that the mother enjoys (ADA, 1989). Nutrition counseling is more likely to be successful when the teenager's present diet is used as the basis for the diet during pregnancy and when she is urged to gradually add nutrient-dense foods that had previously been inadequate. Bringing a partner, relative, or friend with her for the counseling will help build mutual nutritional support. Chapter 16 contains additional information on nutrition during pregnancy.

Various public and private agencies have programs to help pregnant teenagers. Many school districts operate special classes in parenting, nutrition, infant care, and similar topics of concern to young mothers. These programs are often known as "SAM" (School-Age Maternity) or "SAP" (School-Age Parent) programs. Many services include day-care assistance to help the young mother complete her high school courses and earn a diploma. The March of Dimes provides information and counseling in health and nutrition for prospective parents and often provides referral to other agencies when special assistance is needed. Nutrition services are also available through the WIC program, which will be discussed in the upcoming section on nutrition assistance.

Nutrition Challenges for Teens

Compared with teenagers in the developing countries, American teenagers are relatively well-nourished. But compared with what *optimal* nutrition would be, the diets of many teens are short on certain nutrients and long on kcalories, sugar, fat, cholesterol, and sodium (Story, 1989).

Although this assessment comes from data collected in the late 1970s and the RDAs have changed since that time, today's findings probably would be similar: the nutrients most likely to be deficient are iron, calcium, magnesium, zinc, and vitamin B-6. Teens of low socioeconomic status and females are prone to having the lowest nutrient intakes (Story, 1989).

Girls ages 11–16 tend to have the poorest diets of any age/sex group in the United States; this is accentuated in those on weight-reduction diets. The diets of teenage boys usually are somewhat better, although when their intakes fall short of the RDA, they are generally low in the same nutrients as girls. Eating one of the day's meals away from home significantly decreases the intake of calcium, iron, vitamin C, and thiamin for people aged 13–21 (Bunch, 1984).

The 1990 RDA table (inside the back cover of this book) gives the recommended intakes of nutrients for teens in the 11- to 14-, 15- to 18-, and 19- to 24-year-old age groups. Figure 17.3 (earlier in the chapter) shows how the nutrient recommendations for 15- to 18-year-old males compare with those of younger and older males; from this comparison, you can see that recommended intakes of some nutrients are higher during the adolescent years than at any other age. For teenage girls, the same generalization holds, with the reminder that pregnancy, whenever it occurs, adds to nutrient needs.

Table 17.3 suggests intakes for the teenager and the pregnant teenager as recommended by the Basic Food Guide. Remember that the numbers in the Basic Food Guide represent *minimums* that should be consumed to reach RDA intakes; in many cases, teenagers will eat more. If the teenager is tall or physically active, more may be what he or she needs; if he or she is overweight or inactive, more would not be better.

Nutrition for Living: The Teen Years offers some suggestions about intake of foods from the various food groups.

Table 17.3 Basic Food Guide for Teenagers

	Include at Least This Many Servings Daily	
	Teen (Nonpregnant)	Pregnant Teen
Fruits and vegetables		
Vitamin A rich	1	1
Vitamin C rich	1	2
Others to make a group total of . . .	5	5
Grain products (preferably whole grain; otherwise, enriched or fortified)	6	6 or more
Milk and milk products	3	5
Meats and meat alternates	2	3

The more common nutritional problems of teenagers are discussed below.

Anemia Between 5 and 10% of some subgroups of teenagers have anemia. Low hemoglobin levels have been found more often in 12- to 14-year-old boys than in girls of the same age, but in the later teen years, more girls than boys are anemic (Public Health Service, 1982). Blacks, especially males, are anemic more frequently than whites. Interestingly, there is little correlation between low hemoglobin levels and dietary intake of iron. Other factors—such as iron absorption and utilization, growth rates, and menstrual losses—also are important in determining iron status.

Hypertension High blood pressure may affect up to about 10% of teenagers (Gong and Heald, 1988). Since hypertension is a major risk factor for cardiovascular disease, prompt intervention in the teen years can help forestall or reduce later, more serious problems. As is true for adults, nonpharmacologic methods are recommended for initial treatment of high blood pressure. Those related to nutrition include weight reduction if overweight, moderate dietary restriction of sodium, and reduction of dietary saturated fat.

Obesity Obesity and its incidence and treatment were extensively discussed in the earlier part of the chapter related to younger children. It is a serious problem with teenagers as well: in a 15-year period, the prevalence of obesity among 12- to 17-year-olds increased by 39%, and superobesity increased by 64% (Gortmacher et al., 1987).

The same principles of treatment as those for younger children apply to teenage obesity. It is necessary to encourage greater energy output (more exercise) and less input (especially by decreasing the amount of energy-dense foods consumed and increasing food of lower kcaloric density).

A critically important factor to keep in mind when dealing with overweight teenagers is their extreme sensitivity regarding their bodies. Teens who are obviously fatter than the norm suffer acutely. One of the most important aspects of programs for overweight teenagers is to help them develop a more positive self-image; this develops confidence that they can gain control over their problem.

Group programs can be very helpful. SHAPEDOWN, which also has a program for younger children, is an example of an effective program for teens and their parents. Offered by trained leaders in many parts of the country, it involves a thorough individual assessment. The program guides teens toward gradually improving their eating and exercise habits by helping them change the way they think about themselves, the way they communicate their feelings, and the way they make decisions about their lives (Mellin et al., 1987). In contrast, many commercial programs focus primarily on overly restrictive dieting and ignore the other components; recidivism and dropout from such programs are common (Mellin, 1989).

Some overweight teenagers can tackle their problem without a group,

The Teen Years

Teens are increasingly independent about getting food away from home and about food selection and preparation at home. Although parents have probably already made their major impact on their children's eating habits by this time, they still can directly influence their teenager's intake by keeping convenient, nutrient-dense, appealing foods in the house so that even a quick meal or snack can be nourishing.

- **Fruits and vegetables** are a food group teens often eat less of, especially when they are away from home. It may help to have fruit available to take along. At home, dinners are a good opportunity to include a couple of items from this group, such as both a salad and a cooked vegetable, or a mixed dish that contains a generous amount of vegetables. Having juices and vegetables (ready to eat) in the refrigerator may increase their appeal and use.
- **Grain products** are usually more popular with teens, especially boys. Breads, cereals, pastas, and grain-based snack foods are frequent choices. One precaution is that certain types of grain products—particularly fried snack chips and many snack crackers—are high in fat; although there is no reason to totally avoid those higher-fat foods, they should not be a mainstay of the daily diet. However, the consumption of most whole-grain and enriched products should be encouraged.

  To increase the absorption of iron from whole-grain and enriched products (such as crackers or breakfast cereal), consume a good source of vitamin C with them (such as orange juice).
- **Dairy products** should be emphasized, since diet surveys show inadequate calcium intakes among some groups, especially girls. People are less inclined to drink milk when away from home or when on a weight-reduction diet; therefore, it is important to have plenty of skim or low-fat milk, low-fat yogurt, cheese, and ice milk on hand to promote better calcium intake from meals and snacks eaten at home. A pregnant teen should try to consume one more serving of dairy product per day than her nonpregnant peers.
- **Meats and alternates** are important in a teenager's diet, not only for their protein content but also because iron and zinc intakes may be low. This is especially true for girls. Feasible snacks from this group might be cold chicken or water-packed tuna. Eating a small amount of meat when you eat starchy beans and peas increases the bioavailability of iron from those plant sources.
- **Combination foods** can be convenient and provide good nutrition at the same time. Pizza and submarine sandwiches are examples of foods that can include all the basic groups. At home, it may help to keep some single-serving meals or entrees in the freezer for quick, nutritious meals.
- Certain of the **limited extras** tend to be very popular with teens. Especially away from home, carbonated beverages tend to be more frequent choices than juice or milk; therefore, it makes sense not to have too much available at home or to provide them just for special occasions.

although not alone. Books such as *Winning Weight Loss for Teens* by Joanne Ikeda (1987) recommend a comprehensive individual program and suggest how parents and friends can be important allies instead of adversaries as teens try to normalize their weight.

Eating Disorders Chapter 11 is exclusively devoted to eating disorders, but since these conditions are more prevalent during the teen years than at any other time of life, they demand at least some mention here. In an eating disorder, a person dramatically departs from recommended levels of food intake as a means of dealing with life problems, such as making a career choice or reacting to family or other personal strife. Most people who develop eating disorders suffer from a paralyzing sense of ineffectiveness.

The most common eating disorder is frequent binge-eating (often called *bulimia*) until the person vomits or falls asleep. This acting-out behavior may be accompanied by other forms of self-abuse such as alcohol and other drug abuse, by socially unacceptable behavior such as stealing, or by abuse from family members.

Some people severely restrict their eating (often called *anorexia nervosa*) and self-impose excessive exercise. This behavior is often a way of proving to themselves that they do indeed have self-control. Women with anorexia nervosa often lose so much body weight that they cease to menstruate.

Other people exhibit their eating disorders by alternating between binging and starving behaviors. In any variation, eating disorders are dangerous because they threaten health and life itself. If people with eating disorders do not die, they will probably suffer from various other health problems. Eating disorders also take time away from important life issues. Optimally, people in whom an eating disorder is suspected should be directed promptly to diagnosis and treatment; the earlier the intervention, the more likely the treatment will be successful.

Food Assistance Programs Can Help Nourish Children and Teens

In 1986, data were collected on a large U.S. population sample of children ages 1–5 and women ages 19–50. Women and their children were categorized into three groups: the top group had incomes in excess of 300% of the poverty standard; the incomes of the middle group ranged from 131% to 300% of the poverty standard; and the poorest had incomes below 131% of the standard. When the nutritional intakes of these groups of women were compared, significant differences were seen between the middle- and lowest-income groups: the nutrient intakes of the lowest-income group averaged approximately 10% lower than that of the middle group.

The children did not fare as badly as their mothers. The children in the lowest-income group averaged only about 2% lower in nutrient intakes than the middle group; and for a few nutrients, their average intakes were actually higher.

The more moderate effect of poverty on the nutrition of children can be attributed, in part, to various government programs that help provide food for low-income children. This section discusses domestic food programs that benefit children. Some also help low-income adults.

The National School Lunch Program Since the 1940s, the National School Lunch Program has provided full-price, reduced-cost, or free lunches to millions of U.S. school children according to nationwide eligibility criteria. One of the original goals of the program was to improve the nutritional intakes of American children, and data consistently show that it has done that.

According to a study by the U.S. Department of Agriculture's Consumer Nutrition Center and the University of North Carolina, the lunches from the National School Lunch Program were superior in nutrient content to other options (Figure 17.6). Children ages 6–11 in school lunch programs were found to consume 70% more vitamin A, 6% more energy, and 19–21% more calcium, iron, and vitamins B-6 and C than those who ate other kinds of lunches. The positive impact of the school lunch program was even greater for low-income children (Akin et al., 1983).

The high nutritional quality of meals served in the National School Lunch Program is no accident: the meals are required to provide about a third of the RDAs for protein, vitamins, minerals, and energy. This is not to say that the National School Lunch Program is the only possible nutritious choice. The

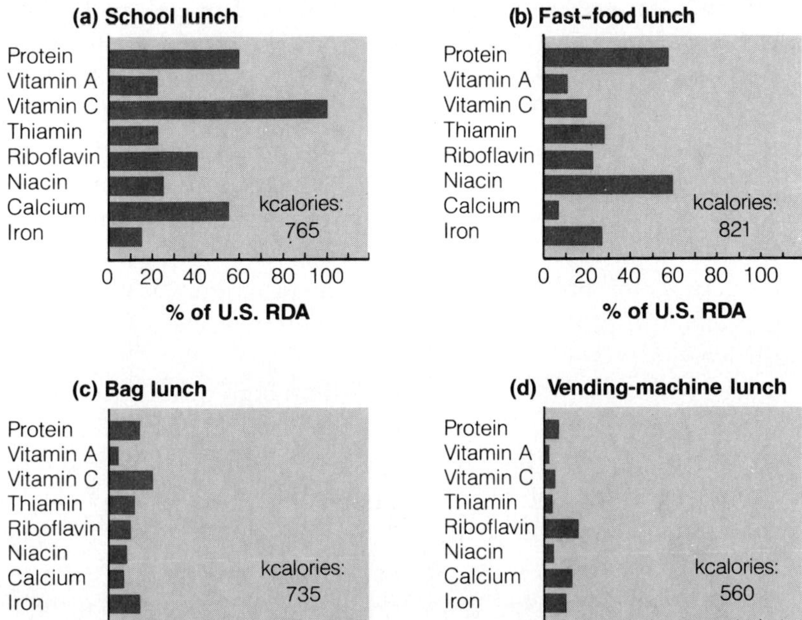

Figure 17.6 Nutrient and kcalorie profiles of various lunches. (a) Profile of a typical school lunch: turkey-and-cheese sandwich, celery sticks, cranberry sauce, fried potatoes, mixed fruit, whole milk, million dollar cookie. (b) Profile of a typical fast-food lunch: quarter-pound hamburger, fries, cola beverage. (c) Profile of a typical bag lunch: bologna sandwich, cookies, sweetened fruit drink. (d) Profile of a typical vending-machine lunch: potato chips, chocolate candy bar, soda. (Courtesy: National Dairy Council.)

typical fast-food lunch (quarter-pound hamburger, fries, cola beverage) has many strengths but would be improved by replacing the cola beverage with milk. A typical sack lunch (bologna sandwich, cookies, sweetened fruit drink) could be improved by substituting fruit for the drink and purchasing milk at school. It is more difficult to suggest how to improve the vending machine lunch because the items stocked are so variable.

Another attractive feature of the School Lunch Program is that it is often significantly less expensive to the recipients than the other types of lunches, since USDA partly subsidizes it. Finally, many school lunch operations are modifying their menus to offer foods more appealing to students. Methods have included using student taste panels; incorporating salad bars, family-style lunches, ethnic foods, and fresh fruits and vegetables; and hiring a gourmet chef. The results of these changes have been satisfactory to both the students and the school lunch management (Tufts, 1985).

Other Child Nutrition Programs The *School Breakfast Program* began in the late 1960s. It provides breakfast at full price, reduced cost, or no cost according to specific eligibility criteria, but the number of meals it serves per year is approximately 15% of the number of meals served by the School Lunch Program (Matsumoto and Smith, 1989). A recent study indicated that participants in the School Breakfast Program improved their scores on basic skills tests and had fewer absences and tardiness (Meyers et al., 1989).

The *Special Milk Program* provides milk to schoolchildren. It expanded in 1987 when federal legislation included kindergartners who attend school for just a half-day and do not have access to other meal-service programs. The *Child Care Food Program* provides cash and commodity assistance to non-profit child-care centers and day-care homes. This program has shown the greatest growth of any of the child nutrition programs during the 1980s, with almost 125,000 sites participating in 1988 (Matsumoto and Smith, 1989).

The Supplemental Food Program for Women, Infants, and Children (WIC) The WIC program provides nutrition education and vouchers for certain foods to high-risk pregnant women, nursing mothers, and children up to the age of 5 who meet the program criteria. Most pregnant teenagers qualify for this program. Studies have shown the program was effective in decreasing premature births, stillbirths, and maternal anemia and in increasing birth weight.

Participation in WIC reached an all-time high in 1989, when it increased 13% over 1988 figures. This occurred with only about a 5% increase in cost (Matsumoto, 1989). This efficiency was possible because infant formula manufacturers had entered into agreements with various states to provide rebates in exchange for being the sole providers of the formula in their region.

The situation changed in 1990 when states with expiring contracts sought new bids from formula manufacturers; the producers all offered *lower* rebates than formerly. This threatened to increase the program cost per client and to force the program to reduce services. Congress acted quickly to maintain the service level by passing legislation allowing state WIC programs to spend a portion of the funds allotted for the next fiscal year, but this was only a stop-gap measure. (This situation is a good example of how economic and political factors can affect nutrition.)

The Food Stamp Program Another important program affecting the food intake of low-income families is the food stamp program. The federal government sponsors a program that issues food stamps that can be used to buy food at any approved grocery store. The monetary value of the food stamps issued depends on the income and size of the family. The amount of money granted is designed to be sufficient for a family to meet its basic nutritional needs when carefully choosing from economical foods. Average monthly benefits in 1989 were approximately $52 per person (Matsumoto, 1989).

A program that provides access to food can make a critical difference to the developing child. Nutrition is important throughout life, of course, but inadequate nutrition during childhood can have lifelong consequences. Physiological, psychological, sociological, political, and economic factors all affect a child's nutritional intake and status—and, in turn, nutritional well-being affects the functioning of each child's mind and body.

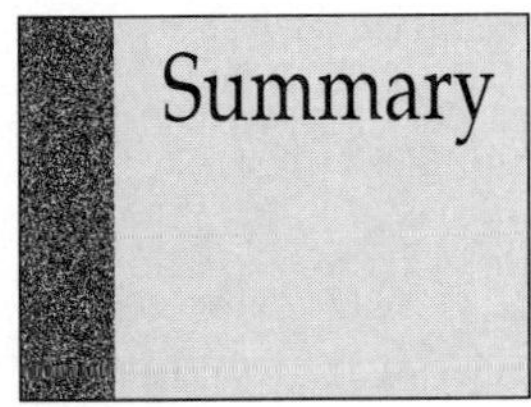

▶ The most important influence that caregivers can have on a child's nutrition during the growing years is to assist him or her in developing sound eating habits. This challenge demands patience, a sense of humor, and some knowledge about what is normal during these transitional times.

▶ The food intake of young children is extremely variable and is not strictly proportional to their weight. As children's motor skills and coordination improve, they should be encouraged to participate in food preparation. Children often assert themselves by rejecting certain foods or using their eating behavior as a negotiating tool. Advertising, family circumstances, and peer influence all contribute to a child's nutrition socialization. Anticipating a child's behavior and the many influences on it can help put this issue in perspective.

▶ Compared with children in other parts of the world, children in North America do not have the same nutritional deficiencies; in general, they are more likely to be *over*nourished than *under*nourished. Obesity is a common and increasing problem for children, and it can predispose an individual to various health problems both during childhood and in the future. Iron deficiency anemia and dental caries, although decreasing in prevalence, continue to be significant problems.

▶ Recommended diets for children are similar in many ways to those for adults and should include a wide variety of nutritionally dense foods. Since children tend to like familiar foods more than unfamiliar ones, it is important to expose them to an increasing assortment of foods that can *become* familiar. As at other ages, the child's sense of hunger and satiety should determine the amount of food consumed. Keeping a growth chart for a child can help provide reassurance that he or she is eating enough.

▶ Many popular articles have attempted to link a child's diet and behavior, although no meaningful scientific evidence supports such claims. There does not appear to be an association between sugar consumption and negative behavior in normal children, nor do food colorings and salicylates prove to cause **hyperactivity,** except in a very few cases.

▶ The dramatic growth of the adolescent years produces high nutrient demands at the very time when many other factors seem to adversely affect nutrition. Intense preoccupation with physical appearance can inspire strange eating habits, compromised growth, or—in extreme cases—eating disorders. **Acne** afflicts many teens, who sometimes try to deal with it by restricting certain foods. The desire to improve athletic performance also motivates adolescent eating behavior, as do peer pressure, the time demands of outside activities, and the use of alcohol and other drugs.

▸ Teenage pregnancies present many medical and nutrition problems for both the mother and the baby and are often considered high-risk situations. Nutritional status both before and after conception is very important to the baby's health. Many public and private agencies sponsor programs to counsel teenage mothers about health, nutrition, and child care and to allow them to finish school.

▸ The diets of teenage boys appear to be better than those of girls; teenage girls on weight-reduction diets tend to be less well-nourished than almost any other North American population group. Iron deficiency anemia, hypertension, obesity, and eating disorders are nutrition and health problems seen during the teen years.

▸ Because nutrition during the childhood and teen years has such an impact on current and future health and well-being, it is fortunate that there are programs that provide food assistance to children at risk for malnutrition. Some of these programs are the National School Lunch Program, the School Breakfast Program, the Special Milk Program, the Child Care Food Program, the Supplemental Food Program for Women, Infants, and Children, and the Food Stamp Program.

References

Akin, J.S., J.S. Bass, D.K. Guilkey, P.S. Haines, and B.M. Popkin. 1983. Evaluating school meals. *The Community Nutritionist* 2(no. 1):4–7.

American Dietetic Association. 1989. Position of the American Dietetic Association: Nutrition management of adolescent pregnancy. *Journal of the American Dietetic Association* 89:104–109.

Bigler-Doughten, S. and R.M. Jenkins. 1987. Adolescent snacks: Nutrient density and nutritional contribution to total intake. *Journal of the American Dietetic Association* 87:1678–1679.

Briley, M.E., A.C. Buller, C.R. Roberts-Gray, and A. Sparkman. 1989. What is on the menu at the child care center? *Journal of the American Dietetic Association* 89:771–774.

Bunch, K.L. 1984. Food away from home and the quality of the diet. *National Food Review* 25:14–16.

Committee on Nutrition. 1989. Iron-fortified infant formulas. *Pediatrics* 84:1114.

Cotugna, N. 1988. TV ads on Saturday morning children's programming—what's new? *Journal of Nutrition Education* 20:125–127.

Dietz, W.H. 1988. Childhood and adolescent obesity. In *Obesity and weight control,* ed. R.T. Frankle. Rockville, MD: Aspen Publishers, Inc.

Dietz, W.H. and S.L. Gortmaker. 1985. Do we fatten our children at the TV set? Television viewing and obesity in children and adolescents. *Pediatrics* 75:807–812.

Dietz, W.H. and R. Hartung. 1985. Changes in height velocity of obese preadolescents during weight reduction. *American Journal of Diseases of Children* 139:705–707.

FDA (Food and Drug Administration) and BBB (Better Business Bureau). 1988. Quackery targets teens. *FDA Consumer,* February, 1988.

Feldman, W., E. Feldman, and J.T. Goodman. 1988. Culture versus biology: Children's attitudes toward thinness and fatness. *Pediatrics* 81:190–194.

Gans, D.A. 1989. Behavioral disorders associated with food components. In *Food toxicology: A perspective on the relative risks,* ed. S.L. Taylor and R.A. Scanlon. New York: Marcel Dekker, Inc.

Garn, S.M. 1986. Maturational timing as a factor in female fatness and obesity. *American Journal of Clinical Nutrition* 43:879–883.

Gong, E.J. and F.P. Heald. 1988. Diet, nutrition, and adolescence. In *Modern nutrition in health and disease,* ed. M.E. Shils and V.R. Young. Philadelphia: Lea & Febiger.

Gortmaker, S.L., W.H. Dietz, A.M. Sobol, and C.A. Wehler. 1987. Increasing pediatric obesity in the United States. *American Journal of Diseases of Children* 141:535–540.

Greenwood, C. 1989. The role of diet in modulating brain metabolism and behavior. *Contemporary Nutrition* 14(no. 7). Minneapolis: General Mills.

HNIS (Human Nutrition Information Service). 1988. *CSFII: Continuing survey of food intakes by individuals.* Washington, DC: U.S. Department of Agriculture.

Ikeda, J. 1987. *Winning weight loss for teens.* Palo Alto: Bull Publishing Company.

Ikeda, J.P. 1989. *If my child is too fat, what should I do about it?* Oakland, CA: ANR Publications.

Jacobs, C. and J.T. Dwyer. 1988. Vegetarian children: Appropriate and inappropriate diets. 1988. *American Journal of Clinical Nutrition* 48:811–818.

King, S.W. 1989. Nutrition information: Reaching the young athlete. In *Report of the Ross symposium: The theory and practice of athletic nutrition: Bridging the gap,* ed. A.M. Cameron. Columbus, OH: Ross Laboratories.

Kris-Etherton, P.M. 1989. Nutrition and athletic performance. *Contemporary Nutrition* 14(no. 8). Minneapolis: General Mills.

Kruesi, M.J. and J.L. Rapoport. 1986. Diet and human behavior: How much do they affect each other? *Annual Reviews of Nutrition* 6:113–130.

Loosli, A.R. 1990. Athletes, food and nutrition. *Food & Nutrition News* 62(no. 3):15–18. Chicago: National Livestock and Meat Board.

Loucks, A.B. and S.M. Horvath. 1985. Athletic amenorrhea: A review. *Medicine and Science in Sports and Exercise* 17:56–72.

Lucas, B., J.M. Rees, and L.K. Mahan. 1989. Nutrition and the adolescent. In *Nutrition in infancy and childhood,* ed. P.L. Pipes. St. Louis: Times Mirror/Mosby.

Matsumoto, M. 1989. Recent trends in domestic food programs. *National Food Review* 12(no. 4):34–36.

Matsumoto, M. and M. Smith. 1989. Food assistance. *National Food Review* 12(no. 2):33–39.

Mayo Clinic Nutrition Letter. 1989a. Fast food: More food options make it easier to elude excess fat. *Mayo Clinic Nutrition Letter,* July, 1989.

———. 1989b. Fast food: When you order breakfast, opt for less fat. *Mayo Clinic Nutrition Letter,* June, 1989.

Mellin, L.M. 1988. *SHAPEDOWN: Just for kids: Level 1 (6–8 years); Level 2 (8–12 years); Parent's guide: A guide for supporting your child.* Anselmo, CA: Balboa Publishing.

Mellin, L.M. 1989. Adolescent obesity: Implications for action. *Food and Nutrition News* 61(no. 5):32–33. Chicago: National Livestock and Meat Board.

Mellin, L.M., L.A. Slinkard, and C.E. Irwin. 1987. Adolescent obesity intervention: Validation of the SHAPEDOWN program. *Journal of the American Dietetic Association* 87:333–338.

Meyers, A.F. 1989. Undernutrition, hunger, and learning in children. *Nutrition News* 52(no. 2):5–7. Rosemont, IL: National Dairy Council.

Meyers, A.F., A.E. Sampson, M. Weitzman, B.L. Rogers, and H. Kayne. 1989. School breakfast program and school performance. *American Journal of Diseases of Children* 143:1234–1239.

Morgan, K.J., M.E. Zabik, and G.A. Leveille. 1981. The role of breakfast in nutrient intake of 5- to 12-year-old children. *American Journal of Clinical Nutrition* 34:1418–1427.

Moses, N., M. Banilivy, and F. Lifshitz. 1989. Fear of obesity among adolescent girls. *Pediatrics* 83:393–398.

National Research Council. 1989. *Diet and health.* Washington, DC: National Academy of Sciences.

NCHS (National Center for Health Statistics). 1982. Diet and iron status, a study of relationships: United States, 1971–1974. DHHS Publication No. (DHS)83-1679. Hyattsville, MD: U.S. Department of Health and Human Services.

Nutrition Reviews. 1985. Megavitamins and the hyperactive child. *Nutrition Reviews* 43:105–107.

Nutrition Reviews. 1986. Manipulation of children's eating preferences. *Nutrition Reviews* 44:327–330.

Olson, C.M. 1987. Pregnancy in adolescents: A cause for nutritional concern? *Professional Perspectives* no. 1:1–5. Ithaca, NY: Cornell University Division of Nutritional Sciences.

Pollit, E., R.L. Leibel, and D. Greenfield. 1981. Brief fasting, stress, and cognition in children. *American Journal of Clinical Nutrition* 34:1526–1533.

Rozin, P. 1988. Cultural approaches to human food preferences. In *Nutritional modulation of neural function,* eds. J.E. Morley, M.B. Sterman, J.H. Walsh. Academic Press, Inc.

Satter, E. 1986. Childhood eating disorders. *Journal of the American Dietetic Association* 86:357–361.

Satter, E. 1987. *How to get your kid to eat . . . but not too much.* Palo Alto: Bull Publishing Company.

Schultz, L.O. 1990. Nutrient supplement use by athletes. *Food and Nutrition News* 62(no. 3):19–20.

Shear, C.L., D.S. Freedman, G.L. Burke, D.W. Harsha, L.S. Webber, and G.S. Berenson. 1988. Secular trends of obesity in early life: The Bogalusa heart study. *American Journal of Public Health* 78:75–77.

Spedding, P. 1989. Day care: Safe or sorry? *Human Ecology Forum* 17(no. 3):16–18.

Steen, S.N., R.A. Oppliger, and K.D. Brownell. 1988. Metabolic effects of repeated weight loss and regain in adolescent wrestlers. *Journal of the American Medical Association* 260:47–50.

Stevens-Simon, C. and E.R. McAnarney. 1988. Adolescent maternal weight gain and low birth weight: A multifactorial model. *American Journal of Clinical Nutrition* 47:948–953.

Story, M. 1989. A perspective on adolescent lifestyle and eating behavior. *Nutrition News* 52(no. 1):1–3. Rosemont, IL: National Dairy Council.

Story, M. and J.E. Brown. 1987. Do young children instinctively know what to eat? The studies of Clara Davis revisited. *The New England Journal of Medicine* January 8, 1987:103–105.

Tufts University Diet and Nutrition Letter. 1985. Good grades for school lunch program? *Tufts University Diet and Nutrition Letter* 3(no. 2) April.

Williams, M.H. 1989. Nutritional ergogenic aids and athletic performance. *Nutrition Today* 24:7–14.

Yip, R., N.J. Binkin, L. Fleshood, and F.L. Trowbridge. 1987. Declining prevalence of anemia among low-income children in the United States. *Journal of the American Medical Association* 258:1619–1623.

18

Nutrition for Adults: Promoting Good Health in Maturity

In This Chapter

- Changes in Health Status and Nutrition Needs Take Place Gradually
- Nutrition and Lifestyle Affect Health and Longevity
- Drugs and Alcohol Interact with Nutrients and Affect Health
- Medications and Nutrients Can Interfere with Each Other
- Alcohol Influences Nutrition and Health
- Live Well in the 1990s
- How Have You Done So Far?

What can good nutrition do for adults? Although the emphasis in the last two chapters was on the role of nutrients in *growth*, good nutrition is vitally important during all of the adult years as well. What are the mental images you have of yourself in the future? Are you training for a profession? Headed for a career in business? Hoping to raise a family? Looking forward to involvement in the performing arts? Expecting to participate in sports? No matter what choices you make in your life, good nutrition is among the factors that can help equip you physically and mentally to accomplish your goals.

The issue of how we can maximize good health during adulthood is exceptionally important, because we have more adult years ahead of us than at any time in history. Demographic forecasters predict that the proportion of our population that will live to be over the age of 65 will increase progressively during the next century (Figure 18.1). Currently, one out of *eight* Americans is at least 65 years old; in 100 years, 1 in *four* are predicted to be 65 or older.

As we noted in the beginning of this book, nutrition has three basic functions throughout life. First, our body cells need nutrients for energy production; second, they use nutrients for regulation of metabolic processes. These processes of living cause some wear and tear on cells. Gradually they deteriorate, and new cells are produced to replace them. Some cells need replacement every couple of days; others function for years at a time. These remodeling processes are the third reason we need adequate amounts of nutrients during adulthood.

Eventually, cell replacement has trouble keeping up with deterioration; the mass of various types of tissue is reduced, and the level of tissue function decreases. It is apparent that these processes are influenced simultaneously by genetic and environmental factors, of which nutrition is one.

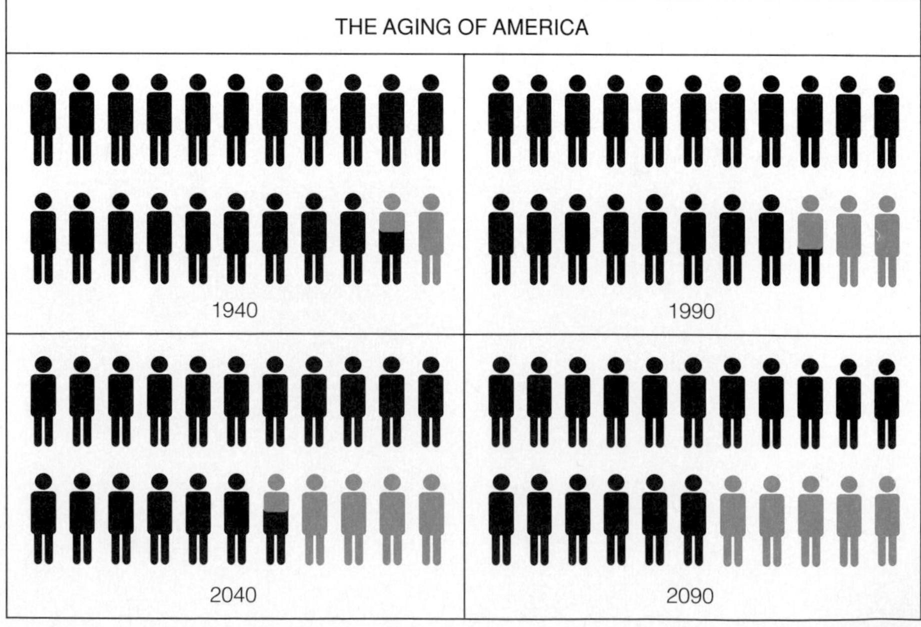

Figure 18.1 The aging of America. In 1940, 6.8% of the population was 65 or older. By 1990, 12.7% of us will have reached age 65; by 2040, 21.7%; and a century from now, nearly one out of four Americans will be 65 and older. An estimated 25,000 Americans now living are 100 years old or older. Source: Flieger, 1988. U.S. Bureau of Census.

Scientists have found that there is no rigid timetable for the rate at which the changes of aging take place. In fact, the variable rates at which individuals experience these changes cause us to become more different from our peers during the elder years than we are at any other phase of life (Chernoff and Lipschitz, 1988). Clearly, there are some 75-year-old people who are healthier than some 50-year-olds.

Scientists in the field of aging research (called *gerontology)* are working to discover how various environmental factors—including nutrition—can influence our physical fitness, the function of the immune system, the presence or absence of disease, one's psychological state, and even the ability to think and learn. Much remains to be learned on these topics. Some researchers suggest that optimizing these factors may make the difference between "successful aging" and "usual aging" (Rowe and Kahn, 1987).

Changes in Health Status and Nutrition Needs Take Place Gradually

The status of body cells, tissues, organs, systems, and their functions changes with time. Although many people consider 21 years of age as the *chronological* beginning of "adulthood," 40 as the start of "middle age," and 65 as the year in which a person becomes "elderly," the *physiological* changes during adulthood are neither so abrupt nor so uniform.

Physical Changes Observed During Adulthood

Figure 18.2 shows some of the changes in body composition that occur with aging. There you see that levels of body calcium, potassium, and protein are likely to remain fairly stable, or decrease slowly, for decades and then rather quickly decrease in mass (Heymsfield et al., 1989). Similarly, losses in function do not usually follow a straight line (Figure 18.3).

From age 30 to age 75, various body systems decrease in function by from less than 10% to more than 50% of young adult values.

Overall, the most influential change is probably the decrease in lean body mass and the concurrent reduction in energy need. Other changes have more specific effects on nutrition. With aging, many changes occur in the gastrointestinal tract. Reduced production of saliva and decreased function of taste buds occur during aging and may change food preferences. People with missing teeth or ill-fitting dentures may avoid chewy, crunchy, or hard foods.

Gastric secretions of acid and enzymes decrease with age, so digestion and absorption become less efficient. The reduction of stomach acid may make dietary iron, calcium, and some other nutrients less absorbable. Decreased production of intrinsic factor impairs the absorption of vitamin B-12. Lower amounts of bile are secreted by the liver and may make fat absorption

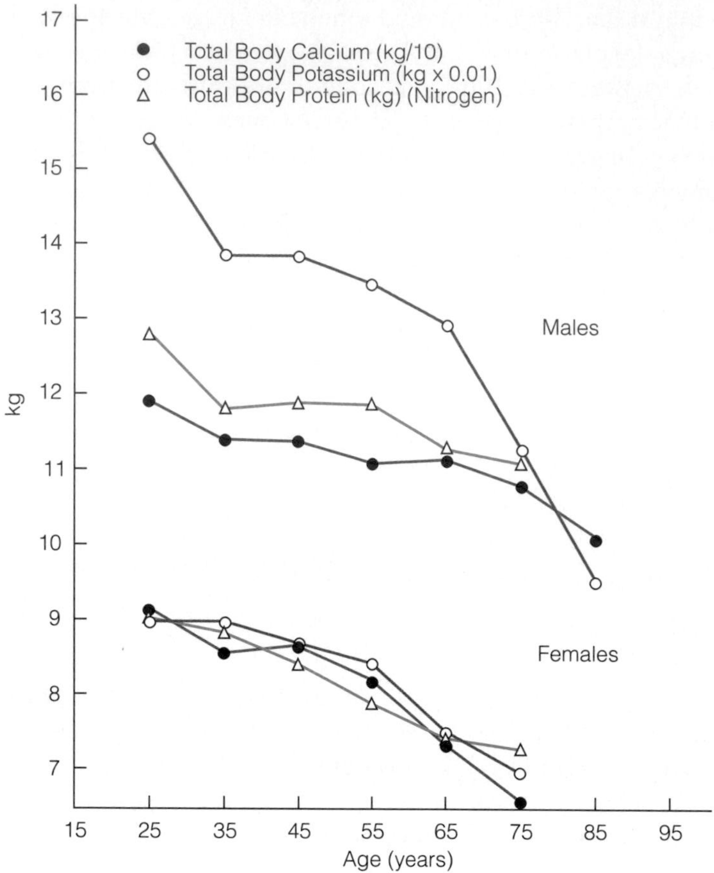

Figure 18.2 Body composition changes during adulthood. This figure shows how average levels of certain substances differ among groups of people of different ages. Calcium is an indicator of bone mass; potassium and protein are indicators of lean tissue.

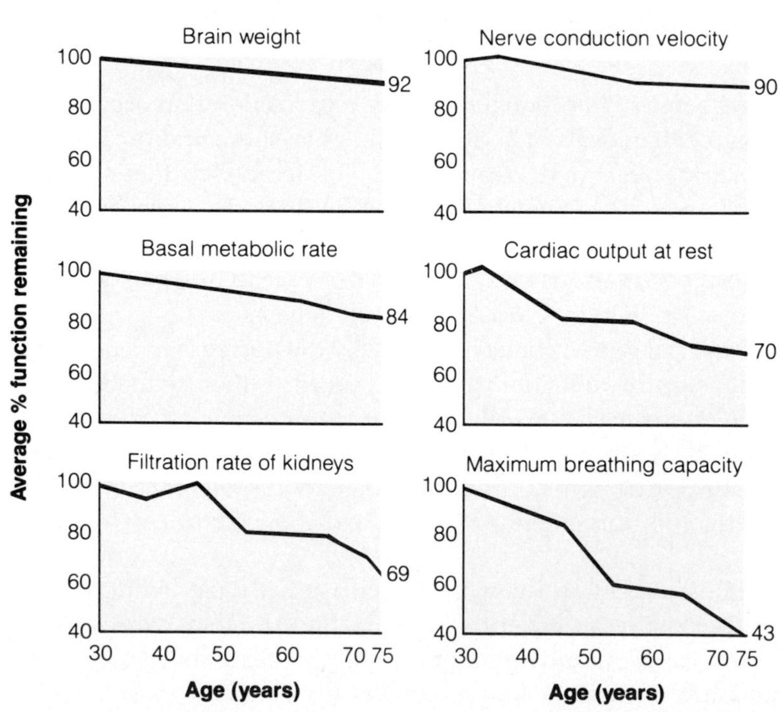

Figure 18.3 Average loss of function with age. (From *Growing old* by Alexander Leaf. Copyright © 1973 by Scientific American, Inc. All rights reserved.)

less efficient in older people. With age, muscles in the lower gastrointestinal tract become weaker and peristalsis slows, so constipation may become a problem. Kidneys function less efficiently with age so that electrolyte and water balance are more difficult to maintain. This effect is more pronounced during periods of physical stress, such as during illness. Some elderly people have a diminished sense of thirst that may result in dehydration.

Theories Concerning Age-Related Changes

Although we can observe many physical changes as people age (as shown in Figures 18.2 and 18.3) we are not sure to what extent these changes are *inevitable*. To explain what we mean by this, let us consider the two general classes of theories about why and how we age. One is that our bodies start making physiological "mistakes" in cell production and function owing to metabolic errors or to repeated external assaults from such factors as viruses, malnutrition, pollutants, or solar radiation. The other theory is that the changes of aging are genetically programmed.

The first theory suggests that you can do something to reduce the rate at which the changes of aging occur, such as nourishing yourself well, getting enough exercise and sleep, not smoking, avoiding excessive environmental and psychological stresses, having a good attitude about life, and getting medical help when you need it. The second theory suggests that your fate is controlled by your genetic makeup and that you can't alter your course of aging no matter what you do.

Which theory is correct? Actually, scientists find evidence that a combination of these factors affect the aging process (Flieger, 1988).

Nutritional Needs During Adulthood

More research has been done on the nutrient needs of young and middle-aged adults than on the needs of older adults (Freeland-Graves and Bales, 1989). Therefore, nutritional recommendations for young and middle-aged adults are probably of higher reliability than those for older adults. Moreover, older populations are generally more heterogeneous than younger ones, which further complicates the application of dietary advice to older adults.

Energy Population studies have shown that lean body mass generally declines after early adulthood at a rate of 2–3% per decade and that *resting metabolic rates* decline proportionately. A study of healthy men showed that beginning in their twenties, their *total energy usage* declined by about 12 or 13 kcalories per day each year. Of this amount, approximately 5 kcalories were accounted for by falling basal metabolic rate, and the remainder were attributable to declining physical activity levels (McGandy et al., 1966). In keeping with this decrease in usage, men and women tend to naturally reduce their total *intake* of kcalories as they age (Figure 18.4).

The energy RDA for men ages 19–50 is 2900 kcalories; for women, it is 2200 kcalories. For adults over age 50, the RDA for energy is only 80–85% of that for younger adults (National Research Council, 1989). Keep in mind that energy RDAs are average figures; some people will need more kcalories, others fewer.

It is also possible that the same person will experience dramatically different energy needs and intakes within the broad age range of 19–50. Think, for example, of a college student in his early 20s who walks everywhere—to classes, to his part-time job, to his apartment—and then participates in sports for recreation. If, after graduation, he gets a job that demands long hours at a desk, after which he drives himself home for an evening of reading in front of the TV, his energy expenditure will be greatly reduced from what it was as a student.

Although population studies generally show energy usage to decrease with advancing age, in recent years, a small but increasing number of people have been enjoying vigorous activity late into adulthood. Consider that many community sports events—such as competitive running, swimming, and tennis—now include a "masters" category for older adults . . . and it is not uncommon for some of these participants to cross the finish line ahead of some of the younger competitors.

Other Nutrients for Young and Middle-Aged Men and Women Most nutrient needs decline somewhat or remain constant from the late teen years into the early and middle adult years because the major periods of growth are over. However, since the accumulation of bone mass can continue through the 20s and possibly into the 30s, the experts who developed the 1989 RDAs

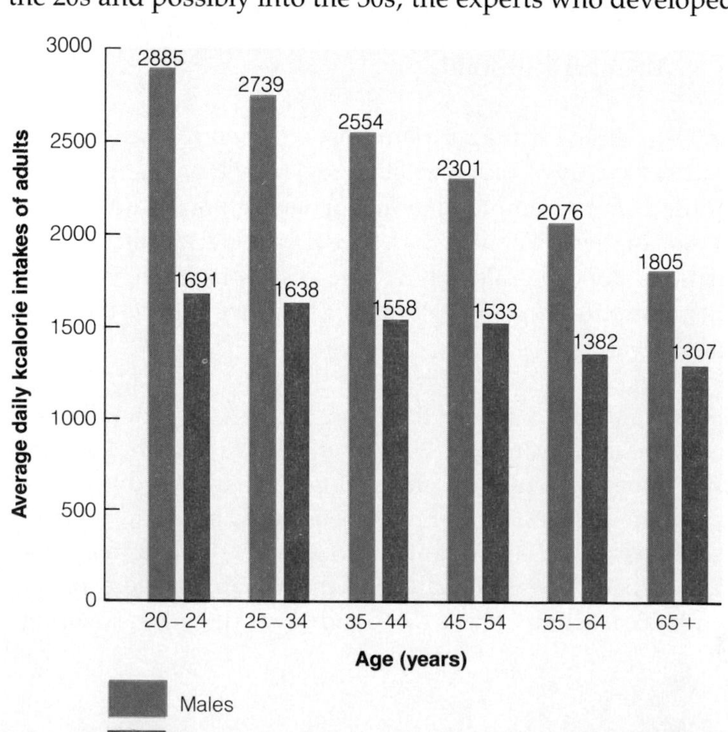

Figure 18.4 Average daily kcalorie intakes of adults. (Data source: National Center for Health Statistics. 1977. *Dietary intake findings: United States, 1971–74.* Data from the National Health Survey, Series 11, No. 202. DHEW Publications No. [HRA]77-1647. Hyattsville, MD: Public Health Service.)

determined that the highest calcium, phosphorus, and vitamin D recommendations for the teen years should also apply through age 24. This level of intake may help people reach their genetic potential for bone mass and thereby reduce their risk of osteoporosis in later years.

Because women are typically smaller than men, and because women have proportionately less lean tissue, RDAs for many nutrients are lower for women than for men. Generally, the difference is 20–25%, similar to the difference in energy needs. Of course, a major increase in nutrient needs occurs if a woman is pregnant or lactating; the RDAs for pregnant and lactating women are higher than the RDAs for men. The specific needs during those unique times are discussed in Chapter 16.

Other Nutrients for Older Adults How do the needs of older adults change? Many factors can affect nutrient requirements with advancing age (Greger, 1989). For example, some people's bodies may become less efficient at absorbing a particular nutrient; they may need to consume more to get enough. If, over the years, people change the food sources from which they get a certain nutrient, its absorption may be different. And even though a nutrient is needed by tissues that have decreased in mass with age, the body may now need less of it. The rates at which nutrients are excreted in urine and feces—rates that can go either up or down—also need to be considered. If people are chronically ill and/or routinely taking medications, their nutrient needs also may be affected.

With such a complex set of interactions, any of these three scenarios is possible: the need for a particular nutrient may go up, it may stay the same, or it may go down. And because of usual physiological and dietary changes, the needs of 50-, 70-, and 90-year-olds are likely to be different.

What, then, should be recommended to older adults regarding nutrient intake? Scientists really don't know for sure, because the amount of research on this issue, especially that regarding the micronutrients, has been inadequate (Bales, 1989). Nonetheless, RDAs have to be given for people of all ages, so scientists have made estimates. The table inside the back cover of this textbook shows what judgments the 1989 RDA Subcommittee made. In general, they recommended that most intakes for older adults should be the same as for 25- to 50-year-old adults. There were exceptions to this, however: Recommended intakes of thiamin, riboflavin, and niacin were reduced somewhat because of decreased energy metabolism; and the RDA for iron was lower for women over age 50, when menopause halts the monthly iron losses previously occurring during menstruation.

Are U.S. Adults Well-Nourished?

How do the diets of American adults compare with the RDAs? Just as energy intake declines with age, so do the intakes of most vitamins and minerals. Average intakes of calcium, magnesium, zinc, and vitamin B-6 were reported to be less than 100% of the 1980 RDAs for men and women included in the Nationwide Food Consumption Survey (NFCS) in the late 1970s. For women in their reproductive years, iron was also low; however, since women need less iron after menopause, inadequate intakes of this nutrient are not as frequent in elderly women.

The results of a 1986 survey, which focused on the intakes of women 19–50 years of age, were more alarming. For this group of almost 1200 women, average intakes were below the 1980 RDAs for the following: energy, vitamin E, vitamin B-6, folic acid, calcium, magnesium, iron, and zinc. This study indicates that the poor dietary habits of many teenage girls continue into adulthood. Nutrient intakes generally are also lower than the average for women who are poor and nonwhite (HNIS, 1988).

It is more difficult to say what the nutritional status of older adults is; in fact, it is meaningless to talk about the nutritional status of the elderly as a whole group. The RDAs for elderly people are based on limited information; in addition, the health, lifestyle, pharmaceutical use, and nutrient intakes of elderly individuals vary greatly.

A striking demonstration of the difference between groups of elderly adults involves protein status. Whereas clinical protein deficiency is unusual among the community-dwelling elderly in the United States, it is much more frequently seen in the hospitalized elderly and those living in nursing homes (Zheng and Rosenberg, 1989). Further, people who are shut-in are much more likely to have low vitamin D status than people who freely go outdoors.

The National Health and Nutrition Examination Survey II (NHANES II) collected data from noninstitutionalized elderly people between 1976 and 1980. Analysis of this survey shows that living arrangements and economic conditions can have a substantial impact on nutrient intakes. Men who lived with spouses had much better nutrient intakes than those who did not, and low-income men without a spouse were at highest risk of dietary inadequacy (Ryan et al., 1989). For women, the factor most closely associated with lower nutrient intakes was poverty.

The use of supplements is another variable in the nutritional status of the elderly. Surveys indicate that from one-third to two-thirds of the elderly, especially women, regularly use vitamin and mineral supplements (Ranno et al., 1988; McIntosh et al., 1990). Although a multiple-nutrient supplement that supplies up to 100% of the U.S. RDA may be useful for many older adults, supplementation also carries some risks. Non-institutionalized elderly often self-prescribe supplements, overestimate the potential benefits of the products they ingest, and may take doses that are potentially toxic. For this reason, nutrient toxicity is a possible problem among the elderly, especially among older women with health problems who live alone (Ranno et al., 1988).

Programs to Improve the Status of Adults at Nutritional Risk

The Supplemental Food Program for Women, Infants, and Children (WIC) provides nutrition education and vouchers for certain nutritious

Congregate meals for the elderly. The Nutrition Program for Older Americans provides a nutritious meal and a social opportunity for many mobile people.

foods to low-income pregnant and lactating women and their children. See Chapter 17 for more detailed information on this program.

The Food Stamp Program serves low-income individuals and families. Refer to Chapter 17 for more discussion of this program.

The Nutrition Program for Older Americans (Title III-C), established in 1973 by the federal government, is specifically targeted for the elderly population. It provides to people over age 60 community-based noon meals at a nominal fee that is often optional. The largest component of this program is the congregate meal service at senior-citizen centers, churches, schools, and other locations. These meals are designed to provide one-third of the RDAs; health and welfare counseling and nutrition education are also provided regularly. Another major benefit to the participants is the regular social interaction (Schlenker, 1988).

The elderly who cannot leave their homes are helped to meet their nutritional needs in various ways by local organizations. Often using a combination of federal and local funds, some deliver ready-to-eat meals; others supply frozen dinners; and others provide grocery service to people in their homes. Some local programs also serve the needs of younger home-bound adults who do not qualify for programs for the elderly (Roe, 1989).

A study of the use of community services by the elderly showed that approximately 10% of noninstitutionalized older adults made use of meals programs, either at senior centers or by receiving home-delivered meals (Stone, 1986). The greatest value of such programs is that they help older people remain in their own homes. The Slice of Life on p. 624 gives an example of how one meal delivery program benefits both its clients and a volunteer driver.

Nutrition and Lifestyle Affect Health and Longevity

Good health is more than the absence of obvious physical and mental illness; it also involves minimizing the modifiable risk factors for chronic diseases and, in addition, achieving and maintaining physical fitness. Other hallmarks of good health are resistance to contagious diseases, ability to reproduce, and enjoyment of life.

Research shows how important and how interrelated some of these factors are. For example, adequate exercise can help achieve and maintain physical fitness and also help reduce many risk factors. Even late in life, weight lifting and low-impact aerobic exercise enhance strength, flexibility, and cardio-respiratory fitness (Work, 1989). Further, large epidemiological studies in recent years suggest that getting enough exercise helps us to live longer.

In one such study, approximately 17,000 Harvard alumni were categorized according to the amount of exercise they had done in ordinary daily activities, such as walking and stair climbing, as well as in sports; then, death rates of the group were compared. Death rates declined steadily as energy expended on activity increased; death rates were one-fourth to one-third lower among alumni expending 2000 or more kcalories during exercise per week than among less active men (Paffenbarger et al., 1986).

In a more recent study, over 13,000 men and women were evaluated for fitness using a maximal treadmill exercise test at the Institute for Aerobics Research in Dallas, Texas. Anybody with obvious present or past illness (such as hypertension, diabetes, or a heart attack) was excluded from the

Slice of Life

A Delivery Service with Mutual Benefits

Nearly every weekday morning Ed Meyer can be found loading warm lunches and cold dinners into the back of his Mercury Marquis. Ed, who is 78, drives a regular route for the Milwaukee, Wisconsin, Visiting Nurse Association's Mobile Meals program, which provides meal service to people for whom this program makes the big difference. Without it, they might not be able to live independently.

At his age, he is older than almost everybody on his route. He explains why he does it: "My wife and I were married 50 years, and after she died two years ago I couldn't stay home alone. Doing this every day is what keeps me alive."

With meals, Ed delivers his own brand of humor and concern. After Rosalie did not answer her door for two days in a row, Meyer greeted her with, "I'm gonna scold you! Where were you Thursday? Where were you yesterday? With your boyfriend?" She holds up her arm in quiet protest, revealing a cast. "I broke my wrist," she explains.

At another stop along his 25-mile route, Ed lets himself in. The thin man in the chair brightens immediately. "How are you, Ed? Any snow on the highway?" he asks. "No," Meyer tells him, "but if you want me to bring you snow, I'll bring it." After a minute or two of visiting, Ed is on his way to the next stop. "Take care now," the man in the chair says. "Don't slip. Thanks. I'll see you later."

Traveling with Ed for a day makes it clear—essential as his services are to the clients on his route, the help he provides adds an important element to his own life at the same time.

(Adapted from *The Milwaukee Journal*, Monday, December 8, 1986.) ▲

study. In the eight years of followup, approximately 280 deaths occurred. When the deaths were evaluated based on fitness quintiles, the death rate among the least fit was several times higher than that of the most fit; the least fit men were 3.4 times more likely to die than the most fit; the least fit women were at 4.6 times greater risk (Blair et al., 1989).

Some of the other factors that have positive effects on health are obtaining a nutritious diet, adequate sleep, and prompt medical help; pursuing worthwhile activities; avoiding tobacco and abuse of alcohol and other drugs; and avoiding excessive physical and psychological stresses. People who don't do these things are less likely to enjoy good health.

Nutrition, Health, and Disease

Some nutrition experts believe that the most important thing good nutrition can do is to help delay the onset of chronic diseases (those persisting over a long period of time). One noted nutritionist estimates that future application of research should some day enable people to forestall the onset of such diseases by 10 to 20 years (Hegsted, 1985). With fewer years of disease, people could enjoy a better *quality* of life and perhaps a somewhat longer life.

Good nutrition . . . health enhancing at every age. What you eat now affects your health not only today but also in the future.

Many of the effects of nutrition on chronic diseases have already been discussed in this text:

- **atherosclerosis** (see capsule in the front matter)
- **cancer** (see capsule in the front matter)
- **constipation** (see Chapter 6, section on fiber)
- **diverticular disease** (see Chapter 6, section on fiber)
- **diabetes** (see Chapter 6)

- **obesity** (see Chapter 10)
- **hypertension** (see Chapter 13, section on sodium, potassium, and chloride)
- **osteoporosis** (see Chapter 13, section on calcium)

In addition to the conditions listed above, those discussed below are also very evident in older adults. The following sections summarize what we know about how nutrition affects them.

Infectious Diseases In the early part of this century, infectious diseases caused the greatest number of deaths. By the middle of the century, improved sanitation and nutrition and the development of antibiotics and immunization had moved such diseases to a very low place on the list of direct causes of death. Now, with no widespread effective treatment for infection with the human immunodeficiency virus (HIV) available, deaths due to Autoimmune Deficiency Syndrome (AIDS) are causing the number of deaths from infections to rise.

The degree to which nutrition influences the ability of the immune system to combat all bacterial and viral diseases continues to be studied. Scientists know that inadequate intake of many of the micronutrients weakens the function of the immune system, making infections of all kinds more likely; however, there is no evidence that taking doses larger than the RDA is any more protective. In fact, for certain nutrients there is evidence to the contrary: zinc, which is an important requirement for immune system function, actually *interferes* with immune function when taken in large doses (Chandra, 1989). The same is true with excessive doses of selenium, vitamin E, vitamin A, and others. In short, for best immune function, consume levels of nutrients around the RDA and follow the rule that more is not better.

Currently, some unscrupulous promoters are marketing megavitamin and mineral supplements to people infected with HIV. With no scientific proof, they claim that such supplements will restore and bolster immune function, inhibit or delay progression of Kaposi's sarcoma, or act as anti-infective agents (Dwyer et al., 1988). Rather, appropriate nutritional support consists of eating a nutritious diet that will prevent malnutrition and maintain weight and normal gastrointestinal function. Health care providers have developed guidelines for nutritional support for patients in various stages of HIV infection (Task Force, 1989).

A recent review states that although immune system function generally decreases in older people making them more vulnerable to all types of infection, this change may not be totally inevitable (Chandra, 1989). When nutritional status and immune responses have been assessed simultaneously, studies have suggested that impaired immunity in the elderly may be associated with nutritional deficiencies in some cases. Further, a few studies of undernourished adults whose intakes were subsequently improved showed an increase in immune function (Chandra, 1989). Interestingly, the reviewer of these studies also points out that adequate exercise has a positive effect on immune function, and loss of a spouse has a negative effect (Chandra, 1989).

Nervous System Function The general public has been asking questions about how nutrition affects nervous system function. Some of these questions involve short-term effects of nutrition on cognitive functioning (perception, thinking, and memory); others have to do with whether nutrition can prevent or relieve psychological stress; and still others relate to long-term mental disability in the elderly.

Most of the information on nutrition and *mental acuity* centers on amino acid and carbohydrate metabolism. This was discussed in Chapter 8 (the effect of dietary amino acids on neurotransmitters) and Chapter 17 (the effect of sugar on children's behavior). In addition, a study of college-age women compared the effects of a sugar-sweetened beverage with the effects of water and an aspartame-sweetened drink; it was found that the sugared beverage produced sleepiness and reduced alertness to a greater extent than was seen after drinking the unsugared drinks (Pivonka and Grunewald, 1990). Although the popular press has used such research to recommend that everybody should eat a low-carbohydrate, high-protein "power lunch" to be mentally sharp in the afternoon, there may be gender-related, age-related, and individual differences in people's responses to a carbohydrate load.

Psychological stress can affect people throughout the adult years as they make life-shaping decisions and experience social, occupational, and health changes. Little scientific information suggests that nutrition can be used to allay *mental and emotional stress,* even though nutrient needs can increase in response to certain *physical stresses* such as illness or injury (see Chapter 12 on vitamin supplements). Therefore, there is no basis for recommending unusual diets or nutrient supplements for people dealing with the psychological ups and downs of everyday life. Nutritional supplements are on the market that claim to do just that; not only are such products of unknown benefit, but many also may cause risk due to megadoses of vitamins. If people want to take a supplement, a multiple-nutrient supplement containing levels that do not exceed 100% of the U.S. RDA would be the best choice.

Before we discuss the role of nutrition on the *long-term mental condition of the elderly,* some background is in order. As is suggested by Figure 18.3, small changes in brain mass and function typically occur in the healthy adult between ages 30 and 75. The normal situation is that reasonably good nervous system function continues into the elder years. Among some individuals, however, pathological changes that result in **dementia** may occur. Up to 6% of the elderly over age 65 have severe dementia, and up to 15% may have a mild form (Gray, 1989). Dementia can be caused by various problems.

dementia—impairment of memory, thinking, and/or judgment to a degree that affects daily activities and relationships with others; may be accompanied by personality changes

Over half of the cases represent individuals with *Alzheimer's Disease (AD),* a progressive, incurable loss of mental function. The cause of AD is unknown, although a genetic component exists. Accumulation of certain proteins, accumulation of aluminum, and decreases in the neurotransmitter acetylcholine have been observed in brains of people with AD (Greger, 1989; Marx, 1989). But increasing the dietary intake of choline and lecithin (precursors of acetylcholine) has not been found to relieve the condition. Several scientists speculate that a *nerve growth factor* might be a useful therapy, but to date there is no successful treatment (Marx, 1990).

The second most common type of dementia in the elderly is *multi-infarct dementia,* the result of multiple strokes. Reducing risk of this condition through nutrition therapy can be done in ways similar to those used to reduce hypertension: treatment of obesity and moderate restriction of sodium intake (Gray, 1989). Third in prevalence is *dementia associated with alcoholism;* abstinence from alcohol use is a sure preventive technique. Severe, prolonged nutritional deficiencies are an additional, but very rare, cause of dementia (see Chapter 12 on vitamins) in the United States.

arthritis—painful condition resulting from the distortion or inflammation of joint surfaces due to degeneration or mineral deposits

Arthritis The major symptom of **arthritis** is pain in the joints, which fluctuates in severity from time to time without obvious reason (Bollet, 1988). Although arthritis is an ancient and common disease, its causes have not been clearly defined. The disease cannot be cured, but patients can usually be helped.

Over 100 different forms of arthritis exist. *Osteoarthritis,* the type very common among the elderly, is characterized by the distortion of joint surfaces apparently due to lifelong wear and tear. *Rheumatoid arthritis,* which is less common and more prevalent in young adults, is characterized by joint inflammation and other systemic changes of unknown origin. The only widely accepted dietary treatment is that overweight arthritics should lose weight to relieve stress on joints (Johns Hopkins Medical Letter, 1989).

Other dietary modifications have often been promoted in the popular press, but they have not usually proved to be effective treatments in controlled studies. (One expert suggests that most popular books on arthritis should be listed in the "fiction" category [Bollet, 1988].) Further, many popular programs do not take overall nutritional needs into account: they may be either nutritionally inadequate or excessive in some regard (Jarvis, 1990). Any arthritic person contemplating the use of a special diet or dietary product should check first with a dietitian who can analyze it for adequacy and possible nutritional toxicity (Wolman, 1987).

Gout is a type of arthritis that has been thought to have a closer relationship to diet. In this condition, crystals of uric acid (a breakdown product of certain protein components) form in the joints, causing pain. In the past, foods containing certain chemicals from which large amounts of uric acid are produced were limited in the diet. However, we now know that the body can produce uric acid precursors from fragments of any of the macronutrients. Even for gout, then, diet is not the primary cause or treatment method: genetic factors are probably the major cause, and drug therapies are the most effective treatment.

periodontal disease—degeneration of the gum and bone tissues supporting the teeth

Periodontal Disease Degeneration of the tissues supporting the teeth is referred to as **periodontal disease.** It generally affects both gum tissue and the bony arches in which the teeth are situated.

Periodontal disease is the major cause of tooth loss in Americans. It is important to our discussion of adult nutrition for two main reasons: first, the bone loss has been hypothetically related to poor diet (as in osteoporosis), and second, the deterioration of the bony arches makes it difficult to fit dentures properly. This results in chewing problems that make meats and some high-fiber foods less appealing.

The origin of periodontal disease is not known, although its initiation and progression correlate with the presence of bacterial plaque. Nutritionally, a diet deficient in vitamin C for several months can lead to symptoms of periodontal problems. Since vitamin C nutriture is not a problem for most people in North America, good dental hygiene is a primary recommendation for avoiding or controlling this problem.

The Impact of Nutrition on Length of Life

The search for a way to live longer is as ancient as the quest for the Fountain of Youth. Periodically we hear stories of people in remote places like the mountains of Soviet Georgia, Pakistan, or Ecuador who achieve a vigorous old age. To try to understand what might be responsible for their longevity, the cultures of these people have been studied.

Another type of research on aging has been the study of the effects of nutrition and various other lifestyle factors on laboratory animals. Each species of animal—including humans—has a **maximum life span,** which is the *oldest age* to which some members of the species have been known to survive (approximately 115 years for humans). Life span appears to be limited genetically and is therefore unlikely to be influenced by nutrition.

maximum life span—potential oldest age to which an animal can survive

Life expectancy, or *average life span* on the other hand, is the *average length of life* statistically shown for a given group of animals; for people in the United States in 1987, life expectancy at birth was almost 76 years; it is actually somewhat more for women and less for men (NCHS, 1988). **Longevity** is the length of time actually lived by an individual member of a species. It has been suggested that nutrition may have a role in life expectancy and longevity.

life expectancy or average life span—average length of life for a given group of animals

longevity—length of time an individual animal actually lives

Human Epidemiological Studies on Longevity Regions of the world in which a high proportion of the inhabitants are claimed to live to a very old age have been studied in an attempt to determine what factors might account for their longevity. In such regions of Russia, Pakistan, and Ecuador, several cultural characteristics stand out. First, all are agrarian societies in which people labor in the fields all their lives to sustain themselves; second, they all consume largely vegetarian diets, out of necessity rather than choice; and third, all of these communities provide strong psychological support for the elderly (Leaf, 1988).

As early epidemiological information was published, many people in our culture hoped that consumption of foods indigenous to these areas would prolong their own lives. This led to an increase in the popularity of yogurt, certain exotic fruits and juices, and other products. However, when dietary comparisons were made among these particular cultures, no uniformity of

Diet and longevity. Claims have been made that in certain isolated regions of the world many people live to extraordinary ages. Investigation casts doubt on whether these people are as old as first thought and on the theory that their diets may have been responsible. The Russian men pictured are from a district legendary for its inhabitants' longevity; these five men claim that their ages total over 600.

nutrition was apparent. Researchers then began to look at other factors for explanations of longevity.

Further doubt was cast on the early theories when a research team in Vilcabamba, Ecuador, discovered that many people older than 65 routinely exaggerated their ages, sometimes by as much as 20 to 40 years. This practice was socially acceptable in a culture where village elders were esteemed in proportion to their ages.

Studies demonstrated that the life expectancy of Vilcabambans was actually the same as for other Ecuadorans; that is, approximately 15% lower than for Americans. In addition, the higher concentration of elderly people in this village was explained by the fact that many of them had gravitated there for the sake of sociability with others of their own age, and younger people had left.

Thus the initial excitement regarding a provable association between diet and human longevity collapsed. Neither these investigations nor any other scientifically valid studies have ever shown that supplements or special foods will prolong human life more than a balanced diet of ordinary foods.

All of that notwithstanding, researchers in Vilcabamba noted that the older adults there enjoyed apparent good health: they were not overweight and had hypertension only rarely, and they had lower than usual blood cholesterol values, lower heart rates, and fewer fractures from osteoporosis. Although their longevity was not impressive, these aspects of health were. For this reason, research on these populations continues to be of interest.

Animal Studies About Longevity A number of animal studies, conducted over more than half a century, have shown that feeding animals a diet that supplied only about half the energy it would take for them to achieve maximal growth but was nutritious in all other respects increased the average age to which the animals lived and slowed down many of the physiological changes seen with aging (Weindruch and Westford, 1988; Masoro, 1989).

The studies also showed that underfeeding had drawbacks. Severely restricted animals had increased infant mortality and growth retardation. In several studies, certain aspects of immune function were improved; in others, certain aspects were depressed (Good and Lorenz, 1988). On physical bases alone, then, severe energy restriction is not recommended for humans at this time; negative psychological consequences could occur as well. Nonetheless, this animal research is extremely important in that it provides information that may help scientists uncover the mysteries of the aging process. Once these are understood, we can progress further in learning how nutrition can be used to improve the health and extend the lives of humans (Masoro, 1989).

Drugs and Alcohol Interact with Nutrients and Affect Health

Two commonly consumed categories of substances that interact with nutrients are medications and alcohol. Although we tend to think of nutrients, medications, and alcohol as three very separate categories, these substances have shared characteristics. All are chemicals we ingest that can have either beneficial or toxic effects depending on the dosage, the time frame in which we consume them, and the other chemicals that are present in our bodies at the same time. To further blur the distinctions between them, some nutrients can be used as drugs; drugs may have some of the properties of nutrients; alcohol is a drug; and alcohol has an energy value just as some nutrients do (Roe, 1988).

Nonetheless, we will be true to tradition in this section and discuss them separately. First we will deal with how medications and nutrients interact with each other. Then we will discuss how alcohol interacts with nutrition and affects health.

Medications and Nutrients Can Interfere with Each Other

Medications can affect nutrition by influencing appetite, decreasing the absorption of nutrients, interfering with nutrient metabolism, and/or affecting excretion. People whose nutrition is most at risk for experiencing negative effects of drugs are 1) individuals who use certain medicines for long periods of time; 2) those who take several kinds of drugs at the same time (whether prescription or over-the-counter types); and 3) persons who have marginal nutritional status to begin with.

Nutrient intake and general nutritional status can affect the body's use of drugs in many ways, such as how well the drug dissolves and is absorbed, transported, and distributed; how rapidly it is metabolized; and how readily it is excreted.

People of any age may need medications from time to time, but older adults are more likely to develop chronic conditions that require ongoing treatment with drugs. For this reason, the elderly are generally more likely to experience negative effects from nutrient/drug interactions than are people in other age groups.

Commonly Used Medications That Can Interfere with Nutrition

Many medications affect nutrient utilization. Common drugs with consequences for nutrition are aspirin, oral contraceptives, laxatives, diuretics, and antacids.

Aspirin Aspirin is one of the medicines used most frequently in America by people of all ages. Many people are chronic users of high doses of aspirin because its anti-inflammatory and pain-relieving properties are helpful in treating arthritis. Some people also take it routinely to slow down blood clot formation, especially if they have had a heart attack, because the aspirin reduces the risk of further blockage of coronary vessels.

Aspirin use causes a small amount of blood (and therefore iron) loss via the gastrointestinal tract. People who routinely use aspirin should fortify their diets with sources of iron.

Oral Contraceptives Most women who take oral contraceptives have approximately the same requirement for vitamins and minerals as those who are not taking them; therefore, routine supplementation is not called for. Oral contraceptives can, however, influence the body's metabolism of nutrients in some cases. A small proportion of the women taking them develop biochemical evidence of vitamin B-6 deficiency. This is occasionally accompanied by mental depression, high blood glucose levels, and/or general malaise. These symptoms may be prevented or reversed when a diet with generous amounts of vitamin B-6 is consumed or a modest vitamin B-6 supplement is taken.

Antacids People often take antacids to treat indigestion or stomach discomfort. Certain antacids contain aluminum or magnesium hydroxide, which combine with phosphorus and fluoride in the gut to form salts that cannot be absorbed. Chronic use of these antacids by some individuals may eventually result in the loss of phosphorus from bone, possibly hastening the course of bone disease.

Laxatives Because constipation becomes more common with age, many elderly people use laxatives frequently. This practice can have negative effects on nutrition. Repeated use of certain types of laxatives can cause calcium, potassium, and fat depletion. Mineral oil should not be used as a laxative, since it prevents the absorption of fat-soluble vitamins, including vitamin D. Losses of vitamin D and minerals could be especially damaging to people with osteoporosis. Dietary alternatives with fewer potential problems are often recommended to increase the fiber and fluid content of the diet. (However, keep in mind that very high fiber intakes will reduce mineral absorption as discussed in Chapter 13.) Adequate exercise can also help.

Diuretics Diuretics cause the kidneys to excrete increased amounts of sodium and water. People who suffer from edema (accumulation of water in the tissues) or hypertension may become chronic users of diuretics.

Many diuretics cause potassium to be excreted along with the sodium and water, which can lead to severe electrolyte imbalance. For this reason, people taking certain diuretics are advised to eat several good sources of potassium daily or take potassium supplements. People who regularly use diuretics may also become depleted in other minerals; they should be sure to ask the physician or druggist about possible nutrient/drug interactions.

Drugs to Lower Blood Cholesterol Some medications can lower blood cholesterol by reducing the usual absorption of cholesterol-containing bile acids from the gastrointestinal tract, causing them to be excreted in the feces. The body is then forced to draw from internal cholesterol to make more bile acids; this, in turn, reduces the overall blood cholesterol level. Cholestyramine (Questran) is a drug commonly used for this purpose.

A possible unfortunate side-effect of such drugs may occur if the absorption of fat-soluble vitamins A, D, E, and K, which are normally carried into the body with the bile acids, is blocked. For this reason, physicians may recommend supplements containing the fat-soluble vitamins and folic acid, which is also partially lost.

Anticoagulants Cardiovascular diseases in which there is a high risk of clot formation are often treated with anticoagulants (other than aspirin) to reduce the likelihood of blood cells sticking together and blocking the artery; omega-3 fatty acids, found in deep-water fish oil capsules, also reduce clotting. A person who consumes both may tend to bleed too easily. The unsupervised use of fish oil capsules is not recommended for anyone, much less for a person already taking anticoagulants (see Slice of Life in Chapter 7 on p. 207). Eating fish while on anticoagulant therapy, on the other hand, is not likely to supply enough omega-3 fatty acids to cause a bleeding problem.

Anticonvulsants Anticonvulsants, which are taken by people prone to epileptic seizures, increase the liver's capacity to metabolize and then eliminate vitamin D. Because vitamin D is needed to absorb calcium, a calcium deficiency can occur in a person taking anticonvulsants. Therefore, people using these medications need to be sure to consume enough vitamin D or have sufficient sun exposure to make up for the losses.

Some anticonvulsants, such as Dilantin, may also interfere with the absorption of folic acid. Patients should ask their doctors whether they need supplements of folic acid to avoid megaloblastic anemia.

The Effect of Nutrients on Drugs

Nutrients can also affect drug utilization. The timing of meals and levels of certain food components including protein, alcohol, dietary fiber, and methylxanthines can have strong effects on drug absorption and metabolism. The following sections provide some examples of these effects. This information certainly is not complete; it is designed to make the point that interactions can occur with commonly used drugs; in some situations, nutrient/drug interactions can have drastic consequences.

Effects on Absorption Foods and beverages that are present in the gastrointestinal tract with a medication may affect the drug's absorption in various ways. Particular components of food can reduce the amount of medicine absorbed, or simply slow it down. For example, the absorption of the antibiotic tetracycline can be *blocked* by calcium from milk; the drug and the calcium form a complex, and absorption of both substances is prevented. With aspirin, food both slows down the rate of absorption and reduces the amount absorbed.

In other cases, food increases the proportion of medicine absorbed or hastens the absorption rate. Darvon, lithium, Valium, and Inderal are examples of drugs that have a greater effect when taken with meals (Tufts, 1989). Another reason you might be advised to take a drug with food is that if the drug has an irritating effect to the stomach, having food present may lessen the irritation.

Effects on Metabolism After a drug has been absorbed, nutrients present in the body can affect the drug's metabolism. Protein is most likely to be influential in this regard: high-protein diets generally enhance drug metabolism, and low-protein diets slow drug metabolism (Roe, 1988). Excessive consumption of foods high in vitamin K, such as liver and green vegetables, can hinder the effectiveness of some anticoagulant drugs. In one case, the anticoagulant drug dicoumarol was rendered ineffective because the patient customarily ate almost a pound of broccoli per day (Tufts, 1989). This makes another good argument for why it is better to eat a varied diet than excessively using a few foods—even if they are very nutritious ones.

A group of antidepressant drugs called monoamine oxidase inhibitors (examples: Parnate, Marplan, and Nardil) can interact with certain components of fermented foods (such as aged cheese) to produce a sudden elevation in blood pressure. If people taking these drugs do not avoid cheese and other offending foods, they may experience a potentially fatal hypertensive crisis. Physicians who prescribe and pharmacists who dispense this drug are careful to educate people about which foods to avoid.

Alcohol is a dietary substance that affects the metabolism of over 100 medications. In some instances, alcohol exaggerates the effect of a drug; in some other cases, it diminishes it. The consequences can be extreme: alcohol and certain medications can be a fatal mix. An upcoming section will discuss other effects of alcohol in the body.

Guidelines for People Who Take Medications

To avoid undesirable food/drug interactions, consumers should carefully follow instructions for use. This applies to both prescription and over-the-counter drugs. Your doctor, a pharmacist, and product labels and package inserts are all important sources of information.

- Follow recommendations regarding dosage and timing for taking medications. This is necessary for reaching and maintaining an effective dose in the body (Figure 18.5).
- Follow recommendations about whether to take a medication with meals or on an empty stomach. Find out whether there are any particular foods or beverages that are contraindicated with particular medications you use.
- If a medication is to be taken with a liquid, take it with a generous amount of water unless otherwise instructed. Absorption of the drug will be more efficient if it is dilute (Roe, 1988).
- If you are likely to consume alcoholic beverages during the course of drug therapy, find out whether your drug is one of the many that interacts negatively with alcohol.
- Advise your health care professionals of *all* medications, both prescription and over-the-counter, that you take. This is important not only for helping you avoid nutrient/drug interactions but also for avoiding drug/drug interactions.
- Eat a nutritionally balanced diet from a variety of foods. Medications cannot, by themselves, restore or maintain good health. Good nutrition is a necessary part of good health, and a balanced diet reduces the risk of drug/nutrient interactions.

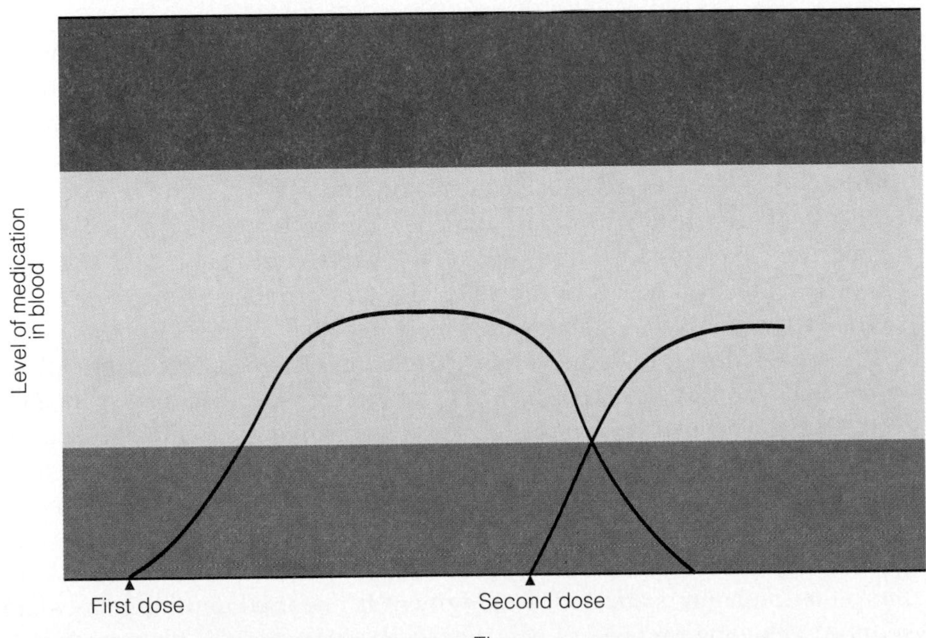

Figure 18.5 Medication, dose, and interval. Medications can help only when they are in the effective range in your blood, which depends on taking them at the recommended amount and intervals of time. Other substances in your body—food, beverages, alcohol—can also affect whether or not an effective level is reached and how long it persists (see text).

Alcohol Influences Nutrition and Health

Although the alcohol in alcoholic beverages has one characteristic of a nutrient—it provides energy (7 kcal/gram)—it is primarily categorized as a drug. It influences health both by affecting nutrition and by producing direct toxic effects on the body. An estimated one-tenth of American adults drink heavily; one-fourth are moderate drinkers; one-third are light drinkers; and the remaining one-third abstain (National Research Council, 1989). This means that there are over 100 million adult drinkers in the United States. Consumption figures indicate that alcohol accounts for 4.5% of the energy value of the average American diet (Shaw and Lieber, 1988).

Many younger people also consume alcohol. Sixty-six percent of high school seniors interviewed by the National Institute on Alcohol Abuse and Alcoholism reported that they had consumed alcohol within the past month, and 5% said they drank daily. In another study, 37% said they had had five or more drinks on at least one occasion in the previous two weeks (National Research Council, 1989).

Beer and ales, wines, and liquors are the common sources of alcohol. Although they differ in the percentage of alcohol they contain, a standard sized serving of any one of them puts approximately half an ounce of absolute alcohol into the consumer (Table 18.1).

The consumption of alcohol affects the body within minutes; if ingested regularly in large amounts over a period of years, it will have serious long-range effects on health.

Short-Term Effects of Alcohol Consumption

Alcohol needs no digestion. It is a simple molecule that is readily absorbed and circulated through the body in the bloodstream. Like some other drugs, it can be absorbed from the stomach; whatever passes into the small intestine is readily absorbed from there. Although its own entry into the body is uncomplicated, it can disturb the digestion and absorption of foods; and, particularly after heavy drinking, diarrhea can occur.

Because alcohol is a toxic substance, the body's normal reaction is to get rid of it or to metabolize it into harmless end-products. Enzymes in the stomach have the first opportunity to metabolize alcohol (Frezza et al., 1990). The kidneys and the lungs excrete predictable percentages of it, which explains why the "breathalizer" test can provide a measure of alcohol in the body. The liver, which plays the major role in detoxification, begins to metabolize alcohol as quickly as it circulates through. In most people, it takes the liver anywhere from 1 to 2 hours to change one-half ounce of alcohol into harmless metabolites.

Alcohol has an anaesthetic (depressant) effect on the nervous system. First, the forebrain is affected, so judgment is impaired and inhibitions are reduced, allowing for feelings of euphoria and relaxation. With greater consumption, the midbrain also becomes involved, and muscular coordination, reflexes, and speech are impaired. At even higher intakes, the hindbrain is affected: senses are dulled and stupor results. Unconsciousness and death can follow if the part of the brain that controls vital functions is sufficiently depressed.

For any given individual in a particular instance, the effects of alcohol depend on body size (a person with a larger body mass is less affected), the time frame within which the individual drank the alcohol, other foods or beverages that were consumed, and drinking history (people who drink routinely tend to be less affected, unless they have liver damage). Over the years, various studies have shown that women are more severely affected than men (Mezey et al., 1988; Witteman et al., 1990). Recent research helps explain why: in women, enzymes in the stomach metabolize less alcohol than they do in men. Therefore, more alcohol reaches the bloodstream of a woman than of a man (Frezza et al., 1990). Because of these many variables, it is almost impossible to generalize about how many drinks it takes to reach a particular level of impairment.

Alcohol intake has an effect on food consumption. A small amount of alcohol usually stimulates the appetite and fosters social interaction. For this reason, an increasing number of hospitals and nursing homes in the United States serve a small amount of wine or beer before meals. On the other hand, a large amount of alcohol depresses appetite. When alcoholic beverages displace food, nutrient intakes are likely to be low since alcoholic beverages are poor sources of nutrients themselves. Some heavy consumers of alcohol get as much as half of their kcalories from alcohol. Alcohol also alters the metabolism of many different nutrients, but moderate alcohol intake has little effect on nutritional status (Shaw and Lieber, 1988).

Strategies for Preventing Short-Term Problems from Alcohol People can *moderate* (not eliminate) the effects of alcohol in a number of simple ways. If you expect to have several drinks during a social event but do not want to experience effects beyond those of mild euphoria and relaxation, you can employ some methods to help delay and thus reduce the impact of the drinks.

First, eat something before you start drinking. The presence of any food in the stomach delays the absorption of alcohol. Second, pace your consumption so that you are not drinking faster than the rate at which your liver can detoxify the alcohol. If you limit your intake to approximately one drink per $1\frac{1}{2}$ hours, you are not likely to become seriously impaired. If you are thirsty and want to drink more than that, alternate alcoholic beverages with nonalcoholic beverages; ask for just a mixer every other time. Or drink more dilute beverages, such as wine coolers (wine with sparkling water). However, "lite" beers and wines, although lower in kcalories, are not necessarily much lower in alcohol than the regular versions. Table 18.1 compares the alcohol and kcalorie content of various alcoholic drinks. If you are the host or hostess, be sure that you provide an acceptable nonalcoholic alternative to your guests.

Table 18.1 Alcohol and Kcalorie Content of Alcoholic Drinks[a]

Beverage	Alcohol (% by volume)	Serving Size (ounces)	Alcohol (grams per serving)	Kcalories per Serving
Beer	4.5	12	13	150
Light beer	3.7	12	11	100
Wine	11.5	5	14	110
Light wine	6–10	5	7–12	65
Wine cooler	3.5–6	12	10–17	220
Sherry	19	3	14	125
Gin, vodka, rum, rye, whiskey (80 proof)	40	1.5	14	100
Cordials, liqueurs (25–100 proof)	12.5–50	1	3–16	50–100
Martini		2.5	22	156
Bloody Mary		5	14	116
Tom Collins		7.5	16	121
Daiquiri		2	14	111

[a]All figures are for drinks without ice. One serving of any listed drink contains approximately one-half ounce of alcohol.

Adapted from Tufts University Diet and Nutrition Letter. 1986. To drink or not to drink? That's one of the questions. *Tufts University Diet and Nutrition Letter* 4(no. 1):4.

Be aware that there is no way to hasten anybody's detoxification of alcohol once it has been overconsumed: neither cold showers, nor coffee, nor exercise, nor sleep can substantially speed up the process. In this case, ounces of prevention may be worth hours of cure.

Long-Term Effects of Alcohol Consumption

Regular consumption of excessive amounts of alcohol over a period of many years is likely to have direct toxic effects and possibly cause poor nutrition as well. The nutrient inadequacies most often seen in chronic consumers of alcohol are in thiamin, folic acid, niacin, and vitamin B-6. These inadequacies result from interruptions in the body's normal processes anywhere from ingestion through excretion.

Health Problems Health problems attributable to chronic alcohol consumption are:

- liver diseases (fatty liver, alcoholic hepatitis, cirrhosis)
- pancreatitis
- heart degeneration
- hypertension and stroke
- hyperlipidemia

- nervous system diseases
- cancer of the alimentary canal (mouth, pharynx, larynx, esophagus [National Research Council, 1989]; colon and rectum [Klatsky et al., 1988])
- fetal alcohol syndrome

Liver diseases associated with chronic alcohol intake have been shown to be the result of direct toxic effects, but this does not totally explain their occurrence; not everybody who regularly drinks gets liver disease. There is also a nutrition component: an inverse relationship has been observed between the intake of nonalcoholic kcalories and the severity of the disease. That is, when more nonalcoholic kcalories are consumed, the less severe the liver disease is likely to be.

In the first phase of liver disease, fat accumulates in the liver *(fatty liver)* because of many alcohol-induced changes in the metabolism of energy nutrients and fat mobilization. The second phase is *alcoholic hepatitis*—inflammation of the liver. Both of these conditions can be reversed if alcohol is avoided and sound health practices are substituted. **Cirrhosis,** an irreversible condition, occurs when fibrous deposits scar the liver, interfering with its function. Since the liver is the primary site for many metabolic reactions, its progressive destruction by cirrhosis can be eventually fatal.

cirrhosis—scarring of the liver by fibrous deposits that interfere with its function; an irreversible condition

There is also a great deal of interest in the effect of alcohol on diseases of the cardiovascular system. The consequences are not easily predictable, because alcohol affects various parts of the cardiovascular system in different ways. Although effects are negative in general (see list above), some research in the last decade seemed to suggest that alcohol could have favorable effects in certain circumstances.

For example, some studies showed that inactive people who consumed one or two drinks per day experienced a rise in the level of HDL cholesterol in their blood, which is thought to be protective against coronary heart disease (see Chapter 7). However, HDL cholesterol consists of various subfractions that have different physiological effects, and the particular subfraction of HDL that is increased by alcohol ingestion plays no proven role against heart disease (Mayo Clinic Nutrition Letter, 1990a).

Another study that received wide publicity noted that people who had a couple of drinks per day seemed to live longer than those who didn't drink at all or than those who drank excessively. A subsequent study may explain why these results were seen. As people get older, they generally tend to drink less or give up drinking altogether; the latter was found to be true especially of people who knew they had heart disease. These people are thought to have died in larger numbers, then, because of their pre-existing heart disease—not because they didn't drink (Harvard Health Letter, 1989).

Alcoholism Another serious concern about alcohol intake is that some people who consume alcohol develop a dependency on it and become alcoholics. This effect is not necessarily related to the problems of physical health in the preceding section, although both types of problems can occur in the same individual. People who are alcoholics *feel that they need to have alcohol to function,* although in actuality it interferes with their interpersonal relationships, their schoolwork or job, and their health. It is estimated that one in ten Americans who drinks is an alcoholic.

Heredity and environment are both believed to play a role in the development of alcoholism. In 1990, scientists isolated a gene much more likely to be found in alcoholics: 78% of the alcoholic subjects in their study had this particular gene, and only 28% of those without the gene were alcoholic (Blum et al., 1990). The fact that the gene did not explain all cases of alcoholism suggests that environment also plays a role and that there may be additional genetic factors. Knowing that there is a physical basis for alcoholism may help people who are alcoholic to accept treatment. In the future, genetic probes may be used to identify children at risk; they could then be educated about conditions that could trigger alcoholism.

Once a person has a dependency, most experts believe that the only effective way to deal with the disease is to quit drinking. There are many drug treatment centers that help affected people and their families cope with this disease.

Live Well in the 1990s

Each of us creates our own lifestyle, and it is a matter of personal choice whether the practices that compose it are healthy. We hear the information loud and clear in public health messages and in the many books about healthy living styles:

- If you smoke, quit. Smoking is the single most preventable cause of death in America, responsible for one death in six. Even if you gain weight when you quit (those who do usually gain less than 10 pounds), the *health benefits of not smoking* are much greater than the negative impact of the gain in weight (Mayo Clinic, 1989b).
- Get regular exercise. Get involved in activities that enhance strength, flexibility, and cardiorespiratory fitness.
- Eat in a way that provides the nutrients you need, maintains your best weight, and reduces risk factors for disease.
- Get adequate sleep. Scientists don't know exactly why we need sleep, but normal function and health deteriorate if we don't get enough.
- Keep your stress level under control. Although psychologists have found that a certain amount of stress is beneficial, too much is damaging. Exercise is a good stress-reducer; learn what other healthy techniques work for you.
- Avoid substance abuse, whether alcohol or other drugs. If you find yourself hooked, get help. There are many types of intervention programs available as well as groups for continuing support.
- Get medical help when you need it.

Yearning for Easy Solutions to Difficult Problems

All of the preceding advice is familiar, but it may not seem easy to accomplish. After all, you have other things to do with your time—such as going to school, earning a living, or caring for a family—that may already make life as full as you think you can handle. You may think that you simply *don't have the time* for regular exercise or eating right, for example; but the feelings of health and well-being you can gain from healthy living can more than make up for the time it takes.

There may be times when you will hear what seem to be easy ways to get around eating well. We remind you that there is a great deal of nutrition quackery targeted at people who have money, who hope for a dramatic change in their lives, and who want to get results easily when, in some cases, the results may not even be attainable. Major targets for quackery among the adult population are people who want to lose weight, people with arthritis, people with terminal illness, and healthy but fearful elderly. Table 18.2 identifies some of the popular claims of nutrition quacks and what they falsely promise nutrition can do. Knowledge is your best defense against this health fraud (Renner, 1989).

Assuming Self-Responsibility for Nutrition

Good nutrition does not depend on eating a certain number of times per day or eating a particular amount at each meal. You might eat "three square

Table 18.2 Nutrition Quacks Have a Familiar Sound

Their promises all sound appealing and genuine, but they are hollow. These are among the more common claims and practices of nutrition hucksters:

- Suggesting that most people are poorly nourished
- Claiming that most disease is due to faulty diet, which can be remedied by the product they sell
- Claiming that diseases for which medical science does not yet have highly effective treatment (such as AIDS and certain forms of cancer) can be cured through their nutrition program
- Claiming that emotional stress can be relieved by taking high doses of nutrients
- Recommending that everybody take vitamin and mineral supplements or eat "health" foods
- Claiming that natural vitamins are better than synthetic ones
- Claiming that megavitamins can improve the function of the immune system
- Claiming that modern processing methods and storage remove all nutritive value from our food
- Claiming that all additives and preservatives are poisons
- Warning that sugar is a deadly poison
- Telling you that it is easy to lose weight with their method
- Using anecdotes and testimonials as the only support for their claims
- Claiming that the medical establishment refuses to acknowledge their nutrition "cures" because doctors would lose business
- Displaying credentials not recognized by responsible scientists or educators

meals" per day, or you might pick up smaller amounts more often, a practice that has been dubbed "grazing." You can nourish yourself well either way, provided your total intake follows the principles of variety, balance, and moderation that characterize a healthy diet. Table 18.3 reviews the Basic Food Guide recommendations for total daily intake for adults; if you eat *at least* these amounts from a variety of foods within the basic food groups and combination foods, you are likely to be adequately nourished. The Nutrition for Living section emphasizes some points about the food groups that are especially relevant to adults.

The following sections suggest what to keep in mind in the various locations in which we make decisions about what to eat.

At the Grocery Store Despite the fact that we eat an increasing number of meals *away* from home, most people still eat most meals *at* home. This calls for grocery shopping.

According to market research, the average consumer goes to the grocery store 2.3 times per week and makes most decisions at the shelf (Opinion Research Corporation, 1989; Light et al., 1989). Knowing this, many processors use food product labels to attract consumers' attention, provide information about the product, and make the product seem more appealing. There also may be separate promotional/informational materials near the product or at store information centers.

As you survey product literature and items on the shelf, you can get your best information about a food's nutritional quality by using food composition data. This is found on nutrition labels rather than in vague terms that may be elsewhere on the label, such as "light," "improved," or "low cholesterol." Many descriptive terms printed on product labels as of July, 1990 were not yet defined by regulations, although they suggest a lot; but that may change soon for some (Federal Register, 1990). Other terms *do* have special definitions (for example, "lean" and "lower fat"), but it's hard to

Table 18.3 Basic Food Guide for Adults

	Include at Least This Many Servings Daily	
	Through Age 24	Middle-Aged and Older Adult
Fruits and vegetables		
Vitamin A rich	1	1
Vitamin C rich	1	1
Others to make a group total of	5	5
Grain products (preferably whole grain; otherwise, enriched or fortified)	6	6
Milk and milk products	3	2
Meats and meat alternates	2	2

keep up with what they are. If you want your purchases to be moderate or low in fat, make your decisions about what to buy based on the fat contents given on the nutrition label. Similarly, you can get information about sodium, protein, and available carbohydrate from the same label.

We know that nutrition labeling is due for a change; the changes should make information about food products more accessible than it currently is. The government intends to make the label format easier to understand, to provide information about food components of greatest current interest, and to require labels on more products. (In 1989, approximately 60% of packaged foods carried nutrition labels.) We look forward to these developments. It is likely that new labeling will be implemented sometime while this edition is in use.

Nutrition for Living

Throughout adulthood, you can achieve good nutrition by eating the types and amounts of foods recommended by the Basic Food Guide. Choosing a variety from within each group increases the likelihood that you will get the nutrients you need, avoid dangerous levels of toxicants, and reduce the risk of drug/nutrient interactions.

- Eat generous amounts of **fruits and vegetables;** the minimum is five servings. Fruits and vegetables are good sources of vitamins A and C. They are high in fiber if you eat the whole form rather than drink their juices. When you want more to eat but do not want more fat, cholesterol, or sodium—eat more of these.
- Eat plenty of **grain products.** Six servings are just the minimum. Most adults could benefit from more of the complex carbohydrate and fiber that grains contain. Whole-grain products are the best choices, because their fiber helps maintain normal intestinal function, which may diminish as you age. When you increase your fiber intake, increase your fluid intake as well.
- Get enough **milk and milk products.** Through age 24, people should get at least three servings daily to help build peak bone mass; people age 25 and older need two or more servings each day. If you have lactose intolerance, try cheese, yogurt, or low-lactose forms of milk.
- Use two servings of lean **meats and meat alternates** each day; they are rich in protein, vitamins, and minerals. When you eat meat alternates, include a good source of vitamin C at the same time to increase your absorption of iron.
- Drink plenty of **fluids.** Drink more water and other beverages than usual when you increase your fiber intake and on days when you perspire noticeably.
- Gradually reduce your intake of **limited extras** such as fats, concentrated sugars, and alcohol. The extras are high in kcalories, and energy needs gradually diminish with the years. You may want to try some products with fat and sugar substitutes. Another alternative is to maintain a more active lifestyle, which will enable you to continue to use some limited extras—and the activity will help maintain fitness as well.

Whenever possible, eat your meals with somebody. When people share mealtime with others, they usually eat better than when they eat alone. And the pleasure of someone's company at a meal adds another healthy dimension to *nutrition for living*.

An alternative to doing all of your thinking in the store is to do some planning before you go shopping. If you are not a cook, you may intend to do nothing more challenging than making a sandwich, pouring a glass of milk or bowl of cereal, washing a piece of fruit, or heating a prepared entree. Here are some things to keep in mind when making food choices.

When looking for prepared main dishes, look for one of the newer, lower-fat and/or lower-salt varieties. If you cannot find products that feature more moderate levels, try to reduce your intake of fat and salt in your other choices for the day. Prepared entrees can be found in the frozen-food section, in cans, and in the new shelf-stable plastic containers.

Many people who don't cook often bypass the fruit and vegetable section. Without these foods, it is hard to get enough vitamins A and C and fiber, so they are important to include. Many fresh fruits just require washing, and you don't even have to dirty a plate or fork to eat them; others need just peeling and eating. Frozen vegetables that you cook for a few minutes on the stove top or in the microwave oven are usually easy to deal with and may even be more nutritious than fresh ones.

If you do cook, you need to decide what you want to make so you can get the ingredients you don't already have on hand. We have many more thoughts for you in the next section.

At Home Most people who cook regularly are interested in getting good-tasting, nourishing food to the table within a reasonable amount of time. They are probably also interested in the cost issue; even if you assign a cost to your time, home-cooked food usually costs less than buying a similarly prepared product. Other reasons people may prefer cooking their own food are to be able to individualize the product and have control over the ingredients, or to economize on the total energy use that goes into the product (Gussow, 1988).

Some newer cookbooks incorporate many of these goals. Look for those that are designed to conform to the Dietary Guidelines; their recipes will include good sources of nutrients and fiber; at the same time, they will be moderate in fat, cholesterol, salt, and sugar. Some of these cookbooks are written by nutrition professionals such as registered dietitians or nutritionists or are produced by their professional associations; others are published by health groups such as the American Heart Association. The U.S. Department of Agriculture also has prepared a booklet called *Shopping for Food and Making Meals in Minutes* that offers some quick and good recipes (USDA/HNIS 232-10). In addition, there are magazines dedicated to a nutritious eating style that provide you with more than enough new recipes to try in a month. Some feature foods of interesting ethnic origins or take advantage of seasonal foods.

Some people have favorite recipes that they may now suspect do not fit well with dietary principles for good health. Does this mean you should throw away the whole file? Not at all. Some recipes may be fine as they are (for example, $\frac{1}{4}$ cup of fat in a recipe that serves 8 people is hardly a problem). Some might be for foods that are high in fat, sugar, and/or salt, but they may be important family traditions; if you don't have them often or eat much of them, they won't affect your overall nutrition significantly.

Finally, some recipes that are staples for you may be able to be modified. In casserole dishes, you can often cut down or eliminate added fat. In baked goods, fat may be able to be cut by one-fourth to one-third of the original amount; the same often can be done for sugar, and even larger cutbacks may be possible for salt. Fiber can be increased by substituting whole grain pasta, rice, and other grains and flour. If you plan to do much recipe modification, get a good set of guidelines for doing so; some products will tolerate change better than others (Stark, 1988).

The Slice of Life on page 646 is an example of a system two sisters developed for preparing good-tasting, healthy food for their own families and their parents—all in a way that was enjoyable, economical, and time-efficient.

In Your Briefcase or Backpack It would be very difficult to obtain a good diet for the whole day from foods that can be carried easily, can be eaten by hand, and can do without refrigeration for several hours, but some types of things pack quite well. Fresh fruit, dried fruit, and juice boxes are very portable. So are crackers, bagels, and pretzels. Nuts, seeds, and cereals also qualify. You can combine a variety of dried fruit, cereal, pretzels, and smaller amounts of nuts and seeds into a mix.

At Your Worksite The kinds of food available to you where you work may range from nothing at all to a vending machine to a full cafeteria line. If the available food does not provide for healthy choices, find out who makes decisions about the food service within your organization and talk with them. They are likely to listen, because employers are concerned about the health of their employees; employers pick up approximately 30% of America's medical bill (Mayo Clinic Nutrition Letter, 1990). There is a trend toward employers providing various types of health-enhancing activities. In a survey of private sector employers with more than 50 employees, 66% had had one or more of the following types of programs within the last five years: smoking cessation, general health risk assessment, care of the back, coping with stress, exercise, accident prevention, nutrition education, blood pressure control, and weight control (Fielding and Piserchia, 1989).

Having a positive attitude about health promotion, most employers are willing to listen to suggestions for improvement in their on-site food service. Some actually seek employee opinion: one innovative program in the public sector involved having firefighters taste-test recipes that were lower in fat, cholesterol, and sodium than their usual fare. As a result, the men learned about the potential benefits of these changes in diet, and they began to use new recipes at the firehouse.

At Restaurants When ordering from a restaurant menu, select foods prepared by methods that retain nutrients and minimize fat, such as broiling, baking, poaching, grilling, stir-frying, and steaming. It is better to avoid frequent consumption of things that are described as deep-fried, creamed, battered, or rich, or served with gravy, cheese sauce, hollandaise sauce, or pastry. Sometimes a restaurant will accommodate special requests for people on modified diets; for example, omitting the salt on broiled meat or fish is an easy way to satisfy a customer.

Soup and salad bars, healthy as they sound, call for careful selection as well. Enjoy all the fresh vegetables and fruit you want, but go easy on the salads with mayonnaise and regular salad dressings; both are very high in fat. If there is a low-fat or low-kcalorie salad dressing, it is a better choice. As far as soups are concerned, broth-based soups are a better choice than are

Slice of Life

Benefits of a Family Food Factory

Paulette Smith and Patty Paulson are sisters; each is married and has children. They have found they can double both flavor and fun when they team up in the kitchen. Every Wednesday, they spend the day shopping, cooking, and planning menus for the following week. By the end of the day, they have packed four tasty and nutritious entrees, in quantities large enough to serve their families and their parents, into reusable food containers. Then the freezer-ready creations are labeled, dated, and delivered.

"With leftovers, we have enough food prepared to last all week," Patty said. "That's important to me because the reason I don't work (out of the home) is so I can be with my kids. I don't want to be intensely involved in the kitchen when they are home. But on the weekend we like to make something fresh, not from the freezer. That's when we grill hamburgers or cook a roast."

The Wednesday cooking project originated as a Christmas gift to their parents. "We were looking for something original, although neither one of us likes cooking that much." But their mother likes cooking even less, and their dad is supposed to be on a special diet, so they thought their idea could help. By choosing recipes carefully, they have found foods that fit their dad's diet and that everybody likes. This is quite an achievement, because they are feeding three generations.

Their recipes come from a variety of cookbooks and magazines that feature healthy cooking such as *Living Fit* magazine and *Jane Brody's Good Food Book.* "We adapt all our recipes. We take a basic idea and make it simpler. We look for low-calorie, low-cholesterol recipes," Paulette said. "And we always double the vegetables." Each weekly menu includes beef, chicken, fish, and vegetarian entrees. (One of the children has chosen to be a vegetarian.)

Many of the entrees include vegetables such as beans, peppers, and tomatoes, which both sisters grow in their own gardens and freeze for year-round use. They supplement their own supply with produce from the Farmers' Market. Of course, there is more shopping to do.

"We meet at Woodman's Food Market, and we have our system down so well, we shoot through the store," Patty said. But the Wednesday cooking bees aren't all work. "We have fun, and we get a chance to catch up on the latest while we get our week's cooking out of the way," Patty said. (Adapted from *The Wisconsin State Journal,* May 27, 1990.) ▲

Lifestyle improvement in the workplace. An increasing number of employers are providing facilities in which their workers can exercise, get nutritious meals, and learn about stress reduction. Such programs can benefit both employees and employers.

creamed, but both are quite salty. If salt is of concern to you, have only a small portion.

Ethnic restaurants can provide healthful and adventurous eating, but you still need to keep the principles of good nutrition in mind. There is no cuisine that gets a blanket recommendation for good nutrition: every cuisine seems to have some items that are stellar examples of healthy food but others that are higher in fat, cholesterol, or salt than is recommended.

A booklet published by the U.S. Department of Agriculture, *Eating Better When Eating Out* (USDA/HNIS No. 232-11), provides many other suggestions for restaurant eating. Some restaurants have gained the privilege of using the seal of the American Heart Association (AHA) on menu items that are low in fat and cholesterol. You can call the local AHA office to find out which restaurants in the area provide that service.

From Carry-out Places Carry-out foods are increasing in popularity faster than any other type of food service. More and more people want to eat at home but not cook. Of course, the same nutritional principles we have discussed above for selecting food in other settings apply here as well. There is tremendous variety in the types of food available this way: from the usual fast-food fare to Oriental or Cajun take-out; and from standard chilled delicatessen food prepared on-site to commercially prepared **sous-vide** items that might be held under refrigeration for a couple of weeks before they are consumed.

sous-vide—literally, "under vacuum"; relatively unregulated type of food processing for prepared, chilled foods

Food safety may be a special concern for some of these foods, because there is always greater opportunity for microbiological contamination of mixed or cooked items and because these foods may be in and out of the temperature danger zone a number of times before they are eaten. Further, since a few types of pathogenic microorganisms thrive even at refrigerator temperatures, items held under refrigeration for long periods (sous-vide) could become sources of food-borne illness. A cautious approach when using such foods would be to buy only as much as you expect to eat at the upcoming meal. It is expected that future standards for production of these foods will provide greater confidence about microbiological safety.

How Have You Done So Far?

During the time you have been using this book, you may have been inspired to try making some changes in the way you nourish yourself as you learned about the benefits of available carbohydrates, fiber, fluids, protein, and other important dietary substances. Learning of the dangers of various excesses may have prompted other changes.

We hope that besides learning some basic facts about nutrition as you used this book, you also have learned how to think critically about nutrition questions. This skill will help you screen what you read and hear about nutrition in the future; nutrition will continue to make news, as scientists uncover more information about how our diets can affect the quality and possibly the length of our lives. We hope that your introduction here to the science of nutrition has heightened your interest and will make you alert to unfolding information about nutrition in the years to come.

We wish you the best in using your nutrition for living.

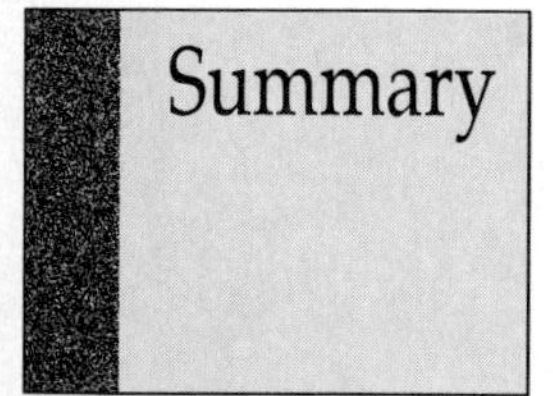

▶ Nutrition, along with other lifestyle factors, affects health during the adult years; these practices assume greater importance as more of us are likely to live longer. Although genetic influences are also involved, lifelong habits of nutrition can modify health and longevity within inherited limits. Because of the cumulative effects of lifestyle practices, there are greater differences between the health conditions of elderly adults than of any other age peers.

▶ The changes of aging take place gradually, and their rate and sequence vary in different individuals. The nutrition-related effects include a decreased need for energy, and possible changes in digestion, absorption, and metabolism of nutrients. More research is needed to clarify these changes and the specific nutrient needs that result from them.

▶ Some of the health problems seen in some adults are atherosclerosis, cancer, constipation, diverticular disease, diabetes, obesity, hypertension, osteoporosis, **periodontal disease, arthritis,** and **dementia.** AIDS is causing deaths from infectious diseases to increase. Nutrition is one of the factors that plays a role in the development and the course of these conditions.

▶ Every species of animals, including humans, has a **maximum life span,** which appears to be set genetically. **Life expectancy,** or average life span, is the statistical average length of life for a given group of animals, and **longevity** is the length of time an individual actually lives. Nutrition may play a role in determining life expectancy and longevity, although no scientifically valid studies have ever shown that supplements or special foods will prolong human life more than an ordinary well-balanced diet.

▶ Medications can influence nutrition by affecting appetite, the absorption of nutrients, their metabolism, and/or excretion. Individuals who use any drug for a long period of time, who use several drugs in combination, or who have marginal nutritional status are at greatest risk of drug-induced nutritional problems. Examples of commonly used drugs that can have consequences for nutrition are aspirin, oral contraceptives, antacids, laxatives, diuretics, cholesterol-lowering drugs, anticoagulants, and anticonvulsants. Nutrients can also affect drug utilization. Nutrient-drug interactions can be minimized by eating a balanced diet and carefully following the instructions for use of medications.

▶ Alcohol is a widely used drug that can influence short-term and long-term health both by affecting nutrition and by producing direct toxic effects on the body. People who use alcohol heavily over long periods of time are much more likely to suffer health problems, including liver diseases such as **cirrhosis,** heart problems, and alcoholism; genetics also plays a role. Treatment is available for people with indications of alcohol dependency.

▶ Research shows that adopting practices such as adequate exercise, good nutrition, and not smoking pays you back in better health and possibly also longer life. There are no short-cuts to good health, although quacks are eager to exchange their empty promises for your money.

▶ No matter how many meals you eat per day or where you get your food, you can eat in a healthful way. Learning how to make better choices at the grocery store, at home, at work, at restaurants, and on the run can help equip you for doing what you want to do in life.

References

Bales, C.W. 1989. Preface. *Current Topics in Nutrition and Disease,* vol. 21 New York: Alan R. Liss, Inc.

Blair, S.N., H.W. Kohl, R.S. Paffenbarger, D.G. Clark, K.H. Cooper, and L.W. Gibbons. 1989. Physical fitness and all-cause mortality: A prospective study of healthy men and women. *Journal of the American Medical Association* 262:2395–2401.

Blum, K., E.P. Noble, P.J. Sheridan, A. Montgomery, T. Ritchie, P. Jagadeeswaran, H. Nogami, A.H. Briggs, and J.B. Cohn. 1990. Allelic association of human dopamine D-2 receptor gene in alcoholism. *Journal of the American Medical Association* 263:2055–2060.

Bollet, A.J. 1988. Nutrition and diet in rheumatic disorders. In *Modern nutrition in health and disease,* eds. M.E. Shils and V.R. Young. Philadelphia: Lea & Febiger.

Chandra, R.K. 1989. Nutritional regulation of immunity and risk of infection in old age. *Immunology* 67:141–147.

Chernoff, R. and D.A. Lipschitz. 1988. Nutrition and aging. In *Modern nutrition in health and disease,* eds. M.E. Shils and V.R. Young. Philadelphia: Lea & Febiger.

Dwyer, J.T., R.L. Bye, P.L. Holt, and S.R. Lauze. 1988. Unproven nutrition therapies for AIDS: What is the evidence? *Nutrition Today* 23:25–33, March/April.

Federal Register. 1990. Food labeling; definitions of the terms cholesterol free, low cholesterol, and reduced cholesterol. *Federal Register* 55 (no. 139), July 19, 1990:29456–29473.

Fielding, J.E. and P.V. Piserchia. 1989. Frequency of worksite health promotion activities. *American Journal of Public Health* 79:16–20.

Flieger, K. 1988. Why do we age? *FDA Consumer,* October, 1988:20–25.

Freeland-Graves, J.H. and C.W. Bales. 1989. Dietary recommendations of minerals for the elderly. *Current Topics in Nutrition and Disease* 21:3–14.

Frezza, M., C. diPadova, G. Pozzato, M. Terpin, E. Baraona, and C.S. Lieber. 1990. High blood alcohol levels in women. *New England Journal of Medicine* 322:95–99.

Good, R.A. and E. Lorenz. 1988. Nutrition, immunity, aging, and cancer. *Nutrition Reviews* 46 (no. 2):62–67.

Gray, G. 1989. Nutrition and dementia. *Journal of the American Dietetic Association* 89:1795–1802.

Greger, J.L. 1989. Potential for trace mineral deficiencies and toxicities in the elderly. In *Current Topics in Nutrition and Disease* 21:171–199.

Gussow, J.D. 1988. Does cooking pay? *Journal of Nutrition Education* 20:221–226.

Harvard Medical School Health Letter. 1989. Alcohol, heart disease, and mortality. *Harvard Medical School Health Letter* 14(no. 7):1–2.

Hegsted, D.M. 1985. Nutrition: The changing scene. *Nutrition Reviews* 43:357–367.

Heymsfield, S.B., J. Wang, S. Lichtman, Y. Kamen, J. Kehayias, and R.N. Pierson, Jr. 1989. Body composition in elderly subjects: A critical appraisal of clinical methodology. *American Journal of Clinical Nutrition* 50:1167–1175.

HNIS (Human Nutrition Information Service). 1988. *Nationwide food consumption survey: Continuing survey of food intakes by individuals.* Washington, DC: U.S. Department of Agriculture.

Jarvis, W.T. 1990. Arthritis: Folk remedies and quackery. *Nutrition Forum* 7(no. 1):1–8.

Johns Hopkins Medical Letter. 1989. Osteoarthritis. *Health After 50,* June, 1989:4–6.

Klatsky, A.L., M.A. Armstrong, G.D. Friedman, and R.A. Hiatt. 1988. The relations of alcoholic beverage use to colon and rectal cancer. *American Journal of Epidemiology* 128:1007–1015.

Leaf, A. 1988. The aging process: Lessons from observations in man. *Nutrition Reviews* 46(no. 2):40–44.

Light, L., B. Portnoy, J.E. Blair, J.M. Smith, A.B. Rodgers, E. Tuckermanty, J. Tenney, and O. Mathews. 1989. Nutrition education in supermarkets. *Family and Community Health* 12(1):43–52.

Marx, J. 1989. Brain protein yields clues to Alzheimer's disease. *Science* 243:1664–1666.

Marx, J. 1990. NGF and Alzheimer's: Hopes and fears. *Science* 247:408–410.

Masoro, E.J. 1989. Food restriction research: Its significance for human aging. *American Journal of Human Biology* 1:339–345.

Mayo Clinic Nutrition Letter. 1989a. Alcohol and heart disease. *Mayo Clinic Nutrition Letter* 3(no. 1):1–2.

Mayo Clinic Nutrition Letter. 1989b. When you stop smoking. *Mayo Clinic Nutrition Letter* 2(no. 7):1–2.

Mayo Clinic Nutrition Letter. 1990. Wellness programs at work. *Mayo Clinic Nutrition Letter* 3(no. 2):2–3.

McGandy, R.B., C.H. Barrows, A. Spanias, A. Meredith, J.L. Stone, and A.H. Norris. 1966. Nutrient intakes and energy expenditure in men of different ages. *Journal of Gerontology* 21:581–587.

McIntosh, W.A., K.S. Kubena, J. Walker, D. Smith, and W.A. Landmann. 1990. The relationship between beliefs about nutrition and dietary practices of the elderly. *Journal of the American Dietetic Association* 90:671–676.

Mezey, E., C.J. Kolman, A.M. Diehl, M.C. Mitchell, and H.F. Herlong. 1988. Alcohol and dietary intake in the development of chronic pancreatitis and liver disease in alcoholism. *American Journal of Clinical Nutrition* 48:148–151.

Montoye, H.J., J.L. Christian, F.J. Nagle, and S.M. Levin. 1988. *Living fit.* Redwood City, CA: The Benjamin/Cummings Publishing Company.

National Research Council. 1989. *Diet and health.* Washington, DC: National Academy Press.

NCHS (National Center for Health Statistics). 1988. *Health, United States: 1987,* DHHS Pubn. No. (PHS) 88–1232.

Opinion Research Corporation. 1989. Trends: Consumer attitudes and the supermarket—1989. Washington, DC: Food Marketing Institute.

Paffenbarger, R.S., R.T. Hyde, A.L. Wing, and C.C. Hsieh. 1986. Physical activity, all-cause mortality, and longevity of college alumni. *New England Journal of Medicine* 314:605–613.

Pivonka, E.E. and K.K. Grunewald. 1990. Aspartame- or sugar-sweetened beverages: Effects on mood in young women. *Journal of the American Dietetic Association* 90:250–254.

Ranno, B.S., G.M. Wardlaw, and C.J. Geiger. 1988. What characterizes elderly women who overuse vitamin and mineral supplements? *Journal of the American Medical Association* 88:347–348.

RDA Subcommittee. 1989. *Recommended dietary allowances.* Washington, DC: National Academy of Sciences.

Renner, J.H. 1989. Knowledge best defense against health fraud. *Food and Nutrition News* 61(no. 4):21–23.

Roe, D.A. 1988. Diet, nutrition and drug reactions. In *Modern nutrition in health and disease,* eds. M.E. Shils and V.R. Young. Philadelphia: Lea & Febiger.

Roe, D.A. 1989. Nutritional surveillance of the elderly: Methods to determine program impact and unmet need. *Nutrition Today* 24(no. 5):24–29.

Rowe, J.W. and R.L. Kahn. 1987. Human aging: Usual and successful. *Science* 237:143–149.

Ryan, A.S., G.A. Martinez, J.L. Wysong, and M.A. Davis. 1989. Dietary patterns of older adults in the United States, NHANES II 1976–1980. *American Journal of Human Biology* 1:321–330.

Schlenker, E.D. 1988. Nutrition for aging and the aged. In *Nutrition throughout the life cycle,* eds. S.R. Williams and B.S. Worthington-Roberts. St. Louis: Times Mirror/Mosby.

Shaw, S. and C.S. Lieber. 1988. Nutrition and diet in alcoholism. In *Modern nutrition in health and disease,* eds. M.E. Shils and V.R. Young. Philadelphia: Lea & Febiger.

Stark, C. 1988. Revitalize your recipes for better health. *Food for Health,* April, 1988. Ithaca, NY: Cornell Cooperative Extension.

Stone, R. 1986. Aging in the eighties, age 65 years and over—use of community services. *Advancedata* 124:1–5.

Task Force on Nutrition Support in AIDS. 1989. Guidelines for nutrition support in AIDS. *Nutrition Today* 24:27–33, July/August.

Tufts University Diet and Nutrition Letter. 1989. Why food and medicine don't always make a good mix. *Tufts Diet and Nutrition Letter* 7(no. 5):3–6.

USDA/HNIS. *Shopping for food & making meals in minutes.* Home and Garden Bulletin No. 232–10. Washington, DC: U.S. Government Printing Office.

USDA/HNIS. *Eating better when eating out.* Home and Garden Bulletin No. 232–11. Washington, DC: U.S. Government Printing Office.

Weindruch, R. and R.L. Wilford. 1988. The retardation of aging and disease by dietary restriction. Springfield, IL: Charles C. Thomas.

Witteman, J.C., W.C. Willett, M.J. Stampfer, G.A. Colditz, F.J. Kok, F.M. Sacks, F.E. Speizer, B. Rosner, and C.H. Hennekens. 1990. Relation of moderate alcohol consumption and risk of systemic hypertension in women. *American Journal of Cardiology* 65:633–637.

Wolman, P.G. 1987. Management of patients using unproven regimens for arthritis. *Journal of the American Dietetic Association* 87:1211–1214.

Work, J.A. 1989. Strength training: A bridge to independence for the elderly. *The physician and sports medicine* 17(no. 11):135–138.

Zheng, J.J. and I.H. Rosenberg. 1989. What is the nutritional status of the elderly? *Geriatrics* 44(no. 6):57–64.

Appendices

Appendix A

Estimated Safe and Adequate Daily Dietary Intakes of Selected Vitamins and Minerals[a]

Category	Age (years)	Vitamins: Biotin (μg)	Vitamins: Pantothenic Acid (mg)
Infants	0–0.5	10	2
	0.5–1	15	3
Children and adolescents	1–3	20	3
	4–6	25	3–4
	7–10	30	4–5
	11+	30–100	4–7
Adults		30–100	4–7

Category	Age (years)	Trace Elements[b]: Copper (mg)	Man-ganese (mg)	Fluoride (mg)	Chromium (μg)	Molybdenum (μg)
Infants	0–0.5	0.4–0.6	0.3–0.6	0.1–0.5	10–10	15–30
	0.5–1	0.6–0.7	0.6–1.0	0.2–1.0	20–60	20–40
Children and adolescents	1–3	0.7–1.0	1.0–1.5	0.5–1.5	20–80	25–50
	4–6	1.0–1.5	1.5–2.0	1.0–2.5	30–120	30–75
	7–10	1.0–2.0	2.0–3.0	1.5–2.5	50–200	50–150
	11+	1.5–2.5	2.0–5.0	1.5–2.5	50–200	75–250
Adults		1.5–3.0	2.0–5.0	1.5–4.0	50–200	75–250

[a] Because there is less information on which to base allowances, these figures are not given in the main table of RDA and are provided here in the form of ranges of recommended intakes.

[b] Since the toxic levels for many trace elements may be only several times usual intakes, the upper levels for the trace elements given in this table should not be habitually exceeded.

Appendix B

Summary of Examples of Recommended Nutrients Based on Energy Expressed as Daily Rates

Age	Sex	Energy kcal	Thiamin mg	Riboflavin mg	Niacin NE[b]	n-3 PUFA[a] g	n-6 PUFA g
Months							
0–4	Both	600	0.3	0.3	4	0.5	3
5–12	Both	900	0.4	0.5	7	0.5	3
Years							
1	Both	1100	0.5	0.6	8	0.6	4
2–3	Both	1300	0.6	0.7	9	0.7	4
4–6	Both	1800	0.7	0.9	13	1.0	6
7–9	M	2200	0.9	1.1	16	1.2	7
	F	1900	0.8	1.0	14	1.0	6
10–12	M	2500	1.0	1.3	18	1.4	8
	F	2200	0.9	1.1	16	1.1	7
13–15	M	2800	1.1	1.4	20	1.4	9
	F	2200	0.9	1.1	16	1.2	7
16–18	M	3200	1.3	1.6	23	1.8	11
	F	2100	0.8	1.1	15	1.2	7
19–24	M	3000	1.2	1.5	22	1.6	10
	F	2100	0.8	1.1	15	1.2	7
25–49	M	2700	1.1	1.4	19	1.5	9
	F	2000	0.8	1.0	14	1.1	7
50–74	M	2300	0.9	1.3	16	1.3	8
	F	1800	0.8[c]	1.0[c]	14[c]	1.1[c]	7[c]
75 +	M	2000	0.8	1.0	14	1.0	7
	F[d]	1700	0.8[c]	1.0[c]	14[c]	1.1[c]	7[c]
Pregnancy (additional)							
1st Trimester		100	0.1	0.1	0.1	0.05	0.3
2nd Trimester		300	0.1	0.3	0.2	0.16	0.9
3rd Trimester		300	0.1	0.3	0.2	0.16	0.9
Lactation (additional)		450	0.2	0.4	0.3	0.25	1.5

[a] PUFA, polyunsaturated fatty acids

[b] Niacin Equivalents

[c] Level below which intake should not fall

[d] Assumes moderate physical activity

SOURCE: Scientific Review Committee. *Nutrition Recommendation*, Ottawa, Canada: Health and Welfare, 1990.

Appendix B (continued)

Summary Examples of Recommended Nutrient Intake Based on Age and Body Weight Expressed as Daily Rates

Age	Sex	Weight kg	Protein g	Vit. A RE[a]	Vit. D μg	Vit. E mg	Vit. C mg	Folate μg	Vit. B_{12} μg	Calcium mg	Phosphorus mg	Magnesium mg	Iron mg	Iodine μg	Zinc mg
Months															
0–4	Both	6.0	12[b]	400	10	3	20	50	0.3	250[c]	150	20	0.3[d]	30	2[d]
5–12	Both	9.0	12	400	10	3	20	50	0.3	400	200	32	7	40	3
Years															
1	Both	11	19	400	10	3	20	65	0.3	500	300	40	6	55	4
2–3	Both	14	22	400	5	4	20	80	0.4	550	350	50	6	65	4
4–6	Both	18	26	500	5	5	25	90	0.5	600	400	65	8	85	5
7–9	M	25	30	700	2.5	7	25	125	0.8	700	500	100	8	110	7
	F	25	30	700	2.5	6	25	125	0.8	700	500	100	8	95	7
10–12	M	34	38	800	2.5	8	25	170	1.0	900	700	130	8	125	9
	F	36	40	800	5	7	25	180	1.0	1100	800	135	8	110	9
13–15	M	50	50	900	5	9	30	150	1.5	1100	900	185	10	160	12
	F	48	42	800	5	7	30	145	1.5	1000	850	180	13	160	9
16–18	M	62	55	1000	5	10	40[e]	185	1.9	900	1000	230	10	160	12
	F	53	43	800	2.5	7	30[e]	160	1.9	700	850	200	12	160	9
19–24	M	71	58	1000	2.5	10	40[e]	210	2.0	800	1000	240	9	160	12
	F	58	43	800	2.5	7	30[e]	175	2.0	700	850	200	13	160	9
25–49	M	74	61	1000	2.5	9	40[e]	220	2.0	800	1000	250	9	160	12
	F	59	44	800	2.5	6	30[e]	175	2.0	700	850	200	13	160	9
50–74	M	73	60	1000	5	7	40[e]	220	2.0	800	1000	250	9	160	12
	F	63	47	800	5	6	30[e]	190	2.0	800	850	210	8	160	9
75+	M	69	57	1000	5	6	40[e]	205	2.0	800	1000	230	9	160	12
	F	64	47	800	5	5	30[e]	190	2.0	800	850	210	8	160	9
Pregnancy (additional)															
1st Trimester			5	100	2.5	2	0	300	1.0	500	200	15	0	25	6
2nd Trimester			20	100	2.5	2	10	300	1.0	500	200	45	5	25	6
3rd Trimester			24	100	2.5	2	10	300	1.0	500	200	45	10	25	6
Lactation (additional)			20	400	2.5	3	25	100	0.5	500	200	65	0	50	6

[a] Retinol Equivalents

[b] Protein is assumed to be from breast milk and must be adjusted for infant formula.

[c] Infant formula with high phosphorus should contain 375 mg calcium.

[d] Breast milk is assumed to be the source of the mineral.

[e] Smokers should increase vitamin C by 50%.

SOURCE: Scientific Review Committee. *Nutrition Recommendations*, Ottowa, Canada: Health and Welfare, 1990.

Appendix B (continued)

Canada's Food Guide (1983)

Variety	Choose different kinds of foods from within each group in appropriate numbers of servings and portion sizes.
Energy balance	Needs vary with age, sex, and activity. Balance energy intake from foods with energy output from physical activity to control weight. Foods selected according to the Guide can supply 1000–1400 kilocalories. For additional energy, increase the number and size of servings from the various food groups and/or add other foods.
Moderation	Select and prepare foods with limited amounts of fat, sugar, and salt. If alcohol is consumed, use limited amounts.

Food Group	**Recommended Number of Servings (adults)**	**Some Examples of One Serving**
Milk and milk products	2[a]	1 cup milk; ¾ cup yogurt; 1½ oz cheddar or processed cheese
Meat, fish, poultry, and alternates	2	2–3 oz cooked lean meat, fish, poultry, or liver; 4 T peanut butter; 1 cup cooked dried peas, beans, or lentils; ½ cup nuts or seeds; 2 oz cheddar cheese; ½ cup cottage cheese; 2 eggs
Breads and cereals[b]	3–5	1 slice bread; ½ cup cooked cereal; ¾ cup ready-to-eat cereal; 1 roll or muffin; ½–¾ cup cooked rice, macaroni, spaghetti, or noodles; ½ hamburger or wiener bun
Fruits and vegetables	4–5[c]	½ cup vegetables or fruits—fresh, frozen, or canned; ½ cup juice—fresh, frozen, or canned; 1 medium-sized potato, carrot, tomato, peach, apple, orange, or banana

[a]For children up to 11 years, 2–3 servings; adolescents, 3–4 servings; pregnant and nursing women, 3–4 servings.

[b]Whole grain or enriched Whole grain products are recommended.

[c]Include at least two vegetables. Choose a variety of both vegetables and fruits—cooked, raw, or their juices. Include yellow, green, or green leafy vegetables.

SOURCE: Adapted from "Canada's Food Guide," Health and Welfare Canada, 1983 with permission of the Minister of Supply and Services Canada.

Appendix C

Measurements Used in Nutrition

In the science of nutrition, metric units are usually used to describe levels of nutrients. This system offers the simplicity of dealing in multiples of ten. Since the metric system is not yet widely used in the United States, we have provided conversion factors for the commonly used metric units and U.S. measures.

Metric Prefixes

Prefix	Abbreviation	Value
micro-	μ	one-millionth
milli-	m	one-thousandth
centi-	c	one-hundredth
deci-	d	one-tenth
deka-	da	ten
hecto-	h	one-hundred
kilo-	k	one-thousand

U.S. Household Measurements and Equivalents

1 quart = 4 cups (c)
1 cup = 8 fluid ounces = 16 tablespoons (T)
1 T = 3 teaspoons (t)
1 t = 5 grams dry weight (such as sugar or salt)

Metric and U.S. Equivalents

Metric Unit	U.S. Equivalent
Mass and Weight	
1 microgram (μg)	0.00000004 ounce (oz)
1 milligram (mg)	0.00004 ounce
1 gram (g)	0.04 ounce
28.35 grams[a]	1 ounce
1 kilogram (kg)	2.2 pounds (lb)
0.454 kilogram	1 pound
Liquid capacity	
1 milliliter (ml)	0.035 fluid ounce
29.6 milliliters	1 fluid ounce
1 liter (l)	1.06 quarts (qt)
0.946 liter	1 fluid quart
Heat	
1 kilojoule	0.239 kilocalorie (kcal)
4.18 kilojoules	1 kilocalorie

[a] This is commonly rounded to 30 grams/ounce, except for calculations in which considerable exactness is required.

Appendix D

Reliable Sources of Nutrition Information

Semitechnical Periodicals

These materials contain reviews that are suitable for people without a strong science background. Most of them are available by subscription, except those indicated with an asterisk (*), which are available to health and education professionals on request.

***Contemporary Nutrition**
A monthly newsletter. Contains one referenced nutrition review topic by recognized expert per issue.

General Mills, Inc.
P.O. Box 5588
Stacy, MN 55079

Dairy Council Digest
A bimonthly newsletter. Contains one referenced nutrition review topic per issue.

National Dairy Council
6300 North River Road
Rosemont, IL 60018-4233

***Dietetic Currents**
A bimonthly newsletter. Contains one referenced nutrition review topic by recognized expert per issue.

Ross Laboratories
Director of Professional Services
625 Cleveland Avenue
Columbus, OH 43216

Environmental Nutrition
A newsletter published ten times per year. Contains reviews of current issues and books and a readers' forum.

2112 Broadway
New York, NY 10023

FDA Consumer
A monthly magazine. Contains articles on concerns and actions of the FDA.

Superintendent of Documents
Government Printing Office
Washington, DC 20402

***Food and Nutrition News**
A newsletter published five times per year. Contains one referenced article by recognized expert per issue; other features.

National Livestock and Meat Board
444 North Michigan Avenue
Chicago, IL 60611

Harvard Medical School Health Letter
A monthly newsletter. Contains information on a variety of health topics including nutrition.

Department of Continuing Education
Harvard Medical School
Boston, MA 02115

National Council Against Health Fraud Newsletter
A monthly newsletter. Contains information concerning health misinformation, faddism, and fraud.

NCAHF
P.O. Box 1276
Loma Linda, CA 92354

Tufts University Diet and Nutrition Letter
A monthly newsletter. Contains reviews of current issues and books; questions and answers.

Tufts Diet and Nutrition Letter
80 Boylston Street
Suite 353
Boston, MA 02116

Appendix D (continued)

Respected Professional Journals

Although this listing includes the journals that are most likely to carry original nutrition research, many other journals occasionally do also. Several of these journals feature technical review articles.

American Journal of Clinical Nutrition
American Society for Clinical Nutrition
9650 Rockville Pike
Bethesda, MD 20814

American Journal of Public Health
American Public Health Association
1015 Fifteenth Street NW
Washington, DC 20005

Food and Chemical Toxicology
Pergamon Press, Inc.
Maxwell House, Fairview Park
Elmsford, NY 10523

Food Technology
Institute of Food Technologists
221 North LaSalle Street
Chicago, IL 60601

Gastroenterology
W.B. Saunders Co.
The Curtiss Center
Independence Square West
Philadelphia, PA 19106–3399

Journal of the American Dietetic Association
American Dietetic Association
216 West Jackson Boulevard, Suite 800
Chicago, IL 60606–6995

Journal of the American Medical Association (JAMA)
American Medical Association
535 North Dearborn Street
Chicago, IL 60610

Journal of Applied Physiology
American Physiological Society
9650 Rockville Pike
Bethesda, MD 20814

Journal of Nutrition
American Institute of Nutrition
9650 Rockville Pike
Bethesda, MD 20814

Journal of Nutrition Education
Society for Nutrition Education
1700 Broadway, Suite 300
Oakland, CA 94612

Lancet (British)
Williams and Wilkins
428 East Preston Street
Baltimore, MD 21202-3993

Medicine and Science in Sports and Exercise
American College of Sports Medicine
401 West Michigan Street
Indianapolis, IN 46202

Nature (British)
Macmillan Magazines Ltd.
Subscription Department
P.O. Box 1733
Riverton, NJ 08077-7333

New England Journal of Medicine
Massachusetts Medical Society
10 Shattuck Street
Boston, MA 02115-6094

Nutrition Reviews
Springer-Verlag New York, Inc.
175 Fifth Avenue
NY, NY 10010

Nutrition Today
Williams & Wilkins
428 East Preston St.
Baltimore, MD 21202

Pediatric Research
International Pediatric Research Foundation, Inc.
428 East Preston Street
Baltimore, MD 21202

Pediatrics
American Academy of Pediatrics
P.O. Box 927
Elk Grove Village, IL 60009-0927

Science
American Association for the Advancement of Science
1333 H Street, NW
Washington, DC 20005

Appendix D (continued)

Professional and Service Organizations

These are organizations that publish various nutrition-related materials but do not publish any of the journals just listed.

American Cancer Society
1599 Clifton Road
Atlanta, GA 30329

American Council on Science and Health
1995 Broadway, 16th Fl.
New York, NY 10023

American Dental Association
211 East Chicago Avenue
Chicago, IL 60611

American Geriatrics Society
770 Lexington Avenue, Suite 400
New York, NY 10021

American Heart Association
7320 Greenville Avenue
Dallas, TX 75231

American Home Economics Association
2010 Massachusetts Avenue NW
Washington, DC 20036

Food and Nutrition Board
National Research Council, National Academy of Sciences
2101 Constitution Avenue NW
Washington, DC 20418

March of Dimes Birth Defects Foundation
1275 Mamaroneck Avenue
White Plains, NY 10605

Office of Cancer Communications
National Cancer Institute
Bldg. 31, Room 10A29
9000 Rockville Pike
Bethesda, MD 20892

Federal Government Resources

These agencies will furnish lists of their nutrition-related government publications.

Consumer Information Center
U.S. General Services Administration
Washington, DC 20405

Food and Nutrition Information
National Agricultural Library
10301 Baltimore Blvd., Room 304
Beltsville, MD 20705

Local Resources

These are people whom you can contact in your own geographical area who are familiar with science-based nutrition information.

Cooperative extension agents
in county extension offices

Dietitians
in clinical positions in local hospitals or nursing homes

Home economists
employed in business (supermarkets, utilities, food processing companies, and so on)

Nutrition faculty
affiliated with a reputable department of nutritional science

Nutritionists
in city, county, or state public health departments

Appendix E

Table of Food Composition—Common Foods

About the Data Base

This composition of food table is compiled by ESHA Research in Salem, Oregon. It includes data from over 250 sources of information, including the most recent U.S. Department of Agriculture (USDA) data available: the Handbook 8 series and the latest Home and Garden Bulletin 72 published in 1985. Even with the USDA data, however, there are missing values, and as the various government data are updated, conflicting values are reported for some items.

To resolve conflicting values and minimize missing information, other sources have been used as well: scientific journal articles, unpublished data from both the USDA and research scientists, composition of food tables from Canada and England, manufacturers' data, and information from other data banks. When estimates of nutrient amounts in cooked foods were derived from reported amounts in raw foods, published retention factors were applied.

You should know that there can be many different nutrient values reported for the same foods. Many factors influence the amounts of some nutrients in foods, including the mineral content of the soil, the diet of the animal, the fertilizer used, genetics, the season of the year, the method of processing, methods of analysis, difference in the moisture content of the samples analyzed, length of storage, method of storage, the number of samples tested, and methods of cooking the food.

Therefore, when the USDA reports a single value for a nutrient, it is in most cases an average of a range of data. There will be different nutrient values reported from reliable sources for the same food, so nutrient data should be viewed and used only as a guide, an approximation of nutrient content.

The reference numbers for the foods are listed for your convenience. They represent the code numbers of the foods in the computer software, The Food Processor nutrition system, from ESHA Research in Salem, Oregon. Where the food item does not have a reference number, the nutrient data can be added to the nutrient data base of the computer program.

Appendix E Table of Food Composition—Common Foods

Item No.	Food*	Approximate Measure	Weight (g)	Food Energy (kcal)	Protein (g)	Total Fat (g)	Unsat Fat[†] (g)	Carbohydrate (g)	Calcium (mg)	Phosphorous (mg)	Sodium (mg)	Potassium (mg)	Iron (mg)	Zinc (mg)	Vitamin A (IU)	Thiamin (mg)	Riboflavin (mg)	Niacin (mg)	Vitamin B_6 (mg)	Vitamin B_{12} (µ)	Folic Acid (µ)	Vitamin C (mg)
290	Alfalfa sprouts	1 cup	33	10	1	tr[‡]	tr	1	11	23	2	26	.3	.3	51	.03	.04	.2	.01	0	12	3
544	Apple butter	2 T	35	66	tr	tr	tr	17	5	13	1	89	.3	tr	0	tr	.01	.1	.01	0	tr	1
—	Apples:																					
	Raw, cored (2¾-in. diam):																					
315	With peel	1 apple	138	80	.27	.5	.2	21	10	10	1	159	.3	.1	74	.02	.02	.1	.07	0	4	8
316	Without peel	1 apple	128	72	.2	.4	.1	19	5	9	0	144	.2	.1	56	.02	.01	.1	.06	0	.5	5
317	Dried, rings	10 rings	64	155	.5	.2	.1	42	9	24	56	288	.9	.1	0	0	.10	.6	.08	0	1	3
—	Apple juice:																					
319	Bottled, canned	1 cup	248	116	.2	.3	.1	29	17	17	7	295	.9	.1	2	.05	.04	.2	.07	0	1	2
823	Frozen concentrate (6-oz can = ¾ cup)	¾ cup	211	349	1	1	.3	87	43	52	54	945	1.9	.3	10	.02	.11	.3	.25	0	2	4
321	Diluted with 3 parts water by volume	1 cup	239	111	.3	.3	.1	28	14	16	17	301	.6	.1	3	.01	.04	.1	.08	0	1	1
—	Applesauce:																					
820	Sweetened	1 cup	255	195	.5	.5	.2	51	10	18	8	156	1.0	.1	28	.03	.07	.5	.07	0	2	4
318	Unsweetened	1 cup	244	106	.4	.1	tr	28	7	18	5	183	.3	.1	70	.03	.06	.5	.06	0	2	3
—	Apricots:																					
827	Raw (about 12/lb with pits)	3 apricots	106	51	1	.4	.3	12	15	21	1	313	.6	.3	1660	.03	.04	.6	.06	0	9	11
324	Dried halves	10 halves	35	83	1	.2	.1	22	16	41	4	482	1.7	.3	2534	tr	.05	1.1	.06	0	4	1
	Canned, fruit and liquid:																					
323	Heavy syrup	1 cup	258	214	1	.2	.1	55	23	33	10	361	.8	.3	3174	.05	.06	1.0	.14	0	4	8
824	Juice pack	1 cup	248	119	2	.1	.1	31	30	50	9	409	.7	.3	4195	.05	.05	.9	.18	0	5	12
825	Light syrup	1 cup	253	160	1	.1	.1	42	28	34	10	349	1.0	.3	3344	.04	.05	.8	.14	0	4	7
325	Apricot nectar, canned	1 cup	251	141	1	.2	.1	36	18	23	8	286	1.0	.2	3304	.02	.04	.7	.16	0	3	2
—	Artichokes, globe or French:																					
171	Cooked (300g whole, 120g edible)	1 artichoke	120	60	4.2	.2	.1	13	54	103	114	425	1.6	.6	212	.08	.08	1.2	.13	0	61	12
909	Hearts, frozen packaged, cooked	9 oz	240	108	7	1	1	22	50	146	127	634	1.3	.9	394	.15	.38	2.2	.21	0	285	12
908	Hearts, marinated (6 oz)	6 oz	170	168	4	14	11	13	39	102	900	438	1.6	.5	278	.06	.17	1.4	.15	0	149	52
—	Asparagus:																					
172	Raw pieces	½ cup	67	15	2	.1	.1	2	15	35	1	202	.5	.5	609	.08	.08	.8	.10	0	70	22
	Cooked, cuts and tips:																					
173	From raw	½ cup	90	23	2	.3	.1	4	22	55	4	279	.6	.4	746	.09	.11	.9	.13	0	88	25
174	From frozen	1 cup	180	50	5	1	.4	9	41	99	7	392	1.2	1.0	1472	.12	.19	1.9	.16	0	176	44
175	Canned spears, ½-in. diam at base	4 spears	80	15	2	1	.2	2	11	30	278	122	.5	.3	380	.05	.07	.7	.04	0	69	13
—	Avocados, average of varieties:																					
326	Whole fruit (272g, 201g edible)	1 avocado	201	324	4	31	23	15	22	83	21	1204	2.0	.9	1230	.22	.25	3.9	.56	0	124	16
327	Mashed	1 cup	230	370	5	35	27	17	25	95	24	1378	2.3	1.0	1407	.25	.28	4.4	.64	0	142	18
—	Bacon:																					
81	Regular, cooked	3 pieces	19	109	6	9	6	.1	2	64	303	92	.3	.6	0	.13	.05	1.4	.05	.33	1	6
	Canadian-style:																					
82	Cooked	2 pieces	47	86	11	4	2	1	5	138	719	181	.4	.8	0	.38	.09	3.2	.21	.36	2	10
1033	Unheated	2 pieces	57	89	12	4	2	1	5	138	799	195	.4	.8	0	.43	.10	3.5	.22	.38	2	12
1034	Pork breakfast strips, cooked	3 pieces	34	156	10	13	7	.4	5	90	714	158	.7	1.3	0	.25	.13	2.6	.12	.60	1	15
639	Bagel, plain (3½-in. diam)	1 bagel	68	180	7	1	1	35	20	61	300	65	2.1	.6	0	.26	.20	2.4	.03	0	16	0
573	Baking powder (sodium aluminum sulphate with monocalcium phosphate monohydrate)	1 T	11	20	0	0	0	4	694	171	1100	15	0	0	0	0	0	0	0	0	0	0
589	Baking soda	1 t	3	0	0	0	0	0	0	—	821	—	—	—	0	0	0	0	0	0	0	0
1384	Bamboo shoots, raw, sliced	1 cup	151	41	4	.5	.2	8	20	89	7	805	.8	1.7	30	.23	.11	.9	.09	0	11	6
—	Bananas:																					
328	Whole (8¾ in. long, 175g with peel, 114g edible)	1 banana	114	105	1	1	.1	27	7	22	1	451	.4	.2	92	.05	.11	.6	.66	0	24	10

329	Mashed	1 cup	225	205	2	1	.3	53	13	44	2	890	.7	.4	182	.10	.23	1.2	1.30	0	47	20
330	Dehydrated powder/flakes	1 cup	100	346	4	2	.5	88	22	74	3	1491	1.2	.6	305	.18	.24	2.8	.54	0	40	7
528	Barbecue sauce	1 cup	250	160	4	6	4	24	53	50	2038	435	2.0	.4	2240	.03	.03	.8	.25	0	10	13
	Barley:																					
452	Pearled, cooked	1 cup	157	193	3.6	1	.4	44	17	85	5	146	2	1.3	11	.13	.02	3	.2	0	25	0
450	Whole, cooked	1 cup	200	200	6	2	1	44	19	170	1	170	1.6	1.2	0	.12	.04	2.1	.14	0	12	0
1095	Bass, baked or broiled	3½ oz	100	125	24	4	3	0	86	216	75	385	1.6	.7	116	.1	.03	2.4	.35	3.4	9	0
	Beans:																					
	Baked beans:																					
918	Pork and beans in sweet sauce	1 cup	253	282	13	4	2.1	53	155	266	849	673	4.2	3.8	289	.12	.15	1	.20	.06	95	7.7
185	Pork and beans in tomato sauce	1 cup	253	247	13	2.6	1.5	49	141	297	1113	759	8	2.6	313	.13	.12	1.3	.18	.03	57	8
195	Black beans, cooked	1 cup	172	227	15	1	1	41	47	241	1	611	3.6	1.9	10	.42	.1	.9	.19	0	256	0
910	Broad beans, cooked	½ cup	100	56	5	.5	.3	10	18	73	41	193	1.5	.9	270	.13	.09	1.2	.03	0	104	20
181	Garbanzo beans/chickpeas, cooked	1 cup	164	269	15	4	3	45	80	275	11	477	5	2.5	44	.18	.10	.9	.2	0	282	2
911	Great Northern beans, cooked	1 cup	177	210	15	1	.4	37	121	293	4	692	4	1.5	2	.25	.13	1.2	.2	0	181	2
	Green/snap beans:																					
176	Raw	1 cup	110	34	2	.1	.1	8	41	42	6	230	1.4	.3	735	.09	.12	.8	.08	0	40	18
	Cooked:																					
177	From fresh	1 cup	125	44	2	.4	.2	10	58	48	4	373	1.6	.5	833	.09	.12	.8	.07	0	42	12
178	From frozen	1 cup	135	36	2	.2	.1	8	61	33	17	151	1.1	.8	713	.07	.10	.6	.08	0	42	11
	Canned:																					
179	Drained solids	1 cup	135	26	2	.1	.1	6	36	26	339	147	1.2	.4	471	.02	.08	.3	.05	0	43	6
184	Solids and liquid	1 cup	240	36	2	.2	.1	8	58	46	883	235	2.1	.5	778	.06	.12	.5	.07	0	44	10
	Kidney beans, red:																					
189	Cooked from dry	1 cup	177	225	15	1	1	40	50	252	4	713	5	2.0	10	.3	.11	1.4	.2	0	229	2
190	Canned, with liquid	1 cup	256	216	13	1	1	40	62	240	873	658	3	1.4	0	.3	.23	1	.05	0	129	3
	Lima beans:																					
193	Cooked from frozen, baby	½ cup	90	94	6	.3	.15	18	25	101	26	370	1.8	.5	150	.06	.05	.7	.10	0	58	5
192	Cooked from dry	1 cup	188	217	15	1	.4	39	32	208	4	955	5	1.8	0	.25	.11	.8	.29	0	156	0
	Canned:																					
913	Drained solids	1 cup	170	164	9	1	1	31	48	120	402	378	2.9	1.6	322	.06	.08	.8	.04	0	40	10
194	Solids and liquid	½ cup	121	96	6	.2	.1	18	25	89	405	266	2.0	.8	214	.04	.04	.3	.1	0	61	11
912	Navy beans, cooked from dry	1 cup	182	259	16	1	1	48	128	285	2	669	4.5	2.0	3	.4	.13	1.3	.3	0	255	2
196	Pinto beans, cooked from dry	1 cup	171	235	14	1	1	44	82	273	3	800	4.5	2	3	.33	.15	.7	.33	0	294	3.5
1338	Refried beans, canned, primarily pinto beans	1 cup	253	270	16	3	2	47	118	214	1071	994	4.5	3.5	0	.14	.1	1.2	.3	.14	150	15
198	Soybeans, cooked from dry	1 cup	172	298	29	15	12	17	175	421	1	886	9	2.1	15	.3	.5	.7	.4	0	93	3
183	White beans, cooked from dry	1 cup	179	253	16	1	1	46	131	302	4	828	5.0	1.9	0	.4	.13	.5	.2	0	245	0
	Yellow wax beans:																					
914	Cooked from raw	1 cup	125	44	2	.4	.2	10	58	48	4	373	1.6	.5	101	.09	.12	.8	.07	0	42	12
915	Cooked from frozen	1 cup	135	36	2	.2	.1	8	61	33	17	151	1.1	.8	151	.07	.10	.6	.08	0	42	11
916	Canned, drained solids	1 cup	135	26	2	.1	.1	6	36	26	339	147	1.2	.4	143	.02	.08	.3	.05	0	43	6
	Bean sprouts (mung beans):																					
199	Raw	1 cup	104	31	3	.2	.1	6	14	56	6	154	.9	.4	22	.09	.13	.8	.09	0	63	14
200	Cooked, boiled, drained	1 cup	124	26	3	.1	.1	5	15	34	12	125	.8	.6	17	.06	.13	1.0	.05	0	35	14
917	Canned, drained	1 cup	125	16	2	.1	.04	3	18	40	175	34	.5	.35	20	.04	.09	.3	.04	0	12	.4
	Beef, cooked:																					
	Braised, simmered, or pot roasted:																					
	Relatively fat (e.g., chuck blade):																					
51	Lean and fat	3 oz	85	325	22	26	13	0	11	162	53	190	2.5	6.7	.3	.06	.19	2.0	.26	2	5	0
52	Lean only	3 oz.	85	230	26	13	6	0	11	200	60	223	3	9	.3	.07	.2	2.3	.26	2	5	0
	Ground beef, broiled patty (3 by ⅝ in.):																					
63	Lean	3 oz	85	230	21	16	8	0	9	134	65	256	1.8	4.9	3	.04	.18	4.4	.24	2.60	3	0
64	Regular	3 oz	85	245	20	18	8	0	9	144	70	248	2.1	5.1	3	.03	.16	4.9	.24	2.60	3	0
1020	Heart, cooked pieces	1 cup	145	239	142	8	4	1	9	363	92	338	10.9	.5	29	.21	2.23	5.8	.3	21	3.4	2
67	Liver, fried	3 oz	85	184	23	7	3	7	9	392	90	309	5.3	5	30690	.18	3.52	12.3	.31	95	187	19
	Roast, oven-cooked, no liquid added:																					
	Relatively fat, rib roast:																					
53	Lean and fat	3 oz	85	324	19	27	13	0	10	144	54	250	2.0	4.4	1	.06	.15	3.1	.20	1.72	6	0
54	Lean only	3 oz	85	204	23	12	6	0	10	181	63	320	2.4	6	1	.07	.18	3.5	.26	2.5	7	0

Item No.	Food*	Approximate Measure	Weight (g)	Food Energy (kcal)	Protein (g)	Total Fat (g)	Unsat Fat† (g)	Carbohydrate (g)	Calcium (mg)	Phosphorous (mg)	Sodium (mg)	Potassium (mg)	Iron (mg)	Zinc (mg)	Vitamin A (IU)	Thiamin (mg)	Riboflavin (mg)	Niacin (mg)	Vitamin B_6 (mg)	Vitamin B_{12} (µ)	Folacin (µ)	Vitamin C (mg)
	Relatively lean, heel of round:																					
55	Lean and fat	3 oz	85	205	23	12	6	0	5	177	50	388	1.6	4.9	17	.07	.14	3.0	.20	2.16	4	0
56	Lean only	3 oz.	85	153	25	6	3	0	3	193	52	337	1.7	5.0	6	.08	.15	3.2	.28	2.84	4	0
	Steak, broiled:																					
	Round:																					
59	Lean and fat	3 oz	85	233	22	16	8	0	6	179	51	311	2	4	6	.08	.2	3.2	.4	2.3	8	0
60	Lean only	3 oz	85	165	24	7	3	0	5	201	54	352	2	4	3	.09	.2	3.5	.43	2.5	9	0
	Sirloin:																					
57	Lean and fat	3 oz	85	238	22	16	8	0	7	168	54	299	2	4	1	.07	.15	4	.32	1.65	6	0
58	Lean only	3 oz	85	172	24	8	3	0	7	185	57	336	2	4	1	.08	.17	5	.4	1.7	7	0
	T-Bone (yield from ½-lb raw):																					
61	Lean and fat	3 oz	85	276	20	21	10	0	8	150	51	288	2.2	3.8	1	.08	.18	3.3	.3	1.8	6	0
62	Lean only	3 oz	85	182	24	9	4	0	6	177	56	346	2.5	4.6	1	.09	.21	3.9	.33	1.9	7	0
1021	Tongue, cooked	3 oz	85	241	19	18	9	.28	6	121	51	153	3	4	0	.03	.28	1.8	.14	5	4	.4
65	Beef, corned, canned	3 oz	85	213	23	13	6	0	17	94	855	116	2	3	0	.02	.13	2.1	2.1	1.4	5	1.3
1355	Beef, hash, corned, canned	1 cup	220	382	18	10	5	22	29	147	1354	440	4.4	4.4	0	.12	.40	4.6	.41	1.54	15	8
66	Beef, dried, chipped	2.5 oz.	71	117	21	3	1	1	5	122	2456	314	3	4	0	.13	.6	7	.4	3	10	0
	Beef, macaroni, and tomato sauce casserole:																					
1463	Recipe	1 cup	226	189	10	6	3	25	30	118	974	562	2.4	2.1	1111	.19	.17	3.5	.30	.77	23	16
	Beef pot pie:																					
1350	Recipe (⅓ of 9-in. pie)	1 piece	210	515	21	30	20	39	29	149	596	334	3.8	3.2	4220	.29	.29	4.8	.24	1.20	29	6
1349	Frozen (serving for one)	1 pie	234	426	16	23	15	39	20	121	1093	14	3.6	2.6	1525	.18	.15	3.1	.27	1.30	17	2
	Beef vegetable stew:																					
1351	Recipe	1 cup	245	220	16	11	5	15	29	184	292	613	2.9	5.3	5690	.15	.17	4.7	.28	1.60	37	17
1353	Frozen entree	7 oz.	200	208	20	8	4	13	26	216	793	418	3.7	3.9	1478	.13	.19	4.9	.23	1.64	28	10
1352	Canned	1 cup	245	194	14	8	3	18	23	56	992	417	3.2	4.2	2616	.07	.12	2.4	.20	1.59	31	7
203	Beet greens, cooked from raw, drained	1 cup	144	40	4	.3	.2	8	165	58	346	1308	2.7	.7	7344	.17	.42	.7	.19	0	47	36
—	Beets:																					
201	Cooked from raw, diced	½ cup	85	26	1	.04	.02	6	9	26	42	266	.5	.2	11	.03	.01	.2	.03	0	49	5
202	Canned, diced, drained	½ cup	85	27	1	.12	.1	6	13	15	233	126	1.6	.2	10	.01	.04	.2	.05	0	22	4
—	Beverages, alcoholic:																					
604	Gin, rum, vodka, whiskey, 86 proof (2 fl oz = ¼ cup):	2 fl oz	56	140	0	0	0	.06	0	2	1	1	.02	.02	0	tr	tr	.01	0	0	0	0
	Beer:																					
603	Regular (12 fl oz)	12 fl oz	356	146	1	0	0	13	18	44	19	89	.1	.1	0	.02	.09	1.6	.18	.06	21	0
1501	Light (12 fl oz)	12 fl oz	354	100	1	0	0	5	18	43	10	64	.1	.1	0	.03	.11	1.4	.12	.02	15	0
1210	Brandy (2 fl oz = ¼ cup)	2 fl oz	56	137	0	0	0	21	5	2	2	2	.02	.04	0	tr	tr	.01	tr	0	0	0
609	Champagne	½ cup	119	91	.2	0	0	3	7	8	7	95	.4	.1	0	0	.01	.1	.02	0	.2	0
	Sherry:																					
1212	Dry	4 fl oz	142	142	tr	0	0	2	11	13	11	89	.3	.1	0	.01	.01	.1	.01	0	.12	0
610	Medium	4 fl oz	120	168	.3	0	0	10	10	8	9	100	.3	.1	0	.01	.03	.1	.01	0	.12	0
	Vermouth:																					
1213	Dry	4 fl oz	120	144	.12	0	0	7	8	8	20	48	.4	.04	0	tr	tr	.1	.01	0	.5	0
1214	Sweet	4 fl oz	120	186	.1	0	0	19	7	7	34	36	.4	.04	0	tr	tr	.1	.01	0	.5	0
	Wine:																					
1211	Dessert, sweet	4 fl oz	118	181	.24	0	0	14	9	11	11	109	.2	.1	0	.02	.02	.3	0	0	.5	0
605	Red	4 fl oz	118	85	.23	0	0	2	9	16	6	131	.5	.1	0	.01	.03	.1	.04	.02	2	0
606	Rosé	4 fl oz	118	84	.23	0	0	2	10	17	5	117	.4	.1	0	.01	.02	.1	.03	.01	1	0
607	White, dry	4 fl oz	119	79	.12	0	0	1	11	7	5	73	.4	.1	0	tr	.01	.1	.02	0	.23	0
608	White, medium	4 fl oz	118	80	.12	0	0	1	10	16	6	94	.4	.1	0	.01	.01	.1	.02	0	.23	0
—	Beverages, nonalcoholic (12 fl oz = 1½ cups):																					
	Carbonated:																					
592	Assorted fruit-flavored soda pop	12 fl oz	372	170	0	0	0	42	15	2	48	20	.3	.3	0	0	0	.02	0	0	0	0

591	Club soda	12 fl oz	355	0	0	0	0	0	17	0	75	6	.2	.4	0	0	0	0	0	0	0	0
590	Cola beverage, regular	12 fl oz	370	151	0	0	0	39	11	45	15	4	.1	.04	0	0	0	0	0	0	0	0
593	Diet soda, assorted	12 fl oz	355	2	0	0	0	.3	14	38	32	7	.1	.1	0	0	0	0	0	0	0	0
594	Ginger ale	12 fl oz	366	124	.1	0	0	32	12	1	25	5	.7	.2	0	0	0	0	0	0	0	0
595	Root beer	12 fl oz	370	152	.1	0	0	39	19	2	48	3	.2	.3	0	0	0	0	0	0	0	0
1502	Lemon-lime soda	12 fl oz	368	149	0	0	0	38	9	1	41	4	.3	.2	0	0	0	.1	0	0	0	0
596	Tonic/quinine water	12 fl oz	366	125	0	0	0	32	4	0	15	0	.04	0.37	0	0	0	0	0	0	0	0
	Coffee:																					
597	Brewed	1 cup	240	2	.14	.01	.01	1	4	3	5	130	.12	.1	0	0	tr	.5	0	0	.24	0
598	Dry instant powder	1½ t	1.8	2	.01	.01	.01	1	3	5	1	64	.1	.03	0	0	tr	.5	tr	0	0	0
	Kool-Aid, prepared drink:																					
1373	Low calorie, with Nutrasweet	1 cup	240	4	0	0	0	0	0	0	0	0	0	0	0	0	0	0	0	0	0	6
1372	Regular, prepared with sugar	1 cup	240	100	0	0	0	25	0	0	0	0	0	0	0	0	0	0	0	0	0	6
364	Lemonade, prepared from frozen concentrate	1 cup	248	100	.2	.1	.04	26	4	5	2	38	.4	.1	53	.02	.05	.04	.02	0	6	10
369	Limeade, prepared from frozen concentrate	1 cup	247	102	.1	.1	.02	27	3	3	.01	32	.1	.03	1	.01	.01	.1	.03	0	6	7
	Tea:																					
599	Brewed	1 cup	240	2	.01	.02	.01	1	0	1	7	89	.1	.1	0	0	.03	.1	0	0	12	0
1371	Dry instant powder	8 t	5.6	14	.6	.02	.01	3	3	25	7	369	.23	.18	0	tr	.04	.7	.04	0	6	0
	Biscuits:																					
640	Homemade/recipe	1 biscuit	28.4	100	2	5	3	13	48	36	195	32	.7	.2	10	.08	.08	.8	.01	.04	2	tr
641	From mix	1 biscuit	28	94	2	3	2	14	59	129	262	57	.6	.2	20	.12	.11	.9	.01	.05	2	tr
1503	From refrigerated dough	1 biscuit	20	65	1	2	2	10	4	78	249	18	.5	.1	0	.08	.05	.7	.01	0	1	0
	Blackberries:																					
331	Fresh	1 cup	144	74	1	1	.26	18	46	30	0	282	.8	.4	237	.04	.06	.6	.08	0	49	30
333	Frozen (measured frozen)	1 cup	151	97	2	1	.3	24	44	46	2	211	.9	.4	172	.04	.07	.6	.09	0	51	5
332	Canned, fruit and liquid	1 cup	256	236	3	.4	.2	59	54	36	7	254	1.7	.5	561	.07	.10	.7	.09	0	68	12
	Blueberries:																					
334	Fresh	1 cup	145	82	1	1	1	21	9	15	9	129	.2	.2	145	.07	.07	.7	.05	0	9	20
336	Frozen (measured frozen)	1 cup	155	78	1	1	1	19	12	18	1	83	.3	.1	126	.05	.06	.8	.09	0	10	4
335	Canned, fruit and liquid	1 cup	256	225	2	1	1	57	14	26	9	102	.8	.2	164	.09	.14	.3	.10	0	7	3
	Bluefish:																					
1097	Baked/broiled	3½ oz	100	159	26	5	3.4	0	9	290	77	477	.6	1.0	422	.08	.11	7.8	.53	7.1	2	.01
1098	Fried in crumbs	3½ oz	100	205	23	10	7	5	8	285	367	413	.5	1.0	400	.06	.08	5.5	.37	5	2	.01
1099	Steamed	3½ oz	100	148	24	5	4	0	10	275	50	431	.6	1.0	422	.06	.08	5.8	.4	5	2	.01
	Boysenberries:																					
338	Frozen (measured frozen)	1 cup	132	66	1	.4	.2	16	36	36	2	183	1.1	.3	89	.07	.05	1.0	.07	0	84	4
337	Canned, fruit and liquid	1 cup	256	225	3	.3	.2	57	46	25	9	230	1.1	.5	102	.07	.07	.6	.10	0	88	16
1030	Brains, calf, pan-fried	3 oz	85	167	11	14	5	0	8	328	134	301	2	1.2	0	.11	.22	3.2	.33	13	5	3
	Bran:																					
1520	Oat Bran	1 cup	94	231	16	7	5	62	55	690	4	532	5	3	0	1	.21	1	.2	0	49	1
942	Rice	1 cup	83	262	11	17	12	42	47	1392	4	1233	15	5	0	2.3	.24	28	3.4	0	52	0
472	Wheat	½ cup	30	65	5	1	1	19	22	304	1	355	3.2	2.2	0	.16	.2	4	.4	0	24	0
	Breads:																					
1446	Banana nut bread, home recipe, ½-in. slice	1 slice	50	161	3	7	5	22	18	48	115	104	.8	.3	140	.10	.08	.8	.13	.08	11	1
	Cornbread: *see* Muffin, cornmeal																					
657	Cracked wheat	1 slice	25	65	2	1	1	13	16	32	106	34	.7	.4	0	.10	.10	.8	.02	0	12	tr
658	French, 5 by 2½ by 1 in.	1 slice	35	100	3	1	1	18	39	30	203	32	1.1	.2	0	.16	.12	1.4	.02	0	13	tr
659	Italian, 4½ by 3¼ by ½ in.	1 slice	30	83	3	.3	.1	17	5	23	176	22	.8	.2	0	.12	.07	1.0	.02	0	11	0
1504	Mixed grain	1 round	25	65	2	1	1	12	27	55	106	56	.8	.3	1	.10	.10	1.1	.03	0	16	0
662	Pita bread, 6½-in. round	1 slice	60	165	6	1	1	33	49	60	339	71	1.5	.5	0	.27	.13	2.3	.01	0	12	0
661	Pumpernickel (⅔ rye flour, ⅓ enriched white flour, 5 by 4 by ⅜ in.)	1 slice	32	80	3	1	1	15	23	71	177	141	.9	.4	0	.11	.17	1.1	.05	0	16	0
663	Raisin bread	1 slice	25	68	2	1	1	13	25	22	92	59	.8	.2	1	.08	.16	1.0	.01	0	9	tr
660	Rye bread, light (⅔ enriched white flour, ⅓ rye flour)	1 slice	25	65	2	1	1	12	20	36	175	51	.7	.4	0	.10	.08	.8	.02	0	10	0
	White bread, enriched:																					
664	Soft crumb, 28g	1 slice	28	75	2	1	1	14	35	30	144	31	.8	.2	1	.13	.09	1.1	.01	0	10	tr
1218	Soft crumb, toasted	1 slice	24	78	2	1	1	14	35	30	142	31	.9	.2	1	.10	.09	1.1	.01	0	10	tr
665	Firm crumb, 33g	1 slice	33	88	3	1	1	16	42	36	170	37	.9	.2	1	.16	.10	1.2	.01	0	12	tr
1216	Firm crumb, toasted	1 slice	29	86	3	1	1	16	42	36	170	37	.9	.2	1	.12	.11	1.2	.01	0	12	tr

Appendix E *(Continued)*

Item No.	Food*	Approximate Measure	Weight (g)	Food Energy (kcal)	Protein (g)	Total Fat (g)	Unsat Fat† (g)	Carbohydrate (g)	Calcium (mg)	Phosphorous (mg)	Sodium (mg)	Potassium (mg)	Iron (mg)	Zinc (mg)	Vitamin A (IU)	Thiamin (mg)	Riboflavin (mg)	Niacin (mg)	Vitamin B_6 (mg)	Vitamin B_{12} (μ)	Folacin (μ)	Vitamin C (mg)
666	Wheat (½ enriched white flour, ½ whole-wheat flour, 1 oz)	1 slice	28	72	3	1	1	13	35	52	151	39	1.0	.3	1	.13	.09	1.3	.03	0	13	tr
1219	Wheat, toasted	1 slice	25	71	3	1	1	13	35	51	150	38	1.0	.3	1	.11	.09	1.3	.03	0	9	tr
	Whole wheat:																					
667	Firm crumb (35g)	1 slice	35	86	4	2	1	16	25	91	222	62	1.2	.6	1	.12	.07	1.3	.07	0	20	tr
1217	Firm crumb, toasted	1 slice	29	81	4	2	1	15	23	86	209	58	1.1	.6	1	.09	.07	1.3	.06	0	14	tr
656	Bread crumbs, white, dry, grated	1 cup	100	390	13	5	3	73	122	141	736	152	4.1	.5	0	.35	.35	4.8	.02	0	28	0
—	Bread sticks:																					
1223	With salt coating (6½ by 1¼-in. diam)	1 stick	35	106	3	1	1	20	16	31	548	33	.3	.2	0	.02	.03	.3	.01	0	4	tr
1224	Without salt coating (7¾ by ¾-in. diam)	10 sticks	100	384	12	3	2	75	28	99	700	92	.9	.6	0	.06	.07	1.0	.02	0	11	tr
—	Bread stuffing:																					
1225	Prepared from dry bread	1 cup	140	500	9	31	23	50	92	136	1254	126	2.2	.5	910	.17	.20	2.5	.02	0	14	0
1226	Prepared from dry bread with egg	1 cup	203	420	9	26	19	40	81	134	1023	118	2.0	.8	850	.10	.18	1.6	.04	18.0	20	.01
—	Broccoli:																					
204	Raw chopped	1 cup	88	24	3	.3	.2	5	42	58	24	286	.8	.4	1356	.06	.10	.6	.14	0	62	82
205	Cooked from raw, chopped	1 cup	156	46	5	.6	.3	8	72	92	40	456	1.3	.6	2168	1	.2	1	.22	0	78	116
206	Cooked from frozen, chopped	1 cup	184	51	6	.6	.3	10	91	101	44	331	1.1	.6	3481	.10	.15	.8	.2	0	55	74
—	Brussels sprouts:																					
208	Cooked from fresh	1 cup	156	60	6	1	.5	14	56	87	17	491	1.9	.5	1122	.17	.12	1	.31	0	94	97
209	Cooked from frozen	1 cup	155	65	6	1	.4	13	38	84	36	504	1.2	.6	912	.16	.18	.8	.27	0	157	71
476	Bulgur wheat, cooked	1 cup	182	151	6	.4	.2	34	18	73	9	124	2	1	0	.1	.05	1.8	.15	0	33	0
—	Burritos, with 3 oz of either beans, beef, or combination:																					
1330	Bean	1 burrito	174	322	13	10	6	47	181	243	1030	427	2.5	2.4	300	.26	.23	2.4	1	.16	55	5
1331	Beef	1 burrito	177	463	29	25	13	32	148	306	382	363	2.9	5.8	276	.26	.36	6.4	.30	2.72	35	3
1332	Beef-and-bean combination	1 burrito	175	390	21	18	9	40	165	274	516	388	2.7	3.3	300	.26	.29	4.4	.73	1.59	48	5
1333	Beef-and-bean deluxe combination	1 burrito	198	424	22	21	10	41	183	289	537	433	2.8	3.9	386	.27	.32	4.4	.67	1.48	51	7
—	Butter:																					
1	One stick (½ cup)	½ cup	113	813	1	92	30	.07	27	26	933	29	.2	.1	3460	.01	.04	.1	tr	tr	3	0
1	One tablespoon	1 T	14.2	100	.12	12	4	.01	3	3	116	4	.02	.01	430	tr	.01	.01	†	†	tr	0
1	One pat (about 1 t)	1 pat	5	34	.04	4	1	tr	1	1	41	1	.01	tr	150	†	tr	tr	†	†	tr	0
1469	Butter oil-ghee	1 T	13	114	.04	13	4	0	.5	.4	.2	1	—	—	488	—	—	—	tr	—	—	0
—	Cabbage:																					
	Common varieties:																					
210	Raw, shredded	1 cup	70	16	1	.1	.1	4	32	16	12	172	.4	.1	88	.04	.02	.2	.07	0	40	33
211	Cooked	1 cup	150	32	1	.4	.2	7	50	38	29	308	.6	.2	130	.09	.08	.4	.10	0	31	36
213	Bok choy, raw, shredded	1 cup	70	9	1	.1	.1	2	74	26	.5	176	.6	.3	2100	.03	.05	.4	.07	0	69	32
212	Pe-tsai, raw, chopped	1 cup	76	11	1	.2	.1	3	59	22	7	181	.2	.2	910	.03	.04	.3	.18	0	60	21
214	Red cabbage, raw, chopped	1 cup	70	19	1	.2	.1	4	36	29	8	144	.4	.2	30	.05	.02	.2	.15	0	19	40
	Savoy:																					
215	Raw, chopped	1 cup	70	20	1	.1	.04	4	25	29	20	161	.3	.3	700	.05	.02	.2	.13	0	56	22
216	Cooked	1 cup	145	35	3	.13	.07	8	44	48	34	267	.6	.3	1290	.07	.03	.04	.22	0	67	25
1354	Cabbage rolls, stuffed with rice and ham	8 oz	228	218	8	11	7	23	56	110	668	354	1.7	1.2	334	.32	.13	2.1	.26	.18	27	28
—	Cakes (cupcake weighs 42g):																					
1257	Angel food cake from mix (1/12 of 10-in. tube cake)	1 piece	53	125	3	.2	.1	29	44	91	269	71	.2	.1	0	.03	.11	.1	.01	0	4	0
1253	Boston cream pie (⅛ cake)	1 piece	120	260	3	8	5	44	26	70	225	40	.6	.2	252	.01	.18	.7	.05	.32	7	0
1256	Carrot cake with cream-cheese frosting (2.5 by 3 in. piece)	1 piece	112	406	4	21	16	52	27	65	146	116	1.2	.5	3700	.11	.14	.9	.1	.12	12	1
1263	Cheesecake (1/12 cake)	1 piece	92	278	5	18	7	26	52	81	204	90	.4	.4	234	.03	.12	.4	.06	.46	17	5
	Chocolate cake with chocolate icing (1/16 of cake):																					
1234	From recipe	1 piece	67	260	3	11	6	37	47	87	157	103	1.2	.3	105	.08	.10	.7	.02	.14	7	.1
1259	From mix	1 piece	69	235	3	8	4	40	41	72	181	90	1.4	.5	100	.07	.10	.6	.02	.10	4	.1

1258	Coffee cake from mix (1/6 of cake)	1 piece	72	230	5	7	4	38	44	125	310	78	1.2	.6	120	.14	.15	1.3	.02	.11	5	.2
1254	Fruitcake, dark (2/3-in. arc)	1 piece	43	165	2	7	5	25	41	50	67	194	1.2	.2	50	.08	.08	.5	.05	.05	2	16
	Gingerbread cake (3-by-3-in. piece):																					
1236	Home recipe	1 piece	110	351	5	11	8	59	47	52	386	214	2.7	.4	451	.16	.15	1.8	.06	.09	8	.1
1260	From mix (1/9 of 9-in. square cake)	1 piece	63	174	2	4	3	32	57	63	192	173	1.2	.6	0	.10	.11	.8	.01	.07	4	.1
1237	Pound cake from mix (1/2-in. slice)	1 piece	30	120	2	5	4	15	20	28	98	28	.5	.2	200	.05	.06	.5	.02	.13	3	.1
1238	Sponge cake (1/12 of 10-in. tube cake)	1 piece	66	194	5	3	2	37	25	70	210	50	1.2	.5	130	.10	.11	.8	.03	.33	11	.2
1264	Sponge snack cake with filling	1 cake	42	155	1	5	3	27	14	44	155	37	.6	.2	30	.07	.06	.6	.02	.12	4	0
	White cake from mix:																					
1261	With chocolate frosting	1 piece	77	291	4	12	8	44	38	122	176	102	1.4	.3	42	.20	.15	1.8	.01	.04	8	0
1255	With coconut frosting, commercial	1 piece	70	270	3	10	7	42	34	106	177	73	1.1	.2	40	.10	.13	1.7	.01	.04	4	0
	Yellow cake with chocolate frosting (2 layers, 1/16 of cake):																					
1235	Home recipe	1 piece	67	254	3	9	4	41	46	75	140	73	1.2	.3	97	.08	.10	.7	.03	.10	6	.2
1262	From mix	1 piece	69	235	3	8	4	40	63	126	157	75	1.0	.2	100	.08	.10	.7	.03	.10	5	.1
	Candy:																					
766	Almond Joy candy bar	1 oz	28	151	2	8	1	19	20	42	48	92	.5	.4	10	.01	.05	.14	.05	0	2	.1
	Chocolate:																					
751	Bittersweet chocolate	1 oz	28	141	2	10	4	16	13	60	2	129	1.0	1.1	10	.02	.05	.3	.01	0	14	0
577	Semisweet chocolate chips	1 cup	170	860	7	61	22	97	51	178	24	593	5.8	2.4	30	.10	.14	.9	.04	0	22	.01
721	Caramel, plain or chocolate	1 oz	28	115	1	3	.4	22	42	35	64	54	.4	.2	1	.01	.05	.1	tr	.02	0	tr
	Chocolate coated:																					
725	Almonds	1 cup	165	935	23	74	58	47	278	627	12	1011	6.3	4.2	26	.30	1.08	4.2	.13	0	128	0
738	Coconut candy	1 oz	28	133	1	7	2	18	8	29	7	75	.6	.4	3	.01	.02	.2	.10	0	5	0
728	Mints	1 oz	28	116	1	3	1	23	16	15	52	26	.3	.2	1	.01	.02	.1	tr	0	1.5	0
726	Peanuts	1 cup	170	954	30	70	47	59	197	507	102	857	4.1	4.5	64	.52	.26	16	.42	0	171	—
727	Raisins	1 cup	187	733	7	18	6	136	81	197	26	1153	4.4	1.3	44	.23	.17	1.3	.34	0	17	4
	Chocolate fudge:																					
730	Plain	1 oz	28	115	1	3	1	21	22	24	54	42	.3	.2	66	.01	.03	.1	tr	.04	2	tr
731	With nuts	1 oz	28	114	1	5	3	19	22	31	48	46	.3	.2	64	.02	.03	.1	.03	.03	4	.12
1444	Divinity, with nuts	1 piece	20	80	1	2	2	16	5	12	19	16	.1	.1	4	.01	.01	.03	.03	0	3	.1
739	English toffee candy bar	1 bar	32	220	1	19	10	11	0	0	90	50	.2	.2	21	.05	.05	.1	.04	0	1	0
729	Fondant candy (candy corn, mints, etc.)	1 oz	28	105	0	0	0	27	2	2	57	1	.1	.1	0	tr	tr	.01	tr	0	0	0
734	Gumdrops	1 oz	28	98	0	.2	.2	25	2	—	10	1	.1	0	0	0	tr	.01	0	0	0	0
735	Hard candy, all flavors	1 oz	28	109	0	0	0	28	6	2	7	1	.1	0	0	0	0	0	0	0	0	0
736	Jelly beans	1 oz	28	104	†	.1	.1	26	1	1	7	11	.3	0	0	0	tr	.01	—	0	0	0
765	M & M's peanut chocolate candies	1.7 oz	47.3	240	5	12	7	28	59	64	29	162	.7	.7	1	.03	.09	1.5	.03	0	5	0
764	M & M's plain chocolate candies	1.7 oz	48	237	3	10	5	33	79	65	41	171	.8	.6	50	.03	.12	.3	.01	0	5	0
740	Mars bar	1 bar	50	240	4	11	5	30	85	63	85	176	.6	.6	1	.02	.16	.5	.01	0	5	.1
	Milk chocolate:																					
722	Plain	1 oz	28	145	2	9	3	16	50	61	23	96	.4	.4	30	.02	.10	.1	.02	0	.3	tr
723	With almonds	1 oz	28	150	3	10	6	15	61	77	23	125	.5	.5	30	.03	.13	.3	.02	0	4	.1
724	With peanuts	1 oz	28	155	5	12	8	10	32	87	19	155	.7	.7	30	.11	.07	2.2	.05	0	16	tr
741	Milky Way bar	1 bar	60	260	3	9	3	43	86	80	140	167	.5	.4	95	.03	.15	.2	.01	0	7	1
750	Reese's peanut butter cup	2 cups	45	240	6	14	9	22	35	87	92	168	.7	.7	31	.03	.05	2.1	.06	0	17	0
742	Snickers bar	1 bar	61.2	290	7	14	8	37	70	75	170	209	.5	.7	19	.03	.11	1.8	.02	0	6	.02
737	Sugar-coated almonds	7 almonds	28	146	3	9	8	15	40	86	1	132	.8	.5	0	.04	.16	.6	.02	0	16	0
	Vanilla fudge:																					
732	Plain	1 oz	28	118	1	3	2.4	22	30	24	50	36	.03	.1	120	.01	.03	.01	tr	.05	1	.1
733	With nuts	1 oz	28	122	1	5	4	18	25	26	36	38	.2	.2	120	.02	.03	.05	.04	.04	4	.1
	Carrots:																					
	Raw:																					
217	Whole (7½ by 1⅛ in.)	1 carrot	72	31	1	.1	.1	7	19	32	25	233	.4	.1	20253	.07	.04	.7	.11	0	10	7
919	Grated	½ cup	55	24	1	.1	.1	6	15	24	19	178	.3	.1	15471	.05	.03	.5	.08	0	8	5
218	Cooked from fresh, sliced	½ cup	78	35	1	.1	.1	8	24	24	52	177	.5	.2	19152	.03	.04	.4	.19	0	11	2

Item No.	Food*	Approximate Measure	Weight (g)	Food Energy (kcal)	Protein (g)	Total Fat (g)	Unsat Fat† (g)	Carbohydrate (g)	Calcium (mg)	Phosphorous (mg)	Sodium (mg)	Potassium (mg)	Iron (mg)	Zinc (mg)	Vitamin A (IU)	Thiamin (mg)	Riboflavin (mg)	Niacin (mg)	Vitamin B_6 (mg)	Vitamin B_{12} (μ)	Folacin (μ)	Vitamin C (mg)
	Canned:																					
921	Drained	½ cup	73	17	.5	.1	.1	4	19	17	176	131	.5	.2	10055	.01	.02	.4	.08	0	7	2
920	Solids and liquid	½ cup	123	28	1	.2	.1	6	31	25	297	213	.8	.4	16196	.02	.03	.03	.52	0	10	3
1018	Carrot juice	½ cup	123	49	1	.2	.1	11	29	51	36	358	.6	.2	31587	.11	.07	.5	.27	0	5	11
529	Catsup	1 T	17	18	.3	1	.04	5	3	7	202	82	.12	.04	173	.02	.01	.23	.03	0	3	3
——	Cauliflower:																					
219	Raw pieces	½ cup	50	12	1	.1	.1	3	14	23	7	178	.3	.1	8	.04	.03	.3	.12	0	33	36
220	Cooked from fresh	½ cup	62	15	1	.1	.1	3	17	22	4	200	.3	.1	9	.04	.04	.3	.13	0	32	34
221	Cooked from frozen	1 cup	180	34	3	.4	.2	7	31	43	33	250	.7	.2	40	.07	.10	.6	.16	0	74	56
1102	Caviar (6.25 Tnsp = 100g)	3½ oz	100	252	25	18	10	4	276	355	1500	180	12	1	—	.19	.62	.12	.32	20	50	0
922	Celeriac/celery root, cooked	3½ oz	100	25	1	.2	.11	6	26	66	61	173	.4	.2	0	.03	.04	.4	.10	0	3	4
——	Celery:																					
222	Raw, chopped (large outer stalk 8 by 1½ in. weighs 40g)	½ cup	60	10	.5	.1	.1	2	24	15	52	172	.2	.1	80	.03	.03	.2	.05	0	17	4
223	Cooked, diced	1 cup	150	27	1	2	.2	6	63	30	137	426	.6	.2	198	.07	.07	.5	.13	0	33	9
——	Cereals:																					
485	All-Bran	⅓ cup	28.4	70	4	.5	.4	22	23	264	260	320	4.5	3.7	1250	.37	.43	5.0	.50	0	100	15
951	Alpha Bits	1 cup	28	111	2	1	.5	25	9	57	100	59	2.7	1.5	1250	.40	.40	5.0	.50	1.50	100	0
952	Apple Jacks	1 cup	28	110	2	.1	.1	26	3	30	125	23	4.5	3.7	1250	.40	.40	5.0	.50	0	100	15
953	Bran Buds	1 cup	84	217	12	2	2	64	56	729	516	930	13.4	11.1	3704	1.10	1.30	14.8	1.50	0	297	45
949	Bran Chex	1 cup	49	156	5	1	1	39	29	327	455	394	7.8	2.1	107	.60	.26	8.6	.90	2.60	173	26
1378	Buc Wheats	¾ cup	28	110	2	1	1	24	60	60	235	—	8.1	.3	2250	.68	.77	9.0	.90	2.70	—	27
954	C.W. Post, plain	1 cup	97	444	7	14	3	72	38	208	256	222	15.4	3.4	1250	1.30	1.50	17.1	1.70	5.10	342	0
956	Cap'n Crunch	1 cup	37	156	2	3	1	30	6	47	278	48	9.8	4.0	53	.66	.71	8.6	1.00	2.30	238	0
958	Cap'n Crunch, peanut butter	1 cup	35	154	3	5	2	27	7	49	268	57	9.1	3.8	0	.60	.70	9.0	1.6	2.30	244	—
486	Cheerios	1 cup	23	89	3	1	1	16	38	109	246	82	3.6	.6	1012	.32	.32	4.0	.40	1.20	5	12
959	Cocoa Krispies	1 cup	36	139	2	tr	tr	32	6	47	275	53	2.3	1.9	1587	.50	.50	6.3	.60	0	127	19
960	Corn Bran	1 cup	36	124	3	1	1	30	41	52	310	70	12.2	4.0	—	.38	.70	10.9	.86	1.39	232	—
962	Corn Chex	1 cup	28	111	2	tr	1	25	3	11	271	23	1.8	.1	143	.40	.07	5.0	.50	1.50	100	15
487	Cornflakes, Kellogg's	1¼ cups	28	110	2	tr	tr	24	1	18	351	26	1.8	.1	1250	.37	.43	5.0	.51	0	100	15
	Corn grits, cooked:																					
458	Enriched, yellow	1 cup	242	145	4	.5	.3	31	0	29	0	53	1.6	.2	145	.24	.15	2.0	.06	0	2	0
1011	Unenriched, yellow, cooked	1 cup	242	145	4	.5	.3	31	0	29	0	53	.5	.2	145	.05	.02	.5	.06	0	2	0
1012	Fortified instant with bacon bits, prepared	⅔ cup	141	104	3	.5	.4	22	6	28	531	60	1.3	.2	87	.20	.12	1.6	.04	0	8	0
	Cornmeal, degermed, enriched:																					
454	Dry	1 cup	138	505	12	2	1	107	7	116	4	224	5.7	1	570	.61	.56	7	.35	0	66	0
455	Cooked	1 cup	240	120	3	.5	.4	26	2	34	1	38	1.5	.2	140	.14	.10	1.2	.06	0	6	0
963	Cracklin' Oat Bran	1 cup	60	229	6	9	6	41	40	332	280	320	3.8	3.2	1500	.80	.90	10.6	1.10	0	212	32
1008	Cream of Rice, cooked	1 cup	244	126	2	.1	.1	28	8	42	2	49	.4	.4	0	.10	0	1.0	.07	0	8	0
1009	Cream of Wheat, cooked	1 cup	244	140	4	1	.3	29	54	43	5	46	10.9	.3	0	.24	.07	1.5	.02	0	9	0
488	Farina, enriched, cooked	1 cup	233	116	3	.2	.1	25	4	28	0	30	1.2	.2	0	.19	.12	1.3	.02	0	5	0
489	40% Bran Flakes, Kellogg's	1 cup	39	125	5	1	1	35	19	192	330	250	11.2	5.2	1741	.51	.59	6.9	.70	2.07	138	0
965	Fortified oat flakes	1 cup	48	177	9	1	1	35	68	176	429	343	13.7	1.5	2116	.60	.70	.4	.90	2.50	169	0
966	Froot Loops	1 cup	28	111	2	1	.2	25	3	28	125	30	4.5	3.7	750	.40	.40	5.0	.50	0	100	15
967	Frosted Mini-Wheats	4 biscuits	31	111	3	.3	.2	26	10	81	9	106	2.0	1.6	1367	.40	.50	5.5	.60	0	109	16
969	Fruity Pebbles	⅞ cup	28	113	1	1	1	24	4	16	157	22	1.8	1.5	1250	.40	.40	5.0	.50	1.50	100	0
	Fruit & Fiber:																					
1379	With apples	½ cup	28	90	3	1	1	22	10	150	195	168	4.5	1.5	1250	.38	.43	5.0	.50	1.50	100	0
1380	With dates	½ cup	28	90	3	1	1	21	10	100	170	168	4.5	1.5	1250	.38	.43	5.0	.50	1.50	100	0
1381	Fruitful Bran	¾ cup	34	110	3	0	0	27	10	150	240	150	8.1	3.8	1250	.38	.43	5.0	.50	1.50	100	0
970	Golden Grahams	1 cup	39	156	2	2	3	33	23	56	390	82	6.2	.3	1720	.52	.60	6.9	.70	0	137	8
	Granola:																					
490	Nature Valley	1 cup	113	503	12	20	6	76	71	354	232	389	3.8	2.2	81	.39	.19	.8	.32	0	85	0
971	Home recipe	1 cup	122	595	15	33	27	67	76	494	12	612	4.8	4.5	43	.73	.31	2.1	.43	0	99	1
491	Grape Nuts cereal	½ cup	57	210	6	.2	.2	46	20	153	341	183	16	2	2509	.7	.9	10.0	1.00	3.00	200	0
972	Grape Nuts flakes	⅞ cup	28	105	2	.3	.1	23	11	83	160	95	8	1	1250	.40	.40	5.0	.50	1.50	100	0
973	Honey & Nut Cornflakes	¾ cup	28	113	2	2	1	23	3	13	225	36	1.8	.1	1250	.40	.40	5.0	.50	0	100	15
974	Honey Nut Cheerios	1 cup	33	129	4	1	1	27	23	118	293	113	5.2	.05	1470	.44	.50	6	.60	1.70	0	18
975	Honey Bran	1 cup	35	119	3	1	1	29	16	132	202	151	5.6	.9	1543	.50	.50	6.2	.60	1.90	23	19

492	Kix	1 cup	19	74	2	.6	.3	16	27	27	192	23	5.4	.2	838	.25	.29	3.4	.34	1.00	67	10
493	Life	1 cup	43	168	8	3	2	28	141	245	235	260	12	1.3	0	.78	1.00	9.4	.06	0	32	0
496	Malt-O-Meal, cooked	1 cup	240	122	4	.2	.1	26	5	24	2	31	9.6	.2	0	.48	.24	5.8	.02	0	5	0
497	Maypo, cooked	¾ cup	180	128	4	2	1	24	94	186	6	158	6.3	1.1	1754	.50	.60	7.0	.65	2.10	7	21
	Nutri-Grain:																					
980	Barley	1 cup	41	153	5	.3	.2	34	11	126	277	108	1.5	5.4	1808	.50	.60	7.2	.70	2.20	145	22
981	Corn	1 cup	42	160	3	1	1	36	1	120	276	98	.9	5.5	1852	.50	.60	7.4	.75	2.20	148	22
982	Rye	1 cup	40	144	4	.3	.2	34	8	104	272	72	1.1	5.3	1764	.50	.60	7.0	.70	2.10	141	21
983	Wheat	1 cup	44	158	4	.5	.4	37	12	164	299	120	1.2	5.8	1940	.60	.70	7.7	.80	2.30	155	23
	Oatmeal (rolled oats):																					
459	Dry	1 cup	81	311	13	5	4	54	42	384	3	284	3.4	2.5	81	.59	.11	.6	.11	0	26	0
460	Cereal cooked, regular, quick or instant, not fortified	1 cup	234	145	6	2	2	25	19	178	2.3	131	1.6	1.2	37	.26	.05	.3	.05	0	9	0
	Instant, fortified:																					
1001	Plain, prepared	¾ cup	177	104	4	2	1	18	163	133	285	99	6.3	1.0	1510	.53	.29	5.5	.74	0	150	0
1002	With apples	⅞ cup	149	135	4	2	1	26	158	117	222	107	6.1	1.0	1450	.48	.28	5.1	.70	0	137	0
1006	With raisins and spice	⅞ cup	158	161	4	2	1	32	165	133	225	150	6.6	1.1	1466	.51	.36	5.5	.75	0	150	.01
984	100% Bran	1 cup	66	178	8	3	2	48	46	801	457	824	8.1	5.7	0	1.60	1.80	20.9	2.10	6.30	200	63
	100% Natural:																					
991	Regular	¼ cup	28	136	3	6	2	18	43	101	12	134	.8	.6	0	.09	.08	.4	.05	.28	14	0
992	With apples and cinnamon	1 cup	104	484	11	18	4	70	125	260	42	524	2.7	2.2	80	.37	.45	1.6	.11	.21	17	0
993	With raisins and dates	1 cup	110	504	12	20	5	71	155	385	46	562	3	2.2	0	.32	.22	1.6	.15	0	45	0
494	Product 19	1 cup	33	126	3	.2	.13	27	4	47	378	51	21.0	.5	5893	1.70	2.00	23.3	2.30	7.00	466	70
501	Puffed rice	1 cup	14	55	1	.1	.1	13	1	14	.4	16	.2	.1	0	.02	.01	.4	.01	0	3	0
506	Puffed wheat	1 cup	12	44	2	.1	.1	10	3	43	0	42	.6	.3	0	.02	.03	1.3	.02	0	4	0
495	Raisin Bran, Kellogg's	1 cup	49	158	5	1	1	37	25	200	293	307	24.0	5.0	1666	.51	.57	6.7	.67	2.00	133	0
995	Raisins, Rice & Rye	1 cup	46	155	3	.1	1	39	10	50	350	144	5.6	4.7	1558	.50	.60	6.3	.60	1.90	125	0
950	Rice Chex	¾ cup	19	75	1	1	5	17	3	19	158	22	1.2	.3	11	.27	.20	3.3	.33	1.00	67	10
500	Rice Krispies	1 cup	29	112	2	.2	.1	25	4	34	340	30	1.8	.5	1295	.40	.40	5.0	.50	0	100	15
499	Roman Meal, cooked	¾ cup	181	111	5	1	.4	25	22	162	2	227	1.6	1.3	0	.18	.09	2.3	.09	0	18	0
	Shredded wheat:																					
505	Bite-sized	¾ cup	32	115	3	1	.5	25	12	112	3	115	1.4	1.1	0	.08	.09	1.7	.08	0	16	0
990	Large biscuits	2 biscuits	38	130	4	1	.4	22	15	137	1	124	1.2	1.0	0	.11	.10	1.7	.10	0	19	0
502	Special K	1½ cups	32	125	6	.1	.1	24	9	62	298	55	5.1	4.2	1429	.45	.45	5.6	.56	0	112	17
996	Sugar Corn Pops	1 cup	28	108	1	.1	.1	26	2	8	90	20	1.8	1.5	750	.40	.40	5.0	.50	0	100	15
503	Sugar-frosted flakes	1 cup	35	133	2	.1	.1	32	1	26	284	22	2.2	.1	1543	.50	.50	6.2	.60	0	124	19
997	Sugar Smacks	¾ cup	28	106	2	.5	.3	25	3	31	75	42	1.8	.3	1250	.37	.43	5.0	.50	0	100	15
999	Tasteeos	1 cup	24	94	3	1	1	19	11	96	183	71	3.8	.7	1058	.30	.40	4.2	.40	1.30	9	13
1000	Team	1 cup	42	164	3	1	.5	36	6	65	259	71	2.6	.6	1852	.55	.63	7.4	.80	2.20	6.7	22
504	Total	1 cup	33	122	3	1	.5	26	56	137	330	123	21.0	15	5893	1.70	2.00	23.3	2.30	6	400	70
986	Trix	1 cup	28	109	1	1	.2	25	6	23	169	27	4.5	.1	1235	.40	.40	5	.50	1.50	99	15
988	Wheat Chex	1 cup	46	169	5	1	1	38	18	182	308	174	7.3	1.2	0	.60	.17	8.1	.80	2.40	162	24
478	Rolled wheat, cooked	1 cup	240	142	4	1	.4	32	17	130	2	165	1.5	1.2	0	.17	.06	2.2	.08	0	27	0
1010	Wheatena, hot, cooked	1 cup	243	135	5	1	1	29	11	146	5	187	1.4	1.7	0	.02	.05	1.3	.05	0	17	0
507	Wheaties	1 cup	29	110	3	1	.3	23	38	82	276	110	4.6	.6	1295	.40	.44	5.1	.52	1.50	101	15
498	Whole-wheat cereal, cooked	1 cup	242	150	5	1	.4	33	17	168	1	171	1.5	1.2	0	.17	.12	2.1	.07	0	25	0
	Chard, Swiss:																					
224	Raw, chopped	1 cup	36	7	1	.1	.04	1	18	17	77	136	.6	.1	1900	.01	.03	.1	.03	0	12	11
225	Cooked	1 cup	175	35	3	.1	.1	7	102	58	313	961	4.0	.6	11980	.06	.15	.6	.15	0	36	32
	Cheese:																					
	American cheese products:																					
2	Processed cheese	1 oz	28	106	4	9	3	.5	174	211	406	46	.1	.9	343	.01	.10	.02	.02	.20	2.2	0
3	Cheese food, refrigerated	1 oz	28	94	6	7	2	2	145	118	274	104	.2	.9	200	.01	.13	.02	.04	.36	2	0
885	Cheese food, pasteurized, in a jar	1 oz	28	93	6	7	2	2	163	130	337	79	.2	.9	259	.01	.13	.04	.02	.32	2	0
4	Cheese spread	1 oz	28	82	5	6	2	2	159	201	381	69	.1	.8	223	.01	.12	.04	.03	.11	2	0
5	Blue	1 oz	28	100	6	8	2	1	150	110	396	73	.1	.8	204	.01	.11	.3	.05	.35	10	0
860	Brick	1 oz	28	105	6	8	3	1	191	128	159	38	.1	.7	307	tr	.10	.03	.02	.36	6	0
6	Brie	1 oz	28	95	6	8	3	.1	52	53	178	43	.1	.7	189	.02	.15	.1	.07	.47	18	0
7	Camembert	1 oz	28	85	6	7	2	.1	110	98	236	53	.1	.7	262	.01	.14	.2	.06	.37	18	0
861	Caraway	1 oz	28	107	7	8	3	1	191	139	196	28	.1	.83	299	.01	.13	.1	.02	.08	2	0
	Cheddar:																					
8	Hard	1 oz	28	114	7	9	3	.4	204	146	176	28	.2	.9	300	.01	.11	.02	.02	.23	5	0
862	Shredded	1 cup	113	455	28	38	12	1	815	579	701	111	.8	3.5	1197	.03	.42	.1	.08	.94	21	0
9	Colby	1 oz	28	112	7	9	3	1	194	129	171	36	.2	.9	293	tr	.11	.03	.02	.23	5	0
	Cottage cheese:																					

Item No.	Food*	Approximate Measure	Weight (g)	Food Energy (kcal)	Protein (g)	Total Fat (g)	Unsat Fat† (g)	Carbohydrate (g)	Calcium (mg)	Phosphorous (mg)	Sodium (mg)	Potassium (mg)	Iron (mg)	Zinc (mg)	Vitamin A (IU)	Thiamin (mg)	Riboflavin (mg)	Niacin (mg)	Vitamin B_6 (mg)	Vitamin B_{12} (μ)	Folacin (μ)	Vitamin C (mg)
10	Creamed, small curd	1 cup	210	215	26	9	3	6	126	277	850	177	.3	.8	340	.04	.34	.3	.14	1.31	26	tr
865	Dry curd	1 cup	145	123	25	1	.2	3	46	151	19	47	.3	.7	44	.04	.21	.2	.12	1.20	21	0
11	Low fat, 2%	1 cup	226	205	31	4	1	8	155	340	918	217	.4	1.0	158	.05	.42	.3	.17	1.61	30	0
864	Low fat, 1%	1 cup	226	164	28	2	1	6	138	302	918	193	.3	.9	84	.05	.37	.3	.15	1.43	28	†
866	With fruit	1 cup	226	279	22	8	2	30	108	236	915	151	.3	.7	278	.04	.29	.2	.12	1.12	22	tr
12	Cream cheese	1 oz	28	99	2	10	3	1	23	30	84	34	.3	.2	405	.01	.06	.03	.01	.12	4	0
867	Edam	1 oz	28	101	7	8	2	.4	207	152	274	53	.1	1.1	260	.01	.11	.02	.02	.44	5	0
13	Feta	1 oz	28	75	5	6	1	1	140	96	316	18	.2	.8	130	.04	.23	.3	.02	.30	3	0
870	Gouda	1 oz	28	101	7	8	2	1	198	155	232	34	.1	1.1	183	.01	.10	.02	.02	.44	6	0
871	Limburger	1 oz	28	93	6	8	3	.1	141	111	227	36	.04	.6	363	.02	.14	.05	.02	.30	16	0
14	Monterey jack	1 oz	28	106	7	9	3	.2	212	126	152	23	.2	.8	269	.03	.11	.03	.02	.30	3	0
	Mozzarella:																					
	With part skim milk:																					
15	Low moisture	1 oz	28	80	8	5	2	1	207	149	150	27	.1	.9	180	.01	.10	.03	.02	.26	3	0
874	Regular	1 oz	28	72	7	5	1	1	183	131	132	24	.1	.8	166	.01	.09	.03	.02	.23	3	0
	With whole milk:																					
873	Low moisture	1 oz	28	90	6	7	2	.4	163	117	119	21	.1	.7	256	.01	.08	.03	.02	.21	2	0
872	Regular	1 oz	28	80	6	6	2	1	147	105	106	19	.1	.6	225	tr	.07	.02	.02	.19	2	0
16	Muenster	1 oz	28	104	6	8	3	.3	203	133	178	38	.1	.8	318	tr	.09	.03	.02	.42	3	0
875	Neufchatel	1 oz	28	74	3	7	2	1	21	39	113	33	.1	.2	321	tr	.06	.04	.01	.08	3	0
	Parmesan:																					
17	Grated (1 T weighs 5g)	1 oz	28	129	12	9	3	1	390	229	528	30	.3	1.0	199	.01	.11	.1	.03	.42	2	0
876	Hard	1 oz	28	111	10	7	2	1	336	197	454	26	.2	.8	171	.01	.09	.1	.03	.42	2	0
882	Processed, with pimiento	1 oz	28	106	6	9	3	.5	174	211	405	46	.1	.8	358	.01	.10	.02	.02	.20	2	.6
18	Provolone	1 oz	28	100	7	8	2	1	214	141	248	39	.2	.9	231	.01	.09	.04	.02	.42	3	0
	Ricotta:																					
19	Made with part skim milk	1 cup	246	340	28	20	6	13	669	449	307	307	1.1	3.3	1063	.05	.46	.2	.05	.72	14	0
878	Made with whole milk	1 cup	246	428	28	32	10	7	509	389	207	257	.9	2.9	1205	.03	.48	.3	.11	.83	14	0
	Romano:																					
880	Grated (1T weighs 5g)	1 oz	28	128	11	9	3	1	351	250	395	33	.3	1.2	188	.01	.12	.03	.03	.42	2	0
879	Hard	1 oz	28	110	9	8	2	1	302	215	340	26	.2	1.0	162	.01	.11	.02	.03	.42	2	0
20	Roquefort	1 oz	28	105	6	9	3	1	188	111	513	26	.2	.6	297	.01	.17	.2	.04	.18	14	0
21	Swiss	1 oz	28	107	8	8	2	1	272	171	74	31	.1	1.1	240	.01	.10	.03	.02	.48	2	0
883	Swiss, processed cheese	1 oz	28	95	7	7	2	1	219	216	388	61	.2	1.0	229	tr	.08	.01	.01	.35	2	0
884	Swiss, processed cheese food	1 oz	28	92	6	7	2	1	205	149	440	81	.2	1.0	243	tr	.11	.03	.01	.65	2	0
709	Cheese puffs (e.g., Cheetos)	1 oz	28	158	2	10	4	14	18	29	344	23	.2	—	90	.01	.03	.2	—	0	—	0
1413	Cheese sauce	½ cup	101	216	10	17	8	6	281	207	539	127	.4	1.2	635	.05	.22	.3	.05	.46	9	1
——	Cherries, sour:																					
829	Frozen (measured frozen)	1 cup	155	72	1	1	.5	17	20	25	1	192	.8	.2	1349	.07	.05	.2	.10	0	7	3
339	Canned, water pack	1 cup	244	90	2	.2	.1	22	27	25	17	240	3.3	.2	1840	.04	.10	.4	.11	0	20	5
——	Cherries, sweet:																					
340	Fresh, pitted	1 cup	145	104	2	1	1	24	21	28	1	325	.6	.1	310	.07	.09	.6	.05	0	8	10
828	Frozen (measured thawed)	1 cup	259	232	3	.3	.2	58	31	41	3	514	.9	.1	489	.07	.12	.5	.08	0	8	13
341	Canned, heavy-syrup pack, fruit and liquid	1 cup	257	213	2	.4	.2	55	23	46	7	373	.9	.3	396	.05	.10	1.0	.23	0	7	9
——	Chicken, cooked:																					
	All types:																					
68	Roasted	1 cup	140	266	41	10	6	0	21	273	120	340	1.7	2.9	73	.10	.25	12.8	.65	.46	8	0
1064	Stewed	1 cup	140	248	38	9	5	0	20	210	98	252	1.6	2.8	70	.07	.23	8.6	.37	.31	8	0
	Breast, meat and skin:																					
1072	Batter-fried	1 breast	140	364	35	19	12	13	28	258	385	282	1.8	1.3	90	.16	.20	14.7	.60	.41	8	0
72	Flour-fried	1 breast	98	218	31	9	5	2	16	228	74	253	1.2	1.1	50	.08	.13	13.5	.57	.34	4	0
69	Roasted	1 breast	98	193	29	8	5	0	14	210	69	240	1.0	1.0	91	.07	.12	12.5	.54	.32	3	0
74	Breast meat only, roasted	1 breast	86	142	27	3	2	0	13	196	64	220	.9	.9	18	.06	.10	11.8	.52	.29	3	0
	Drumstick:																					
1065	Flour-fried	1 drumstick	49	120	13	7	4	1	6	86	44	112	.7	1.4	40	.04	.11	3.0	.17	.16	4	0
1066	Roasted	1 drumstick	52	112	14	6	4	0	6	91	47	119	.7	1.5	52	.04	.11	3.1	.18	.17	4	0
	Thigh, meat and skin:																					
1067	Flour-fried	1 thigh	62	162	17	9	6	2	8	116	55	147	.9	1.6	61	.06	.15	4.3	.21	.19	5	0
1068	Roasted	1 thigh	62	153	16	10	6	0	8	108	52	137	.8	1.5	102	.04	.13	4.0	.19	.18	4	0
1070	Thigh meat only, roasted	1 thigh	52	109	14	6	3	0	6	95	46	124	.7	1.3	34	.04	.12	3.4	.18	.16	4	0

71	Wing (meat and skin), roasted	3 wings	102	297	27	20	12	0	15	153	84	186	1.3	1.9	162	.04	.13	6.8	.42	.30	3	0
76	Liver, simmered	7 livers	140	219	34	8	3	1	20	437	71	196	11.9	6.1	22890	.21	2.45	6.2	.82	27.1	1077	22
1075	Canned, boned with broth	5 oz	142	235	31	11	7	0	20	158	714	196	2.2	2.1	170	.02	.18	9.0	.50	.42	4	3
	Chicken a la king:																					
1456	Recipe	1 cup	245	470	27	34	20	12	127	358	760	404	2.5	1.8	1130	.10	.42	5.4	.23	.31	11	12
1457	Frozen entree	1 cup	224	255	25	14	8	8	46	182	895	307	1.2	.9	680	.16	.16	5.5	.16	.02	7	0
	Chicken and noodles:																					
1466	Recipe	1 cup	240	365	22	18	11	26	26	247	600	211	2.4	2.1	430	.05	.17	4.3	.16	.53	9	1
1467	Frozen entree	¾ cup	195	217	15	9	6	17	108	123	728	147	2.7	1.9	338	.07	.13	3.2	.10	.41	6	1
1468	Chicken chow mein, recipe	1 cup	250	231	23	11	7	10	58	293	718	473	2.5	2.1	280	.08	.23	4.3	.41	.22	19	10
1455	Chicken curry, recipe	1½ cups	337	305	26	18	13	8	30	223	970	410	2.0	1.8	517	.11	.23	10.2	.35	.48	5	.1
1367	Chicken pot pie from frozen	1 pot pie	230	430	15	23	16	41	30	177	907	16	3.1	1.2	1135	.17	.17	3.9	.46	.23	29	1
1266	Chicken salad with celery	½ cup	78	266	11	25	19	1	16	80	199	137	.7	.8	115	.03	.08	3.3	.17	.12	4	1
—	Chili: *see* Soups																					
—	Chili sauce:																					
530	Hot red-pepper base	2 T	31	6	.3	.2	.1	3	3	5	3	46	.2	.1	2940	tr	.03	.2	.04	0	3	9
531	Mild, tomato-based	1 cup	273	284	7	1	.4	68	55	142	3653	1010	2.2	.7	3820	.25	.19	4.4	.33	0	20	44
—	Chocolate: *see also* Candy																					
576	Baking chocolate	1 oz	28	145	4	15	5	7	22	109	1	235	1.9	1.0	10	.02	.10	.4	.01	0	18	0
—	Chocolate beverage powders:																					
580	Contains dry milk and is prepared with water	1 oz	28.4	100	4	1	.4	23	89	88	139	223	.3	.5	3	.03	.17	.2	.04	.44	3	1
581	Contains chocolate flavor and is prepared with milk	¾ oz	21.6	75	1	1	.2	20	8	28	45	128	.7	.3	4	.01	.03	.1	tr	0	4	.2
—	Chocolate topping:																					
579	Fudge topping	1 cup	300	1020	14	40	15	153	300	490	336	645	4.3	3.1	320	.16	.66	.6	.03	0	23	0
578	Thin syrup	1 cup	300	680	10	4	2	176	45	390	248	680	6.0	3.2	60	.06	.15	.9	.03	0	24	0
—	Clams:																					
127	Steamed, meat only	3½ oz	100	148	26	2	1	5	92	338	111	628	28	2.7	105	.01	.4	3	.10	99	4	4
128	Canned, drained	3 oz	85	125	22	2	1	4	79	287	95	534	24	2.0	90	.01	.4	3	.07	84	4	3
1104	Minced, canned with liquid	½ cup	100	79	14	1	.4	3	55	179	160	333	15	1.2	22	.01	.2	2	.04	54	2.3	2
582	Cocoa powder	1 cup	86	224	15	16	7	42	124	618	17	1000	11.7	6.5	68	.07	.46	1.8	.06	0	33	0
—	Cod:																					
129	Baked with butter	3½ oz	100	132	23	3	2	0	20	140	224	245	.5	.6	90	.09	.08	3.0	.28	1	10	0
130	Batter-fried	3½ oz	100	199	20	10	6	8	80	200	100	370	.5	.5	77	.04	.04	2.2	.24	.9	9	.01
131	Poached	3½ oz	100	102	22	1	.4	0	14	138	78	244	.5	.6	46	.09	.08	2.5	.28	1	11	.1
1109	Smoked	3½ oz	100	79	18	1	.3	0	14	190	1170	390	.4	.4	0	.08	.07	1.4	.27	1.70	5	.01
—	Collards:																					
226	Fresh/raw	1 cup	36	11	1	.1	.1	3	10	4	7	61	.1	.1	1200	.01	.02	.1	.02	0	40	8
227	Cooked from fresh	1 cup	128	35	2	.2	.2	8	29	10	21	168	.2	.1	3491	.03	.07	.4	.07	0	55	16
228	Cooked from frozen	1 cup	170	63	3	1	1	14	54	19	37	307	.4	.3	6378	.05	.1	.7	.12	0	129	28
1267	Coleslaw, recipe	1 cup	120	84	1	3	3	15	54	38	28	218	.7	.2	762	.08	.07	.3	.18	.03	32	39
—	Cookies:																					
754	Butter cookies	5 cookies	25	115	2	4	1	18	32	24	105	15	.2	.1	165	.01	.02	.1	.02	.01	2	0
	Brownies:																					
744	With nuts, recipe	1 brownie	20	95	1	6	4	11	9	26	51	35	.4	.3	20	.05	.05	.3	.04	.04	4	.01
746	With icing, frozen	1 brownie	25	103	1	8	4	15	10	31	49	44	.4	.3	50	.03	.03	.2	.01	.05	2	.01
745	With nuts and frosting, commercial	1 brownie	25	100	1	4	3	16	13	26	59	50	.6	.4	70	.08	.07	.3	.04	.05	5	.01
	Chocolate chip:																					
749	Recipe	4 cookies	40	185	2	11	6	26	13	34	82	82	1.0	.2	16	.06	.06	.6	.03	.04	4	0
747	Commercial	4 cookies	42	180	2	9	6	28	16	41	140	56	.8	.3	50	.10	.23	.9	.02	.02	4	tr
748	Home recipe, with nuts, small	1 cookie	16	108	1	10	8	12	9	25	85	46	.6	.2	126	.03	.03	.3	.03	.02	4	.04
758	Ladyfingers	4 cookies	44	158	3	3	2	28	18	72	50	52	.8	.6	250	.03	.06	.1	.05	.53	20	0
752	Oatmeal-raisin	4 cookies	52	245	3	10	7	36	18	58	148	90	1.1	.5	40	.09	.08	1.0	.03	.03	6	0
761	Peanut butter, recipe	4 cookies	48	245	4	14	9	28	21	60	142	110	1.1	.4	20	.07	.07	1.9	.04	.02	12	0
753	Sugar cookies from refrigerated dough	4 cookies	48	235	2	12	9	31	50	91	261	33	.9	.2	40	.09	.06	1.1	.02	.02	4	0
755	Sandwich-type cookies, assorted	4 cookies	40	195	2	8	6	29	12	40	189	66	1.4	.2	0	.09	.07	.8	.01	.02	1	0
759	Sandwich cookie, peanut butter filling	4 cookies	49	232	5	9	5	33	21	57	85	86	.4	.2	100	.03	.04	1.4	.02	.02	3	0
1265	Snickerdoodles	1 cookie	20	110	1	5	2	16	12	11	93	18	.6	.1	176	.04	.05	.5	.01	.01	2	.2
756	Shortbread, commercial	4 cookies	32	155	2	8	4	20	13	39	123	38	.8	.2	30	.10	.09	.9	.01	0	3	0

Item No.	Food*	Approximate Measure	Weight (g)	Food Energy (kcal)	Protein (g)	Total Fat (g)	Unsat Fat† (g)	Carbohydrate (g)	Calcium (mg)	Phosphorous (mg)	Sodium (mg)	Potassium (mg)	Iron (mg)	Zinc (mg)	Vitamin A (IU)	Thiamin (mg)	Riboflavin (mg)	Niacin (mg)	Vitamin B_6 (mg)	Vitamin B_{12} (μ)	Folacin (μ)	Vitamin C (mg)
757	Vanilla wafers	10 wafers	40	185	2	7	5	29	16	36	150	50	.8	.1	50	.07	.10	1.0	.01	.02	4	0
——	Corn:																					
230	Cooked on cob, from raw (5- by 1¾-in. ear)	1 ear	77	83	3	1	1	19	2	79	13	192	.5	.4	167	.17	.06	1.2	.18	0	36	5
231	Cooked from frozen	½ cup	82	67	2	tr	tr	17	2	39	4	114	.2	.3	204	.06	.06	1.1	.18	0	19	2
	Canned:																					
234	Cream-style	½ cup	128	93	2	1	.4	23	4	65	365	172	.5	.7	124	.03	.07	1.2	.08	0	57	6
233	Kernels, vacuum pack	1 cup	210	166	5	1	1	41	11	134	572	390	.9	1.0	510	.09	.15	2.5	.12	0	104	17
232	Kernels, regular pack, drained	½ cup	82	66	2	1	1	15	4	65	190	126	.4	.4	128	.03	.04	.7	.04	0	30	3
923	Kernels, regular pack, with liquid	½ cup	128	79	2	1	.4	19	5	65	324	196	.4	.5	153	.03	.08	1.2	.26	0	49	9
710	Corn Chips: *see also* Tortilla chips	1 oz	28	155	2	9	7	16	35	52	233	52	.5	.4	110	.04	.05	.4	.04	0	3	1
815	Corn dog	1 corn dog	111	330	10	20	11	27	34	303	1252	164	1.9	1.4	1	.28	.17	3.3	.11	.58	2	3
	Corn grits and cornmeal: *see* Cereals																					
574	Cornstarch	1 T	8	20	.01	tr	.01	5	.12	.7	.5	.2	.1	tr	0	0	0	0	0	0	0	0
——	Corn syrup:																					
1405	Dark	1 cup	328	944	0	0	0	246	151	52	223	16	3.3	0	0	0	0	0	0	0	16	0
546	Light	1 cup	328	912	0	0	0	246	146	39	148	54	.3	0	0	0	0	0	0	0	12	0
——	Crab:																					
133	Dungeness, cooked from fresh	¾ cup	101	85	18	2	2	.5	46	184	299	359	.4	4.3	50	.04	.2	3.0	.33	10.0	20	2
134	Canned	1 cup	135	133	28	2	1	0	137	351	450	505	1.1	5.4	50	.11	.11	2	.41	.6	22	0
——	Crackers:																					
697	Armenian cracker bread: Ak-Mak, 4¼ by 1¾ in., thin	4 piece	28	117	5	2	2	19	21	1	—	77	.5	.9	14	.06	.04	1.1	.03	0	12	2
699	Cheese crackers with peanut-butter filling	4 crackers	30	150	4	8	4	19	26	94	338	64	1.2	.1	10	.16	.12	2.4	.03	0	—	0
698	Cheese crackers, 1-in square	10 crackers	10	50	1	3	2	5	11	17	112	17	.4	.1	20	.05	.04	.4	.01	0	—	0
700	Graham crackers	2 crackers	14	60	1	1	1	11	6	20	86	36	.4	.1	0	.02	.03	.6	.01	0	2	0
763	Graham cracker crumbs	1 cup	120	514	9	13	9	93	51	171	737	309	3.2	1.0	0	.17	.26	5.1	.09	0	15	0
701	Round crackers (e.g., Ritz)	3 crackers	9	45	1	2	2	6	13	23	73	11	.2	.1	0	.03	.03	.4	tr	0	1	0
702	Rye wafers, whole grain	2 wafers	14	55	1	1	.7	10	7	44	115	65	.5	1.6	0	.06	.03	.5	.03	0	10	0
703	Saltines	4 crackers	12	50	.4	1	1	9	3	12	155	17	.5	.1	0	.06	.05	.6	.01	0	2	0
704	Sesame crackers	4 crackers	12	60	1	3	2	7	20	14	108	17	.4	.1	4	.06	.04	.3	—	0	5	0
705	Soda crackers	6 crackers	17	75	2	2	2	12	4	15	187	20	.3	.1	0	tr	.01	.2	—	0	2	0
706	Triscuits	2 crackers	9	42	1	2	1	6	3	26	50	25	.2	.2	0	.2	.01	.4	—	0	—	0
707	Wheat crackers, thin	4 crackers	8	35	1	1	1	5	3	15	69	17	.3	.2	0	.04	.03	.4	.01	0	3	0
708	Whole-wheat crackers	2 crackers	8	35	1	2	1	5	3	22	59	31	.2	.2	0	.02	.03	.4	.01	0	3	0
342	Cranberries, raw, whole	1 cup	95	46	.4	.2	.2	12	7	8	1	67	.2	.1	44	.03	.02	.1	.06	0	2	13
344	Cranberry juice cocktail	1 cup	253	145	.1	.1	.1	36	8	5	5	45	.4	.2	10	.02	.02	.1	.05	0	.5	90
343	Cranberry sauce, canned, strained	1 cup	277	419	1	.4	.4	108	11	17	80	72	.6	.1	55	.04	.06	.3	.05	0	3	6
——	Cream, imitation products:																					
	Coffee whitener/creamer:																					
29	Frozen, liquid	1 T	15	20	.2	2	.02	2	1	10	12	29	.01	tr	13	0	0	0	0	0	0	0
28	Powdered	1 T	6	32	.3	2	.06	3	1	25	12	48	.1	.03	12	0	.01	0	0	0	0	0
	Dessert topping, nondairy:																					
30	Frozen, semisolid, nondairy	1 T	5	15	.1	1	.1	1	.3	.4	1	1	.01	tr	40	0	0	0	0	0	0	0
31	Mix, prepared with whole milk	1 T	5	9	.2	.6	.1	1	5	4	3	8	tr	.01	18	tr	.01	tr	tr	.01	2	.03
891	Pressurized	1 T	4	12	.04	1	.1	1	.3	.8	2.7	.8	tr	tr	330	0	0	0	0	0	0	0
——	Cream, sweet:																					
22	Half-and-half (cream and milk)	1 T	15	20	.5	2	1	1	16	14	6	20	.01	.1	66	.01	.02	.01	.01	.05	.4	.1
23	Light, coffee or table	1 T	15	29	.4	3	1	1	14	12	6	18	.01	.04	108	.01	.02	.01	.01	.03	.3	.1
	Whipped cream:																					
886	Whipped topping, pressurized	1 T	4	10	.1	1	.3	.5	4	3	5	6	tr	.01	34	tr	tr	tr	tr	.01	.1	0
25	Whipping cream, whipped	1 T	7	26	tr	3	1	tr	5	5	3	6	tr	tr	109	tr	.01	tr	tr	.01	tr	tr
	Whipping cream, liquid (volume about double when whipped):																					

24	Heavy	1 T	15	51	.3	6	2	.4	10	9	6	11	tr	.03	219	tr	.02	.01	tr	.03	1	.1
888	Light	1 T	15	44	.3	5	1	.4	10	9	5	14	tr	.04	168	tr	.02	.01	tr	.03	1	.1
	Cream, sour:																					
26	Cultured	1 T	14	31	.5	3	1	1	17	12	8	21	.01	.04	114	.01	.02	.01	tr	.04	2	.1
1406	Half-and-half	1 T	15	20	tr	2	1	1	16	14	6	19	.01	.1	68	.01	.02	.01	tr	.05	2	.1
27	Imitation, nondairy	1 T	14	30	.4	3	.1	1	.4	6	15	23	.1	.2	0	0	0	0	0	0	0	0
696	Crepe, without filling	1 crepe	26.8	47	2	1	1	7	24	36	115	34	.4	.2	52	.04	.07	.4	.02	.14	5	.1
668	Croissant, 4½ by 4 by 2 in.	1 croissant	57	235	5	12	8	27	20	64	452	68	2.1	.3	50	.17	.13	1.3	.03	.04	18	0
669	Croutons, dry	1 cup	30	111	4	1	1	22	37	57	399	52	1.1	.2	1	.11	.11	1.4	.01	0	3	tr
236	Cucumber slices, with peel	7 slices	28	4	.2	.04	.02	1	4	5	1	42	.1	.1	13	.01	.01	.1	.02	0	4	1
1387	Currants, dried, Zante	1 cup	144	407	6	.4	.3	107	124	180	11	1285	4.7	.9	104	.23	.20	2.3	.43	0	15	7
345	Dates, chopped	1 cup	178	489	4	1	tr	131	58	70	5	1161	2.1	.5	89	.16	.18	3.9	.34	0	29	0
—	Desserts (*see also* Cakes, Candy, Cookies, Pies, and individual fruits):																					
1445	Cherry and cream-cheese torte	1 serving	161	451	7	23	4	57	162	174	337	298	1.5	.9	824	.08	.30	1.1	.07	.30	15	4
1348	Chocolate mousse	¾ cup	178	345	8	30	11	14	152	182	107	253	1.2	1.0	1006	.08	.30	.2	.09	.90	30	1
1232	Chocolate éclair with custard filling	1 éclair	94	262	4	15	6	30	62	92	101	90	.9	.5	582	.06	.14	.3	.04	.43	14	.4
1233	Cream puff with custard filling	1 cream puff	110	280	5	18	7	27	64	104	122	85	1.1	.6	733	.06	.16	.4	.05	.53	18	.2
619	Custard, baked	1 cup	265	305	14	15	6	29	297	310	209	387	1.1	1.5	530	.11	.50	.3	.13	.09	24	1
1228	Danish pastry, plain, round	1 pastry	57	220	4	12	7	26	60	58	218	53	1.1	.5	60	.16	.17	1.4	.02	.18	14	.01
	Doughnuts:																					
1229	Cake type (3¼-in. diam)	1 doughnut	50	210	2	12	8	25	23	111	192	58	.8	.3	20	.12	.12	1.1	.02	0	4	tr
1231	Jelly-filled	1 doughnut	65	226	3	9	4	30	28	42	40	30	.8	.2	121	.12	.10	.9	.30	0	6	.2
1230	Yeast-leavened, glazed (3¾-in. diam)	1 doughnut	60	235	4	13	6	26	17	55	222	64	1.4	.3	1	.28	.12	1.8	.28	0	13	0
—	Duck, domestic, roasted:																					
1080	Meat and skin (½ duck)	2.7 cups	382	1287	73	108	63	0	43	595	227	780	10.3	7.1	804	.67	1.03	18.4	.70	1.13	25	0
1079	Meat only (½ duck)	1.6 cups	221	445	52	25	11	0	26	449	143	557	6.0	5.8	170	.57	1.04	11.3	.55	.88	22	0
237	Eggplant, cooked	1 cup	160	45	1	.4	.2	11	10	35	5	397	.6	.2	102	.12	.03	1.0	.14	0	23	2
—	Eggs:																					
	Raw:																					
44	Large, whole	1 egg	50	75	6	5	2	1	25	89	61	60	.7	.6	322	.03	.3	.04	.07	.5	25	0
45	White only	1 white	33	17	4	0	0	.3	2	4	55	48	.01	0	0	tr	.2	.03	tr	.07	1	0
46	Yolk only	1 yolk	17	59	3	5	3	.3	23	81	7	16	.7	.6	323	.03	.11	.01	.07	.5	24	0
47	Fried egg in margarine	1 egg	46	91	6	7	4	.6	25	89	162	61	.7	6	394	.03	.2	.04	.07	.4	18	0
	Hard-cooked:																					
48	Entire egg	1 egg	50	77	6	5	3	1	25	86	62	63	.6	.6	280	.03	.3	.03	.06	.6	22	0
904	Chopped	1 cup	136	210	17	14	8	2	68	233	169	172	2	1	762	.10	.7	.1	.16	1.5	60	0
49	Scrambled, with milk and butter	1 egg	61	101	7	8	4	2	44	104	171	84	.7	.6	416	.03	.3	.1	.07	.5	18	.1
50	Poached	1 egg	50	74	6	5	3	1	25	89	61	60	.7	.6	316	.03	.2	.03	.06	.4	18	0
1268	Egg salad	1 cup	183	438	19	39	27	3	94	282	428	211	3.4	2.2	858	.12	.45	.2	.18	1.97	74	0
—	Enchilada:																					
1334	Beef	1 enchilada	120	292	13	14	7	16	255	159	157	193	1.8	2.3	549	.07	.16	2.1	.15	1.02	11	9
1335	Cheese	1 enchilada	120	330	13	18	8	16	457	260	311	135	1.4	1.5	872	.07	.21	.6	.09	.39	15	8
1336	Chicken	1 enchilada	120	269	14	11	6	16	256	170	160	176	1.5	1.2	563	.08	.15	3.2	.21	.25	12	9
1337	Enchirito	1 enchirito	207	441	23	22	11	24	376	303	463	449	3.0	4.0	868	.11	.27	3.1	.70	1.56	33	15
—	Fats:																					
508	Bacon fat	1 T	14	126	0	14	8	0	.02	.8	140	.01	0	.03	1	0	0	0	0	0	0	0
509	Beef fat/tallow, drippings	1 T	12.8	115	0	13	6	0	.13	2	.1	.1	.03	—	.1	0	0	0	0	0	0	0
510	Chicken	1 T	12.8	115	0	13	8	0	—	—	—	—	—	—	65	—	—	—	0	—	—	—
511	Lard (pork fat)	1 T	13	115	0	13	7	0	.01	.4	tr	tr	0	.14	0	0	0	0	0	0	0	0
512	Vegetable shortening	1 T	13	115	0	13	9	0	0	0	0	0	0	.01	0	0	0	0	0	0	0	0
—	Figs:																					
831	Fresh, medium	1 fig	50	37	.4	.2	.1	10	18	7	1	116	.2	.1	71	.03	.03	.2	.06	0	2	1
833	Dried	10 figs	187	477	6	2	2	122	269	128	21	1331	4.2	.9	250	.13	.17	1.3	.42	0	16	1
832	Canned in heavy syrup	3 figs	85	75	.3	.1	.1	20	23	9	1	85	.2	.1	31	.02	.03	.4	.05	0	1	1
	Fish: *see* Bass, Bluefish, Cod, Flounder, Haddock, Halibut, Herring, Perch, Pollock, Salmon, Sardines, Sea Trout, Shad, Snapper, Swordfish, Tuna, Trout, etc.																					

Item No.	Food*	Approximate Measure	Weight (g)	Food Energy (kcal)	Protein (g)	Total Fat (g)	Unsat Fat† (g)	Carbohydrate (g)	Calcium (mg)	Phosphorous (mg)	Sodium (mg)	Potassium (mg)	Iron (mg)	Zinc (mg)	Vitamin A (IU)	Thiamin (mg)	Riboflavin (mg)	Niacin (mg)	Vitamin B_6 (mg)	Vitamin B_{12} (µ)	Folacin (µ)	Vitamin C (mg)
135	Fish sticks, frozen, heated	2 sticks	57	155	9	7	4	14	11	103	332	149	.4	.38	60	.07	.10	1.2	.03	1	10	0
—	Fish cakes, fried:																					
1113	From frozen	3½ oz	100	213	9	12	9	16	70	110	500	260	1.0	.4	65	.06	.06	1.2	.05	1.00	8	.02
1112	From recipe	3½ oz	100	172	15	8	6	9	90	143	500	330	1.0	.5	65	.08	.08	1.2	.07	.69	8	.02
—	Flounder/sole:																					
1123	Steamed	3½ oz	100	93	19	1	1	0	16	246	89	292	.3	.6	35	.07	.11	2	.2	2.00	11	.01
1122	Batter-fried	3½ oz	100	214	16	11	7	14	93	170	228	230	.8	1.0	35	.20	.15	2.0	.15	1.00	6	.01
1121	Fried in crumbs	3½ oz	100	195	18	9	6	9	67	180	228	280	.6	.7	35	.23	.18	2.9	.36	1.00	17	.01
—	Flour:																					
	Buckwheat flour:																					
945	Dark	1 cup	98	338	12	3	2	71	32	298	1	490	2.5	2.7	0	.58	.16	2.8	.41	0	125	0
946	Light	1 cup	98	340	6	1	1	78	11	86	1	314	1.0	2.6	0	.09	.05	.5	.09	0	100	0
941	Corn flour	1 cup	117	422	8	5	3	90	8	318	6	369	3	2	549	.3	1	2	.4	0	29	0
456	Masa Harina enriched flour	1 cup	114	416	11	4	3	87	161	254	6	340	8	2	0	1.56	.87	11	.4	0	21	0
	Rye flour:																					
470	Dark	1 cup	128	415	18	3	2	88	72	809	1	934	8	7	0	.4	.32	6	.57	0	77	0
471	Light	1 cup	102	361	9	1	1	82	21	198	2	238	2	2	0	.3	.09	.8	.2	0	22	0
1014	Medium	1 cup	102	374	10	2	1	79	25	211	3	347	2	2	0	.34	.12	2	.27	0	38	0
	Soy flour:																					
484	Whole	1 cup	85	364	32	18	14	27	175	420	11	2138	5.4	3	102	.5	1	4	.4	0	293	0
948	Low fat	1 cup	88	326	45	6	5	30	165	522	16	2262	5.3	1	35	.3	.25	2	.5	0	361	0
	Wheat flour:																					
480	All-purpose, white, enriched, unbleached	1 cup	125	455	13	1	1	95	19	135	3	134	6	1	0	1	.62	7.4	.06	0	33	0
643	Cake, sifted, enriched	1 cup	96	348	8	1	.5	75	13	82	2	101	7	.6	0	.86	.4	6.5	.03	0	18	0
483	Self-rising, enriched	1 cup	125	442	12	1	1	93	423	744	1587	155	6	.8	0	.84	.52	7.3	.06	0	53	0
947	Semolina flour	1 cup	167	601	21	2	1	122	28	227	2	311	7	2	0	1.4	1	10	.17	0	120	0
482	Whole-wheat flour	1 cup	120	407	16	2	1	87	41	415	6	486	5	4	0	.5	.3	8	.41	0	53	0
—	Fruit cocktail, canned:																					
346	Heavy syrup	1 cup	255	185	1	.2	.1	48	16	28	15	224	.7	.2	522	.05	.05	1.0	.11	0	1	5
836	Juice pack	1 cup	248	115	1	.03	.02	29	20	34	10	235	.5	.2	760	.05	.04	1.0	.13	0	2	7
835	Light syrup	1 cup	252	145	1	.2	.1	38	16	28	15	225	.7	.2	524	.05	.05	1.0	.11	0	1	5
—	Mixed fruit:																					
840	Dried mixture	11 oz	293	712	7	1	1	188	110	226	52	2332	7.9	1.5	7155	.13	.46	5.7	.47	0	13	11
841	Frozen (measured thawed)	1 cup	250	245	4	.5	.1	61	18	30	8	327	.7	.1	806	.04	.09	1.0	.06	0	22	188
834	Fruit pie filling canned	1 can	595	565	2	.01	tr	149	107	53	178	470	3.0	.5	0	.02	.06	.6	.40	0	6	.02
1245	Gelatin salad or dessert, plain	½ cup	120	70	2	0	0	17	2	23	55	91	.1	.03	0	.01	.01	.2	tr	0	0	0
—	Gooseberries:																					
1399	Fresh	1 cup	150	67	1	1	1	15	38	40	1	297	.5	.2	435	.06	.05	.5	.12	0	8	42
1400	Canned, fruit and liquid	1 cup	252	185	2	.5	.3	47	40	17	6	194	.8	.3	348	.05	.13	.4	.03	0	8	25
—	Goose, domestic, roasted:																					
1082	Meat and skin	½ goose	774	2362	195	170	99	0	104	2091	543	2546	21.9	20	541	.60	2.50	32.3	2.89	3.81	17	0
1081	Meat only	½ goose	591	1406	171	75	35	0	84	1828	447	2291	17.0	19	238	.54	2.31	24.1	2.8	3.81	13	0
—	Grapefruit																					
	Fresh half (3¾-in. diam, 241g with refuse):																					
347	Pink/red	1 fruit	123	37	1	.12	.1	10	13	11	0	158	.1	.1	318	.04	.03	.2	.05	0	15	47
348	White	1 fruit	118	39	1	.12	.04	10	14	9	0	175	.1	.1	12	.04	.02	.3	.05	0	12	39
350	Canned sections	1 cup	254	152	1	.3	.1	39	36	25	4	328	1.0	.2	0	.10	.05	.6	.05	0	22	54
—	Grapefruit juice:																					
353	Prepared from frozen	1 cup	247	102	1	.3	.1	24	20	34	2	337	.3	.1	22	.10	.05	.5	.11	0	52	83
	Canned:																					
352	Unsweetened	1 cup	247	93	1	.2	.1	22	17	27	2	378	.5	.2	20	.10	.05	.6	.05	0	26	72
837	Sweetened	1 cup	250	115	1	.2	.1	28	20	28	5	405	.9	.2	20	.10	.06	.8	.05	0	26	67
—	Grape juice:																					
357	Prepared from frozen	1 cup	250	128	.5	.2	.1	32	10	11	5	53	.3	.1	19	.04	.07	.3	.11	0	4	60
356	Bottled/canned	1 cup	253	155	1	.2	.1	38	22	27	8	334	.6	.1	20	.07	.09	.7	.16	0	7	.2
—	Grapes, fresh:																					
354	Thompson seedless, European type, with skin	1 cup	160	114	1	1	.3	28	17	21	3	296	.4	.1	117	.15	.09	.5	.18	0	11	17
355	Slip skin, with seeds	1 cup	92	58	1	.3	.1	16	13	9	2	176	.3	.04	92	.09	.05	.3	.10	0	6	4

—	Gravy:																			
1177	Beef, homemade	½ cup	135	151	2	13	5	6	9	24	392	73	.5	.1	0	.05	.06	1.3	.01	.30	7	0
1176	Chicken, homemade	½ cup	130	163	3	14	10	6	6	43	388	112	.5	.2	70	.06	.07	2.1	.03	.12	2	—
1402	Guava, raw	1 fruit	90	45	1	1	.3	11	18	23	2	256	.3	.2	713	.05	.05	1.1	.13	0	13	165
—	Haddock:																					
139	Breaded, fried	3 oz	85	175	17	9	6	7	34	183	123	270	1.0	.6	60	.06	.10	2.9	.13	.79	14	0
141	Smoked/steamed	3½ oz	100	116	25	1	.5	0	49	251	763	415	1.4	.5	73	.05	.05	5.1	.4	1.6	.5	0
—	Halibut:																					
143	Broiled in butter and lemon juice	3 oz	85	140	23	6	2	0	51	242	100	490	.9	.4	610	.06	.07	6.1	.3	1.2	6	.01
1126	Smoked	3½ oz	100	224	21	15	12	0	48	222	480	450	.8	.4	150	.05	.07	5.8	.38	.9	5	.01
142	Steamed	3½ oz	100	131	22	3	2	0	60	285	69	576	1.1	.53	179	.07	.1	7.2	.4	1.4	11	.01
—	Ham, cured pork:																					
	Roasted (1 cup measure weighs just under 5 oz)																					
89	Lean and fat	1 cup	140	341	30	24	14	0	10	300	1661	400	1.2	3.3	0	.91	.31	6.2	.53	.90	4	0
90	Lean only	1 cup	140	219	35	8	4	0	10	318	1858	443	1.3	3.6	0	.95	.36	7.0	.66	.98	6	0
91	Unheated measure, lean ham	1 cup	140	206	31	8	5	.06	10	325	2122	519	1.1	2.9	0	1.30	.32	7.4	.74	1.21	11	0
	Canned:																					
92	Measured heated	1 cup	140	234	29	12	7	1	10	309	1495	491	1.5	3.3	0	1.34	.35	7.0	.56	1.16	7	32
1036	Measured unheated	1 cup	140	202	25	10	6	0	8	290	1787	468	1.3	2.6	0	1.23	.32	6.4	.64	1.12	8	35
1049	Chopped	1 piece	21	50	3	4	3	.06	1	29	287	60	.2	.4	0	.11	.04	.7	.07	.15	1	8
	Lunch meats:																					
1050	Ham and cheese loaf or roll	2 pieces	57	147	9	12	6	1	33	143	762	166	.5	1.1	170	.34	.11	2.0	.15	.46	3	14
104	Minced ham	1 piece	21	55	3	4	3	.4	2	33	261	65	.2	.4	0	.15	.04	.9	.06	.20	1	6
103	Sliced ham (1 oz piece = 6 by 4 by 1⁄16 in.; wafer-thin slice = about 9g)	1 piece	28	37	5	[illegible]	1	.3	2	62	405	99	.2	.6	0	.26	.06	1.4	.13	.21	2	7
1041	Patty, cooked	1 patty	60	203	8	18	11	1	5	60	632	145	1.0	1.1	0	.21	.11	1.9	.10	.42	2	0
—	Herring:																					
1131	Grilled	3½ oz	100	203	23	12	8	0	74	303	115	419	1.5	1.3	102	.1	.3	4.0	.4	13	5	.7
1129	Canned, with liquid	3½ oz	100	208	20	14	10	0	147	297	466	480	3.1	1.7	130	.03	.18	3.8	.16	8.50	5	.01
1130	Canned, with tomato sauce	3½ oz	100	173	16	11	8	4	150	296	370	420	2.7	1.6	95	.02	.20	3.8	.10	8.50	5	.02
144	Pickled	3½ oz	100	262	14	18	14	10	77	89	870	69	7.2	.53	861	.04	.14	2.8	.11	4.3	2	.1
145	Smoked, kippered	3½ oz	100	217	25	12	8	0	84	325	918	447	1.5	1.4	128	.13	.3	4.4	.41	19	14	1
1418	Hollandaise sauce, recipe	1 cup	160	867	12	91	64	2	138	366	1905	115	3.9	2.4	4083	.12	.25	.1	.17	2.20	60	4
547	Honey	1 T	21	65	.06	0	0	17	1	1	1	11	.11	.02	0	tr	.01	.1	tr	0	2	.2
532	Horseradish, prepared	1 T	15	6	.2	.03	.02	1	9	5	14	44	.1	.2	0	.01	tr	.1	.01	0	2	1
1306	Hot-dog sandwich (frankfurter and bun)	1 sandwich	85	260	8	15	9	21	59	83	745	113	1.7	1.2	1	.29	.19	2.5	.07	.58	17	12
—	Ice cream, vanilla:																					
613	Regular, about 10% fat	1 cup	133	269	5	14	5	32	176	134	116	257	.1	1.4	543	.05	.33	.1	.06	.63	3	1
614	Rich, about 16% fat	1 cup	148	349	4	24	8	32	151	115	108	221	.1	1.2	897	.04	.28	.1	.05	.54	2	1
615	Soft serve, about 10% fat	1 cup	173	377	7	23	8	38	236	199	153	338	.4	2.0	794	.08	.45	.2	.10	1.00	9	1
—	Ice milk, vanilla:																					
616	Hardened, about 4% fat	1 cup	131	184	5	6	2	29	176	129	105	265	.2	.6	214	.08	.35	.1	.09	.88	3	1
617	Soft serve, about 3% fat	1 cup	175	223	8	5	2	38	274	202	163	412	.3	.9	175	.12	.54	.2	.13	1.36	5	1
1244	Ice slushy	1 cup	193	247	0	0	0	37	0	0	0	6	0	0	0	0	0	0	0	0	0	2
548	Jam or preserves	1 T	20	54	.12	.02	.01	14	4	2	2	18	.2	.01	2	tr	.01	.04	.01	0	2	.4
549	Jelly	1 T	18	49	.02	.02	.01	13	2	1	4	16	.1	0	2	tr	.01	.04	.01	0	2	1
240	Jerusalem artichoke, raw slices	1 cup	150	114	3	.02	.01	26	21	117	6	644	5.1	.1	30	.30	.09	2.0	.11	0	20	6
1016	Jicama	3½ oz	100	41	1.4	.2	.01	9	15	18	6	175	.6	.33	0	.04	.03	.3	.02	0	55	20
—	Kale, chopped:																					
928	Fresh	1 cup	67	33	2	.5	.3	7	90	38	29	299	1.1	.3	5963	.07	.09	.7	.18	0	20	80
238	Cooked from fresh	1 cup	130	42	3	1	.3	7	94	36	30	296	1.2	.3	9620	.07	.09	.7	.18	0	30	53
239	Cooked from frozen	1 cup	130	39	4	1	.4	7	179	36	20	417	1.2	.2	8260	.06	.15	.9	.11	0	31	33
358	Kiwifruit, medium	1 fruit	76	46	1	.34	.3	11	20	30	4	252	.3	.1	130	.02	.04	.4	.05	0	17	75
—	Kohlrabi:																					
241	Raw slices	1 cup	140	38	2	.14	.1	9	34	64	28	490	.6	.3	50	.07	.03	.6	.21	0	14	87
242	Cooked slices	1 cup	165	48	3	.2	.1	11	41	74	34	561	.7	.3	58	.07	.03	.6	.14	0	13	89
—	Lamb, cooked:																					
	Lamb chop:																					
77	Lean and fat	1 chop	80	235	22	16	7	0	16	162	62	272	1.4	3.7	10	.09	.21	5.5	.12	1.24	2	0
78	Lean only	1 chop	64	140	19	6	3	0	12	145	54	241	1.3	3.0	4	.08	.18	4.4	.14	1.16	2	0

Item No.	Food*	Approximate Measure	Weight (g)	Food Energy (kcal)	Protein (g)	Total Fat (g)	Unsat Fat† (g)	Carbohydrate (g)	Calcium (mg)	Phosphorous (mg)	Sodium (mg)	Potassium (mg)	Iron (mg)	Zinc (mg)	Vitamin A (IU)	Thiamin (mg)	Riboflavin (mg)	Niacin (mg)	Vitamin B_6 (mg)	Vitamin B_{12} (μ)	Folacin (μ)	Vitamin C (mg)
	Leg of lamb, roasted:																					
79	Lean and fat	3 oz	85	205	22	13	6	0	8	162	57	273	1.7	3.8	6	.09	.25	5.5	.17	1.52	3	0
80	Lean only	3 oz	85	163	23	7	3	0	7	175	58	288	1.8	3.9	3	.09	.23	5.4	.19	1.62	3	0
1025	Cutlet, grilled	3 oz	85	189	24	9	5	0	8	204	64	323	1.9	3.6	1	.13	.26	5.1	.19	1.70	3	0
	Shoulder, roast:																					
1023	Lean and fat	3 oz	85	297	27	20	9	0	21	178	62	263	2.0	3.9	1	.05	.22	5.9	.14	1.48	3	0
1024	Lean only	3 oz	85	239	30	12	5	0	21	197	64	287	2.3	4.2	1	.05	.23	5.3	.19	1.48	3	0
——	Lasagna, vegetarian:																					
1356	From recipe	1 serving	218	316	20	14	5	30	457	345	760	424	2.4	1.9	1356	.21	.28	2.0	.22	.48	14	7
1368	Frozen entree	1 serving	205	275	17	12	5	19	246	253	967	437	2.5	1.3	974	.19	.33	2.7	.29	1.45	25	6
1505	Lasagna, with meat, recipe	1 serving	245	398	26	20	9	30	460	393	783	507	3.1	3.2	1122	.22	.33	3.6	.35	1.5	16	7
——	Leeks, chopped:																					
926	Raw	1 cup	104	63	2	.3	.2	15	61	36	21	187	2.2	.2	99	.06	.03	.4	.24	0	67	13
925	Cooked	½ cup	52	16	.4	.1	.1	4	16	9	5	45	.6	.1	24	.01	.01	.1	.08	0	16	2
——	Lemon juice:																					
361	Fresh	1 T	15	4	.06	0	0	1	1	1	.12	19	.01	.01	3	.01	tr	.02	.01	0	2	7
362	Bottled	1 T	15	5	.06	.04	.13	1	2	1	3	15	.02	.01	2	.01	tr	.03	.01	0	2	4
363	Frozen, single strength	1 T	15	3	.07	.05	.02	1	1	1	.15	14	.02	.01	3	.01	tr	.02	.01	0	1	5
360	Lemon peel	1 T	6	3	.1	.02	.01	1	8	1	0	10	.1	—	3	tr	.01	.02	.01	0	—	8
187	Lentils, cooked	1 cup	200	230	16	.7	.47	40	37	356	4	731	7	3	2	.3	.2	2.1	.35	0	358	3
——	Lettuce, chopped:																					
243	Butterhead	1 cup	56	7	1	.1	.1	1	19	13	3	144	.2	.1	543	.03	.03	.2	.03	0	41	5
244	Iceberg	1 cup	56	7	1	.1	.1	1	11	11	5	89	.3	.1	185	.03	.02	.1	.02	0	31	2
924	Escarole, curly endive	1 cup	50	9	1	.1	.1	2	26	14	11	157	.4	.4	1025	.04	.04	.2	.01	0	71	3
245	Loose leaf	1 cup	56	10	1	.17	.1	2	38	14	5	148	.8	.2	1064	.03	.05	.2	.03	0	60	10
246	Romaine	1 cup	56	9	1	.11	.1	1	20	25	4	162	.6	.2	1456	.06	.06	.3	.03	0	76	13
——	Lime juice:																					
367	Fresh	1 cup	246	65	1	.3	.1	22	22	18	2	268	.1	.2	25	.05	.03	.2	.11	0	21	72
368	Bottled	1 cup	246	50	1	1	.2	16	30	25	39	185	.6	.2	40	.08	.01	.4	.07	0	20	16
	Liver:																					
	see Beef, Chicken, Veal																					
——	Lobster:																					
146	Boiled	3½ oz	100	98	21	.6	.25	1.3	61	184	380	351	.39	2.9	87	.07	.07	1.1	.08	3.1	11	.01
147	Canned meat	3½ oz	100	95	19	.6	1	1.3	61	185	380	340	.4	2.9	82	.07	.06	1.1	.06	3.1	9	.01
——	Loganberries:																					
371	Fresh	⅔ cup	100	70	2	.3	.2	13	30	26	1	145	.6	.3	80	.05	.03	.8	.07	0	26	35
372	Frozen (measured frozen)	1 cup	147	80	2	.5	.2	19	38	38	1	213	.9	.5	52	.07	.05	1.2	.10	0	38	23
838	Lychees, canned	3½ oz	100	68	.4	0	0	18	4	12	2	75	.7	.2	0	.03	.03	.2	—	0	—	8
——	Macaroni, cooked:																					
694	Cooked firm	1 cup	130	190	7	1	.4	39	14	85	1	74	2	.9	0	.23	.13	1.8	.10	0	4	0
695	Cooked tender	1 cup	140	155	5	1	.3	32	15	90	1	80	1.8	.9	0	.20	.11	1.5	.09	0	4	0
——	Macaroni and cheese:																					
1458	From recipe	1 cup	200	430	17	22	11	40	362	322	1086	240	1.8	1.2	860	.20	.40	1.8	.05	.30	10	1
1459	Frozen entree	1 cup	200	254	11	12	5	26	181	238	460	294	1.0	1.2	801	.10	.36	1.0	.05	.29	12	2
1460	Canned	1 cup	240	230	9	10	4	26	199	182	730	139	1.0	1.2	260	.12	.24	1.0	.02	.20	8	.01
1269	Macaroni salad, no cheese	1 cup	141	371	3	33	27	18	27	50	315	162	1.1	.3	164	.10	.07	.7	.07	0	7	3
381	Mandarin oranges, canned, fruit and liquid	1 cup	252	155	1	.1	.04	41	18	25	15	197	.9	.1	1055	.13	.11	1.1	.17	0	20	50
373	Mango, fresh slices	1 cup	165	108	1	.5	.3	28	17	18	3	257	2.1	.3	6425	.10	.09	1.0	.22	0	31	46
——	Manicotti:																					
1452	With meat and tomato sauce, from recipe	1 serving	233	320	22	14	5	28	378	321	487	395	2.2	1.8	1055	.16	.36	.6	.11	.36	8	7
1453	Frozen entree, no meat	1 serving	225	271	15	11	4	27	274	264	795	347	2.2	2.0	956	.24	.39	2.7	.22	.54	28	4
552	Maple syrup	1 T	20	50	0	0	0	13	21	2	2	35	.2	.01	0	.03	.01	.02	—	0	—	0
——	Margarine:																					
	Regular (about 80% fat):																					
32	One stick (½ cup)	½ cup	113	812	1	91	69	1	34	26	1066	48	.1	.2	3740	.01	.04	.03	.01	.11	1	.2
32	One tablespoon	1 T	14	100	.13	11	9	.13	4	3	133	6	.01	.03	460	tr	.01	tr	tr	.01	.2	.02
32	One pat (about 1 t)	1 pat	5	25	.03	3	2	0	1	1	50	2	0	.01	167	0	tr	tr	0	tr	.04	.01
1506	Soft spread (about 60% fat)	1 T	14	75	.08	9	6	0	3	2	139	4	0	.02	463	.01	tr	tr	tr	.01	.12	.02
1507	Imitation (about 40% fat)	1 T	14.2	50	.07	6	4	.06	3	2	136	4	0	.03	470	tr	tr	tr	tr	.01	.1	.01

550	Marmalade	1 T	20	52	.1	0	0	14	7	2	4	7	.1	—	10	tr	tr	.02	tr	0	1	1.2
551	Marshmallows	4 marshmal-lows	28	90	1	0	0	23	1	2	25	2	.5	tr	0	0	tr	.01	tr	0	0	0
533	Mayonnaise	1 T	13.8	100	.2	11	9	.4	3	4	80	5	.1	.02	40	tr	.01	tr	tr	.04	.4	0
1450	Meat loaf (about 3-oz slice)	1 piece	87	193	16	12	6	4	29	123	340	227	1.9	3.5	136	.06	.19	3.2	.18	1.89	8	1
—	Melon:																					
374	Cantaloupe, cubes	1 cup	160	57	1	.5	.2	13	18	27	14	494	.3	.3	5158	.04	.03	.9	.18	0	48	68
375	Casaba, cubes	1 cup	170	45	2	.2	.1	11	9	12	20	357	.7	.1	51	.10	.03	.7	.10	0	40	27
376	Honeydew, cubes	1 cup	170	60	1	.2	.1	16	10	17	17	461	.1	.1	68	.13	.03	1.0	.10	0	51	42
839	Melon balls, mixed (measured frozen)	1 cup	173	55	1	.1	.2	14	17	22	53	484	.1	.3	3069	.03	.04	1.1	.18	0	45	11
—	Milk:																					
36	Skim	1 cup	245	86	8	.4	1	12	302	247	126	406	.1	.9	500	.09	.34	.2	.10	.93	14	2
35	1% low fat	1 cup	244	102	8	3	1	12	300	235	123	381	.1	1.0	500	.10	.41	.2	.11	.90	12	2
34	2% low fat	1 cup	244	121	8	5	2	12	297	232	122	377	.1	1.0	500	.10	.40	.2	.11	.89	12	2
33	Whole	1 cup	244	150	8	8	3	11	291	228	120	370	.1	.9	307	.09	.40	.2	.10	.87	12	2
37	Buttermilk	1 cup	245	99	8	2	1	12	285	219	257	371	.1	1.0	81	.08	.38	.1	.08	.54	12	2
38	Instant nonfat dry milk powder	1 cup	68	244	24	1	.2	36	837	670	373	1160	.2	3.1	1612	.28	1.19	.6	.24	2.72	34	4
	Canned:																					
40	Evaporated, skim	½ cup	128	99	10	.3	.1	15	369	248	147	423	.4	1.1	500	.06	.39	.2	.07	.31	11	2
39	Evaporated, whole	½ cup	126	169	9	10	3	13	329	255	133	382	.2	1.0	306	.06	.40	.2	.06	.21	9	2
41	Sweetened, condensed	1 cup	306	982	24	27	8	166	868	775	389	1136	.6	2.9	1004	.28	1.27	.6	.16	1.36	34	8
—	Milk beverages: *see also* Chocolate beverage powders																					
	Chocolate milk:																					
893	1% low fat	1 cup	250	160	8	3	1	26	287	256	152	425	.6	1.0	500	.10	.42	.3	.10	.86	12	2
892	2% low fat	1 cup	250	180	8	5	2	26	284	254	151	422	.6	.9	500	.09	.41	.3	.10	.85	12	2
894	Whole	1 cup	250	210	8	8	3	26	280	251	149	417	.6	1.0	302	.09	.41	.3	.10	.84	12	2
895	Cocoa, hot, prepared drink	1 cup	250	218	9	9	3	26	298	270	123	480	.8	1.2	318	.10	.44	.4	.11	.87	12	2
898	Instant breakfast powder	1 packet	37	130	7	0	0	23	10	15	166	0	7.9	3.0	1750	.30	.07	5.0	.40	.60	100	27
	Prepared instant breakfast:																					
901	With 1% milk	1 cup	281	232	15	3	1	35	310	250	289	381	8.0	4.0	2250	.40	.48	5.2	.51	1.50	112	29
900	With 2% milk	1 cup	281	251	15	5	2	35	307	247	289	377	8.0	4.0	2250	.40	.47	5.2	.51	1.49	112	29
899	With whole milk	1 cup	281	280	15	8	3	34	301	243	286	370	8.0	4.0	2057	.39	.46	5.2	.50	1.97	112	29
889	Eggnog, commercial	1 cup	254	342	10	19	7	34	330	278	138	420	.5	1.2	894	.09	.48	.3	.13	1.14	2	4
897	Goat's milk	1 cup	244	168	9	10	3	11	326	270	122	499	.1	.7	451	.12	.34	.7	.11	.16	2	3
896	Human milk	1 cup	246	171	3	11	5	17	79	34	42	126	.1	.4	593	.03	.09	.4	.03	.11	18	12
1215	Kefir	1 cup	233	122	9	5	1	9	350	319	50	205	.5	.9	465	.45	.44	.3	.09	.90	20	6
	Malted milk, powder only:																					
902	Natural-flavored powder	4 t	21	87	2	2	1	16	63	75	103	159	.2	.2	61	.11	.19	1.1	.09	.16	10	1
903	Chocolate-flavored powder	4 t	21	79	1	1	.3	18	13	37	53	130	.5	.2	19	.04	.04	.4	.03	.04	4	.3
944	Millet, cooked	½ cup	120	143	4	1	1	28	4	120	2.4	74	1	1.1	0	.13	.1	1.6	.13	0	23	0
1521	Miso	¼ cup	69	141	8	4	3	19	46	105	2507	113	1.9	2	60	.07	.17	.6	.15	.14	23	0
—	Molasses:																					
554	Blackstrap	1 T	20	43	0	0	0	11	137	17	19	586	5.1	0	0	.02	.04	.4	.06	0	3	0
553	Light	1 T	20	43	0	0	0	11	33	9	3	183	1.1	3	0	.01	.01	.01	.05	0	3	0
1415	Mornay sauce	½ cup	172	380	11	32	16	13	307	251	1022	233	1.1	1.3	1254	.10	.30	.5	.12	.84	20	2
1454	Moussaka, lamb and eggplant entree	1 cup	250	250	21	11	6	16	129	245	485	695	2.8	3.3	623	.25	.32	4.8	.35	1.42	44	7
—	Muffins:																					
671	Blueberry, recipe	1 muffin	45	135	3	5	3	20	54	46	198	47	.9	.3	40	.10	.11	.9	.01	.13	12	1
672	Bran, recipe	1 muffin	45	125	3	6	4	19	60	125	189	99	1.4	.4	230	.11	.13	1.3	.01	.13	9	3
	Cornmeal:																					
674	From mix	1 muffin	45	145	3	6	4	22	30	128	291	31	1.3	.3	90	.09	.09	.8	.04	.13	5	tr
673	From recipe	1 muffin	45	145	3	5	4	21	66	59	169	57	.9	.3	80	.11	.11	.9	.04	.13	5	tr
670	Plain, from recipe	1 muffin	45	133	3	5	3	19	50	60	176	50	.6	.2	45	.10	.12	.9	.01	.13	6	1.3
—	Mushrooms, sliced:																					
247	Fresh	½ cup	35	9	1	.15	.1	2	2	36	1	130	.4	.3	0	.04	.16	1.4	.03	0	7	1
248	Cooked from fresh	½ cup	78	21	2	.4	.2	4	5	68	2	278	1.4	.7	0	.06	.23	3.5	.07	0	14	3
249	Canned, drained	½ cup	78	19	1	.2	.1	4	9	52	332	101	.6	.6	0	.05	.17	1.3	.06	0	10	0
—	Mustard greens:																					
927	Fresh, chopped	1 cup	56	15	2	.1	.1	3	58	24	14	198	.8	.1	2968	.05	.06	.4	.10	0	105	39
250	Cooked from fresh	1 cup	140	21	3	.3	.2	3	104	57	22	283	1.6	.15	4244	.06	.09	.6	.14	0	102	35
251	Cooked from frozen	1 cup	150	29	3	.4	.2	5	152	36	38	209	1.7	.3	6705	.06	.08	.4	.16	0	104	21
534	Mustard, prepared	1 T	16	12	1	1	1	1	13	12	196	20	.3	.1	0	.01	.03	.2	.01	0	0	0

Item No.	Food*	Approximate Measure	Weight (g)	Food Energy (kcal)	Protein (g)	Total Fat (g)	Unsat Fat† (g)	Carbohydrate (g)	Calcium (mg)	Phosphorous (mg)	Sodium (mg)	Potassium (mg)	Iron (mg)	Zinc (mg)	Vitamin A (IU)	Thiamin (mg)	Riboflavin (mg)	Niacin (mg)	Vitamin B_6 (mg)	Vitamin B_{12} (µ)	Folacin (µ)	Vitamin C (mg)
377	Nectarine slices (1 fruit = about 1 cup of slices)	1 cup	138	68	1	1	1	16	6	22	0	292	.2	.1	1016	.02	.06	1.4	.04	0	5	7
——	Noodles:																					
693	Chow mein, dry	1 cup	45	237	4	14	11	26	14	72	197	54	2.1	.6	38	.26	.2	2.7	.05	0	10	0
692	Egg noodles, cooked	1 cup	160	213	8	2	1	40	19	110	11	45	2.5	1	32	.3	.13	2.4	.06	.14	11	0
——	Nuts:																					
	Almonds:																					
427	Dried, whole	1 cup	142	837	28	74	64	29	378	738	15	1034	5.2	4.2	0	.30	1	4.8	.16	0	83	1
428	Oil-roasted, unsalted	1 cup	157	970	32	91	78	25	367	859	16	1073	6.0	7.7	0	.20	1.55	5.5	.13	0	100	1
429	Slivered, packed measure	1 cup	135	795	27	71	61	28	359	702	15	988	4.9	3.9	0	.28	1.05	4.5	.15	0	79	1
430	Brazil nuts, dry (about 7)	1 oz	28.4	186	4	19	13	4	50	170	.4	170	1.0	1.3	.2	.28	.04	.5	.07	0	1	.2
	Cashews:																					
441	Dry-roasted, salted	1 cup	137	787	21	64	48	45	62	671	877	774	8.2	7.7	0	.27	.27	1.9	.35	0	95	0
1508	Oil-roasted, salted	1 cup	130	748	21	63	48	37	53	554	814	689	5.3	6.2	0	.55	.23	2.3	.33	0	88	0
	Coconut:																					
432	Raw, grated	1 cup	80	283	3	27	1	12	12	90	16	285	1.9	.9	0	.05	.02	.4	.04	0	21	3
433	Dried, unsweetened	1 cup	78	515	5	50	3	19	20	161	29	423	2.6	1.6	0	.05	.08	.5	.23	0	7	1
434	Shredded, sweetened	1 cup	93	466	3	33	2	44	14	100	244	313	1.8	1.7	0	.03	.02	.4	.29	0	9	1
435	Filberts (hazelnuts), chopped	1 cup	115	727	15	72	63	18	216	359	3	512	3.8	2.8	77	.6	.13	1.3	.70	0	83	1
436	Macadamia nuts, dried	1 cup	134	940	11	99	80	18	94	182	7	493	3.2	2.3	12	.47	.15	2.9	2.6	0	56	0
	Peanuts:																					
1522	Dried, unsalted	1 cup	146	827	38	72	58	24	85	559	23	1047	4.7	4.8	0	.97	.19	20.7	.43	0	153	0
438	Oil-roasted, salted	1 cup	144	837	38	71	58	27	126	744	624	982	2.6	9.6	0	.36	.16	21	.37	0	181	0
440	Pecans, dried, chopped	1 cup	119	794	9	81	70	22	43	346	1	466	2.5	6.5	152	1.01	.15	1.1	.22	0	47	2
856	Pine nuts/pignolia, dried	1 oz	28.4	146	7	14	12	4	7	144	1	170	2.6	1.2	9	.23	.05	1.0	.03	0	19	1
442	Pistachios, dried, shelled	1 cup	128	739	26	62	51	32	173	644	8	1399	8.7	1.7	299	1.05	.22	1.4	.32	0	74	0
443	Pumpkin kernels, dried, unsalted	1 cup	138	747	34	63	49	25	59	1620	25	1114	20.7	10.3	525	.29	.44	2.4	.31	0	79	tr
445	Sesame seed kernels, dried	1 cup	150	882	40	82	67	14	197	1164	59	611	11.7	14.8	100	1.1	.13	7.0	1.2	0	138	0
446	Sunflower seeds, dried, shelled	1 cup	144	821	33	71	61	27	167	1015	4	992	9.8	7.3	72	3.30	.36	6.5	1.83	0	339	.01
	Walnuts:																					
447	Black, chopped	1 cup	125	759	30	71	63	15	73	580	1	655	3.8	4.3	370	.27	.14	.9	.70	0	83	1
448	English, chopped	1 cup	120	770	17	74	64	22	113	380	12	602	2.9	3.3	148	.46	.18	1.3	.67	0	79	4
——	Oils, vegetable and nut:																					
514	Corn	1 T	14	125	0	14	12	0	0	0	0	0	0	.03	0	0	0	0	0	0	0	0
513	Olive	1 T	14	125	0	14	12	0	.02	.2	0	0	.1	.01	0	0	0	0	0	0	0	0
1172	Peanut	1 T	14	125	0	14	11	0	.01	0	0	0	tr	tr	0	0	0	0	0	0	0	0
515	Safflower	1 T	14	125	0	14	12	0	0	0	0	0	0	.03	0	0	0	0	0	0	0	0
1173	Sesame	1 T	14	120	0	14	11	0	0	—	—	—	0	.1	.06	0	0	0	0	0	—	0
517	Soybean	1 T	14	125	0	14	11	0	.01	.06	0	0	0	.03	0	0	0	0	0	0	0	0
1174	Soybean/cottonseed	1 T	14	120	0	14	11	0	0	0	0	0	0	.03	.06	0	0	0	0	0	0	0
516	Sunflower	1 T	14	125	0	14	12	0	.03	0	.01	0	0	0	0	0	0	0	0	0	0	0
——	Okra, cooked:																					
252	Cooked from fresh, pods	8 pods	85	27	2	.2	.1	6	54	48	4	274	.4	.5	489	.11	.05	.7	.16	0	39	14
253	Cooked from frozen, slices	½ cup	92	34	2	.3	.1	8	88	42	3	215	.6	.6	473	.09	.11	.7	.04	0	134	11
——	Olives, pitted:																					
539	Black, ripe, large	10 olives	45	52	.4	5	4	3	40	1.4	392	4	2	.1	181	tr	tr	.02	tr	0	.3	.4
538	Green	10 olives	39	45	.5	6	4	.5	24	6	936	21	.6	.03	120	tr	tr	.01	.01	0	.3	tr
——	Onions:																					
254	Raw, chopped	1 cup	160	61	2	.3	.1	14	32	53	5	251	.4	.3	0	.1	.03	.2	.19	0	30	10
256	Cooked from raw	½ cup	105	46	1	.2	.1	11	23	37	3	174	.3	.2	0	.04	.02	.2	.14	0	16	6
258	Onions, green, chopped	½ cup	50	16	1	.1	.1	4	36	19	8	138	.7	.2	193	.03	.04	.3	.03	0	32	9
713	Onion rings, frozen, heated	2 rings	20	81	1	5	3	8	6	16	75	26	.3	.1	45	.06	.03	.7	.02	0	3	.3
378	Orange, medium (2⅝-in. diam, 180g with peel)	1 orange	131	60	1	.2	.1	15	52	18	tr	237	.1	.1	270	.11	.05	.4	.08	0	40	70
380	Orange peel, grated	1 T	6	5	.1	.01	tr	2	10	1	0	13	.1	—	25	.01	.01	.1	.01	0	—	8
——	Orange juice:																					
382	Fresh	1 cup	248	111	2	.5	.2	26	27	42	2	496	.5	.1	500	.22	.07	1.0	.10	0	109	124
383	Prepared from frozen concentrate	1 cup	249	110	2	.1	.1	27	22	40	2	474	.3	.1	190	.20	.04	.5	.11	0	109	97
385	Canned, unsweetened	1 cup	249	105	1	.4	.2	25	20	35	5	436	1.1	.2	440	.15	.04	.4	.1	0	15	86

386	Prepared from dry crystals (e.g., Tang)	1 cup	248	114	.3	.5	.03	29	60	37	12	50	.2	.1	500	.20	.04	0	0	0	140	121
842	Orange grapefruit juice, canned	1 cup	247	105	1	.2	.1	25	20	35	7	390	1.1	.2	293	.14	.07	.8	.06	0	20	72
——	Oysters:																					
	Raw:																					
1139	Eastern	1 cup	248	170	18	6	3	10	111	344	277	568	62	226	740	.34	.4	3	.12	48	25	24
149	Western/Pacific	1 cup	248	200	23	6	3	12	20	402	262	417	13	41	740	.2	.6	5	.12	39.6	24	24
	Simmered:																					
1140	Eastern	3½ oz	100	137	14	5	2	8	89	278	224	458	13	182	564	.3	.3	2.5	.1	38	18	9
150	Western/Pacific:	3½ oz	100	135	18	2	1	7	16	322	210	334	10	33	268	.14	.5	4	.1	32	17	7
151	Fried, breaded, Eastern	1 oyster	45	89	4	6	4	5	28	72	188	110	3	39	150	.07	.10	.7	.03	7	6	4
——	Pancakes (4-in. diam):																					
686	Buckwheat, from mix	1 each	27	55	2	2	1	6	59	91	125	66	.4	.5	60	.04	.05	.2	.06	.05	6	tr
688	Plain, from mix	1 each	27	60	2	2	1	8	36	71	160	43	.7	.2	30	.09	.12	.8	.01	.05	3	tr
687	Plain, home recipe	1 each	27	60	2	2	1	9	27	38	115	33	.5	.2	30	.06	.07	.5	.02	.05	4	tr
743	Pancake syrup	¼ cup	84	244	0	0	0	64	2	8	38	14	.1	.1	0	0	0	0	0	0	.01	0
843	Papaya, whole	1 fruit	304	117	2	.4	.2	30	72	16	8	780	.3	.2	6122	.08	.10	1.0	.06	0	48	188
389	Papaya nectar, canned	1 cup	250	142	.4	.4	.2	36	24	1	14	78	.9	.4	277	.02	.01	.4	.02	0	5	8
——	Parsnips:																					
931	Raw slices	1 cup	133	100	2	.4	.2	24	47	94	13	499	.8	.8	0	.12	.07	.9	.12	0	89	23
932	Cooked slices	1 cup	156	125	2	1	.3	30	58	108	16	573	.9	.4	0	.13	.08	1.1	.15	0	91	20
1395	Passion fruit	1 fruit	18	18	.4	.1	.1	4	2	12	5	63	.3	—	126	—	.02	.3	—	0	—	5
——	Passion fruit juice:																					
1396	Purple	1 cup	247	126	1	.1	.1	34	9	31	7	343	.6	—	1771	—	.32	3.6	—	0	—	74
1397	Yellow	1 cup	247	149	2	.4	.2	36	9	61	15	687	.9	—	5953	—	.25	5.5	—	0	—	45
——	Peaches:																					
390	Fresh (2½-in. diam)	1 peach	87	37	1	.1	.1	10	4	10	0	171	.1	.1	470	.02	.04	.9	.02	0	3	6
	Canned (1 half = about 80g):																					
393	Heavy syrup	1 cup	256	190	1	.3	.2	51	8	29	16	235	.7	.2	849	.03	.06	1.6	.05	0	8	7
845	Juice pack	1 cup	248	109	2	.1	.1	29	15	43	11	317	.7	.3	940	.02	.04	1.4	.05	0	8	9
844	Light syrup	1 cup	251	136	1	.1	.1	37	9	27	13	244	.9	.2	888	.02	.06	1.5	.05	0	8	6
394	Dried halves	10 halves	130	311	5	1	1	80	37	155	9	1295	5.3	.7	2812	tr	.28	5.7	.09	0	6	6
395	Peach nectar, canned	1 cup	249	134	1	.1	.1	35	13	16	10	101	.5	.2	643	.01	.04	.7	.03	0	2	13
439	Peanut butter	1 T	16	95	4	8	6	3	5	52	75	116	.3	.4	0	.02	.02	2.1	.06	0	13	0
——	Pears:																					
396	Fresh, with skin, 180g with core	1 pear	166	98	1	1	.3	25	19	18	1	208	.4	.2	33	.03	.07	.2	.03	0	12	7
	Canned (1 half = about 77g):																					
398	Heavy syrup	1 cup	255	188	1	.3	.2	49	13	18	13	166	.6	.2	10	.03	.06	.6	.04	0	3	3
847	Juice pack	1 cup	248	123	1	.2	.1	32	22	29	10	238	.7	.2	14	.03	.03	.5	.04	0	5	4
846	Light syrup	1 cup	251	144	.5	.1	.03	38	13	17	13	165	.7	.2	0	.03	.04	.4	.04	0	3	2
400	Pear nectar, canned	1 cup	250	149	.3	.03	.02	39	11	7	8	33	.6	.2	1	.01	.03	.3	.03	0	2	3
——	Peas:																					
	Black-eyed peas:																					
933	Cooked from raw	1 cup	165	160	5	.6	.3	34	211	84	7	690	2	2	1305	.2	.2	2	.11	0	210	4
259	Cooked from frozen	1 cup	170	224	8	1	.4	47	290	117	9	860	3	2.4	900	.2	.3	3	.15	0	220	5
262	Cooked from dry	1 cup	171	198	13	1	.5	35	42	266	6	476	4	2	26	.3	.10	1.0	.17	0	356	1
260	Canned, with liquid	1 cup	240	184	11	1	1	33	48	167	718	413	2	2	32	.2	.2	.8	.11	0	123	7
	Edible pod peas:																					
267	Fresh/raw	1 cup	145	61	4	.3	.2	11	62	77	6	290	3.0	.6	300	.22	.12	.9	.23	0	44	87
268	Cooked from fresh	1 cup	160	67	5	.4	.2	11	67	89	6	383	3.2	.6	298	.21	.12	.9	.23	0	48	77
	Green peas:																					
263	Fresh, raw	1 cup	145	118	8	1	3	21	36	157	7	354	2.1	1.8	928	.39	.19	3.1	.25	0	95	58
264	Cooked from fresh	1 cup	160	134	9	.3	.2	25	44	187	4	434	2.5	1.9	1370	.41	.24	3.2	.25	0	101	23
265	Cooked from frozen	½ cup	80	63	4	.2	.12	11	19	72	70	134	1.3	.8	766	.23	.14	1.2	.09	0	47	8
	Canned:																					
266	Drained	½ cup	85	59	4	.3	.2	11	17	57	186	147	.8	.6	653	.10	.07	.6	.05	0	38	8
934	Solids and liquid	½ cup	124	61	4	.4	.2	11	22	66	340	108	.1	.9	470	.14	.09	1.0	.08	0	35	14
271	Peas and carrots, cooked from frozen	½ cup	80	38	2	.3	.2	8	18	39	55	127	.8	.4	6209	.18	.06	.9	.07	0	21	7
270	Dried peas, split, cooked	1 cup	196	230	16	1	.5	41	26	195	4	710	2.5	2	14	.37	.11	1.7	.09	0	127	.8
——	Peppers:																					
229	Hot green, canned	½ cup	68	17	1	.1	.04	4	5	12	700	127	.3	.12	415	.01	.03	.5	.1	0	7	46
	Sweet green:																					
272	Raw, chopped	½ cup	50	14	.5	.1	.2	3	5	10	1	89	.23	1	316	.03	.02	.3	.12	0	11	45
273	Cooked, chopped	½ cup	68	19	.6	.1	.1	5	6	12	1	113	.31	.1	403	.04	.02	.3	.16	0	10	51

Item No.	Food*	Approximate Measure	Weight (g)	Food Energy (kcal)	Protein (g)	Total Fat (g)	Unsat Fat† (g)	Carbohydrate (g)	Calcium (mg)	Phosphorous (mg)	Sodium (mg)	Potassium (mg)	Iron (mg)	Zinc (mg)	Vitamin A (IU)	Thiamin (mg)	Riboflavin (mg)	Niacin (mg)	Vitamin B_6 (mg)	Vitamin B_{12} (µ)	Folacin (µ)	Vitamin C (mg)
274	Sweet red (mature green), raw, chopped	½ cup	50	14	.5	.1	.2	.32	5	10	1	89	.23	.1	2850	.03	.02	.26	.12	0	11	95
1370	Pepper, green stuffed, entree	1 pepper	172	217	10	13	6	16	15	91	210	227	2.3	2.6	294	.11	.10	3.0	.22	1.16	14	83
153	Perch, ocean, breaded, fried	3 oz	85	185	16	11	7	7	92	191	138	241	1.2	.4	66	.10	.11	2.0	.22	.8	6	0
——	Persimmon, raw:																					
1388	Large, Japanese	1 fruit	168	118	1	.3	.2	31	13	28	3	270	.3	.2	3640	.05	.03	.2	—	0	13	13
1389	Small, native	1 fruit	25	33	.2	.1	.1	8	7	7	0	78	.6	—	—	—	—	—	—	0	2	17
——	Pickle:																					
540	Dill, whole (3¾ in. long by 1¼ in. diam)	1 pickle	65	12	.4	.12	.04	3	6	14	833	199	.4	.1	214	.01	.02	.04	.01	0	1	1
542	Sweet, small (about 2½ in. long by ¾ in. diam)	1 pickle	15	20	.1	.1	.04	5	3	2	107	30	.3	.01	10	0	tr	tr	tr	0	0	1
541	Fresh pack, 1½ in. diam by ¼ in. thick	4 pieces	30	20	.3	.1	.02	5	3	6	201	20	.2	0	42	tr	.01	tr	tr	0	0	2
543	Pickle relish	1 T	15	20	.1	.1	.04	5	3	2	107	30	.1	.01	20	0	tr	tr	0	0	0	1
——	Pie crusts:																					
762	Graham cracker crust, 9 in.	1 crust	325	1636	14	87	65	205	103	276	1910	502	4.8	1.7	2813	.26	.42	7.7	.14	.08	24	.1
	Regular, single shell:																					
767	From recipe	1 crust	180	900	11	60	42	79	25	90	1100	90	4.5	1.5	0	.54	.40	5.0	.17	0	32	0
771	From mix	1 crust	180	835	12	52	37	79	74	153	1462	101	5.2	.8	0	.60	.44	5.6	.15	0	32	0
	Regular, double crust:																					
768	From recipe	1 double crust	320	2005	20	107	74	141	49	191	2202	208	9.6	2.6	0	1.12	.74	10.9	.30	0	31	0
769	From mix	1 double crust	320	1485	21	93	66	141	131	272	2600	179	9.3	1.2	0	1.07	.79	9.9	.27	0	57	0
——	Pies (pieces are ⅙ of 9-in. pie)																					
1239	Apple	1 piece	158	405	4	18	13	60	28	50	476	100	1.7	.3	50	.18	.13	1.6	.08	tr	8	.3
1246	Banana cream, made from vanilla pudding, 2 bananas	1 piece	152	333	7	14	8	47	100	125	294	308	1.2	.9	385	.13	.26	1.2	.46	.60	22	1
1240	Blueberry	1 piece	158	380	4	17	12	55	26	46	423	126	2.1	.3	140	.17	.14	1.7	.07	tr	14	6
1241	Cherry	1 piece	158	410	4	18	13	61	37	58	480	153	3.2	.3	700	.19	.14	1.6	.08	tr	16	1
1250	Coconut custard	1 piece	165	384	10	22	9	36	146	195	430	289	1.8	1.2	350	.17	.32	1.1	.24	.76	25	1
1247	Custard	1 piece	152	293	8	13	9	34	124	147	333	173	1.4	.8	350	.14	.27	.9	.08	.62	15	.2
1248	Lemon meringue	1 piece	140	355	5	14	10	53	25	69	395	70	1.4	.5	240	.10	.14	.8	.05	.33	13	4
1249	Mincemeat	1 piece	160	395	4	12	8	73	39	70	330	349	2.0	.3	11	.16	.14	1.6	.15	0	9	3
1242	Peach	1 piece	158	405	4	18	13	61	27	55	423	235	1.9	.4	1150	.18	.16	2.3	.07	tr	12	5
1252	Pecan	1 piece	138	583	6	24	18	92	35	130	304	130	1.9	1.5	153	.22	.17	1.1	.08	.31	18	0
770	Pumpkin	1 piece	200	367	9	16	9	51	212	211	338	400	2.6	1.0	18237	.14	.29	1.2	.11	.32	20	1
1251	Strawberry chiffon, from recipe	1 piece	162	372	5	20	10	46	44	54	259	151	1.5	.3	470	.12	.13	1.3	.06	.05	21	31
1382	Pimento, canned	2 oz	57	13	.6	.2	.1	3	3	10	8	90	.9	.11	1513	.01	.03	.35	.12	0	3.4	48
——	Pineapple:																					
401	Fresh chunks	1 cup	155	76	1	1	.3	19	11	11	2	175	.6	.1	40	.14	.06	.7	.14	0	16	24
403	Frozen, sweetened	1 cup	245	208	1	.3	.1	54	22	10	5	245	1.0	.3	74	.25	.07	.7	.18	0	12	20
	Canned, chunks, tidbits, or crushed (one ring = about 58g):																					
402	Heavy syrup	1 cup	255	199	1	.3	.1	52	36	18	3	265	1.0	.3	37	.3	.06	.7	.19	0	12	19
849	Juice pack	1 cup	250	150	1	.2	.1	39	35	15	3	305	.7	.3	95	.24	.05	.7	.19	0	12	24
848	Light syrup	1 cup	252	131	1	.3	.1	34	36	17	3	266	1.0	.3	37	.23	.06	.7	.19	0	12	19
——	Pineapple juice:																					
404	Prepared from frozen concentrate	1 cup	250	129	1	.1	.03	32	28	20	3	340	.8	.3	25	.18	.05	.5	.19	0	64	30
405	Canned, unsweetened	1 cup	250	140	1	.2	.1	34	43	20	3	335	.7	.3	12	.14	.06	.6	.24	0	58	27
1369	Pizza, cheese (⅛ of 15-in. pie)	1 piece	120	290	15	9	4	39	220	216	699	230	1.6	1.8	750	.34	.29	4.2	.04	.48	40	2
——	Plantain:																					
1390	Raw slices	1 cup	148	181	2	1	.2	47	4	50	6	739	.9	.2	1668	.08	.08	1.0	.44	0	33	27
1391	Cooked slices	1 cup	154	179	1	.3	.1	48	3	43	8	716	.9	.2	1400	.07	.08	1.2	.37	0	40	17
——	Plums:																					
406	Raw, medium (2⅛-in. diam)	1 plum	66	36	1	.4	.4	9	3	7	.4	114	.1	.1	213	.03	.06	.3	.05	0	3	6
	Canned:																					
408	Heavy syrup	1 cup	258	230	1	.3	.2	60	23	34	49	235	2.2	.2	668	.04	.10	.8	.07	0	7	1
850	Juice pack	1 cup	252	146	1	.1	.1	38	25	38	3	388	.9	.3	2542	.06	.15	1.2	.10	0	8	7

851	Light syrup	1 cup	252	158	1	.3	.2	41	24	33	50	233	2.2	.2	666	.04	.10	.8	.07	0	6	1
1383	Poi	1 cup	240	269	1	.3	.2	65	37	94	28	439	2.1	.5	48	.31	.10	2.6	.7	0	51	10
	Pollock:																					
1146	Poached	3½ oz	100	128	23	1	.7	0	60	252	98	400	.5	.5	32	.04	.2	3	.3	3.1	12	0
154	Baked/Broiled	3½ oz	100	113	23	1	1	0	6	482	116	387	.28	.6	76	.07	.08	1.7	.07	4	4	tr
1393	Pomegranate juice, fresh	½ cup	125	55	.3	tr	—	15	4	10	1	250	.3	—	0	.03	.04	.3	—	0	—	10
1392	Pomegranate, raw (3½-in. diam)	1 fruit	154	104	1	.5	.2	26	5	12	5	399	.5	—	0	.05	.05	.5	.16	0	—	9
	Popcorn:																					
716	Cooked in oil, salted	1 cup	11	55	1	3	3	6	3	31	86	19	.3	.3	20	.01	.02	.1	.02	0	3	0
715	Plain, air-popped	1 cup	8	30	1	.4	.3	6	1	22	.5	20	.2	.2	10	.03	.01	.2	.02	0	3	0
717	Sugar syrup–coated	1 cup	35	135	2	1	1	30	2	47	.5	90	.5	.3	30	.13	.02	.4	.03	0	3	0
676	Popovers	1 each	51	96	4	4	1	12	42	58	101	69	.9	.4	140	.09	.12	.8	.03	.24	8	.2
1243	Popsicle (3 oz when fluid)	1 each	95	70	0	0	0	18	0	0	11	4	.01	0	0	0	0	0	0	0	0	0
	Pork:																					
	Roast, oven-roasted, average cut:																					
85	Lean and fat	3 oz	85	271	20	21	12	0	7	188	54	270	.9	2.2	7	.61	.27	4.6	.32	.74	4	.3
86	Lean only	3 oz	85	204	23	12	7	0	8	216	59	312	1.0	2.6	6	.68	.31	5.1	.38	.79	5	.3
	Chop, average cut:																					
83	Lean and fat	3 oz	88	304	22	23	13	0	4	188	62	317	.7	1.7	8	.90	.24	4.5	.35	.65	4	.3
84	Lean only	2.4 oz	70	172	21	9	6	0	3	177	56	303	.7	1.6	5	.83	.22	2.5	.34	.52	4	.3
	Shoulder roast, braised:																					
87	Lean and fat	3 oz	85	293	23	22	12	0	6	162	74	286	1.4	3.4	8	.46	.26	4.4	.23	.59	3	.3
88	Lean only	2.4 oz	67	166	22	8	5	0	5	151	68	271	1.3	3.3	5	.40	.24	4.0	.28	.48	3	0
1035	Spareribs, cooked (yield from 1 lb raw)	6¼ oz	177	703	51	54	31	0	83	462	165	566	3.3	8.1	18	.72	.68	9.7	.62	1.91	7	0
	Potato:																					
1805	Baked (4¾ by 2⅓-in. diam): With peel	1 each	202	220	5	.2	.1	51	20	115	16	844	2.8	.7	0	.22	.07	3.3	.70	0	22	26
275	Flesh only	1 each	156	145	3	2	.1	34	8	78	8	610	.6	.5	0	.16	.03	2.2	.47	0	14	20
	Boiled, flesh only (2½-in. diam):																					
276	Peeled after cooking	1 each	136	119	3	.1	.1	27	7	60	6	515	.4	.4	0	.14	.03	2.0	.41	0	14	18
277	Peeled before cooking	1 each	135	116	2	.1	.1	27	10	54	7	443	.4	.4	0	.13	.03	2	.36	0	12	10
	French fried, 2–3½ in. long:																					
255	Prepared from raw	10 strips	50	137	2	7	4	18	8	56	15	199	.7	.1	0	.07	.04	1.6	.09	0	11	11
281	Frozen, oven heated	10 strips	50	111	2	4	2	17	4	43	15	229	.7	.2	0	.06	.02	1.2	.12	0	8	6
282	Hash brown potatoes, prepared from frozen	1 cup	156	340	5	18	10	44	24	112	53	680	2.4	.5	0	.17	.03	3.8	.20	0	26	10
	Mashed potatoes:																					
278	Prepared from fresh, with milk	1 cup	210	162	4	1	.4	37	55	100	636	628	.6	.6	40	.19	.08	2.4	.49	.11	17	14
279	Prepared from instant	1 cup	220	239	5	13	.9	28	92	108	733	428	.4	.5	1741	.3	.1	2	.3	.2	15	23
935	Dried potato flakes, unprepared	1 cup	45	159	4	.2	.6	37	11	69	48	488	.5	.3	0	.5	.1	3	.2	0	18	38
714	Potato chips	14 chips	28.4	148	2	10	7	15	7	43	133	369	.3	.3	0	.04	.01	1.2	.14	0	13	12
1270	Potato salad, with mayonnaise and eggs	1 cup	250	358	7	21	16	28	48	130	1323	635	1.6	.8	523	.19	.15	2.2	.35	.39	17	25
1271	Potato salad, hot German-style	¾ cup	182	209	5	8	5	33	19	98	702	616	1.1	.7	6	.18	.08	2.6	.27	.11	25	25
1083	Poultry sandwich spread	1 T	13	25	2	2	1	1	1	4	49	24	.1	.1	18	tr	.01	.2	.01	.05	1	.2
155	Prawns, cooked	3½ oz	100	99	21	1	1	0	39	137	224	182	3	1.6	60	.03	.03	3.0	.13	2	4	0
	Pretzels:																					
719	Thin sticks, 2¼ in. long	10 each	3	10	.3	.1	.1	2	1	3	48	3	.1	.03	0	.01	.01	.1	tr	0	.5	0
718	Thin twists	10 each	60	240	6	2	1	48	16	55	966	61	1.2	.4	0	.19	.15	2.6	.01	0	10	0
1394	Prickly pear, raw	1 fruit	103	42	[illegible]	1	.3	10	58	25	6	226	.3	—	53	.01	.06	.5	—	0	—	14
	Prunes:																					
409	Dried (97g with pits)	10 each	84	201	2	.4	.4	53	43	66	3	626	2.1	.4	1669	.07	.14	1.7	.22	0	3	3
410	Cooked from dry (250g with pits)	1 cup	212	227	2	.5	.4	60	49	74	4	708	2.4	.5	649	.05	.21	1.5	.46	0	.1	6
411	Prune juice, bottled	1 cup	256	181	2	.1	.1	45	31	64	10	707	3.0	.5	9	.04	.18	2.0	.56	0	1	11
	Pudding:																					
	Chocolate:																					
623	Prepared from mix, cooked	1 cup	260	300	9	8	2	50	292	240	334	380	.4	1.2	280	.10	.39	.3	.13	.20	8	2
624	Instant, prepared	1 cup	260	310	8	8	3	54	260	658	880	352	.6	1.2	260	.08	.36	.2	.13	.20	10	2
1509	Canned	5 oz	142	205	3	11	1	30	74	117	285	254	1.2	.7	100	.04	.17	.6	.03	.07	3	tr
1510	Rice, prepared from mix	½ cup	132	155	4	4	1	27	133	110	140	165	.5	.6	140	.10	.18	.6	.05	.40	6	1
1511	Tapioca, prepared from mix	½ cup	130	145	4	4	1	25	131	103	152	167	.1	.5	140	.04	.18	.1	.05	.40	6	1

Item No.	Food*	Approximate Measure	Weight (g)	Food Energy (kcal)	Protein (g)	Total Fat (g)	Unsat Fat† (g)	Carbohydrate (g)	Calcium (mg)	Phosphorous (mg)	Sodium (mg)	Potassium (mg)	Iron (mg)	Zinc (mg)	Vitamin A (IU)	Thiamin (mg)	Riboflavin (mg)	Niacin (mg)	Vitamin B_6 (mg)	Vitamin B_{12} (μ)	Folacin (μ)	Vitamin C (mg)
	Vanilla:																					
1512	Prepared from mix, cooked	½ cup	130	145	4	4	1	25	132	102	178	166	.1	.5	140	.04	.18	.1	.05	.40	6	1
1513	Instant, prepared	½ cup	130	150	4	4	1	27	129	273	375	164	.1	.5	140	.04	.17	.1	.05	.40	6	1
1514	Canned	5 oz	142	220	2	10	.4	33	79	94	305	155	.2	.7	.3	.03	.12	.6	.03	.07	3	tr
283	Pumpkin, canned, usually a mixture of squash and pumpkin	½ cup	123	42	1	.4	.1	10	32	43	6	252	1.7	.2	27019	.03	.07	.5	.07	0	15	5
1357	Quiche Lorraine (¼ of 8-in. pie)	1 piece	242	496	22	33	18	27	460	418	811	332	2.4	2.6	667	.23	.54	2.1	.18	1.54	35	2
1090	Rabbit, cooked meat	3½ ounces	100	154	23	6	3	0	15	206	37	300	2	2	10	.07	.2	7	.4	7	9	0
284	Radishes, red	10 each	45	7	.3	.2	.03	2	9	8	11	104	.1	.1	3	tr	.02	.1	.03	0	12	10
412	Raisins, seedless (measured packed)	1 cup	165	494	5	1	.3	131	81	159	19	1239	3.5	.5	13	.26	.15	1.4	.41	0	7	6
——	Raspberries:																					
413	Fresh	1 cup	123	60	1	1	.5	14	27	15	0	187	.7	.6	160	.04	.11	1.1	.07	0	33	31
415	Frozen (measured thawed)	1 cup	250	255	2	.4	.3	65	38	43	3	285	1.6	.5	150	.05	.11	1.5	.09	0	65	41
414	Canned, with liquid	1 cup	256	234	2	.3	.2	60	27	23	9	241	1.1	.4	85	.05	.08	1.1	.11	0	27	22
416	Rhubarb, cooked with sugar	1 cup	240	279	1	.1	.1	75	348	19	2	230	.5	.2	166	.04	.06	.5	.05	0	13	8
——	Rice:																					
462	Brown, cooked	1 cup	195	217	5	2	1	45	20	162	10	84	.8	1.1	0	.19	.05	2.7	.29	0	8	0
466	White, converted parboiled	1 cup	175	200	4	.5	.3	43	33	74	5	65	2	.5	0	.4	.03	2.5	.03	0	7	0
464	White, regular, cooked	1 cup	205	264	6	.6	.3	57	23	96	4	80	2.3	.94	0	.33	.03	3	.2	0	6	0
468	White, instant, prepared	1 cup	165	162	3	.3	.2	35	13	23	5	7	1	.4	0	.12	.08	1.5	.02	0	7	0
469	Wild rice, cooked	½ cup	164	66	5	.6	.4	35	5	135	5	166	1	2.2	0	.09	.14	2.1	.22	0	43	0
——	Rolls:																					
	Dinner roll:																					
679	Homemade	1 roll	35	120	3	3	2	20	16	36	98	41	1.1	.3	30	.12	.12	1.2	.01	0	12	0
678	Commercial	1 roll	28	85	2	2	1	14	33	44	155	36	.8	.2	1	.14	.09	1.1	.01	0	11	tr
681	Hamburger bun	1 bun	45	129	4	2	2	23	61	50	271	63	1.3	.4	1	.22	.15	1.8	.02	0	17	tr
682	Hard roll, white	1 roll	50	155	5	2	1	30	24	46	313	49	1.4	.4	0	.20	.12	1.7	.02	0	17	0
680	Hot dog bun	1 bun	40	115	3	2	1	20	54	44	241	56	1.2	.4	1	.20	.13	1.6	.01	0	15	tr
1221	Submarine roll/hoagie roll	1 roll	135	400	11	8	5	72	100	115	683	128	3.8	1.2	0	.54	.33	4.5	.09	0	49	0
——	Rutabaga, cubed pieces:																					
937	Raw	1 cup	140	51	2	.3	.2	11	65	81	28	471	.7	.5	0	.13	.06	1.0	.14	0	29	35
938	Cooked	½ cup	85	29	1	.2	.1	7	36	42	15	244	.4	.3	0	.06	.03	.5	.08	0	13	19
——	Salad dressings:																					
518	Blue cheese	1 T	15	75	1	8	6	1	12	11	164	6	.03	.04	32	tr	.02	.02	.01	.04	3	.3
	French:																					
520	Regular	1 T	16	67	.1	9	5	3	2	1	188	2	.1	.01	30	tr	tr	tr	tr	.02	.7	0
519	Low calorie	1 T	16	22	.03	2	1	4	6	2	128	13	.07	.03	1	0	0	0	0	0	0	0
	Italian:																					
522	Regular	1 T	14.7	69	.1	9	6	1	1	1	116	5	.03	.02	35	tr	tr	0	tr	.02	.7	0
521	Low calorie	1 T	15	8	.02	1	.3	1	.3	1	120	2	.03	.02	0	0	0	0	0	0	0	0
	Mayonnaise-type salad dressing:																					
524	Regular	1 T	15	58	.13	5	4	4	2	4	105	1	.03	0	30	tr	tr	tr	tr	.03	.9	0
523	Low calorie	1 T	15	35	.04	3	2	2	3	4	75	1	.03	.02	34	tr	.01	0	—	0	0	—
1420	Ranch-style	1 T	14.9	54	.5	6	5	1	15	13	65	20	.04	.05	36	.01	.02	.01	.01	.04	1	.1
525	Russian	1 T	15.3	76	.2	8	6	2	3	6	133	24	.1	.1	106	.01	.01	.1	.01	0	.0	1
	Thousand Island:																					
527	Regular	1 T	16	60	.2	6	5	2	2	3	110	18	.1	.02	50	tr	tr	tr	tr	.03	1	.3
526	Low calorie	1 T	15	25	.1	2	.1	3	2	3	153	17	.1	.03	50	tr	tr	tr	tr	.03	1	.4
——	Salmon:																					
157	Baked or broiled	3 oz	85	183	23	9	7	0	6	234	56	319	.5	.4	178	.18	.15	5.7	.2	5.10	14	0
158	Canned, pink, with liquid	3 oz	85	118	17	5	3	0	182	280	471	278	.7	.8	60	.02	.15	6	.3	4	13	0
159	Smoked, Chinook	3 oz	85	99	16	4	3	0	9	139	666	149	.7	.3	75	.02	.09	4	.2	3	2	0
156	Steamed, Coho	3½ oz	100	185	27	8	5	0	29	300	59	534	.9	.5	320	.20	.11	7.8	.83	6.00	20	1
939	Salsify, slices, cooked	1 cup	135	92	4	.2	.1	21	64	75	21	381	.7	.4	0	.04	.23	.5	.3	0	21	6
——	Sardines, canned:																					
160	In mustard	3½ oz	100	208	24	12	9	2	382	490	505	397	3	1	224	.08	.2	5	.2	9	12	.01
1154	In oil, Atlantic sardines	3 oz	85	177	21	10	8	0	324	417	430	337	2.6	1	190	.07	.2	4.5	.14	8	10	0

1153	In oil, Pacific sardines	3½ oz	100	245	25	15	12	0	382	490	505	397	2.9	1.3	224	.03	.23	5.3	.17	9	12	0
1156	In tomato sauce	3½ oz	100	178	16	12	8	1	240	366	414	341	2.3	1.4	365	.04	.23	4.2	.12	9	24	1
285	Sauerkraut, canned with liquid	1 cup	236	44	2	.3	.2	10	72	46	1561	401	3.5	.4	42	.05	.05	.3	.31	0	56	35
	Sausages and lunch meats:																					
1046	Barbecue loaf, pork and beef (6 by 3¼ by 1⁄16 in.)	1 piece	23	40	4	2	1	1	13	30	307	76	.3	.6	0	.08	.06	.5	.06	.39	1	4
93	Beef, wafer-thin sliced lunch meat	1 ounce	28.4	50	8	1	.5	2	3	48	408	122	.76	1.1	0	.02	.05	1.5	.1	.73	1.2	4
	Beerwurst/beer salami (4-in. diam by ⅛ in.):																					
1043	Beef	1 piece	23	75	3	7	3	.4	2	24	214	42	.3	.6	0	.03	.03	.7	.05	.49	1	3
1039	Pork	1 piece	23	55	3	4	3	.5	2	24	285	58	.2	.4	0	.13	.04	.7	.08	.20	1	7
94	Berliner (2½-in. diam by ¼ in.)	1 piece	23	53	4	4	2	1	3	30	298	65	.3	.6	0	.09	.05	.7	.05	.61	1	2
	Bologna (23g slice = 4-in. diam by ⅛ in.):																					
95	Beef	1 piece	23	72	3	7	3	.5	3	19	230	36	.3	.5	0	.01	.03	.6	.04	.32	1	4
96	Beef and pork	1 piece	28.4	89	3	8	4	1	3	26	289	51	.4	.6	0	.05	.04	.7	.05	.38	1	6
1040	Pork	1 piece	23	57	4	5	3	.2	3	33	272	65	.2	.5	0	.12	.04	.9	.06	.21	1	8
97	Turkey (28g piece = 4½-in. diam)	1 piece	28.4	56	4	4	3	.3	23	37	248	56	.4	.5	0	.02	.05	1.0	.06	.08	2	tr
98	Braunschweiger	1 piece	18	65	2	6	3	1	2	30	206	36	1.7	.5	2529	.05	.28	1.5	.06	3.62	5	2
	Breakfast sausage:																					
108	Link, cooked	1 link	13	48	3	4	2	.1	4	24	168	47	.2	.3	0	.10	.03	.6	.04	.22	1	.2
107	Patty, cooked (from 2 oz raw)	1 patty	27	100	5	8	5	.3	9	50	349	97	.3	.7	0	.20	.07	1.2	.09	.47	2	.5
1060	Turkey	1 patty	28	65	6	4	3	0	5	52	191	76	.5	1.0	0	.03	.08	1.4	.08	.50	1	—
1044	Bratwurst, raw link	1 link	70	226	10	20	11	2	34	94	778	197	.7	1.5	0	.18	.16	2.3	.09	1.44	2	20
1045	Cheesefurter/cheese smokie	1 link	43	141	6	13	7	1	25	76	465	89	.5	1.0	12	.11	.07	1.3	.05	.74	1	8
1047	Corned beef loaf, jellied	1 piece	28	46	7	2	1	0	3	18	294	25	.6	1.1	0	tr	.03	.5	.04	.33	1	2
1048	Dutch loaf	1 piece	28	68	4	5	3	2	24	46	354	107	.4	.5	0	.09	.08	.7	.06	.37	1	5
	Frankfurters:																					
99	Beef (57g each, 8 per package)	1 link	57	184	6	17	9	1	7	47	584	90	.8	1.2	0	.03	.06	1.4	.06	.94	2	14
100	Beef and pork (57g each, 8 per package)	1 link	57	183	6	17	9	1	6	49	639	95	.7	1.1	0	.11	.07	1.5	.08	.74	2	15
101	Chicken (10 per package)	1 link	45	115	6	9	6	3	43	48	616	38	.9	4.7	60	.03	.05	1.4	.09	.58	2	0
102	Turkey (10 per package)	1 link	45	102	6	8	5	1	48	70	454	84	.8	1.0	60	.02	.08	1.9	.10	.13	4	0
106	Italian sausage link, cooked	1 link	67	216	13	17	10	1	16	114	618	204	1.0	1.6	0	.42	.16	2.8	.22	.87	4	1
1051	Keilbasa, 6 in. by 3¾ in. by 1⁄16 in.	1 piece	26	81	3	7	4	1	11	38	280	70	.4	.5	0	.06	06	.7	.05	.42	1	6
1052	Knockwurst sausage (4-in. link by 1⅛-in. diam)	1 link	68	209	8	19	11	1	7	67	687	136	.6	1.1	0	.23	.10	1.9	.11	.80	2	18
1078	Liver pâté, canned	1 T	13	41	2	4	2	.2	9	26	91	18	.7	.5	429	tr	.08	.4	.01	.42	8	0
109	Liverwurst, pork (2½-in. diam by ¼ in.)	1 piece	18	59	3	5	3	.4	5	41	55	30	1.2	.5	2430	.05	.19	1.4	.03	2.42	5	tr
1053	Luncheon meat, canned (3- by 2- by ¼-in. piece)	1 piece	21	70	3	6	4	.4	1	17	271	45	.2	.3	0	.08	.04	.7	.04	.71	1	.2
1054	Luncheon sausage (4-in. diam by ⅛ in.)	1 piece	23	60	4	5	3	tr	3	28	272	56	.3	.6	0	.05	.05	.8	.05	.45	1	4
1055	Luxury loaf (4-in. square by 3⁄32 in.)	1 piece	28	40	5	2	1	2	11	53	347	107	.3	.9	0	.20	.09	1.0	.09	.39	1	6
1056	Mortadella	1 piece	15	47	2	4	2	.5	3	15	187	24	.2	.3	0	.02	.02	.4	.02	.22	.5	4
1057	Olive loaf (4-in. square by 3⁄32 in.)	1 piece	28	67	3	5	3	2	31	36	421	85	.2	.4	0	.09	.08	.5	.07	.35	1	3
110	Pastrami, cured turkey	2 pieces	57	74	11	4	2	1	5	142	569	155	.9	1.5	0	.05	.15	2.5	.15	.14	3	tr
1058	Pepper loaf (4-in. square by 3⁄32 in.)	1 piece	28	42	5	2	1	1	15	48	432	112	.3	.9	0	.11	.09	.9	.08	.56	1	7
111	Pepperoni, small slice (1⅜-in. diam by ⅛ in.)	4 pieces	22	109	5	10	6	1	2	26	449	76	.3	.6	0	.07	.06	1.1	.06	.55	.9	tr
1059	Pickle and pimiento loaf (4-in. square by 3⁄32 in.)	2 pieces	57	149	7	12	7	3	54	79	787	193	.6	.8	.1	.17	.14	1.2	.11	.67	1	8
112	Polish sausage (4 oz piece = 4 in. long by 1¼-in. diam)	1 oz	28.4	92	4	8	5	.5	3	39	248	67	.4	.6	0	.14	.04	1.0	.05	.28	1	0
	Salami:																					
113	Beef (4-in. diam by ⅛ in.)	1 piece	23	58	3	5	2	1	2	23	266	52	.5	.5	0	.03	.06	.8	.05	1.11	2	3

Item No.	Food*	Approximate Measure	Weight (g)	Food Energy (kcal)	Protein (g)	Total Fat (g)	Unsat Fat† (g)	Carbohydrate (g)	Calcium (mg)	Phosphorous (mg)	Sodium (mg)	Potassium (mg)	Iron (mg)	Zinc (mg)	Vitamin A (IU)	Thiamin (mg)	Riboflavin (mg)	Niacin (mg)	Vitamin B_6 (mg)	Vitamin B_{12} (μ)	Folacin (μ)	Vitamin C (mg)
114	Pork and beef (4-in. diam by ⅛ in.)	2 pieces	57	143	8	11	6	1	7	65	604	112	1.5	1.2	0	.14	.21	2	.12	2.1	1.1	7
116	Pork and beef, dry (3-in. diam by 1/16-in. thick)	2 pieces	20	85	5	7	4	1	2	28	372	76	.3	.6	0	.12	.06	1.0	.10	.38	0	6
115	Turkey	2 pieces	57	111	9	8	5	.3	11	73	535	125	1	1	0	.06	.15	2.2	.14	.12	2.3	tr
	Smoked link sausage (a little link weighs 16g):																					
118	Beef and pork (large link = 4 in. long by 1⅛-in. diam)	1 link	68	229	9	21	12	1	7	73	642	129	1.0	1.4	0	.18	.12	2.2	.12	1.03	2	13
117	Pork, large link	1 link	68	265	15	22	13	1	20	110	1020	228	.8	1.9	0	.48	.18	3.1	.24	1.11	2	1
1062	Turkey	1 oz	28.4	55	5	4	3	.3	5	37	219	59	.4	.7	0	.02	.06	1.2	.06	.56	1	0
	Summer sausage																					
119	Thuringer	1 piece	23	80	4	7	4	1	2	23	334	53	.5	.5	0	.04	.07	.9	.07	1.06	1	5
1061	Turkey, cured	1 oz	28.4	50	5	3	2	.3	4	68	304	65	.5	.7	0	.03	.12	1.4	.08	1.15	1	0
105	Turkey ham	2 oz	57	73	11	3	2	1	5	138	548	163	1.6	1.6	0	.04	.15	2.8	.16	1.29	3	0
1063	Vienna sausage, canned	1 sausage	16	45	2	4	2	.3	2	8	152	16	.1	.3	0	.01	.02	.3	.02	.16	.4	0
—	Scallops:																					
1160	Breaded, cooked from frozen	6 scallops	93	200	17	10	7	9	39	219	431	310	.76	1	70	.04	.1	1.4	.18	1.2	11	0
161	Steamed	3½ oz	100	113	23	1	.4	3	30	267	197	393	.35	1.2	70	.02	.08	1.4	.21	1.9	18	0
1157	Scampi, fried in crumbs	3½ oz	100	242	21	12	9	12	67	218	344	225	1.3	1.4	82	.13	.14	3.1	.1	1.9	8	0
166	Sea trout/steelhead, cooked	3½ oz	100	131	21	5	2	0	20	288	67	393	.3	.5	138	.09	.23	9.7	.8	6	10	.01
1158	Shad, baked with bacon	3½ oz	100	201	23	11	7	0	24	313	78	377	.6	.3	30	.13	.26	8.6	.20	1.40	8	.01
618	Sherbet	1 cup	193	270	2	4	1	59	103	74	88	198	.3	1.3	185	.03	.09	.1	.03	.16	14	4
—	Shrimp:																					
162	Boiled	3½ oz	100	99	21	1	1	0	39	137	224	182	3	2	220	.03	.03	2.6	.13	1.5	3.5	2
164	Canned, drained	1 cup	128	154	30	3	1	1	75	299	216	269	4	1.6	75	.04	.05	3.5	.14	1.4	2.3	3
163	Fried in bread crumbs	12 shrimp	90	206	19	11	8	10	60	196	310	203	1.1	1.2	168	.12	.12	2.8	.09	1.7	7	1
165	Snapper, baked	3½ oz	100	128	26	1.7	1	0	40	201	57	522	.24	.4	40	.05	.08	3.5	.27	1.60	9	.1
—	Sole/flounder:																					
137	Batter-fried	3 oz	85	250	13	15	10	12	50	161	194	191	.7	.4	30	.17	.13	2.1	.13	1.4	7	1
136	Fried	3½ oz	100	188	18	9	7	9	40	210	200	250	.5	.5	35	.13	.12	2.1	.17	1.8	9	1
138	Steamed	3½ oz	100	92	20	1	1	0	16	250	89	280	.3	.5	30	.06	.09	1.8	.2	2.1	10	.01
—	Soups (canned unless otherwise stated):																					
625	Bean and bacon	1 cup	253	173	8	6	4	23	81	132	952	403	2.1	1.0	890	.09	.03	.6	.04	.05	1.9	2
	Beef broth/bouillon:																					
626	Prepared from canned	1 cup	240	16	3	1	.2	.1	14	31	782	130	.4	.3	0	.01	.05	1.9	.02	.17	5	0
1197	Prepared from cube	1 cup	241	8	1	.2	.1	1	.3	11	1152	20	.1	.01	0	.01	.01	.2	0	0	2	.3
1196	Prepared from dry	1 cup	244	19	1	1	.3	2	10	24	1362	37	.02	.1	8	.01	.02	.4	.02	0	2	.01
627	Beef noodle	1 cup	244	84	5	3	2	9	15	46	952	100	1.1	1.5	630	.07	.06	1.1	.04	.20	4	.24
	Chicken broth/bouillon:																					
628	Prepared from canned	1 cup	244	39	5	1	1	1	9	73	776	210	.5	.2	0	.01	.07	3.4	.02	.24	5	0
1199	Prepared from cube	1 cup	243	13	1	.3	.2	2	12	12	792	24	.1	.01	16	.01	.02	.3	0	.02	2	0
1198	Prepared from dry	1 cup	244	21	1	1	1	1	15	12	1484	24	.1	.01	40	.01	.03	.2	0	.02	2	0
	Chicken noodle:																					
629	Prepared from canned	1 cup	241	75	4	3	2	9	17	36	900	55	.8	.6	711	.05	.06	1.4	.03	.15	2	.2
1201	Prepared from dry mix	1 cup	252	53	3	1	1	7	32	33	1284	31	.5	.2	50	.07	.06	.9	.01	0	2	.3
1184	Chicken rice	1 cup	241	60	4	2	1	7	17	22	815	101	.8	.3	660	.02	.02	1.1	.02	.15	1	.2
1202	Chicken vegetable	1 cup	251	49	3	1	.5	8	15	33	808	68	.6	.2	25	.07	.05	.7	.09	.1	3	1.2
631	Chili beef	1 cup	250	169	7	7	3	22	43	148	1035	525	2.1	1.4	1510	.06	.08	1.1	.16	.32	18	4
1195	Chili con carne with beans	1 cup	255	286	15	14	7	30	119	393	1330	932	9	5	860	.12	.27	.91	.34	.03	41	4
	Clam chowder:																					
1185	Manhattan-style, tomato-based	1 cup	244	78	2	2	2	12	27	41	578	188	2	1	964	.03	.04	.82	.1	4	10	4
632	New England-style, white-sauce based	1 cup	248	163	10	7	3	17	187	157	992	300	1.5	1.3	160	.07	.24	1.0	.13	10.3	11	4
	Celery, cream of:																					
1181	Condensed	1 cup	251	180	3	11	8	18	80	75	1899	246	1.3	.3	613	.06	.10	.7	.03	.1	5	.5
1179	Prepared with whole milk	1 cup	248	165	6	10	5	15	186	151	1010	309	.7	.2	461	.07	.25	.4	.06	.5	9	1

	Chicken, cream of:																					
1183	Condensed	1 cup	251	233	7	15	4	19	68	75	1973	174	1.2	1.3	1121	.06	.12	1.6	.03	.18	3	.3
630	Prepared with whole milk	1 cup	248	191	8	12	6	15	180	152	1046	273	.7	.7	710	.07	.26	.9	.07	.45	8	1
1200	Dehydrated mix, prepared with water	1 cup	261	107	2	5	2	13	76	96	1184	215	.3	2	123	.1	.20	3	.05	.3	5	.5
	Mushroom, cream of:																					
634	Condensed	1 cup	251	257	4	19	13	19	64	84	2032	167	1.1	1.2	0	.06	.17	1.6	.03	.3	7	2
635	Prepared with milk	1 cup	248	205	6	14	8	15	178	156	1076	270	.6	.6	154	.08	.28	.8	.06	.5	11	2
1203	Dehydrated mix, prepared with water	1 cup	253	96	2	5	4	11	66	76	1019	200	.5	.1	7	.28	.11	.5	.03	.3	5	1
1190	Potato, cream of	1 cup	248	148	6	7	2	17	166	160	1060	323	.5	.7	443	.08	.24	.6	.09	.5	9	1
1209	Vegetable, cream of, prepared from dry mix	1 cup	260	105	2	6	4	12	31	54	1171	96	.5	.3	26	1.22	.11	.5	.03	.13	8	4
633	Minestrone	1 cup	241	80	4	3	2	11	34	56	911	312	.9	.7	2340	.05	.04	.9	.10	0	16	1
	Onion:																					
1186	Prepared from canned	1 cup	241	57	4	2	1	8	26	11	1053	69	.7	.6	0	.03	.02	.6	.05	0	15	1
1204	Prepared from dry packet	1 cup	246	27	1	.4	.4	5	12	29	849	64	.2	.06	0	.03	.06	.5	0	0	2	.2
1188	Oyster stew	1 cup	245	134	6	8	2	10	167	162	1040	235	1.0	10.3	225	.07	.23	.3	.06	2.63	10	4
	Split pea, with ham:																					
1189	Prepared from canned	1 cup	253	189	10	4	2	28	22	213	1008	399	2.3	1.3	454	.15	.08	1.5	.07	.3	3	1
1205	Prepared from dry mix	1 cup	255	133	8	2	1	23	20	.25	1147	224	1.0	.6	49	.21	.14	1.3	.05	.3	40	0
	Tomato:																					
636	Prepared with whole milk	1 cup	248	160	6	6	3	22	159	148	932	450	1.8	.3	850	.13	.25	1.5	.16	.44	21	68
1191	Prepared with water	1 cup	244	86	2	2	1	17	13	34	872	263	1.8	.2	688	.09	.05	1.4	.11	0	15	67
1206	Prepared from dry mix	1 cup	265	102	3	2	1	19	54	66	943	295	.4	.2	832	.06	.05	.8	.10	0	7	5
1207	Tomato vegetable, prepared from dry mix	1 cup	253	55	2	1	.4	10	7	29	1146	103	.6	.2	200	.06	.05	.8	.09	0	10	6
	Vegetable beef:																					
638	Prepared from canned	1 cup	244	79	6	2	1	10	17	41	956	173	1.1	2.0	1890	.04	.05	1.0	.07	.32	11	2
1208	Prepared from dry mix	1 cup	253	53	3	1	1	8	13	35	1000	76	.9	.3	238	.03	.04	.5	.05	.3	8	1
637	Vegetarian vegetable	1 cup	241	70	2	2	2	12	21	35	823	209	1.1	.5	3010	.05	.05	.9	.06	0	11	1
535	Soy sauce (wheat & soy)	1 T	18	9	1	.01	.01	2	3	20	1029	32	.4	.1	0	.01	.02	.6	.03	0	3	0
—	Spaghetti entree, spaghetti and sauce casserole:																					
	With cheese:																					
1515	Canned	1 cup	250	190	6	2	.9	39	40	88	955	303	2.8	1.12	930	.35	.28	4.5	.131	0	6	10
1516	Recipe	1 cup	250	260	9	9	4.8	37	80	135	955	408	2.3	1.3	1080	.25	.18	2.3	.197	0	8	13
	With meat:																					
1517	Canned	1 cup	250	260	12	10	7	39	53	113	1220	245	3.3	2.39	1000	.15	.18	2.3	.119	.822	5	5
1518	Recipe	1 cup	248	330	19	12	6.6	39	124	236	1009	665	3.7	2.45	1590	.25	.3	.4	.2	1.2	10	22
	Spaghetti noodles: *see* Macaroni																					
	Spaghetti sauce, plain:																					
1358	From recipe	1 cup	220	179	6	10	8	23	52	86	900	915	3.0	.6	2350	.20	.13	3.0	.39	0	23	20
1359	Canned	1 cup	249	272	5	12	9	40	70	90	1236	957	1.6	.5	3055	.14	.15	3.8	.40	0	39	28
	Spaghetti sauce, with meat:																					
1360	From home recipe	1 cup	248	297	15	19	12	20	30	136	846	615	2.5	2.1	2500	.19	.20	3.5	.53	3.52	26	24
1361	Canned	1 cup	250	267	9	12	7	33	44	129	1268	539	3.4	1.3	2288	.20	.19	4	.32	2.13	16	3
	Spaghetti sauce with meatballs:																					
1362	Home recipe	1 cup	248	352	19	14	9	39	124	235	1009	665	4.1	3.1	2440	.27	.29	4.3	.51	3.70	22	22
1364	Frozen	1 cup	248	294	16	13	9	27	3	188	1468	617	2.9	2.7	2415	.17	.26	4.0	.45	3.24	20	8
1363	Canned	1 cup	250	255	12	10	6	29	53	113	1106	245	3.3	2.3	2200	.16	.19	2.4	.32	2.36	14	5
	Spaghetti sauce with mushrooms:																					
1365	Home recipe	¾ cup	185	137	3	7	6	18	41	79	1180	717	2.3	.7	2340	.15	.14	2.4	.31	0	24	18
1366	Canned	¾ cup	185	162	2	5	4	9	22	45	744	500	1.5	.5	3624	.12	.12	1.4	.24	0	19	14
—	Spices:																					
561	Cinnamon	1 T	6.8	18	.3	.2	.1	5	84	4	2	34	2.6	.1	18	.01	.01	.1	.06	0	—	2
	Garlic:																					
563	Cloves	4 cloves	12	18	1	.1	.03	4	22	18	2	48	.2	.14	0	.02	.01	.1	.15	0	.4	4
564	Powder	1 T	8.4	28	1	.1	.03	6	7	35	2	93	.2	.2	0	.04	.01	.1	1.70	0	5	.01
565	Onion powder	1 T	6.5	15	1	.1	.04	5	24	21	3	60	.2	.2	0	.03	tr	.04	.10	0	9	1
567	Paprika	1 T	6.9	20	1	1	1	4	12	24	2	162	1.6	.3	4182	.05	.12	1.1	—	0	—	5
	Parsley:																					
568	Freeze-dried	¼ cup	1.4	4	.4	.1	.04	1	2	8	5	88	.8	.1	885	.02	.03	.1	.02	0	22	2
569	Fresh, chopped	½ cup	30	10	1	.1	.1	2	39	12	12	161	1.9	.2	1560	.02	.03	.2	.05	0	55	27
572	Pepper, black	1 T	6.4	16	1	.2	.2	4	28	11	3	81	1.9	.1	12	.01	.02	.1	0	0	—	0
1430	Pepper, red cayenne	1 T	5.3	17	1	1	1	3	8	16	7	107	.4	.1	2205	.02	.05	.5	—	0	—	4

Item No.	Food*	Approximate Measure	Weight (g)	Food Energy (kcal)	Protein (g)	Total Fat (g)	Unsat Fat† (g)	Carbohydrate (g)	Calcium (mg)	Phosphorous (mg)	Sodium (mg)	Potassium (mg)	Iron (mg)	Zinc (mg)	Vitamin A (IU)	Thiamin (mg)	Riboflavin (mg)	Niacin (mg)	Vitamin B_6 (mg)	Vitamin B_{12} (μ)	Folacin (μ)	Vitamin C (mg)
570	Salt	1 T	16.5	0	0	0	0	0	42	9	6396	1	.02	.1	0	0	0	0	0	0	0	0
——	Spinach:																					
286	Fresh, chopped	1 cup	56	12	2	.2	.1	2	55	27	44	312	1.5	.3	4480	.04	.11	.4	.11	0	109	16
287	Cooked from fresh	1 cup	180	41	5	.5	.2	7	244	100	126	838	6.4	1.4	17500	.17	.43	.9	.44	0	262	40
288	Cooked from frozen, leaf	1 cup	190	53	6	.4	.1	10	277	91	163	566	2.9	1.3	17557	.11	.32	.8	.28	0	204	23
289	Canned, drained	1 cup	214	50	6	1	.5	7	271	94	683	740	4.9	1.0	18780	.03	.30	.8	.21	0	209	31
1448	Spinach souffle	1 cup	136	218	11	18	10	3	230	231	763	202	1.3	1.3	3461	.09	.31	.5	.12	.68	62	3
——	Squash:																					
	Summer (crookneck, scallop zucchini):																					
291	Fresh, raw	1 cup	130	26	2	.3	.1	6	26	46	3	253	.6	.3	255	.08	.05	.7	.14	0	33	19
292	Cooked	1 cup	180	36	2	1	.3	8	48	69	2	346	.6	.7	517	.08	.07	.9	.12	0	36	9
	Winter (acorn, butternut, Hubbard, spaghetti):																					
295	Baked, mashed	1 cup	245	96	2	2	.3	21	34	49	3	1071	.8	.6	8715	.21	.06	1.7	.18	0	69	24
293	Boiled, mashed	1 cup	240	83	3	.4	.2	20	44	44	7	1469	1.2	.3	6033	.16	.05	1.1	.05	0	30	13
294	Frozen, cooked	1 cup	240	95	3	.2	.1	24	46	34	5	319	1.4	.3	8014	.12	.06	1.1	.22	0	38	8
——	Strawberries:																					
417	Fresh	1 cup	149	45	1	1	.4	11	21	28	2	247	.6	.2	40	.03	.10	.3	.09	0	28	85
418	Frozen (measured frozen)	1 cup	149	52	1	.2	.1	14	23	20	3	220	1.1	.2	66	.03	.06	.7	.04	0	28	61
419	Frozen, sweetened (measured thawed)	1 cup	255	245	1	.3	.2	66	28	33	8	250	1.5	.2	61	.04	.13	1.0	.08	0	42	106
——	Sugar:																					
555	Brown	1 cup	220	820	0	0	0	212	187	56	97	757	4.8	.1	0	.02	.07	.2	0	0	0	0
556	White granulated	1 cup	200	770	0	0	0	199	3	.1	5	7	.1	.04	0	0	0	0	0	0	0	0
557	White powdered, sifted	1 cup	100	385	0	0	0	99	0	0	3	4	.1	tr	0	0	0	0	0	0	0	0
296	Succotash, cooked from frozen	1 cup	170	158	7	2	1	34	25	119	77	451	1.5	.8	393	.13	.12	2.2	.16	0	57	10
——	Sweet potato:																					
297	Baked in skin, peeled after (5- by 2-in. diam)	1 potato	114	118	2	.13	.06	28	32	63	12	397	.5	.3	24877	.08	.15	.7	.28	0	26	28
298	Boiled, peeled before cooking	1 potato	151	160	2	.5	.2	37	32	41	20	278	.8	.4	25752	.08	.21	1.0	.36	0	22	26
	Canned:																					
299	Mashed	½ cup	128	129	3	.3	.1	30	39	67	95	268	1.7	.3	19285	.03	.12	1.2	.24	0	21	7
300	Vacuum pack, mashed	1 cup	255	233	4	.5	.3	54	56	125	136	796	2.3	.5	20355	.09	.15	1.9	.49	0	42	67
301	Candied (2½-in. by 2-in. diam)	1 piece	105	144	1	3	1	29	27	27	73	198	1.2	.2	4399	.02	.04	.4	.17	0	12	7
1169	Swordfish, broiled with butter	3½ oz	100	155	25	5	3	0	6	337	115	369	1	2	137	.04	.12	12	.4	2	16	1
——	Turnips, cubed:																					
309	Raw	1 cup	130	35	1	.13	.1	8	39	35	88	248	.4	.4	0	.05	.04	.5	.12	0	19	27
310	Cooked from raw	½ cup	78	14	1	.1	.04	4	18	15	39	106	.2	.1	0	.02	.02	.2	.05	0	7	9
——	Taco:																					
1339	Beef	1 taco	78	207	14	13	7	10	85	141	141	183	1.3	2.9	136	.03	.13	2.5	.16	1.36	13	1
1340	Chicken	1 taco	78	172	15	8	5	10	87	156	145	158	.9	1.3	157	.04	.12	4.2	.24	.20	14	1
1013	Tahini (sesame butter)	1 T	15	91	3	8	7	3	21	119	5	69	.8	1.6	10	.24	.02	.8	.06	0	15	1
420	Tangerine, fresh	1 fruit	84	37	1	.2	.1	9	12	8	1	132	.1	.4	773	.09	.02	.1	.06	0	17	26
——	Tangerine juice:																					
423	Prepared from frozen	1 cup	241	110	1	.3	.1	27	18	20	2	272	.2	.1	1382	.13	.05	.2	.10	0	11	58
422	Canned, sweetened	1 cup	249	125	1	.5	.1	30	45	35	2	443	.5	.1	1050	.15	.05	.2	.08	0	8	55
536	Tartar sauce	1 T	14	74	.2	8	7	1	3	4	182	11	.1	.02	30	tr	tr	tr	.01	0	1	tr
1175	Teriyaki sauce	1 T	18	15	1	.1	.1	3	4	28	690	41	.3	.02	0	.01	.01	.2	.02	0	4	0
1227	Toaster pastry, fortified	1 pastry	54	210	2	6	4	38	104	104	248	91	2.2	.3	500	.17	.18	2.3	.21	0	43	4
308	Tofu, soybean curd	1 cup	124	94	10	6	5	2	130	120	9	150	8	.9	105	.1	.06	.24	.06	0	19	0
——	Tomato:																					
303	Whole, 2⅗-in. diam	1 tomato	123	26	1	.4	.2	6	6	30	11	273	.5	.1	766	.07	.06	.7	.09	0	19	22
304	Cooked from fresh	1 cup	240	65	3	1	.6	14	14	74	26	670	1.3	.3	1783	.17	.14	1.8	.23	0	32	55
305	Canned with liquid & added salt	1 cup	240	47	2	1	.3	10	63	46	390	529	1.5	.4	1450	.11	.07	1.8	.22	0	35	36
425	Tomato juice, canned	1 cup	244	42	2	.15	.08	10	22	46	881	537	1.4	.3	1357	.12	.08	1.6	.27	0	49	45
	Tomato products, canned:																					
307	Paste	1 cup	262	220	10	2	1	49	92	207	170	2442	7.8	2.1	6466	.41	.50	8.4	1.00	0	59	111

1017	Puree	1 cup	250	102	4	.3	.2	25	37	99	49	1051	2.3	.5	3402	.18	.14	4.3	.38	0	39	88
306	Sauce	1 cup	245	74	3	.4	.2	18	34	78	1481	908	1.9	.6	2399	.16	.14	2.8	.4	0	39	32
	Tostada:																					
1342	Beef and bean, deluxe	1 tostada	192	332	18	21	10	20	186	247	483	442	2.2	3.6	778	.08	.24	2.9	.67	1.66	37	6
1343	With beans and chicken	1 tostada	157	249	19	11	6	19	162	242	474	358	1.7	1.9	494	.07	.19	4.5	.73	.44	34	3
1341	With refried beans only	1 tostada	157	212	10	9	5	26	177	195	618	422	1.9	1.6	471	.06	.14	.8	1.01	.32	47	6
	Tortilla chips:																					
720	Plain	1 oz	28.4	139	2	8	6	17	82	74	140	30	1.0	.4	7	.01	.02	.2	.08	0	1	tr
711	Doritos, nacho flavor	1 oz	28.4	139	2	7	5	18	17	98	107	109	.4	.4	127	.04	.03	.4	.10	0	—	0
712	Doritos, taco flavor	1 oz	28.4	140	3	7	5	18	45	91	191	72	.7	.4	151	.08	.09	.8	.10	0	—	0
	Tortillas:																					
1222	Corn tortilla, enriched, fried	1 tortilla	30	87	2	3	3	13	42	40	16	43	.6	.3	80	.05	.03	.4	.02	0	5	0
685	Taco shell	1 shell	13.6	59	1	3	2	9	26	33	62	25	.3	.2	6	tr	.01	.2	.03	0	2	0
684	Flour tortilla (8-in. diam, 10½-in. round weighs 1 oz)	1 tortilla	35.4	105	3	3	2	19	21	59	134	35	.5	.3	0	.13	.08	1.2	.01	0	16	0
167	Trout, broiled	3 oz	85	129	22	4	2	.01	73	272	29	539	2	1	63	.07	.19	2.3	.42	3	6	3
	Tuna:																					
168	Canned in oil, drained	3 oz	85	169	25	7	5	0	11	265	301	176	1.2	.8	70	.03	.09	10.1	.09	2.8	5	0
169	Canned in water, drained	3 oz	85	111	25	.4	.2	0	10	158	303	267	1.2	.7	110	.03	.10	13.2	.32	2.89	4	0
1465	Tuna noodle casserole, home recipe	1 cup	202	251	21	7	5	24	37	182	869	224	1.9	1.0	115	.14	.17	8.6	.24	1.78	13	1
1274	Tuna salad	1 cup	205	383	33	19	14	19	35	365	824	365	2	1.2	199	.06	.14	13.3	.17	3.59	15	5
	Turkey, roasted meat:																					
121	All types	1 cup	140	238	41	7	4	0	35	298	99	418	2.5	4.3	0	.09	.26	7.6	.64	.52	10	0
123	Dark meat	1 cup	140	262	40	10	5	0	45	286	110	406	3.3	6.3	0	.09	.35	5.1	.50	.52	13	0
122	Light meat	1 cup	140	219	42	5	2	0	27	307	89	426	1.9	2.9	0	.09	.18	9.6	.75	.52	8	0
1462	Turkey pot pie, from frozen	1 pie	233	416	15	23	13	38	64	137	1000	138	2.1	1.5	1415	.17	.17	3.8	.46	.20	24	4
	Turnip greens:																					
311	Cooked from raw	1 cup	144	29	2	.3	.2	6	198	41	41	293	1.2	.3	7917	.07	.10	.6	.26	0	171	40
312	Cooked from frozen	½ cup	82	24	3	.4	.2	4	125	27	12	184	1.6	.3	6540	.04	.06	.4	.06	0	32	18
	Veal:																					
124	Cutlet, braised/broiled	3½ oz	100	181	33	4	2	0	9	295	85	439	1.1	3.7	1	.09	.41	13	.4	2	17	0
126	Liver, simmered	3 oz	85	222	25	11	6	3	11	456	100	385	12.1	5.23	21330	.22	3.56	14.0	.62	74	272	31
426	Vegetable juice cocktail, canned	1 cup	242	46	2	.2	.1	11	27	41	883	467	1.0	.5	2831	.10	.07	1.8	.34	0	38	67
313	Vegetables, mixed, cooked from frozen (corn, green beans, limas, carrots, peas)	1 cup	182	107	5	.3	.1	24	46	93	64	308	1.5	.9	7784	.13	.22	1.6	.14	0	35	6
537	Vinegar, cider	1 cup	240	29	0	0	0	14	14	12	2	240	1.4	.3	0	0	0	0	tr	0	0	.01
	Waffles:																					
689	Home recipe, 9-in. square	1 waffle	75	245	7	13	8	26	154	135	445	129	1.5	.7	140	.18	.24	1.5	.03	.10	13	tr
690	Prepared from mix, 9-in. square	1 waffle	75	205	7	8	4	27	179	257	515	146	1.2	.5	170	.14	.23	.9	.03	.10	4	tr
691	Frozen, 4-in. square	1 waffle	35	98	2	3	2	15	29	134	242	73	1.7	.3	436	.15	.19	1.9	.09	.05	1	tr
1273	Waldorf salad	1 cup	142	424	4	42	34	13	44	88	246	279	1.0	.7	203	.10	.0[illegible]	.27	.16	0	19	6
314	Water chestnuts, canned, sliced	½ cup	70	35	[illegible]	.04	.03	9	3	14	6	82	.6	.3	3	.01	.0[illegible]	.3	.11	0	5	1
940	Watercress, raw, chopped	½ cup	17	2	.4	.02	.01	.2	20	10	7	56	.03	.02	799	.02	.0[illegible]	.03	.02	0	34	7
424	Watermelon, diced pieces	1 cup	160	50	1	1	.5	12	13	14	3	186	.3	.1	585	.13	.0[illegible]	.3	.23	0	3	15
	Wheat germ:																					
473	Raw	1 cup	100	360	23	10	7	52	39	842	12	892	6.2	12	0	1.9	.51	7	1.3	0	281	0
474	Toasted	1 cup	113	432	33	12	9	56	51	1295	5	1070	10	18.9	0	1.89	.93	6.3	1.13	0	398	0
989	Toasted with brown sugar and honey	¼ cup	28	107	6	2	2	17	9	244	1	201	1.9	3.5	0	.35	.18	1.2	.21	0	75	4
1178	White sauce, home recipe	1 cup	250	395	10	30	19	24	292	238	888	381	.9	1.2	1190	.15	.43	.8	.12	.83	15	2
170	Whiting, fried	3½ oz	100	190	18	6	4	7	40	220	102	334	.7	.4	87	.08	.07	2	.15	2	12	0
1015	Whole-grain wheat, cooked	⅓ cup	50	28	1	.14	.08	7	3	26	.2	33	.3	.2	0	.04	.01	.5	.03	0	6	0
	Yeast:																					
588	Brewer's	1 T	8	25	3	.1	.04	3	17	140	10	152	1.4	.6	1	1.3	.34	3.2	.40	0	313	tr
587	Dry active	4 T	30	80	11	.5	.2	1	24	387	15	600	5.9	1.8	4	.71	1.64	12.0	.60	0	1140	tr
	Yogurt:																					
43	Low fat with fruit	1 cup	227	231	10	3	1	43	345	325	125	442	.2	1.7	104	.08	.40	.2	.09	1.06	21	2
42	Low fat, plain	1 cup	227	144	12	4	1	16	415	326	159	531	.2	2.0	150	.10	.49	.3	.11	1.28	25	2
1519	Frozen, Aug, low fat	½ cup	87	110	4	2	.5	17	120	980	45	148	.1	1	74	.03	.14	.1	.03	.4	7	.5

*Values pertain to edible portions unless indicated otherwise.

†Mono- and polyunsaturated fats combined

—Data are unreliable

tr = Trace

Reprinted with permission from ESHA Research—Nutrition Systems, P.O. Box 13028, Salem, OR 97309. Developer of the Food Processor® Nutrition Software.

Appendix F Table of Food Composition—Fast Foods

ARBY'S

		Weight	Calories	Protein	Total FAT	Unsaturated FAT	Carbohydrates	Cholesterol	Calcium	Phosphorus	Sodium	Potassium	Iron	Zinc	Vitamin A	Thiamin	Riboflavin	Niacin	Vitamin B_6	Folacin	Vitamin C	Vitamin B_{12}
		(g)		(g)	(g)	(g)	(g)	(mg)	(mg)	(mg)	(mg)	(mg)	(mg)	(mg)	(RE)	(mg)	(mg)	(mg)	(mg)	(mcg)	(mcg)	(mg)
1523	Roast beef san-regular	147	353	22.2	14.8	7.5	31.6	39	80	120	588	368	3.6	3.75	20	.23	.43	7.00	.2	—	14	1.20
1549	Roast beef san-Giant	227	531	35.2	23.1	—	45.8	65	100	—	908	597	5.40	6.00	20	.38	.68	12.0	—	—	—	2.40
1530	Roast beef san-King	192	467	28.6	19.2	9.9	43.6	49	100	—	766	468	4.50	5.25	20	.30	.60	10.0	—	—	—	2.40
1524	Roast beef san-Junior	86	218	12.4	8.5	4.6	22.4	20	40	60	345	197	1.8	1.5	—	.15	.25	4.0	.1	—	7	—
1525	Roast beef san-super	234	501	25.1	22.1	13.6	50.4	40	100	190	798	503	4.50	3.75	150	.38	.60	9.00	.3	—	21	3.60
1526	Beef 'n cheddar san	197	455	25.7	26.8	19.2	27.7	63	60	260	955	335	3.60	3.75	80	.38	.51	8.0	.22	—	19	—
1550	Philly beef'n swiss san	197	460	24.4	28.4	—	26.7	107	450	—	1300	367	2.70	3.75	100	.30	.34	3.0	—	—	—	2.40
1533	Turkey sandwich-deluxe	197	375	23.8	16.6	12.5	32.5	39	80	250	1047	346	2.70	1.50	60	.23	.43	12.0	.52	—	20	4.80
1527	Chicken breast sandwich	184	493	23.0	25.0	23.6	47.9	91	80	180	1019	330	3.6	.15	—	.23	.51	8.0	.38	—	18	4.80
1543	Chicken cordon bleu	216	630	31.5	36.7	—	50.3	138	150	—	1824	375	3.60	2.25	—	.38	.51	9.0	—	—	—	—
1537	Roast chicken club san	234	610	31.0	33.0	—	40.0	80	150	—	1500	430	3.60	2.25	—	.53	.60	9.0	—	—	—	—
1539	Reuben sandwich	200	450	30.0	18.0	—	36.0	55	300	—	1900	420	19.8	5.25	—	.15	.60	5.0	—	—	—	2.40
1540	Corned beef sandwich	158	400	28.0	15.0	—	32.0	45	300	—	1440	330	4.50	4.50	40	.23	.60	6.0	—	—	—	3.60
1574	Steak'n cheddar san	203	640	23.0	37.0	—	53.0	45	60	—	960	320	3.60	3.00	—	.23	.51	4.00	—	—	—	—
1531	Bac'n cheddar-san-delux	226	526	26.9	36.5	26.8	32.7	83	150	—	1672	422	4.50	3.00	100	.38	.51	8.0	—	—	—	9.0
1532	Ham'n cheese sandwich	156	292	22.9	13.7	9	19.2	45	200	405	1350	312	2.70	.90	50	.15	.26	6.00	.31	—	26	24
1545	Sub deluxe sandwich	226	540	24.0	29.0	—	38.0	50	150	—	1600	420	3.60	3.75	—	.38	.51	5.0	—	—	—	2.40
1546	Fish fillet sandwich	193	537	21.5	29.1	—	46.6	79	80	—	994	345	3.60	2.25	—	.30	.43	4.0	—	—	—	—
1528	Potato cakes	85	204	1.8	12.0	6	19.8	0	—	—	397	289	1.44	—	0	.06	—	1.60	—	—	—	21.0
1529	French fries-serving	71	246	2.1	13.2	4.7	29.8	0	3.01	—	114	240	1.08	—	0	.006	—	2.0	—	—	—	6
1542	Cheddar fries	142	399	6.2	21.9	—	46.2	9	80	—	454	742	1.44	.90	—	.08	.17	2.0	—	—	—	—
1544	Curly fries	99	337	4.2	17.2	—	43.2	0	20	—	167	724	1.26	.60	—	.08	.09	1.80	—	—	—	—
1534	Vanilla shake	312	330	10.5	11.5	7.6	46.2	32	300	350	281	686	2.70	1.50	100	.23	.85	4.0	.14	—	37	2.40
1535	Chocolate shake	340	451	10.2	11.6	8.7	76.5	36	250	350	341	410	2.70	1.5	40	.06	.85	.80	.14	—	14	4.80
1536	Jamocha shake	326	368	9.3	10.5	8	59.1	35	250	350	262	525	2.70	1.50	60	.06	.77	5.00	.14	—	14	2.40
1541	Garden salad	247	149	11.5	8.6	—	1.6	74	150	—	99	428	.90	.90	300	.03	.24	1.20	—	—	—	6.0
1576	Chicken cashew salad	376	590	34.0	37.0	—	23.0	65	250	—	1140	660	2.70	3.75	200	.90	.51	6.00	—	—	—	4.80
1571	Side salad	150	25	2.0	0	—	4.0	0	40	—	30	290	.72	.60	200	.03	.10	.40	—	—	—	3.60
1570	Chef salad	312	210	21.0	11.0	—	3.0	115	150	—	720	590	1.44	2.25	300	.15	.34	3.00	—	—	—	6.0
1551	Buttrmlk ranch dressing	71	210	0.6	48.8	—	2.1	3	20	—	598	17	—	—	—	—	—	—	—	—	—	—
1552	Croutons	14	59	1.6	2.2	—	8.5	1	—	—	155	0	—	—	—	.030	.034	—	—	—	—	2.40
1553	Honey French dressing	71	350	0.3	27.2	—	23.8	0	—	—	532	263	.36	—	—	—	—	—	—	—	—	—
1554	Light Italian dressing	56	25	0.1	1.0	—	3.3	0	—	—	255	126	—	—	—	—	—	—	—	—	—	—
1555	1000 island dressing	71	345	0.5	33.2	—	11.0	13	—	—	576	4	—	—	—	—	—	—	—	—	—	—
1556	Blue cheese dressing	71	390	2.7	38.8	—	3.0	28	40	—	766	34	—	—	—	—	.07	—	—	—	—	—
1557	Horsey sauce	28	110	0.2	10.0	—	5.1	2	40	—	210	28	—	—	—	—	—	—	—	—	—	—
1561	Arby's sauce	28	30	0.2	0.3	—	6.5	0	—	—	227	56	1.80	—	—	—	—	—	—	—	—	—
1573	Cinnamon nut danish	99	340	7.0	9.5	—	59.0	0	40	—	230	130	2.70	1.20	—	.23	.26	1.60	—	—	—	—
1558	Ham platter	241	719	22.3	24.2	—	46.2	404	60	—	1192	553	4.32	2.10	—	.50	.36	4.0	—	—	—	6.0
1559	Sausage platter	221	816	19.2	38.6	—	50.8	428	80	—	841	486	3.96	.90	80	.12	.51	3.40	—	—	—	6.0
1560	Croissant-plain	63	260	6.0	15.6	—	28.0	49	40	—	300	95	2.70	.30	—	.15	.14	2.0	—	—	—	—
1562	Croissant-bacon/egg	105	469	11.4	24.7	—	30.2	280	50	—	580	171	3.42	1.20	40	.26	.22	2.40	—	—	—	—
1563	Croissant-ham/cheese	119	345	16.0	20.4	—	30.0	100	140	—	960	225	3.06	1.50	—	.27	.20	3.20	—	—	—	—
1564	Croissant-mushroom/chz	113	337	10.9	17.5	—	34.0	98	200	—	625	200	1.08	.60	150	.23	.43	4.00	—	—	—	—
1565	Croissant-sausage/egg	133	600	16.4	37.5	—	29.3	406	50	—	619	231	4.14	1.20	40	.30	.26	2.80	—	—	—	—
1566	Biscuit-plain	82	280	6.0	14.9	—	34.0	0	100	—	730	130	2.70	—	—	.23	.14	3.00	—	—	—	—
1567	Biscuit-bacon	90	330	7.0	19.0	—	36.0	10	100	—	960	165	2.70	.90	—	.23	.14	3.40	—	—	—	—
1568	Biscuit-ham	124	325	13.0	16.8	—	35.0	30	—	—	1190	250	3.06	.90	—	.32	.20	4.20	—	—	—	—
1569	Biscuit-sausage	118	460	12.0	31.9	—	35.0	60	100	—	1000	225	3.42	.90	—	.51	.31	6.80	—	—	—	—
1538	French toast syrup	43	219	0	0.2	—	54.2	0	—	—	48	20	—	—	—	—	—	—	—	—	—	—
1572	Toastix	99	420	8.0	25.0	—	43.0	20	—	—	440	110	2.70	.90	—	.12	.17	.80	—	—	—	—
1547	Apple turnover	85	303	4.4	18.3	—	27.5	0	—	—	178	51	.72	—	20	.03	.03	.40	—	—	—	1.20
1548	Cherry turnover	85	280	4.6	17.8	—	25.4	0	—	—	200	68	.72	—	—	.03	.07	.40	—	—	—	4.80
1575	Chocolate chip cookie	27	130	2.0	4.0	—	17.0	0	—	—	95	50	.36	—	—	—	.03	—	—	—	—	—

BURGER KING

1577	Whopper sandwich	265	640	27	41	23	42	94	80	237	842	547	4.9	4.5	60	.33	.41	7	.4	—	35	14
1578	Whopper with cheese	289	723	31	48	23	43	117	210	360	1126	570	4.9	5.1	85	.34	.48	7	.4	—	35	14
1579	Whopper-double beef	351	850	46	52	29	52	188	91	387	1080	760	7.3	8.5	60	.34	.56	10	.5	—	45	14
1580	Whopper-dbl beef + chez	374	950	51	60	32	54	211	222	510	1535	730	7.3	9.1	85	.35	.63	10	.5	—	45	14
1581	Whopper-Junior	136	370	15	17	9.4	31	41	40	127	486	275	2.8	2.3	30	.23	.25	4	.2	—	17	6
1582	Whopper + cheese-Junior	158	420	17	20	8.8	32	52	105	189	628	287	2.8	2.6	85	.23	.29	4	.2	—	17	6
1583	Hamburger	109	275	15	12	—	29	37	37	124	509	235	2.7	2.4	15	.23	.25	4	.12	—	18	3
1584	Cheeseburger	120	317	17	15	7	30	48	102	186	651	247	3.8	2.6	70	.23	.29	4	.13	—	24	3
1585	Dbl cheeseburger + bacon	159	510	33	31	22	27	104	168	328	728	363	3.8	5.1	85	.31	.42	6	.3	—	30	1
1595	Ham + cheese sandwich	230	471	24	23	12	44	70	195	384	1534	419	3.2	2.4	85	.87	.42	6	.31	—	25	7
1593	Whaler fish sandwich	189	488	19	27	19	45	84	84	249	592	366	2.2	.09	20	.28	.21	4	.13	—	3	2
1594	Whaler + cheese sandwich	201	530	21	30	19	46	95	112	311	734	378	2.2	1.1	40	.27	.24	4	.13	—	3	2
1596	Chicken sandwich	230	688	26	40	27	56	82	79	274	1423	375	3.3	1.2	13	.45	.31	10	.4	—	18	1
1597	Chicken tenders-1 svg	95	204	20	10	5.6	10	47	18	236	636	200	.7	.6	5	.08	.08	7	.34	—	10	.4
1586	French fries-reg serv	74	227	3	13	5	24	14	9	114	160	360	.5	.34	0	.1	.3	7.5	.23	—	20	4
1587	Onion rings-reg serv	79	274	4	16	11	28	0	124	195	665	173	.8	.4	0	.056	.028	.72	.07	—	8	.5
1589	Chocolate shake-medium	273	320	8	12	—	46	—	260	262	202	567	1.6	1	60	.13	.55	.13	—	—	—	0
1592	Choc shake plus-medium	284	374	8	11	—	60	—	248	264	225	590	1.6	1.05	60	.12	.51	.14	—	—	—	0
1590	Vanilla shake-medium	273	321	9	10	—	49	—	295	284	205	505	—	1	80	.11	.57	.13	—	—	—	0
1591	Vanilla shake plus-med	284	334	9	10	—	51	—	—	—	213	524	—	—	80	—	—	—	—	—	—	—
1598	Croissant + egg + bcn + chez	119	335	15	24	10	20	249	136	249	762	182	2	1.5	150	.32	.3	2	.06	—	24	2
1599	Croissant + egg + saus + chz	163	538	19	41	15	20	293	145	292	1042	284	2.9	2.4	150	.36	.32	4	.06	—	24	.2
1600	Croissant + egg + ham + chez	145	335	18	20	8	20	262	136	317	987	256	2.2	1.9	150	.49	.32	3	.06	—	24	10
1601	Scrambled egg platter	195	468	14	30	—	33	370	102	271	808	487	2.7	1.5	94	.31	.35	3	—	—	—	3
1602	Scrambled egg + sausage	247	702	22	52	—	33	420	112	335	1213	623	3.7	2.7	94	.42	.4	5	—	—	—	3
1603	Scrambled egg + bacon	206	536	18	36	—	33	378	103	299	975	532	2.8	1.9	94	.39	.38	4	—	—	—	3
1604	French toast + bacon	117	469	11	30	—	41	73	59	118	448	151	2.7	1.3	0	.24	.24	3	—	—	—	2.0
1605	French toast + sausage	158	635	16	46	—	41	115	70	164	686	242	3.7	2.3	0	.29	.27	6	—	—	—	.2
1606	Salad-plain	148	28	2	0	—	5	0	37	57	23	382	1.2	.42	200	.06	.12	1	—	—	—	42
1607	Salad + house dressing	176	159	3	13	—	8	11	44	74	293	402	1.3	.52	205	.06	.15	1	—	—	—	42
1608	Salad + blue cheese drsg	176	184	3	16	—	7	22	66	83	333	382	1.3	.59	212	.06	.15	1	—	—	—	42
1609	Salad + french dressing	176	152	2	11	—	13	0	40	60	330	410	1.4	.45	212	.06	.12	1	—	—	—	43
1610	Salad + golden italian	176	162	2	14	—	7	0	40	60	292	389	1.3	.43	200	.05	.12	1	—	—	—	42
1611	Salad + creamy italian	176	159	3	13	—	8	11	44	74	293	402	1.3	.52	212	.06	.15	1	—	—	—	42
1612	Salad + low cal italian	176	42	2	1	—	7	0	40	59	430	390	1.4	.42	200	.05	.12	1	—	—	—	42
1613	Cherry pie	128	357	4	13	—	55	6	12	37	204	166	1.1	.2	15	.24	.16	.5	.03	—	4	8
1614	Pecan pie	113	459	5	20	15.4	64	4	24	84	374	204	1.1	.6	16	.28	.18	.6	.06	—	15	0
1588	Fried apple pie	125	305	3	12	—	44	4	15	31	412	122	1.2	.2	4	.27	.16	.6	.03	—	7	5

DAIRY QUEEN

1615	Ice cream cone-small	85	140	3	4	—	22	10	100	100	45	134	.4	.47	25	.03	.17	.06	.04	.36	2	.001
1616	Ice cream cone-regular	142	240	6	7	—	38	15	150	200	80	220	.7	.7	49	.06	.34	.11	.06	.6	3	.001
1617	Ice cream cone-large	213	340	9	10	—	57	25	250	300	115	330	1.4	1.0	98	.12	.51	.167	.09	.9	4	.001
1618	Dipped cone-small	92	190	3	9	—	25	10	100	100	55	134	.4	.47	25	.03	.17	.06	.04	.36	2	.001
1619	Dipped cone-regular	156	340	6	16	—	42	20	150	200	100	220	.7	.7	49	.06	.34	.11	.06	.6	3	.001
1620	Dipped cone-large	234	510	9	24	—	64	30	250	300	145	330	1.4	1.0	98	.12	.51	.167	.09	.9	4	.001
1621	Sundae-small	106	190	3	4	—	33	10	100	150	75	145	.4	.45	25	.03	.17	.17	.03	.36	2	.001
1622	Sundae-regular	177	310	5	8	—	56	20	200	200	120	290	1.1	.9	49	.06	.34	.3	.06	.6	4	.001
1623	Sundae-large	248	440	8	10	—	78	30	250	300	165	435	1.4	1.35	98	.12	.43	.4	.09	.9	6	.001
1624	Shake-small	291	490	10	13	—	82	35	350	400	180	480	1.8	.1	123	.15	.6	.3	.14	1.2	3	.001
1625	Shake-regular	418	710	14	19	—	120	50	450	500	260	690	2.7	.14	184	.23	.77	.4	.2	1.8	4	.001
1626	Shake-large	489	831	16	22	—	140	60	550	600	304	807	3.6	.16	200	.3	.94	.4	.23	2.1	5	.001
1627	Malt-small	291	520	10	13	—	91	35	350	400	180	480	2.7	.1	123	.15	.6	.4	.14	1.2	3	.001
1628	Malt-regular	418	760	14	18	—	134	50	450	600	260	690	4.5	.14	184	.3	.85	.8	.2	2.1	4	.001
1629	Malt-large	489	889	16	21	—	157	60	550	700	304	807	5.4	.16	200	.37	.90	.8	.23	2.7	5	.001
1630	Float	397	410	5	7	—	82	20	200	200	85	—	1.1	—	40	.06	.26	.05		.6	—	.001

Appendix F Table of Food Composition—Fast Foods

No.	Food	Weight	Calories	Protein	Total FAT	Unsaturated FAT	Carbohydrates	Cholesterol	Calcium	Phosphorus	Sodium	Potassium	Iron	Zinc	Vitamin A	Thiamin	Riboflavin	Niacin	Vitamin B_6	Folacin	Vitamin C	Vitamin B_{12}
		(g)		(g)	(g)	(g)	(g)	(mg)	(mg)	(mg)	(mg)	(mg)	(mg)	(mg)	(RE)	(mg)	(mg)	(mg)	(mg)	(mcg)	(mcg)	(mg)
1631	Banana split	383	540	9	11	—	103	30	250	350	150	670	1.8	2.1	160	.15	.51	.4	.8	.9	9	15
1667	Blizzard-Heath flavor	404	800	15	24	—	125	65	500	350	325	—	2.7	—	60	.3	.42	1.2	—	.48	—	4.8
1665	Fudge nut bar	142	406	8	25	—	40	10	100	250	167	—	1.08	—	20	.12	.17	2.0	—	.36	—	—
1632	Ice Cream Parfait	283	430	8	8	—	76	30	250	300	140	—	1.4	—	98	.09	.43	.3	—	.9	—	3.6
1633	Peanut Buster Parfait	305	740	16	34	—	94	30	250	450	250	500	1.8	1.5	74	.15	.43	2	.1	.9	7	—
1634	Double Delight	255	490	9	20	—	69	25	200	300	150	—	1.4	—	74	.15	.34	.4	—	.9	—	—
1635	HotFudgeBrownieDelight	266	600	9	25	—	85	20	200	300	225	300	1.8	.9	74	.12	.34	.3	.06	.6	4	—
1636	Strawberry shortcake	312	540	10	11	—	100	25	250	300	215	—	1.8	—	98	.23	.51	1	—	.24	—	12
1637	Freeze	397	500	9	12	—	89	30	300	350	180	—	1.8	—	98	.15	.51	—	—	.9	—	—
1638	Mr. Misty-small	248	190	0	0	—	48	0	—	—	10	—	—	—	0	—	—	—	—	—	—	—
1639	Mr. Misty-regular	330	250	0	0	0	63	0	—	—	10	—	—	—	0	—	—	—	—	—	—	—
1640	Mr. Misty-large	439	340	0	0	—	84	0	—	—	10	—	—	—	0	—	—	—	—	—	—	—
1641	Mr. Misty kiss	89	70	0	0	0	17	0	—	—	10	—	—	—	0	—	—	—	—	—	—	—
1642	Mr. Misty freeze	411	500	9	12	—	91	30	300	200	140	—	1.4	—	98	.12	.51	—	—	.60	—	—
1643	Mr. Misty float	411	390	5	7	—	74	20	200	200	95	—	.7	—	49	.06	.26	—		.6	—	—
1644	Buster bar	149	460	10	29	—	41	10	100	250	175	—	1.1	—	25	.12	.17	2	—	.36	—	—
1645	Dilly bar	85	210	3	13	—	21	10	100	100	50	—	.4	—	25	.03	.17	—		.24	—	—
1646	DQ ice cream sandwich	60	140	3	4	—	24	5	60	60	40	—	.04	—	15	.03	.07	.4	—	.12	—	—
1647	Single hamburger	148	360	21	16	8	33	45	100	150	630	290	3.6	4.5	10	.3	.17	5	.18	1.5	16	1
1648	Double hamburger	210	530	36	28	15	33	85	100	300	660	410	6.3	6.4	20	.45	.34	9	.28	2.7	23	1
1649	Triple hamburger	272	710	51	45	25	33	135	100	450	690	532	9	8.2	28	.6	.51	14	.33	4.2	29	1
1650	Single cheeseburger	162	410	24	20	9	33	50	200	250	790	300	3.6	5.0	110	.3	.17	5	.2	1.8	20	1
1651	Double cheeseburger	239	650	43	37	16	34	95	350	500	980	443	6.3	7.3	160	.45	.43	9	.3	3	30	1
1652	Triple cheeseburger	301	820	58	50	23	34	145	350	700	1010	550	9	9.2	200	.6	.6	14	.55	4.8	37	1
1659	Fish filet sandwich	177	430	20	18	—	45	40	150	150	674	—	3.6	—	15	.6	.42	8.0	—	.9	—	—
1660	Fish sandwich + cheese	191	483	23	22	—	46	49	250	200	870	—	3.6	—	60	.67	.51	8.0	—	1.2	—	—
1661	Chicken sandwich	202	608	27	34	—	46	78	150	250	725	—	5.4	—	20	.6	.59	8.0	—	.06	—	2.4
1668	Chicken san w/cheese	216	661	30	38	—	47	87	250	300	921	—	5.4	—	150	.68	.68	8.0	—	.90	—	2.4
1669	Chicken nuggets-svg	99	276	16	18	—	13	39	—	300	505	—	1.0	—	0	.15	.17	2.0	—	1.2	—	—
1666	Chipper sandwich	113	318	5	7	—	56	13	100	80	170	—	2.7	—	20	.09	.34	1.2	—	.12	—	1.2
1670	BBQ sauce-packet	28	41	—	—	—	9	—	20	—	130	—	.36	—	150	.06	.10	—	—	—	—	—
1653	Hotdog	100	280	11	16	9	21	45	80	100	830	130	1.4	1.4	0	.12	.14	3	.08	.9	20	.01
1654	Hotdog with chili	128	320	13	20	10	23	55	80	150	985	170	1.8	1.8	60	.15	.26	4	.17	1.29	30	.01
1655	Hotdog with cheese	114	330	15	21	10	21	55	150	200	990	140	1.4	1.9	85	.12	.17	3	.08	1.2	24	.01
1656	Super hotdog	175	520	17	27	15	44	80	150	150	1365	210	2.7	2.8	0	.23	.26	5	.14	1.5	35	.01
1657	Super hotdog w/chili	218	570	21	32	16	47	100	150	250	1595	250	2.7	2.5	60	.23	.43	6	.25	1.8	45	.01
1658	Super hotdog w/cheese	196	580	22	34	16	45	100	250	300	1605	220	1.4	2.5	100	.23	.26	5	.16	1.8	39	.01
1671	DQ Hounder	151	480	16	36	—	21	80	150	150	1800	—	4.5	—	.5	.45	.34	7.0	—	0.9	—	—
1672	DQ Hounder w/chili	208	575	22	41	—	25	89	200	200	1900	—	4.5	—	19	.37	.42	10	—	1.5	—	—
1673	DQ Hounder w/cheese	165	533	19	40	—	22	89	250	200	1995	—	4.5	—	41	.52	.42	7.0	—	1.2	—	—
1662	French fries-small svg	71	200	2	10	—	25	10	10	60	115	450	.34	.3	0	.06	.02	.8	.16	0	15	9
1663	French fries-large svg	113	320	3	16	6	40	15	15	100	185	700	1.08	.3	0	.09	.03	1.2	.3	0	25	15
1664	Onion rings-1 serving	85	280	4	16	11	31	15	20	60	140	110	.72	.3	15	.09	.05	.4	.08	0	10	2.4
	DOMINO'S PIZZA																					
1674	Cheese pizza	169	376	21.6	10.0	4.52	56.3	18.5	221	—	482	—	2.75	—	72.2	.48	.43	4.64	—	—	—	.52
1675	Pepperoni pizza	187	460	24.1	17.5	9.14	55.6	28.0	239	—	825	—	3.08	—	93.0	.63	.55	5.49	—	—	—	.64
1676	Sausage/mushroom pizza	201	430	24.2	15.8	8.08	55.2	28.1	227	—	552	—	3.01	—	94.2	.61	.63	6.07	—	—	—	.46
1677	Veggie pizza	261	498	31.0	18.5	8.34	60.0	36.5	435	—	1035	—	4.74	—	102	.57	.97	5.58	—	—	—	.26
1678	Deluxe pizza	234	498	26.7	20.4	11.1	59.2	39.8	233	—	954	—	4.66	—	90.3	.57	.50	6.6	—	—	—	.82
1679	Dbl cheese/pepprn pizza	227	545	32.1	25.3	12.1	55.2	47.7	458	—	1042	—	4.02	—	91	.57	.62	5.69	—	—	—	1.32
1680	Ham pizza	186	417	23.2	11.0	5.07	58.0	26.0	226	—	805	—	4.61	—	46.7	.60	.39	5.8	—	—	—	.63

HARDEE'S

1703	Hamburger	99	264	5.9	9.6	5.4	39	25.3	101	—	500	198	3	—	14	—	—	—	—	—	—	—
1704	Cheeseburger	110	310	16.8	13.1	6.8	32	27.8	142	—	681	142	3	—	47	—	—	—	—	—	—	—
1705	Quarter lb cheeseburger	184	509	32	29.2	15	29	60.4	211	—	1076	430	4.5	—	128	—		—	—	—	—	—
1706	Big deluxe burger	226	495	27	26.8	17	33	58	190	—	824	394	4.1	—	104	—	—	—	—	—	—	—
1707	Bacon cheeseburger	229	610	32	39.1	23.5	33	59	130	—	973	492	4.7	—	47	—	—	—	—	—	—	—
1708	Mushroom & swiss burger	197	516	29	28.3	14.9	36	55	239	—	1032	390	4.1	—	47	—	—	—	—	—	—	—
1709	Reg roast beef sandwich	141	338	20.7	14.7	8.9	31	34	68	—	967	277	4.1	—	30	—	—	—	—	—	—	—
1710	Big roast beef sandwich	174	396	27	18.3	10.7	31	52	76	—	1277	484	5	—	30	—	—	—	—	—	—	—
1711	Hot ham'n cheese san	140	316	20.5	10.6	6.3	35	42	222	—	1497	216	2.5	—	94	—	—	—	—	—	—	—
1712	Turkey club sandwich	224	374	28	14.3	10.4	33	46	140	—	1296	505	2.9	—	104	—	—	—	—	—	—	—
1713	Chicken fillet sandwich	182	416	24	15	12.7	47	61	82	—	1384	324	3.4	—	30	—	—	—	—	—	—	—
1714	Fisherman's fillet san	206	510	26.7	25	18.7	44	40	157	—	861	397	3.7	—	22	—	—	—	—	—	—	—
1715	Beef hotdog sandwich	124	306	12.2	16.1	9	29	22.5	70	—	776	263	2.4	—	0	—	—	—	—	—	—	—
1716	Side salad	112	19	1.8	.8	.31	1	0	22	—	14	172	0.5	—	37	—	—	—	—	—	—	—
1717	Garden salad	241	208	13.7	13.7	5.3	3	103	289	—	266	426	1.2	—	584	—	—	—	—	—	—	—
1718	Chef salad	294	248	28	14.6	6.1	.6	114	279	—	932	588	1.8	—	584	—	—	—	—	—	—	—
1719	Chicken fiesta salad	297	286	24	13.8	5.2	6	128	297	—	533	578	1.2	—	584	—	—	—	—	—	—	—
1720	Chicken stix-6 pce svg	100	210	18.7	9.1	7.4	13	35	20	—	678	258	.8	—	0	—	—	—	—	—	—	—
1681	Rise 'n shine biscuit	84	319	4.9	18.5	14.7	33.5	0	124	—	722	86	2	—	139	—	—	—	—	—	—	—
1682	Cinnamon/raisin biscuit	79	315	4.4	16.7	12.2	37.1	0	125	—	514	79.4	1.7	—	129	—		—	—	—	—	—
1683	Sausage biscuit	115	448	11.6	29.5	20.5	34.5	19.3	122	—	1053	173	2.8	—	0	—	—	—	—	—	—	—
1684	Sausage & egg biscuit	151	530	16.2	37	25.6	33.4	141	134	—	1123	205	3.4	—	88	—	—	—	—	—	—	—
1685	Bacon biscuit	84	315	7.2	16.6	12	34	3.8	141	—	848	106	2.3	—	0	—	—	—	—	—	—	—
1686	Bacon and egg biscuit	136	449	14.5	24.2	16.8	43	89.2	192	—	983	221	2.5	—	88	—	—	—	—	—	—	—
1687	Bacon/egg/cheeseBiscuit	149	492	16.5	26.6	18	47	125	276	—	1049	225	2.8	—	158	—	—	—	—	—	—	—
1688	Ham biscuit	115	321	11.8	15.4	11.8	34	11.3	135	—	1075	196	2.5	—	70	—	—	—	—	—	—	—
1689	Ham and egg biscuit	155	404	17.2	22	16.6	34	159	170	—	1132	259	3.1	—	167	—	—	—	—	—	—	—
1690	Ham/egg/cheese biscuit	171	455	20.4	24.7	17.4	38	148	225	—	1418	293	3	—	227	—	—	—	—	—	—	—
1691	Country ham biscuit	103	348	11.7	18	15.3	35	17	121	—	1282	168	2.5	—	70	—	—	—	—	—	—	—
1692	Country ham&egg biscuit	134	404	16	21.5	16	37	106	151	—	1435	230	2.7	—	167	—	—	—	—	—	—	—
1693	Can Rise'nShine biscuit	158	478	20	28.2	22.3	36	187	195	—	1550	243	3.4	—	70	—		—	—	—	—	—
1694	Steak biscuit	150	521	13.8	30.4	24.9	48	17	129	—	1376	226	3.6	—	70	—	—	—	—	—	—	—
1695	Steak 'n egg biscuit	171	563	22	34.4	24.7	42	103	134	—	1425	225	4	—	167	—	—	—	—	—	—	—
1696	Chicken biscuit	152	448	15.3	25.1	20	41	9	157	—	1308	226	2.3	—	0	—	—	—	—	—	—	—
1697	BCB-sausage	313	1005	32	73.3	57.6	55	280	126	—	1950	552	6.3	—	247	—	—	—	—	—	—	—
1698	BCB-bacon	240	754	23.3	53.7	44.4	45	350	149	—	1661	467	4.8	—	247	—	—	—	—	—	—	—
1699	BCB-ham	284	768	28	47	35.6	58	265	182	—	2021	576	4.6	—	247	—	—	—	—	—	—	—
1700	BCB-country ham	276	764	32	47	40.9	52	269	133	—	2493	562	4.8	—	247	—	—	—	—	—	—	—
1701	Hash Rounds	79	232	3.3	13.7	11	24	0	15	—	558	398	1	—	0	—	—	—	—	—	—	—
1702	Biscuit 'n gravy	210	420	8.6	21.4	18.1	48	9.7	132	—	1379	187	3	—	0	—	—	—	—	—	—	—
1721	French fries-reg svg	71	226	2.7	10.5	8.5	30	0	12	—	83	348	.9	—	0	—	—	—	—	—	—	—
1722	French fries-large svg	113	361	4.3	16.7	13.5	48	0	19	—	133	557	1.4	—	0	—	—	—	—	—	—	—
1723	Big fry	156	496	5.9	23	18.6	66	0	26	—	182	766	1.9	—	0	—	—	—	—	—	—	—
1724	Cheese slice	13	46	2.4	4.0	1.4	.6	5	68	—	226	14	.1	—	38	—	—	—	—	—	—	—
1725	Vanilla shake	239	280	9.3	6.2	2.1	46	23	339	—	225	532	.1	—	76	—	—	—	—	—	—	—
1726	Chocolate shake	335	447	10.6	7.7	2.6	83	25	389	—	338	616	1.4	—	76	—	—	—	—	—	—	—
1727	Strawberry shake	317	410	10	7.0	2.3	76	24	387	—	274	475	.1	—	76	—	—	—	—	—	—	—
1728	Cool Twist cone-vanilla	124	192	4.9	6.1	2	29	17	168	—	81	161	.1	—	55	—	—	—	—	—	—	—
1729	Cool Twist cone-chocolt	138	208	5.5	6.4	2.2	32	18	169	—	82	232	.5	—	55	—	—	—	—	—	—	—
1730	Cool Twist cone-van/chc	131	203	5.1	6.4	2.1	31	21	184	—	84	205	.3	—	55	—	—	—	—	—	—	—
1731	Cool Twist sundae-HtFdg	134	245	6	7.8	—	37	17	152	—	147	173	.4	—	70	—	—	—	—	—	—	—
1732	Cool Twist sundae-carml	141	271	5.3	6.5	2.1	47	20	184	—	175	211	.3	—	55	—	—	—	—	—	—	—
1733	Cool Twist sundae-straw	152	241	4.7	5.5	1.8	43	17	187	—	87	220	.4	—	54	—	—	—	—	—	—	—
1734	Apple turnover	91	268	2.9	11.7	8.4	38	0	8	—	245	74	1.3	—	2.8	—	—		—	—	—	—
1735	Big cookie	49	250	2.6	13.1	9.1	31	0	5	—	239	46	.7	—	0	—	—	—	—	—	—	—

Appendix F Table of Food Composition—Fast Foods

JACK IN THE BOX

No.	Food	Weight (g)	Calories	Protein (g)	Total FAT (g)	Unsaturated FAT (g)	Carbohydrates (g)	Cholesterol (mg)	Calcium (mg)	Phosphorus (mg)	Sodium (mg)	Potassium (mg)	Iron (mg)	Zinc (mg)	Vitamin A (RE)	Thiamin (mg)	Riboflavin (mg)	Niacin (mg)	Vitamin B_6 (mg)	Folacin (mcg)	Vitamin C (mcg)	Vitamin B_{12} (mg)
1736	Hamburger	98	276	13	12	—	30	29	70	115	521	165	2.7	1.8	9	.36	.24	3.2	.1	.73	—	1.2
1737	Cheeseburger	113	323	16	15	—	32	42	160	194	749	177	2.7	2.3	57	.36	.27	3.3	.1	.87	—	1.2
1759	Double cheeseburger	149	467	21	27	—	33	72	400	—	842	—	2.7	—	200	.15	.34	6.0	—	—	—	—
1738	Jumbo Jack burger	205	485	26	26	—	38	64	97	208	905	390	6.9	3.7	50	.51	.21	7.03	.25	2.1	—	5.1
1739	JumboJack burger + chees	246	630	32	35	—	45	110	250	411	1665	499	4.5	4.8	107	.53	.34	12	.31	3.05	—	4.8
1740	Cheeseburger + bcn-suprm	231	724	34	46	—	44	70	310	—	1307	—	4.9	—	86	.56	.51	8.8	—	—	—	3
1741	Swiss + bacon burger	230	643	33	43	—	31	99	230	—	1354	—	4.7	—	57	.45	.41	6.8	—	—	—	3
1742	Taco-super	135	288	12	17	—	21	37	150	198	765	347	1.6	1.8	85	.12	.08	1.4	.18	.74	—	1.8
1751	Taco salad	402	503	34	31	13.5	28	92	410	—	1600	—	3.8	—	270	.29	.52	5.8	—	—	—	9
1769	Mexican chicken salad	413	442	28	23	10.7	30	89	39	—	1500	—	2.0	—	250	.25	.46	6.0		—	—	18
1762	Beef Fajita Pita	175	333	24	14	7.5	27	45	250	—	635	—	1.08	—	100	.37	.51	5	—	—	—	—
1763	Chicken Fajita Pita	189	292	24	8	5	29	34	250	—	703	—	2.7	—	100	.75	.17	6	—	—	—	—
1764	Grilled chicken fillet	205	408	31	17	10.6	33	64	170	—	1130	—	2.2	—	57	.27	.37	14.4	—	—	—	7.8
1765	Fish supreme sandwich	228	554	20	32	18.4	47	.66	45	—	1047	—	2.7	—	72	.15	.26	5	—	—	—	—
1743	Chicken supreme	228	601	31	36	—	39	60	240	—	1582	—	3	—	64	.52	.37	10.6	—	—	—	4.2
1772	Chicken strips	125	349	29	14	6.6	28	68	10	—	748	—	1.4	—	0	.06	.14	2.0	—		—	—
1773	Fried shrimp	84	370	10	16	8.4	22	84	20	—	669	—	1.1	—	0	.03	.10	1.2	—		—	—
1774	Taquitos-pieces	140	363	16	16	8	40	37	17	—	467	—	3.2	—	0	.06	.14	2.2	—	—	—	—
1775	French fries-jumbo svg	136	442	4	24	13.2	54	16	—	—	328	—	1.1	—	0	.15	.06	2.4	—	—	—	6.0
1771	Egg rolls	171	405	15	19	9.9	42	30	50	—	903	—	2.7	—	80	.23	.17	3.0	—	—	—	4.8
1752	French fries-reg svg	109	353	3	19	10.5	43	13	—	—	262	—	.9	—	0	.12	.05	1.8	—	—	—	4.8
1753	Onion rings-serving	108	382	5	23	—	39	27	30	69	407	109	1.4	.4	.01	.21	.12	1.8	.06	.2	—	3
1768	Chef salad	369	295	32	18	6.2	3	107	15	—	812	—	4.5	—	136	.23	—	8	—	—	—	—
1770	Side salad	111	51	7	3	1	—	—	60	—	84	—	—	—	15	.06	.10	—	—	—	—	—
1766	Mayo-Onion sauce-servg	21	143	.3	15	—	1	20	—	—	140	—	—	—	16	—	—	—	—	—	—	—
1767	Mayo-Mustard sauce-svg	21	124	.5	13	—	2	10	—	—	247	—	—	—	14	—	—	—	—	—	—	—
1744	Supreme crescent	146	547	20	40	—	27	178	150	—	1053	—	2.7	—	78	.64	.54	4.2	—	—	—	.001
1745	Sausage crescent	156	584	22	43	—	28	187	170	—	1012	—	2.9	—	78	.6	.51	4.6	—	—	—	.001
1750	Canadian crescent	134	472	18.6	31	—	24.6	226	125	—	851	—	3.4	—	135	.5	.4	3.6	—	—	—	3.1
1746	Pancake platter	231	612	15	22	11.1	87	99	100	633	888	237	1.8	1.9	69	.03	.75	7	.19	.56	3	6
1747	Scrambled egg platter	249	662	24	40	20.7	52	354	200	483	1188	635	5.4	3.0	252	.3	.77	5	.34	1.31	30	4.8
1748	BreakfastJack sandwich	126	307	18	13	—	30	203	170	310	871	190	3.1	1.8	120	.47	.41	3	.11	1	—	.001
1749	Bacon strips	12	70	3	6	—	0	10	1	—	226	—	.38	—	0	.03	.03	.8	—	—	—	4
1754	Hash browns-serving	62	116	2	7	3.6	11	3	40	—	211	—	.36	—	0	.06	.03	1.2	—	—	—	3.6
1755	Vanilla shake	317	320	10	6	—	57	25	350	312	230	599	.3	1	.1	.15	.34	.4	.2	1.36	—	.01
1756	Strawberry shake	328	320	10	7	—	55	25	350	328	240	613	.4	1.1	.1	.15	.43	.4	.16	1.1	—	3.3
1757	Chocolate shake	322	330	11	7	—	55	25	350	330	270	650	.7	1.2	.1	.15	.59	.6	.18	.98	—	3.2
1758	Apple turnover	119	410	4	24	—	45	15	11	33	350	69	1.4	.2	0	.23	.12	2.5	.03	.17	—	.01

KENTUCKY FRIED CHICKEN

No.	Food	Weight (g)	Calories	Protein (g)	Total FAT (g)	Unsaturated FAT (g)	Carbohydrates (g)	Cholesterol (mg)	Calcium (mg)	Phosphorus (mg)	Sodium (mg)	Potassium (mg)	Iron (mg)	Zinc (mg)	Vitamin A (RE)	Thiamin (mg)	Riboflavin (mg)	Niacin (mg)	Vitamin B_6 (mg)	Folacin (mcg)	Vitamin C (mcg)	Vitamin B_{12} (mg)
793	Chicken wing/original	42	136	9.60	9.1	6.1	4.2	54.6	21.6	76	302	86	.68	.58	2.7	.030	.040	2.28	.097	.316	3.8	.85
794	Chicken leg/original	47	117	12.1	6.5	4.21	2.6	63	12.1	95	207	122	.8	1.29	2.7	.040	.090	2.38	.085	.405	4.2	1
795	Chick side-brst/orig	69	199	16.2	11.7	7.58	7.1	69.8	50.1	151	558	176	.98	.774	4.2	.060	.080	5.66	.2	.455	6.4	1.4
796	Chicken thigh/originl	88	257	18.4	17.5	11.3	6.5	109	34.2	169	566	217	1.45	1.65	5.4	.080	.16	4.03	.167	.968	8.60	1.8
797	Chicken breast/orig	95	236	23.9	14	8.13	7.4	86.7	29.8	205	631	267	1.17	.72	5.7	.080	.11	7.57	.313	.398	7.8	1.9
798	2-pce dinner/white	322	604	30.4	32.1	21.6	48.3	133	142	326	1528	643	3.31	1.88	76.5	.22	.19	10	.504	.925	39.1	36.6
799	2-pce dinner/dark	346	643	35.1	35.2	23.4	46.2	180	116	363	1441	720	3.9	3.47	76.5	.25	.32	8.46	.459	1.53	41.7	36.6

800	2-pce dinner/combo	341	661	32.6	37.8	25.2	47.8	172	126	344	1536	684	3.78	2.76	76.5	.24	.27	8.36	.471	1.44	41.3	36.6
801	Chicken wing/crispy	53	201	11.2	13.5	9.1	8.7	58.7	15.5	77	312	100	.65	.673	3.3	.060	.090	2.94	.112	.336	5.3	1.1
802	Chicken leg/crispy	58	155	13.3	9	5.83	5.1	65.5	11	100	263	147	.95	1.32	3.6	.070	.11	3.07	.157	.434	5.9	1.2
803	Chicken side-breast/C	84	286	17.2	17.8	11.5	14.1	65.1	56.8	157	564	188	1.12	.879	5.1	.12	.13	5.37	.237	.541	8.5	1.7
804	Chicken thigh/crispy	107	343	20.4	23.4	15.1	12.6	109	49	185	549	228	1.49	1.73	6.6	.12	.19	5.35	.171	.973	11	2.2
805	Chicken breast/crispy	104	297	23.6	16.4	10.8	13.6	78.8	62.2	218	584	244	1.29	.77	6.3	.11	.11	7.89	.302	.478	10.8	2.1
806	2-pce dinner/white/C	348	755	33	42.6	28.6	59.9	132	143	333	1544	689	6.03	2.08	76.5	.31	.29	10.4	.556	1.03	42.7	36.6
807	2-pce dinner/dark/C	375	765	38.3	53.7	28.8	54.7	183	130	383	1480	776	4.09	3.58	76.5	.32	.38	10.4	.535	1.56	45.8	36.6
808	2-pce combo dinner/C	371	902	36.2	48.2	32	58.4	176	135	361	1529	729	6.4	2.93	76.5	.31	.35	10.3	.49	1.46	45.2	36.6
1776	Kentucky nuggets	16	46	2.82	2.88	2.12	2.2	11.9	2.4	29	140	33	.13	.22	30	.02	.03	1	.037	.12	1.4	1.5
1777	Barbeque sauce	30	35	.3	.57	.48	7.1	1	6.05	10	450	75	.24	.05	37	.01	.014	.19	.02	—	3	.36
1778	Sweet & sour sauce	30	58	.1	.56	.47	13	1	4.66	5	148	39	.16	.02	6	.01	.02	.04	.01	—	.6	.31
1779	Honey sauce	15	49	0	.01	—	12.1	—	.581	—	10	6	.11	.001	0	.01	.003	.04	—	—	1	2.5
1780	Mustard sauce	30	36	.88	.91	—	6.04	—	10.2	15	346	23	.26	.09	.9	.02	.008	.16	.015	—	3	1
1786	Chicken Little Sandw	56.7	177	6.1	9.15	6.55	17.1	19.7	38.8	105	398	114	1.4	.934	6	.152	.138	1.65	.067	.062	10.5	.001
809	Mashed potatoes	80	60	1.9	.6	.41	11.6	.2	20.6	41	228	218	.28	.16	5	.010	.038	.96	.11	.059	7	4.5
810	Chicken gravy	78	59	2	3.7	2.6	4.4	2	8.58	10	398	21	.48	.036	1	.007	.028	.47	.005	.059	1.54	.385
1782	Mashed potatoes + gravy	86	62	2.1	1.4	.43	10.3	1	19.1	28	297	137	.35	.106	5	.01	.036	1	.08	.07	8	1
811	Dinner roll	21	61	1.8	1.1	.77	10.9	.64	21.3	28	118	29	.53	.2	1	.1	.040	.98	.014	.022	6.6	.25
812	Corn-on-the-cob	143	176	5.1	3.1	2.46	31.9	.15	7.19	134	21	323	.39	.986	27	.14	.113	1.8	.219	.117	71	2.3
813	Coleslaw	79	103	1.3	5.7	4.8	11.5	4	28.5	20	171	115	.19	.127	28	.030	.026	.20	.07	.04	9.5	18.7
1781	Kentucky fries-srving	119	268	4.8	12.8	9.2	33.3	1	24.3	78	81	606	.94	.31	0	.17	.057	2.7	.18	0	20	2.7
1783	Buttermilk biscuit	75	269	5.1	13.6	6.65	31.6	1	77	264	521	95	1.22	.292	30	.28	.13	1.8	.03	.1	7.5	.5
1784	Potato salad	90	141	1.8	9.27	7.65	12.6	11	10.4	32	396	256	.32	.293	27	.07	.023	.6	.19	—	7.2	2.7
1785	Baked beans	89	105	5.1	1.2	.74	18.4	1	53.6	90	387	229	1.43	1.29	9.8	.06	.039	.5	.073	.017	32.2	2.1

LONG JOHN SILVER'S®

1787	Fish + fryes-3pc-batrfr	350	853	43	48	—	64	106	—	—	2025	—	—	—	—	—	—	—	—	—	—	—
1788	Fish + fryes-2pc-batrfr	260	651	30	36	—	53	75	—	—	1352	—	—	—	—	—	—	—	—	—	—	—
1789	Fish & more	—	978	34	58	—	82	88	—	—	2124	—	—	—	—	—	—	—	—	—	—	—
1790	Fish din-3pce-batrfrd	540	1180	47	70	—	93	119	—	—	2797	—	—	—	—	—	—	—	—	—	—	—
1791	ChickenPlank din-3pce	370	885	32	51	—	72	25	—	—	1918	—	—	—	—	—	—	—	—	—	—	—
1792	ChickenPlank din-4pce	440	1037	41	59	—	82	25	—	—	2433	—	—	—	—	—	—	—	—	—	—	—
1793	ChicknNugget din-6pce	300	699	23	45	—	54	25	—	—	853	—	—	—	—	—	—	—	—	—	—	—
1794	Fish & chicken dinner	460	935	36	55	—	73	56	—	—	2076	—	—	—	—	—	—	—	—	—	—	—
1795	Seafood platter	410	976	29	58	—	85	95	—	—	2161	—	—	—	—	—	—	—	—	—	—	—
1796	Clam dinner	460	955	22	58	—	100	27	—	—	1543	—	—	—	—	—	—	—	—	—	—	—
1797	Shrimp dinner-batrfrd	300	711	17	45	—	60	127	—	—	1297	—	—	—	—	—	—	—	—	—	—	—
1798	Scallop dinner	320	747	17	45	—	66	37	—	—	1579	—	—	—	—	—	—	—	—	—	—	—
1799	Oyster dinner	360	789	17	45	—	78	55	—	—	763	—	—	—	—	—	—	—	—	—	—	—
1800	Fish dinner 3pce-brdd	450	940	35	52	—	84	101	—	—	1900	—	—	—	—	—	—	—	—	—	—	—
1801	Fish dinner 2pce-brdd	400	818	26	46	—	76	76	—	—	1526	—	—	—	—	—	—	—	—	—	—	—
1802	Fish sandwich platter	400	835	30	42	—	84	75	—	—	1402	—	—	—	—	—	—	—	—	—	—	—
1803	Seafood salad	480	426	19	30	—	22	113	—	—	1086	—	—	—	—	—	—	—	—	—	—	—
1804	Ocean chef salad	320	229	27	8	—	13	64	—	—	986	—	—	—	—	—	—	—	—	—	—	—
1805	Fish-batter fried-svg	86	202	13	12	—	11	31	—	—	673	—	—	—	—	—	—	—	—	—	—	—
1806	Fish-breaded-serving	58	122	9	6	—	8	23	—	—	374	—	—	—	—	—	—	—	—	—	—	—
1807	ChickenPlank-alacarte	62	152	9	8		10	—	—	—	515	—	—	—	—	—	—	—	—	—	—	—
1808	Fried shrimp-alacarte	17	47	2	3	—	3	17	—	—	154	—	—	—	—	—	—	—	—	—	—	—
1809	Clam chowder-alacarte	185	128	7	5	—	15	17	—	—	611	—	—	—	—	—	—	—	—	—	—	—
1810	Cole slaw	98	182	1	15	—	11	12	—	—	367	—	—	—	—	—	—	—	—	—	—	—
1811	Fryes-serving	85	247	4	12	—	31	13	—	—	.6	—	—	—	—	—	—	—	—	—	—	—
1812	Hush puppies	47	145	3	7	—	18	—	—	—	405	—	—	—	—	—	—	—	—	—	—	—

Appendix F Table of Food Composition—Fast Foods

	McDONALDS®	Weight (g)	Calories	Protein (g)	Total FAT (g)	Unsaturated FAT (g)	Carbohydrates (g)	Cholesterol (mg)	Calcium (mg)	Phosphorus (mg)	Sodium (mg)	Potassium (mg)	Iron (mg)	Zinc (mg)	Vitamin A (RE)	Thiamin (mg)	Riboflavin (mg)	Niacin (mg)	Vitamin B_6 (mg)	Folacin (mcg)	Vitamin C (mcg)	Vitamin B_{12} (mg)
774	Big Mac sandwich	215	560	25.2	32.4	22.4	42.5	103	256	338	950	268	4	5.04	35	.48	.41	6.81	.285	1.9	22.6	1.68
775	Quarter-Pounder	166	410	23.1	20.7	12.6	34	86	142	258	660	334	3.68	5.30	40	.36	.29	6.70	.276	1.95	23.9	3.24
776	Quarter-Pounder w/chz	194	520	28.5	29.2	18	35.1	118	296	315	1150	356	3.72	5.95	134	.37	.39	6.73	.243	2.24	24	3.24
1833	McDLT sandwich	234	580	26.3	36.8	29.7	36	109	225	321	990	414	3.91	5.98	159	0.39	0.36	6.87	.26	2.24	30	7.38
1834	McChicken sandwich	190	490	19.2	28.6	—	39.8	42.6	143	—	780	—	2.61	—	—	0.96	0.21	8.92	—	—	—	2.42
777	Filet-O-Fish sandwich	142	440	13.8	26.1	21	37.9	50	165	227	1030	149	1.83	.884	22	.30	.15	2.68	.094	.814	19.9	.06
778	Hamburger	102	260	12.3	9.5	5.86	30.6	37	122	129	500	145	2.29	2.13	21.2	.28	.16	3.84	.124	.822	17.3	2.15
779	Cheeseburger	116	310	15	13.8	8.59	31.2	53	199	205	750	157	2.3	2.6	74	.29	.21	3.86	.115	.908	21	2.15
280	French fries-sml svg	68	220	4	12.0	8.19	25.6	0	9.92	101	70	564	.51	.32	2	.13	0	1.83	.218	.027	19	2.17
1832	French fries-med-svg	97	320	4	17.2	7.01	36.5	0	14.2	144	100	804	.73	.66	2.9	.19	0	2.61	.311	.038	27	3.10
1839	French fries-lrg serv	122	400	6	21.6	—	45.9	0	17.8	—	170	—	0.92	—	0	0.24	0	3.29	—	—	—	3.90
1408	Chicken McNuggets	112	270	20	15.4	12.2	17.2	56	13.5	293	580	313	1.05	.923	0	.12	.12	8.34	.394	.373	11.4	0
1409	Hot mustard sce-paket	30	70	.5	3.6	3.09	8.2	5	15	15	250	23	.22	.09	1.6	.01	.01	.15	.01	.02	3	.45
1410	Barbecue sauce-packet	32	50	.3	.5	.41	12.1	0	12.8	10	340	75	.31	.05	15.3	.01	.01	.17	.02	.13	3	2.34
1411	Sweet&sour sce-packet	32	60	.2	.2	.22	13.8	0	10.9	5	190	39	.17	.02	32.4	0	.01	.08	.01	.01	.6	.64
1835	Honey-packet	14	45	0	0	—	11.5	0	.70	—	0	—	.07	—	—	0	.01	.04	—	—	—	.14
1819	Chef salad	283	230	20.5	13.3	7.65	7.5	128	256	200	490	400	1.51	1.4	411	.31	.29	3.6	.04	—	60	13.6
1836	Chunky chicken salad	250	140	23.1	3.4	—	5.3	78	33.8	—	230	—	1.02	—	—	0.22	0.17	8.5	—	—	—	19.9
1818	Sausage McMuffin + egg	167	440	22.6	26.8	18	27.9	263	263	291	980	298	3.34	2.39	150	.64	.42	4.82	.200	1.39	33.4	0
1820	Garden salad	213	110	7.1	6.6	3.91	6.2	83	149	80	160	280	1.26	.4	391	.10	.16	.59	.06	—	60	13.5
1821	Side salad	115	60	3.7	3.3	.94	3.3	41	76.3	20	85	140	.67	.24	217	.05	.08	.32	.04	—	60	7.4
1837	Ranch dressing-1pkt	57	332	.68	34.4	—	5.20	20	26.6	—	520	—	.16	—	4	.04	.08	.04	—	—	—	.24
1838	Peppercorn dress-1pkt	71	400	.85	43.5	—	2.5	35	15.6	—	425	—	.25	—	5	0	0	0	—	—	—	.45
1824	Bleu chz dresing-1pkt	71	350	2.50	34.5	—	6.0	30	73	—	750	—	.15	—	9	0	.1	.15	—	—	—	.15
1825	Red French dres-1 pkt	57	160	.28	7.6	—	20.8	0	12.5	—	440	—	.40	—	30	0	0	.2	—	—	—	2.56
1826	1000 Isl dresng-1pkt	71	390	1.00	37.5	—	12.0	40	12.7	—	500	—	.40	—	25	0	0	.15	—	—	—	2.25
1827	Lt vingrt dress-1pkt	57	60	.92	2.0	.323	8.0	0	13	—	300	—	.16	—	37	0	0	.08	—	—	—	1.40
1822	Croutons-serving	11	50	1.39	2.17	1.43	6.8	0	6.48	—	140	—	.35	—	0	.05	.03	.42	—	—	—	.14
1823	Bacon bits-serving	3	16	1.3	1.19	1.19	.1	0	0	—	95	—	0	—	0	0	0	0	—	—	—	0
1828	Apple danish	115	390	5.8	17.9	12.8	51.2	25	14	—	370	—	1.37	—	32	.28	.2	2.2	—	—	—	16.1
1829	Iced cheese danish	110	390	7.4	21.8	13.9	42.3	47	32.9	—	420	—	1.42	—	52	.29	.23	2.1	—	—	—	1.1
1830	Cinnamon raisn danish	110	440	6.4	21	14.6	57.5	34	35.1	—	430	—	1.81	—	31	.32	.24	2.8	—	—	—	3.2
1831	Raspberry danish	117	410	6.1	15.9	11.3	61.5	26	14.2	—	310	—	1.47	—	33	.33	.21	2.1	—	—	—	3.2
1847	Apple bran muffin	85	190	5	0	—	46	0	31	—	230	—	.60	—	1	.02	.08	.40	—	—	—	0.7
675	English muffin w/btr	59	170	5.4	4.6	2.18	26.7	9	151	69.3	270	66.5	1.61	.466	31	.33	.14	2.47	.041	.019	15.9	0
788	Egg McMuffin	138	290	18.2	11.2	8.04	28.1	226	256	322	740	168	2.77	1.92	122	.47	.33	3.71	.211	.75	30	0
1817	Sausage McMuffin	117	370	16.5	21.9	14.1	27.3	64	235	189	830	219	2.3	1.71	72	.60	.29	4.8	.153	.691	23.4	0
789	Hotcakes + butter syrup	176	410	8.2	9.2	5.6	74.4	21	114	412	640	154	2.08	.563	43	.32	.33	2.82	.099	.156	7.4	0
790	Scrambled eggs-1 svg	100	140	12.4	9.8	7.77	1.2	399	57	269	290	138	2.08	1.69	148	.07	.26	.05	.204	.95	66.3	0
791	Pork sausage-1 serv	48	180	8.4	16.3	10.4	0	48	8.24	86	350	115	.67	1.33	0	0.27	0.10	2.31	.165	.48	.906	0
792	Hashbrown potatoes	53	130	1.4	7.3	4.03	14.9	9	5.58	64.6	330	238	.27	.164	0	.06	.02	.85	.124	.013	5.78	1.59
1813	Biscuit + BiscuitSpread	75	260	4.6	12.7	9.28	31.9	1	75	264	730	95.3	1.31	.292	0	.23	.11	1.65	.03	.098	7.5	0
1814	Biscuit with sausage	123	440	13.0	29.0	19.7	31.9	49	83.2	359	1080	235	1.98	1.33	0	.49	.21	3.96	.123	.529	12.3	0
1815	Biscuit w/sausage + egg	180	520	19.9	34.5	24.2	32.6	275	116	490	1250	321	3.16	3.16	88	.53	.35	3.99	.199	1.37	36	0
1816	Biscuit + bacon + egg + chz	156	440	17.5	26.4	18.9	33.3	253	185	496	1230	250	2.56	1.67	160	.36	.33	2.47	.110	1.14	46.8	0
1844	Van lowfat milkshake	293	290	10.8	1.3	—	60	10	327	—	170	—	.10	—	92	.13	.48	.31	—	—	—	0
1845	Choc lowfat milkshake	293	320	11.6	1.7	—	66	10	323	—	240	—	.84	—	92	.13	.50	.40	—	—	—	0
1846	Strwbry lwfat mlkshke	293	320	10.7	1.3	—	67	10	—	—	170	—	.09	—	92	.13	.48	.31	—	—	—	0
1840	Vanilla cone	80	100	4	0.75	—	22	3	112	—	80	—	0.23	—	40	0.04	0.18	0.37	—	—	—	0
1841	Strawberry sundae	171	210	5.7	1.1	—	49.2	5	191	—	95	—	0.16	—	65	0.07	0.29	0.25	—	—	—	1.3
1842	Hot fudge sundae	169	240	7.3	3.2	—	50.5	6	235	—	170	—	0.48	—	65	0.08	0.35	0.30	—	—	—	0
1843	Hot caramel sundae	174	270	6.6	2.8	—	59.3	13	222	—	180	—	0.08	—	88	0.08	0.35	0.26	—	—	—	0
784	Apple pie	83	260	2.2	14.8	9.98	30	0	10.7	26.4	240	38.1	.71	.158	0	.06	.02	.32	.020	.033	4.88	11.4
786	McDonaldland cookies	56	290	4.2	9.2	7.32	47.1	0	8.91	71.8	300	50.4	2.07	.325	0	.25	.18	2.54	.027	.033	5.82	0
787	Chocolaty chp cookies	56	330	4.2	15.6	10.6	41.9	4	23.9	102	280	160	2.18	.468	0	.18	.21	2.47	.029	.072	5.65	0

PIZZA HUT

1848	Pan pizza-cheese	205	492	30	18	9	57	34	630	470	940	320	5.4	4.0	90	.56	.60	5.2	1.8	—	—	7
1849	Pan pizza-pepperoni	211	540	29	22	12.3	62	42	520	440	1127	405	6.3	4.2	100	.63	.44	5.4	1.8	—	—	8
1850	Pan pizza-supreme	255	589	32	30	16.2	53	48	500	460	1363	580	5.0	5.6	120	.81	.78	6.0	2.3	—	—	10
1851	Pan pizza-super suprm	257	563	33	26	14	53	55	540	470	1447	.532	6.7	5.4	120	.75	.66	6.4	2.4	—	—	11
1852	Thin/crispy pizza-chez	148	398	28	17	7	37	33	660	470	867	261	3.2	3.6	70	.4	.4	4.8	1.5	—	—	4.8
1853	Thin/crispy pizza-pepr	146	413	26	20	9	36	46	450	370	956	287	3.2	3.5	70	.4	.4	5.2	1.5	—	—	6
1854	Thin/crisp pizza-suprm	200	459	28	22	11	41	42	430	400	1328	544	5.9	4.7	100	.6	.5	5.4	1.8	—	—	9.6
1855	Thin/crisp pizza-Ssprm	203	463	29	21	11	44	56	460	420	1336	463	4.9	4.5	100	.6	.4	5.4	2.1	—	—	8.4
1856	Hand tossed pizza-chez	220	518	34	20	6.4	55	55	750	550	1276	396	5.4	4.7	100	.5	.5	5.4	1.8	—	—	10
1857	Hand tossed pizza-pepr	197	500	28	23	10.1	50	50	440	390	1267	415	6.8	4.8	100	.5	.5	5.6	2.0	—	—	7
1858	Hand tossed pizza-supr	239	540	32	26	12.2	50	55	480	460	1470	578	8.1	5.7	110	.7	.5	7.2	2.4	—	—	12
1859	Hand tossd pizza-Ssprm	243	556	33	25	12	54	54	440	420	1648	516	6.8	4.8	110	.7	.6	7.4	2.5	—	—	12
1860	Pers Pan pizza-pepprni	256	675	37	29	16.5	76	53	730	450	1335	408	5.8	3.8	120	.6	.7	8.2	1.3	—	—	10
1861	Pers Pan pizza-supreme	264	647	33	28	16.8	76	49	520	400	1313	487	6.7	3.8	120	.6	.7	8.0	1.4	—	—	11

TACO BELL

1878	Taco	78	183	10.3	10.8	—	10.6	31.8	84	—	276	159	1.07	—	24	.05	.142	1.2	—	—	—	1.15
1879	Taco Bellgrande	163	355	18.3	23.1	—	17.7	55.9	182	—	472	334	1.9	—	40	.107	.29	2.02	—	—	—	5.5
1880	Taco Light	170	410	19	28.8	—	18.1	55.6	155	—	594	316	2.4	—	60	.2	.33	2.5	—	—	—	4.7
1881	Soft Taco	92	228	11.9	11.8	—	17.9	31.8	116	—	516	178	2.27	—	30	.39	.223	2.74	—	—	—	1.22
1890	Soft taco supreme	124	275	—	16.3	—	19.1	31.9	142	—	516	226	2.31	—	88	.40	.268	2.9	—	—	—	3
1891	Super combo taco	142	286	—	15.9	—	20.9	39.8	165	—	462	288	1.77	—	140	.1	.217	1.42	—	—	—	14.6
1883	Fajita (steak taco)	135	234	14.6	10.9	—	19.5	14.2	117	150	485	207	3	3.18	107	.403	.341	3.71	.171	—	15	2.7
1897	Chicken fajita	136	226	13.6	10.2	—	19.8	43.7	123	—	619	201	2.16	—	103	.384	.318	2.94	—	—	—	3.61
1863	Bean Burrito w/red sce	191	357	13.1	10.2	—	54.4	9.35	147	—	888	428	3.47	—	50	.037	2.02	1.98	—	—	—	52.6
1884	Bean burrito w/grn sce	191	351	13	10.2	—	53	9.35	136	—	763	393	3.47	—	18	.37	2.03	2.15	—	—	—	51.9
1864	Beef Burrito w/red sce	191	403	22.5	17.3	—	39.1	56.7	114	—	1051	313	3.73	—	72	.398	2.14	3.44	—	—	—	1.77
1865	Beef + bn burrito-red sc	191	381	17.1	14.1	7.1	46.1	36.2	111	220	958	370	2.15	2.67	80	.486	.415	3.09	.588	—	38	1.6
1885	Beef burrito w/grn sce	191	397	22.4	17.3	—	37	56.7	102	—	926	278	3.73	—	33	.4	2.14	3.61	—	—	—	1.07
1866	Burrito Supreme-red sc	241	413	18	18.0	—	46.6	32.6	153	227	921	432	3.6	—	125	.41	2.12	2.89	—	—	—	25.6
1886	Burrito supreme + grn sc	241	407	17.8	17.5	—	45.2	32.6	142	—	796	399	3.6	—	140	.41	2.13	3.06	—	—	—	24.9
1867	Dbl BfBurritoSuprm-red	255	457	23.6	21.8	—	41.7	56.8	145	230	1053	431	4.0	4.0	136	.43	2.2	3.68	.30	—	30	8.7
1887	Dbl beef burrito + gr sc	255	451	23.4	21.8	—	40.3	56.8	133	—	928	396	4	—	155	.43	2.19	3.9	—	—	—	7.9
1868	Tostada-red sauce	156	243	9.5	11.1	—	26.6	16.0	179	—	596	401	1.53	—	95	.061	.169	.626	—	—	—	45.1
1888	Tostada w/green sauce	156	237	9.3	11.1	—	25.2	16	168	—	471	366	1.5	—	99	.06	.17	.8	—	—	—	44.4
1869	Beefy Tostada	198	322	15.1	19.6	8.89	22	40.3	185	206	764	408	1.96	2.97	152	.235	.286	1.61	.557	—	31	5.86
1870	Bellbeefer	177	312	16.5	13.2	5.7	32	38.6	174	125	855	299	2.36	2.10	121	.164	.304	1.73	.12	—	.1	5.41
1876	Pintos&cheese + red sce	128	190	8.97	8.72	4.33	19	16.2	156	156	642	385	1.42	2.17	87	.05	.146	.396	.21	—	68	51.7
1889	Pintos & cheese-grn sc	128	184	8.8	8.7	—	17.5	16.2	144	—	518	349	1.4	—	68	.05	.15	.57	—	—	—	51
1875	Mexican Pizza	223	575	21.3	36.8	—	39.7	52	257	400	1031	408	3.74	5.4	215	.319	.326	2.96	1.11	—	60	30.9
1862	Nachos-serving	107	346	7.5	18.5	9.68	37.5	8.8	191	260	399	159	.9	1.68	87	.17	.16	.68	.189	.776	9.5	1.9
1877	Nachos Bellgrande-svg	287	649	21.6	35.3	—	60.6	36.3	297	—	997	674	3.48	—	40	.104	.34	2.17	—	—	—	57.8
1871	Enchirito-red sauce	213	382	19.8	19.7	—	31.0	54.2	269	—	1243	423	2.84	—	100	.256	.418	2.3	—	—	—	28.1
1901	Meximelt	106	266	13	15.5	—	18.8	38	247	—	689	115	2	—	115	.381	.244	2.42	—	—	—	1.61
1898	Sour cream-serving	21.3	45.7	.647	4.44	—	.924	—	25.8	—	—	31.6	.009	—	51	.017	.031	.019	—	—	—	.285
1899	Pico de Gallo-serving	28.4	7.76	.349	.224	—	1.19	.539	5.61	—	88.8	0	.253	—	91	.011	.013	.268	—	—	—	1.53
1900	Guacamole-serving	21.3	34	.427	2.37	—	3	0	9.52	—	113	110	.128	—	12	.038	.028	.466	—	—	—	3.16
1873	Taco Sauce-packet	3.7	2.06	.115	.011	—	.377	0	1.78	—	126	13.1	.069	—	19	.001	.004	.063	—	—	—	.272
1894	Hot taco sauce-packet	.4	2.52	.194	.2	—	.315	0	2.1	—	82	14.6	.115	—	15	0	.002	.052	—	—	—	.828
1874	Salsa-serving	9.7	18.1	1.1	.091	—	3.6	0	36	—	376	376	.6	—	7	.018	.14	0	—	—	—	1.8
1896	Jalapeno peppers-srvg	100	20	1	.28	—	4	0	40	—	1370	110	.332	—	25	0	0	.475	—	—	—	2.23
1882	Taco Salad + salsa + shell	595	941	36	61.3	—	63.1	80.4	398	—	1662	1212	7.1	—	400	.508	.753	4.8	—	—	—	77
1892	Taco salad + sals-no shl	530	520	30.6	31.5	—	30	79.8	367	—	1431	1151	5.14	—	504	.264	.648	3.27	—	—	—	76.2
1893	Taco salad-no shell	530	502	29.6	31.3	—	26.3	79.9	332	—	1056	988	4.54	—	392	.256	.50	3.27	—	—	—	74.3
1895	Ranch dressing-serving	73.7	236	1.19	24.9	—	1.57	35.6	29.5	—	572	44.2	.587	—	48	0	.06	.198	—	—	—	0
1872	Cinnamon Crispas-serv	47.3	259	2.7	15.3	—	27.5	.831	37	—	127	36	1.26	—	0	.138	.084	.966	—	—	—	.653

Appendix F Table of Food Composition—Fast Foods

	WENDY'S	Weight	Calories	Protein	Total FAT	Unsaturated FAT	Carbohydrates	Cholesterol	Calcium	Phosphorus	Sodium	Potassium	Iron	Zinc	Vitamin A	Thiamin	Riboflavin	Niacin	Vitamin B_6	Folacin	Vitamin C	Vitamin B_{12}
		(g)		(g)	(g)	(g)	(g)	(mg)	(mg)	(mg)	(mg)	(mg)	(mg)	(mg)	(RE)	(mg)	(mg)	(mg)	(mg)	(mcg)	(mcg)	(mg)
1931	Hamburger-small-plain	106	260	13	9	—	31	30	100	—	510	210	2.7	—	20	.38	.26	4	—	—	—	2.4
1903	Single burger/white bun	119	350	21	16	—	29	65	100	—	420	265	4.5	—	0	.38	.34	6	—	—	—	—
1935	Single burger deluxe	227	430	22	22	—	36	70	100	—	805	485	4.5	—	150	.45	.34	6	—	—	—	15
1932	Cheeseburger-small	124	320	17	15	—	31	50	100	—	805	210	2.7	—	20	.38	1.36	4	—	—	—	2.4
1939	Single cheeseburger	137	410	25	22	—	29	80	100	—	—	265	4.5	—	40	.38	1.36	6	—	—	—	—
1934	Single cheeseburger dlx	245	490	26	28	—	36	85	100	—	1100	485	4.5	—	150	.45	1.53	6	—	—	—	15
1904	Double hamburger + bun	197	560	41	34	21	32	125	48	339	575	431	6.3	8.35	0	.22	.43	9	.473	1.8	28.8	.04
1927	Dbl Cheeseburger + all	291	735	48.3	47.5	23.9	27	165	180	470	883	620	5.4	8.8	112	.36	.53	10	.46	4.6	31	5.5
1902	Dbl cheeseburger deluxe	215	548	29.7	33.3	17.2	32.2	84	177	339	864	430	4.0	4.41	111	.337	.353	5.29	.248	1.23	28	5.5
1905	Bacon cheeseburger + bun	147	460	29	28	15.8	23	65	136	296	860	332	3.6	5.14	82	.265	.28	5.7	.235	1.76	25	1
1925	Big Classic burger	241	470	26	25	—	36	80	40	—	900	470	4.5	—	60	.3	.255	5	—	—	—	12
1933	Big Classic burger + chez	288	640	28	40	—	47	100	150	—	1310	580	5.4	—	200	.45	1.53	6	—	—	—	15
1937	Philly swiss burger	201	510	30	24	—	46	65	100	—	—	360	4.5	—	46	.45	.34	6	—	—	—	6
1938	Bacon swiss burger	261	710	37	44	—	58	90	150	—	—	560	5.4	—	150	.6	.42	8	—	—	—	18
1906	Chick san/multigrn bun	219	430	26	19	—	41	60	100	—	705	460	14.4	—	100	.45	.34	14	—	—	—	9
1930	Kid's meal-hamburger	99	260	13	9	—	30	30	100	—	510	195	2.7	—	20	.38	.26	4.0	—	—	—	1.2
1907	Kid's Meal cheeseburger	117	320	17	15	—	30	50	100	—	805	195	2.7	—	20	.38	1.36	4.0	—	—	—	1.2
1909	French fries-serving	106	306	4.2	15.2	7	37.8	15	13.1	197	105	689	1.02	.508	0	.148	.036	2.96	.265	—	32.8	12.2
1948	French fries-large svg	159	459	6.30	22.8	—	56.7	22.5	19.7	296	158	1034	1.53	.76	0	.22	.05	4.44	.39	—	49.2	18.3
1923	Home fries	103	360	4	22	—	37	20	20	—	745	615	.720	—	0	.12	.03	.8	—	—	—	4.8
1951	Crispy chicken nuggets	93	310	15	21	—	14	50	20	—	660	230	1.1	—	0	.15	.14	9	—	—	—	—
1941	Special sauce	15	40	—	3	—	3	—	—	—	120	10	—	—	40	—	—	—	—	—	—	—
1952	Fish fillet-meat only	92	210	14	11	—	13	45	—	—	475	255	.7	—	20	.09	.07	2	—	—	—	—
1942	California coleslaw-svg	57	60	—	6	—	9	10	20	—	140	95	—	—	150	—	—	—	—	—	—	15
1943	Red Bliss potato salad	57	100	—	9	—	6	—	—	—	265	150	.36	—	9	.03	—	4	—	—	—	6
1944	Pasta deli salad	57	35	2	—	—	6	—	—	—	120	—	.36	—	5	—	.03	4	—	—	—	—
1908	Chili-serving	256	230	21	9	—	16	—	60	—	960	565	4.5	—	200	.12	.17	3	—	—	—	9
1947	Cheddar chips	28.4	160	3	11	—	12	—	60	—	445	—	.36	—	5	.03	—	.8	—	—	—	
1910	Taco salad (take out)	791	660	40	37	—	46	—	800	576	1110	1330	6.3	7.8	800	.45	.77	5	.735	2.05	137	48
1936	Chef salad (take out)	331	180	15	9	—	10	120	250	—	—	590	2.7	—	1100	.23	.42	1.2	—	—	—	66
1940	Garden salad(take out)	227	102	7	9	—	9	—	200	—	110	560	1.8	—	1100	.15	.36	1.2	—	—	—	66
1912	Baked potato-plain	250	250	6	.2	.09	51.7	0	40	169	60	1360	2.7	.65	0	.275	.102	3.82	.7	.15	67.5	36
1913	Potato + sour cream + chive	310	460	6	24	6	53	15	40	185	230	1420	2.7	.90	100	.225	.136	3	.79	.20	32	36
1924	Bkd potato + bacon + cheese	350	570	19	30	16	57	22	200	406	180	1380	3.7	2.53	150	.225	.170	4.64	.866	.386	33	36
1914	Baked potato + cheese	350	590	16.5	34	19.9	55	22	350	49.7	2.22	1380	3.6	.609	200	.225	.255	3.3	.80	.213	33	36
1915	Bkd potato + chili + cheese	400	510	22	20	15.3	63	22	250	498	810	1590	6.13	3.78	172	.3	.26	4.1	.9	.22	50	36
1916	Potato + broccoli + cheese	365	500	12.9	25	12.8	54	22	250	373	2.19	1550	3.6	.865	350	.3	.255	4	.861	.355	65.7	90
1958	Apple danish	95	360	6	14	—	53	—	60	—	380	—	.72	—	0	.09	.06	1.6	—	—	—	—
1959	Cheese danish	95	430	8	21	—	52	—	80	—	500	—	.72	—	10	.12	.12	2.0	—	—	—	—
1953	Cinnamon raisin danish	95	410	7	18	—	55	—	60	—	430	—	.72	—	119	.06	.14	1.6	—	—	—	—
1957	Buttermilk biscuit	94	320	5	17	—	37	—	100	—	860	125	1.08	—	0	.12	.06	.8	—	—	—	—
1956	Breakfast potatoes-svg	103	360	4	22	—	37	20	20	—	745	615	.72	—	0	.12	.03	3	—	—	—	4.8
1954	Sausage gravy	214	440	17	36	—	13	85	40	—	1300	340	1.8	—	0	.23	.26	4	—	—	—	—
1955	Sausage patty	45	200	8	18	—	—	45	—	—	405	115	1.1	—	0	.15	.07	3	—	—	—	—
1917	Omelet-ham + cheese + mushr	114	250	18	17	—	6	450	100	—	405	180	2.7	—	200	.15	.6	.8	—	—	—	—
1918	Omelet-ham and cheese	118	290	18	21	—	7	355	100	—	570	190	2.7	—	200	.23	.6	1.2	—	—	—	—
1919	Omelet-Denver	128	280	19	19	—	7	525	150	—	485	200	2.7	—	200	.15	.6	.8	—	—	—	6
1921	Omelet-msrm + onion + peppr	114	210	14	15	—	7	460	60	—	200	190	2.7	—	150	.09	.51	.3	—	—	—	6
1920	Breakfast sandwich	129	370	17	19	—	33	200	150	—	770	155	3.6	—	200	.45	.43	3	—	—	—	—

1922	French toast	135	400	11	19	—	45	115	80	—	850	175	1.8	—	100	.6	.51	3.9	—	—	—	—
1928	White toaster bun-4 in	54	160	5	3	—	28	—	80	—	265	65	1.4	—	0	.3	.17	2.0	—	—	—	—
1929	Kaiser toaster bun	69	200	6	3	—	36	—	100	—	330	115	1.8	—	0	.38	.17	2.0	—	—	—	—
1949	Frosty dairy desrt-med	281	460	9.23	16.5	—	68.5	57.9	334	309	252	673	1.12	1.20	186	.13	.58	.40	.15	1.04	21.6	.01
1950	Frosty dairy dessert-lg	367	602	12.1	25	—	89.6	75.7	437	405	330	881	1.46	1.57	243	.18	.77	.527	.209	1.36	28.2	.017
1911	Frosty dairy dessert-sm	216	354	7.1	12.7	5	52.7	44.5	257	238	194	518	.863	.924	143	.107	.453	.31	.123	.8	16.6	.01
1926	Chocolate chip cookies	64	320	2.56	16.6	10.7	39.7	5	9.6	62	235	100	1.09	.46	0	.06	.068	.4	.03	.03	5.8	0
1945	Chocolate pudding	57	90	—	4	—	12	—	150	—	70		.36	—	0	.03	.03	—	—	—	—	—
1946	Butterscotch pudding	57	90	1	4	—	11	—	60	—	85	—	.36	—	0	—	—	—	—	—	—	—

WHITE CASTLE

1960	Hamburger sandwich	58	161	5.9	7.9	—	15.4	—	—	—	266	—	—	—	8	—	—	—	—	—	—	—
1961	Cheeseburger sandwich	65	200	7.8	11.2	—	15.5	—	—	—	361	—	—	—	28	—	—	—	—	—	—	—
1965	Chicken sandwich	64	186	7.99	7.45	—	20.5	—	—	—	497	—	—	—	6.5	—	—	—	—	—	—	—
1962	Fish san-no tartar sce	59.3	155	5.8	5.0	—	20.9	—	—	—	201	—	—	—	5.2	—	—	—	—	—	—	—
1964	Sausage sandwich	49	196	6.67	12.3	—	13.3	—	—	—	488	—	—	—	0	—	—	—	—	—	—	—
1963	Sausage & egg sandwich	96	322	12.6	22.0	—	16.1	—	—	—	698	—	—	—	86.2	—	—	—	—	—	—	—
1966	Cheese only-slice	8.7	30.7	1.5	1.64	—	2.27	—	—	—	154	—	—	—	15.2	—	—	—	—	—	—	—
1967	Bun only	25	74.4	2.16	.92	—	13.9	—	—	—	131	—	—	—	.2	—	—	—	—	—	—	—
1968	French fries-serving	96.8	301	2.49	14.7	—	37.7	—	—	—	193	—	—	—	0	—	—	—	—	—	—	—
1969	Onion rings-serving	60.2	246	2.91	13.4	—	26.6	—	—	—	566	—	—	—	.5	—	—	—	—	—	—	—
1970	Onion chips-serving	93.4	329	3.72	16.6	—	38.8	—	—	—	823	—	—	—	.8	—	—	—	—	—	—	—

VARIOUS BEVERAGES

1971	Coca Cola classic-no ice	360	144	—	—	—	38	0	—	60	14	2	—	—	0	—	—	—	—	—	—	0
1972	Diet Coke	360	.9	—	—	—	.3	0	—	28	16	34	—	—	0	—	—	—	—	0	0	0
1973	Pepsi-regular	240	110	0	0	0	27.5	0	8.1	32.2	10.7	2.68	.08	.03	0	0	0	0	0	0	0	0
1974	Diet Pepsi	240	2.4	.24	0	0	.24	0	9.6	21.6	14.4	40	.07	.19	0	.01	.06	0	0	0	0	0
1975	Sprite	360	144	—	—	—	36	0	—	—	15	—	—	—	0	—	—	—	—	0	0	—
1976	Diet sprite	360	3	—	—	—	0	0	—	0	9	57	—	—	0	—	—	—	—	0	0	0
1977	7-UP Gold	180	78	0	0	—	19	0	—	34	35	—	—	—	0	—	—	—	—	0	0	—
1978	Diet 7-UP Gold	180	2	0	0	—	1	0	—	34	35	—	—	—	0	—	—	—	—	0	0	—
1979	7-Up-regular	360	144	0	0	—	38	0	—	—	10	27	—	—	0	—	—	—	—	0	0	—
1980	Diet 7-Up	360	3.6	.36	—	—	.36	0	—	—	10	27	—	—	0	—	—	—	—	0	0	—
1981	Tab	360	1	—	—	—	1	0	—	45	30	20	—	—	0	—	—	—	—	0	0	0
1982	Hi-C grape drink	360	164	—	—	—	40	0	—	—	12	—	—	—	0	—	—	—	—	0	0	120
1983	Hi-C lemon	360	142	—	—	—	36	0	—	148	100	—	—	—	0	—	—	—	—	0	0	120
1984	Hi-C orange	360	152	—	—	—	38	0	—	—	12	—	—	—	0	—	—	—	—	0	0	120
1985	Hi-C punch	360	154	—	—	—	40	0	—	—	12	—	—	—	0	—	—	—	—	0	0	120
1986	Mello Yello-no ice	360	172	—	—	—	44	0	—	—	28	8	—	—	0	—	—	—	—	0	0	—
1987	Mr. Pibb-no ice	360	142	—	—	—	37	0	—	42	21	2	—	—	0	—	—	—	—	0	0	0
1988	Fanta ginger ale	360	126	—	—	—	32	0	—	—	26	—	—	—	0	—	—	—	—	0	0	0
1989	Fanta grape	360	168	—	—	—	42	0	—	—	12	—	—	—	0	—	—	—	—	0	0	0
1990	Fanta orange	360	164	—	—	—	42	0	—	—	12	—	—	—	0	—	—	—	—	0	0	0
1991	Fanta root beer	360	158	—	—	—	42	0	—	—	18	—	—	—	0	—	—	—	—	0	0	0
1992	Root Beer	370	152	.1	0	0	39.2	0	19	2	49	3	.18	.26	0	0	0	0	0	0	0	0
1993	Slice-lemon lime flavor	240	100	—	—	—	24	0	—	—	10	40	—	—	0	—	—	—	—	0	0	—
1994	Slice-mandarin orange	240	110	—	—	—	32	0	—	—	10	40	—	—	0	—	—	—	—	0	0	—

Appendix G

Cholesterol Content of Foods

Food	Approximate Measure	Weight (g)	Cholesterol (mg)
Beef, oven-cooked; separable lean, composite of retail cuts	2 oz	57	51
Beef potpie	1 piece	210	42
Beef stew	1 cup	245	72
Butter	1 pat	5	11
Cakes:			
Pound[1]	1 slice	33	68
White, 2 layer with chocolate icing[2]	1 piece	71	8
Yellow, 2 layer with chocolate icing[1]	1 piece	69	36
Cheese:			
American, pasteurized, process	1 oz	28	27
Blue	1 oz	28	21
Camembert	1 oz	28	20
Cheddar	1 oz	28	30
Cottage:			
Creamed, Small curd	1 cup	210	31
Low fat, 1% fat	1 cup	226	10
Uncreamed, dry curd, less than ½% fat	1 cup	145	10
Cream	1 oz	28	31
Mozzarella, made with part skim milk	1 oz	28	16
Muenster	1 oz	28	27
Parmesan, grated	1 tbsp	5	4
Ricotta, made with part skim milk	1 oz	28	9
Swiss	1 oz	28	26
Chicken, roasted, no skin			
Dark meat	2 oz	57	54
Light meat	2 oz	57	48
Chicken à la king	1 cup	245	220
Chicken potpie	1 piece	232	56
Chili with beef	1 cup	255	28
Chocolate, milk (20% milk solids)[3]	1 oz	28	5
Coconut oil	1 tbsp	14	0
Coffee whitener (nondairy)			
Liquid, frozen (contains coconut or palm kernel oil)	½ fl oz	15	0
Powdered (contains coconut or palm kernel oil)	1 tbsp	6	0
Cookies:			
Brownies, with chocolate icing[1]	1 brownie	25	13
Chocolate chip[4]	4 cookies	40	21
Vanilla wafers[4]	10 cookies	40	25
Corn oil	1 tbsp	14	0
Crackers			
Graham	2 crackers	14	0
Saltines[5]	4 crackers	11	3

[1]Major sources of cholesterol are eggs and butter.
[2]Major sources of cholesterol are milk and butter.
[3]Source of cholesterol is milk solids.
[4]Major source of cholesterol is eggs.

Appendix G (continued)

Food	Approximate Measure	Weight (g)	Cholesterol (mg)
Cream, sour, cultured	1 tbsp	12	5
Cream, sweet			
Half-and-half (cream and milk)	1 tbsp	15	6
Light, coffee, or table	1 tbsp	15	10
Heavy, whipping, unwhipped	1 tbsp	15	21
Cupcakes, with chocolate icing[1]	1 cupcake	36	15
Desert toppings (nondairy):			
Powdered, made with whole milk	1 tbsp	4	trace
Pressurized	1 tbsp	4	0
Doughnuts, cake type[4]	1 doughnut	25	10
Doughnuts, yeast-leavened[4]	1 doughnut	50	13
Eggnog	1 cup	254	149
Eggs, large	1 egg	50	213
Fish:			
Cooked:			
Flounder or sole (a lean fish), cooked, dry heat	2 oz	57	39
Salmon, red (a fatty fish) baked	2 oz	57	50
Canned:			
Salmon, pink, water pack, solids and liquid	2 oz	57	25
Sardines, Atlantic, oil pack, drained solids	1 can	92	131
Tuna, chunk light, oil pack, drained solids	2 oz	57	10
Tuna, light, water pack, drained solids	2 oz	57	24
Ice cream:			
Regular (about 10% fat)	1 cup	133	59
Rich (about 16% fat)	1 cup	148	88
Ice milk:			
Hardened (about 4.3% fat)	1 cup	131	18
Soft serve (about 2.6% fat)	1 cup	175	13
Lamb, loin chop:			
Lean only	2 oz	57	54
Lean and fat	2 oz	57	55
Lard	1 tbsp	13	12
Liver, beef, fried	2 oz	57	222
Margarine, regular (at least 80% fat):			
Stick:			
Corn oil, hydrogenated	1 tbsp	14	0
Soybean oil, hydrogenated	1 tbsp	14	0
Tub:			
Corn oil	1 tbsp	14	0
Soybean oil	1 tbsp	14	0
Margarine, diet (about 40% fat), tub	1 tbsp	14	0
Mayonnaise	1 tbsp	14	8
Milk, fluid			
Whole, 3.3% fat	1 cup	244	33
Low fat, 2% fat	1 cup	244	18
Low fat, 1% fat	1 cup	244	10
Nonfat, skim	1 cup	245	5
Buttermilk, cultured	1 cup	245	9
Milkshake, thick, vanilla	11 oz	313	37

[5]Major source of cholesterol is animal shortening.

Appendix G (continued)

Food	Approximate Measure	Weight (g)	Cholesterol (mg)
Olive oil	1 tbsp	14	0
Palm kernel oil	1 tbsp	14	0
Palm oil	1 tbsp	14	0
Peanut butter	1 tbsp	16	0
Peanut oil	1 tbsp	14	0
Pizza with cheese[6]	1 slice	48	7
Pork:			
Ham, roasted	2 oz	57	54
Bacon, fried crisp	2 slices	13	11
Potatoes, french-fried (fried in edible tallow)[7]	10 strips	50	6
Poultry:			
Dark meat, fried	2 oz	57	55
Light meat, fried	2 oz	57	51
Safflower oil	1 tbsp	14	0
Sausages and cold cuts:			
Bologna (beef and pork)	1 slice	28	16
Braunschweiger	1 slice	28	44
Frankfurters (beef)	1 frank	57	27
Salami, cooked (beef and pork)	1 slice	28	18
Shellfish:			
Raw:			
Clams, mixed species	2 oz	57	19
Oysters, Eastern	6 medium oysters	84	31
Canned:			
Crabmeat, blue	2 oz	57	51
Shrimp, dry pack or drained solids of wet pack	2 oz	57	98
Sherbet (about 2% fat)	1 cup	193	14
Shortening (animal and vegetable fat)	1 tbsp	13	7
Shortening (vegetable)	1 tbsp	13	0
Soybean oil (partially hydrogenated)	1 tbsp	14	0
Soybean-cottonseed oil blend (partially hydrogenated)	1 tbsp	14	0
Sunflower oil	1 tbsp	14	0
Tallow, edible	1 tbsp	13	14
Turkey, roasted, no skin			
Dark meat	2 oz	57	64
Light meat	2 oz	57	49
Veal cutlet	2 oz	57	58
Yogurt, plain:			
With added milk solids:			
Made with low fat milk	8 oz	227	14
Made with nonfat milk	8 oz	227	4
Without added milk solids, made with whole milk	8 oz	227	29

[6]Source of cholesterol is cheese.
[7]Source of cholesterol is tallow.

Data sources for Appendix G (Cholesterol Content of Foods)

1) U.S. Department of Agriculture (USDA). 1976–1990. *Revised agricultural handbook no. 8 series.* Washington, DC: USDA.

2) Human Nutrition Information Service. 1989. *Agricultural handbook no. 8, 1989 supplement.* Washington, DC: USDA.

3) Weihrauch, J.L. 1984. Provisional table on the fatty acid and cholesterol content of selected foods. Washington, DC: Data Research Branch, Consumer Nutrition Division, USDA.

Appendix H

Weight Control Resources in Print

CONSUMER SELF HELP/WORKBOOKS

Bibliographic	Approach	Target Audience	Organization and Format	Accuracy of Information	Behavior Modification	Nutrition Overall	Diet Recommended	Dietary Guidelines	Menu/Recipes Included	Stress Management	Psychosocial Intervention	Weight Maintenance	Exercise Overall	Forms and Tools
Diet To Lose and Win: The Game That Pays When You Lose, 1987. M. Cummings, R.D.	primary diet	adults; fairly educated	B+	B+	C+ 1	A 2–3	Y	Y	N	0	0	0	C 1	Y
The Fat Book: A Comprehensive Self-help Workbook Offering a Three-fold Approach to Lifestyle Change, 1982. H. Lamb, Ed.D.	behavioral, psychological (problem solving) spiritual	"fat persons"	B	C	B 2–3	D+ 1	N	N	N	B 2–3	B+ 2	C 1–2	D+ 1	Y
How To Be Slimmer, Trimmer, and Happier, 1983. F. Berg, M.S., family social science and anthropology; extension home economist	consumer self help	young adults	A	B+	A 3	B+ 3	N	Y	N	B+ 3	A 3	B+ 2	B+ 2	Y
Making Peace With Food: A Step-by-Step Guide to Freedom From Diet-weight Conflict, 1985. S. Kano	behavioral, psychological	compulsive eaters, chronic dieters	B	C	B 1–2	D 1	N	N	N	C+ 2–3	B+ 2–3	C 1	D+ 1	Y
Safe Slimming: Participant's Workbook, 1985. L. Hamilton, M.S., R.D.	diet and exercise	any weight losers, esp. those in weight loss program	B	B	B 3	A 3	Y	Y	N	0	0	C 1–2	B+ 2–3	Y
Slimming Only Sensibly, 1983. D. Schusterman	comprehensive	consumers; home study groups	B+	A	A 2–3	A 3	Y	Y	Y	B 1–2	A 2	B+ 2	B+ 2	Y
Winning Weight Loss for Teens, 1987. J. Ikeda, M.A., R.D.	comprehensive	teens and parents	B	A	A 3	B+ 3	N	Y	Y	C+ 2	A 3	A 2–3	A 3	Y
You're SomeBODY: How To Be a Slim Kid, 1985. L. Corby, M.Sc., R.D., P. Clarke, P.Dt.	comprehensive	children aged 9 to 12	A	A	A 3	A 3	N	Y	Y	B 2	A 3	B 2	A 3	Y

From *National Weight Control Resource Directory*, 1988. S.A. Berkowitz, ed.
Society for Nutrition Education
The American Dietetic Association
Office of Disease Prevention—U.S. Dept. of Health and Human Services

KEY TO CHART RATINGS (For specific questions, refer to Appendix B)

A = Excellent B+ = Good-Excellent B = good C+ = Fair-Good C = Fair D+ = Poor-Fair D = Poor
3 = Extensive 2–3 = Moderate-Extensive 2 = Moderate 1–2 = Brief-Moderate 1 = Brief 0 = Not Covered Y = Yes N = No

DIET BOOKS

Bibliographic	Approach	Target Audience	Organization and Format	Accuracy of Information	Behavior Modification	Nutrition Overall	Diet Recommended	Dietary Guidelines	Menu/Recipes Included	Stress Management	Psychosocial Intervention	Weight Maintenance	Exercise Overall	Forms and Tools
Are You Hungry?, 1985. J. Hirschmann, M.S.W., L. Zaphiropoulos, M.S.W.	behavioral, psychological	parents of children w/food-related problems	B	D+	A 3	D 1	N	N	N	C 1	0	0	0	N
The Best Chance Diet, 1982. J. Goldstrich, M.D., F.A.C.C.	comprehensive	educated adults interested in health promotion	B	D	D+ 1,	C+ 3	Y	Y	Y	B 2	C 1–2	C 2	C 1–2	N
Breaking The Diet Habit, 1985. J. Polivy, professor of psychology and psychiatry, C. Herman, professor of psychology	behavioral, psychological	overweight adults, dieters	D+	C	0	0	N	N	N	D+	C 1	C 1	0	N
The "Can-Have" Diet, P. Stein, M.S., M.A., R.D., N. Winn, M.S., R.D.	primarily diet	motivated, educated adults	C	B	D 1	C 1	Y	Y	Y	D 1	0	D 1	D+ 1	N
Childhood Obesity, 1986. P. Collip, M.D., ed.	diet and exercise, behavioral	families of overweight children	C+	B	A	B	N	Y	N	A	A 3	0	B 2	N
The Diet Alternative, 1984. D. Hampton, recovered overeater	spiritual	overeaters, binge eaters	C	D	D 1–2	D 1	N	N	N	D+ 1	D 1	D+ 1	D 1	N
Diet and Exercise Made Easy, 1987. S. Lewis, M.D.	diet and exercise	young, educated adult women	C+	C+	0	C 2	Y	Y	N	0	0	0	C 1–2	N
The Diet Center Program: Revised and updated, 1983. S. Ferguson, founder of the Diet Center	primarily diet	"every overweight man, woman, and child"	C+	D	C 1–2	D+ 1	Y	Y	N	C 1–2	C+ 1	D+ 1–2	C+ 1–2	N
The Dieter's Dilemma, W. Bennett, M.D., J. Gurin, editor American Health magazine	reporting research and theories	overweight general public	C	B	0	0	N	N	N	0	0	0	C+	N
Diets Don't Work, 1982. B. Schwartz, founder of DIETS DON'T WORK Seminar	behavioral, psychological	literate adults, unsuccessful yo-yo dieters	B	D+	C+ 2	D 1	N	N	N	D 1	C+ 1–2	C+ 1–2	0	Y
Dr. Berger's Immune Power Diet, 1985. S. Berger, M.D., diet and recipes by M. Clark of the Food Consulting Group	primarily diet	anyone who wants to feel better and lose weight	C	D+	D 1–2	C	Y	Y	Y	D 1	0	C 1	D+ 1	Y
The Dr. DeBetz Champagne Diet, 1987. B. DeBetz, M.D., and S. Baker, professional writer	behavioral diet	adults	B+	C+	B 2	C+ 2	Y	Y	Y	B 1–2	B 2	B+ 2–3	B 1–2	N
Eating Awareness Training, 1983. M. Groger, personal experience with weight loss	behavioral, psychological	overweight adults with 3 to 30 pounds to lose	D	D	C 1	D	N	N	N	0	0	C 1	0	Y
Escape the Fat Trap! 1986. L. Webber, personal experience with weight loss.	behavioral, psychological	overweight adults, unsuccessful dieters	B	C+	B 2	C 1	N	N	N	B+ 3	C+ 1–2	C+ 1–2	C 2–3	Y

KEY TO CHART RATINGS (For specific questions, refer to Appendix B)
A = Excellent B+ = Good-Excellent B = good C+ = Fair-Good C = Fair D+ = Poor-Fair D = Poor
3 = Extensive 2–3 = Moderate-Extensive 2 = Moderate 1–2 = Brief-Moderate 1 = Brief 0 = Not Covered Y = Yes N = No

DIET BOOKS (continued)

Bibliographic	Approach	Target Audience	Organization and Format	Accuracy of Information	Behavior Modification	Nutrition Overall	Diet Recommended	Dietary Guidelines	Menu/Recipes Included	Stress Management	Psychosocial Intervention	Weight Maintenance	Exercise Overall	Forms and Tools
The Fat Chance Diet Book, 1983. J. Quail, self-proclaimed "doctor"	humorous	middle-aged white adults	D+	D	0	0	N	N	N	0	0	0	0	N
Fat Free Forever: The natural way to conquer persistent fat, 1987. Melville, self-proclaimed "doctor" and C. Johnson, "holistic health expert"	primarily diet, behavioral	adults with PRF (Persistant Fat Retention) syndrome	B	D	0	C 2	Y	Y	Y	C 1	C 1	D+ 1–2	0	N
Fit For Life, 1985. H. and M. Diamond, certificate from American College of Health Sciences	primarily diet, spiritual	adults with high school education	B	D	D 1	D 2	Y	N	Y	D 1	0	0	C 1	N
Free To Be Thin Daily Planner, 1983. N. Coyle, Founder of Overeaters Victorious	spiritual	Christian adults	C+	0	D+ 2	D+ 1	Y	N	N	D 1	0	0	D 1	Y
Freedom From Fat, 1985. M. Bircoll, M.D.	diet and exercise, liposuction	women who want to lose weight in specific body areas	C+	C	D 1	C+ 2	N	N	N	B 1	0	0	B 1–2	N
Getting Your Family On Your Side, 1987. N. Coyle, founder of Overeaters Victorious and D. Dixon, Ph.D.	spiritual, psychological	dieters and their families	C+	0	C 3	0	N	N	N	C 1	C 1	C 1	0	N
The Harvard Square Diet, 1987. F. Stare, M.D., E. Whelan, Sc.D.	diet and exercise	anyone who wants to lose a few pounds in a short time	B	C	D+ 1	D+ 1	Y	N	N	0	D+ 1	D+ 1	D+ 1	N
A Healthy Life: Exercise, behavior, nutrition, 1986. F. Drews, P.E.D.	comprehensive	all adults	B	A	B+ 3	A 3	N	Y	N	B+ 1–2	C+ 2	B 2–3	A 3	Y
Hilton Head Metabolism Diet, 1983. P. Miller, Ph.D., clinical psychology	diet and exercise	primarily women	C	C	D+ 1	D+ 1–2	Y	N	Y	D+ 1	C 1–2	D+ 1	C 2–3	Y
How I Lost Weight, 1985. A. Printup, personal experience with weight loss	psychological, spiritual, behavioral	adults "struggling to lose weight"	D+	D	D+ 1–2	D 1–2	N	N	N	C 1	D+ 1–2	C 1	C 1	N
How To Lower Your Fat Thermostat, 1983. D. Remington, M.D., A. Fisher, Ph.D., E. Parent, Ph.D.	check	adults who have failed at previous diets	B	C	C 2	C+ 1–2	Y	Y	Y	0	0	C 1	B+ 3	Y
The Hungry Self: Women, eating, and identity, 1985. K. Cherin, author and counselor of women with eating disorders	pschological, problem solving and behavioral	all women and those with eating disorders	B	D+	A 3	0	N	N	N	B 2	0	0	0	N
Intelligent Dieting for Weight Loss and Prevention of Disease, 1982. D. Price, Ph.D., animal nutritionist	primarily diet	general public	D+	D	D+ 1	D+ 2	N	N	N	0	0	0	C 2	N

KEY TO CHART RATINGS (For specific questions, refer to Appendix B)

A = Excellent B+ = Good-Excellent B = good C+ = Fair-Good C = Fair D+ = Poor-Fair D = Poor

3 = Extensive 2–3 = Moderate-Extensive 2 = Moderate 1–2 = Brief-Moderate 1 = Brief 0 = Not Covered Y = Yes N = No

DIET BOOKS (continued)

Bibliographic	Approach	Target Audience	Organization and Format	Accuracy of Information	Behavior Modification	Nutrition Overall	Diet	Recommended Dietary Guidelines	Menu/Recipes Included	Stress Management	Psychosocial Intervention	Weight Maintenance	Exercise	Overall Forms and Tools
Jane Brody's Good Food Book: Living the high carbohydrate way, 1985. J. Brody, M.S., health columnist, New York Times	primarily diet	health concerned consumers	B	B	0	B+ 2	N	Y	Y	0	0	B 2	B 2	Y
Just The Weight You Are, 1986. Eileen Wegelben, R.N.	diet and exercise, behavioral and psychological	overweight adults with low self-esteem	B+	B	C+ 1–2	C 1–2	N	Y	N	B 1	C+ 1–2	C 1	B 2	Y
The Life Extension Weight Loss Program, 1987. D. Pearson, degrees in physics, biology, and psychology and S. Shaw, degree in chemistry	diet and exercise	body builders and overweight adults	C+	C	D+ 1–2	D+ 1	Y	N	Y	D 1	D 1	D 1	C 1	Y
Living Health, 1987. H. and M. Diamond, certificate from American College of Health Science	primarily diet, spiritual	anyone including children	D+	D	0	D 1	Y	N	Y	D 1	C 1	0	C 1	N
The Living Heart Diet, 1984. M. DeBakey, M.D., A. Gotto, L. Scott, and J. Foreyt, Ph.D.	diet and exercise	anyone, especially wanting to reduce heart disease	B+	B+	B+ 3	A 3	Y	Y	Y	B 2	B 1–2	B+ 1		Y
Living Thin: 305 ways to eat less, 1986. E. Schneider, M.S.	behavioral, psychological	adults; junior high school education	B+	B	B 2–3	0	N	N	N	B+ 2–3	C+ 2–3	C 1	C 1	N
Lowfat Lifestyle, 1987. V. Parker, M.S.	diet and exercise	most Americans	C+	C+	D+ 1	C+ 1	Y	Y	Y	0	1	C 1	B+	N
Maintenance For Compulsive Overeaters: The twelve step way to on-going recovery, 1986. B. Bill, fellow overeater	spiritual, metaphysical	all individuals	B	C	C+ 1–2	0	N	N	N		B+ 3	B 2–3	0	N
Maybe It's Not Your Fault You're Fat, 1985. A. Pilgrim, Doctor of Chiropratic	underlying causes of obesity; diet and exercise	moderately overweight adults	D+	C	0	D 2	N	N	Y	0	C 2	C 1	C 2–3	N
The Mollen Method: A 30-day program to lifetime health addiction, 1986. A. Mollen, doctor unspecified	primarily exercise	professional adults, upper, middle class	C	D	0	C+ 2	Y	Y	Y	0	0	0	B 3	N
Natural Weight Loss, 1985. Prevention magazine editors	diet and exercise	anyone	B+	B+	B+ 2	B 2	N	Y	Y	C+ 2	B 2	C+ 2	B+ 3	Y
Not Another Diet Book: A right brain program for successful weight management, 1987. B. Sommer, Ph.D.	psychological, problem solving, behavioral	adults	B	B	C 2	D+ 1	N	N	N	C+ 2	C 1–2	C+ 1–2	D+ 1	Y
The Original Natural Hygiene Weight Loss Diet Book, 1986. Shelton, H. Doctorate in Chiropractic and Naturopathy, J. Willard, hygenic teacher, J. Oswald, teacher	primarily diet	healthy adults who are frustrated with mainstream approach to weight loss	D+	D	0	D 1	Y	N	Y	0	0	0	D 1	0
The Pasta Diet, 1984. E. Celli, actress and gourmet cook	primarily diet	adults who want rapid weight loss	C+	C	0	C+ 2	Y	N	Y	0	0	0	C 1	N

KEY TO CHART RATINGS (For specific questions, refer to Appendix B)
A = Excellent B+ = Good-Excellent B = good C+ = Fair-Good C = Fair D+ = Poor-Fair D = Poor
3 = Extensive 2–3 = Moderate-Extensive 2 = Moderate 1–2 = Brief-Moderate 1 = Brief 0 = Not Covered Y = Yes N = No

DIET BOOKS (continued)

Bibliographic	Approach	Target Audience	Organization and Format	Accuracy of Information	Behavior Modification	Nutrition Overall	Diet	Recommended Dietary Guidelines	Menu/Recipes Included	Stress Management	Psychosocial Intervention	Weight Maintenance	Exercise Overall	Forms and Tools
The Rochester Diet, 1983. P. Cherasky, M.D.	diet and exercise, behavioral	college educated overweight adults	B	B+	B 2	B+ 3	Y	Y	Y	B+ 2	C 1	C + 1–2	A 2–3	N
The Rotation Diet, 1986. M. Katahn, Ph.D.	combined diet and exercise	healthy adults, prevention	B+	C+	0	B 3	Y	Y	Y	0	0	0	B 1–2	Y
Sculpturing Your Body: Diet, exercise, and lipto(fat) suction, 1987. J. McCurdy, M.D.	diet and exercise, surgery	mildly obese and normal weight adults	C	C+	0	C 1	N	Y	N	0	0	0	C+ 2–3	N
The 35-Plus Diet for Women: The breakthrough metabolism diet developed at Kaiser Permanente for women over 35, 1987. J. Spodnik, M.S., R.D., and B. Gibbons, author	primarily diet	women over 35 years	C+	D+	D+ 1	D+	Y	N	Y	D 1	D 1	D 1	D 1	N
The 200 Calorie Solution: How to burn an extra 200 calories a day and stop dieting, 1982. M. Katahn, Ph.D.	comprehensive diet & exercise, behavioral	overweight individuals	B+	C+	B 3	B 3	Y	Y	Y	B 2	B 2	A 3	A 3	Y
There's More To Being Thin Than Being Thin, 1984. N. Coyle, founder Overeaters Victorious, M. Chapian, Ph.D.	spiritual	overweight Christians	C	0	0	0	Y	N	N	0	C 1–2	1	0	Y
The Thinking Person's Guide To Permanent Weight Loss, 1986. J. Perlow, successful weight loss experience	consumer self-help	obese males	C+	C	B 3	D+ 1	N	N	N	C 1–2	D+ 1	C 2	D 1	N
Thinning While Grinning: 30 day diet handbook, 1985. F. Gott, M.D. and K. Terry, writer	behavioral, diet and exercise	educated middle class adults	B	C	C+ 2–3	C 1	Y	N	N	C 1	D 1	C 1	C 1–2	Y
Time Calorie Displacement: Approach to weight control, 1985. R. Weinseir, Ph.D., M.D. and M. Johnson, M.S., R.D., and D. Doleys, Ph.D.	diet, exercise, behavioral	all people who have tried fad weight loss schemes	C+	B	A 2–3	B+ 2–3	Y	Y	Y	B 2	C+ 1–2	B 1–2	A 3	Y
Weight Loss to Super Wellness, 1982. T. Edwards, M.D.	comprehensive	overweight stressed adults	B	B	B+ 2–3	A 3	Y	Y	Y	B+ 1–2	C 1	B 2	B 2	Y
Weight No More, 1984. K. Darling, counselor	behavioral, psychological	primarily women, weight loss for life	B+	B	B+ 2–3	C+ 1	N	N	N	B+ 2–3	B 2	B 1	B 2	Y
Weight, Sex, and Marriage: A delicate balance, 1987. R. Stuart, marriage therapist and professor, B. Jacobsen, counselor	behavioral, psychological	obese women	B+	A	B+ 2	B 1	N	Y	N	B+ 3	B 2	C 1	D 1	N
You Can Do It! Kids Diet, 1985. D. Matthews, previous yo-yo dieter, A. Zullo, editor and writer, B. Nash, author	primarily diet, behavioral	overweight teens and their parents	B+	B+	B 2	C 1	Y	Y	Y	0	A 2	B+ 2	B 1	Y

KEY TO CHART RATINGS (For specific questions, refer to Appendix B)

A = Excellent B+ = Good-Excellent B = good C+ = Fair-Good C = Fair D+ = Poor-Fair D = Poor
3 = Extensive 2–3 = Moderate-Extensive 2 = Moderate 1–2 = Brief-Moderate 1 = Brief 0 = Not Covered Y = Yes N = No

Appendix I

Chemical Structures of the Vitamins

The fat-soluble vitamins

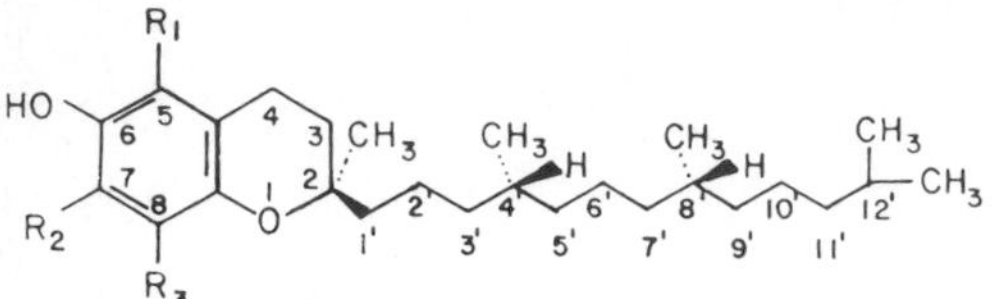

Vitamin E

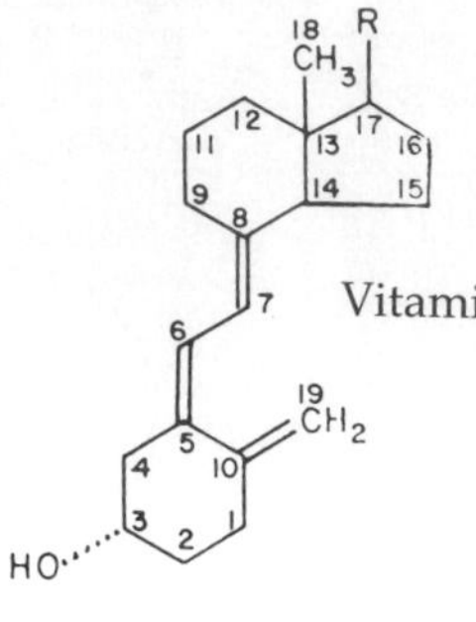

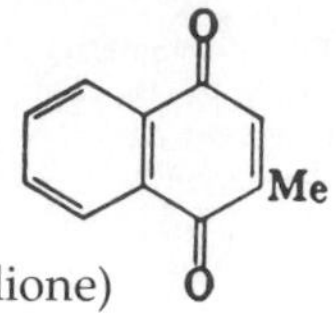

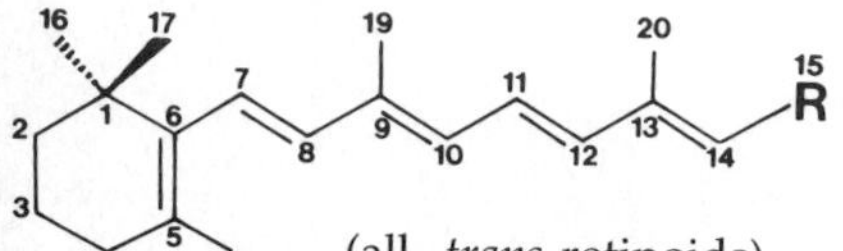

(all- *trans* retinoids)
Vitamin A

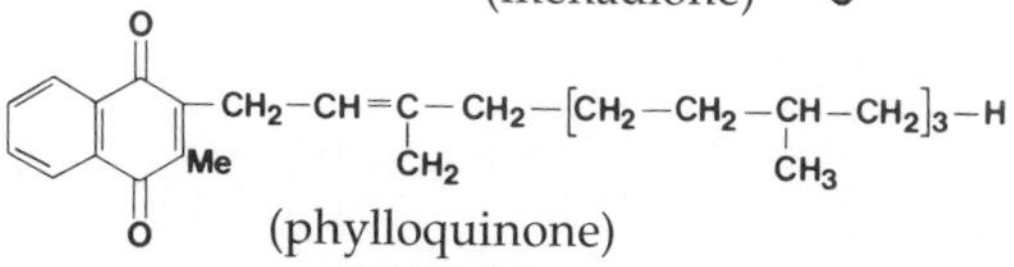

Vitamin D

(menadione)

(phylloquinone)
Vitamin K

The water-soluble vitamins

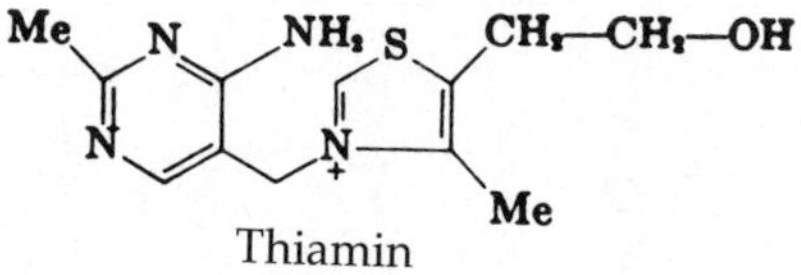

Thiamin

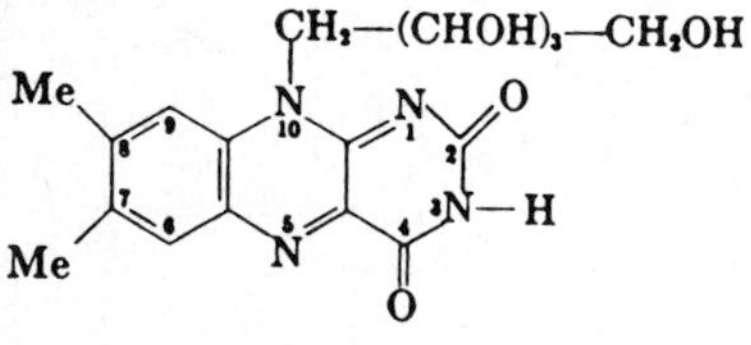

Riboflavin

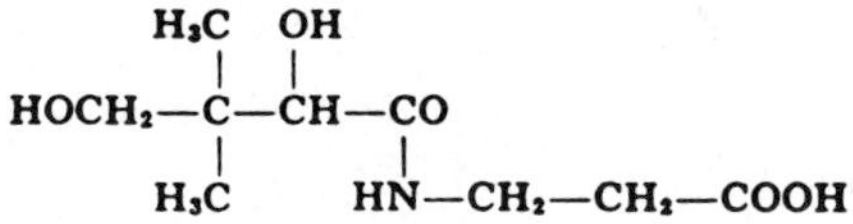

Pantothenic acid

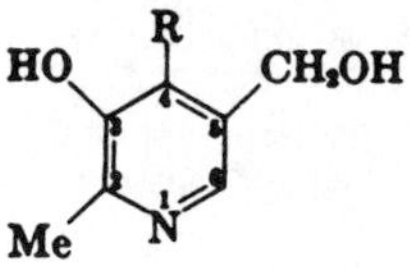

Vitamin B-6

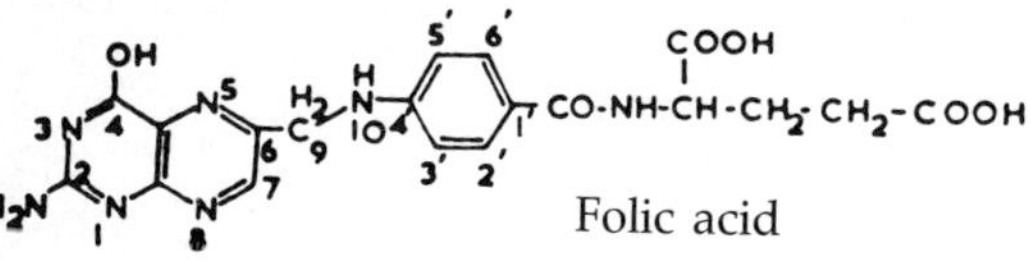

Folic acid

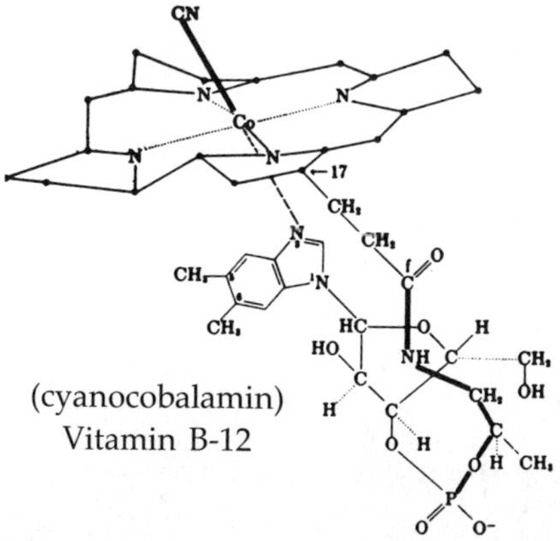

Niacin

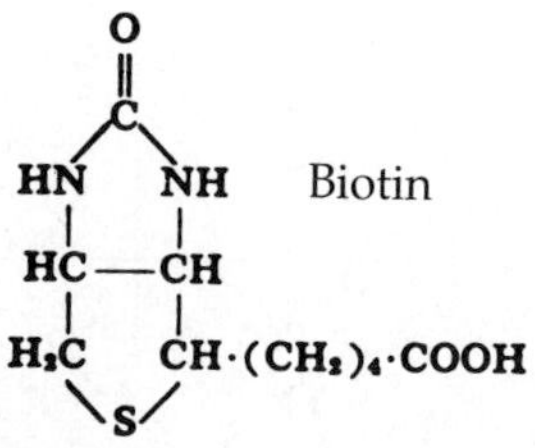

Biotin

(cyanocobalamin)
Vitamin B-12

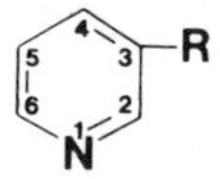

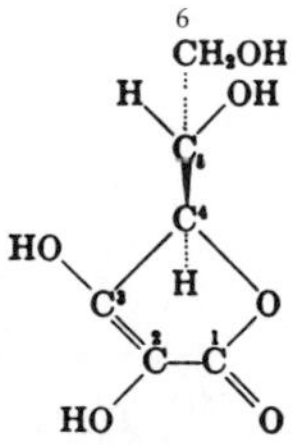

Vitamin C

Me = methyl group (CH_3) R = group that can vary

Reprinted from Journal of Nutrition. 1990. Nomenclature policy: generic descriptors and trivial names for vitamins and related compounds.

Appendix J

(Proposed) Reference Daily Intakes (RDIs) [1,2]

(to replace the U.S. RDAs)

Nutrient	Unit of measurement[1]	Adults and children 4 or more years of age	Children less than 4 years of age[2]	Infants[3]	Pregnant women	Lactating women
Vitamin A	Retinol equivalents[4]	875	400	375	800	1300
Vitamin C	Milligrams	60	40	33	70	95
Calcium	Milligrams	900	800	500	1200	1200
Iron	Milligrams	12	10	8.0	30	15
Vitamin D	Micrograms[5]	6.5	10	9.0	10	10
Vitamin E	*alpha*-Tocopherol equivalents[4]	9.0	6.0	3.5	10	12
Vitamin K	Micrograms	65	15	7.5	65	65
Thiamin	Milligrams	1.2	0.7	0.4	1.5	1.6
Riboflavin	Milligrams	1.4	0.8	0.5	1.6	1.8
Niacin	Niacin equivalents[4]	16	9.0	5.5	17	20
Vitamin B_6	Milligrams	1.5	1.0	0.5	2.2	2.1
Folate	Micrograms	180	50	30	400	280
Vitamin B_{12}	Micrograms	2.0	0.7	0.4	2.2	2.6
Biotin	Micrograms	60	20	13	65	65
Pantothenic acid	Milligrams	5.5	3.0	2.5	5.5	5.5
Phosphorus	Milligrams	900	800	400	1200	1200
Magnesium	Milligrams	300	80	50	320	355
Zinc	Milligrams	13	10	5.0	15	19
Iodine	Micrograms	150	70	45	175	200
Selenium	Micrograms	55	20	13	65	75
Copper	Milligrams	2.0	0.9	0.6	2.5	2.5
Manganese	Milligrams	3.5	1.3	0.6	3.5	3.5
Fluoride	Milligrams	2.5	1.0	0.5	3.0	3.0
Chromium	Micrograms	120	50	33	13	130
Molybdenum	Micrograms	150	38	26	160	160
Chloride	Milligrams	3150	1000	650	3400	3400

[1] The following abbreviations are allowed: "mg" for "milligrams"; "mcg" for "micrograms"; "mcg RE" for "retinol equivalents"; "mg *a*-TE" for *alpha*-tocopherol equivalents"; "mg NE" for "niacin equivalents."

[2] The term "children less than 4 years of age" means persons 13 through 47 months of age.

[3] The term "infants" means persons not more than 12 months of age.

[4] 1 retinol equivalent = 1 microgram retinol or 6 micrograms *beta*-carotene; 1 *alpha*-tocopherol equivalent = 1 milligram *d-alpha*-tocopherol; 1 niacin equivalent = 1 milligram niacin or 60 milligrams of dietary tryptophan.

[5] As cholecalciferol.

Appendix J (continued)

(Proposed) Daily Reference Values (DRVs)[1,2]

(to provide intake guidelines for substances not included in the 1989 RDAs)

Food component	Unit of measurement[1]	DRV
Fat	Grams	75
Saturated fatty acids	Grams	25
Unsaturated fatty acids	Grams	50
Cholesterol	Milligrams	300
Carbohydrate	Grams	325
Fiber	Grams	25
Sodium	Milligrams	2400
Potassium	Milligrams	3500

[1]The following abbreviations are allowed: "g" for "grams" and "mg" for "milligrams."

[1]From *The Federal Register,* July 19, 1990, pp. 29485–29486.

[2]Written comments on these proposals were accepted until November 11, 1990. Many comments were received; therefore changes are possible. After the problems identified in the comments are resolved, final rules will be published. The RDIs and DRVs will each become effective one year after publication of their final rules.

Photo Credits

Text Photos: 5 left California Prune Board, **5** right © Diana Lyn/Shooting Star, **7** © Billy E. Barnes/Jeroboam, **8** © Milton Potts/Photo Researchers, **11** © Mark Boulton/Photo Researchers, **66** From *Tissues and Organs; A Text-Atlas of Scanning Electron Microscopy,* by Richard G. Kessel and Randy H. Kardon. W.H. Freeman and Company. Copyright 1979, **71** Peter Arnold, **103** © Kent Reno/Jeroboam, **106** © Olaf Kallstrom/Jeroboam, **117**(a) © Owen Franken/Stock Boston, (b) © Kent Reno/Jeroboam, (c) © Bob Daemmrich/Stock Boston, (d) © Bob Daemmrich/Stock Boston, (e) © Agence Vandystadt/Photo Researchers, **120** © Tom Carter/Jeroboam, **142** © Grant Heilman, **180** © Ed Reschke, **198** © Ed Reschke, **238** M. Murayama, Murayama Research Laboratories/BPS, **252** © Omikron/Photo Researchers, **257** © Teri Stratford/ Photo Researchers, **272** © Steve McCurry/Magnum, **275** left © Cary Wolinsky/Stock Boston, **275** right © Grant Heilman, **208** © Ira Kirschembaum/Stock Boston, **285** top © Lawrence Migdale/Stock Boston, bottom © Jack Coletti/Stock Boston, right © Ronny Jaques/Photo Researchers, **289** © Alexander Lawry/Photo Researchers, **293** © Billy Barnes/Jeroboam, **296** left © Jeff Persons/Stock Boston, right Wayland Lee, bottom Wayland Lee, **317** © Spencer Grant/Stock Boston, **321** Bettmann Archive, **323** left to right Art Resource, Bettmann Archive, Cooper Hewitt Museum Picture Library, UPI/ Bettmann Newsphotos, **349** Bettmann Archive, **367** © Susan Rosenberg/Photo Researchers, **373** © Jeff Persons/Stock Boston, **375** UPI/Bettmann Newsphotos, **392** J. Christopher Bauernfeind, *Nutrition Today* March/April 1988, p. 36, **418** © Dion Ogust/Image Works, **429** © Peter L. Chapman/Stock Boston, **433** Gjon Mili/LIFE Magazine © Time Inc., **444** © Stephen L. Feldman/Photo Researchers, **451** Panamerican Health Organization, **454** K.M. Hambidge, P.A. Walravens, and K.H. Neldner. In *Zinc and Copper Clinical Medicine,* eds. K.M. Hambidge and B.L. Nichols. New York: Spectrum Publishers, 1978., **456** © Bob Daemmrich/Stock Boston, **472** © Guy Gillette/Photo Reserchers, **474** National Livestock and Meat Board, **477** © Larry Lefever/Grant Heilman **478** © Martin J. Heade/Bettmann Archive, **491** Wayland Lee, **494** © Jeffry W. Myers/Stock Boston, **500** © Newsweek, **507** © L.S. Stepanowicz/Photo Researchers, **508** © Charles Gupton/Stock Boston, **515** © Eugene Smith/Magnum, **543** left © Lennart Nilsson/Boehringer Ingelheim International, middle © Lennart Nilsson, right © Lennart Nilsson, **552** Streissguth, A.P., Clarren, S.K., and K.L. Jones, Natural History of the Fetal Alcohol Syndrome: A ten-year follow-up of eleven patients. *Lancet* 2 (July 1985):85–92, **558** © A. Menashe/Photo Researchers, **566** David Johnsen, Case Western Reserve University, **568** © Martha Cooper/Peter Arnold, **601** J.G. Ruggiero, Virginia Polytechnic Institute and State University photographer, and Ann Hertzler, **583** top UPI/Bettmann Archive, bottom © Wally McNamee/Woodfin Camp, **587** © Mike Douglas/Image Works, **625** top © Charles Gupton/Stock Boston, left © Lawrence Migdale/Photo Researchers, bottom © Mike Mazzaschi/Stock Boston, **630** AP/Wide World Photos, **647** © Spencer Grant/Photo Researchers, **Part and Chapter Opener Photos:** Part I © Jeffrey Mark Dunn/Stock Boston, Chapter 1 © Bob Daemmrich/Stock Boston, Chapter 2 © John Elk III/Photo Researchers, Chapter 3 © Will and Deni McIntyre/Photo Researchers, Part II © Spencer Grant/Photo Researchers, Chapter 4 © John Dommers/Photo Researchers, Chapter 5 © Frank Keillor/Jeroboam, Chapter 6 © Luca Gavagna/Photo Researchers, Chapter 7 © Stephen Frisch, Chapter 8 © Ken Gagham/Jeroboam, Part III © Sepp Seitz/Woodfin Camp, Chapter 9 © Ann Chatsky/Jeroboam, Chapter 10 © David Conklin/Photo Edit, Chapter 11 © Lara Hartley, Part IV © Gerd Ludwig/Woodfin Camp, Chapter 12 © Jerry Howard/ Stock Boston, Chapter 13 © John Carter/Photo Researchers, Part V Calgene, Chapter 14 © Larry Lefever/Grant Heilman, Chapter 15 © John Coletti/Stock Boston, Part VI © Stephen Frisch/Stock Boston, Chapter 16 © Edward Lettau/Photo Researchers, Chapter 17 © Ellis Herwig/Stock Boston, Chapter 18 © Will McIntyre/Photo Researchers

Index